T0120089

The CAESAR OF PARIS

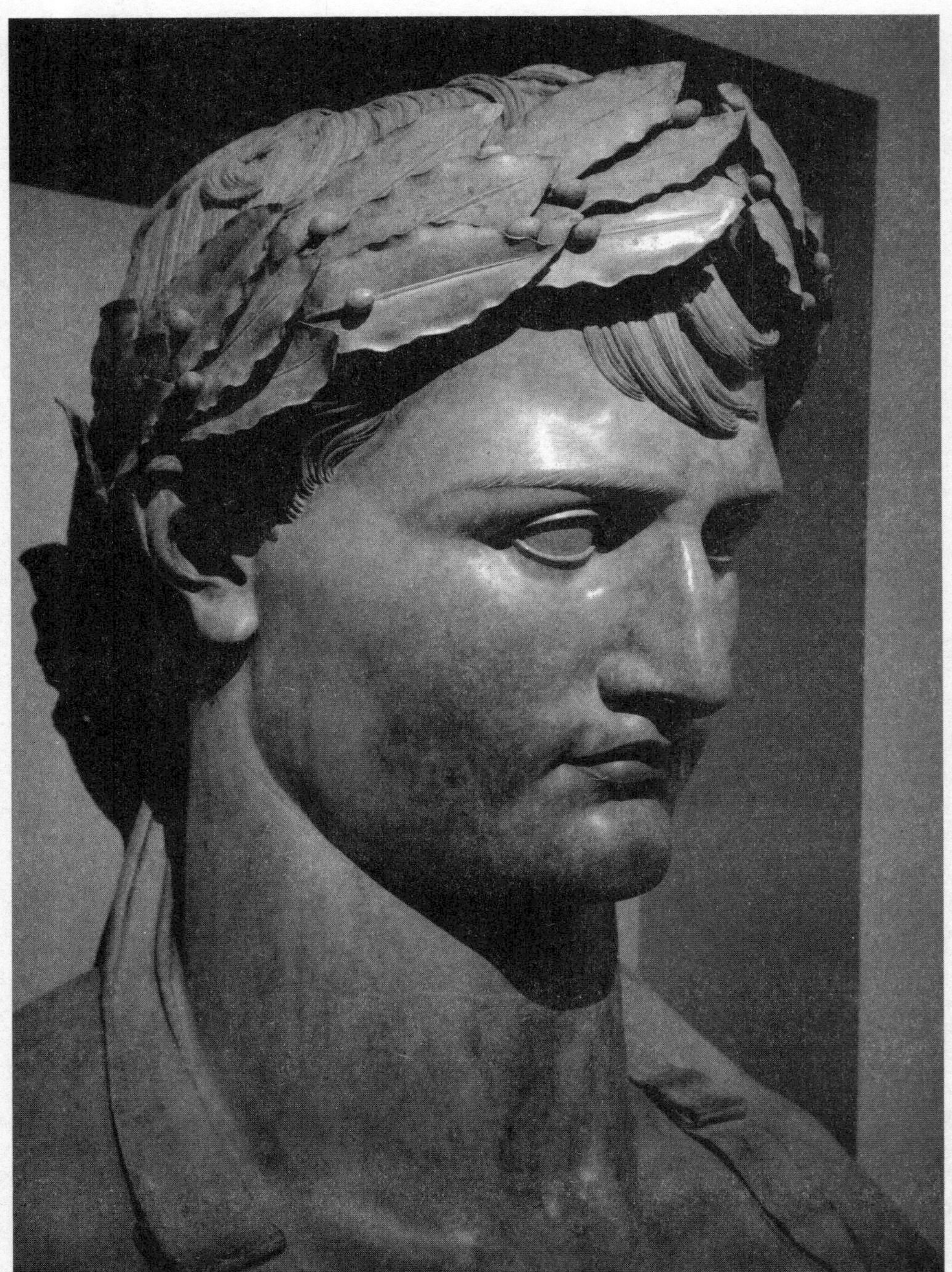

The CAESAR OF PARIS

NAPOLEON BONAPARTE, ROME, AND THE ARTISTIC OBSESSION THAT SHAPED AN EMPIRE

SUSAN JAQUES

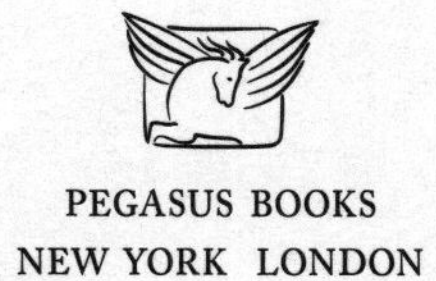

PEGASUS BOOKS
NEW YORK LONDON

THE CAESAR OF PARIS

Pegasus Books Ltd.
148 W 37th Street, 13th Floor
New York, NY 10018

First Pegasus Books edition December 2018

Frontispiece: Bust of Napoleon I by Lorenzo Bartolini at the Louvre Museum, Paris.

Interior design by Maria Fernandez

Library of Congress Cataloging-in-Publication Data is available.

ISBN: 978-1-68177-869-3

10 9 8 7 6 5 4 3 2 1

Printed in the United States of America
Distributed by W. W. Norton & Company

For Doug,

to another thirty-four years

CONTENTS

"I am of the race of the Caesars, and of the best of their kind, the founders."

—Napoleon Bonaparte

INTRODUCTION

As a young boy growing up on the island of Corsica, Napoleon Buonaparte begged his older brother to switch places with him in a mock combat pitting Romans and Carthaginians. The skinny youngster couldn't stand being on the losing side.[1]

In May 1779, the nine-year-old arrived as a scholarship student at the Brienne military college in the Champagne region, speaking a Corsican dialect and bad French. Napoleon escaped his classmates' bullying by reading, especially biographies of antiquity's great military commanders. His fascination with antiquity continued at the Military Academy in Paris. Napoleon was so well versed in Greek and Roman history that Corsican leader Pasquale Paoli told him: "There is nothing modern in you; you are entirely out of Plutarch."[2]

Early in his career as commander of the Army of Italy, Napoleon looked to his ancient heroes for military strategy. "Caesar's principles were Hannibal's, and Hannibal's were Alexander's: keep your forces together, don't be vulnerable on any front, strike very fast with full strength on a given point," he told his officers during the Italian campaign.[3] En route to invading Egypt in 1799, Napoleon invoked the legendary Roman army: "Roman legions that you have sometimes imitated but not yet equaled fought

Carthage first on this same sea and then on the plains of Zama. . . . Soldiers, the eyes of Europe are upon you."[4] The Egypt campaign was a military failure, but Napoleon cleverly spun it into a political and cultural victory. The French army was promoted as a successor to the Roman legions; the Egyptian Revival style became the rage in decorative art and architecture.

Antiquity exerted an equally powerful influence on Napoleon off the battlefield, where he waged a parallel campaign. After returning from Egypt, Napoleon took advantage of France's power vacuum and staged a coup, replacing the corrupt Directory regime with the Consulate, named for a Roman institution. Just as Rome's Caesars returned from campaigns with spoils of war, Napoleon brought wagonloads of art back to Paris from his military victories. Napoleon most prized the antiquities, many stripped from the Vatican. As Alex Potts puts it, the exhibition of Napoleonic war booty in Paris was a cruder version of the ancient Romans giving distinction to the ideal statuary of ancient Greece.[5]

Tellingly, Napoleon gave the famed actor François-Joseph Talma advice on how to play Nero in Racine's *Britannicus* and Julius Caesar in *La Mort de Pompée*. "Emperors aren't like that," the first consul told the star after seeing his performance as the notorious Roman emperor.[6] About Talma's portrayal of Caesar, Napoleon advised: "You use your arms too much: men in power are more restrained in their movements; they know that a gesture is an order, a look is death. So limit your gestures and looks. . . . In your first scene with Ptolemy, there's a line whose meaning escapes you. . . . You say it with too much sincerity. . . . At that moment, Caesar is not saying which he thinks. Caesar is not a Jacobin."[7]

Napoleon soon cast himself in the real-life role. In May 1804, the Senate proclaimed the thirty-four-year-old emperor, bringing the French Republic to an end. Napoleon invited Pope Pius VII to officiate at his December coronation, then shocked everyone by crowning himself. As he famously told a confidant, "I have dethroned no one. I found the crown in the gutter. I picked it up and the people put it on my head." Two years earlier, Napoleon's Concordat with the newly elected Pius VII reestablished the Catholic Church in France. But the rapprochement did not last long.

The battle for control of the Catholic Church was just one of Napoleon's obsessions with Rome. As the repository of 2,500 years of art and architecture, Rome had become Europe's cultural capital—a magnet for painters, sculptors, tourists, and archeologists. During his fifteen-year rule, Napoleon reshaped Paris into the new Rome, Europe's culture capital. As Paris shined, the rest of Rome faded, first as the Roman Republic and later as a marginalized French dominion. Napoleon kept the uncooperative Pius VII under house arrest for nearly five years. During this time, he appropriated the Palazzo del Quirinale, the papal summer residence, turning it into his own lavish imperial palace.

Antiquity inspired all aspects of Napoleon's imperium—from his short Augustus-like haircut to his choice for the symbol of his Empire, the eagle of Jupiter. From ancient Rome, he borrowed images and symbols of power and authority, along with its powerful rituals. Yet as Diana Rowell notes, "Napoleon was not simply reinventing the Roman world; he and his entourage were simultaneously manipulating former Rome-inspired traditions to reinforce the impact of his own form of power over the past, the present, and the future."[8]

Without any hereditary claim to rule, Napoleon sought legitimacy by associating himself with antiquity's greats and his rule with the great civilizations of ancient Egypt, Greece, and Rome. Napoleon's heroes were many and variable, writes Matthew Zarzeczny, his "personal pantheon constantly changed with the circumstances."[9] Just before his coronation, Napoleon added Charlemagne to the group, the Frankish king and military leader who unified medieval Europe after the Roman model. To drum up support for his planned invasion of England, Napoleon promoted William the Conqueror, the man behind the Norman Conquest, with an exhibition in Paris of the famous Bayeux Tapestry.

Travel continued to be a touchstone experience. Like his heroes Alexander, Julius Caesar, Augustus, and Charlemagne, Napoleon was rarely in his capital. Occupied on foreign campaigns, waging some sixty battles, the peripatetic ruler spent just two and a half years in Paris between 1804 and 1814. Extended visits to cities like Vienna, Berlin, Venice, and Genoa influenced Napoleon's ambitious vision for Paris. Between battles, Napoleon dictated thousands of instructions for his projects to turn Paris into the "rendezvous of all Europe."

A frequent recipient of these dispatches was Dominique-Vivant Denon, director of the Musée Napoléon, who traveled with the Grande Armée overseeing art confiscations and curating the ever-growing collection. As Napoleon's de facto culture minister, the urbane Denon also commissioned art to enforce his patron's heroic image. To lend authenticity to a series of monumental battlefield scenes, Denon embedded draftsmen in the army to take notes on everything from uniforms to topography. Denon's A-list painters included Antoine-Jean Gros, and Jean-Auguste-Dominique Ingres, as well as their teacher Jacques-Louis David.

In paintings, sculpture, medals, and porcelain, Napoleon was portrayed in the guise of Roman gods and as a modern Caesar. As Christopher Lloyd writes, "his personal iconography is one of the most extensive ever created for an individual and is a perfect demonstration of the way in which art could be harnessed to political and military ambition."[10]

A far less enthusiastic propagandist was the celebrated Italian sculptor Antonio Canova. Resentful of France's treatment of Italy, Canova had a complex relationship with Napoleon. He designed the tomb of the patriotic Italian poet Vittorio Alfieri for Santa Croce in Florence, along with a funerary monument for Napoleon's archnemesis, British admiral Horatio Nelson, yet kept a bust of Napoleon in his bedroom until his death. Dispatched to Paris twice to model portraits of the Bonapartes, Canova doubled as papal envoy. In 1815, Pius entrusted Canova with retrieving the Papal States's stolen art in Paris, forcing a face-off with the wily Denon.

Like Rome's emperors, Napoleon adorned his capital with heroic, monumental architecture inspired by surviving masterworks of ancient Rome. Declaring that "Men are only as great as the monuments they leave," he ordered the construction of icons like the Vendôme Column, the Arc de Triomphe, the Arc de Triomphe du Carrousel, and Temple to the Glory of the Grande Armée, today's Madeleine Church. Augustus boasted of building his Forum from the spoils of war; Napoleon too financed his building spree with indemnities from his many conquests.

In the same way that Rome's emperors represented the Empire and its wealth with aqueducts, forums, and temples throughout the provinces, Napoleon left his mark on the places he conquered. Anxious to demonstrate loyalty to the emperor, officials designed grandiose projects for the cities of Milan, Vienna, and Venice. Like the Caesars in Rome, Napoleon modernized Paris's infrastructure with new roads, canals, bridges, sewers, and quays. To improve public health and hygiene, he ordered a series of fountains fed by the canals to bring fresh drinking water to Paris. A vast Roman-style catacomb and cemeteries on the outskirts of Paris replaced overflowing church graveyards.

Napoleon's favorite architects Charles Percier and Pierre Fontaine conceived a bold, assertive spin on classicism known as the Empire style. Furniture, silver, textiles, and porcelain combined imperial Roman motifs such as laurel wreaths, trophies, and sphinxes with First Empire symbols such as *N*, eagles, and bees. As Bette Oliver writes, "The empire style applied to everything from architecture and the decorative arts to clothing and hairstyles, helped promote cultural unity and to lend an air of legitimacy and grandeur."[11]

Desperate for an heir, Napoleon divorced Joséphine, his wife of thirteen years, and married the teenage Habsburg archduchess Marie Louise in 1810. His dynastic ambition was realized with the birth of their son, the King of Rome. The "Eaglet" inspired a barrage of dynastic imagery drawing on Roman mythology and imperial art. By 1811, Napoleon ruled over eighty million people. Controlling most of continental Europe, the French Empire was a world power, rivalling that of ancient Rome. Napoleon planned a triumphant entry into Rome and a spectacular third coronation at St. Peter's Basilica.

But he never got there. Napoleon's catastrophic invasion of Russia in late 1812 and final defeat at Waterloo in 1815 put an end to the First Empire. When the Allies led by the Duke of Wellington arrived in Paris to claim their plundered artworks at the Louvre, the antiquities gallery brimmed with some four hundred statues; over eleven hundred paintings lined the Grand Gallery from floor to ceiling.

The British shipped Napoleon off to the remote Atlantic island of St. Helena where he surrounded himself with reminders of his ancient heroes. Napoleon dictated accounts of his campaigns and weighed in on Caesar and Alexander the Great. Meanwhile, the restored Bourbon kings Louis XVIII and Charles X launched a campaign to erase public memory of Napoleon, like the Roman *damnatio memoriae*. In spite of this, Napoleon's legend continued to grow.

Toward the end of his life, the exiled Caesar of Paris saw himself as a mythological hero. After his death in 1821, a torn scrap of paper was discovered in his handwriting: "A new Prometheus, I am nailed to a rock to be gnawed by a vulture. Yes, I have stolen the fire of Heaven and made a gift of it to France. The fire has returned to its source, and I am here!"[12]

PART ONE
DIRECTORY

"If I were master of France, I would make Paris not only the most beautiful city which has existed, but the most beautiful that could exist . . . to combine all the admirable aspects of Athens, Rome, Babylon, and Memphis."

—Napoleon Bonaparte en route to Egypt, 1798

ONE
TRIUMPHUS

Preparations began in the early hours, northwest of Rome's city walls in the swampy Campus Martius, the mosquito-ridden military camp named for the war god Mars. In April, 46 B.C.E., after years of fighting abroad, Julius Caesar returned to Rome and unprecedented power.

Thanks to Caesar's fearsome legions, Rome controlled most of Western Europe and Northern Africa. To celebrate, Caesar was to stage the first of four triumphs marking his victory over Gaul, roughly comprising today's France, Belgium, and Switzerland. For six years, Caesar battled the Gallic tribes, culminating with the siege at Alesia (Burgundy). According to an ancient estimate, the campaign claimed the lives of one million Gauls with another two million taken prisoner.[1]

Caesar spent the night before the Gallic triumph at the Temple of Isis in the Campus Martius. When he awoke, crowds of Romans and out-of-towners were already lining the triumphal route. As musicians played, standard-bearers with captured enemy flags led the way, crossing the pomerium, Rome's sacred boundary, through the special gateway known as the *porta triumphalis*.

Senators and magistrates followed. Perfume wafted through the air as cartloads of gold and silver rolled by, along with elephants and sacrificial animals. Elaborate floats, decorated with citrus and acanthus wood, ivory, and tortoiseshell, hauled replicas of captured buildings and statues personifying the Rhine and Rhône rivers.

The procession continued past the Circus Flaminius and Circus Maximus before winding its way around the tony Palatine Hill along the Via Sacra (Sacred Way), the city's oldest, most fabled street. Following the Via Sacra, the parade arrived at the ancient Roman Forum, filled with temples and markets. Half a dozen Vestal Virgins tended the city's sacred fire at the circular Temple of Vesta, goddess of the hearth. After years of war, the gates of the small shrine of Janus, the god of beginnings, were finally closed to commemorate the new peace.

The crowds cheered as monumental triumphal paintings rolled by, including an image of conquered Massilia, along with captured artillery from its renowned arsenal.[2] But their enjoyment dimmed as canvases depicting the suicides of their fellow Romans came into view—those of Cato disemboweling himself and Lucius Scipio stabbing himself in the chest and throwing himself into the sea.[3]

Next up came Caesar's seventy-two lictors, each carrying a fasces—a bundle of rods and an axe wreathed with laurel. Behind his bodyguards was Caesar himself, in a gilded chariot drawn by four white horses. His face was painted blood red like the cult statue of Jupiter Optimus Maximus. Dressed in a toga, a purple robe woven with gold thread, tall red boots, and a crown of gold and precious stones, Caesar held a sprig of laurel and an ivory scepter topped by the eagle, Jupiter's bird. A slave stood behind him, balancing a gold oak leaf crown over his head and eerily repeating: "Look behind you; remember you are mortal."[4]

Following Caesar's quadriga were equestrian military officers and Romans rescued from slavery. Caesar's soldiers brought up the rear, chanting "*Io triumphe!*" and singing bawdy songs about their commander's legendary sexual appetite. "Romans, watch your wives," they are thought to have chanted, "see the bald adulterer's back home."[5] The men would soon have more to celebrate. Following the triumphal procession, each would receive a piece of the campaign booty, according to his rank. To build goodwill, Caesar also doled out tokens to spectators, which may have explained the turnout. According to Roman historian Suetonius, the crowds were so big that two senators and several spectators were trampled to death by the mob.

At the Roman Forum, the procession made a dramatic stop. The prisoners of war were led out in chains and thrown into the nearby *Tullianum*, Rome's most infamous jail. Built in the seventh century B.C.E., the prison publicly displayed the tortured corpses of its inmates on a flight of steps, the *Scalae Gemoniae* (Stairs of Mourning). Caesar's star prisoner was Gaul's king and chieftain Vercingetorix who had surrendered at the Battle of Alesia. On Caesar's orders, the charismatic Gallic leader would be strangled in the dark, putrid underground cell.[6]

Bordering the Roman Forum was Caesar's own grandiose Forum Julium. In the colonnaded square stood a marble temple to Venus Genetrix who Caesar claimed as his divine ancestress through the Trojan prince Aeneas. Adorning the temple were numerous portraits of Caesar, a golden statue of his Egyptian lover Cleopatra as the goddess Isis, and Timomachus's paintings of Ajax and Medea. It's thought that *Equus Caesaris* was installed outside, depicting Caesar atop his favorite horse, described by Pliny and Suetonius as having almost human forefeet.[7]

Somewhere between the Palatine and Capitoline Hill, the axle of Caesar's chariot broke, nearly tossing him out onto the street. But the mishap was not going to rain on his triumphal parade. Flanked by forty elephants, each toting a torch in its trunk, Caesar climbed the steep steps to the Capitoline, the most sacred of Rome's seven hills.

In the late sixth century B.C.E., the last kings of Rome, the Tarquins, built the Temple of Jupiter Optimus Maximus at the summit of the Capitoline. After the Tarquins's expulsion from Rome, the Temple was dedicated to the Capitoline Triad—Jupiter, chief god of the Roman pantheon, his wife Juno, and Minerva, goddess of wisdom, on September 13, 509 B.C.E., the first year of the Roman Republic. Decorated lavishly in Etruscan style, the shrine became Rome's religious and political center, copied in new cities across the Republic.

As *pontifex maximus*, head priest of the state religion, Julius Caesar now paid homage to the god who had endowed him with power. After Caesar laid the victory wreath and a laurel branch in the lap of Jupiter's painted terra-cotta statue, two white bulls with garlands and gilded horns were sacrificed to Rome's state god.

Over the next month, Caesar would also mark his victories over Egypt, Asia Minor, and Africa, part of a civil war begun when the republican opposition fled Rome under Pompey Magnus. After defeating Pompey at Pharsalus in northern Greece, Caesar pursued his rival to Egypt. It's there that the fifty-two-year-old commander fell for the captivating twenty-one-year-old Cleopatra, with whom he had a son, Caesarion. After spending just a few weeks in Rome at the end of 47 B.C.E., Caesar departed for North Africa to deal with his rivals Scipio and Cato. In 46, Caesar left for Spain where he defeated Pompey's sons Gnaeus and Sextus.

Julius Caesar's sensational homecoming was part of a long tradition that dated back to Romulus, Rome's mythical founder. The triumph, one of ancient Rome's most important institutions, was the ultimate honor. Awarded by the Senate to generals for major victories, the rules required a *triumphator* to have defeated a foreign enemy with at least five thousand enemies killed in a single battle. The tradition of the four-horse chariot, or *quadriga,* introduced by Rome's Etruscan kings continued after the founding of the Republic. Pompey tried replacing the horses with elephants in 61 B.C.E., but his chariot got stuck in the *porta triumphalis.*

The *quadriga*, from the Latin for four (*quad*) and yoke (*iugum*), was also used in Roman chariot races in the Circus Maximus. Skilled charioteers could earn top dollar, but controlling the four-horse vehicle was challenging. The reins of two horses were bound around the body of the driver, who was highly motivated not to crash.

With Rome's sack of the Etruscan city of Veii in 396 B.C.E., followed by its victory over Pyrrhus in 275 B.C.E., spoils were added to the Roman triumph, including gold statues and painted panels. Plutarch tells us that Lucullus's triumph over Mithridates showcased "a large gold statue of Mithridates himself, six feet high, a long shield set with stones, twenty loads of silver vessels."[8]

Subsequent Roman generals followed suit, returning from foreign conquests with tons of silver coin, bullion, and luxury objects. As part of their triumphs, they paraded their war booty through Rome, often selling the loot to finance buildings and future military campaigns.

As Rome expanded across the Mediterranean during the Punic Wars (264–146 B.C.E.), triumphs became more frequent. So did a building spree of public monuments along the triumphal route by returning generals. These columns, arches, porticoes, and temples helped make the triumph a central institution of Roman society.[9]

Parading war booty through the streets of Rome reached new heights when M. Claudius Marcellus returned in 211 B.C.E. after capturing the celebrated Greek city of Syracuse. Because Marcellus's army was still in Sicily, the Senate offered him an ovation rather than a full triumph. The ovation, from the Latin word *ovis* for the sheep sacrificed at the end of the procession, was bestowed in lieu of a triumph if a defeated rival was seen as inferior or if less than five thousand enemies were killed.[10]

Rather than riding a chariot, Marcellus walked, accompanied by flautists. In lieu of the triumphator's traditional costume of a laurel wreath and gold embroidered purple toga, the general wore a wreath of Venus's myrtle and his magistrate's toga. Marcellus's procession began with an allegorical painting of Syracuse made prisoner. Spanish and Syracusan allies with golden wreaths followed along with eight elephants. Enemy artillery designed by the renowned scientist Archimedes was paraded along with silver, gold, royal ornaments, statuary, paintings, and opulent furniture. According to Plutarch, Marcellus showed off "many of the most beautiful public monuments from Syracuse, realizing that they would both make a visual impression in his triumph and also be an ornament for the city."[11]

The Greek art booty earned Marcellus a reputation as a man of culture, and he is credited with turning elite Romans into collectors of Greek art. But the pilfering of sculptures from Syracuse's temples also caused a protest. As Ida Östenberg explains, because statues were believed to embody the gods they represented, taking statues from temples was seen as not just stealing from the gods, but stealing the gods themselves from their abodes.[12] A year after Marcellus's ovation, a delegation from Syracuse arrived in Rome complaining that the gods themselves had been carried away and accusing the general of rejecting peace offers so that he could occupy and loot the city. After great debate, the Senate ultimately supported Marcellus.

Anti-looting sentiment continued when M. Fulvius Nobilior emptied the Aetolian city of Ambracia of its sculptures and paintings, many from the palace of Pyrrhus. Livy and Cicero criticized Verres for plundering Sicily; his art seizures, including famous temple paintings, were sent to a storehouse in Messana while a ship was built to transport the statues, tapestries, gold rings, decorated goblets, and elegant furniture to Rome. Again, the Senate upheld *ius belli*, the rights of war, allowing Rome's generals to confiscate everything as long as a city had been captured in a justly fought war.

After Titus Quinctius Flamininus defeated Macedonia's Philip V in 197 B.C.E., Livy tells us that "gold and silver, worked, unworked, and coined was carried in procession." "The unwrought silver came to 43,270 pounds, while wrought silver included vessels of every sort, most embossed, some works of outstanding craftsmanship. . . ." Eight years later, Livy reported on a staggering parade of loot from Scipio's victory over Antiochos III. In addition to silver and gold, the haul included 1,200 ivory tusks, gold crowns, coins, and engraved silver vases.[13]

Rome's looting reached its height after 146 B.C.E. when Scipio Aemilianus captured Carthage and Lucius Mummius captured mainland Greece, including Athens. Greek masterpieces poured into Rome, along with Greek architects, sculptors, and painters. Around this time, returning military leaders began building marble Greek-style temples in the Campus Martius, often decorated with war booty.

Greek art had a dramatic impact on Roman society. As Paul Zanker writes, Rome's appropriation of Greek culture led to an enthusiasm for Hellenistic art and "paved the way for the development of a new and specifically Roman system images."[14] During the early Republic, triumphs had functioned as purification rituals and moments of glory for Roman generals returning from war. By displaying show-stopping booty from Syracuse and Carthage, Marcellus and Scipio Africanus turned the triumph into a powerful propaganda tool.

War spoils introduced Romans to new art genres and materials, like bronze and marble statues, paintings, arms and armor, gold and silver tableware, pearls and gemstones, and textiles woven with gold. Pliny reports that during Pompey's 61 B.C.E. triumph, he presented variegated agate Myrrhine ware for the first time, dedicating the beautiful bowls and cups to Jupiter Capitolinus.

In February 44 B.C.E., two years after his extravagant triumphs, Julius Caesar was named Rome's dictator for life. Rumors flew that he wished to be king—Rome's first in nearly five centuries. With Cleopatra beside him in the capital, Caesar was preparing an offensive against the Parthians (modern Iran) when he was attacked outside the Senate House in the Forum on March 15, the Roman calendar's Ides of March. L. Junius Brutus and his fellow regicides stabbed Caesar to death at the foot of a statue of his rival Pompey, then fled to the Capitoline's holy Temple of Jupiter.

To Brutus and his coconspirators, Caesar's power grab represented an ominous threat to republican liberty. But Caesar's assassination triggered a civil war resulting in Rome's transformation from a republic to an empire by his great-nephew and heir, Octavian (Gaius Julius Caesar Octavianus). The first order of business for the triumvirate of Octavian, Mark Antony, and Lepidus was to avenge Caesar's murder. After a lengthy battle in Macedonia, Brutus and Cassius committed suicide. The same fate awaited the popular general Mark Antony in Alexandria.

When Octavian returned to Rome in 29 B.C.E., he celebrated a triple triumph over three days in mid-August for victories in Dalmatia, Actium, and Egypt.[15] As Rome's first emperor, Octavian took the name Augustus, and turned the triumph into a glorification of imperial power and authority. Not wanting to be upstaged by his military commanders, Augustus decreed that only members of the imperial family could celebrate triumphs.

Early in his reign, Augustus transformed an ancient temple of Apollo in the Campus Martius into a Hellenistic-style museum for Greek art booty. Among the masterworks installed inside were a cedar-wood Apollo from Seleucia, a dozen statues by Rhodian sculptor Philiscus, Athenian sculptor Timarchides's *Apollo Citharoedus* (harp player), a group sculpture of Niobe and her children by Praxiteles or Scopas, and a picture by Aristeides of Thebes.[16]

Rome's zeal for Greek art continued to grow during the Augustan era, with the wealthy competing with the ruling class for statues, bronzes, and silver for their luxurious homes. "This obsession with the past remained a characteristic of artistic culture throughout the . . . whole Julio-Claudian epoch," writes Ranuccio Bandinelli. "It also crops up again later, giving rise to a series of 'neo-classical' movements which form a basic ingredient in all Roman art up to the time of Constantine and Theodosius . . ."[17]

A canon of the most famous Hellenistic works, the *opera nobilia*, inspired Roman copies for public monuments and private homes. Especially prized were statues of athletes by Polykleitos and Aphrodites by Praxiteles and paintings by Zeuxis. Soon, Roman connoisseurs were not just commissioning copies, but were having artists combine elements from various periods to create a uniquely Roman style. Marble furniture and table legs were often carved with mythological figures based on Greek originals.[18]

In 71 C.E., Romans were treated to a jaw-dropping display of war spoils when Flavian dynasty founder Vespasian and his son Titus paraded treasures taken from the Second Temple of Jerusalem. Among the shimmering booty was the seven-branched Menorah, table of the shewbread, and sacred silver trumpets. "Silver and gold and ivory in masses, made in all kinds of forms, might be seen, not as if carried in procession, but flowing so to speak like a river . . ." wrote Jewish historian Flavius Josephus.[19]

Following a triumph, many of the spoils were put on public display in theaters, porticoes, and temples, joining other looted objects. In this way, the triumphator ensured his legacy for future generations. Many looted objects found a permanent home in the Roman Forum, the city's bustling hub, which John Henry Merryman calls "the world's first great outdoor art museum."[20]

In its final centuries, Rome remained the symbolic heart of the Empire but it lost its prominence as capital. In the late thirrd century, the imperial court moved to Milan, followed by Ravenna in the early fifth century. In between, Constantinople stole much of Rome's thunder. In 410, Rome was sacked and plundered by Alaric and the Goths; Gaiseric and the Vandals followed in 455.

During the ensuing Gothic and Byzantine periods, it was standard practice for victors to strip the treasures of the vanquished. From Ravenna, Byzantine emperor Justinian dispatched his general Belisarius to Carthage in 535 to defeat the Vandals and capture the loot they had stolen from Rome.[21] During this period, war spoils lost their original political function, becoming instead a way to bankroll military campaigns.

Art plunder as cultural enrichment reemerged in the Renaissance. When the Gonzagas seized Mantua in 1433, they saw themselves as modern Caesars. In the latter part of the century, Francesco II Gonzaga commissioned Andrea Mantegna's *The Triumphs of Caesar* for the halls of the massive Ducal Palace in Mantua. Drawing on ancient texts by Plutarch, Appian, and Suetonius, Mantegna reimagined Caesar's famous triumphs on nine monumental tempera on canvas panels, concluding with Caesar in his chariot.

The epic cycle, which took the artist at least six years, was among the most celebrated, copied works of the sixteenthth and early seventeenth centuries. To legitimize their own reigns, European rulers ordered reproductions in engravings, friezes, paintings, tapestries, and porcelain. (Acquired by England's Charles I in 1629, *The Triumphs of Caesar* has been displayed since at Hampton Court Palace.)

The staging of Roman-style triumphs continued. After leading the papal armies, Pope Alexander VI's son Cardinal Cesare Borgia made a triumphal entry into Rome in 1500. Pope Julius II (1503–13), known as the warrior pope for his efforts to expand the papal empire, fashioned himself as an imperial Caesar, a triumphator. Italy's foreign invaders—from France's Charles VIII and Louis XII to Holy Roman Emperor Charles V—also appropriated the Roman triumph.

In France, Henri II's spectacular entry into Rouen in 1550 was compared to Pompey's third triumph, "magnificent in riches and abounding in the spoils of foreign nations."[22] A triumphal arch made for Louis XIII's royal entry into Paris in 1628 carried a depiction of Pompey.[23] In the seventeenth century, Swedish King Gustavus Adolphus turned his court into a "cultural center" with plundered European artworks.[24]

But nothing, not even the plunder of Syracuse or Athens, matched what came next.

⚜

Rain did not deter Parisians from turning out in force for the start of the two-day Festival of Liberty. The date had been chosen for its symbolic associations. July 27, 1798, marked the fourth anniversary of the Republic's

Directory government, and with it the fall of Robespierre and the end of the infamous Terror that followed the French Revolution.

That morning, on the Quai du Louvre by the Museum of Natural History, forty-five cases were loaded onto wagons decorated with garlands and tricolors. To the sound of marching bands, the procession began, with the first wagons hauling a collection of natural specimens and exotic trees from Trinidad. Camels, ostriches, caged lions, gazelles, and a bear from a German zoo followed, evoking the animals of ancient's Rome's triumphs and gladiator games. Following a detachment of troops came half a dozen wagons filled with rare books, manuscripts, and medals.

After a banner reading, "The Arts seek the land where laurels grow," twenty-five wagons rumbled by. Big floats bore two enormous statues representing the Nile and Tiber rivers. Wooden packing cases housed many of the world's most coveted antique marble statues, including the *Laocoön*, the *Apollo Belvedere*, the *Capitoline Venus*, and the *Dying Gaul*. On the cart carrying the *Apollo Belvedere* and *Clio*, the inscription read: "Both will reiterate our battles, our victories." Another banner read: "Monuments of Antique Sculpture. Greece gave them up; Rome lost them; Their fate has twice changed; it will not change again."[25]

Six horses drew the next wagon sporting the banner: "Horses transported from Corinth Rome to Constantinople, from Constantinople to Venice and from Venice to France. They are finally in a free land."[26] The precious cargo, four bronze horses, had stood watch over Venice's St. Mark's Basilica since their looting by the Venetians from Constantinople nearly six centuries earlier. St. Mark's medieval lion followed.

Bringing up the rear were two wagons packed with painted masterpieces of the Renaissance and Baroque periods. The banner read: "Artists, hurry! Your masters have arrived."[27] Among the precious cargo was Raphael's final work, *Transfiguration*, removed from the altarpiece of San Pietro in Montorio. According to Renaissance art critic Giorgio Vasari, when the thirty-seven-year-old artist died suddenly in 1520, the painting was placed at the head of his funeral procession "breaking the heart of all who look upon it."[28] Vasari called the painting "the most famous, the most beautiful and most divine."[29]

Also inside the crates was Paolo Veronese's *Wedding at Cana* from Venice, three of his canvases from San Sebastiano, and two from the Doge's

Palace.[30] From the Vatican painting gallery came *The Mass of Saint Gregory* by Andrea Sacchi; from the papal Roman summer residence, the Palazzo del Quirinale, came Nicolas Poussin's *The Martyrdom of Saint Erasmus* and Guercino's *Saint Petronilla*.

After passing the Botanical Gardens, the procession of masterpieces wound its way along the Seine. By late afternoon, the wagons and marching bands arrived at the Champs de Mars, Paris's version of Rome's Campus Martius. There, before an imposing Altar of Victory, an antique bust of Julius Caesar's assassin Brutus was placed on a pedestal. As Patricia Mainardi explains, the inscription, "Rome was first governed by kings: Junius Brutus gave it liberty and the Republic," was a reference to the recent overthrow of the Bourbon kings by the French Republic.[31]

The Directory had commissioned a special festival song; lyrics were handed out to the crowd. Accompanied by cavalry and military bands, Parisians sang the refrain: "*Rome is no more in Rome. It is all in Paris.*"[32]

Among the spectators that day were the Goncourt brothers who raved: "And as if twenty-nine carts of divine monuments were not enough, more carts followed laden with plants, fossils, animals, bears from Bern, lions, camels, African dromedaries, carts with manuscripts, coins, musical scores, and books. . . . The Eternal City itself had never seen such a colossal spectacle, nor had any emperor's victory parade passing through its proud streets ever brought in its triumphant wake an army of such prisoners."

The reenactment of a Roman triumphal procession was made possible by France's military sensation, twenty-six-year-old Napoleon Bonaparte.

Three years earlier, on October 5, 1795, the Corsican-born officer made headlines by quashing a major royalist insurrection in Paris. The following year, he was given command of the dejected army of Italy. That spring, as a newlywed, Napoleon led his troops across the Alps into Piedmont and Lombardy, stunning Europe with a series of victories over Austria. "On 15 May 1796, General Bonaparte made his entry into Milan at the head of that youthful army which had just crossed the bridge at Lodi, and let the world know that after all these centuries, Caesar and Alexander had a successor," Stendhal famously wrote.[33]

As Napoleon's army marched across northern and central Italy, its young general added clauses to peace treaties demanding precise quantities and often specific works of art. With his organized plunder, Napoleon institutionalized a policy begun by the Directory. After occupying Belgium in 1794, the Directory packed off seven convoys of painting and sculptures. Among the treasures were Peter Paul Rubens's *The Descent from the Cross* and *Erection of the Cross* (from Antwerp Cathedral), the crucifixion scene *Le Coup de Lance*, a sculpture of the *Madonna of Bruges* by Michelangelo, and the central panels of Jan van Eyck's altarpiece from Ghent's St. Bavo Cathedral, *Adoration of the Mystic Lamb.*

Weeks after pilfering the famous fifteenth century altarpiece, librarian Antoine Alexandre Barbier addressed the National Convention: "Too long have these masterpieces been sullied by the gaze of serfs. . . . These immortal works are no longer in a foreign land. . . . They rest today in the home of the arts and of genius, in the motherland of liberty and sacred equality, in the French Republic."[34]

Opposition to the looting was deemed unpatriotic. In October 1796, the official government newspaper *Le Moniteur* justified the action by invoking the Romans: "We form our taste precisely by long acquaintance with the true and the beautiful. The Romans, once uneducated, began to educate themselves by transplanting the works of conquered Greece to their own country. We follow their example when we exploit our conquests and carry off from Italy whatever serves to stimulate our imagination."[35]

To oversee the selection and transfer of Italy's "monuments of interest," the Directory appointed a Commission of Arts and Sciences. Members included the mathematician Gaspard Monge, botanist André Thouin, chemist Claude Louis Berthollet, painters Jean-Baptiste Wicar and Jean-Simon Berthélemy, sculptors Jean-Guillaume Moitte and Claude Dejoux, naturalist Jacques-Julien Labillardière and artist Jean-Pierre Tinet, who was assigned to join the Grande Armée in Tuscany. These commissioners followed Napoleon's army, shipping the finest artworks to Paris.

An armistice with the art-rich duchy of Parma and Piacenza in May 1796 yielded over twenty paintings including Correggio's masterwork, *Madonna with St. Jerome*. The Duke of Modena ceded twenty paintings plus seventy manuscripts from his library. Bologna, part of the papal dominion, lost thirty-one paintings, one hundred prints, and over five hundred manuscripts. Ferrara gave up ten paintings. Milan, Verona, Perugia, Loreto,

Pavia, Cento, Cremona, Pesaro, Fano, and Massa fell to France and were forced to give up art.

In May 1797, Napoleon's troops occupied Venice. On October 17, 1797, after five months of negotiations from his headquarters at the Villa Manin in Udine, Napoleon and the Austrians signed the Treaty of Campo Formio. The treaty validated the new Cisalpine Republic that adopted the French Constitution; the Venetian Republic was reduced to a province of the Austrian empire. Before the Austrians took possession of Venice, France's commissars arrived to remove its treasures.

Veroneses, Titians, and Tintorettos were ripped from the ceilings of the meeting rooms of the Council of Ten. Giovanni Bellini's *The Madonna and Child Enthroned* from the Church of San Zaccaria and Titian's masterpiece *The Death of St Peter Martyr* from Santi Giovanni e Paolo were also removed. The four bronze horses were lowered from the loggia of St. Mark's by ropes onto carts, along with the winged lion of St. Mark's square. By 1799, when France extended its reach to Florence and Turin, Napoleon boasted to the Directory: "We will have everything beautiful in Italy."

But the greatest prize of Napoleon's Italian campaign was Rome. By the terms of the Armistice of Bologna on June 23, 1796: "The Pope shall deliver to the French Republic one hundred pictures, busts, vases, or statues at the choice of the commissioners who shall be sent to Rome, among which articles shall be particularly included the bronze bust of Junius Brutus and that in marble of Marcus Brutus, the two placed upon the Capitol, and five hundred manuscripts at the choice of the same commissioners."[36] The following February, the Treaty of Tolentino confirmed the terms of the plunder.

In addition to recognizing the Directory as France's legitimate government, Pope Pius VI was forced to pay an indemnity of twenty-one million livres (some sixty million dollars today), and surrender one hundred of Rome's greatest artworks—eighty-three sculptures and seventeen paintings. Sixty-three of the sculptures would come from the Vatican; twenty from the Capitoline Museum (on the Capitoline Hill). Six paintings were removed from the Pinacoteca Vaticana, one from the Quirinale, two from the Capitoline Museum, five from Rome's churches, and three from Umbria.

To add insult to injury, Napoleon required the octogenarian pope to pay for the shipping of the art to Paris—another 800,000 livres (about

2.3 million dollars). That December, the murder of the popular French general Mathurin-Léonard Duphot gave the Directory an excuse to occupy Rome and proclaim it a republic. Napoleon demanded the pope erect a monument to Duphot along with a French diplomat killed in Rome in 1793, Nicolas de Basseville.

On February 15, 1798, French troops marched into the city—the first foreign invasion since Charles V sacked Rome in 1527. Five days later, the partially paralyzed Pius VI was carted off over the Alps to Valence's citadel, where he died the following August. After a reign of nearly a quarter of a century, his death certificate simply read: "Name: John Braschi. Occupation: pontiff."[37]

Along with his eighteenth-century predecessors, Pius VI had helped Rome reinvent itself as Europe's undisputed cultural mecca. By the second half of the century, tourists, artists, and architects flocked to Rome, lured by the rediscovery of classical antiquity through archeological digs, monuments, and magnificent ruins. With its classical models, the papal capital was a must for the day's artists and architects. As they had during the Renaissance and Counter-Reformation, popes became avid art collectors and patrons.

In the ensuing neoclassical craze, Rome lost many of its antiquities to foreign art collectors. To protect its cultural patrimony, Pope Clement XII opened the Capitoline Museum in 1734 with the acquisition of the renowned sculptures of his nephew, Cardinal Alessandro Albani. After restricting the export of antiquities, Pope Benedict XIV added more antiquities and founded the Capitoline picture gallery with the Sacchetti and Pio collections. Benedict also created the Museo Sacro at the Vatican's Apostolic Library to house ivory and gold treasures from early Christianity. Pope Clement XIII formed the Profane Museum to showcase the Vatican's secular treasures.

Inspired by discoveries in Herculaneum and Pompeii, Pope Clement XIV began planning a museum devoted to antiquities in the Vatican's Belvedere Villa where Leonardo da Vinci had lived for several years. Various thematic galleries branched out from Michelangelo Simonetti's Octagonal Courtyard, including the Hall of Animals, Hall of the Muses, and Gallery of the Candelabra. The elegant Pio-Clementino opened in 1784, named for Clement and Pius VI who completed its twelve galleries. In

1790, Pius VI combined paintings from the Capitolina (founded in 1748 by Benedict XIV) and Quirinale to create the Vatican Pinacoteca, or picture gallery.

Just eight years later, Rome was pillaged. Within two weeks of the signing of the Treaty of Tolentino, France's cultural commissars arrived to pack up treasures from the Vatican and Capitoline Museums, along with churches, palaces, and private collections. In the same way ancient Rome's generals had absconded with works by celebrated Greek sculptors like Praxiteles, Lysippos, and Pheidias, Paris now claimed Rome's most famous statues, paintings, manuscripts, and jewelry.

Archivist Pierre Claude François Daunou was sent to Rome to supervise the removal of manuscripts from the Vatican Archives. Like the Roman general Sulla who sacked Athens in 86 B.C.E. and seized its finest library including works by Aristotle, Napoleon's haul was spectacular. The loot included the *Codex Vaticanus*, a fourth-century parchment manuscript containing almost the entire Christian canon in Greek. The illustrated *Vatican Virgil*, created in Rome around 400 C.E., contained one of the oldest surviving copies of the *Aeneid*, the epic tale of Aeneas's journey from Troy to Italy where he founded Rome. The manuscripts were confiscated on July 24, 1799, along with Pius VI's private collection of manuscripts and incunabulum that he had boasted rivaled all private libraries of the day.[38]

The Vatican's Profane Museum was emptied of its coins, precious gems, and classical cameos. Among the prizes was the *Apollo Belvedere,* discovered in 1489 near Grottaferrata, Rome, and named for its specially designed niche in the Belvedere Courtyard. A second-century copy of a fourth-century B.C.E. bronze by the Greek sculptor Leochares, the marble depicts Apollo as an archer. Sketched and copied by Renaissance artists like Michelangelo and Dürer, the statue achieved icon status by the eighteenth century when it was seen as the ideal of aesthetic perfection. "Before this miracle of art I forget the entire universe," raved German art historian Johann Winckelmann.[39]

Also from the Belvedere, French commissars packed the monumental masterpiece *Laocoön* that Pliny the Elder called the most extraordinary work of painting or sculpture he'd ever seen. When it was accidentally discovered in a vineyard on Rome's Esquiline Hill in 1506, the *Laocoön* was immediately recognized as the "miraculous" first-century Hellenistic work described by the Roman naturalist. Pope Julius II took Michelangelo's advice and bought it. Carved out of a single marble slab, the work depicts the Trojan priest Laocoön and his two sons being strangled by sea serpents sent by Apollo—punishment for the priest's warning to the Trojans not to let the enormous wooden horse into their city.

Snatched from the Sala Rotunda of the Vatican's Pio-Clementino Museum was *Jupiter d'Otricoli*, a monumental marble bust of the king of the gods. Unearthed in a 1782 excavation sponsored by Pius VI at the ancient Ocriculum colony on Via Flaminia, the bust dates to the first half of the first century B.C.E. Thought to be the work of Paros with late eighteenth-century restorations, Jupiter is depicted with deep-set eyes, a deep horizontal wrinkle on his forehead, long strands of hair, and a thick beard. The model was one of the Seven Wonders of the World, Phidias's ivory and gold Zeus from the temple of Olympia.

Rome's Capitoline Museum provided another twenty-one ancient masterworks. Among these was *The Dying Gaul*, an ancient Roman copy of a lost Hellenic sculpture (first or second century C.E.). Unearthed around 1622 in the gardens of the Villa Ludovisi on the Pincian Hill, the expressive statue carved in Greek marble depicts a warrior in his final moments, his face twisted in pain from the wound to his chest. The *Capitoline Venus*, discovered in the 1670s on the Quirinal Hill, was among the best preserved sculptures from Roman antiquity. Standing six feet six inches, the marble goddess sports a more elaborate coif and reversed pose than her celebrated model—Praxiteles's *Aphrodite of Cnidos* (circa 360 B.C.E.). For centuries, Praxiteles's masterpiece adorned a shrine dedicated to the goddess of love at Cnidos on the Aegean Sea's eastern shore. Later taken to Constantinople, Praxiteles's statue was destroyed in a fire that swept the Byzantine capital in 475 C.E.

Rome's villas were also alluring targets. After the sale of his first antiquities collection to the Vatican in 1728, Cardinal Alessandro Albani assembled an even larger trove. To show off his new collection, he built the stately Villa Albani on the Via Solaria. French troops carted off 294 of the best works to Paris, including the Cardinal's cherished *Antinous* bas-relief excavated at Hadrian's Villa in 1735. A decade later, Jean-François de Troy, director of the French Academy in Rome, called the marble relief "of its kind one of the finest pieces of antiquity that can be found."[40]

Some of Rome's finest altarpieces were also seized. These include Raphael's *Transfiguration,* Caravaggio's *Deposition* from the Chiesa Nuova, Andrea Sacchi's *Vision of Saint Romuald*, Reni's *Martyrdom of Saint Peter,* and Domenichino's *Last Communion of Saint Jerome.* To the disappointment of French officials, Daniele da Volterra's fresco *Descent from the Cross* could not be removed from the wall of Santissima Trinita dei Monti.[41]

As in ancient Rome, not everyone in Paris was a fan of the state-sponsored plunder. The most eloquent opponent was Antoine Quatremère de Quincy. During the Revolution, he had overseen the transformation of the Church of Ste-Geneviève into the secular Panthéon. In *Letters on the Plan to Abduct the Monuments of Italy,* Quatremère protested "the removal of the art monuments from Italy, the dismemberment of her schools of art, and the despoiling of her collections, galleries, museums, etc. . . ." "Moreover, I believe it equally injurious to the 18th century to suspect it of being capable of reviving this Roman right of conquest that renders men and things the property of the strongest."[42]

Quatremère secured the signatures of some four dozen artists and architects for a petition urging the Directory to reconsider its appropriation of Italian art. Ironically, the supporters of the petition included a handful of Napoleon's future propagandists—Dominique-Vivant Denon, painters Jacques-Louis David and his pupil Anne-Louis Girodet, and architects Charles Percier and Pierre-François Fontaine. A counter-petition was assembled, signed by a group of artists backing the art confiscations. "The French republic, by virtue of its strength, its superior enlightenment, and superior artists, is the only country in the world that can provide inviolable sanctuary for these masterpieces," read the counter-petition published in the *Moniteur Universel.* At stake was "the instruction of the French people as a whole."[43]

In the end, the Directory's confiscations continued. Many of Italy's greatest paintings were removed from their stretchers, layered with padding, and rolled onto waxed cylinders; its renowned statues wrapped in plaster and straw. Specially built carts transported the irreplaceable cargo by land to Livorno, where a frigate carried the art to Marseilles. From there, the canvases traveled by barge up the Rhône, then the Centre and Brione canals, and the Seine. The outside of the cases were tarred and covered with wax cloth to protect against humidity and other conditions. The first of four wagon convoys left Rome in April, accompanied by painter Antoine-Jean Gros.[44]

As a model for the upcoming Paris festival, organizers looked to Aemilius Paulus's lavish three-day Roman triumph in 167 B.C.E. As Plutarch describes, on the first day of the triumph, crowds climbed scaffolding in the Circus Maximus and Forum to get a better view of the 250 wagons brimming with Macedonian booty, enemy armor, gold plate, and coins. The biggest prize was Macedonian king Perseus and his family. In arguing for the triumph, M. Servilius emphasized the ritual's importance to Roman identity:

"Are the many triumphs which have been celebrated over the Gauls, over the Spaniards, over the Carthaginians spoken of as pertaining merely to the generals themselves, or to the Roman People? Just as triumphs are celebrated, not merely over Pyrrhus or Hannibal, but over the people of Epirus or Carthage, so not Manius Curius or Publius Cornelius alone, but the Romans themselves celebrated the triumph."[45]

After four years of fighting and a battered economy, the Directory hoped that a parade of Italian war booty would improve morale and patriotism among Parisians just as it had for the Romans. "What could be more appropriate to revive and strengthen public spirit than to exhibit ceremonially to the French people this striking witness of its grandeur and its power?" the Institut asked.[46]

France's plunder was justified as part of a long historical tradition dating back to the Romans. In a speech to interior minister François de Neufchâteau, Thouin, one of the commissioners, described the looting as the continuation of a long historical tradition. "The Romans plundered the Etruscans, the Greeks, and the Egyptians, accumulated [the sculptures] in Rome and other Italian cities; the fate of these productions of genius is to belong to the people who shine successively on earth by arms and by wisdom, and to follow always the wagons of the victors."[47]

The Directory also claimed that as heir to the ancient civilizations, only France could liberate art from tyranny and save the treasures from decay. "The Romans, once an uncultivated people, became civilized by transplanting to Rome the works of conquered Greece. . . . Thus the French people, naturally endowed with exquisite sensitivity, will, by seeing the models from antiquity, train its feeling and its critical sense. . . . The French Republic, by its strength and superiority of its enlightenment and its artists is the only country in the world which can give a safe home to these masterpieces."[48]

On the second day of the festival, with only military officials present, Neufchâteau presented the inventories of stolen art to the Directory at the Altar of Victory. From there, the sculpture and paintings were deposited at the Louvre. Natural history specimens went to the Jardin des Plantes; books and manuscripts to the Bibliothèque Nationale. The festival ended with a salvo of artillery, orchestras, fireworks, and speeches.

But the triumphator wasn't in Paris to accompany the parade of his war spoils. Like Julius Caesar and his successor Octavian, Napoleon Bonaparte was on his way to conquer Egypt.

TWO

THE LAND OF THE NILE

On the morning of May 19, 1798, crowds gathered at the port of Toulon in southern France, waving goodbye to their loved ones. It was a scene no one would forget. To deafening canon fire and military marches, seventeen thousand soldiers boarded one hundred eighty ships anchored in the crowded bay. Convoys from other French ports would soon join the fleet, bringing the total military personnel to some thirty-four thousand soldiers and sixteen thousand sailors.

A brisk wind blew across the deck of the *Junon* as the dapper Dominique-Vivant Denon observed the chaotic scene. "Thousands of men leaving their country, their fortunes, their friends, their children, and their wives, almost all of whom knew nothing of the course they were about to steer, nor indeed of anything that concerned their voyage, except that Bonaparte was the leader," he recorded in his journal.[1]

It was here five years earlier that Napoleon Bonaparte notched his first military victory. In defiance of France's new republic, Toulon had opened its port to the English. The young artillery captain led his soldiers in an assault on the fort above the harbor, suffering a bayonet wound in the thigh. Napoleon's troops bombarded the British fleet, destroying ten ships. The British fled and Napoleon was promoted to brigadier general.

Now fresh from a series of stunning victories in Northern Italy, the twenty-eight-year-old military hero had returned to Toulon with his eye on a far bigger prize. Since the 1600s, France had been vying with England for economic control around the world. Rather than risk an invasion of Britain, Napoleon proposed to hurt its lucrative trade with India by invading Egypt, gateway to Africa and Asia. With Egypt's ruling Mamelukes controlled by the distant Ottomans, Napoleon sensed an opportunity.

Egypt was also tantalizing for personal reasons. "Europe presents no field for glorious exploits; no great empires or revolutions are to be found, but in the East where there are six hundred million men," wrote the ambitious general, "My glory is declining. This little corner of Europe is too small to supply it. We must go East. All the great men of the world have there acquired their celebrity."[2]

Though France's state coffers were depleted from years of war, the government green-lighted Napoleon's campaign. The five members of the Directory were more than happy to get rid of the young star who they viewed as a political threat. "The general in chief of the Army of the Orient will seize Egypt; he will chase the English from all their possessions in the Orient," read Napoleon's marching orders. "He will then cut the Isthmus of Suez and take all necessary measures in order to assure the free and exclusive possession of the Red Sea for the French Republic."[3]

Bidding farewell to his wife Joséphine de Beauharnais, Napoleon set sail from Toulon on the flagship *L'Orient* with several thousand crew members and soldiers. In addition to tons of explosives and 120 cannons, the former royal navy's *Dauphin Royal* featured a ballroom, an elegant red damask suite for Napoleon, and a shipboard library of several hundred volumes.

Among the works were Napoleon's favorite ancient writer Plutarch, along with Livy, Virgil, and Homer, Arrian's account of Alexander the Great's campaigns, and the Koran. Interestingly, the Koran was shelved with political titles along with the Bible and Montesquieu.[4] In preparing for the invasion, Napoleon had studied the Comte de Volney's description of his years in Egypt.[5] During the Italian campaign, he had permanently checked out all the books about the Orient from the Milan library.

Napoleon jotted down book passages he found especially interesting. According to biographer Emil Ludwig, his notes ranged from foot-racing in ancient Crete and Hellenic fortresses in Asia Minor to the military exploits of Prussia's Frederick the Great. Tellingly one of the passages he copied, from Raynal's *Philosophical History of the Two Indies,* addressed why Alexander the Great had chosen Egypt as the center of his empire. Napoleon memorized the passage so well, writes Ludwig, he could still recite it by heart three decades later.[6]

With the invasion, Napoleon was deliberately following in some of history's largest footsteps. Starting with Alexander the Great, superstars of the Greco-Roman worlds had conquered Egypt. When the twenty-four-year-old Macedonian king invaded today's Middle East in the fall of 332 B.C.E., Egypt was part of the Persian Empire. Virtually unopposed, Alexander led forty thousand soldiers across the Nile to the capital, Memphis. He founded a city on the Mediterranean in his name, Alexandria, Egypt's future capital.

In addition to his army, Alexander brought along a team of philosophers, geographers, and historians. Fascinated by the Nile, he sent a small exploratory expedition accompanied by Callisthenes, the campaign's official historian. Alexander's tutor Aristotle reported on the Nile's magical properties, crediting the river for the fertility of Egyptian women who supposedly often had twins after just eight months of pregnancy. Soon after the conquest of Egypt, Alexander marched east in pursuit of Persia's Darius III.

In 323 B.C.E., when Alexander died of an unknown disease in Babylon, the thirty-three-year-old ruled most of the known world. His brilliant general and childhood friend Ptolemy went on to found the Ptolemaic dynasty in Egypt, a wealthy kingdom that would also control modern-day Libya, Israel, Jordan, Lebanon, Syria, and Cyprus, as well as the entire southern coast of Asia Minor. Under Ptolemy, the former fishing village of Alexandria became a cultural and commercial powerhouse.

After Julius Caesar's assassination, Cleopatra left Rome and took up with the popular general Mark Antony, married to Octavian's sister Octavia. Together they would have three children. Joining forces against Octavian, the power couple endured a months-long standoff with their rival in 31 B.C.E. at Actium on the northwest coast of Greece. Cleopatra finally sailed back to Alexandria with her forces, followed by Anthony, handing Octavian an easy win. Octavian pursued his rivals to Egypt, capturing Alexandria in 30 B.C.E.

With his soldiers deserting him and believing Cleopatra was dead, Antony committed suicide by stabbing himself. He died in the arms of Cleopatra, who soon ended her own life and the Ptolemaic dynasty. Egypt became a Roman province under Octavian, who had Cleopatra's son with Caesar assassinated and her children with Antony removed.[7]

While visiting Alexander the Great's tomb in his eponymous city, Octavian asked to view the mummified body. After crowning Alexander's head with a gold diadem, Octavian bent down to kiss his forehead, reportedly breaking off part of his nose.[8] Alexander was lauded by the Romans who gave him the sobriquet "Great" around 200 B.C.E. According to Plutarch, Julius Caesar wept at the sight of Alexander's statue in Spain. Caesar's head was placed atop a statue of Alexander in Rome. During Rome's late imperial period, Alexander's portraits continued to circulate on coins.[9]

Egypt joined Sardinia and Sicily as Rome's breadbasket, supplying a third of the Empire's requirements. Following harvests in April and May, grain ships from Alexandria reached Rome's ports by early June—some five million bushels a year.[10] The Romans also imported water from the Nile for religious rites.

With its promise of immortality, Egypt's religion was another popular export. The Triumvirate erected a temple to Isis, wife of Osiris, on Capitoline Hill.[11] Caligula rebuilt the Iseum on the Campus Martius that featured temples to Isis and serapeums to her consort, the Greco-Egyptian deity Serapis. Nero introduced Isiac feast days into the Roman calendar, Vespasian visited Alexandria's Serapeum, and Titus traveled to the Serapeum in Memphis. Isiac cults peaked during the Severan era, starting with Emperor Septimius Severus who converted in Egypt. Caracalla built a temple to Serapis on the Quirinal, decorated his baths with the heads of Isis and Serapis, and had himself depicted wearing the *nemes*, headdress of the pharoahs.

Like the ancient Greeks, Romans were infatuated with Egyptian art and culture. Egyptian art reached Rome as early as the third century B.C.E., first as gifts from the ruling Ptolemies and later as exotic home décor for Rome's elite. The new temples in Rome dedicated to Isis and Serapis displayed statues imported from Egypt as well as Egyptian-style sculptures made in Italy. After Rome's conquest in 30 B.C.E., Augustus brought back many spoils as symbols of his victory, along with artists and scribes.

Their work inspired copies by Roman artists. Frescoes of the Nile covered walls of villas; furniture, silverware, and glass vessels sported Egyptian motifs. Private gardens boasted sculptures of hippopotami, crocodiles, and Egyptian deities.[12] Romans incorporated Egyptian art and culture, combining references to Egyptian motifs and fashion with Roman traditions like the portrait bust.

Egyptomania quickly spread beyond Rome. Private villas in Pompeii, Herculaneum, and Stabiae were also decorated with frescoes evoking Egypt's exotic landscape, religion, and people. As the cult of Isis took off in southern Italy, sanctuaries dedicated to the goddess sprung up. For example, a temple of Isis in Pompeii featured works imported from Egypt along with Roman statues and wall paintings with Egyptian themes.

In 18 C.E., a Roman geologist discovered a dark purple stone called porphyry in the remote eastern desert of Egypt. Rome's emperors built imperial stone quarries at Mons Porphyrites and nearby Mons Claudianus, known for its stunning black marble. From the mountainsides, stone columns were quarried and hauled across the desert to the Nile for voyages to Rome. Nero appears to have been the first Roman emperor to be entombed in a porphyry sarcophagus. Hadrian's Pantheon was built with gray granite from Mons Porphyrites; its porphyry decorated the inlaid panels.

Of all Rome's emperors, Hadrian was the most smitten by Egypt. Two visits (117 and 129–130 C.E.) inspired him to dedicate a Serapeum at the Roman port of Ostia and recreate the Canopus, a sanctuary in the Nile Delta near Alexandria, at his sprawling imperial palace in Tivoli some twenty miles outside of Rome. Dedicated to Isis and Serapis, Canopus had become a cult center of the Ptolemaic Kingdom and Roman Egypt. Hadrian's replica featured a long pool representing a branch of the Nile surrounded by a colonnade with a Temple of Serapis dug into the hillside.

During Hadrian's second visit to Egypt, his handsome young lover Antinous drowned in the Nile under mysterious circumstances. Born in

Claudiopolis (today's Bolu, Turkey) in the Roman province of Bithynia, Antinous had met the forty-something emperor as a teenager. The bereft Hadrian founded a new Roman cult featuring his companion as a semi-divine hero equated with Osiris, Egyptian god of the underworld. On the site where Antinous died, Hadrian built the city of Antinoöpolis that became a cult center for the worship of Osiris-Antinous. Games commemorating Antinous were held in various locations including Antinoöpolis and Athens. For his villa at Tivoli, Hadrian commissioned numerous statues of Antinous as an Egyptian deity, and dozens more with pharaonic themes.

Also in his lover's memory, Hadrian installed an obelisk in the villa's sanctuary. The arrival of spectacular obelisks from pharaonic sanctuaries helped fuel Rome's Egyptomania. Just before Egypt's annexation by Rome in 30 B.C.E., Cleopatra had an obelisk brought to Alexandria. To celebrate the twentieth anniversary of Rome's conquest of Egypt, Augustus ordered two additional obelisks moved from Heliopolis near Cairo to Alexandria. To get the two-hundred-plus-ton Aswan granite monoliths to Italy, Roman engineers used Egyptian technology to build a seagoing version of Nile vessels. Rowed by three hundred oarsmen, the double-ship with three hulls was so long that it took up a large part of the left side of the harbor at Ostia.[13]

Often dedicated to sun gods and inscribed with hieroglyphics, obelisks held great religious meaning for ancient Egyptians. Augustus used the soaring monuments to proclaim his own divine descent. According to Pliny, an obelisk on the Campus Martius served as the pointer for a colossal open-air sundial positioned to cast its shadow on the Ara Pacis (Altar of Peace) on Augustus's birthday. The message, explains Susan Sorek, was that Augustus's reign of peace was predestined at his birth; that his rule was divine.[14] Augustus installed the second obelisk at the central barrier of the Circus Maximus horse and chariot racetrack. After Augustus's death, two more Egyptian obelisks were placed by his circular mausoleum near the Ara Pacis.

Rome's obelisk craze continued under Augustus's successors. Eleven more were transported to Rome, six of which were ordered by Roman emperors.[15] But with the fall of Rome and the rise of Christianity, the neglected monuments fell into ruin. In the sixteenth and eighteenth centuries, Popes

Sixtus V and Pius VI turned the ancient monuments into powerful Church symbols. They added crosses to the tops of many obelisks, moving them to key sites throughout the city like the Lateran Palace, St. Peter's Square, and the Piazza del Quirinale.

⚜

In his youth, Napoleon preferred the ancient Spartans to Alexander the Great. But before landing his fleet at Alexandria, Napoleon informed his soldiers that "the first city [they would] encounter had been built by Alexander [who did everything in a day] and [that they would find] at each footstep great memories worthy of exciting the imagination of the French." In a letter to his brother Joseph, he invoked the Macedonian king again, writing, ". . . this land so fertile can witness the rebirth of the centuries of Alexander and Ptolemy."[16]

Like Alexander, Napoleon saw himself as a civilizing hero, liberating the people of the Middle East with a new kingdom created "from the ruins of an ancient one." Before the Egypt campaign, Napoleon wrote a childhood friend: "This country seems to offer me the most fortunate chances; the people who inhabit it, cruelly harassed by the Beys and the Mamelukes, will see with delight a brave army and a renowned general labour to extricate them from the encroachment of their oppressors. Milder laws, better treatment, a general affranchisement, will easily bind them to my standard."[17]

Though ancient Egypt had long captivated the imagination of Europe, the civilization millennia older than ancient Greece and Rome remained a mystery. Between the Crusades and Napoleon's invasion, few Europeans had actually explored the region. Little was known about the Land of the Nile except for its powerful pharaohs and their monumental pyramids and obelisks.

Like Alexander the Great, Napoleon brought to Egypt a civilian force known as the savants. Mathematician Gaspard Monge and chemist Claude-Louis Berthollet, fresh from seizing art for Napoleon in Italy, spent two months conscripting colleagues for the Scientific and Artistic Commission of Egypt. The 150 member brain trust included the inventor Nicolas-Jacques Conté, physicist Jean-Baptiste Joseph Fourier, and engineer Edme-François Jomard. The small cadre of artists included Pierre-Joseph

Redouté and Dominique-Vivant Denon. Napoleon's soldiers would dub the scholars "the mules."

On June 9, 1798, after three rocky weeks at sea, the French armada made a brief detour at Malta. Since the Crusades, the Mediterranean island had been ruled by the Knights of Saint John, a religious-military order. Malta's port, Valletta, was protected by a heavily armored fortress. The Knights commanded some ten thousand conscripted, unmotivated Maltese. After just a day of fighting, Malta surrendered. Within a week, Napoleon issued dozens of edicts, declared religious equality, and freed the slaves (some of whom became translators for his Egypt campaign). To finance the upcoming campaign, Monge and Berthollet looted art, weapons, silver plate, and gold.

When the French fleet neared Alexandria on June 22, Napoleon finally disclosed the top secret mission to his troops. Aboard each ship, his captains read the proclamation: "Soldiers! You are going to begin a conquest of which the effects on civilization and world commerce are incalculable! You will give the English a most sensible blow, which will be followed up with their destruction."[18] Like Rome's generals, Napoleon promised his soldiers acres of land upon their return.

Before this, his new Army of the Orient would need to defeat a historic fighting force. Since 1517, the Mamelukes had been surrogate rulers of Egypt under the Ottoman sultan. Torn from their families as children by the Ayyubid Dynasty in the twelfth century, the Eurasians were sold in Damascas, Istanbul, and Cairo and trained as professional slave soldiers. Elite horsemen, the Mamelukes had defended Islam against the Mongols and Crusaders. But their rule was inefficient and unpopular, a fact working in Napoleon's favor, writes Ronald Fritze.[19]

On the afternoon of July 1, the French fleet arrived at the bay of Alexandria. As the capital of Ptolemaic Egypt, the city had been the intellectual center of the ancient world with a celebrated library and a half a million people. Peering through a telescope at Pompey's Column and the minarets, Denon could not contain his excitement. "It was there, said I, thinking of Cleopatra, of Caesar, and of Anthony, that the empire of glory was sacrificed to the empire of voluptuousness," he wrote.[20]

In one regard, Napoleon's timing was fortunate. Britain's admiral Horatio Nelson had left just two days earlier in pursuit of the French fleet.

But with its granite boulders and thrashing sea, Alexandria's harbor was notorious for destroying ships. To help guide sailors, Ptolemy had built a soaring lighthouse on the island of Pharos, one of the Seven Wonders of the Ancient World. Napoleon made the fatal decision of disembarking his soldiers in a thunderstorm. As thousands of his soldiers climbed down ladders and ropes, many of the rowboats capsized, throwing the men into the swells to drown. Napoleon didn't flinch. According to Denon, "not a muscle moved" on the general's face.[21]

After two days in the harbor, Denon and his fellow savants disembarked. They found the fabled city of antiquity impoverished, reduced to a population of six thousand. Like Alexander, Napoleon was met with little interest from the locals, and proceeded to march his army across the Sahara to Cairo. During the five-day trek across the desert, hundreds of his soldiers died of heatstroke in the scorching sun.[22]

On July 21, three weeks after landing in Alexandria, Napoleon's army faced the Mamelukes at the Battle of the Pyramids. The fact that the pyramids were not actually visible from the battlefield did not stop him from rallying his troops with the famous line: "Soldiers! From atop these pyramids, forty centuries of history look down upon you!" Led by Murad Bey, six thousand Mameluke fighters charged at the French, sabers and pistols drawn. But their bravery and equestrian skills were no match for French weapons. Organized in squares with rifles at the sides, artillery at the corners, and cavalry inside, the French waited until the last moment before crushing the Mamelukes. In the one-hour battle, the French lost thirty men; the Mamelukes five to six thousand.

Three days later, Napoleon's army entered Cairo in a victory procession through a triumphal arch in the city's main square depicting the Battle of the Pyramids. As booty, Napoleon was presented with magnificent Mameluke harnesses upholstered in red velvet with gold embroidery, and red cotton saddle seats dotted with flowers and crescents and bordered with gilt copper studs. The gilt copper spurs were so sharp that the Mamelukes used them as weapons.[23]

One week after the victory, disaster struck. On the night of August 1, Admiral Horatio Nelson caught the French fleet by surprise at Aboukir Bay, a few miles east of Alexandria. In the ensuing Battle of the Nile, eleven

French warships and two frigates were blown to pieces; 1,700 men were killed and another 1,500 wounded (only two warships and two frigates escaped). The victory confirmed Nelson's status as England's greatest hero and Napoleon's greatest nemesis.

Without naval support and reinforcements, Napoleon and his troops were marooned. Food and ammunition would need to come from Egypt. Replicating the political model he'd used in Italy, Napoleon founded the Egyptian republic with provinces headed by generals. He became the benefactor of holidays and festivals—like Muhammad's birthday and the festival of the Nile. Like Alexander, Napoleon tried to achieve his goals by using religion.

By late October, a mob of several thousand staged a bloody uprising in Cairo. The rebellion ended when Napoleon turned his cannons on the Al-Azhar mosque. Meanwhile, the Ottoman sultan declared war on France. He dispatched two armies, one by sea to Alexandria with British support and a second by land from Syria. In February 1799, Napoleon marched into Syria with twelve thousand soldiers. On March 7, he conquered Jaffa, massacring some 2,400 men.[24] After this, Napoleon continued onto Acre. In the ensuing defeats, hundreds of French soldiers were killed; hundreds more were victims of bubonic plague.

⚜

After the Battle of the Pyramids, the surviving Mamelukes retreated south with their leader Murad Bey. In August, Napoleon ordered General Louis-Charles Desaix to chase Bey to Upper Egypt where he was raising a new army. With three thousand soldiers, Desaix embarked on a nine-month manhunt up the Nile past Aswan, over to the Red Sea, and back to Cairo. Vivant Denon enthusiastically went along, sketchpad in hand.

At fifty-one, Denon was among the eldest savant. Born in January 1747 at Givry near Chalon-sur-Saône in Burgundy to a family of minor nobility, Vivant de Non studied drawing in Lyon before moving to Paris to learn etching. There he landed a position as Louis XV's Gentleman of the King's Chamber. He was also curator of the medal and gemstone collection of the king's mistress, Madame de Pompadour, to whom he gave drawing lessons. De Non's charm and wit helped him advance in a series of diplomatic positions. He met Frederick the Great at Potsdam, Voltaire at Ferney, and Catherine the Great in St. Petersburg where he was recalled after a failed attempt to free a jailed French actress. During a posting at Naples, Denon became an avid art collector, filling the French embassy with ancient Etruscan vases, paintings, sculptures, and medals (he sold over five hundred Etruscan vases to Louis XVI).

In the fall of 1788, Denon arrived in Venice where he taught engraving and collected drawings. He also fell in love with the married Greek-born *saloniste* Isabella Teotochi Albrizzi. When the French Revolution erupted, he was expelled from Venice as a suspected spy. Denon returned to France to try to save his family's property from government confiscation. Denon himself was saved from the guillotine thanks to painter Jacques-Louis David. He quickly shifted his allegiance to the republican cause, changing the spelling of his aristocratic name to Denon.

While frequenting the Paris Salons, Denon befriended Joséphine de Beauharnais, recently married to the up-and-coming General Napoleon Bonaparte. The former diplomat wangled an invitation to be the official artist of the Egypt campaign. The chance to explore and sketch Egypt's fabled monuments was the thrill of a lifetime. "I had from my infancy wished to make a voyage to Egypt," he would write.[25]

Since the collapse of the Roman Empire, few Westerners had seen the ruins of Upper Egypt. The site of the ancient monuments left Denon completely awestruck. So did Egyptian women, who he compared to statues of the Egyptian goddess Isis. Often Denon would be up by dawn, drawing before the troops marched south. Other times, he worked on a pad held on a drawing board across his saddle, dodging enemy musket balls. "I most often made [drawings] on my knee, or standing, or even on horseback," he recalled. "I never finished a single one to my satisfaction, as for an entire year I never once had a table straight enough to set a ruler on."[26]

Among Denon's subjects was Antinoöpolis, built by Hadrian on the east bank of the Nile (the well-preserved city was dismantled in the nineteenth century to build a sugar refinery). "At last I have beheld the portico of Hermopolis. Its massive ruins provided me with my first view of the splendour of Egypt's colossal architecture," he raved. "On every stone of this edifice, I seem to see the words posterity and eternity engraved."[27]

Denon wasn't the only one impressed. At the ruins of ancient Thebes, he recorded that "The whole army, suddenly and with one accord, stood in amazement at the sight of its scattered ruins, and clapped their hands in delight, as if the end and object of their glorious toils, and the complete conquest of Egypt, were accomplished and secured by taking possession of the splendid remains of this ancient metropolis."[28]

The artist's fascination for the ruins was contagious. "I made a drawing of this first sight, as if fearing that this image of Thebes would elude me," wrote Denon. "And through their good-natured enthusiasm, the soldiers provided their knees as a worktable and their bodies as protection from the sun's ardent rays beating down on the scene I intended to paint for my readers, so that they could partake of my emotion in the presence of such great objects, and share the spectacle of an atmosphere charged with the passion of an army of soldiers whose delicate sensibility made me happy to be their companion, proud to be French."[29]

Denon discovered another awe-inspiring sight, the Temple of Dendera, half-buried in sand. Begun by the Ptolemies in the first century B.C.E. and finished by the Romans, the massive temple featured columns and capitals representing the goddess Hathor. "I felt that I was in the sanctuary of the arts and sciences . . ." wrote Denon. "Never did the labour of man show me the human race in such a splendid point of view. In the ruins of Tentyra [Roman for Dendera] the Egyptians appeared to me giants."[30] In a small chapel, Denon found a circular zodiac adorning the ceiling.

General Desaix's troops moved south to Esna, then Edfu, where Denon saw "the sublime temple of Apollinopolis . . . the most beautiful of all Egypt." In Denon's opinion, the Egyptians had surpassed the Greeks in architecture. He noted that the capitals on their columns "borrowed nothing from other peoples," but used local material, like papyrus, lotus, palm, and reed for ornament.

By early February 1799, the regiment arrived at Syene (Aswan), and Denon finally had time to sketch. From Elephantine, the lush island opposite Syene before the Nile's first cataracts, he saw a nilometer mentioned by the Greek geographer and historian Strabo. Next came the small island of

Philae, the ancient entry point into Egypt. After the locals were evicted, Denon drew the island's temples. "The next day was the finest to me of my whole travels," he wrote. "I possessed seven or eight monuments in the space of six hundred yards, and could examine them quite at my ease . . . I was alone in full leisure, and could make my drawings without interruption."

Of all the monuments, Denon was most enamored with Philae's Kiosk of Trajan. Standing over fifty feet tall, the rectangular pavilion boasted fourteen columns with elegantly carved flower capitals originally supporting a wood roof. Decorations on two screen walls depicted the Roman emperor Trajan making offerings to Isis, Osiris, and Horus (along with the temple of Isis, the Kiosk was relocated in the 1960s from Philae to Agilika Island after construction of the Aswan High Dam).

"If ever the French were to take a monument back to Paris, this would be the one," Denon wrote, for "it would give a palpable proof of the noble simplicity of Egyptian architecture, and would show, in a striking manner, that it is character, and not extent alone, which gives dignity to an edifice."[31]

By late February, Desaix's soldiers headed back north, with Murad Bey ahead of them. This gave Denon another chance to sketch. In May, Denon revisited Dendera and drew the zodiac. "It would appear to be the lot of Egyptian monuments of every description to resist alike the ravages of time and man," he concluded.[32]

Later that month, Denon ran into a scientific expedition dispatched by Napoleon. Headed by engineer Pierre-Simon Girard, the group was making a hydrographic study of the upper Nile. After a trip over to the Red Sea and other excursions, Denon arrived back in Cairo in July 1799. Napoleon too had retreated to Cairo, after failing to capture Acre in Syria. The general was so impressed with Denon's sketches and watercolors, he immediately authorized a survey of Upper Egypt.

But as the architects and engineers traveled up the Nile on double-masted boats, their leader was sailing the opposite direction toward France.

While Napoleon was in Egypt, France had returned to war with Austria, Britain, and Russia. In November 1798, Ferdinand IV of Naples had taken advantage of the power vacuum and seized Rome. With its kidnapping of Pius VI, the Directory had managed to turn the elderly pontiff into a martyr. At home, there were rumors of an impending coup against the

Directory. On top of the political turmoil, Napoleon was embroiled in a personal crisis. Devastated by word that Joséphine was cheating on him, he had taken up in Egypt with the wife of one of his cavalrymen.

Before leaving Cairo at midnight on August 23, Napoleon left General Jean-Baptiste Kléber a note promoting him to commander of the campaign. It was a very different goodbye than that of Alexander the Great, who after six months in Egypt, reviewed his forces and bid them farewell. Napoleon slipped away, leaving an army decimated by casualties and plague.

After three days on the Nile, Napoleon sailed from the coast in the small ship *Muiron*. Among the handful of trusted companions were his brother-in-law Joachim Murat, Monge, Berthollet, and Denon who brought with him amulets and ancient fragments. Also onboard was a gift from the Sheikh of Cairo—eighteen-year-old Raza Roustam, a Mameluke kidnapped in the Caucasus and sold in the slave markets of Constantinople. For the next fifteen years, Roustam would be Napoleon's bodyguard and valet.

In early October, after crossing along the coast of Tunisia, the *Muiron* arrived in the harbor at Ajaccio, Corsica. An hour later, Napoleon disembarked and visited his family's home, admiring improvements made by his mother and Joseph. The grape and fig harvest was underway. The weeklong visit to his birthplace would be his last. With English ships near Toulon, the *Muiron* set a course for Fréjus in Provence.

From the destruction of the French naval fleet, defeats by the Ottomans, and bubonic plague, Napoleon's fourteen months in the Middle East were an abject military disaster. Yet in an echo of the great military leaders of ancient Greece and Rome, he arrived home to cheering crowds. Like Octavian turning the long standoff at Actium into an epic victory, Napoleon spun his Army of the Orient's blunders into triumphs over both the Ottomans and the British. As he had after his Italian campaign in 1796, Napoleon ordered commemorative medals struck of the Egypt campaign, portraying himself as Mercury.

The self-promotion was so effective that when Napoleon returned to Paris, he was seen as a national hero, the only person who could save France from invasion, economic disaster, and the corrupt Directory regime. Collaborating with two disaffected Directors, Emmanuel Sieyès and Roger Ducos, Napoleon agreed to supply military force for a coup d'état.

Using the threat of a conspiracy as a pretext, France's national assemblies were moved from Paris to the formal royal palace of Saint-Cloud; the Council of the Ancients to the Apollo Gallery, and the Council of Five Hundred to the Orangery. On November 9, 1799, Napoleon's younger brother Lucien Bonaparte, president of the Council of Five Hundred, announced the resignation of Paul Barras, the incompetent head of the Directory since 1795.

Wearing a saber inscribed "Armée d'Égypte," Napoleon marched into the chambers with four uniformed grenadiers and declared that he was staging a coup. Enraged council members shouted "Down with the dictator! Outlaw!" As men approached him with knives and called for his death sentence, Napoleon was hustled out by his grenadiers. Napoleon ordered his bayonet-wielding soldiers back to the Orangery, causing the legislators to flee, some jumping out of the windows.

With the coup spiraling downward, Lucien took control, delaying a vote against his brother. He managed to turn the attack on Napoleon into a vote of confidence. By the end of the night, Lucien convinced the Elders of the council to replace the Directory with a Consulate. A few hours later, Napoleon accepted the appointment as a consul in a new triumvirate, like Rome's triumvirate of Caesar, Pompey, and Crassus.

On December 13, over three million voters ratified a new constitution. Drawing on terminology from the Roman Republic, the constitution created a three-man Consulate along with a Tribunate to debate laws and a senate with the power to change the constitution. Consuls Sieyès and Ducos were replaced with legal expert Jean-Jacques-Régis de Cambacérès and politician Charles-François Lebrun. The following February, a referendum confirmed Napoleon as first consul. He was the most powerful person in France with complete executive authority.

Meanwhile, the three-year Egypt expedition was coming to a costly, embarrassing end. In August 1801, General Jacques Menou surrendered to the British, handing over all archeological finds. The most important object was the Rosetta Stone, discovered by the French near the town of Rosetta on the Nile river delta. The three-foot gray granite slab was carved with the same text in Greek, demotic (Egyptian script), and hieroglyphics. The French also handed over a sarcophagus from Alexandria, which they believed to be that of Alexander the Great. A rumor spread that Napoleon planned to be buried in the coffin, which was later determined to have belonged to Pharaoh Nectanebo II. With its naval fleet destroyed by Nelson, French forces had to be evacuated on British ships.

In the spring of 1800, when Napoleon was asked by his private secretary Bourrienne to name his favorite ancient commander, he chose Alexander. "I look upon the siege of Tyre, the conquest of Egypt, and the journey to the Oasis of Ammon, as a decided proof of the genius of that great captain. . . . By persevering in the taking of Tyre, he secured his communications with Greece, the country he loved as dearly as I love France, and in whose glory he placed his own. By taking possession of the rich province of Egypt, he forced Darius to come to defend or deliver it, and, in so doing, to march halfway to meet him. By representing himself as the son of Jupiter, he worked upon the ardent feelings of the orientals in a way that powerfully seconded his designs. Though he died at thirty-three, what a name he has left behind him!"[33]

In his apartment at Saint-Cloud, Napoleon would hang a painting from the Louvre. Stolen from Munich in 1800, *The Battle of Alexander at Issus* by the sixteenth century German painter Albrecht Altdorfer depicted the Macedonian's victory over Persia's Darius III. After Issus, Alexander conquered Egypt.

Napoleon would call his time in Egypt the best years of his life.[34] "In Egypt, I found myself freed from the obstacles of an irksome civilization," Napoleon told Madame de Rémusat, Joséphine's lady-in-waiting. "I was filled with dreams. I saw myself founding a new religion, marching into Asia, riding an elephant, a turban on my head and in my hand a new Koran that I would have composed to suit my needs."[35]

THREE
PONTIFEX MAXIMUS

On a brisk December morning with wind whipping his robes, Barnaba Chiaramonti, Bishop of Imola took a seat in the bobbing black gondola. As the boat pulled away from the Riva degli Schiavoni, the diminutive prelate glanced back at the columns of San Todaro, the Lion of St. Mark, and the Doge's Palace, minus a doge.

Before him lay the stretch of sea known as St. Mark's basin, between the Doge's Palace and St. Mark's square on one side and the islands of San Giorgio Maggiore and Giudecca on the other. Once Europe's busiest port, all merchant ships headed to and from Europe had to pass through here. Now gondolas and sailing ships dotted the water.

Though many had tried to invade Venice, it had always been saved by its unusual geography and location—islands two and a half miles off the mainland, surrounded by two hundred square miles of water.[1] Now behind its beautiful façade, Venice was crumbling. In April 1797, the French fleet had arrived at the Lido. A month later, after eleven proud centuries, the ancient Republic of Venice surrendered.

That fall, with French troops approaching Vienna, Austria signed the Treaty of Campo Formio. Without consulting the Directory, Napoleon dictated the terms, preserving most of his conquests in northern Italy. To compensate for its losses in Lombardy, the Austrians gained Istria, Dalmatia, and the Republic of Venice less the Ionian Islands. After a millennium, Napoleon Bonaparte had reduced the former naval and commercial power to a Habsburg province.

From the gondola, Barnaba Chiaramonti took in the splendid view of the tiny island of San Giorgio Maggiore. With its classical white stone façade gleaming above the blue water, Andrea Palladio's church appeared to float on the lagoon. Like the church, San Giorgio Maggiore's bell tower was also classical—but of a more recent vintage. Rebuilt eight years earlier after the original fifteenth-century campanile collapsed and killed a monk, the tower was said to have the best view in all of Venice. On a clear day, one could even make out the snow-covered Alps. The brick and marble bell tower was a visual counterpart to the more famous campanile of St. Mark's across the basin. Yet from the start, the abbey's Benedictines had always operated independently from the Bishop of Venice.

During the reign of Emperor Augustus, small rivers led from the mainland to San Giorgio Maggiore, then called "the island of Memmia" after its Roman owner, the Memmo family. A small church was built here, across from Piazza San Marco, called San Giorgio Maggiore. In the late tenth century, Venice's doge gave the marshy, cypress-covered island to the Benedictines. Over the next eight centuries, San Giorgio Maggiore became one of the wealthiest Benedictine monasteries with collections of art and manuscripts.

Along with riches, Venice endured its share of tragedy. As Palladio's church on San Giorgio Maggiore was going up in 1576, the maritime power was struck by a plague that wiped out one third of its population. To mark the unspeakable loss, the Paduan architect was hired to design a church for the nearby island of Guidecca dedicated to Christ the Redeemer, Redentore. Venice's deliverance from the plague was commemorated with an annual festival in which the doge and his court crossed the water in a flotilla of boats to visit the church. Together, the islands of San Giorgio Maggiore and Guidecca and their remarkable Palladian churches marked Venice's southernmost boundary.

Flanking the central portal of San Giorgio Maggiore were statues of Saint George and Saint Stephen, to whom the church was dedicated. Instead of a cross, the dome was topped with a copper and wood figure of St. George, some thirteen feet tall. Inside the church were the relics of St. Stephen, the first Christian martyr, given to the Benedictines in 1109. Until the recent invasion, St. Stephen's feast day, December 26, had been an even bigger holiday in the Republic than Christmas. The doge had led the annual ceremonial procession, rowing out to the Church for Mass sung by the resident Benedictine monks and choristers from nearby St. Mark's.

Through the centuries, the beautiful abbey had welcomed many celebrities—from King Henri III of France and Queen Casimira of Poland to Austrian emperors Joseph II, Francesco I, and Frederick I. In 1443, exiled Cosimo de' Medici took refuge here with his court and friends, including architect Michelozzo Michelozzi who built a library for the Benedictines. Now Barnaba Chiaramonti's visit would also prove historic.

Though the papacy had been vacant for three months, Cardinal Chiaramonti had only learned of Pius VI's death in early October. He had arrived in Venice ahead of the conclave to attend Pius's Novena. Nine days of public Masses were held at St. Mark's Basilica for the repose of the pontiff's soul.[2] French troops had taken the elderly pope from Rome to Sienna in February 1798, just days after the Republic of Rome was proclaimed. From there, Pius was moved to Florence in May, then to Valence in July where he died a month later. On January 30, 1800, Pius was buried in an unadorned grave in a cemetery in Valence.

Since the great Western Schism ended in 1417, every papal conclave had been held in Rome. But with Neapolitan king Ferdinand II occupying the Eternal City since the end of September, the College of Cardinals had to find an alternative location. Some cardinals fled Rome for Venice. Others, including Cardinal Albani, Dean of the Sacred College, sought refuge in Naples.

Habsburg emperor Francis II, head of Catholic Austria, offered the isolated San Giorgio Maggiore to the cardinals, agreeing to pay for most of the conclave, along with Spain, and to guarantee its safety. Because of the political turmoil, the turnout was the lowest since 1534. Only thirty-four of the forty-six living cardinals made it to Venice. For many, the trip posed serious risks and challenges. Twenty-four votes were required to elect a new pope. The Benedictine monks moved into temporary quarters to make room for the arriving cardinals. Monsignor Ercole Consalvi was appointed secretary of the conclave.

Barnaba Chiaramonti entered the dignified church with its lofty transept, enormous dome, and colossal Corinthian columns. Palladio, who did not live to see the church finished, considered white the color most pleasing to God. In the 1590s, the decade after the architect's death, the Benedictines began decorating its simple interior. Jacopo Tintoretto and his workshop created a series of altarpieces placed in Palladio's marble frames. One of Tintoretto's last works, the *Entombment* (1594), was hung in the Chapel of the Dead where the abbots of the monastery were buried.

Before commissioning Palladio to replace the Gothic-style church, the Benedictines hired him to design a new dining room. A low wide flight of stairs led to the vestibule where an imposing door recalled the Roman basilica, San Salvatore di Spoleto. Inside the impressive hall featured a barrel-vaulted ceiling and three large windows. Now the east wall above the abbot's head table was empty.

In September 1797, French troops stormed into the monastery and ripped the *Wedding at Cana* off the wall of the refectory. To get Paolo Veronese's monumental one-and-a-half-ton work (22 by 32.5 feet) to Paris, it was cut in half and stitched back together in France, where it was displayed at the Louvre on November 8, 1798. Venice was still in shock by the plunder of its art treasures, which included the four magnificent bronze horses from the façade of St. Mark's Basilica. The monastery also lost Rocco Marconi's *Christ and the Adulteress*, Cima da Conegliano's *Saint Jerome in the Desert* (1495), and two small panels depicting four pairs of saints.

The Benedictines had specified the subject of the purloined painting, the wedding banquet at Cana in Galilee when Jesus miraculously turned water into wine. The contract called for Veronese to fill the entire wall opposite the room's entrance, using precious pigments like ultramarine, and complete the canvas in time for the September 1563 "*festa de la madona*." By adding columns and other classical architectural elements, Veronese created the impression that the picture was an extension of the space. Palladio's cornice created a framing device for the top of Veronese's canvas.

Veronese set his colorful composition in Renaissance Venice, complete with lavish table settings and ornate costumes, music and conversation. Guests and servants surround the serene central figures of Jesus and Mary who are joined at the table for dessert by twenty-one men and four women, including contemporaries of the artist.[3] The work features a staggering 132 figures. The orchestra is made up of artists with Veronese playing the viola, Tintoretto on the violin, and Jacopo Bassano the flute. The bearded man leaning toward Veronese and playing the viola may be the architect Palladio.[4]

The refectory was a no-talking zone, a place for silence and contemplation. Above the entrance to the dining room, Veronese painted two angels, now lost, that are thought to have held a card inscribed SILENTIUM.[5] Finished in a year, *Wedding at Cana* earned the thirty-four-year-old painter 324 ducats, food, and a barrel of wine. After the collaboration, Palladio asked Veronese to work with him again at the Villa Barbaro at Maser.

Accolades soon began for the work. Two years after the painting's completion, a resident monk named Benedetto Guido wrote: "[a]ll the sculptors come and the painters to admire it three, four, and six times . . . and PAOLO [sic] is praised with eternal fame."[6]

Wedding at Cana was so renowned that people went to San Giorgio just to see it. Cosimo III de' Medici claimed it alone was worth a trip to Venice. Princes requested copies. In December 1705, to avoid the crowds, the friars limited the number of visitors to the island traveling to see the painting. Almost a century later, visitors headed to Paris to experience the masterpiece with similar gusto.

⚜

Bergamo carver Gaspare Gatti furnished the large choir facing the Sacristy of San Giorgio Maggiore with some eighty-two walnut stalls. Flemish sculptor Albert Van der Brulle carved four dozen spectacular panels narrating the life of Saint Benedict, which included dolphin-riding cherubs. To the right of the choir, a door led to a dark, narrow spiral staircase.

Up this flight of stairs, Barnaba Chiaramonti and his fellow cardinals convened in a private chapel hidden from view. The chapel was originally conceived as a choir for the monks to pray at night. In the 1730s, an organ was acquired for the room. The high wooden seats folded down allowing the cardinals to stand with arm rests. The chairs are still inscribed with the names of each of the cardinals.

Above the high altar hung Venetian artist Vittore Carpaccio's 1516 *St. George and the Dragon*. Eight years earlier, Carpaccio had depicted St. George for a painting at the Scuola di San Giorgio degli Schiavoni, the seat of a confraternity built by wealthy Dalmatian merchants. Carpaccio created nine paintings depicting the lives of St. George, patron saint of the scuola, and St. Jerome, patron saint of Dalmatia.

For the chapel at San Giorgio Maggiore, Carpaccio took inspiration from Jacopo da Varazze's chronicle of the lives of the saints, the *Golden Legend*, a hugely popular religious work from the Middle Ages. Carpaccio included references to the monastery including St. Jerome in the upper left corner and St. Stephen being stoned to death on the top right. For the predella, Carpaccio depicted the martyrdom of St. George. According to legend, after converting to Christianity, the officer in the Guard of Emperor Diocletian was tortured by his fellow Roman soldiers.

The cardinals arrived at San Giorgio Maggiore deeply divided on the selection of a new pope. Austria's support for the conclave had come at a price. The Habsburgs wanted a pope who would not challenge its occupation of Venice and territories of the Papal States. As special envoy of the Austrian emperor, Cardinal Francesco Herzan von Harras's December 12 arrival was a major event. As reported by the *Venetian Gazette*, most of the prelature, along with many prominent Venetian and foreign figures, accompanied the cardinal in an afternoon procession of numerous gondolas from the Procuratie to San Giorgio Maggiore.[7]

Pius VI's nephew, Cardinal Braschi, led another faction promoting Cardinal Carlo Bellisomi, Bishop of Cesena, a protégé of Pius and Spain's first choice. Braschi garnered the support of Albani, Dean of the Sacred College, along with Cardinal York and Cardinal Chiaramonti. He also lobbied Cardinal Hertzan for his vote. Unbeknownst to Braschi, Herzan was secretly developing a bloc backing Cardinal Alessandro Mattei. The Austrians' first choice for pope, Mattei had signed the onerous Treaty of Tolentino on behalf of the papacy. Mattei and Bellisomi ended up locked in a stalemate. Meanwhile a minority bloc emerged led by Cardinal Leonardo Antonelli, supported by France's only representative, Jean-Sifrein Maury, the personal envoy of the future Louis XVIII, brother of France's beheaded king Louis XVI.

France's new first consul Napoleon Bonaparte also tried to influence the papal election. In February 1800, Prime Minister Talleyrand wrote to the Spanish Ambassador in Paris, asking the king of Spain to exercise his right of royal veto. The conclave, Talleyrand complained, was entirely under the domination of Austria with the non-Catholic governments of Britain and Russia participating. He reminded the Spaniards that the selection of the right candidate was in the interest of both France and Spain.

The Spanish minister replied that Spain's Cardinal Lorenzana was working under the king's instructions. In a March 30 letter to Talleyrand, the French Ambassador to the Spanish Court Charles-Jean-Marie Alquier repeated the king of Spain's reaction to Talleyrand's letter: "You don't know my people: I would be stoned to death and shred to pieces if I were to do what the First Consul is asking."[8]

After nearly three months of wheeling and dealing and threats of vetoes, the various factions fell apart. The impasse was almost unprecedented in the history of papal conclaves.[9] Finally in March, conclave secretary Consalvi proposed a compromise candidate, fifty-eight-year-old Barnaba Chiaramonti.

Like his relative Pius VI, Chiaramonti was born in the small northern Italian town of Cesena in Romagna. At fourteen, he entered the local Benedictine order taking the name Don Gregorio. Ordained a priest in 1765, Gregorio taught theology and philosophy at the abbey of S. Giovanni of Parma, a duchy that was undergoing political and ecclesiastical reforms under the Bourbons. After the accession of his relative Giovanni Angelo Braschi as Pius VI, Gregorio's career took off. He returned to Rome in 1775 as theology professor at the college of S. Anselmo. Three years after Pius VI named him Bishop of Tivoli, the forty-two-year-old was elevated to Cardinal and Bishop of Imola in Romagna. For the past several years, Chiaramonti had been carefully navigating the Papal States crisis.

When Napoleon's army invaded northern Italy in 1797, the Cardinal advised his diocese to submit to the new Cisalpine Republic. In his Christmas homily that year, he argued that there was no conflict between a democratic form of government and being a good Catholic: "Christian virtue makes men good democrats. . . . Equality is not an idea of philosophers but of Christ . . . and do not believe that the Catholic religion is against democracy." When Austrian forces replaced the French two years later, Chiaramonti called on his congregation to submit to the authority "of the victorious Austro-Russian armies" and the "unvanquished defender of the laws of the Church and of the Throne, the Most Pious Emperor Francis II."[10] At the same time that he counseled submission to the new regime, Chiaramonti called on authorities to protect the clergy and their flocks, referencing the captivity of his elderly relative, Pius VI.

Now, Chiaramonti's republican views about faith and democracy alarmed some of the conclave's older cardinals. On top of that, the former Benedictine monk was happy as a bishop; the papacy wasn't a position he sought. After persuading him not to prolong "the widowhood of the Church," the Cardinals broke the stalemate on March 14, unanimously electing Barnaba Chiaramonti (Chiaramonti himself voted for his supporter Cardinal Dean). The scholarly prelate was considered pragmatic and conciliatory, someone who would remain neutral in future European conflicts.

In memory of his predecessor, Chiaramonti took Pius VII as his pontifical name. In addition to Bishop of Rome, he was pontifex maximus. Originally the title of ancient Rome's pagan high priest, literally the "greatest bridge-builder," pontifex maximus metaphorically connected mortals and gods.[11] The holders of the prestigious position, typically members of prominent Roman families, interpreted omens, managed the calendar, and advised the Senate. In 63 B.C.E., Julius Caesar was elected pontifex maximus. His successor Augustus made the position of high priest an imperial prerogative; successive Roman emperors automatically inherited the esteemed title.[12]

According to Christopher Lascelles, when Christianity replaced paganism as Rome's imperial state religion in the late fourth century, Emperor Gratian relinquished the title and granted it to the Bishop of Rome. From then on, the Bishop of Rome became the high priest or pontifex maximus of the Catholic Faith. As Lascelles explains, "The term 'pontiff', by which the pope is sometimes known, is derived from

Pontifex, and various churches and papal tombs in Rome bear the inscription 'Pont. Max.'"[13]

Trading his black Benedictine habit for white vestments, Pius VII was carried on the portable throne, *sedia gestatoria*, to the altar of the Abbey Basilica for a public "adoration." But because they had not supported Francis II's candidate Mattei, the cardinals were locked out of the prestigious St. Mark's Basilica for the papal coronation. Instead, the ceremony was held in San Giorgio Maggiore on March 21, the Feast of St. Benedict.

The tiara, an emblematic sign of the papacy, was a conical-shaped metal cap decorated with three crowns. This unique headwear is mentioned for the first time by the *Uber Pontificalis,* which describes the entry of Pope Constantine (710) in Constantinople wearing a cap, the camelaucum. In the twelfth and thirteenth centuries, the papal tiara evolved to feature a three crown design, the *triregne.*

As part of the Treaty of Tolentino, the Vatican had been forced to cede the papal tiaras from the sacrarium.[14] During his kidnapping, Pius VI's crown with its spectacular emerald was also seized. In lieu of the real thing, Antonio Cardinal Doria-Pamfilj, the Cardinal Protodeacon, placed a papier-mâché tiara of cardboard and gilt paper on Pius VII's head.

From the window of the great hall, Pius delivered his *"Urbi et Orbi"* blessing. Representatives of various princes, including Austria's emperor, did not attend. Crowds overflowed onto the piazza outside the abbey; thousands more watched Pius's public crowning on the balcony from boats in the canal and St. Mark's square across the water. After a six and a half month vacancy and nearly four months of contention, the Church had a new pope.

When the late Pius VI visited Venice in 1782, he had met Doge Paolo Renier at San Giorgio in Alga. His successor would enjoy no such meeting. Venice's last doge, Ludovico Manin, abdicated in May 1797 when Napoleon invaded the city. Many blamed him for surrendering to France too easily. In May, Pius VII issued his first encyclical, *Diu satis.* He praised his predecessor as a martyr pope, like Martin I who was exiled to Crimea by the Byzantine emperor. In a passage about France, he referred to the "strength and constancy" of the episcopate, the clergy, and the faithful in the face of a "cruelty revisited from former times."[15]

⚜

While the College of Cardinals convened in Venice, Napoleon was busy planning an encore in Italy. The Treaty of Campo Formio had left the Habsburgs hungry for revenge. In early 1800, the Austrian army crossed into northern Italy. After defeating a French regiment near Genoa, they organized a siege to starve the remaining French troops. Austrian troops advanced to Nice in southeastern France, coming close to Fréjus where Napoleon had landed the previous fall.

In March, Napoleon gave orders to General André Masséna, commander of the Army of Italy, about the Genoa siege and sent supply trains down the Rhône. In early May, Napoleon embarked on the Second Italian campaign. He had returned from Egypt determined to divorce Joséphine for her affair, but the two reconciled. While in Milan, he took another mistress, the singer Giuseppina Grassini, who he subsequently installed in Paris.

Surprising the Austrians in Lombardy required Napoleon's army to cross the Great St. Bernard, a fifty-mile-long, eight-thousand-foot elevation pass. The steep trail had been opened up for Julius Caesar some two thousand years earlier. No one since Carthaginian general Hannibal had attempted such a bold offensive. Napoleon led forty thousand soldiers through the icy pass.

At the summit, Napoleon and his army took a three-day break at the Monastery at Col Du St. Bernard, famous for its lifesaving dogs. Since its founding in the eleventh century by an Augustinian monk, the monastery and hospice had supported monks, travelers, pilgrims, and soldiers along the treacherous journey. In the monastery library, Napoleon read Livy's account of Hannibal's famous crossing with elephants and his victories over the Romans.

After descending into Aosta, Italy, Napoleon's army captured Milan and Pavia before moving west. The decisive battle took place on June 14 south of the Po River near the village of Marengo. With his army outnumbered and on the verge of defeat, General Desaix appeared at the last moment with six thousand reinforcements. Napoleon's counterattack was successful, but the thirty-one-year-old veteran of the Egypt campaign was killed in the battle. Also that month, General Kléber, France's commander in Egypt, was assassinated.

Napoleon immediately ordered a monumental tomb for Desaix in the chapel of the Grand St. Bernard hospice. Napoleon renamed his new Arab stallion from Egypt "Marengo" (over the next fifteen years, this trusty light gray steed survived numerous battle wounds). With the second Italian campaign, France regained northern Italy from Austria and expanded its eastern border to the Rhine River. For maximum impact, Napoleon postponed his entry into Paris to coincide with Bastille Day on July 14.

Meanwhile Pius VII was spending his post-coronation days receiving delegations and traveling to various churches, monasteries, and convents across Venice in a gilded gondola. Francis II invited him to visit Vienna, but he declined, wary of being pressured into recognizing Austria's rule over the papal dominions.[16] Instead, Pius set sail for Pesaro on the Adriatic coast onboard the *Bellona*, a rickety Austrian ship. After a twelve-day voyage, the papal entourage continued by land. At Ancona, they learned of Napoleon Bonaparte's stunning victory at Marengo.

At Fano, Pius VII celebrated Mass in the convent church where his mother was buried. On July 3, the pope entered Rome, escorted by Austrian troops. There was no triumphant *possesso* through the city, no commemorative coins or medals, and no appointment of a symbolic Camerlengo. One of Pius's first decisions was to promote Ercole Consalvi, conclave secretary, to Cardinal (Deacon of Sant'Agata dei Goti) and Secretary of State. In mid-November, Pius took possession of the Lateran Basilica. The Austrians sent Ferdinand IV's troops back to Naples.

Shortly after the conclave, Napoleon declared he would be an Attila for Venice. For centuries, the luxurious state barge, the *Bucintoro*, was used in a special ceremony each Ascension Day when the doge, accompanied by his court and some two hundred guests, threw a gold ring into the Adriatic to renew the symbolic marriage of the Republic and the sea. To mark his victory, Napoleon ordered the barge destroyed in January 1798.

After removing the *Bucintoro*'s elaborate carvings and gilded statues, French soldiers hauled the booty to San Giorgio Maggiore where it was burned. The ashes were transferred to Milan to extract the melted gold.[17] Stripped of its gold leaf and decorations, the 115-foot-long ship was taken from its berth in the Arsenale and set on fire. The barge reportedly burned for three days. Only the stripped hull was saved, fitted with cannons to patrol the lagoon. The vessel was later stored at the Arsenale and demolished in 1824 (a few surviving gilded wood fragments are housed at Venice's Correr Museum).

At the Arsenale, Napoleon built a warehouse for artillery and a dock with two small towers. San Giorgio Maggiore was suppressed; its monks dispersed. San Giorgio Maggiore remained an armory for over a century. Its library, archive, and most of its art were removed.

Before the Battle of Marengo, Napoleon told aides that he had decided to come to an agreement with the new pope. With Catholicism gaining popularity in France, Napoleon recognized that religion was his best means for social control. "The people need a religion;" he said, "this religion must be in the hands of the government." At the same time, he declared that "The Church must be within the State, and not the State within the Church."[18]

France's alliance with the papacy dated back to its early Frankish monarchs—Clovis I, Pepin the Short, and Charlemagne. In 1516, Francis I and Pope Leo X signed the Concordat of Bologna, regulating church and state relations for over 270 years until the French Revolution. The 1790 Civil Constitution of the Clergy, condemned by Pius VI, stripped the Catholic Church in France of its property and hierarchy, and transferred control from the Vatican to the Republic. Thousands of French priests, nuns, and monks were killed or exiled.

Now a decade later, Pius sent Ercole Consalvi to Paris to negotiate the restoration of Catholicism in France. Negotiating on behalf of France were François Cacault, French plenipotentiary minister in Rome and Cardinal Joseph Fesch, stepbrother of Napoleon's mother. The day after his arrival, Cardinal Consalvi had his first audience at the Tuileries Palace. Talleyrand led Consalvi to an audience room filled with the three consuls, Senate members, the Tribunate, the legislative corps, generals, officers, and dignitaries. Without letting Consalvi speak, Napoleon began hounding him to sign the agreement immediately.

Despite several late-night sessions, the parties remained far apart and Napoleon threatened that he would follow the example of Henry VIII (who made Protestantism England's official religion). In the middle of the deliberations, Napoleon told his private secretary Louis-Antoine Fauvelet de Bourrienne, "Guess what they are holding out to me. The salvation of my soul! But as far as I'm concerned, there is no immortality but the memory that is left in the minds of men."[19]

As Robin Anderson puts it, "Napoleon saw the Church as something like an army, and bishops as generals whom he could command. . . . He therefore went to any lengths to have the bishops whom he wanted, and whom he thought would be subservient to him in furthering his plans, regularly put in command by the Church's head."[20] Pius was equally adamant about holding onto his power to ratify bishops. In the epic power struggle that ensued, this issue would remain a major point of contention.

On the evening of December 24, 1800, the consular couple and their entourage left by carriage from the Tuileries for the opera. As the first consul's carriage pulled out of the Carrousel onto rue Sainte-Nicaise, a mounted escort noticed a wagon with a large barrel partly blocking the road. The escort stopped and ordered the wagon removed. Instead of waiting for the road to be cleared, Napoleon's coachman maneuvered through the narrow passageway. Seconds later, a bomb exploded behind them.

Following in a second carriage, Joséphine, her daughter Hortense and sister-in-law Caroline heard the explosion just after entering the Place du Carrousel. Hortense, who suffered cuts on her arms from the window's broken glass, wrote: "We felt a violent shock. The carriage seemed to be blown away . . . our horses, terrified at the noise, reared and dashed back with us to the Tuileries."[21]

Napoleon and Joséphine were unhurt, but the bomb killed twenty-four and wounded one hundred; some fifty houses and shops were destroyed. After learning that Joséphine was unharmed, Napoleon enjoyed Haydn's *Creation* from his opera box. Chouan conspirators, royalists from Brittany, designed the bomb with cases of grapeshot and barrels of gunpowder placed on a cart. Two of "the scoundrels," as Napoleon called them, were tried and executed for the crime.

From the start of the Consulate, Napoleon enacted measures to restore social order after a decade of revolution. "There has been too much tearing down; we must rebuild," he declared. "A government exists, yes and power, but the nation itself—what is it? Scattered grains of sand. . . . We must plant a few masses of granite as anchors in the soil of France."[22] "Masses of granite" referred to several of Napoleon's new institutions.

In the face of a financial crisis, Napoleon created the Banque de France in January 1800. Bonaparte was a shareholder, and made his family members and notables shareholders. The Banque was funded with some state funds, but the majority came from private capital. By giving the central bank exclusive right to issue paper money and stabilizing the value of the currency with gold and silver, Napoleon managed to restore confidence in France's financial system.

The same year, Napoleon replaced the elected position of Mayor of Paris with a Prefect of the Seine. The first prefect, Louis Nicolas Dubois, held the position for a decade. Each of the twelve arrondissements had its own mayor. For police prefect, Napoleon appointed Joseph Fouché who cracked down on government critics, both royalists and republicans. About his police chief, Napoleon wrote: "Intrigue was as necessary to Fouché as food; he intrigued all the time, everywhere, in every way and with everyone."[23]

For further protection, some one hundred Mamelukes who had defected and joined the French army in Egypt were attached to Napoleon's Household Guard. Forming the Tenth Squadron, the elite fighters dressed in exotic "Turkish" style clothes and carried curved scimitars or sabers. Unlike Julius Caesar, Napoleon would survive some thirty assassination attempts.

Voltaire observed that a traveler in France "changes his law almost as often as he changes his horses." In addition to royal decrees and Roman and feudal laws, marriage and domestic matters were controlled by the canon law of the Catholic Church. Between 1801 and 1803, Napoleon spearheaded three dozen legal statutes to supersede Church law. In 1804, these statutes were combined into the Code Civil des Français, renamed the Code Napoléon several years later. Primogeniture, hereditary nobility, and class privilege were out; the Church lost control over civilian institutions. The dramatic reforms did not include French women who remained at the mercy of fathers and husbands in regard to property, divorce, and child custody.

Napoleon considered religion a valuable tool for maintaining social order. On July 15, 1801, the first consul and Pius VII signed the Concordat. The agreement legalized public Catholic worship in France while giving

Napoleon political and financial gains. Pius recognized the French Republic and accepted its laws on civil status, marriage, and divorce. Bishops nominated by Napoleon were required to pledge allegiance to the state before being consecrated by the pope. Church property confiscated after 1790 would not be returned.[24]

The Concordat became official on Easter 1802 with a Te Deum at Notre Dame Cathedral. Masses resumed in churches across France and priests donned ecclesiastical clothing. But no sooner had the ink dried, France added an addendum. The so-called Organic Articles gave the French Republic control over most church matters. The pope, who felt double-crossed, immediately wrote Napoleon in protest. Despite Napoleon's promise to investigate, no remedies were made.

The battle between Napoleon and Pius VII had begun.

PART TWO
CONSULATE

"I will be the Brutus of kings and the Caesar of the Republic."

—Napoleon Bonaparte

ONE
THE ETRUSCANS

In early October, 1795, General Paul Barras, head of the Army of the Interior, called on twenty-six-year-old Napoleon Bonaparte to suppress an insurrection of thirty thousand National Guard soldiers and royalists in Paris. On October 5, in the pouring rain, the young artillery officer fired forty canons at the crowd. In less than an hour, the revolt was over. Over three hundred lay dead by the Church of Saint-Roch.

As a reward, Napoleon was made a full general, head of the Army of the Interior, Governor of Paris, and head of the local police. The promotion included a raise, a coach with four horses, and lodging in the rue des Capucines. Meanwhile General Barras became the most important member of the Directory, France's new government.

Following the insurrection, residents of Paris's royalist neighborhoods were required to surrender their weapons. When Napoleon allowed young Eugène de Beauharnais to keep his deceased father's sword, his mother called on him to express her thanks. Napoleon was smitten. "Everyone knows [her] extraordinary grace . . . her irresistibly sweet, attractive manners," he wrote. "The acquaintance soon became intimate and tender . . . I was not insensible to women's charms, but I was shy with them. [She] was the first to give me confidence."[1]

Born in 1763 at Port Royal in the French colony of Martinique, Marie-Josèphe Rose Tascher de la Pagerie was sent to Paris at age sixteen to live with a relative. Within a year, she married Viscount Alexandre de Beauharnais with whom she had a son and daughter. During the Terror in 1794, Joséphine's estranged husband was guillotined; she barely escaped the same fate. Released from the Carmelites prison after the fall of Robespierre, Joséphine struggled to make ends meet. She became one of several mistresses of Paul Barras, Napoleon's mentor.

Joséphine did not share Napoleon's passion, but marriage offered the thirty-two-year-old an escape from her financial worries. She had always been known as Rose or Marie, but disliking these names, Napoleon called her Joséphine. On the evening of March 9, 1796, the couple wed in a civil service. For the marriage certificate, the bride lessened their six-year age gap by making herself four years younger; the groom added eighteen months. As a wedding gift, Napoleon gave Joséphine a gold enamel medallion inscribed "To Destiny."

Two days later, the groom left Paris to lead the Army of Italy in a military campaign against Austria. Between a series of stunning victories, he penned a flurry of romantic letters. "Not a day goes by without my loving you, not a night without holding you in my arms," he wrote Joséphine. "Never has a woman been loved with more devotion, fire and tenderness."[2]

Meanwhile Napoleon's soulmate was having an affair with the handsome, young lieutenant Hippolyte Charles, ignoring her husband's invitation to join him in Italy. After weeks of pleading letters, Joséphine reluctantly left for Milan where Napoleon filled the elegant Serbelloni Palace with flowers. The following spring, the couple settled into the palace at Mombello, outside Milan. There Joséphine received Napoleon's disapproving mother and sisters. They would never warm up to Joséphine, referring to her as "that Beauharnais woman."

Just months before meeting Napoleon, Joséphine had leased a modest residence on rue de Chantereine. Before her trip to Milan, she began redecorating the home, hiring the fashionable Jacob brothers. In honor of Napoleon's victories in Italy, rue de Chantereine was renamed rue de la

Victoire in December 1797. The following March, Napoleon bought the property for 52,400 livres. It was the only house he privately owned in Paris.

Napoleon would later complain about his wife's exorbitant decorating: "Imagine my surprise, my indignation, my ill-humor when they presented me with the furniture of the drawing-room, which did not seem to me very extraordinary, and which nevertheless rose to the level of 120 to 130,000 francs. In vain I defended myself, shouted, and had to pay."[3]

In April 1799, with Napoleon on campaign in Egypt, Joséphine purchased a new home, a seventeenth-century fixer-upper on one hundred fifty acres northwest of Paris. Short of cash for the deposit, she borrowed fifteen thousand francs from the seller, prominent financier Jean-Jacques Le Couteulx du Molay, a cousin of Napoleon's banker. When Napoleon returned to Paris that fall, he finalized the deal for Château de Malmaison.

Around this time, society portraitist Jean-Baptiste Isabey, a student of Jacques-Louis David, introduced Joséphine to designers Charles Percier and Pierre-François-Léonard Fontaine. In November 1799, Fontaine made the one-hour carriage ride from Paris to inspect her new property. "She [Joséphine] wants me to make this estate a place of delight," he told David. "The gardens are beautiful. The site is very beautiful. The house, as well as all of its dependent buildings, is awful."[4]

A few days later, Percier and Fontaine met Napoleon in Paris where he was discussing with David where to display the recently confiscated art from Italy. When David informed him that the sculptures were already at the Louvre, Napoleon asked why they weren't at the military church of the Invalides. Fontaine responded frankly: "What can these masterpieces of art from Italy have in common with the army that made the conquest? What kind of effect would be achieved by placing the *Apollo*, the *Venus* and the *Laocoön* under the vaults and the dome of the Invalides?"

Napoleon rewarded Fontaine's honesty with the Malmaison project. "I forgot completely the hero," wrote Fontaine. "I saw no more than the little man in the gray redingote."[5]

Like their powerful patron, Percier and Fontaine had come of age during the French Revolution and hailed from modest, non-aristocratic backgrounds. Percier's father worked as a gatekeeper at the bridge between the

Place Louis XV and the Tuileries Garden; his mother did laundry for Marie Antoinette. Fontaine's father was a provincial contractor and plumber.

After meeting as architecture students in Paris, Percier and Fontaine left for Rome in the mid-1780s to study the art and architecture of antiquity at the French Academy. Percier won the highest accolade—a five-year Grand Prix de Rome scholarship for architecture. Fontaine, who had finished second, secured the resources to continue his studies in Rome. Their Rome sojourn coincided with the final years of the ancien régime.

As Europe's "academy," Rome was a mecca for international artists and architects. The city had its own academy system that included the Accademia di San Luca, the Capitoline Accademia del Nudo, the Concorsi Clementini, and numerous studios. In 1666, over two decades into his seventy-two year reign, Louis XIV founded the French Academy in Rome under the direction of Jean-Baptiste Colbert, Charles Le Brun, and celebrated Italian sculptor Gian Lorenzo Bernini. The prestigious Prix de Rome gave France's top painters and sculptors scholarships to study antique and Renaissance masterpieces.

The students, called pensioners, were required to send their works back to Paris to embellish the Louvre, Tuileries, and Versailles. During its first century, the Academy enrolled such talents as Jean-Honoré Fragonard, François Boucher, and Jean-Antoine Houdon. In 1720, French architects joined painters and sculptors at the Academy. As Helen Jacobsen puts it, during pre-Revolutionary Paris "the fashion for architecture in the neoclassical manner reigned supreme. Architects and designers looked to the ruins of Rome and Athens to provide them with inspiration . . ."[6] Elegant neoclassical architectural motifs were incorporated into the decorative arts in gilt bronze furnishings, porcelain, and marble.

The French Academy began in a modest house near Sant'Onofrio Sardinia before moving to the Caffarelli and Capranica palaces. In 1725, the Academy relocated to the Palazzo Mancini on the Corso, just north of Piazza Venezia. Conceived by French Prime Minister Cardinal Jules Mazarin, the Palazzo was built a few decades later in the late seventeenth century by his nephew, Philippe Jules Mancini, Duke of Nevers.

When twenty-two-year-old Charles Percier arrived at the Palazzo Mancini in 1786, he felt overwhelmed. "I went from antiquity to the Middle

Ages, from the Middle Ages to the Renaissance, without being able to settle down anywhere," Percier confided to a colleague. "I was divided between Vitruvius and Vignola, between the Pantheon and the Farnese Palace, wishing to see everything, learn everything, devouring everything and being unable to resolve to study anything."[7]

Over the next five years, Percier produced an astonishing two thousand drawings. This did not include his official assignment—a study of the iconic one-hundred-foot-tall Trajan's Column in the Roman Forum. To get close enough to measure and sketch the towering marble bas-reliefs, Percier spent four months being hoisted up and down in a basket with a scaffold and pulley system. ". . . the cursed column eats all of my time . . ." he complained to his friend Claude-Louis Bernier in April 1789. While Percier was immersed with the column, his friend Pierre Fontaine was studying and sketching ancient Roman aqueducts.

Completely captivated by Rome's ancient ruins and monuments, Percier explored excavation sites, private collections, and museums. In the Capitoline Museum, he sketched sarcophagi and an urn decorated with musical putti. Together, Percier and Fontaine studied Rome's monumental Egyptian obelisks and the Pyramid of Cestius, along with objects from the nearby Etruscan towns of Viterbo and Velletri, prompting their fellow students to nickname them "The Etruscans." The duo was also known as the sobriquets Castor and Pollux, the inseparable mythological twins.[8]

On his way back to Paris, Percier trekked across northern Italy, stopping in Ancona and Ravenna, then northwest to Parma, Cremona, Mantua, Venice, Bologna, and Ferrara. Throughout his journey, the prolific draftsman continued to sketch ruins, monuments, and buildings from different periods. "Venice completely disoriented me," Percier wrote British sculptor John Flaxman. "It struck me as one of the most beautiful cities in Italy . . . the marble, the water, the paintings, everything ravished me. However, in summer the small canals smell bad. That's the other side of the coin."[9]

Percier and Fontaine returned to Paris just in time for the French Revolution. Percier assembled his drawings from Italy in a series of volumes, keeping eight with his most beautiful sketches in his studio as a reference.[10] In Italy, Percier developed an appreciation for combining architecture and decoration. Writes Tom Stammers, "Italy taught Percier to think of fixed structures and their flexible contents as a single entity."[11]

Living together in cramped quarters on the third floor of a building off rue Montmartre, Percier and Fontaine eked out a living designing exotic theater sets for the Paris Opéra. In 1798, they published the first of their two books based on their Rome sojourn—*Palais, maisons, et autres édifices modernes, dessinés à Rome.* During the Directory regime when luxury consumption made a comeback, the duo began renovating interiors for businessmen who had acquired residences of the nobility.

Of all their clients, France's frugal, temperamental first consul and his glamorous, spendthrift wife would prove the most challenging and rewarding. Napoleon, who had grown up in comfortable but modest circumstances on the island of Corsica, often became irate over the renovation bills for Malmaison. To avoid a scene, Joséphine offered to pay an upholsterer an extra ten thousand francs to keep her bedroom's decorative tassels, braid, and fringe simple.[12]

Further complicating matters, the consular couple often disagreed, as was the case with Joséphine's passion for tents. Upon seeing Percier and Fontaine's striped sentry tent at the entrance of Malmaison, Napoleon demanded to know who authorized the structure and told Fontaine that it looked like "a booth for animals on display at the fair."[13]

Working within the constraints of the old château, Percier and Fontaine began with the entrance hall. They created a Roman atrium with four scagliola or faux-marble columns, a ceiling painted to imitate granite, and pale yellow walls adorned with antique trophies. The designers enhanced the Roman ambience with white marble busts and two bronze busts of philosophers. The atrium's quietude was interrupted after Joséphine, perhaps nostalgic for Martinique, installed aviaries with noisy tropical birds.

The addition of sliding mirrors in the central arcades opened the entrance hall onto the billiard and dining rooms. After extending the dining room with a semicircular section, Percier and Fontaine covered the floor with dramatic black and white marble squares (along with the billiard room and adjoining spaces). Inspired by the Villa of Cicero in Pompeii, Percier designed a series of graceful female dancers for the dining room. Artist

Louis Lafitte translated his drawings into a series of decorative wall paintings.

As Napoleon increasingly spent long weekends at the château, it began to double as a country home and seat of government. Over ten dizzying days in July, Percier and Fontaine built a meeting room on the ground floor of the south wing. Shaped like a military tent, the Council Room was covered in blue and white striped cotton trimmed with red and yellow wool fringe. Ancient helmets and swords adorned the doors, capped with eagles, the Roman symbol of victory. Between January 1801 and September 1802, the room hosted some 169 councils. The Concordat and 1803 sale of the Louisiana Territory to the United States were decided here.

Next door, Percier and Fontaine combined three small rooms in the south corner to create a library for Napoleon. Fontaine removed the partition walls and commissioned the Jacob brothers to fashion the teak woodwork. Mahogany paneling, desk, and bookcases held some 4,500 volumes, selected by Fontaine, many bearing the monogram "B-P" for Bona-Parte. Frederic Moench's decoration of the vaulted ceiling after Percier's designs featured Minerva leaning on her spear and Apollo with his lyre. Surrounding Minerva and Apollo were portrait medallions of great authors—Homer with his owl, Virgil with a wolf suckling Romulus and Remus, Dante with the lion of Florence, and Voltaire with the Gallic rooster (probably by Lafitte). According to Alain Pougetoux, Moench did not intend to produce frescoes, but he didn't have time to let the plaster dry. Napoleon ordered the library done quickly.[14]

A hidden staircase behind the mirrors led to Napoleon's two-room apartment upstairs. By mid-September, 1800, Fontaine wrote: "Everything is now in place, and even though the First Consul found that the room looked like a church sacristy, he was nevertheless forced to admit that it would have been difficult to do better in such an unsuitable space."[15]

To realize their heroic new decorative style in chairs, cabinets, and tables, Percier and Fontaine began a collaboration with the Jacob brothers, Paris's foremost *ébeniste* or cabinetmaker. After furnishing many of the royal palaces for Marie Antoinette, Georges Jacob had been saved from the guillotine by his friend Jacques-Louis David. In 1796, he retired, turning over the family business to his sons Georges Jacob II and François-Honoré-Georges Jacob. When his older brother's death in 1803, François-Honoré expanded the firm under the name Jacob-Desmalter & Cie, employing over 330 workers in some sixteen workshops. Among its remarkable furnishings for Malmaison was a bureau for Joséphine, designed with a Roman arch and a golden frieze with four winged figures of Victory.[16]

Ancient Rome also inspired Percier's designs in gilt-bronze. Among the ornamental objects for Malmaison, noted Parisian bronzeur and gilder Pierre-Philippe Thomire created a candelabrum and vase for Napoleon's bedroom with a winged Victory holding a laurel wreath overhead supporting a branched candlestick. Trained initially as a sculptor under Augustin Pajou and Houdon, Thomire switched to his family's bronze-smithing business. After an apprenticeship to Pierre Gouthière, he formed his own atelier in 1776 and worked for the Crown toward the end of Louis XVI's reign. In 1783, Thomire became exclusive supplier of gilt-bronze mounts for the Sèvres porcelain factory. He managed to survive the Revolution by making arms and ammunition. Under the Consulate, Thomire returned to decorative bronze work, employing hundreds in his thriving workshop. Thomire supplied finely chased and gilded mounts for furniture and clocks to the leading ébénistes.

Combining motifs and martial imagery from ancient Rome, Etruria, and Egypt, Percier and Fontaine created a singular style for Malmaison. Joséphine heightened the effect by presenting her collection of antiquities as decorative objects. During the Consulate and the Empire, Malmaison "took on the aura of a Roman domus," write Martine Denoyelle and Sophie Deschamps-Lequime.[17]

But Pierre Fontaine soon clashed with Joséphine over Malmaison's park. The opinionated architect preferred classical French gardens; his patron loved the natural English landscapes. "She wants us to work on the gardens, the waters, the conservatories," wrote Fontaine in 1800, describing her demands as "without measure and without limits."[18] Joséphine's Anglophile gardener Jean-Marie Morel opposed Percier and Fontaine's bold designs. After submitting their resignation, Fontaine expressed relief, noting that Joséphine's "desires are orders that one cannot refuse, and whose outcome even the subtlest would be unable to foresee."[19]

The disagreement hurt the designers' relationship with Joséphine, but not her husband. In 1801, Napoleon appointed Percier and Fontaine co-architects to the government.

⚜

After Napoleon's November coup d'état, he and Joséphine left their modest residence on rue de la Victoire for the Petit Luxembourg. Located just west of the sumptuous Palais du Luxembourg built by Marie de' Medici, Petit Luxembourg's recent tenants included the future Louis XVIII and his wife (before they fled revolutionary Paris in 1791) and four of the five members of the deposed Directory.

Just three months later, Napoleon and Joséphine moved again. On the afternoon of February 19, 1800, a procession of carriages left the Luxembourg accompanied by a military band. The three consuls rode in a coach driven by six white horses—a gift from Habsburg Emperor Francis II after the Treaty of Campo Formio. Some three thousand soldiers lined the streets and crowds cheered as the cortege made its way to the Tuileries Palace, west of the Louvre.

From the balcony, Joséphine watched with her daughter Hortense and sister-in-law Caroline Murat as her husband mounted a horse and conducted a military review in the courtyard below. Recognizing the impressive effect of his soldiers in their elegant uniforms, Napoleon would restage this spectacle twice a month, to a fanfare of drums and trumpets.

Soon after his review, Napoleon learned that George Washington had died at Mount Vernon. He ordered a wreath for the tomb of the American hero. During an official period of mourning, black crepe draped the Republic's flags and pennants. "This great man fought to overthrow tyranny," read the official pronouncement. ". . . His memory will ever be dear to the French People, as to every free man in both hemispheres, and especially to French soldiers who, like him and the other soldiers of America, are fighting for equality and liberty."[20]

During France's own recent revolution, the Tuileries Palace was repurposed as a royal prison. After being driven out of Versailles in 1789, Louis XVI and Marie Antoinette were held under house arrest at the Tuileries before being tried and beheaded. Napoleon had witnessed the occupation of the palace in June 1792 when it was ransacked and looted by a revolutionary mob. Its staircases were still stained with the blood of Swiss Guards who had tried to protect the royal family.

Tuileries had long been associated with royal extravagance. In 1564, recently widowed Catherine de' Medici began building a new palace perpendicular to the Seine. The property overlooked gardens and marshes that were later named the Elysian Fields after the heaven of the heroes of Greek mythology. The palace and garden were named Tuileries after the local tile factories or *tuileries*. But the superstitious queen put the kibosh on the project when her astrologer predicted she would soon die "near Saint Germain." The Church of Saint-Germain-l'Auxerrois was too close for comfort.

Catherine's son-in-law Henri IV finished the palace, constructing the Grand Gallery to connect it to the Louvre. Louis XIV would spend his last night in Paris at the Tuileries before moving permanently to Versailles. In 1715, his five-year-old great grandson and heir, the future Louis XV, moved to the Tuileries from Versailles. Under his rule, the promenade through the Tuileries Garden became a long, broad avenue known as the Champs-Élysées.

Now Napoleon gave architect Étienne-Chérubin Leconte one month to refit the palace. During the Directory, the palace was occupied and subdivided by the Convention and its committees. One of the first changes was to remove the red republican caps and other revolutionary symbols painted on the walls. "Get rid of all these things," Napoleon told his architect. "I don't like to see such rubbish."[21]

On the first floor at the south end of the palace, the Gallery of Diane was replaced by a Gallery of Consuls. Lucien Bonaparte, now Interior Minister, ordered nineteen ancient and contemporary marble portrait busts from nineteen different sculptors including Augustin Pajou, Claude Dejoux, Jean-Joseph Espercieux, and Pierre Cartellier.[22] Lining the gallery walls were busts of Alexander the Great, Julius Caesar, Brutus, Demosthenes, Scipio, Hannibal, Cicero, and Cato. The military pantheon included a number of France's enemies like Frederick the Great, Eugene of Savoy, Gustavus Adolphus, and the First Duke of Marlborough, who served briefly under France's General Turenne against the Dutch. "Brave men impress me, regardless of which land they represent," Napoleon later inscribed in a biography of the Duke of Marlborough.[23]

The first consul's relatively small entourage consisted of aides-de-camp, secretaries, and servants. Géraud-Christophe-Michel Duroc, governor of the palace, oversaw security and general operations. Napoleon's future brother-in-law, Joachim Murat, was named commander of the ten-thousand-man consular guard. Anne-Jean-Marie-René Savary, who had served under General Desaix in Egypt, was entrusted with palace surveillance, commanding the seven hundred member legion of gendarmerie.

Napoleon soon replaced architect Leconte with his favorite designers, Percier and Fontaine. On October 4, 1801, Fontaine wrote: "The First Consul is very much occupied with the decoration of the apartments of the Tuileries. He wants Versailles to be all that can be found in the museums and warehouses, that the great pictures of the battles of Alexander by Lebrun be placed in the gallery of Diana. . . . We visited every detail in detail when, in one of the saloons of the great apartment, he found several members of the Tribunate. 'You see,' he said, 'trying to do honor to the country which I am governing, and now that we have peace, we are going to occupy ourselves with the arts.'"[24]

To realize his designs for the Tuileries Palace, Charles Percier turned again to cabinetmaker François-Honoré-Georges Jacob-Desmalter, along with Alexandre Brongniart, director of Sèvres, and silversmith Martin-Guillaume Biennais. In 1798, Biennais allowed Napoleon to make purchases at his Paris shop on credit. As first consul, Napoleon returned the favor, appointing Biennais as his official goldsmith.

For Napoleon's bedroom, Biennais produced an elegant yew, gilt bronze, and silver washstand known as an *athénienne* after a design by Percier (the ewer and lavabo were made by Marie-Joseph-Gabriel Genu). Its form came from the Greco-Roman three-legged perfume burner or brazier also used for offerings to the gods. The antique brazier was generally made of bronze, but could also be done in copper, silver, stone, or gold. With classical art in vogue, the antique tripod enjoyed a comeback.

Biennais decorated Napoleon's luxe athénienne with gilt bronze antique motifs of swans, dolphins, chimaeras, bees, and eagles. According to

Wolfram Koeppe, dolphins and swans carried an especially powerful message—Napoleon's place as rightful heir to Louis XIV. The firstborn son of the French king was called the Dauphin or dolphin. Louis XIV, the Sun King, linked himself to Apollo, who himself was associated with swans. Dolphins and the winged sea creatures on the frieze around the shelf also evoked Napoleon's birthplace, the island of Corsica.[25] For his business card, Biennais chose a tripod crowned by a swan with spread wings.[26]

Gradually, the rooms of the Tuileries Palace were decorated and furnished. The second floor of the west wing housed Napoleon's private apartments and the state apartments with the state cabinet where the Administrative Council and Cabinet met. Joséphine and her son and daughter occupied Marie Antoinette's rooms on the entresol, or ground floor. Despite the refurbishing, Napoleon and Joséphine never enjoyed the Tuileries, where it was impossible to walk without being seen by the public. Joséphine especially enjoyed the privacy of Malmaison where she was surrounded by her gardens. The Tuileries remained Napoleon's official residence, soon the seat of his imperial court.

With Malmaison too modest for the head of the French Republic, Napoleon took possession of the former royal Château de Saint-Cloud for his main summer residence. During his coup d'état, Napoleon had seized power in Saint-Cloud's Orangery. Located near the Seine some three miles west of Paris, the château had been enlarged in the seventeenth century by Louis XIV's brother Philippe, Duke of Orléans (who died there), and again by Marie Antoinette after Louis XVI acquired the palace for her in 1785. In September 1801, Percier and Fontaine began renovations.

About the six-story palace, Fontaine wrote: "The First Consul fixed, but in a somewhat vague manner, the distribution of the apartments. . . . We do not know what to do with the chapel."[27] Like at the Tuileries, some of Saint-Cloud's furnishings came from the Garde-Meuble Impérial and palaces of the Republic. Much of the furniture for Joséphine's apartments was new. Located in the left wing, her suite included a dining room, music room, two salons, bathroom, boudoir, and bedchamber.

Overlooking the forecourt, the boudoir featured four large mirrors and a fireplace. Percier decorated the room in red, white, and gold, adding white taffeta curtains and cerise drapes. There were two large porcelain

Sèvres Medici vases, goblets made of "oriental agate," and a Lepaute clock supported by two chimeras. Percier also designed an elegant gondola chair incorporating one of Joséphine's favorite motifs, the swan. Made of gilded beechwood and upholstered in cerise silk velvet, the innovative seat was inspired by the ancient klismos chair and featured deep convex backs and swan-shaped armrests painted white.[28] The swan had appeared in various forms during antiquity, often in connection with the myth of Leda, Apollo, or Venus.[29]

Swans reappeared during the Renaissance, especially in the decoration of grotesques. According to Jean-Pierre Samoyault, Percier depicted the swan as it had appeared in Nero's Golden House in Rome and its copy at Raphael's Vatican Loggia.[30] Swans, along with butterflies, dancers, and flowers for Joséphine's furnishings were a dramatic contrast to the masculine Empire style emblems.

Percier's X-shaped stool, painted white and gold, was also based on an antique model. The form recalls numerous chairs on Greek vases, Etruscan and Roman mural paintings, and coins, as well as the curved legs of the "curule" chair. Also for the boudoir, Percier designed a pair of candelabra produced by Thomire in gilt-bronze. Hellenistic winged figures of Victory held floral wreaths from which branched ten candle sockets decorated with acanthus leaves. As symbols of military triumph, these winged figures soon became a key motif for Napoleonic décor.

Percier and Fontaine made quick work at Saint-Cloud. By August 1802, Fontaine wrote, "The renovations at the château de Saint-Cloud are complete. The apartments are finished. We oversaw the selection, fabrication, and placement of every piece."[31] Working at the hourglass-shaped desk, Napoleon penned his frequent dispatches. Saint-Cloud would continue to witness a number of important events during Napoleon's rule, including the proclamation of the Empire on May 18, 1804, in the north wing's Apollo Gallery.

Of the dozens of former royal palaces, Saint-Cloud was the most convenient. The first consul began holding frequent audiences at the château. Lasting for several hours, these were attended by cardinals, bishops, senators, councilors of state, deputies, tribunes, generals, ambassadors, magistrates, and private citizens.[32] On Sundays, Wednesdays, and Fridays, the consular couple also hosted dinners for twelve to fifteen guests, followed by card games. Civil costumes replaced military uniforms at palace functions. For the fete of July 14, 1802, Napoleon exchanged his uniform for a coat embroidered with red silk. But he did don a black military cravat. "There is always something about me which smells of the army; there is no harm in that," he said.[33]

Percier and Fontaine's opulent take on Neoclassicism became known as the Empire style. Their objective was to go beyond mere fashion, writes Hans Ottomeyer, with a unified use of color and fabric, and lasting materials like marble, mahogany, and satinwood.[34]

In 1801, Percier and Fontaine published the first installment of the *Recueil de décorations intérieures*. The book featured seventy-two plates illustrating the furnishings, decorations, and interiors for their celebrity clients. According to the authors, its purpose was to contribute "to the dissemination and upholding of the principles of taste that we have derived from ancient art, and that we believe are linked, albeit by a less apparent chain, to those general laws of truth, simplicity, and beauty."[35]

The *Recueil* proved tremendously influential, establishing an international neoclassical taste and inspiring generations of decorators and designers. Percier's models generated a style across a number of different media. "Jewellers, goldsmiths, engravers, cabinetmakers, and wallpaper manufacturers drew upon the work of Percier," observed the *Journal du Commerce* in 1805, "such that it is not unusual to find in a single apartment a tapestry, a clock, a table service, and a woman's parure in the same design elements."[36]

Percier and Fontaine were opposites in personality. Percier was obsessed with work, with a "compulsive passion for details" and an "unchecked penchant for drawing" writes Jean-Philippe Garric. He wore the same clothes every day and rarely appeared in public, prompting Napoleon to remark to Fontaine, "Your Percier does nothing: I never see him."[37]

In fact, Percier was the creative force behind the successful partnership. As Tom Stammers writes, Percier's "imagination released a bestiary of griffins, chimeras, sphinxes, swans, and lions into French drawing rooms; from tented rooms and 'Etruscan' Sèvres vases, few icons of the First Empire were untouched by his genius for design."[38]

With his ability to execute projects quickly, the confident Fontaine won over Napoleon. Trained in construction and engineering, Fontaine managed the technical aspects of building and the business side. Fontaine described their division of responsibilities: "Percier, whose temperament and taste, indeed his gifts, were ill-suited to the trouble and demands of business, left all practical matters to me," wrote Fontaine. "I handled the correspondence as well as the accounts, and he focused almost exclusively on study drawings and graphic compositions."[39] By 1803 and 1804, Percier and Fontaine were working exclusively for France's consular couple, creating increasingly glamorous takes on antiquity.

During the eighteenth century, excavations of the Roman cities of Pompeii and Herculaneum (buried by Vesuvius in 79 C.E.) revived enthusiasm for the classical past and inspired the neoclassical artistic movement. An early phase of Neoclassicism, the *goût grec* or Grecian style, became the rage in France during the reign of Louis XVI and Marie Antoinette. In a complete departure from the ornate baroque and asymmetrical Rococo styles associated with Louis XIV and Louis XV, goût grec furnishings featured bold, angular shapes of symmetrical design with decoration inspired by classical motifs like ram's heads, urns, and swags.

With the Empire style, Percier and Fontaine created an opulent spin on Neoclassicism based on the splendor of imperial Rome. They enlivened austere classical forms with gilding and redecorated former royal palaces with a dramatic palette of white and gold, purple, red, and emerald green. Roman arabesques, laurel wreaths, trophies, eagles, and sphinxes, along with Napoleon's cypher, appeared on everything from throne-shaped chairs and tented beds to luxe carpets and porcelain dinner services. Perfectly in tune with France's bold new leader, the Empire style took off across the Continent, a powerful symbol of Paris's ascendancy as Europe's cultural capital.

TWO

CAESAR'S FRIEND

Napoleon and Joséphine kicked off 1802 with a two-week trip to Lyon where he was elected chief magistrate of the new Italian Republic. Composed of the Cisalpine Republic and provinces taken from Austria by the Treaty of Lunéville, the Republic represented the first time "Italy" had appeared on Europe's political map since the fall of Rome.[1]

The first couple also visited the city's renowned silk factories. Determined to revive France's luxury industries, Napoleon ordered silk to decorate both the Tuileries Palace and Saint-Cloud from Camille Pernon, formerly the main supplier to the crown. Sumptuous silk panels were hung in the Tuileries's Gallery of Consuls.[2] For Napoleon, getting the silk weavers back to work was a pragmatic issue. "I am afraid of these insurrections based on the lack of bread," Napoleon told Interior Minister Jean-Antoine Chaptal. "I would be less afraid of a battle of 200,000 men."[3]

Napoleon's patronage of the silk industry continued, as he renovated a series of former royal palaces. Over the ensuing decade, silk, brocade, and velvet were ordered to decorate the former royal palaces of Fontainebleau,

Meudon, and Compiègne. Later, for the redecoration of Versailles, a staggering 87,500 yards of silk was delivered to the Mobilier Imperial.[4]

Napoleon continued to appropriate former royal palaces, both physically and symbolically. As Jean-Philippe Garric describes, in addition to the practical need to lodge with his entourage and host guests, Napoleon pursued two other goals: assuming the monumental heritage of the ancien régime and leaving a testimony of his reign for posterity.[5] With some four dozen palaces in his real estate portfolio, most sacked during the Revolution, Napoleon would personally keep France's luxury goods industry busy.

For the Tuileries, Saint-Cloud, Compiègne, and Fontainebleau, Percier and Fontaine ordered enormous carpets from Savonnerie, named for the *savonnier* or weaver. Under the direction of artist Charles Lebrun, the former royal factory had woven hundreds of spectacular carpets for Louis XIV. These included thirteen carpets for the Louvre's Apollo Gallery, followed by a set of ninety-three carpets for the Grand Gallery, each nearly thirty feet long. Now the enormous looms were back in use, producing Empire style designs by architect La Hamayde de Saint-Ange.

With the new year, Napoleon began arranging marriages for his relatives, most of which proved disastrous. Like the Roman emperors who almost exclusively arranged marriages for family members, Napoleon's matchmaking was intended to further his political ambitions. On January 4, his brother Louis married Joséphine's daughter Hortense. In love with someone else, Louis could barely tolerate his young wife. Also that month, Napoleon married off his youngest sister, seventeen-year-old Caroline, to the dashing cavalry officer Joachim Murat, a veteran of his Italian and Egyptian campaigns.

It was at the Murats' Château de Villiers-la-Garenne near Neuilly that Napoleon saw *Cupid and Psyche* and *Psyche Revived by Cupid's Kiss* by the celebrated neoclassical sculptor Antonio Canova. The Scottish colonel who commissioned the works had trouble shipping them to England, and Joachim Murat acquired the pendants after visiting Canova's studio during the French occupation of Rome in 1798. Cupid and Psyche was a popular neoclassical theme and Canova produced many versions of the mythological lovers.

The Murats' standing *Cupid and Psyche* was the embodiment of innocence. With Cupid leaning on her shoulder, the graceful Psyche holds his hand and passes him a butterfly, symbol of the soul to the ancient Greeks. In contrast, his erotic *Psyche Revived by Cupid's Kiss* inspired French novelist Gustave Flaubert to kiss "the armpit of the swooning woman stretching out her long marble arms to Cupid. And then the foot! The head! Her face! Forgive me, but it was my first sensual kiss for so long; indeed it was something more; I was kissing beauty itself."[6]

Napoleon was also smitten. In September 1802, François Cacault, French ambassador in Rome, summonsed Canova to Paris to produce a portrait bust and statue of the first consul. It was Canova's second invitation.

In 1797, then General Napoleon Bonaparte learned that Canova was in financial straits. As a result of the French occupation of Venice, the new democratic municipality froze Canova's pension for his tribute to the naval hero Angelo Emo. Eager to be portrayed by Europe's most sought after artist, Napoleon personally wrote to Canova that August, promising to reinstate his life annuity of one hundred silver ducats a month:

"I have come to understand, Monsieur, from one of your friends, that you have been deprived of [your] Venetian pension. The French Republic acknowledges the great talents that you possess. As a celebrated artist, you have a special right to be protected by the Army of Italy. I am ordering that your pension should be restored to you in full. I hope that you will let me know if this order has not been fulfilled and that you believe the pleasure it gives me to do something useful for you."

Napoleon never made good on his promise. Later that year, he offered Canova a commission to carve a relief portrait of himself for Padua, near Venice. Canova declined, citing health issues and bad roads. Three years earlier, Canova had turned down Catherine the Great's invitation to travel to St. Petersburg. But in the case of Napoleon, his motivation was patriotic. France's recent pillaging of Italy's masterpieces and its ceding of his beloved Venice to Austria were deeply upsetting. "I have St. Mark in my heart and nothing in the world will change me," Canova pronounced after the fall of the millennium-old Venetian Republic to Napoleon.[7]

Later in 1797, when French troops besieged Rome, Canova found himself trapped. A pro-French mob stormed his studio, nearly destroying his model for a statue of Ferdinand IV of Naples. Among the works seized by the French in Rome were some of Canova's prized plaster models. Around this time, Canova expressed his anti-Bonapartist sentiment in a letter to a friend: "I would happily lose anything, even my life, if by it I could help my beloved country, for I shall call it thus till my dying breath."

Though the new governors of French-controlled Rome gave Canova various honors, he sought refuge in his hometown of Possagno. Located north of Venice in the foothills of the Dolomites, the small village was not far from the birthplaces of such Renaissance giants as Bellini, Giorgione, and Titian. Born in November 1757 to a family of stonemasons, Canova was just three years old when his father died. His mother remarried two years later, leaving him in the care of his paternal grandfather Pasino, a stone-cutter. At eleven, Canova was apprenticed to a local sculptor who arranged for him to study drawing, painting, and sculpture in nearby Venice.

During these formative years, Canova formed a special bond with Venice, one that would be reciprocated. As part of his training, Canova drew the terra-cottas and plaster casts of ancient Greek sculptures assembled by collector Filippo Farsetti at Palazzo Farsetti on the Grand Canal. Canova's early works from the 1770s were naturalistic, including his stone figures *Orpheus* and *Eurydice*, and marble *Daedalus and Icarus*. In 1775, the young sculptor left Giuseppe Bernardi's studio and opened his own atelier inside the cloister of the Church of Santo Stefano.

In 1779, the twenty-two-year-old traveled to Rome under the protection of Venetian ambassador Girolamo Zulian. Two years later, Canova settled in Rome permanently, joining a community of artists lured by the city's ancient ruins and monuments. For Canova, like Charles Percier, Rome offered an inexhaustible source of inspiration. He studied and copied Rome's famed statues including the *Apollo Belvedere*, along with its temples, baths, triumphal arches, and bas-reliefs. He immersed himself in the art of Rome's churches and private collections. His library featured archeology, the classics, and biographies of ancient heroes. He mastered correct Italian and learned some English and French, languages that would prove extremely useful. In pursuit of antiquity, Canova traveled to the archeological sites of Naples, Paestum, Pompeii, and Pozzuoli.

In a competition organized by Venetian aristocrat Don Abbondio Rezzonico, Canova produced *Apollo Crowning Himself*, an antiquity-inspired statuette. Its success allowed Canova to obtain a massive block of marble for his 1782 *Theseus and the Minotaur* from Ovid's *Metamorphoses*. Canova took the advice of his friend Gavin Hamilton, the Scottish archeologist and dealer, and portrayed Theseus and the Minotaur *after* their epic struggle.

Canova depicted the legendary Greek hero sitting astride the prostrate Minotaur, holding a club in his left hand and resting his right on his victim's leg. By the leg, Canova carved the coils of thread Theseus used to retrace his steps from the lair. By the time Canova finished the work, his patron Girolamo Zulian had moved to Constantinople. Zulian gave the sculpture to Canova who sold it to a collector in Vienna. The dramatic marble was the talk of Rome. As Canova's acclaim grew, commissions poured in. French critic Quatremère de Quincy called the marble Canova's masterpiece.

In 1782, the twenty-four-year-old sculptor was briefly engaged to Domenica Volpato, the beautiful daughter of the noted Rome engraver Giovanni Volpato. But Canova broke off the engagement after his fiancée seemed more interested in engraver Raffaello Morghen. Canova never married. Art became his true passion. "I love [art] so much that it absorbs me totally without being able to lose a moment," he wrote his early patron, Giovanni Falier.[8]

Among the sculptors the young Canova admired was Rome's seventeenth-century phenom, Gian Lorenzo Bernini. After seeing Bernini's *Apollo and Daphne* at the Borghese Villa, an astonished Canova wrote: "the nude is so beautiful I can scarcely believe it." Under the patronage of the popes, Bernini dominated his era with his theatrical marbles and dazzling architectural projects. Though Canova would share Bernini's celebrity, he broke completely with his predecessor's Baroque style, producing elegant, exquisitely carved neoclassical marbles.

Canova's artistic practice was also strikingly different from that of Bernini, who famously took his scalpel straight to marble. Preparatory drawings and oil paintings were the key first step for Canova—a natural extension of sketching ancient statues and casts during his early training. Renaissance painters Giorgione, Titian, Raphael, Correggio, along with a

Venetian contemporary, Giovanni Battista Tiepolo, were great influences. Canova avidly collected Tiepolo's drawings and oil sketches.[9]

What Canova was after in his sculptures, writes Rachel Spence, was to emulate the exquisite, sensual detail of painting. Canova's "scalpel proceeded like a paintbrush," wrote his secretary and biographer Melchior Missirini.[10] Canova followed his preparatory sketches and paintings with clay and terra-cotta models. These *modelli* allowed him to work out the details of a composition before spending money on marble and labor.

While visiting the Rome studio of sculpture restorer Bartolomeo Cavaceppi, Canova was struck by the excellent quality of the copies produced by his assistants using plaster casts of antiquities. Canova decided to hire *formatore*, specialists in taking molds of antique sculptures, to make plaster molds of his clay models (in the process, the clay models were destroyed). In his 1765 *Encyclopedia*, Denis Diderot described the pointing machine, an innovation developed at the French Academy in Rome. The procedure involved multiplying or dividing measurements of an original to make larger or smaller reproductions. Canova adapted the pointing technique to produce original works, not replicas.

The plaster model was covered with black nails. These were carefully measured and transferred onto the marble block by his studio assistants. The plaster model was key to Canova's practice, allowing him to create numerous copies or variants in marble. According to Johannes Myssok, Canova revolutionized sculptural technique and ". . . adopted the workmanship of antique sculpture far more profoundly than any sculptor before him."[11]

The façade of the building housing Canova's studio was covered in marble fragments from sarcophagi and imperial Roman relief sculptures. "These artifacts reflect the decorative taste prevalent in the early 18th century, the same taste adopted by Canova in designing the Museo Chiaramonti and the Galleria Lapidaria in the Vatican Museums," writes Mario Guderzo. "He even acquired an entire series of eighty pillars and donated them to the museum as bases for the statues, writing, 'said pillars are to be used as an erudite and elegant base for the statues, saving a vast sum of money instead of having them newly created in marble.'"[12]

Canova achieved different textures with a variety of tools. He also had special curved tools made to reach the most inaccessible parts of a work.

In addition, he was renowned for "the final touch" he gave his works, creating the illusion of warm flesh from cold marble. Canova polished every surface and crevice of a marble until it shone. Among his finishing treatments was the application of wax and grind water, adding a stain to the marble surface that gave the appearance of antiquity—similar to the patinas added to bronze. Sculptors in antiquity also added a smooth sheen to their statues by repeatedly rubbing the marble surface with abrasives. Emery, pumice, and sandstone were used in either a handheld form or a powder using fabric or leather.[13]

The success of *Theseus and the Minotaur* led to Canova's breakthrough. In 1783, he was hired to create a neoclassical tomb for Pope Clement XIV at Rome's Church of the Holy Apostles. The high profile commission was secured with the help of well-connected Giovanni Volpato. For inspiration, Canova turned to the pyramid, the ancient Egyptian symbol of grief and transcendence. He may also have been influenced by Rome's own first century Pyramid of Cestius. One hundred Roman feet (ninety-eight feet) high, faced with white Carrara marble, the pyramid tomb for praetor and state priest Gaius Cestius had been built between 18 and 12 B.C.E., not long after Augustus added Egypt to the Roman Empire. Five years after finishing Clement XIV's tomb, Canova produced a second funerary monument for Pope Clement XIII at St. Peter's Basilica in white Carrara marble with a pair of travertine lions at the base.

While executing the gigantic papal tombs, Canova's assistants read aloud texts by Homer, Virgil, and other classical authors. This led to a series of large clay reliefs depicting episodes from these texts. The austere classicism of the papal tombs established Canova as "the new Phidias" after ancient Greece's most famous sculptor. Goethe, Byron, and Wordsworth sang his praises. Stendhal described him as a "simple worker who had received from heaven a beautiful soul and genius."

By the first decade of the nineteenth century, Canova's reputation was soaring. As Robert Hughes writes, "No Italian artist since Bernini had the relations Canova enjoyed with the great and the good of his day: with the popes he served, depicted and memorialized (Clement XIII, Clement XIV, Pius VII), with bankers and politicians, princesses and powerful women, with every sort of foreigner. . . . His very presence in Rome, and his art's relation to Roman prototypes, seemed to confirm that the city had kept an undiminished vitality as a centre of the world's culture."[14]

In 1801, the Vatican acquired Canova's monumental *Perseus* for the space previously occupied by the purloined *Apollo Belvedere*. The acquisition launched an important relationship between Canova and Pius VII that would continue for two decades. Canova collaborated with Pius on an edict on the conservation of Rome's artworks and monuments. In 1802, Pius named him Inspector General of Antiquities and Fine Arts for the Papal States, a position once held by Raphael. Canova's responsibilities included the Vatican museums, Capitoline museums, and the Academy of Saint Luke.

Canova entrusted the Vatican's Museo Chiaramonti and its hundreds of ancient busts and statues to his disciple Antonio D'Este, and his sons Giuseppe and Alessandro. The two sculptors met in 1768 as apprentices in Giuseppe Bernardi's Venice studio and developed a lifelong friendship.[15] Thanks to Canova, the Burano-born sculptor produced a statue after *Apollo Belvedere* for the king of Poland; he also restored sculptures for the Vatican and other prominent collectors. By 1799, D'Este was managing Canova's studio. His duties included the selection of marble, an indication of Canova's confidence in his friend.[16] D'Este himself carved a number of portraits, including a bust of Canova (in 1807, he was named curator of the Vatican museums; he would later become its director).

In 1802, Canova declined Napoleon's summons to Paris, pleading illness, bad weather, and the need to organize his studio. But Pius VII and Cardinal Consalvi insisted he travel to Paris. Despite the Concordat, the pope's relationship with Napoleon was precarious. Both men saw the invitation as a diplomatic opportunity. Canova could no longer say no.

Pius supplied Canova with an elegant carriage for the two-week journey to France, and asked him to deliver the ceremonial pallium to Napoleon's new appointee for Archbishop of Paris, nonagenarian Jean-Baptiste de Belloy. Traveling with his half-brother and a servant, Canova left Rome on September 22.

⚜

It was a rare moment for Napoleon to be in Paris. In February 1801, as a result of his victory at Marengo, Napoleon coerced Austria's Francis II into signing the Treaty of Lunéville. In March 1802, after six months of acrimonious negotiations, his brother Joseph Bonaparte and England's Marquess Cornwallis signed the Peace of Amiens. The war-weary French public was elated by the prospect of peace and Napoleon's popularity surged. Engravings were published of female representations of France crowning busts of the "pacificator" Napoleon wearing laurel leaves.

In May 1802, Napoleon established the Legion of Honor. Unlike the old orders of chivalry based on social status, the institution rewarded merit and bravery to civilians and military men of any background (women were excluded). Borrowing its name from the legions of ancient Rome, the order took as its motto "Honor and Homeland." Structured around legionaires, officers, commanders, regional "cohorts," and a grand council, the order was loosely based on the Roman legion.

Some legislators pushed back against the decoration, arguing that it would be the end of the Revolution's hard fought egalitarianism. Crosses and ribbons, they maintained, were baubles fit for monarchs. To this Napoleon famously replied, "You call these medals and ribbons baubles; well, it is with such baubles that men are led . . . the French are not changed by ten years of revolution; they are what the Gauls were, fierce and fickle. They have only one feeling: honour. We must nourish that feeling . . ."[17]

In 1802, Talleyrand and Cambacérès proposed to the Senate that Napoleon be given the position of consul for life. In a compromise, the senators cut the proposal to a ten-year term plus the seven Napoleon still had left to serve. But Napoleon refused, claiming that the French people needed to grant such an extension. On August 2, Napoleon was declared first consul for life. According to Valérie Huet, Napoleon was a shrewd student of Roman history. Octavian used the same tactic on several occasions leading up to his establishing himself as Augustus, Rome's first emperor. "Bonaparte's decision helped to reassure the mass of citizens that the legitimacy of the French Republic was not contested and that the republic was still in operation," writes Huet. "Bonaparte, just as Octavian had done, required a power which was legitimate."[18] Like Octavian, Napoleon was careful to preserve an illusion of a republic while he consolidated power.

After years of war on the Continent, the Treaty of Amiens was a boon for tourism. Foreign visitors, especially British, flocked to the Louvre to experience the artworks seized from Italy and the famous horses of St. Marks in an inner courtyard. Among the visitors was British painter J.M.W. Turner, who filled a sketchbook. Napoleon was thrilled with the crowds. The goal of his art confiscations was to turn Paris's Louvre into the greatest museum in the world; the embodiment of the French Republic. "A great capital is the homeland of a nation's elite . . . it is the center of opinion, the repository of everything," he declared.[19]

One person not impressed with the purloined art was Antonio Canova, who arrived in Paris and was hosted by Cardinal Giovanni Battista Caprara. Napoleon's recent choice for papal legate, Caprara had helped implement the Concordat, officiating at Notre Dame Cathedral on Easter Day, 1802, the official restoration of public worship in France. A month later, Napoleon named the Bologna-born Caprara archbishop of Milan.

In early October, Canova's friend Quatremère de Quincy presented him to Napoleon and Joséphine at Saint-Cloud. The former residence of the Dukes of Orléans and Marie Antoinette was fresh from a makeover by Percier and Fontaine, who Canova knew from Rome. The château was a dramatic showcase for their bold new Empire style. During this initial meeting, Canova joined the couple for a fork luncheon. Napoleon bore so little resemblance to his portraits that Canova didn't recognize him at first.[20]

During the Italian campaign, Napoleon wore his fine chestnut hair long, cut square and covering his ears in a style called "dogs ears." In Cairo, Napoleon ordered his soldiers to follow his example and cut their hair short, Roman style "à la Titus." His soldiers, who wore their hair tied on the nape, nicknamed their general *Petit Tondu*, Little Shaved/Mowed One. Because of Napoleon's popularity, short hair became the rage for both men and women. As Irene Antoni-Komar writes, Roman emperor Titus's distinctive short hairstyle had a strong advocate in Napoleon whose military style was part of the staging of his political power.[21] Caracalla, emperor from 198–217, the first of the so-called soldier emperors, wore a similar tightly cropped hairdo.

Canova may also have been surprised by the unassuming figure Napoleon cut relative to his status. As the painter Jacques-Louis David observed:

"Nothing let on the man who had overthrown, sustained, or created several states and whose protection four kings and a host of sovereign princes have implored; neither his height, nor his features, nor his manner, nor his attire drew one's attention; and yet, the fame attached to his name being so resplendent, he struck all the onlookers."[22]

After inquiring about the state of Rome, Napoleon asked Canova to sculpt his portrait statue. Canova returned a few days later with clay and modeling tools. Napoleon convinced him to stay for another week, which turned into two, and then a month and a half. Canova was granted a handful of meetings and five sittings with Napoleon—generous for a man who disliked posing and refused to sit for David.[23] During the informal sessions, Napoleon read papers and wrote dispatches from an hourglass-shaped desk topped with busts of Caesar and Hannibal.

Napoleon also chatted with Joséphine and Canova, reportedly calling the sculptor "Caesar's friend."[24] Keenly aware of his role as papal envoy, Canova used the meetings to convey Rome's economic plight and the dire financial situation of the Papal States. According to the sculptor, he did not hold back, expressing his concern about France's treatment of Venice, the "deportation" of the St. Mark's horses, and the removal of Rome's masterworks. In exchange for a superb portrait bust, the first consul seems to have put up with Canova's complaints.

On one occasion, Canova returned to Saint-Cloud to find Napoleon preparing to go hunting. While waiting for him to return, Canova made preliminary sketches for a full-length marble portrait. During their discussions, Napoleon had expressed a strong preference to be portrayed in his military uniform. Canova insisted that he be sculpted nude, like the heroes and rulers of ancient Greece. "God himself would not have been able to create a beautiful work of art if he had represented Your Majesty as you are . . . dressed in French fashion," declared the sculptor.[25]

Because of his celebrity, Canova enjoyed a high degree of artistic freedom with his powerful patrons. Dominique-Vivant Denon supported Canova, telling Napoleon that costumes were rooted in time, while nudity was timeless and fitting for a great military leader. Antiquarian Ennio Visconti also favored Canova's approach. Napoleon wound up deferring to Canova, reportedly saying, "We do not impose a law on Genius."[26] Canova had carte blanche for the statue and a contract for 120,000 francs.

The *Journal de Paris* painted a glowing picture of Canova's visit to Paris, the impressive portrait bust, and the future commission for a heroic, monumental statue of the French leader. But the First Consul's private secretary Bourrienne had a different take. In *Memoirs of Napoleon Bonaparte*, Bourrienne described Canova's sessions with Napoleon and the final portrait bust as less than ideal:

"This great artist came often in the hope of having his model pose for him but it was really making Bonaparte bored, disgusted, and impatient. Therefore he only rarely posed and just for short sessions. You could tell that the likeness suffered from that. However, he really appreciated Canova and every time he was announced, the First Consul sent someone to keep him company until the time he could be available to pose. But he would shrug his shoulders and say, 'Posing again? My God, this is so annoying!' Canova expressed his displeasure to me at not being able to study his model as he would have liked to. Bonaparte's lack of willingness dampened his creativity . . ."[27]

On October 17, Canova asked Quatremère to see Napoleon's bust. Quatremère reported that Canova was "pleased to say that he had found, in the features and physiognomy of his model, forms most favorable to sculpture, and most applicable to the heroic style of the figure that he was envisioning."[28] According to the popular late eighteenth-century theories of physiognomy, the shape of the skull reflected a person's character.

With the larger than life-size head, and hairstyle like Augustus, Canova managed to evoke his sitter's restless intelligence. The bust also conveyed Napoleon's superhuman quality noted by contemporaries like Étienne-Léon Langon. "Though Napoleon was of medium height [about five feet six inches], like Alexander the Great . . . by optical effect he dominated all others with the majesty of his gestures, his irresistible eyes, and seductive smile."[29] Despite Bourienne's criticism, Canova's portrait bust became a canonical image of Napoleon. The new Augustus would be incorporated into Canova's monumental statue, *Napoleon as Mars the Peacemaker.*

During his three-month stay in Paris, Canova reconnected with his colleagues from Rome, including Pierre Fontaine and Jacques-Louis David.

He also befriended François Gérard who painted his portrait. A stickler for how his sculptures were displayed, Canova traveled to the Murat château in Neuilly to visit his two *Cupid and Psyche* groups, taking along Quatremère.[30]

Quatremère was especially taken with the standing version. "I could not refrain from complementing him [Canova] on the visible progress that I saw in the second group," he wrote, "not for its elegance, voluptuousness, or the picturesque composition; but on the contrary, for its simplicity, purity, nobility of style and design, the truth of the nude, the ingenuity of the antique manner, which I saw with please he had so frankly embraced."[31] Quatremère raved that the sensual marble was not carved or polished, but caressed and kissed into life by Canova.

On November 12, Canova joined a group for dinner that included Dominque-Vivant Denon, antiquarians Ennio Visconti and Auguste de Choiseul-Gouffier, Prussian diplomat Girolamo Lucchesini, and musician Johann Friedrich Reichardt. At the recommendation of David, Napoleon had just appointed Denon director of the Louvre, renamed the Central Museum of Arts, passing over Visconti. Denon's best-selling Egypt travel guide had turned his failed military campaign into a triumph. "Denon, very ugly and of a less sympathetic approach, limited himself to recounting his travels with a cheerful good-nature," wrote Reichardt. Visconti was "small in stature, plump, of a certain age, but with an all-around petulance."[32]

Denon was not Napoleon's first choice. He had initially offered the prestigious directorship to Antonio Canova, who promptly declined. The sculptor was already director of the Vatican and Capitoline museums and the Academy of St. Luke.

Canova presented Napoleon's portrait bust on November 21 (today at the Palazzo Pitti, Florence). Napoleon insisted that Canova postpone his departure until Monday so that he could attend a Sunday Mass with a group of dignitaries. With the first consul's clay bust carefully packed in his carriage, Canova and his stepbrother left Paris on November 30. In Lyons, they were hosted by Cardinal Fesch, Napoleon's art-loving uncle. From there, Canova proceeded to Milan where he was welcomed by Joachim Murat, along with Melzi d'Eril, vice president of the Italian Republic and his friend Giuseppe Bossi, secretary of the Academy of Brera. During his stay, Canova dined with Napoleon's stepson Eugène de Beauharnais and sat for his portrait by Andrea Appiani.

Before returning to Rome in December, Canova made a detour to Florence where he was greeted by Louis I, the Bourbon King of Etruria. As part of the March 1801 Treaty of Lunéville, Ferdinand, Duke of Parma surrendered his duchy to France after his death in exchange for the new Kingdom of Etruria, the former Grand Duchy of Tuscany. That summer, Ferdinand's epileptic son was installed as Louis I, King of Etruria; his wife, Marie Louisa, was the daughter of Spanish king Charles VII.

Florentine officials met with Canova to discuss a commission. The treasure of the Uffizi Gallery, the *Medici Venus,* was widely regarded as the standard of female perfection in sculpture. The marble was believed to be a first-century copy of a post-Praxitelean bronze statue dating from around 200 B.C.E. In 1667, the work was moved to Florence from Rome because the pope thought that the sensuous pose encouraged lewd behavior. The erotic depiction of Venus covering her breasts and pubic area with her hands added to its popularity with wealthy travelers on the Grand Tour.

At the time, Venus's lips were painted red, her hair sparkled with gold leaf, and earrings hung from her earlobes.[33] As Hugh Honour writes, ". . . the Parian marble is indeed outstanding both for its colour and texture—and, more surprisingly, the voluptuousness of the form."[34]

In June 1796, while touring the Uffizi with the gallery director Tommaso Puccini, Napoleon saw the celebrated *Medici Venus* in the gallery's Tribuna. At the time, he threatened that he would take the famous marble to Paris if Florence declared war on France. Two years later, when a French invasion of Tuscany seemed imminent, Puccini transferred the prized statue along with other Uffizi masterworks to Palermo for safekeeping. That did not stop Napoleon. In September 1802, French forces seized the *Medici Venus* in Palermo. Napoleon called her a "bride" for the Vatican's *Apollo Belvedere,* already installed at the Louvre.

Distraught over the loss, Florentine officials asked Canova to create a copy of the prized antiquity. He returned to Rome without making a decision. In early February 1803, Canova accepted the commission and requested a cast of the *Medici Venus.*[35] Though Canova repeated the *Medici Venus*'s turn of the head, the rest of his Venus was new. She stood some seven inches taller. Her stance was reversed, with her left knee bent instead of the right. Her coiffure more closely resembled that of the *Capitoline Venus*. Instead of portraying Venus nude, Canova added the cloth that she modestly clutches to her breast.

According to his assistant Adamo Tadolini, Canova conceived the gesture after his beautiful studio model was overcome with shyness when asked to undress. Some contemporary art historians have interpreted the goddess's hunch and closed legs as a political statement by the sculptor, a subtle expression of his feelings about the rape of Italy by the French.

Given Canova's resentment of Napoleon's art confiscations, it's tempting to read the statue politically. Yet the critical literature of the day focuses on the statue's expressiveness and naturalness. It seems more likely that Canova invented the modest pose to distinguish his Venus from her famous antique prototypes. From the start, the commission did take on a patriotic quality when the Florentines thanked Canova for helping ease the painful loss of their beloved *Medici Venus*.

Canova would soon carve a far less modest Venus, creating a scandal with a life-size marble portrait of Napoleon's topless sister Pauline.

THREE

NAPOLEON'S EYE

On November 7, 1800, Napoleon and Joséphine made the short hop from the Tuileries to the Louvre. The occasion was the inauguration of the Musée des Antiques, located on the ground floor in the former summer apartment of Anne of Austria, who, in 1638, over two decades into her marriage and as the thirty-seven-year-old Spanish-born queen consort, gave birth to the future Louis XIV.

Anne of Austria's mid-seventeenth-century royal suite now brimmed with over one hundred antique marble sculptures, mainly hauled off from Rome, Venice, Modena, and Mantua, along with antiquities from the royal collection nationalized during the Revolution.

The gallery's curator, Ennio Visconti, was intimately acquainted with the looted Italian treasures. His father, Giovanni Battista Visconti, was the Papal States's superintendent of antiquities and first director of the Vatican's Pio-Clementino museum. Together, they had worked on a description of the Capitoline and Vatican collections. Visconti, who fled to Paris after Naples occupied Rome, was considered one of the most famous antiquarians of the day.

Inspired by the thematic groupings in the Capitoline and Vatican museums, Visconti tried matching the antiquities with Giovanni Francesco Romanelli's ornate ceiling paintings for the queen's six-room flat. Architect Jean-Arnaud Raymond replaced the walls separating the rooms with columns pilfered from the Palatine Chapel in Aachen (removed ten centuries earlier from Ravenna and Rome by Charlemagne). With its red-and-white marble revetment modeled after a Roman bath, Paris's new antiquities gallery resembled the Pio-Clementino.[1]

Visitors entered via the former Mars Rotunda. The spandrels of its dome sported new reliefs depicting personifications of the great cultures of the past, culminating with modern France. The *Colossus of Memnon*, the *Apollo Belvedere*, and Michelangelo's *Moses* represented Egypt, Greece, and Italy. The rotunda led to the Emperors Room, populated with statues of Rome's imperial rulers. Large imitation bronze medallions of the Po, Tiber, Nile, and Rhine rivers symbolized France's recent military campaigns. History painter Charles Meynier decorated the ceiling with the *Emperors Hadrian and Justinian presenting to the World the Codes of Roman Law*. Three more halls followed, dedicated to the seasons, illustrious men, and the Romans.

The showstoppers were two acclaimed masterpieces from the Vatican. The monumental *Laocoön* was installed in a niche at the end of a long corridor visible from the rotunda. Once displayed in Titus's palace in Rome, the massive marble was described by Pliny the Elder as the work of the sculptor Agesander of Rhodes and his two sons, "superior to any other work of sculpture present in the city." The jury is still out on whether the famed group marble of the priest of Troy and his two sons was a first-century original by the Rhodes father and sons or a copy by them of an earlier bronze model.[2]

Turning right led to the Apollo Hall, the new home for the *Apollo Belvedere*. A second-century C.E. Roman copy of Leochares's fourth-century B.C.E. bronze from the Agora in Athens, the ancient marble depicts the divine archer Apollo nude save his sandals and a draped cloak resting on his right arm. In Paris, the marble tour de force was placed on a high pedestal above a raised platform. Framing the recess, supporting two busts, were two red granite columns from Charlemagne's tomb in Aachen.

Now Napoleon attached a plaque to the pedestal of the *Apollo Belvedere*. The inscription read: "The statue of Apollo/Erected on this pedestal/Found at Antium, at the end of the XV century, placed in the Vatican by Julius II/At the beginning of the XVI century/Conquered in the Year V of the Republic/By the Army of Italy/Under the orders of General Bonaparte/Has been set her on 21 Germinal Year VIII/First year of his Consulate."[3] Two days later, on the first anniversary of Napoleon's coup d'état, the antiquities gallery opened to the public.

Part of the official delegation that day was Dominique-Vivant Denon. Since returning from Egypt, he had been compiling his impressions of Egypt along with engravings of some three hundred of his sketches of the ancient architecture and ornaments. In 1802, he published *Travels in Upper and Lower Egypt during the Campaigns of General Bonaparte*. An instant bestseller, *Travels* was translated into Italian, Spanish, German, and English, enjoying some forty printings. In addition to securing Denon's reputation as an artist, *Travels* promoted France's army as heir to the Roman legions and inspired the Egyptian Revival style in decorative art and architecture. Not since ancient Rome had there been such enthusiasm for Egyptian art.

Denon extolled the originality of ancient Egyptian art and architecture. "Having borrowed nothing from other nations, the Egyptians added not one extraneous ornament, not a single superfluity to the lines dictated by necessity," he wrote. "Order and simplicity were their principles, which they raised to the sublime."[4] His drawings and engravings were especially influential in the decorative arts where Egyptian Revival furniture sported sphinxes, chimera heads, and Egyptian gods and goddesses. As Frederica Todd Harlow notes, Denon brought "the art of the pharaohs into the drawing rooms of Napoleonic France . . . transforming the artistic idiom of an ancient people into the sumptuous decoration of Napoleonic France."[5]

Denon dedicated the travel guide to Napoleon, bolstering the first consul's image as a patron of art and science: "To associate the glory of our name with the splendour of the monuments of Egypt is to combine the grandeur of our century with the mythical eras of history; to rekindle the ashes of Sesostris and Mendes, who, like you, were conquerors and benefactors. When Europe learns that I accompanied you on one of your most memorable expeditions, it will greet my book with keen interest. I have spared no effort in making it worthy of the hero to whom I wish to dedicate it."[6]

The literary sensation was a propaganda boon for Napoleon who rewarded its author by appointing him director of the Musée des Monuments Français (in the former convent of the Petits Augustins), a special museum devoted to the French school at Versailles, and the Louvre. Several weeks after his appointment, on January 1, 1803, Denon wrote his patron:

"I spend my time in execution of all what you've entrusted me in order to engross all and demonstrate in future the opinion that your choice was given to me and every time that I perceive the amelioration in doing what I do with reverence for you and I address you my thanks for my preference to its execution. Accept, General, the homage of my profound respect."[7]

Denon was an inspired choice. Napoleon wasn't a connoisseur; he was known to admire artworks based on their size. As Thomas Gaehtgens puts it, Denon became Napoleon's Colbert, his minister of fine arts, guiding him in all matters of taste.[8]

To novelist Anatole France, the witty and dapper museum director looked like "he had just stepped out of a fête by Watteau."[9] Denon would earn the moniker "Napoleon's Eye" for his ability to pick the finest Western art for the Louvre. Traveling with the French army, he confiscated works from vanquished Italy, Spain, Belgium, Prussia, and Austria. He was so good at his job, French generals dubbed him "the packer" and the "thief on the coattails of the Grande Armée." Indefatigable and driven, Denon devoted himself to making the Louvre the "most beautiful museum in the universe."

To help run the Louvre, Denon assembled a talented team. Athanase Lavallée remained secretary. Léon Dufourny who had seized many renowned works from Italy including the *Medici Venus*, became paintings conservator. Visconti remained antiquities curator, and Morel d'Arleux was named curator of drawings and chalcography. But Denon fired dealer and connoisseur Jean-Baptiste-Pierre Le Brun. The ex-husband of émigré portraitist Élisabeth Vigée Le Brun and grandnephew of Charles Le Brun, Louis XIV's first painter, Le Brun had played a key role in assembling the collection of the Musée National, selecting art from fleeing and condemned nobles.

Though Denon managed to eliminate rivals like Le Brun, a formidable new competitor soon emerged. During his first weeks as museum director, Denon had the first of many run-ins with Napoleon's architect Pierre Fontaine. Though Fontaine was officially Denon's superior, the two competed for Napoleon's approval and often disagreed aesthetically. In November 26, 1801, Fontaine described Denon's lack of cooperation in providing Louvre artworks to decorate the Tuileries.

"The First Consul insisted that not only the public deposits, but also the houses of the ministers, those of the State authorities, should contribute to the furnishing and decoration of the Tuileries apartments," Fontaine wrote. "That is why we are asking the minister for the Savonnerie carpets of the Legislative Body. The administration of the museum of painting, which has a large number of effects, which we ask of it, sees with difficulty draw from its stores the objects committed to its preservation, it believes in giving them to diminish its importance. He dared not refuse, but he appeared to be displeased, a bad grace, which made him wrong in the mind of the First Consul."

The power struggle continued when Fontaine replaced Jean-Armand Raymond as the museum's architect in 1804. Another dispute broke out when Fontaine and Percier demolished the latrines during a project. An irked Denon wrote to Fontaine, urging the reinstallation of the latrines "as promptly as possible, in order to avoid evacuation in the courtyards, on the stairways, and perhaps even in the gallery of the museum, which would surely happen if the guards appointed to safeguard and maintain the propriety of this monument had no place to which to direct those in need."[10]

The Louvre had never been finished. During the Renaissance, François I turned the former medieval fortress into a royal abode, but it did not compare to his magnificent châteaux at Fontainebleau and Blois. Louis XIV's ministers had tried unsuccessfully to keep him in Paris by embellishing the Louvre, even inviting Gian Lorenzo Bernini to draw up plans. But the Louvre was abandoned by the three Louies who continued amassing art for Versailles and other royal palaces. By the mid-eighteenth century, the royal art trove was one of Europe's largest, numbering some 1,800 paintings and an important sculpture collection.

During the Revolution, the royal collection was nationalized, along with art from France's churches and private art collections. The Louvre was chosen for France's national museum. As painter Jacques-Louis David described, "The national museum will embrace knowledge in all its manifold beauty and will be the admiration of the universe. By embodying these grand ideas, worthy of a free people . . . the museum . . . will become among the most powerful illustrations of the French Republic."[11]

Opened to the public in August 1793, the Musée National offered a jumble of paintings, antique busts, clocks, and porcelain. To meet the demand, the museum implemented a ten-day schedule with six days for artists and visitors, three for the public, and one for cleaning. But with the exception of paintings in the Salon Carré, the museum soon closed for a year of improvements. Complicating the project was the arrival of new masterworks—war booty from the Netherlands.

After the Directory government confiscated more art in Italy, the museum closed its doors again in 1796. When it reopened three years later, masterpieces from Rome and Venice hung in the Salon Carré adjoining the Grand Gallery; a selection of the most superb Old Master drawings lined the walls of the Apollo Gallery. Antiquity's most famous marble sculptures were installed below the Grand Gallery in the new Musée des Antiquities.

It was around this time, writes Andrew McClellan, that the museum took on an atmosphere of military conquest. A journalist reviewing an exhibition of plundered Italian art described a museum door decorated with captured arms and battle standards from Napoleon's Italian campaign. "The sight of this trophy warmed my blood, the words brought tears to my eyes," he wrote. "One day we will raise monuments of marble and bronze to our warriors. Unnecessary efforts! The true and lasting monuments to their glory will be in our museums."[12]

When Denon's tenure began in late 1802, art occupied just a fraction of the vast former royal palace. Works were displayed in the Apollo Gallery, Salon Carré, Grand Gallery, and the new Musée des Antiquities below. Henri IV had built the Grand Gallery between 1595 and 1610 to link the Louvre and Tuileries palaces. Until Louis XVI decided to install a sampling of royal art, the Grand Gallery housed the royal collection of relief maps.

But measuring 1,300 feet long with numerous windows, the corridor was not ideal for viewing art.

Denon reorganized the floor-to-ceiling painting display. In his new hang, pictures were organized around masterpieces. For example, Denon placed Raphael's celebrated *Transfiguration* in the center of a bay. Surrounding this final altarpiece were other works from his brief, extraordinary career—from his early years in Perugino and formative period in Florence to his mature phase in Rome. According to Denon, he chose the Raphaels so "one could see at a glance the extent of this artist's genius, the astonishing rapidity of his progress, and the variety of genres which his talent encompassed."[13]

In an invitation to Napoleon to see the installation, Denon further explained his goal. "It is like a life of the master of all painters," he wrote on January 1, 1803. "The first time you walk through this gallery, I hope you will find that this exercise already brings a character of order, instruction, and classification. I will continue in the same spirit for all the schools, and in a few months, while visiting the gallery one will be able to have . . . a history course in the art of painting."[14] By arranging paintings in an art historical dialogue, Denon reinvented museum display, notes Noah Charney.[15]

That summer, Denon added a history course in the art of sculpture. One hundred cases of looted antiquities arrived from Italy, including the Uffizi's *Medici Venus*. In a speech to members of the Institut de France, Denon described the newest treasure: "Dressed in her modesty alone, her nakedness is pure. Her expression of happiness belongs to her perfection, to the plenitude of her being. The smile on her face is not yet that of voluptuousness, and yet happiness is already on her lips." The former diplomat also praised his powerful patron. "The hero of our century, during the torment of war, required of our enemies trophies of peace, and he has seen to their conservation."[16]

Denon informed Napoleon that the *Medici Venus* was safely in Paris and proposed that he inaugurate the new antique halls. Reflecting his admiration for Egypt, he installed Egyptian and Egyptian-inspired sculpture from Italy, including the *Antinous* from Hadrian's Villa. Denon also suggested renaming the Louvre the Musée Napoléon. "There is a frieze on the door waiting for an inscription, I think that Napoleon's Museum is the only one that suits it," he wrote.

In fact, Denon had already ordered the bronze letters. For the museum's main entrance, at the southeast corner of the Cour Napoleon, he also commissioned a colossal bronze bust of Napoleon from Tuscan sculptor Lorenzo Bartolini. Set in a niche above the entrance to the museum, the imposing bust measured over five feet tall and weighed over one ton. To compensate for the viewing angle, Bartolini elongated Napoleon's neck and accentuated his chin and the lock of hair in the middle of his forehead.[17] He captured the bend in his nose, berries in laurel wreath. Ends of the strips tying the wreath fell onto Napoleon's shoulders.

Until the bronze was finished, a mold was installed on August 15, 1805, Napoleon's birthday. The truncated bust format known as a herm hailed from Roman art, and gave the portrait a hieratic quality.[18] As Isabelle Leroy-Jay Lemaistre writes, "The general herm shape, the bare shoulders symmetrically decorated with the ties of the crown and the laurel crown itself, like the Augustan stylization of the features, speak to Bartolini's training in the ateliers of David and François Lemot, and to the zeal of Denon whose artistic preferences are well-known. Denon could not but admire this sculptor driven by such a strong feeling for antiquity."[19]

Denon cosigned Bartolini's *Napoléon Empereur*, cast with bronze from enemy cannons.

Behind his many official titles, Vivant Denon was Napoleon's image maker. With its political message of patriotism and citizenship, Neoclassicism was the ideal artistic style for the public relations campaign, allowing artists to compare Napoleon to history's great military commanders—Alexander the Great, Julius Caesar, Hannibal, and Charlemagne. Denon's A-list painters included Antoine-Jean Gros, Jean-Auguste-Dominique Ingres, and their teacher Jacques-Louis David. "O! My friends, what a beautiful head he has," David raved about Napoleon. "It is pure, it is great, it is as beautiful as the antique. There is a man to whom altars would have been raised in ancient times."

Denon conceived a series of monumental battlefield scenes starring a heroic Napoleon. To lend authenticity to the canvases, Denon sent draftsmen to the battlefields to take notes on everything from costumes to topography. Antiquity's great generals had also invited artists along on their campaigns. Alexander the Great took artists to India. During Trajan's Dacian campaign, artists were embedded in the Roman army, sketching scenes used later by sculptors for the famous column. These include scenes of the emperor supervising the crossing of the Danube, caring for his troops at a battlefield hospital, and demonstrating *clementia* to prisoners brought before him.

One of Denon's go-to artists was Antoine-Jean Gros, who took Jean-Germain Drouais's place as David's favorite student. Gros would later run David's studio when his mentor was forced into exile.[20] While in Genoa in 1796, Gros had the good fortune of meeting Joséphine who invited him to Milan. That December, he started *Napoleon on the Bridge at Arcole*. Thanks to Joséphine, the artist got several sessions with his subject.

After two days of fighting in November 1796, French troops captured Arcole, sealing the conquest of Northern Italy. Gros, who had been on the scene, depicted the young general as a dashing hero with long flowing hair, seizing a flag and leading an attack across the bridge. On Napoleon's drawn sword, Gros inscribed "Armée d'Italie" to symbolize that his real weapon was his brave troops. According to eyewitnesses, the reality was less glamorous.

Napoleon did not actually cross the bridge. Rather, he was stopped before the bridge when he was knocked into a ditch.[21] Despite this, one of his generals, Antoine-François Andréossy, claimed that Napoleon's actions resembled those of Caesar dismounting at Munda and running to the front lines to rally his troops.[22] In a savvy investment, Napoleon paid to have Gros's portrait engraved. The print helped launch his image as one of history's great commanders.

In the spring of 1802, Denon hired Gros to paint *Bonaparte Visiting the Victims of the Plague at Jaffa*. With his soldiers stricken by the plague, Napoleon visited a makeshift hospital in March 1799. In the original pencil sketch, Gros depicted Napoleon standing, holding a plague victim in his arms. The final painting was completely changed, perhaps at Denon's suggestion. Gros portrayed Napoleon touching the sore in the armpit of one of his soldiers in a miraculous gesture of healing—in the tradition of Jesus Christ, the saints Roch and Carlo Borromeo, and the "king's touch" of French and English royals. "The picture made Napoleon appear as a new 'roi thaumatuge' (healing king)," writes Walter Friedlaender.[23]

Gros may have based Napoleon's pose on the *Apollo Belvedere*. In his catalogue of the Museo Pio-Clementino, Visconti posited that the Athenians had commissioned *Apollo Belvedere* in praise of Apollo after a plague during the Peloponnesian War; the serpent at his feet represented medicine, which Apollo taught to men. As David O'Brien notes, Gros was familiar with both Visconti's work and the famed statue that he helped pack up from the Vatican as a member of Napoleon's arts commission.[24]

The picture caused a sensation at the Salon of 1804. Joseph Fouché, Napoleon's formidable police prefect, said it was Napoleon's most beautiful gesture. Artists hung a laurel wreath over the monumental canvas at the Louvre. Declaring the work a masterpiece, Denon wrote Napoleon: "The memory of the expedition to Egypt was still fresh in people's minds, and the glory of the young artist, who had made sacred the memory of one event in this campaign, was as it were involved with the hero who had directed it. You are represented in it in a noble fashion, with the serenity of an exalted soul. . . . Your costume is admirable, your appearance spirited and accurate. Round you everyone is so moved with confidence and hope, that there is no feeling of the horror such a scene could inspire by its representation of all that is most disgusting in nature."[25]

Gros's painting of Napoleon as a caring Samaritan also helped deflect attention from the massacre that coincided with the plague's outbreak. In attacking Jaffa in March 1799, French troops slaughtered women and children in addition to soldiers. Napoleon ordered the massacre of an estimated two thousand Turkish prisoners on a nearby beach.[26]

After his return from Egypt and coup d'état, Napoleon found himself on shaky ground. Advancing across Northern Italy, the Austrians defeated the French near Genoa in April 1800. Napoleon quickly launched the second Italian campaign, marching his army through the snowy Great Saint Bernard Pass crossed by Julius Caesar, Hannibal, and Charlemagne.

After surprising the Austrians, his army defeated them decisively at the Battle of Marengo on June 14, 1800.

Napoleon hurried back to Paris, but postponed his soldiers' entry to stage a dramatic event for Bastille Day on July 14, 1800. News of the crossing spread quickly. Jacques-Louis David commemorated the event for Spain's Charles IV in *Bonaparte Crossing the Great St. Bernard Pass* (1800–1801). Though Napoleon reportedly rode a mule, not a horse, and slid part way down the mountain into Italy on his behind, David portrayed him heroically riding a rearing white steed, his red cloak blowing in the wind.

Like the *adlocutio,* or orator's pose, seen in Roman coins, sculpture, and possibly the equestrian statue of Marcus Aurelius, Napoleon's right arm is raised and index finger pointed. In the left foreground, "Bonaparte" is etched on the rocks by the names of his predecessors, Hannibal and Charlemagne. At Napoleon's feet, David added miniature soldiers hoisting a cannon up the mountain. Since Napoleon refused to pose, David convinced the first consul's valet to lend him his uniform, red cloak, hat, sword, and boots, and dressed up a dummy as a model. The propaganda piece was so popular, Napoleon ordered three more copies.[27]

On August 31, 1801, Interior Minister Jean-Antoine Chaptal proposed the creation of provincial art galleries across France. Napoleon signed the decree the next day, establishing fifteen museums in Rennes, Nancy, Dijon, Lyon, Nantes, Strasbourg, Bordeaux, Lille, Rouen, Marseille, Toulouse, and Caen, along with Mainz, Geneva, and Brussels, annexed in 1797. Each museum was to have a small but encyclopedic collection of art with works from different schools, countries, and periods, along with an art college to develop local talent.[28]

While keeping the most important art for the Louvre, Denon sent many paintings to the new provincial museums. In the process, Denon did not hesitate to dismember altarpieces, like his predecessors who seized the center of the Ghent Altarpiece. Denon would try to acquire the wings and Adam and Eve panels from the bishop and mayor of Ghent. When they refused, he offered to trade paintings by Rubens for the panels. Now Denon sent a Rubens altarpiece from Flanders to the Brera in Milan, and its predella to Dijon and Nancy. Two parts of a Mantegna predella went to Tours; the third stayed in Paris.[29]

Excelling as museum director, Denon soon found himself running four prestigious luxury brands: Sèvres porcelain, Savonnerie carpets, and the Gobelins and Beauvais tapestry factories. He oversaw the minting of coins and medals and palace furniture, and managed major building projects. By 1811, his official responsibilities included "head of the museums of French monuments and of the French school at Versailles, the galleries of government palaces, the studios of chalcography [engravings on copper], gem-engraving and mosaics," and the "buying and transport of works of art, the supervision of modern works ordered by the government and of archaeological digs at Rome."[30]

In addition to the provincial museums, Denon selected large canvases for Napoleon's personal collection. The brilliant conversationalist charmed Joséphine who tapped him as her art adviser. Though the spoils of war were supposedly earmarked for the Louvre, she was given "temporary" custody of many Greco-Roman sculptures to decorate her apartments and parks. Denon also chose paintings for Malmaison where Joséphine formed a picture gallery.

Before the Revolution, Denon had been keeper of the cabinet of carved gems inherited by Louis XV from Madame de Pompadour—miniature divinities, mythological heroes, and historical figures. Now Joséphine asked him to keep an eye out for cameos and turquoise for her on his travels.[31] On one occasion, Joséphine wrote the intendant general of her husband's military household, describing how Denon had a assembled a collection of cameos for her on his travels and asking him "if while on campaign you come across anything unusual in the way of pearls or gems, please buy them for me."

Anxious to please her, generals delivered pilfered cameos.[32] According to Ernest Knapton, Joséphine's collection amounted to "gifts," "plunder and purchases on an extravagant scale."[33] During her own trip to Italy, Joséphine acquired coral and cameos from Naples, glass, mosaics, cameos, and intaglios from Rome, and copies of Greek and Roman jewels excavated from various archeological sites.

First produced in Hellenistic times, cameos were wildly popular in ancient Rome. Early in his reign, Augustus's official seal was an intaglio featuring a sphinx that belonged to his mother, followed by a seal with a portrait of Alexander the Great. The emperor finally commissioned a portrait of himself for his seal from the Greek master carver Dioskourides. His successors used this seal until the end of the Julian-Claudian dynasty.[34] Throughout the Renaissance and Enlightenment, Rome remained the center for cameo production. After Napoleon's first Italian campaign, engraved gems enjoyed new popularity in France. Following the French invasion of Rome, Napoleon presented Joséphine with cameos—most famously the Vatican's extraordinary Gonzaga Cameo.

As a wedding gift, Napoleon had given Joséphine a simple ring with twin hearts. Now the first consul allowed his wife to use pearls and precious stones from the *Trésor de la Couronne* (Crown Jewels), which he began replenishing after the revolutionary dispersals. Joséphine amassed one of Europe's best private jewelry collections, almost all in the symmetrical classical style with ancient motifs. As in ancient Rome, Joséphine's jewels were a symbol of status and power.

Joséphine wore some of the gems in her hair which she cut short like her husband, in a style evocative of antiquity. Worn short, tousled, and close to the head, fashionable hairstyles were named the Titus, à la Agrippine, or à la Phèdre (after the Greek mythological character Phaedra).[35] The popularity of these hairstyles may have been inspired by plays like Racine's *Britannicus* and *Phèdre*. Mozart's *Clemenza di Tito*, based on Suetonius, helped sustain Titus's reputation as one of Rome's best emperors.

Keen on reestablishing the prominence of Parisian jewelers, Napoleon supported his wife's passion for carved gems. The art form was a favorite of the rulers of ancient Greece and Rome who often ascribed magical properties to gemstones. Emperors and elite Romans commissioned their portraits in intaglio, carved into the stone, along with the more labor-intensive cameos, carved in raised relief. Unlike Roman sculpture which went largely unsigned, the names of over seventy Greek and Roman gem engravers are known from their signatures.[36]

In addition to popularizing neoclassical jewelry, Joséphine became an influential fashionista. Jacques-Louis David's history paintings had underscored the parallels between antiquity and the new French Republic. Filled with classical costumes, the popular canvases helped make classical dress fashionable in France. According to E. Claire Cage, by incorporating classical aesthetics into their wardrobes, elite Parisians, such as Joséphine, Thérésa Tallien, and the celebrated *salonnière* Juliette Récamier, "drew upon an ennobling language of the arts and of the virtues and glory of antiquity."[37]

Though Joséphine called the shawls Napoleon brought back for her from Egypt "hideous," she turned them into a signature fashion statement, evoking the drapery of antique statues. She owned several hundred shawls in cashmere, lace, gauze, and muslin embroidered in gold and silver.[38] French women took lessons in how to drape their large scarves antique-style like Joséphine. They also bought her favorite perfume, Á la Cloche d'Argent, and lace from Chantilly and Brussels.[39]

As Aileen Ribeiro writes, "Women so dressed, elegantly draped in the large cashmere shawls in fashion, and with which the most adept could create 'antique' poses, could easily be taken, in a flight of fancy, for those on vases or wall paintings. . . . The neoclassical . . . actually entered the mainstream of fashion, albeit in forms that would have been unrecognized by the ancient Greeks or Romans."[40]

Power dressing goes back to the ancient world when costume conferred legitimacy and authority. As Shelley Hales writes, "Costume would be crucial for imperial families whose claim to power lay, in not inconsiderable measure, in their very visibility. Emperors and their entourage were everywhere: in person around Rome, and in the thousands of images set up around the empire. Whilst portrait heads changed, imperial outfits remained largely constant . . ."[41]

The triumphal costume connected its wearer toward the divine, adds Hales, from robes copied after those of Jupiter to the military cuirass associated with Mars. Triumphal garb was compulsory for Roman emperors at their own funerals.[42] To reflect their position, imperial first ladies created their own looks, which featured jewels.[43]

The quintessential garment for Roman men was the toga; married women wore the stola, often covered with a mantle or palla. But notes Michele George, "Togas, like the Romans who wore them, were not created equal." Rome developed a complex system of dress determined by position and law. For example, the purple bordered toga, the *toga praetexta*, could only be worn by magistrates and children. The embroidered *toga picta* was worn exclusively for triumphant generals (sometimes bestowed on friendly foreign kings).

As *triumvir*, Octavian issued an edict around 35 B.C.E. limiting the color purple to senators and magistrates. After the civil war, he required all citizens to don togas on public occasions in Rome.[44] Later, togas were required dress for the daily morning *salutatio* where clients greeted patrons, along with imperial banquets. Around 162, Septimius Severus, fresh from North Africa, arrived at a banquet in Rome wearing a pallium. Marcus Aurelius reportedly lent the embarrassed future emperor one of his own togas.[45]

Like the Roman hierarchy of togas, France's new Consulate established its own sartorial code to identify rank and office. In reaction to the revealing gowns of the Directory, Napoleon strongly encouraged Joséphine and her entourage to dress more modestly. To bolster the French textile industry, the first consul also banned Indian muslin (imported through England), and made formal dress obligatory for receptions. The result was a dramatic shift to more expensive velvet and satin gowns.[46] Elaborate uniforms were also introduced for men. By decree, consuls and ministers, members of the Council of State and legislature, and prefects and senators were all required to wear heavily embroidered uniforms.[47]

Napoleon would soon instate an even stricter dress code, reinforcing the social structure of his new Empire by evoking imperial Rome.

FOUR

PARISII

In the summer of 53 B.C.E., Julius Caesar visited Parisii on the Île de la Cité and asked the Gallic tribes to support his campaign. Instead, Vercingetorix, king of Gaul, led an uprising against the Romans. The following year, Caesar dispatched a deputy, Titus Labienus, and four legions to crush the rebellion. After victories at the Battles of Lutetia (near today's Eiffel Tower) and Alesia, Labienus rebuilt an abandoned village on the left bank of the Seine River.

Lutetia, probably from the Latin word *luta* for swamp, followed the traditional Roman town design along a north-south axis, the *cardo maximus*. On the left bank, the main street followed today's rue Saint-Jacques. It crossed the Seine and traversed the Île de la Cité on two wooden bridges, the Petit Pont and Grand Pont (today's Pont Notre-Dame). A port was located on the island where the parvis in front of Notre Dame Cathedral is today.

Like other Roman towns in France, Lutetia, capital of Roman Gaul, boasted a forum, theaters, baths, and a governor's palace. The main building of the forum, near today's Pantheon, was over three hundred twenty feet long and featured a temple dedicated to Jupiter, a basilica for civic functions, and a square portico with shops. Nearby, seventeen thousand fans, nearly the entire population of the town, packed an enormous oval amphitheater to watch comedies and dramas, and gladiators fight wild animals. For mock sea battles, the amphitheater was flooded with water.

Also near the forum was a large bath complex, the Thermes de Cluny. As in Rome, an aqueduct carried fresh water some ten miles from the Rungis plateau south of Paris to the baths. In addition to a thirty-foot pool, there was a *frigidarium,* or cold room, a three-room *caldarium,* or hot bath, with heated floors, a *tepidarium* or lukewarm bath, and areas for relaxing and exercise. Besides Roman architecture, the town enjoyed Roman cuisine, including wine, olive oil, and garum, a popular fish sauce similar to ketchup.

Around the mid-third century, Christianity was introduced. When Saint Denis, Bishop of the Parisii, refused to renounce his faith, he was beheaded by the Romans on Mount Mercury. According to legend, Saint Denis picked up his head and carried it to a Christian cemetery some six miles away. The hill where he was executed became known as the Mountain of Martyrs, today's Montmartre. A church was built on the site of his grave, Saint-Denis, the future necropolis of the kings of France.

Early in the fourth century, Lutetia was renamed Civitas Parisiorum, or City of the Parisii after the Celtic tribe that originally settled the area in the third century B.C.E. By the late Roman Empire, the name was simplified to Parisius in Latin and Paris in French. Paris gained importance during the five-year rule of Julian the Apostate, Constantine's nephew. After his soldiers proclaimed him Augustus or Emperor in 360, Paris enjoyed a brief period as capital of the Western Roman Empire (the next imperial coronation here was not until Napoleon's in 1804). Near the end of the Roman Empire, emperors Valentian I and Gratian spent winters in the city.

In 461, Paris was besieged by the Salian Franks led by Merovingian King Childeric I. Saint Geneviève rescued the city from starvation by bringing wheat from Brie and Champagne by barge. Two decades later, Childeric's teenage son Clovis became King of the Franks. In 486, Clovis defeated the last Roman army, taking control of Gaul. With Geneviève's consent, Clovis entered Paris. He was converted to Christianity by his wife Clotilde, and baptized at Reims in 496. Because of Paris's strategic location between the Loire and Rhine, Clovis chose it as his capital in 508.

The city's prestige waned when Carolingian king Charlemagne moved the Frankish capital and Holy Roman Empire to Aix-la-Chapelle or Aachen. At the end of the tenth century, the Capetians came to power, restoring the royal palace on the Île de la Cité and building a church where the Sainte-Chapelle now stands. The big change came in the twelfth century, when the Capetians turned Paris into France's political, economic, religious, and cultural capital.

At Saint-Denis, the Merovingian church built in 775 by Charlemagne's father Pepin the Short was replaced by an abbey church in a dramatic new Gothic style; the Cathedral of Notre Dame soon followed. On the left bank of the Seine, the new University of Paris was founded to train scholars in theology, mathematics, and law. Meanwhile, trade and finance were centered on the right bank (north of the Seine), with a port, central market, and workshops. Boasting a population of roughly one hundred thousand, medieval Paris was western and central Europe's largest city.

To protect against an English attack from Normandy, Philip II erected the massive fortress of the Louvre. Surrounded by a moat, the rectangular fortress sported four towers and a central circular tower nearly one hundred feet tall. Philip rebuilt the wooden Petit-Pont and Grand-Pont in stone, and began construction of a covered market, Les Halles. He also used stone to pave the city's foul-smelling mud streets. Before leaving for the Third Crusade, Philip strengthened Paris's defenses with stone walls on both banks of the Seine.

Charles V built a new wall of fortifications around the city. He also built the Bastille fortress at the eastern end of Paris, and an imposing fortress at Vincennes, east of the city. In 1534, François I became the first French king to live at the Louvre, demolishing the central tower to create an open courtyard. Near the end of his reign, François replaced one of Philip II's wings with a new wing sporting a Renaissance façade. François also reinforced Paris's position as a center of learning.

François's son Henri II continued to decorate Paris in the French Renaissance style. The finest Renaissance fountain in the city, the Fontaine des Innocents, was built to celebrate his official entrance into Paris in 1549.

Like his father, Henri added a new wing to the Louvre, the Pavillon du Roi, to the south along the Seine, which included his first floor bedroom. He also built a magnificent ceremonial hall, the Salle des Cariatides, in his father's Lescot Wing.

After Henri's death from jousting wounds, his widow Catherine de' Medici constructed the Tuileries Palace perpendicular to the Seine, just outside the city's Charles V wall. To the west of the palace, she created a large Italian-style garden. Louis XIV, who transferred his court from Paris to Versailles, commissioned Les Invalides as a hospital and church for war-wounded and retired soldiers.

By 1800, Paris's Roman roots lay buried under fourteen centuries of construction. The Roman aqueduct d'Arcueil that supplied fresh water to the city was long gone. Some six hundred thousand Parisians lived without a sewer system. The neglected capital looked and smelled like the city of Louis XVI. Unlike London, the streets of Paris had no sidewalks. Seagulls fed on heaps of garbage. Not much had improved in the half century since Voltaire described the city as a model of squalor, shapelessness, and disorder.[1]

Fifty-five fountains had potable water—one per every ten thousand Parisians. An estimated twenty thousand Parisian houses and buildings lacked any water supply. Running on a limited schedule, turned off at night, the crowded fountains were supplied by two large seventeenth-century water pumps next to the Seine, the Samaritaine, and Notre-Dame, and by two large steam pumps at Chaillot and Gros Caillou installed in 1781.[2] After filling their buckets at the public fountains or Seine, water carriers traveled from house to house with two buckets hanging from a yoke of wood across their shoulders.

Shortly after taking power, Napoleon asked his interior minister, chemist Jean-Antoine Chaptal, what would be the most useful thing he could do for Paris. Without hesitating, Chaptal replied, "Give it water." That evening, Napoleon ordered studies for an aqueduct from the Ourcq River. On May 19, 1802, Napoleon green lighted construction of the Ourcq canal, diverting the Seine from below the Bassin d'Arsenal to the Bassin de la Villette.

Leading the project was Pierre-Simon Girard, Napoleon's energetic Chief Engineer of Bridges and Highways and head of his service of water and sewers. Born in Caen, Girard was a math and engineering prodigy who served with Napoleon in Egypt. With his team of engineers, Girard had drawn up plans for Alexandria, the port, and surrounding coast. He took part in the study of ancient monuments, including on the island of Elephantine.

Funding for the canal was secured via a grant and wine taxes; the first stone was laid on September 23. Private financiers were awarded the contract to construct and manage the canals. The city of Paris agreed to purchase land and surrender tolls for ninety-nine years to the firms building the canals. Work began in 1805. In addition to the Canal d'Ourcq, Girard supervised the Canal Saint-Denis and Canal Saint-Martin to improve the city's waterways for trade.

Just before the Bassin de la Villette was filled with water on December 2, 1808, Napoleon wrote his new interior minister Emmanuel Crétet about the canal projects: "I made the glory of my reign consist in changing the face of the territory of my empire. The execution of these great works is as necessary to the interest of my people as to my own satisfaction."[3]

Napoleon also ordered the creation of Paris's sanitation system, with sewers built on the model of the ancient Roman sewer system. Thanks to a constant supply of running water, Roman hygiene was the most advanced in the ancient world. Construction of aqueducts was often driven by demand from Rome's popular bath complexes; bathing became a nearly universal practice among Romans of all social levels. Latrines with stone seats and small pipes underneath with running water were added to bath complexes, near forums, and the city's busiest streets. In private homes, people used chamber pots, which were emptied into the streets.

In the sixth century B.C.E., Rome began developing its sewer system. An underground network of conduits carried away the city's waste from public and private latrines, and removed water from the baths and runoff from roads.[4] Starting below the Forum of Augustus, the principal sewer, or Cloaca Maxima, passed between the basilica Julia and temple of Vesta, under the Arch of Constantine, before discharging into the Tiber below the Ponte Rotto through an arch sixteen feet in diameter.[5] Rome's sanitation system became "one of marvels of the world's civil engineering," writes Robert Hughes.[6]

Rome's aqueducts earned it the moniker *regina aquarum*, "the queen of waters."[7] Rome's first aqueduct, the Aqua Appia, was built in 312 B.C.E., and named for Appius Claudius Caecus, one of two powerful magistrates or censors. In 35 B.C.E., Augustus launched a major overhaul of the city's aging water supply. Old aqueducts were repaired and four new aqueducts were built to meet the needs of the growing population, estimated at one million people. Augustus also established a permanent office, the *cura aquarum,* dedicated to maintaining and improving Rome's water supply.[8]

By Trajan's reign in 109 C.E., eight aqueducts including the new Aqua Trajana brought water from the surrounding hills to the right bank of the Tiber. At the height of the Empire, eleven aqueducts supplied water from springs, a river, and a lake. Gravity brought the fresh water across great distances into elevated *castellum* or cisterns, then through both open conduits and underground lead pipes, supplying the city's baths, fountains, and houses. Most aqueducts were built at ground level or in a tunnel below. When the water had to cross the Roman Campagna, it arrived via long arches and bridges.

Distinctively Roman, a symbol of the Empire, the aqueduct was in Pliny's words, "the greatest wonder the world has ever seen."[9] About the system Pliny wrote: "But if anyone will note the abundance of water skillfully brought into the city, for public uses, for baths, for public basins, for houses, runnels, suburban gardens, and villas; if he will note the high aqueducts required for maintaining the proper elevation; the mountains which had to be pierced for the same reasons; and the valleys it was necessary to fill up; he will consider that the whole terrestrial orb offers nothing more marvelous."[10]

With over forty tributaries, flooding was a persistent problem with the 210-plus-mile long Tiber. In an effort to minimize the damage, Julius Caesar proposed changing the river's course by building a canal from the Milvian Bridge that would sweep water to the west, and flow along the slopes of the Vatican and Janiculum hills. Seeking a less drastic solution, Augustus created an office of curator of the Tiber, overseeing programs to clean and widen the riverbed. Augustus's lifelong friend Marcus Agrippa restored Rome's waterworks during his post as Augustus's aedile (the magistrate responsible for public buildings). Agrippa replaced the contractors in charge of the water supply with a new government department, the Statio Aquarium, which cleaned the clogged sewers, repaired the leaking aqueducts, and built the Aqua Julia aqueduct.[11]

The Romans also built aqueducts across the Empire. One of the most spectacular provincial aqueducts was the first century Pont du Gard. Considered a masterpiece of civil engineering, the bridge carried water over thirty miles from the Eure springs near Uzès to Nîmes across the Gard River. With its thirty-five arches, the magnificent aqueduct attracted eighteenth-century tourists, including philosopher Jean-Jacques Rousseau.

"I was expecting to discover a monument worthy of the men who had built it," wrote Rousseau, "but what in fact I saw went, for the only time in my life, well beyond my expectations. Only the Romans were capable of creating such an effect. The silence and solitude of its setting made this austere, noble monument all the more impressive. . . . The immense vaults sent back the echo of my footsteps, and I seemed to hear the voices of those who had built them. Now no more than a tiny insect lost in the vast structure, I felt more and more insignificant, when suddenly something lifted up my spirits and I cried out, 'Why am I not a Roman?'"[12]

Near the end of the Roman Empire, Rutilius sang the praises of its water system: ". . . and what of the streams suspended on aerial arches, higher than the rainbow's reach? One might call them mountains raised to the stars, Giants' work as Greece would say. Rivers are diverted into your precincts and concealed underground; the great Baths swallow up whole lakes. Your walled gardens are irrigated by streams of your own: they echo with the babble of local springs. Thus a cool breath refreshes the summer air; a healthy thirst is relieved by clear waters. . . . What of the groves enclosed by vaulted cloisters, where Rome-bred birds frolic with varied song?"[13]

The Romans were also famous for their bridge building. With the innovation of keystone for arches, they began constructing stone bridges. Among the famous examples was Julius Caesar's bridge over the Rhine. Finished in just ten days, the three-hundred-foot-long bridge sent a powerful message to the Germanic tribes—not even the Rhine could stop Rome. Two centuries later, Trajan's engineer Apollodorus of Damascus designed a legendary bridge across the Danube. Reaching sixty-two feet above the water, with a width of passage of 49 feet and length of 3,723 feet, it remained one of the world's longest arched bridges for over a millennium.[14]

Between 1801 and 1804, Napoleon ordered construction of three new bridges financed by a private company in exchange for toll revenues. To the traditional bridge building materials of granite, marble, and wood, Napoleon's engineers added iron, which had been used for two bridges in England. Architects Percier and Fontaine objected to iron on aesthetic grounds. "The city will gain little from the building of an iron bridge," Fontaine wrote Napoleon's secretary Bourrienne. "Such a bridge will of necessity be very narrow and it will diminish this beautiful stretch of water, often used for fêtes. Nor will it, with its light structure, match the magnificence of the two monuments between which it will be built."[15]

Undeterred, Napoleon approved the Pont des Arts on March 15, 1801, connecting the Louvre and the Collège des Quatre-Nations (today's Institut de France). Designed by engineers Jacques Dillon and Delon de Cessart, inspector general of roads and bridges, Paris's first iron bridge featured wooden planking resting on nine cast iron arches (each with an 18.5-meter span) supported by masonry piles. When the footbridge debuted in November 1803, it became an instant hit, with a reported 64,000 crossings on opening day.[16] Furnished with benches and lanterns, decorated with potted orange trees and rare shrubs along the iron balustrades, the bridge offered splendid views of the Louvre and Île de la Cité for a one-sou toll.

Despite its popularity, the charming Pont des Arts was not a hit with Napoleon. He came to agree with Percier and Fontaine that the iron did not complement the nearby stone bridges. But his biggest issue seemed to be its lack of monumentality. After visiting the Louvre, Napoleon stopped at an intersection leading to the Pont des Arts and turned to Bourrienne: "It [the bridge] has no feeling of solidity about it; it has no grandeur. I can understand that in England where stone is rare they use iron for arches of enormous dimensions; but in France where everything abounds . . ."

Napoleon's concept of monumentality was an ancient one. As a young general in Egypt, he had admired the millennia-old pyramids, sphinxes, and obelisks built by the pharoahs. Rome's emperors were also masters of the monumental. As Edmund Thomas explains, a *monumentum* in second-century Rome was a lasting structure that perpetuated the name of its builder and advertised the wealth and promise of the Antonine society.[17]

With the Pont des Arts underway, work began on a second iron bridge connecting the Jardin des Plantes with Faubourg Saint-Antoine. After several attempts to link the two banks, engineer Becquey de Beaupré proposed a design featuring five cast-iron arches over masonry piles. After the Grande Armée's victory over Austria in December 1805, the bridge would be renamed the Pont d'Austerlitz. The names of the principal officers who died in the battle were inscribed on the bridge. The third bridge built during the Consulate, Cité, featured two arches in a masonry framework and connected the Île de la Cité and Île Saint-Louis (demolished in 1811).

Napoleon's most ambitious iron project was inspired by ancient Rome. In 1802, fire destroyed the dome roof of the Halle aux Blés, Paris's circular grain exchange. Jean-Baptiste Rondelet came upon a glowing description by Caracalla's biographer Spartianus of a "miracle of engineering"—a metal vault in the Baths of Caracalla. Architects, wrote Spartianus, had theorized that "the whole roof was supported by girders of metal dexterity concealed in the thickness of the masonry."[18] French engineers were familiar with Vitruvius's descriptions of structural vaults made with iron bars. Napoleon approved the project and personally dedicated the cast-iron dome, the largest iron structure of its day.

A small bridge across the Crou, a tributary of the Seine near Saint-Denis, was also made of wrought iron. Pierre Fontaine succeeded in stopping construction of two more iron bridges in Paris on aesthetic grounds. Iron was also more expensive than any other building materials, and Napoleon abandoned other projects. Ironically in 1829, Fontaine would design a glazed iron roof for the Galerie d'Orléans in the Palais Royal.[19] Ultimately, Napoleon would complete three bridges, the Pont des Arts footbridge (1804), the Pont d'Austerlitz (1807), and the Pont d'Iéna (1808–1814).

Napoleon wasn't sentimental about "the old Paris." "To beautify Paris," he wrote, "we need to demolish more than build."[20] Determined to modernize and adorn the capital with monumental buildings, Napoleon continued to demolish church property confiscated during the Revolution.

The area around the Tuileries had developed gradually after construction of the palace in 1564 between the Louvre, the rue Saint-Honoré, and the Seine. Napoleon's move here in 1800 and the development of the Louvre into Napoleon's museum inspired his interest in unifying the two former royal palaces into an unmatched imperial palace. Driving this ambition was an element of one-upmanship with the Bourbon kings. "As heir to the Enlightenment and the Revolution, Napoleon . . . wanted to complete a project that a century of royal rule had been unable to bring to fruition," writes Jean-Philippe Garric.[21]

The Grand Gallery along the Seine enclosed the ensemble on the south, but its central area was still occupied by private hotels and the convents of the Assumption, the Capuchins, and the Feuillants. This problem was solved after the Revolution when these private and religious buildings became national property. By decree in October 1801, Napoleon ordered a series of openings cut between the Tuileries Gardens, the Place Vendôme, rue Saint-Honoré and rue Saint-Florentin, the gardens of the convents of the Assumption, the Capucines, and the Feuillants. In January 1802, Napoleon acquired land to be used for the rue de Rivoli, named for his victory against Austria on January 14 and 15, 1797. In addition to this main street, the plan called for the creation of the perpendicular rue Castiglione and rue and place des Pyramides. Demolition and clearing began in 1802.

Napoleon assigned Charles Percier and Pierre Fontaine to design buildings for the new avenue to complement both the Louvre and Tuileries palaces and gardens. After rejecting their first proposal that included a winter walk, pavilion, and amphitheater, Napoleon accepted a plan featuring an elegant neoclassical arcade. All buildings were required to be three stories, built over a ground floor and mezzanines with arcades. The first floor was to feature a light modillioned entablature with balconies bordered in wrought iron. The second, shorter story was to have an attic and balustrade above. But Napoleon's ambition to connect the palaces went unrealized; only the arcades and a few buildings were finished during his watch.[22] The famous rue de Rivoli would be completed by later regimes.

⚜

In January 1804, Paris police uncovered an assassination plot against the first consul, supposedly hatched by the Bourbons. After killing two officers, royalist Georges Cadoudal was tried, convicted, and guillotined along with eleven accomplices. General Jean-Charles Pichegru was found strangled with his cravat in his jail cell; either an assassination or a suicide. Suspicion also fell on the Duke of Enghien, son of the last prince of Condé. In mid-March, Napoleon ordered the duke kidnapped in the Prussian territory of Baden. A week later, after a quick trial for treason, the thirty-one-year-old was executed at Vincennes. When Lucien Bonaparte learned of Enghien's fate, he told his wife, "with the gesture of a togaed senator who braved Tiberius: Alexandrine, let us go away, he [Napoleon] has tasted blood."[23]

That spring, Napoleon used the alleged royalist conspiracy, along with France's resumed conflict with Britain, to justify the reinstatement of a hereditary monarchy with himself as emperor. In a move that recalled Rome's Praetorian Guard, Napoleon warned his co-consuls Charles-François LeBrun and Jean-Jacques-Régis de Cambacérès that if the government didn't take immediate action, the army might take matters into its own hands and proclaim him emperor.[24]

The Senate capitulated. On May 18, a *sénatus-consulte* proclaiming Napoleon and Joséphine Emperor and Empress of the French was approved (with three votes against and two abstentions). Taken from the *senatus consultum,* Latin for "decree of the senate," the term harkened back to opinions issued by the Roman Senate. Under the Consulate and Empire, it carried the authority of law. According to Philip Dwyer, the creation of the First French Empire was not only the result of Napoleon's personal ambition. Moderate conservatives in France's political and military elite and a segment of the French public favored a return to a monarchical form of government.[25]

Later that day at Saint-Cloud, the first consul was officially pronounced Napoleon I, Emperor of the French to a twenty-one-gun salute.

Cambacérès became Arch Chancellor of the Empire. Reviving France's highest military rank of marshal, abolished with the Bourbon monarchy, he promoted sixteen of his generals to Marshal of the Empire.

During the banquet that evening, Joseph and Louis Bonaparte and their male descendants were announced as Napoleon's heirs in the event that he did not have a son. Napoleon made his brothers princes of the Empire; their wives Julie Clary and Hortense de Beauharnais were named princesses. In addition to their titles, Joseph and Louis were each given an annual salary of one million francs a year plus one-third of a million francs for expenses.

Lucien, who played an instrumental role in his brother's coup d'état, was left out of the succession plan, as was the youngest sibling, Jérôme. Instead of a political marriage to Spanish Infanta Maria Luisa, widow of the king of Etruria, Lucien had secretly married Alexandrine Jouberthon over his brother's objections, causing a final rift and his move to Rome. Jérôme was also passed over for marrying wealthy Baltimorean Elizabeth Patterson. Unlike Lucien, Jérôme would ultimately cave to his brother. In 1807, he abandoned his pregnant wife and married German princess Catharina von Württemberg, becoming prince of Westphalia.

Napoleon seemed to be channeling Julius Caesar and his adoptive son Octavian when he formally adopted his stepson, Eugène de Beauharnais two years later. With the adoption, Joséphine's son, the Viceroy of Italy, moved ahead of Napoleon's brothers in the line of succession.[26]

The May 1804 succession announcement infuriated Napoleon's sisters. According to Claire de Rémusat, Joséphine's lady-in-waiting, Elisa and Caroline Bonaparte were "dumbfounded by this distinction between themselves and their sisters-in-law."[27] To placate his sisters, Napoleon made each of them princesses and imperial highnesses. As the wife of Rome's Prince Camillo Borghese, his sister Pauline was already a princess.

The austere family matriarch Letizia Bonaparte, in Rome for the proclamation, was no easier to deal with. Engaged at fourteen to lawyer Carlo Maria Buonaparte, Letizia Bonaparte was widowed with eight children by age thirty-four. After their father's death in 1784, Joseph assumed the role of family head for his four brothers and three sisters. But it was fifteen-year-old Napoleon who took over, demanding an audience to secure the family's pension in Paris.

Now believing she should have a title equal to those of her children, Letizia was unhappy with her son's decision to call her "Madame Mère" of his Majesty the Emperor and not "The Imperial Mother."[28] With a visceral dislike for Joséphine and displeasure with Napoleon's treatment of Lucien and Jérôme, Letizia would boycott the upcoming coronation.

To plan the coronation, Napoleon assembled a Council Commission composed of several members of his Council of State. They were responsible for organizing all aspects of the December ceremony—from the guest list and imperial emblems to decorations and costumes. Napoleon, a micromanager, involved himself in the event's smallest details. On June 12, the Commission met at Saint-Cloud to discuss an emblem for the new Empire to replace the Republic's Phrygian cap and Roman lictor's axe and fasces.

Each commissioner promoted his favorite animal, presenting arguments and scientific references to the emperor. Early in the meeting, Napoleon nixed the rooster as a "barnyard creature." "The rooster has no strength," he declared. "It cannot be the image of an empire such as France. It's necessary to choose between the eagle, the elephant, or the lion."[29]

Interior minister and commission chair Emmanuel Crétet suggested the elephant, a symbolic animal associated with Alexander the Great and Hannibal. It was also the symbol of the Danish order of the Elephant created in the fifteenth century. But Crétet's proposed motto for the Empire, "by mass and spirit" was rejected by Napoleon (four years later, Danish king Frederic VI awarded Napoleon the prestigious Danish order). The lion was a popular choice, despite being part of the British royal family's escutcheon. Louis XII had incorporated a beehive into his coat of arms; Cambacérès suggested a swarm of bees as the nation's emblem, representing a great republic with a single, all-powerful leader. In the end, the lion won the majority of votes.

The memory of Rome and Rome-inspired empires proved irresistible to Napoleon. Ignoring the commission's recommendation, Napoleon chose the eagle with outstretched wings as France's imperial emblem. A July decree specified that the Empire's seal and arms should be "azure with an antique-style eagle in gold bearing a thunderbolt in its claws, also gold." As its battle-standard, the French military adopted the eagle of the Roman legions above the Republican tricolor. Napoleon was called "the Eagle"—symbol of his empire and army.[30]

The powerful bird had captivated ancient cultures, including the ancient Chinese, Egyptians, Aztecs, and Babylonians.[31] By choosing the eagle, Napoleon clearly connected the First Empire to Rome and himself to Jupiter, king of the Olympian gods.[32] Associated since the earliest antiquity with military victory, the eagle, bird of Jupiter, was the symbol of imperial Rome. According to legend, Romulus spotted an eagle on the Aventine Hill and considering it a good omen, had the large bird of prey precede the Roman army instead of a standard.[33]

In his detailed chapter on birds, Pliny the Elder tells us that the eagle is thought to be the only bird never killed by lightning. According to Pliny, Consul Gaius Marius designated the eagle the exclusive military standard of the Roman legion, replacing the wolf, ox with a man's head, horse, and boar (around 104 B.C.E.). Silver or bronze eagles with outstretched wings were attached to staffs and carried into battle. During Rome's imperial period, an eagle would be released at the consecration of an emperor—believed to carry the deified ruler's spirit to heaven.

The eagle continued to be used as imperial symbol after Rome's adoption of Christianity. Mentioned in the Old Testament in relation to Adam, Elijah, and David, the eagle would become associated with Christ's ascension. During the reign of Emperor Isaac I Komnenos, the imperial emblem was changed to a double-headed eagle to represent East and West. The Byzantine Empire continued to use the two-headed eagle, representing the secular and spiritual power of its emperors. After the fall of the Byzantine Empire, Russian rulers instated the title of tsar for Caesar, along with the imperial symbol of the double-headed eagle.

The Holy Roman Empire also made the eagle its heraldic animal. A gold eagle on an azure background appeared on Charlemagne's arms and on top of his palace at Aachen.[34] The Habsburgs, who controlled this title from the sixteenth century, adopted the double-headed eagle with an escutcheon showing their coats of arms.[35]

Besides the imperial symbol, Napoleon needed a personal emblem. The fleur-de-lys had been adopted by Clovis I, France's first Christian king who moved the capital to Paris and united the Frankish tribes. But the lily, like other symbols of the deposed Bourbons, had been purged during the Revolution. Napoleon's commissioners began a search for another historical reference. They found it in an unexpected place.

In 1653, a crew excavating in Tournai (today's Belgium) near the Church of Saint Brice accidentally discovered a royal tomb, identified by the gold ring inscribed with the name and title of Childeric I, father of Clovis I. When Childeric died in 481, he was buried with hundreds of gold and silver coins, a pair of gold buckles, gold and cloisonné jewelry, and a golden bull's head. Beside a horse skeleton were the remains of an ornate harness studded with three hundred gold fluerons adorned with red garnets. The "scratching" under each garnet was a signature of Merovingian cloisonné.

Because Tournai was part of the Austrian Netherlands, the tomb's contents were presented to Habsburg archduke Leopold Wilhelm in Brussels. In an illustrated report, the archduke's physician Jean-Jacques Chifflet concluded that the gold and garnet fluerons represented bees, and were a symbol of the Frankish kings. Alternatively, the buried fleurons may have been cicadas or crickets, symbols of death and resurrection for the Merovingians.[36] In 1656, the royal burial objects were moved from Brussels to the Austrian treasury in Vienna. Nine years later, Austrian Emperor Leopold gave the treasure to France's Louis XIV. Underwhelmed, the Sun King consigned them to the Cabinet of Antiquities in his Bibliothèque Royale (the postrevolutionary Bibliothèque Nationale).

To Napoleon, the industrious, productive bee was an admirable insect, appropriate for his imperial emblem. By adopting Childeric's bee, Napoleon linked his new dynasty with France's ancient Merovingian dynasty—itself a bridge between the Roman Empire and the Carolingian era. The bee was incorporated into Napoleon's coat of arms and the arms of the Princes-Grand-Dignitaries, or the High Officers of the Empire. Embroidered bees decorated Napoleon's clothes and his residences. Bees were woven into carpets, wall hangings, and upholstery fabrics for the imperial residences, and appeared on furniture, ceramics, and wallpaper.

Percier and Fontaine combined bees and eagles with other ancient motifs—Jupiter's oak leaf, Minerva's olive tree, the laurel wreath, palm of Victory, knight's helmet, and a trophy of weapons. As Odile Nouvel-Kammerer writes, the emblems and motifs were repeated wherever

Napoleon exercised power, forming "the framework for a symbolic language that was new and at the same time understood by everyone, since it took its legitimacy from the heritage of ancient Rome, the mother of civilization and a model of political unity."[37]

On July 14, 1804, Napoleon and Joséphine traveled to the Soldiers' Church at Hôtel des Invalides for the first investiture of the Legion of Honor. The original badge design, attributed to Jacques-Louis David, was specified by decree:

"The decoration of the Légion d'Honneur will consist of a five-pointed star, with each point doubled. The center of the star, surrounded by an oak and laurel wreath, shall present, on one side, the head of the Emperor, with this legend: 'Napoléon, Emp. des Français' (Napoleon Emperor of the French) and, on the other, the French eagle holding a thunder bolt, with this legend: 'Honneur et Patrie' (Honor and Fatherland). The decoration will be in white enamel. It will be in gold for 'Grands-Officiers,' 'Commandants,' and 'Officiers,' and in silver for Legionaires; it shall be worn from one of the buttonholes on the jacket and attached to a red moiré ribbon."[38]

For the investiture, Joséphine wore a pale pink tulle dress with gold and silver stars. Based on Roman tradition, she adorned her hair à la Ceres, Roman goddess of the harvest, with diamond ears of wheat. This symbol of fertility was one of many Roman motifs borrowed in Empire style jewelry. As Melanie Sallois writes, based on the tradition of imperial Rome, Napoleon imposed the diadem, symbol of sovereignty and power, for Joséphine and women of his court. Under Joséphine's influence, Empire jewels borrowed antique motifs like wheat ears, lyres, thyrses, palmettes, and honeysuckle.[39]

Wearing the new five-pointed star and his guard's simple mounted grenadier uniform, Napoleon awarded the first insignia of the Legion of Honor. Among the recipients were Jacques-Louis David and Dominique-Vivant Denon; newly promoted marshals Jean-Baptiste Bernadotte, Nicolas Oudinot, Jacques MacDonald, and Auguste de Marmont; Napoleon's uncle Cardinal Fesch, Cambacérès, Talleyrand, mathematicians Monge and Pierre-Simon Laplace, naturalist Georges Cuvier, balloonist Joseph-Michel Montgolfier, composer Étienne Méhul, writer Bernardin de Saint-Pierre, poet Fontanes, wounded veterans, and the grenadier Jean-Roch Coignet.

After the ceremony, Napoleon left Paris for a three-month tour. By mid-August, he arrived at a military camp in Boulogne. The major Roman port for trade and communication with England, Boulogne had later been occupied by England numerous times over the centuries. Now it was a staging area for Napoleon's troops and navy as they prepared an invasion of Great Britain.

The fragile Peace of Amiens was broken. Instead of turning the strategic island of Malta over to the Order of Malta as agreed, the British stayed. In 1803, concerned that France would lose Louisiana to England, Napoleon sold the vast territory gained from Spain to the United States. Napoleon planned to use the fifteen million dollars to finance an invasion of England.

On August 16, before an estimated one hundred thousand officers and soldiers, Napoleon conferred Legion of Honor badges on two thousand members of his Army of England. To add further drama to the event, Denon installed symbolic props on the stage. From the National Library in Paris by way of the Abbey of St. Denis came a small bronze throne of the seventh-century Merovingian king Dagobert who had unified the Franks. His ancient throne, inspired by a Roman campaign stool, stood against a backdrop of medieval armor and enemy flags.[40]

Denon invited along history painter Philippe-Auguste Hennequin to memorialize the seven-hour event with a monumental canvas. "Scarcely was the general seated in the bronze chair that they had carried from the library to the camp when the sky cleared up, the clouds divided and let a ray of light escape that fell on the trophy behind the emperor and distinguished the flags of all the nations conquered by the French army," the painter recalled.[41]

To shore up support, Napoleon left Boulogne for a series of state visits to Ostend, Arras, Mons, Brussels, Rheinberg, Cologne, Coblenz, Mainz, Kaiserslautern, Trier, Luxembourg, and Stenay. But it was a stop in Aachen that became a defining moment for the emperor-to-be.

PART THREE

IMPERIUM

"I am not the successor of Louis XIV but of Charlemagne."

—Napoleon Bonaparte

ONE

CAROLUS MAGNUS

The collapse of the Roman Empire in 400 C.E. plunged Western Europe into chaos. Four centuries later, Charlemagne, king of the Franks, set about recreating that lost empire. From his accession in 770 to his death in 814, Charlemagne doubled his real estate through nearly constant warfare. His conquests were brutal. According to the Franconian annals, Charlemagne ordered the execution of 4,500 Saxons at Verden in 782. Even his own tutor, Alcuin of York, criticized the violence and forced baptisms.

The itinerant warrior-king ruled from many cities, but his favorite was Aachen (Aix-la-Chapelle in French). Strategically located on several hundred acres in the Rhine Valley near today's Belgium (then Northern France), the palace complex became Charlemagne's political power base, the center of a religious and intellectual renaissance, and the seat of medieval Christendom. Constantinople, capital of the Byzantine Empire, now had a serious rival for the title "New Rome."

Charlemagne's choice of Aachen, a former Roman military outpost, may have been influenced by its forested hunting grounds and curative hot springs that helped relieve his rheumatism. According to Einhard, the king's companion and biographer, "Charles enjoyed the exhalations from natural warm springs, and often practiced swimming, in which he was such an adept that none could surpass him; and hence it was that he built his palace at Aix-la-Chapelle, and lived there constantly during his later years until his death."[1]

Six feet tall, fair-haired, with a high squeaky voice, Charlemagne enjoyed life with five wives and several concubines. Einhard describes him as a caring father of at least eighteen children, half of whom predeceased him. "He was so careful of the training of his sons and daughters," wrote Einhard, "that he never took his meals without them when he was at home, and never made a journey without them."[2]

To govern his vast realm, Charlemagne introduced administrative reforms and established a network of territorial units run by kings, prefects, and marquises. Scholars from across Europe came to Aachen to teach Charlemagne and his children grammar, rhetoric and dialectics, arithmetic, geometry, astronomy, and music. Though Charlemagne learned to write late in his life, he was fluent in Latin and understood Greek. Scribes copied the king's collection of classical texts; his palace scriptorium produced exquisitely decorated manuscripts. Through Charlemagne's friendship with Persian king Harun al-Rashid, envoys from Bagdad brought scientific knowledge and gifts to the capital, including an astronomical clock and a white elephant.

Charlemagne's political model was inspired by Rome. Like Clovis in the late fifth century, Charlemagne fashioned himself as heir to the ancient civilization, invoking Roman images and classical forms. The reverse side of Charlemagne's official seal bore an image of the gates of Rome with the inscription *Renovatio Romani Imperii*, Renewal of the Roman Empire. Charlemagne added "auguste" to his title and like the Julians, claimed descent to the Trojan hero Aeneas, Rome's legendary founder. As Charlemagne's courtier Moduin of Autun observed: "Our times are transformed into the civilization of Antiquity. Golden Rome is reborn and restored anew to the world!"[3]

In Aachen, notes Neil MacGregor, Charlemagne "remade Rome on German soil."[4] Even the location of Charlemagne's estate was an ancient Roman site. Situated on the slope of a hill, the royal estate incorporated part of the ancient Roman *thermae* along with its own thermal baths. A one-hundred-meter-long gallery linked the large *aula regalis*, or coronation hall, to the most important building, a three-story domed octagonal chapel, for centuries the tallest building north of the Alps.

Charlemagne may have been inspired by a 787 visit to Ravenna where he saw Justinian I's sixth-century imperial Church of San Vitale. He recruited Frankish architect Odo of Metz and workers from Northern Italy familiar with Roman structural engineering, dome building, and stone laying.[5] The austere exterior with its sixteen corners stood in dramatic contrast to the dazzling interior. Light from eight windows illuminated the dome's colorful mosaic, a popular art form in late antiquity, with *Christ Enthroned with the Elders of the Apocalypse*. The two upper stories were each embellished with sixteen columns, possibly after the clerestory of Rome's Lateran Basilica.[6] An atrium and a portico led to the imperial apartments.

The chapel was filled with references to ancient Rome and Constantine, Rome's first Christian emperor. As Maria Fabricius Hansen suggests, Charlemagne endowed his court with Rome's authority by literally and figuratively taking possession of the ancient civilization.[7] Dependent on Charlemagne for his independence, Pope Hadrian approved his request for marble from Rome and Ravenna, including precious red and green porphyry. Charlemagne reused the ancient marble to embellish his chapel, a practice now called *spolia*. The massive marble columns traveled by oxcarts and perhaps by barge, either across the Alps or along the coasts to Aachen.[8] There, Charlemagne installed the ancient pillars in double tiers under the eight tall arches; marble slabs covered the piers and walls.[9]

In appropriating ancient objects, Charlemagne was following a tradition started five centuries earlier by Constantine. Despite spending little time in Rome, Constantine went on a citywide building spree using material from existing monuments. For his eponymous arch marking his victory over Maxentius at the Milvian Bridge, Constantine removed parts of the triumphal monuments of Trajan, Hadrian, and Marcus Aurelius. He also used spolia to build the Lateran Basilica and the original St. Peter's.

Yet according to the Christian historian Eusebius, Constantine, who legalized Christianity in 313, ordered the temple of Aphrodite in Jerusalem removed before erecting the Church of the Holy Sepulchre at the site, considering the pagan building materials impure.[10] For the first few centuries of Christianity, ancient Roman temples were generally considered idolatrous. Constantine's son Constantius II closed temples and banned sacrifices; pagan tombs and monuments were vandalized.

After Rome's demise, the city experienced more losses during a series of sacks, from the Visigoths and Vandals in the fifth century to the Normans in the eleventh. In the wake of the fifth- and sixth-century invasions, possibly for economic reasons, a series of ancient Roman temples were converted into churches. The most famous is the Pantheon, rebuilt by Hadrian, featuring massive gray granite columns quarried in ancient Egypt. Originally dedicated to the Roman pantheon of gods, the temple was transformed into Santa Maria ad Martyres in 609, reconsecrated to Christian martyrs.

Building with ancient columns, marble panels, and bricks became a common, accepted practice for many of Rome's medieval churches. During the ensuing centuries, a number of Roman churches were also built atop the ruins of ancient temples whose materials had been used as spolia. In the twelfth century, Pope Innocent II had himself buried in what was thought to be the porphyry sarcophagus of Hadrian.

Theodoric, king of the Ostrogoths from 475 to 526, spent a fortune moving ancient marble slabs and columns for his palace in Ravenna, capital of the Western Roman Empire. Ruling with the consent of the Byzantine emperor at Constantinople, Theodoric did not need Roman symbols for legitimacy, writes Beat Brenk. Rather, by transferring material from Roman ruins, he sought to preserve ancient art and architecture. "Nothing but the newness of the buildings must distinguish them from the constructions of the ancients," wrote Theodoric. "Let us renew the works of the ancients faultlessly and unmask the new glory of their venerable antiquity."[11]

What distinguishes Charlemagne's use of spolia from that of Constantine and Theodoric is his deliberate borrowing from the great civilization of Rome to bolster his ambitions and legitimize the Carolingian Empire. Charlemagne, argues Brenk, transported materials from Rome and Ravenna to his court at Aachen and palace at Ingelheim to perpetuate his place in the Christian Roman imperial tradition.[12]

In addition to importing mosaics and marble columns and capitals from Ravenna, Charlemagne removed bronzes—including a life-size bronze equestrian statue of Theodoric—that he installed in the courtyard in front of the palace between the chapel and audience hall. It's not known whether Charlemagne acquired the *She-Wolf,* a tour de force of second-century bronze casting. The hole in the animal's chest suggests that it was originally a fountain, like the wolf in Rome's Lateran.[13]

Charlemagne added to the spolia by reviving the ancient art of bronze casting. A local foundry produced five pairs of solid-cast bronze doors adorned with classical lion head knockers for the chapel. The main entrance, the west door, featured a massive pair of doors, each measuring nearly 13 feet high, 4.5 feet wide, and weighing 2.75 tons.[14] The upper floor was decorated with a Roman-style bronze trellis behind which stood the ancient marble pilasters.[15]

A bronze pine cone fountain in the chapel vestibule, likely a copy of the Vatican's famed fountain, is thought to have been created at Aachen in the tenth century. Made of 129 bronze scales arranged in nine overlapping rows, the pine cone was embedded into a capital and crowned a column that stood in the center of the fountain's basin. The Latin inscription along the base read: "The waters are bestowed upon the world, that always cause it to flourish; the fruitful Euphrates, as swift as an arrow of the Tigris."[16]

A devout Christian, Charlemagne strengthened the papacy, enacting the legal principle that the pope was beyond the reach of temporal justice. On his second trip to Rome in 781, Charlemagne brought his four-year-old son to be baptized as Pepin by Pope Hadrian. In 800, soon after the Palatine Chapel was completed, Charlemagne assumed the title of Roman Emperor and traveled to Rome to be crowned by Pope Leo III. Having survived revolt and an assassination attempt, the pope badly needed an alliance with Charlemagne.

After an entry into Rome worthy of Caesar, Charlemagne was crowned Holy Roman Emperor on Christmas Day 800 C.E. during Mass at the Old St. Peter's Basilica in Rome begun by Constantine. The choice of the Vatican basilica over the Church of Santa Maria Maggiore started a new tradition for the coronation of emperors that continued through the Middle Ages.

At the pope's request, Charlemagne wore a Roman outfit for the ceremony—a long tunic and Roman cloak and shoes. After placing the crown on Charlemagne's head, Leo pronounced a blessing. Then, with Charlemagne kneeling before the Confession of St. Peter, the congregation repeated an acclamation three times: "Long life and victory to Charles Augustus, crowned by God, great and peaceful Emperor of the Romans."[17] As the first Holy Roman emperor, Western Europe's first since the fall of the Western Roman Empire, Charlemagne was equal in power to the emperor in the East. As Robert Folz writes, ". . . the king of the Franks was raised to a title that had been extinct for more than three centuries, and thus seemed to inherit the position of the Caesars of old."[18]

The idea of Rome reborn can be seen in a cycle of pictures or tapestries thought to have been hung before the coronation at Charlemagne's Palace of Ingelheim, a few miles from Mainz. One wall of the hall featured the greats of antiquity—from Romulus and Remus to Hannibal and Alexander the Great and possibly Augustus. On the opposite wall were depictions of Christian rulers starting with Constantine, Theodosius, Charles Martel, Pepin the Short, and finally Charlemagne.[19]

Charlemagne had reformed the Franconian coinage system after the Roman model, adopting Rome's denarius as his empire's currency. Toward the end of his reign, he ordered the minting of a series of portrait coinage—the only definitive image from his lifetime. The right-facing portrait bust shows Charlemagne wearing a Roman military cloak and laurel wreath with the title "*imperator augustus*."

When Charlemagne died on January 28, 814, around age sixty-five, he was buried in his chapel at Aachen, possibly in an ancient Carrara marble sarcophagus that he had brought from Rome. Carved in the first quarter of the third century C.E., the sarcophagus depicted the mythological story of Proserpina's abduction by Pluto, god of the underworld. With its themes of eternal life and resurrection, the legend was popular during early Christianity.

For the first time since the Roman Empire, most of Western Europe was united. Charlemagne left an empire ranging from the Pyrenees in the west to the Elbe and Danube in the east. But hopes for peace across ended in 843 when Charlemagne's three grandsons divvied up the empire. Rulers of the western and eastern realms, roughly today's France and Germany, continued to fight for supremacy. Charlemagne's Carolingian dynasty survived for over 170 years until Hugh Capet, ancestor of a long line of French kings, took the throne and established the Capetian dynasty.

Like Constantinople's Hagia Sophia for the Byzantine emperors, Aachen's Palatine chapel became the favored location for the coronations of Charlemagne's successors.[20] With its ancient marble columns and bronze doors, the chapel hosted the coronations of Germanic kings from Charlemagne's son Louis the Pious in 813 to Ferdinand I in 1531. Only after being anointed at Aachen could a ruler be crowned Holy Roman emperor in Rome.

Over the centuries, stories about the emperor with the flowing white beard took on mythic proportions. Around the turn of the first millennium, the Carolingian ruler became known as Carolus Magnus, Charles the Great. The honorific became part of his name in France which claimed him as their hero, Charlemagne. In the struggle for Charlemagne's inheritance, his chapel and remains became symbolic prizes.

In 1165, Emperor Frederick I Barbarossa of Swabia persuaded Pope Paschal III to canonize Charlemagne. Frederick and his wife Beatrice donated a magnificent octagonal-shaped gilt chandelier for the chapel. Hung from the cupola by an ironwork chain, measuring over thirteen feet in diameter, the chandelier symbolized the heavenly city of Jerusalem. Its eight arches represented Jerusalem's eight city gates. The base plates of the sixteen towers featured engraved scenes from the life of Jesus and the eight beatitudes. Forty-eight candles symbolized the litany of the twelve apostles, twelve martyrs, twelve confessors, and twelve virgins.[21]

Like Charlemagne, Barbarossa's grandson Frederick II of Hohenstaufen was interested in Italy, and chose to live in Sicily and southern Italy. In 1215, he moved Charlemagne's remains to a golden casket, known as the *Karlsschrein*, or Shrine of Charlemagne. Lavishly adorned with gilt silver, gilt copper, filigree, precious stones, and enamel, the church-shaped casket was placed in the center of the chapel below the spectacular chandelier donated by Frederick II's grandparents.

At the front end, Charlemagne is shown sitting enthroned below Christ and flanked by Leo III and the Archbishop of Rheims. On the opposite end, Saint Mary and the Christ Child are enthroned between archangels Michael and Gabriel. Four reliefs on the shrine's roof narrate scenes from Charlemagne's life from the twelfth-century manuscript, the

Pseudo-Turpin. A crest of gilded copper with five towers decorates the roof's ridge and gable. Eight kings of the Holy Roman Empire—from Louis the Pious to Frederick II—decorate each of the casket's long sides.[22]

In the mid-fourteenth century, Charlemagne's remains were disturbed again when a relic revival inspired Holy Roman emperor Charles IV to create reliquaries for some of his illustrious predecessor's bones. A gold reliquary contained a thigh bone; the Bust of Charlemagne housed his skullcap. During coronations, the Bust of Charlemagne was carried toward the king as he entered the cathedral, creating the impression that the illustrious emperor was greeting his successor.[23] Every seven years, the four "great relics" thought to have been brought to Aachen by Charlemagne were shown to the faithful: Christ's swaddling clothes and loincloth, St. Mary's cloak, and a raiment of John the Baptist.

In 1481, France's Louis XI decided to honor Charlemagne as the forefather of France's kings by commissioning a golden Arm Reliquary with a naturalistic hand for parts of Charlemagne's right forearm. He also decreed Charlemagne's birthday a public holiday to be observed upon pain of death.[24] Tradition has it that Charlemagne himself brought some of the most precious relics in Christendom from Jerusalem to Aachen. Their rediscovery in the mid-fourteenth century elevated Aachen to the rank of Rome and Spain's Santiago de Compostela as a sacred pilgrimage destination. Pilgrimages and coronations became key to the town's economic and cultural life.

During the Middle Ages, Charlemagne's original chapel was expanded into a cathedral with a Gothic choir and a circle of surrounding chapels. The largest, a spectacular vaulted chancel with a glass exterior façade, was inaugurated in 1414, the six hundredth anniversary of Charlemagne's death. The inspiration for the soaring 108-foot-tall Gothic choir came from St. Chapelle in Paris.

Royal gifts to the Aachen Cathedral treasury helped make it one of Northern Europe's most illustrious ecclesiastical collections. "Since I have seen every royal marvel, [I know that] no-one living has seen a more marvellous thing," raved artist Albrecht Dürer after attending Charles V's coronation at Aachen in 1520. Eight years earlier, Dürer painted an iconic portrait of a white-bearded Charlemagne in the robes of a Holy Roman emperor.

⚜

In August 1804, Joséphine made her own pilgrimage to Aachen with a fifty-plus-person entourage that included four ladies-in-waiting, two women of the bedchamber, two chamberlains, a comptroller, a master of the horse, two ushers, ten footmen, coachmen, and cooks. Though the original Roman baths were no longer visible, Aachen was a popular spa destination for European royalty, aristocrats, artists, and writers.

Under considerable pressure from her husband to get pregnant, Joséphine took the waters in the mineral rich hot springs. In between treatments, Joséphine visited Aachen's palace and cathedral. On August 12 and 15, she presided over festivals honoring Charlemagne and marking her husband's thirty-fifth birthday.

For centuries, France and Germany had competed for Charlemagne. Aachen had been in the path of the French revolutionary army as it marched across the Rhineland in mid-1794. That August, with French troops approaching, the contents of Aachen's Cathedral Treasury were whisked off to the Capuchin cloister at Paderborn for safekeeping. Among the objects were the Great Relics—the relics of the Lord, the Virgin Mary, and Saint John the Baptist. The Pala d'Oro, a shimmering eleventh-century altarpiece with over eighty-five figures in deep gold relief, possibly made with Charlemagne's own coins, was dismantled and removed. As Annika Elisabeth Fisher observes, "The altar's position in Charlemagne's chapel, proximity to Charlemagne's throne, and the possible material link to Charlemagne's gold, powerfully aligned Henry [Henry II, king of Germany and Italy] with the Frankish emperor."[25]

On September 23, 1794, French troops under General Jean-Baptiste Jourdan invaded Aachen. The lead roof of Aachen chapel was removed to make ammunition, leaving the wooden structure exposed to the elements. Objects from the chapel were confiscated including the Proserpina sarcophagus, and the bronze she-wolf and pine cone.[26]

A month later, French soldiers began hacking out the ancient marble columns from the upper arcade. Renaissance painter Albrecht Dürer was among the pillars' admirers: "In Aachen, I have seen the well-proportioned pillars with their beautiful capitals from porphyry green and red and granite, which Carolus [Charlemagne] ordered to be taken from Rome and placed in this building," he wrote in 1520.[27] Back in Paris, the marble columns were installed in the Louvre's Musée des Antiquities alongside plundered sculptures. For several weeks, a 1620 bronze statue of Charlemagne from Namur was installed in the Tuileries courtyard, after which it was neglected in the basement of the Bibliothèque Nationale.

The 1801 Peace of Lunéville formally transferred ownership of Aachen and the Rhine's entire "left bank" from Germany to France. The Concordat gave Napoleon authority to name bishops and archbishops in France. In April 1802, without Pius VII's consent, Napoleon elevated the Aachen cathedral to a bishop's seat and nominated Alsatian Marc-Antoine Berdolet as its first bishop. Berdolet and Joséphine had known each other for years. During the French Revolution, Berdolet was imprisoned with her first husband, Alexandre de Beauharnais, an officer in the royal army. After Berdolet's release, he delivered the executed viscount's personal belongings and final letters to Joséphine.

Now, Berdolet presented Joséphine with the Talisman of Charlemagne featuring an emerald and a sapphire surrounded by some four dozen gems and pearls. The hair relic of the Virgin Mary behind the jewels had been transferred to the Agnus Dei reliquary and replaced with a cross relic. But Joséphine politely declined a grimy bone said to be from the emperor's right arm, telling Berdolet that she already had "the support of an arm just as strong as Charlemagne's."[28] (The Staufen arm-reliquary is now in the Louvre; the Talisman of Charlemagne is at Reims Cathedral treasury.)

On September 2, Napoleon joined Joséphine in Aachen at the hotel Zur kaiserlichen Krone, the Imperial Crown Hotel on Alexanderstraße near the Kurhaus, or assembly rooms (today's Aachen library). Officially, the visit was a part of Napoleon's tour of the four departments of the Rhine. Unofficially, Napoleon would spend the next week and a half studying Charlemagne's legacy.

Since his stunning victories in Italy, Napoleon had been likened to military greats Alexander, Hannibal, and Caesar. In light of his newly proclaimed dynastic empire, it was now politically advantageous to also claim the inheritance of the Carolingians who had laid the foundation for

France.[29] As Thierry Lentz explains, to Napoleon, there was no contradiction in appropriating both Julius Caesar and Charlemagne. The Frankish king had considered himself a Caesar, restoring the Roman Empire.[30]

In a letter to Napoleon, Talleyrand played up the symbolism of his upcoming visit to Aachen: "It will appear great and just that the city that was the first imperial city for so long, that always bore the special name of the seat and the throne of the emperors, and that was Charlemagne's habitual residence, experience its own magnificence through the presence of Your Majesty and bring out the resemblance in destinies that Europe has already grasped between the restorer of the Roman Empire and the founder of the French Empire."[31]

When he invaded Italy, writes Johannes Fried, Napoleon had ambitions to resurrect Charlemagne's empire.[32] In late 1803, Napoleon conceived a plan for a statue of Charlemagne for either the Place de la Concorde or Place Vendôme. In January 1804, he invoked Charlemagne when talking about the Civil Code before the Legislative Body: "[Charlemagne], just like he who governs us, wrote in the tumult of military camp the laws which were to keep families in peace, and he meditated on new victories when opening the peaceful assemblies of the Champ de Mars."[33]

As Matthew Zarzeczny explains, Napoleon admired Charlemagne's success at unifying Christendom while promoting religious tolerance for political purposes.[34] "[As] I had restored them [Jews] to all their privileges, and made them equal to my other subjects, they must consider me like Solomon or Herod, to be the head of their nation, and my subjects as brethren of a tribe similar to theirs," he wrote. ". . . I wanted to establish a universal liberty of conscience and thought to make all men equal, whether Protestants, Catholics, Mohammedans, Deists, or others . . ."[35]

The connections between the empires of Napoleon and Charlemagne were striking. To start, there was the geographic parallel, with the two empires encompassing France, Spain, Italy, and Germany. Both Charlemagne and Napoleon had unified France after periods of great turmoil. To govern his diverse empire, Charlemagne, like Napoleon, produced social reforms and a new civil code. Charlemagne used Christianity to bring together the disparate populations of the territories he conquered—a policy Napoleon emulated. On his desk at Saint-Cloud, Napoleon kept a bible on parchment belonging to Charlemagne.[36] (Bibliothèque nationale de France).

Charlemagne proved an effective model for Napoleon. As Robert Morrissey writes, "Napoleon's eagerness to cultivate his resemblance to Charlemagne . . . provided him with symbolic capital that he could exploit . . . and legitimate his ascension to the imperial throne. . . . It also made it possible to . . . establish a link with ancient Rome, of which the emperor of the West was the direct heir. Finally, it used history to foreshadow and justify not only a reconciliation with the Church but also a policy of dominating it . . ."[37]

Napoleon took a special interest in Aachen. Though he kept the pilfered marble columns and sarcophagus in Paris, he returned some of the stolen art, including the bronze sculpture of Charlemagne to the fountain on the Market Place, along with the second-century bronze *She-Wolf* and tenth-century pine cone. The Great Relics were brought back to Aachen from Paderborn in 1804.

Charlemagne's original palace was long gone, but Napoleon must have been struck by the towering cathedral that dominated the town. From the belfry, eight bells hung on wooden yokes in a wooden bell frame. The bells were cast three years after the city fire of 1656. In the aftermath of the fire, the cupola mosaic and other walls in the chapel had been covered with white stucco. But it was still possible to experience the sophisticated Carolingian artistic style—a fusion of late Antique, Hellenistic, Byzantine, Italian, Insular, and Frankish models.[38]

From 936 until 1531, Otto I through Ferdinand I, thirty Roman-German kings and twelve queens were crowned at the main altar. Chronicler Petrus Beek described the ceremony: "After the coronation, the king ascends the throne of Charlemagne in the high choir in prayer, after which he receives congratulations. The Te Deum is sung and the consecrator returns with his escort to the altar in order to end the Holy Mass, while the remaining electorates remain with the king. In the meantime, the king is received in the Aachen chapter and upon the old Book of Gospels, swears the oath of allegiance and obedience before the blood of the protomartyr Stephen. Then he accepts the knightly accolades with the Carolingian sword and descends into the Cathedral, where the formal Mass continues."[39]

Napoleon participated in a number of symbolic acts. He had a Te Deum Mass sung and took part in a procession in which Charlemagne's supposed relics were carried to the cathedral. Marie-Jeanne-Pierrette Avrillion, Joséphine's first chambermaid (premiere femme de chamber) recalled the event: "Of all the fetes and ceremonies held for the Emperor in Aix-la-Chapelle, there was one which was really exceptional for the grandeur of the memories it evoked. There was a superb procession in which were solemnly carried the insignia used at the crowning and anointing of Charlemagne and also [. . .] relics such as his skull and the bone of one of his arms; we saw his crown, his sword, his scepter, his hand of justice, his imperial globe, and his gold spurs: all objects that were greatly venerated by the inhabitants of Aix-la-Chapelle and which had only been exhibited so as to celebrate the presence of the Emperor. As for Napoleon, he took every care to express to the inhabitants how pleased he had been by their attentiveness."[40]

Napoleon also paid his respects by Charlemagne's golden shrine, a direct physical link with the emperor. The old monument, the arcosolium, most probably Charlemagne's original tomb, was destroyed in 1786. Excavations in 1803 and 1804 had been unsuccessful in locating his tomb in the middle of the octagon. That winter, Bishop Berdolet placed a large stone plate in the excavated area inscribed "Carolo magno."[41]

Napoleon, who had led two Italian campaigns and an invasion of Egypt, must have felt a special affinity with the warrior-king who had unified much of Western Europe through his military campaigns. When Julius Caesar visited Alexandria, he made a pilgrimage to the tomb of Alexander the Great—one despot paying homage to another, as Roman poet Lucan said.[42]

Now in the upper gallery, Napoleon declined to sit on Charlemagne's throne. The two ancient marble pillars that had flanked the throne for nearly one thousand years were at the Louvre. Considered a relic in its own right, the revered throne was made of four marble slabs, possibly from Jerusalem's Church of the Holy Sepulchre. The right side panel and backrest showed bits of ancient carvings with crosses and cavalries. During Charlemagne's time, it's believed the golden purse of St. Stephen was hidden in a cupboard underneath the back of the throne, holding earth soaked with his blood—possibly a gift from Pope Leo III.

The throne itself sat on ancient marble slabs, including green and red porphyry and gray Egyptian granite. Six red-veined stone steps, like those of King Solomon's throne (described in the First Book of Kings), led up to the seat. From this vantage, Charlemagne symbolically faced east toward the Redeemer and looked down to the main altar and up to Christ's enthroned image depicted in the dome's mosaic.

Before leaving Aachen, Napoleon issued an edict aimed at connecting himself with Charlemagne. The Carolingian Renaissance was noted for learning and science. The edict announced the creation of prizes for the sciences, history, fine arts, and poetry, "having as subject matter the memorable events of our history or the deeds bringing honor to the French character."[43] Like Louis XIV, Napoleon used Charlemagne to legitimize France's military expansion to the east and beyond the Rhine. Napoleon called his new road along the left bank of the Rhine the "route of Charlemagne."

From Aachen, Napoleon and Joséphine embarked down the Rhine, stopping at a dozen towns before reaching Mainz. During their summer separation, Napoleon had penned a series of affectionate letters. "I cover you with kisses," he wrote. "I cannot wait to see you. . . . A bachelor's life is horrid. I miss my good and beautiful wife . . ."[44] But as their entourage progressed, Napoleon turned his attention to Joséphine's lady-in-waiting, Elisabeth de Vaudey, with whom he began an affair.

Napoleon's monthlong state visit was like a Roman triumph, with crowds of new subjects greeting the imperial couple.[45] Like Charlemagne who met the German princes at Mainz en route to be crowned in Rome, Napoleon held court in Mainz on September 21—the first time outside of Paris. The delegation of Rhine princes congratulated Napoleon, describing him as the "first of our Roman Caesars to have crossed the Rhine to drive out the barbarians."[46]

During Napoleon's stay in Aachen, Austrian foreign minister Johann Ludwig von Cobenzl arrived and informed him that Holy Roman Emperor Franz von Habsburg (crowned in 1792) had recognized the new French emperor. Reading the writing on the wall, desperately needing a backup hereditary imperial title, Franz had himself proclaimed Francis II, Emperor of Austria in August. After nearly one thousand years, Charlemagne's revival of the Roman Empire was coming to an end.

TWO
CHARLEMAGNE'S HONORS

Napoleon's visit to Aachen made a deep impression. The imperial seal of 1804 featured Napoleon on one side and a reconstruction of the Carolingian coat of arms on the other. Having experienced the evocative power of Charlemagne's regalia firsthand, he insisted on having the famous objects beside him at his own coronation ceremony.

Kept in the imperial city of Nuremberg and only taken out for coronations, the regalia had carried Charlemagne's aura for centuries. Ironically, the most coveted of the objects—the Karlskrone, or Crown of Charlemagne—had never been worn by its namesake. As Neil MacGregor puts it, "It's not so much a crown, but an echo of a building, Charlemagne's chapel."[1]

German king Otto I was the first to don the gem-studded gold crown for his coronation in 962; successive Holy Roman emperors continued the tradition. A tour de force of champlevé enamel, the crown's eight hinged panels formed an octagon, symbol of regeneration. A trio of Old Testament kings along with Christ enthroned adorned four enamel plaques, conveying the idea of empire as a divine institution.[2] Amethysts, malachite, rubies, quarts, crystals, and pearls embellished the other four panels.

Over the ensuing centuries as Holy Roman emperors were elected from different families, the Crown of Charlemagne traveled from city to city. When the Habsburgs consolidated power around 1500, the crown stayed put in Nuremberg (until its transfer to Vienna for safekeeping in 1796).[3] In the sixteenth century, the coronation ceremony moved from Aachen to Frankfurt; the coronation in Rome by the pope was discontinued.

Not surprisingly, the Habsburgs did not think much of Napoleon's request to borrow Charlemagne's crown, bible, sword, and relics (including part of the Holy Cross) for his upcoming coronation. Undeterred, Napoleon dispatched Vivant Denon to track down royal insignia of medieval France and assemble the so-called "honors of Charlemagne."

Like the Holy Roman emperors, France's kings had bolstered their own claims to Charlemagne by adding his relics to their coronations. But the French Revolution had taken a toll. The few surviving objects of regalia associated with Charlemagne were now housed at the Musée Napoléon, including gold spurs, the sword of Charlemagne and its scabbard, and the scepter of Charles V.

Until the Revolution, Saint Denis was the designated basilica for royal funerals and burials. Thanks to gifts from abbots, princes, and kings, its treasury was the richest in France, with sacred medieval treasures along with the royal regalia. According to legend, the oldest and most precious of Saint Denis's medieval swords was Charlemagne's "La Joyeuse." First mentioned in connection with Philippe III the Bold in 1271, La Joyeuse was received by subsequent French kings in their coronations at Reims.

Another part of the crown jewels, the scepter of Charles V (known as Charlemagne's Scepter), was commissioned by the king for his coronation in the fourteenth century. In 1380, the scepter was embellished and gifted to the abbot of Saint Denis with the other regalia for the coronation of Charles's son, Charles VI.

Capping the two-foot-long golden scepter was a statuette of Charles's namesake Charlemagne, holding an orb and scepter and seated on a throne that rises from a lily, symbol of purity. Beneath a ring of pearls, the gem-studded pommel featured three medallions with scenes of Apostle St. James the Great reportedly seen by Charlemagne. The statuette was part of a public relations effort by the Habsburgs and Valois kings to associate themselves with the Carolingians.[4]

In ancient Greece, the scepter was a staff used by the elderly or by shepherds to lead their flocks. The staff of antiquity evolved into the pastoral staff, associated with Christ the Good Shepherd protecting the flock of the faithful; or in the case of European rulers, protecting one's subjects, writes Paula Rapelli. The scepter's sphere-shaped orb represented a ruler's power over the world.[5]

To restore the famous Charles V scepter, goldsmith Martin-Guillaume Biennais replaced a missing pearl and stones, three small eagles on the throne, and a small cross that once topped the orb. Biennais also regilded and then integrated a late fourteenth-century gold vermeil baton used by Saint Denis's choirmaster into the upper part of the shaft, which had been melted down in 1793.

Like scepters, crowns had been symbols of power and sovereignty since antiquity. In addition to repairing the Charlemagne-related objects, Biennais was asked to recreate a medieval "Charlemagne" crown, melted down for its gold. The goldsmith consulted Bernard de Montfaucon's 1729 *Monuments of the French Monarchy* with engravings showing Charlemagne wearing a cameo-encrusted imperial crown. Another reference may have been a pearl and cameo crown (circa 1349) capping the reliquary Bust of Charlemagne that Napoleon had seen during his trip to Aachen.

The crown's eight branches met under a cruciferous ball topped by a cross. To the headband and arches, Biennais affixed forty cameos and intaglios from the Louvre—antique, medieval, Byzantine, and seventeenth-century—taken by revolutionaries from Bourges, Arpajon, and the abbey of Saint Denis. Roughly half of the ancient gems used by Biennais came from a monumental, early fifteenth-century silver plated gold reliquary bust of Saint Benedict, which held a fragment of his skull and arm. The reliquary had been gifted to Saint Denis in 1401 by Charles V's brother, Jean de Berry.[6]

Carried off in November 1793 with the rest of Saint Denis's treasury, the reliquary was melted down; its carved gems deposited at the Louvre. Among Biennais's choices for the crown were a white chalcedony bust of an emperor wearing a breastplate, a two-layer agate portrait of the Roman emperor Elagabalus, and a two-layer agate cameo head of the mythological Omphale, mistress of Hercules.[7]

Denon also repurposed gems from the reliquary for a new hand of justice by Biennais. These included a medieval oval cameo of Domitian from the base of the reliquary's neck and an ancient intaglio of Victory reading.[8] The original hand of justice that disappeared during the Revolution had featured an ivory hand whose ring finger was loaded with a sapphire mounted on a ring of gold. The wooden stick, covered with gold leaf, featured three circles of foliage. Originally, each circle was adorned by three garnets, three sapphires, and a dozen large pearls.[9]

In keeping with the tradition of two crowns for the coronation of French kings, Biennais also designed a second crown for Napoleon. This time, the jeweler took his inspiration from Rome. The laurel was considered sacred to the worship of the sun; ancient Greek Olympiads received wreaths of laurel. For their triumphal processions, Roman generals wore the *corona triumphalis* of gold laurel leaves, representing the pinnacle of human supremacy. After Augustus established the Roman Empire, the laurel crown became a symbol of eternal power, exclusively for the emperors.[10]

The oak leaf, sacred to Jupiter and Cybele, was another powerful symbol representing strength and endurance. Following his assassination, Alexander the Great's father Philip II of Macedonia was buried with a spectacular crown of oak leaves made with hammered gold. The Roman Republic's most coveted crown, made of three types of oak leaves, was presented to a citizen who had saved someone from an enemy.[11]

On a velvet oval band, Biennais mounted fifty large gold laurel leaves in two rows to form branches, embellished with forty-two golden seeds. A dozen smaller gold leaves crisscrossed the forehead. To achieve the naturalistic details like veins, the goldsmith may have used a real laurel leaf in the casting. After Napoleon complained that the crown was too heavy, Biennais removed half a dozen of its large leaves, leaving forty-four. In the days before the coronation, crowds gathered at the window of Biennais's Paris showroom to ogle the crown, along with Joséphine's dazzling diadem, crown, and jeweled belt.[12] The modern *corona triumphalis* cost 8,000 francs, plus a 1,300-franc storage box.

Napoleon's "honors of Charlemagne" had the desired effect. "In Europe," wrote the *Journal of Paris*, "there is only one hand that is worthy of wielding the sword of Charlemagne, and it belongs to Bonaparte the Great."[13]

⚜

Determined to have a magnificent setting for his sacre, Napoleon dismissed a proposal to use the Champs-de-Mars military grounds. "We are no longer in that period when the people governed the king, and it is no longer necessary for them to meddle in politics," he said.[14] To avoid any reference to the deposed Bourbons, Napoleon also ruled out Reims cathedral where Clovis was baptized in 498 and almost all French kings had been crowned since 1027. Only Louis XI the Fat and Henri IV were crowned elsewhere—Orléans and Chartres in 1108 and 1594, respectively.[15] Napoleon also considered Lyon, the ancient capital of the Gauls, along with Charlemagne's capital of Aachen.

In the end, Napoleon chose his own center of power. On August 13, he announced the selection of Notre Dame Cathedral, then called the Metropolitan Church of Paris. Set on an island in the Seine on the former site of a Roman temple and early Christian churches, the vast Gothic cathedral could accommodate thirty thousand guests. During the ancien régime, the cathedral had hosted some royal occasions, including solemn entries, Te Deums, and weddings such as that of Louis XVI and Marie Antoinette in 1779.

But Napoleon's selection of the Gothic cathedral presented a dilemma. Comparing Notre Dame to "a vast symphony in stone," Victor Hugo later wrote: ". . . it is difficult not to sigh, not to wax indignant, before the numberless degradations and mutilations which time and men have both caused the venerable monument to suffer, without respect for Charlemagne, who laid its first stone, or for Philip Augustus, who laid the last."[16]

During the Revolution, the cathedral suffered extensive damage. Revolutionaries had mistaken twenty-eight Old Testament statues of the kings of Judah for the kings of France, and roped and pulled them down from the west façade. Inside, relics and altars were pillaged and vandalized. Renamed the Chief Temple of Reason, the cathedral hosted a festival in November 1793. As Blake Ehrlich describes, statues of Voltaire and Rousseau replaced figures of saints in niches. The goddess of Reason, played by a Paris Opera star, emerged from a Greek temple and sat on a throne of greenery on a high altar. Holding torches, female attendants in white robes with tricolor sashes and flower wreaths paraded up and down the aisle. Following the lighting of the Flame of Truth by the goddess, the Opera's Corps de Ballet performed.[17] The Chief Temple of Reason became a wine depot.

After Napoleon and Pope Pius VII signed the Concordat, Notre Dame was quickly redecorated for the installment of Jean-Baptiste de Belloy as bishop on Palm Sunday, 1802. Pillars were draped with cloth, the altar was rebuilt, and a figure of Christ was transferred from Arras. In preparation for the ceremony, Napoleon ordered nearby houses demolished to create more room for expected crowds for the coronation. Streets along the cortege route were paved, including the rue de Rivoli, the Place du Carrousel, and the Quai Bonaparte.

To decorate the cathedral, Napoleon again turned to Charles Percier and Pierre Fontaine. Having started their careers designing backdrops for the Opera and the Comédie-Française, the designers had experience producing dramatic visual effects. In addition, Percier embraced medieval architecture as a student at the French Academy and had made numerous drawings of the Gothic basilica of Saint Denis and Chartres Cathedral. This experience came in handy for the coronation décor for Notre Dame. Percier and Fontaine created an elaborate stage set that evoked both ancient and medieval history, helping fashion Napoleon's image as the direct heir to the Caesars and Charlemagne.

At Notre Dame's main entrance, the designers erected an arcaded portico resting on four square pillars. As Jean-François Bédard describes, this portico was divided into three registers matching those of the church's west façade. The lowest level featured statues and niches that corresponded to the location of the statues destroyed during the Revolution. For the middle register, large pointed arches repeated the cathedral's central archway, known as the Portal of Judgement. These were flanked with pillars decorated with niches in the manner of the buttresses that separated the three portals of the church's west façade. The top register replicated Notre Dame's Gallery of Kings with a continuous band of statues in niches surrounded by a parapet.[18]

In front of Notre Dame's main doors, Percier and Fontaine built a huge Gothic pavilion out of wood, papier-mâché, and painted canvas. In addition to hiding Notre Dame's decapitated sculptures, the portico functioned as a grand entrance. According to the official coronation program, the structure featured "four great Gothic arches, supported by four pillars on which were placed statues of the thirty-six cities that were called to participate in the ceremony."

Two of the pillars were topped with statues of Clovis and Charlemagne, each holding scepters. Between the two pillars was a long mast flying a replica of the ancient banner of Saint Denis. During the Middle Ages, the orange-red silk oriflamme became the battle standard of the French kings, carried in crusades and wars. According to legend, Charlemagne himself carried the banner to the Holy Land in response to a prophecy about a knight with a golden lance, from which flames would burn and drive out the Saracens. Capping one of the arches were the arms of Napoleon with figures representing the sixteen cohorts of the Legion of Honor. Percier and Fontaine crowned the entire structure with imperial eagles and gothic pyramids.[19]

From the cathedral entrance to the archbishop's palace, the duo also constructed an enormous rotunda embellished with filigree decoration and large, colorful Gobelins tapestries. Portable tapestries had previously been used as décor for royal coronations at Reims. The long, tent-shaped rotunda, conceived by Percier and Fontaine for the king of Etruria's visit to Malmaison in 1801, was repurposed to provide shelter for Napoleon's VIP guests as they disembarked from their coaches. Another wooden gallery along the side of the cathedral functioned as a dressing room for Pius VII and the imperial couple.

Inside, the designers combined the popular new Empire style with medieval chic. Sumptuous brocaded wall hangings featured the new coats of arms and symbols of the First Empire—golden eagles and bees, laurel wreaths, and garlands of oak leaves. There were also Carolingian-themed tapestries featuring Charles IV's scepter topped with Charlemagne's statuette and the hand of justice crosswise under the imperial crown. The cathedral was carpeted; damage was hidden with gold-fringed crimson silk and velvet drapes. To light the vast cathedral, candelabras embellished with gilt winged Victories were attached to the pillars; two dozen crystal chandeliers hung from the ceiling.

Since seating was at a premium, Percier and Fontaine removed the ironwork choir screen along with two altars to make room for tiers of wooded seats covered with silk and velvet in the clerestories and flanking the nave. On a platform to the left of the high altar, the designers installed a canopied throne adorned with the papal arms for Pius VII. Facing the high altar on a dais of four steps (recycled from the funeral of the former archbishop of Paris, Jean-Baptiste Royer), they placed two chairs of state for the imperial couple.

Near the main entrance, toward the west end of the nave, a dramatic dais was erected with twenty-four red carpeted steps. Beneath a triumphal arch of eight gilded columns, the designers placed the rounded-back throne of Napoleon, reminiscent of a Frankish shield.[20] Joséphine's throne was placed one step below.

In advance of the ceremony, Napoleon ordered sacred vessels, processional crosses, and lace vestments transferred to Notre Dame. He also returned relics formerly in the treasury of the Sainte-Chapelle, which had been sent in 1791 to Saint Denis and later displayed in a cabinet of curiosities in the National Library.[21] Despite these additions, classical décor outweighed Christian symbols.

Percier and Fontaine created a cross between a Greek temple and the grandeur of ancient Rome. "God wouldn't have recognized the place," quipped one observer.[22]

⚜

Letizia Bonaparte boycotted the coronation. For starters, she was angry at her son for excluding brothers Lucien and Jérôme from the succession plan. In addition, Napoleon's devout mother despised her daughter-in-law who she called *la putana,* the whore. She could not bear to see Joséphine crowned Empress of France.[23]

In fact, Napoleon had not yet decided whether Joséphine would be crowned alongside him in December. When his wife complained about his extramarital affairs, Napoleon fired back, accusing her of spying and driving him to marry a woman who could bear him a child.[24] With preparations for the sacre underway, the threat of divorce loomed large.

Ultimately, Napoleon decided to make Joséphine empress. As he told politician Pierre Louis Roederer at Saint-Cloud, "My wife is a good woman who does them [the family] no harm. She is willing to play the empress up to a point, and to have diamonds and fine clothes—the trifles of her age! I have never loved her blindly, yet if I have made her an empress it is out of justice. I am above all a just man. If I had been thrown into prison instead of ascending a throne, she would have shared my misfortune. It is right for her to share my grandeur."[25]

Part of that grandeur were the couple's magnificent coronation costumes designed by Joséphine's good friend Jean-Baptiste Isabey, a former student of Jacques-Louis David. "The coronation of Napoleon was a political pageant such as the world will never see again," writes Herbert Richardson, "simply because we shall never get again such a combination as Napoleon as producer and principal actor, and Isabey, the painter and miniaturist, for master of the robes."[26]

By imperial decree, Napoleon's *grand habillement* included: "white silk pantaloons and stockings; white slippers with gold embroidery; a white silk tunic, bordered and embroidered with gold crepine at the base; a cloak attached at the shoulders, made of purple velvet spotted with golden bees, embroidered around the edges and lined with ermine [a privilege of royalty since the Middle Ages]; white gold-embroidered gloves, a lace cravat; open crown of gold, formed into bay leaves formée; gold scepter and hand of justice; sword with gold handle, encrusted with diamonds, attached to a white sash worn around the waist and decorated with gold crepine."[27]

To Isabey, the Childeric bee that Napoleon had adopted for his personal emblem was too compact to produce the desired effect when embroidered in gilt thread on the purplish-red velvet coronation cloak. In its place, he designed a larger bee with partially open wings. For fifteen thousand francs, the firm of Picot produced three hundred of these embroidered gold bees for the mantle, along with *N*s and olive, laurel, and oak leaves. Russian ermine decorated with tufts of black astrakhan lined the mantle. It was so heavy, Napoleon reportedly nearly fell over from the weight.[28] Napoleon's long classical white satin tunic was embroidered in gold and fringed at the ankles. Napoleon nixed the idea of Roman sandals in favor of shoes. As a compromise, gold embroidery was added to imitate laces.

For inspiration for the imperial mantle, Isabey looked to the ancient *paludamentum*. Purple, the most prized color in ancient Greece, Egypt,

Phoenicia, and Rome, was produced from the juice of Mediterranean shellfish. According to legend, the source was discovered by Heracles's dog whose muzzle turned red after nibbling mollusks. After trying to extract murexes from their shells, Phoenician sailors also noticed their fingers had turned bright red. It took vast quantities of purpura and *murex* to extract the juice to make the purple dye.

Costly purple fabric adorned both ancient rulers and the statues of their gods.[29] In the late Republic, Julius Caesar made a controversial gamble. At official ceremonies, he wore the ceremonial clothing of kings—a purple cloak, long red boots, and a laurel wreath. At the Lupercalia, the Roman fertility festival, Mark Anthony tried crowning Caesar with a diadem with white ribbons. When the crowd protested, Caesar was forced to refuse the monarchial symbol.

In imperial Rome, the color purple was restricted to the emperor, priests, magistrates, and commanders. Violations were considered treason—as the son of Macedonian king Juba II learned the hard way. After wearing a purple outfit in Rome, the young man was arrested and put to death.[30] Roman citizens were allowed to add a band or braid of purple to their ceremonial attire; the width and shade indicating rank and age. Wealthy Romans also decorated their villas with prestigious purple furnishings.[31]

On his way to and from Notre Dame, Napoleon wore a *petit habillement*, a spectacular purple velvet cloak bordered in ermine and elaborately decorated in *point couché* gold and silver embroidery, along with a plumed black velvet hat. From top to bottom, the cloak's facings were embellished with a large motif repeated three times: *N* inscribed in an aureole with twelve stars of glory. The base of the aureole was bordered by ears of wheat, above it, a bee was surrounded by oak branches entangled with vine, olive, and laurel branches. Sewn onto the robe's left breast was a plaque of the Legion of Honor featuring the imperial eagle.[32]

In designing Joséphine's costume, Isabey looked to both classical fashion and a celebrated painting cycle of Marie de' Medici. Flemish Baroque artist Peter Paul Rubens produced two dozen canvases for the Luxembourg Palace, home of the Italian-born French queen. Like Marie de' Medici's collar, Joséphine's silk lace collar stood high behind her head, subtly connecting her with the last woman to be crowned queen of France. Isabey added other historical flourishes to Joséphine's dress, including knuckle-length sleeves, a late Gothic high waistline, and Renaissance-style puffed and embroidered upper sleeves.[33]

To complement Napoleon's fringed tunic, Joséphine's white silk satin and silver brocade gown was trimmed with gold fringe at the hem. Diamonds adorned the bodice and edges of the sleeves; golden bees were embroidered all over the gown. Even her white satin slippers had a golden bee embroidered on each toe, topped by a cluster of gilt bobbin lace.

Joséphine's seventy-two-foot mantle was lined and bordered with ermine. Gold bees, Napoleon's cipher, and oak, laurel, and olive leaves were embroidered onto the crimson velvet. Isabey intended to hang the mantle from Joséphine's left shoulder in a dramatic toga-like style, complementing Napoleon's robe worn open at the left shoulder. But at eighty pounds, the mantle was too heavy and had to be anchored low on Joséphine's back by sturdy shoulder straps. Even with this adjustment, Joséphine still had trouble walking through the cathedral. Both the gown and mantle were produced by Joséphine's favorite *marchand de modes* Louis Hippolyte LeRoy who raved: "These objects were of a magnificence and taste which exceeded all imaginings."[34]

Joséphine's jewelry was equally splendid. Her crown was decorated with black pearls, attached by clips to the diadem.[35] In contrast to Napoleon's ring with an emerald, symbol of divine revelation, the jeweler Marguerite set Joséphine's coronation ring with a ruby, symbol of joy.[36] She also wore Charlemagne's sapphire talisman from Aachen.[37]

"The coronation costumes were clearly intended to impress by virtue of their sheer magnificence, and their evocation of earlier historic periods, from classical antiquity to the 17th century, served to underscore the legitimacy of Napoleon's claim to the throne," write Lourdes Font and Michele Majer.[38]

Isabey also dressed many of Napoleon and Joséphine's A-list guests. Spectators were required to wear court dress made exclusively from French materials, with Isabey dictating the colors to be worn. He dressed the marshals of the Empire in royal blue. The Bonaparte princesses wore embroidered, trained dresses with delicate lace collars à la Catherine de' Medici.[39]

Like the French royal coronations at Reims where "everything was painstakingly fine-tuned to express meaning,"[40] Napoleon's coronation was meticulously staged with the emperor himself as choreographer.

In addition to the costumes, Napoleon ordered Isabey to produce a series of seven drawings, each with more than a hundred figures, elaborating highlights of the upcoming ceremony. But worried about missing the deadline, the artist took a cue from the French painter Nicolas Poussin. Scouring Paris for toy figurines, Isabey dressed the wooden dolls in papal, imperial, and other costumes and placed them in a large model of the cathedral.

Napoleon and his aides used Isabey's faux cathedral to organize and rehearse the upcoming sacre, putting the figures in their proper places.[41]

THREE
THE SACRE

Like Charlemagne, Napoleon sought divine legitimacy for his new Empire. After being proclaimed Emperor Napoleon I by the Senate in May, he sent Pope Pius VII this unusual invitation:

"Most Holy Father:

The happy effect produced upon the character and morality of my people by the reestablishment of religion induces me to beg your Holiness to give me a new proof of your interest in my destiny, and in that of this great nation, in one of the most important conjunctures presented in the annals of the world. I beg you to come and give, to the highest degree, a religious character to the anointing and coronation of the first Emperor of the French. That ceremony will acquire a new lustre by being performed by your Holiness in person. It will bring down upon our people, and yourself, the blessing of God, whose decrees rule the destiny of Empires and families. Your Holiness is aware of the affectionate sentiments I have long borne towards you, and can thence judge of the pleasure that this occurrence will afford me of testifying them anew. We pray God that He may preserve you, most Holy Father, for many years, to rule and govern our mother, the Holy Church.

Your dutiful son, Napoleon."[1]

Pius didn't RSVP at first. It had been over a millennium since a pope had ventured abroad to crown a civil ruler. In 754, Pope Stephen II traveled to Paris to consecrate Charlemagne's father Pepin the Short, king of the Franks. In a splendid ceremony at Saint Denis, Stephen bestowed Pepin with the additional title of *Patricius Romanorum*, Patrician of the Romans. In thanks, Pepin defeated the Lombards and presented Stephen with the former Exarchate of Ravenna, leading to the establishment of the Papal States. In 800, Pepin's son Charlemagne traveled to Rome to be crowned by Pope Leo III at St. Peter's Basilica.

Five months of negotiations ensued, conducted by Napoleon's uncle Cardinal Fesch, ambassador to the Holy See. From the Rhineland, Napoleon sent Arch-Chancellor Cambacérès a French translation of the prescribed coronation ceremony from the Roman Pontifical, asking for changes.

Against the advice of the Curia, Pius agreed to officiate. He hoped that his cooperation would result in concessions including the return of seized papal real estate and changes to the Concordat. In light of the recent experience of his predecessor at the hands of the French, Pius executed his will before departing for Paris. With a forty-person entourage, six cardinals, four bishops, and numerous officials, the pope left Rome on November 2 and crossed the Alps via the Mont Cenis Pass. After a two day stopover in Florence, Pius continued to France.

To give the sixty-four-year old pontiff ample travel time, the original coronation date of November 9, the anniversary of Napoleon's coup d'état, was pushed back to December 2. But the postponement was worth the wait. By requiring Pius to leave Rome for the coronation, Napoleon was about to outdo Charlemagne. For the first time since Charlemagne's 800 coronation, Western Europe would have two emperors.

Napoleon chose the Château de Fontainebleau to host the Pope. Located some thirty-five miles southeast of Paris, the historic château represented what Napoleon called "the real abode of kings, the house of ages." But like most of the royal palaces, Fontainebleau had been ransacked during the Revolution. Charles Percier and Pierre Fontaine, along with Calmelet, administrator of imperial furniture, and Duroc, grand marshal of the Palace, quickly went to work. Percier had a great interest in Fontainebleau, having visited several times after studying in Italy. Jacob-Desmalter produced Empire-style furnishings; the Garde-Meuble also supplied confiscated furniture and second-hand pieces.

At Napoleon's request, Dominique-Vivant Denon chose paintings for Fontainebleau from the Musée Napoléon, including two large canvases by Hubert Robert for Louis XVI's dining room. For the Pope's suite, he selected Caspar Netscher's *Meleager and Atalanta with the Boar's Head,* based on Roman poet Ovid's *Metamorphoses.* Divided into two apartments, the eleven-room papal suite comprised the first floor of the Gros Pavilion and west wing of the Cour de la Fontaine, known as the Queen Mother's Wing.

Fontaine, who had described the château in 1803 as being in a "state of extraordinary degradation and abandonment," congratulated himself on finishing the project in a record time for the Pope's arrival. "The apartments were furnished as though by magic [in nineteen days], thanks to the care and provident foresight of [Grand] Marshal Duroc," wrote Fontaine.[2] "Finally, the inhabitants of Fontainebleau, overwhelmed with so many new things, cannot prevent themselves from admitting that under the monarchy they never saw the castle more brilliant or better furnished."[3] Napoleon would continue refurbishing Fontainebleau in 1807, 1809, and 1810.

It was France's Renaissance king François I who turned the royal hunting lodge into an elegant art-filled château. In 1540, he dispatched painter Francesco Primaticcio to Rome to buy antiquities and have molds made of famous Vatican sculptures. Ironically, Fontainebleau's bronze replicas included many of the famous marbles recently pilfered by Napoleon, including *Ariadnes* (then Cleopatra), the *Laocoön*, *Apollo Belvedere*, *Cnidian Venus*, *Commodus Hercules*, and the *Tiber.* A plaster cast of Marcus Aurelius's horse from the Capitoline was installed in the servants' courtyard at Fontainebleau, later known as the Cour du Cheval Blanc, Court of the White Horse.

Like François I, Napoleon was attracted to the rich forest surrounding the château, over three hundred acres. In a reference to Joséphine's passion for natural English-style gardens, he told Fontaine: "How silly to spend fortunes creating little lakes, little rocks and little rivers . . . my *jardin a l'angalise* is the forest at Fontainebleau and I want no other."[4]

On the afternoon of November 25, 1802, Napoleon rode on horseback through Fontainebleau's forest to meet the papal cortege. As Napoleon dismounted in his green hunting outfit, his honored guest dressed in white robes and silk shoes descended from his carriage into the mud. After exchanging greetings, the two men entered a waiting carriage. Joséphine welcomed Pius on the steps of Fontainebleau.

When Charlemagne received Pope Leo III in his palace at Paderborn, he hosted a great feast complete with sparkling wine and gifts.[5] After his coronation, Charlemagne is believed to have also given the Pope a life-size silver crucifix. Now it was Pius VII who presented gifts to his imperial hosts at a banquet at Fontainebleau.

At Pius's request, sculptor Antonio Canova acquired dozens of presents for the imperial couple and their court. Canova himself created the most important gift—a portrait bust of the pope. "The presentation of such an image to Napoleon was not without an ulterior motive; it was intended to confirm the sitter's sovereignty, which was neither temporal nor limited, but universal," explains Guilhem Scherf. "Perhaps the slight smile of the patient diplomat (the Pope) can be glimpsed . . . the soft, extremely fine way in which the sculpture has been modelled contrasts with the brilliant, almost Bernini-esque carving of the hair."[6]

Despite the political challenges facing his sitter, Canova found Pius serene and gentle. He depicted him with a skullcap on his head, an ermine-lined stole over his buttoned cape embroidered with crosses and stars (the Chiaramonti emblem) with the Benedictine motto PAX. The motto was repeated under each cross, identifying Pius and referring to his role as peacemaker. To emphasize the pope's inner life, Canova left the eyes smooth, without pupils. In Stendhal's opinion, the bust had "too much ideal grace."[7]

Other imperial gifts included cameos set on boxes, medallions, and bracelets, mosaics, silverware, and precious marbles. Joséphine received an alabaster box, a Carrara marble cameo, and the Atlanta Cameo *opera di prima ordine* by Giuseppe Girometti, one of Rome's top engravers. Girometti's antique-style cameos were inspired by the great Hellenistic carvers and original Roman sculptures. Napoleon also received cameos—Girometti's agate cameo medallion of Achilles and a precious onyx cameo depicting the continence of Scipio.

Another ancient Roman art form featured in other gifts for Napoleon. In the sixteenth century, mosaics had been revived by the Vatican Workshops to decorate St. Peter's Basilica and other Rome churches. In the late eighteenth century, the workshops began producing highly prized secular pieces. For the *pietre dure* or hard stones technique, cut marble and rare and semiprecious stones such as agates, amethyst, chalcedony, lapis lazuli, and onyx were used to create colorful mosaics.

For Napoleon's vases, mosaicist Nicola de Vecchis was inspired by ancient Roman mosaics, possibly from Baths of the Seven Sages. Each white marble vase (1795 and 1800) featured a band of vertical acanthus leaves carved in relief below a band inlaid with jasper and lapis lazuli palmettes. Above, a micromosaic frieze depicted two griffins each holding a vase. A candelabrum between the griffins supported two festoons of flowers, the ends of which were carried by a pair of birds. For the waisted neck and volute handles, de Vecchis used the pietre dure technique of inlaid colorful hardstones.

Also for Napoleon, Canova chose a graceful neoclassical triumphal-arch clock (1804) from the studio of Giacomo Raffaelli. The triumphal arch was especially appropriate for the victorious military leader. The clock's white marble, a reference to classical antiquity, set off the micromosaic and pietre dure decoration in amethyst, agate, gasper, lapis lazuli, garnet, and labradorite.

Raffaelli mounted a timepiece by Swiss-born clockmaker Abraham-Louis Breguet on top of a triumphal arch made of red and white antique marble. Four amethyst columns topped by Corinthian capitals flanked the arch. Between these columns were two micromosaic panels depicting military trophies. Raffaelli topped the clock dial with bronzes—a military trophy flanked by winged figures of Victory and Fame, and a cockerel, vulture, wolf, and dog standing watch. In the center and beneath the arch stood a gilt-bronze statuette of Mars, god of war.[8]

Pius's gifts would become part of Joséphine's collection at Malmaison. Impressed by Giacomo Raffaelli's clock, Napoleon encouraged him to set up a workshop near the imperial court in Milan. Micromosaics became fashionable in Rome during the last decade of the eighteenth century. In 1804, Napoleon recruited Vatican Workshop veteran Francesco Belloni to start a mosaics school in Paris that became the École Impériale de Mosaïque.

After three days at Fontainebleau, on November 28, the papal party left for Paris. The pope's quarters at the Tuileries's Pavillon de Flore overlooked the Seine and featured an antechamber, dining room, salon, chapel, throne room, bedchamber, study, and bathroom. On the floors above, his entourage occupied some fifty-six rooms.

Joséphine, who'd almost been left out of the coronation, now scored a personal triumph. She had wed Napoleon in a 1776 civil ceremony, leaving their marriage invalid in the eyes of the newly reestablished Roman Catholic Church in France. At Fontainebleau, Joséphine confided to Pius that she and Napoleon had not had a religious ceremony. The pope assured her that he would insist on one as a condition of his taking part in the Sacre.

On the afternoon of December 1, a reluctant Napoleon tied the knot with Joséphine in a secret religious ceremony in the chapel at the Tuileries. Cardinal Fesch officiated; Talleyrand and Berthier were witnesses. Joséphine wasn't taking any chances. Two days later, she obtained a certificate of legality from Fesch.

⚜

At midnight on December 1, 1804, cannon salvoes announced the coronation at Notre Dame Cathedral. Starting at six o'clock that morning, bells chimed as workers rushed to clear snow from the Tuileries Palace and salt the icy streets along the procession route. Carpenters rushed to put final touches on cathedral decorations and repair the outdoor rotunda, damaged during the night's snow storm.

Around seven o'clock, five hundred musicians and singers arrived and took their places in two orchestras and choirs on the temporary grandstands at both ends of the cathedral's crossing. Directing the large ensemble was Jean-François Le Sueur, who had also composed several marches and motets for the ceremony.[9]

Meanwhile, deputations from the cities of France, the Army and Navy, the legislative assemblies, the judiciary, the administrative corps, the Legion of Honor, the Institute, and chambers of commerce left different meeting places around the city and met at Notre Dame. At eight o'clock, members of the Senate, Council of State, the Legislative body, and Tribunat arrived, followed by the diplomatic corps at nine. Tellingly, Austria's Count Cobenzl was a no-show.

Patriotic red, white, and blue bunting, artificial flowers, and green branches adorned the houses along the procession route: papier-mâché eagles decorated the Champs-Elysées.[10] Half a million Parisians braved the frigid weather to catch a glimpse of the forty carriage procession. Onlookers hung out of windows from rented bedrooms and balconies.

Napoleon had organized the procession from the Tuileries to Notre Dame with military precision. The elaborate coronation would cost three million francs, including about 380,000 francs for the coaches and equipages.[11] At nine, Pius VII descended the steps of the Pavillon de Flore with his retinue. Clad in white robes, he took his place in a decorated carriage topped by a large papal tiara and drawn by eight horses. Two squadrons of cavalry, some 108 dragoons, accompanied his ten carriages. By tradition, the pope's carriage was preceded by a nuncio riding a white mule and carrying the gilt papal crucifix. But found at the last minute, the mule was gray instead of white. Its presence in the midst of the pomp and pageantry caused great amusement among the crowd.

By ten-thirty, the pontifical cortege reached Notre Dame. At the entrance to the archbishop's palace, Pius was welcomed by Cardinal du Belloy, Archbishop of Paris. After donning his tiara and ceremonial robes, Pius made a dramatic entrance into the cathedral to Le Sueur's motet, *Tu es Petrus*. First came the apostolic cross, escorted by seven acolytes carrying golden candlesticks, followed by one hundred bishops and archbishops, then the pope escorted by seven cardinals. On the left hand side of the choir near the high altar, Pius took a seat on the papal throne. He would wait nearly two hours in the frigid sanctuary for the imperial couple to arrive.[12]

Around the same time, the imperial cortege left the Tuileries to a salvo of artillery. Napoleon's brother-in-law Joachim Murat, governor of Paris, led four squadrons of carabinieri, mounted chasseurs, and Mamelukes of the imperial guard. Next came four carriages with high-ranking military officers, three coaches of ministers, a coach for the grand chamberlain, grand squire, and master of ceremonies, a coach for the arch-chancellor and arch treasurer, a coach for the princesses, a coach for Napoleon and his brothers Joseph and Louis, a coach for the chaplain, grand marshal of the palace and grand veneur, and a coach for Joséphine's ladies.

Eight horses drew Napoleon's new imperial coach, adorned with gold, emblazoned with a capital *N* and three gilt eagles holding a golden crown. From the Place du Carrousel, the imperial procession passed rue Saint-Honoré and rue du Roule. Crossing the Pont Neuf, the carriages proceeded along the Quai des Orfèvres leading into the rue Saint-Louis, the rue du Neuf, and finally the rue du Parvis Notre-Dame. It took an hour for all twenty-five carriages to reach the cathedral.

After eleven, Napoleon and Joséphine entered the tent at the entrance to the archbishop's palace to change from their petit habillement into their formal robes. To keep warm, Joséphine and her ladies-in-waiting had worn cashmere shawls, which they removed before entering the cathedral.[13]

At the entrance of Notre Dame, Cardinal du Belloy sprinkled Napoleon and Joséphine with holy water before leading them inside to Le Sueur's Coronation march. At the east end of the cathedral, the imperial couple stopped in front of the high altar in the center of the choir. David watched as Napoleon took his place on a throne at the right of the altar, and Joséphine sat to his right on a smaller throne five steps below.

Among the thousands of invited guests that day was Jacques-Louis David. Napoleon had personally commissioned the artist to memorialize his coronation. Sketchpad in hand, David navigated his way through the cathedral to a ringside seat. But the class-conscious master of ceremonies, Louis-Philippe de Ségur, was not a fan of the revolutionary artist who had voted for Louis XVI's execution in 1792. When Ségur tried moving David into the upstairs galleries where he couldn't see the procession or the crowning, a fight broke out. The irate painter managed to reclaim his seat on the second level of Percier and Fontaine's tribune at the transept, giving him a good view of the ceremony.[14]

As the imperial couple entered the choir, Pius descended from his throne, stood at the altar, and began the *Veni Creator Spiritus*. While this hymn was sung by the choir, Napoleon and Joséphine knelt in prayer. Next, Napoleon gave the regalia he was carrying—the hand of justice, scepter, crown of Charlemagne, sword, necklace of the Legion of Honor, ring, and orb—to his marshals Perignon, Kellerman, LeFevre, Bernadotte, Beauharnais, and Berthier.

David continued sketching as Pius blessed the kneeling couple with the triple benediction taken from the coronation rite of Reims. With the choir singing Le Sueur's motet *Unxerunt Salomonem*, Napoleon and Joséphine approached the high altar where they received the sacred coronation unction on their foreheads and both hands. From there, Mass began to music commissioned from Neapolitan composer Giovanni Paisiello. Recently removed as chapel master of Tuileries for political reasons, Paisiello had suggested Le Sueur as his successor.

After the Mass, Napoleon climbed the steps to the altar alone. Rather than letting Pius do the honors as expected, he seized the Charlemagne crown. Then facing the congregation, he held it in the air before placing it on his own head. By anointing himself, Napoleon declared that he was even more powerful than Charlemagne who had been crowned by the pope. "My crown proceeds from God," Napoleon wrote, "and from the will of the people, and only to God and my people am I answerable for it."[15] For Pius, who had traveled to France against the wishes of his advisers, Napoleon's stunning gesture was a humiliating snub. His role in the coronation was reduced to a benediction.

Returning to the altar, Napoleon replaced the "Charlemagne" crown on his head with Biennais's gold laurel wreath. Next, Napoleon picked up a smaller crown and walked to the kneeling Joséphine. As he held her crown up, Napoleon stated that he was crowning Joséphine Empress of the French as his wife, not by her own right. "After picking up her smaller crown, he first put it on his own head and then transferred it to hers. . . ." wrote Laure Junot, Duchess of Abrantès. "His manner was almost playful. He took great pains to arrange this little crown, which was set over Joséphine's diadem. He put it on, then took it off, and finally put it on again."[16]

Napoleon and Joséphine slowly moved to the west end of the cathedral accompanied by a procession comprised of Pius VII, princes, grand dignitaries, grand officers, princesses, ladies-in-waiting, pages, heralds, and bailiffs bearing the honors of Charlemagne. They climbed the red carpeted steps to the elaborate dais spanning the entire width of the nave. During this process, Napoleon stopped an altercation among his sisters Elisa, Pauline, and Caroline about carrying Joséphine's train. The weight of his own robes nearly caused him to fall backward as he climbed the staircase.

Napoleon and Joséphine took their seats on a pair of thrones under a huge Roman-style triumphal arch with faux marble columns and Corinthian capitals topped by eagles. The princes and princesses, dignitaries and officials gathered below. Climbing to the top of the dais, Pius VII raised his hands and blessed the couple with words from the Reims rite: "May God confirm you upon this throne, and may Christ cause you to reign with Him in His eternal kingdom."

After kissing Napoleon on the cheek, Pius turned toward the congregation and repeated Leo III's words from Charlemagne's coronation: *"Vivat Imperator in aeternum"*—"May the Emperor live forever!"[17] The singing of the Vivat by the Abbé Roze followed and Pius was accompanied back to his throne. The Mass continued with the Te Deum by Paisiello and the Gospel sung in Latin and Greek.

Following the Mass, Pius retired to the sacristy. Surrounded by his court, generals, and dignitaries, Napoleon raised his right hand and placed his left hand on the gospel held by Cardinal Fesch. With the constitutional oath, Napoleon promised to uphold the constitution and preserve the gains of the Revolution. The oath ended with the words: "Napoleon Emperor by the grace of God and the constitution."[18]

The herald proclaimed: "the most glorious, the most august emperor Napoleon, emperor of the French, is crowned and enthroned emperor, Long live the Emperor!" Cries of *"Vive l'Empereur"* rose inside the cathedral, echoed by canon salvoes. With their cortege, France's new emperor and empress returned to the archbishop's palace to change their robes. Pius left the sacristy and returned to the cathedral, proceeding out to *Tu es Petrus*.

Despite the setting and presence of the pope, the religious nature of the sacre had been understated. An enthusiastic crowd waited in the falling snow to see the imperial procession. Around four o'clock, the procession left Notre Dame and headed toward the Place du Chatelet, returning to the Tuileries via the rue and the Place de la Concorde. The streets had been strewn with flowers and paper lanterns. At about six-thirty, the imperial couple reached the palace; Pius arrived about seven. During this time, there was a scramble at the cathedral as some twenty thousand guests tried to leave.

That evening, Napoleon and Joséphine dined together in the Tuileries. The city of Paris presented the couple with the 1,069-piece Grand Vermeil service by goldsmith Henri Auguste, architect Jacques Molinos, painter Pierre-Paul Prud'hon, and sculptor Jacques-Edme Dumont. Among the spectacular gilded silver objects were his and her *nefs*, spice cellars in the shape of ships, long associated with France's royals.

As Odile Nouvel-Kammerer describes, the emperor's nef featured a figurehead on the prow representing Fame on a wolf's head rostrum, holding a laurel wreath. Justice and Prudence sit at the prow on either side of Charlemagne's crown, resting on a helmet. Atop the lid, Napoleonic bees fly toward the prow. Large bas-reliefs adorn the sides—including a depiction of the coronation and the presentation of gifts from the city of Paris. At the base, a male and a female figure representing the Seine and Marne support the spice cellar on their heads while steering the rudder. The nef rests on a base decorated with the initial *N* and imperial eagles in laurel wreaths.[19]

After the meal, Napoleon looked out on the illuminated gardens of the Tuileries. The grande allée was lined with brightly shining columns, reflecting the light from thousands of colored lamps hanging from the tree branches. An unmanned balloon fitted with three thousand lights and shaped like an imperial crown was launched from Notre Dame. Forty-six hours later, the balloon landed in Lake Bracciano near Rome. Considering this an omen of his destiny, Napoleon suggested the balloon be displayed in Rome.

Napoleon used his coronation to garner public support. For several days, Paris celebrated with festivals, military displays, banquets, balls, receptions, and official ceremonies. Lights on the façade of the Tuileries Palace created a magnificent effect, the garden was brilliantly lit with two rows of illuminated arches bordering the great alley and surrounding the parterres. Public entertainments were organized throughout France, from street theater, games, and music to fireworks over the Seine and balloon releases. Medals were distributed with Napoleon's portrait.

On December 5, Napoleon and Joséphine left the Tuileries at eleven A.M. for the parade grounds of the Champs de Mars accompanied by his family, officers of the Empire, and Mamelukes. Two decades earlier, Napoleon drilled here as a student at the École Militaire. Percier and Fontaine designed an elaborate two-story stage. The imperial couple climbed a grand staircase to a monumental portico and colonnade hung with drapery and took their seats on thrones. The entire length of the façade was decorated by a covered gallery. From the parade grounds to the Seine, soldiers stood in tight formation.

Donning his gold laurel leaf crown and coronation robe, Napoleon presented the army regiments and National Guard with the Empire's new emblem—eagles based on the Aquila of the legions of Rome. Designed by Antoine-Denis Chaudet and cast in bronze in six pieces and gilded by Pierre-Philippe Thomire, the 3.5-pound eagles had a 9.5-inch wingspan and measured 8 inches in length. Mounted on top of the blue regimental flagpoles, the eagles were on a plinth, with one claw resting on Jupiter's thunderbolt spindle, wings slightly spread and heads turned to the right. The eagle rested on a box indicating the number of the various regiments, with a dowel to attach the emblem to the flagstaff.

Like Rome's emperors delivering the *adlocutio*, France's new emperor addressed his troops:

"Soldiers, behold your standards! These eagles will always serve as your rallying point. Will you swear to defend them with your life?"

To this, the troops shouted "We Swear!"[20]

Like the Roman legions, Napoleon's Grande Armée would carry the eagle into battle as a symbol of France's imperial power. Standard-bearers were expected to defend the standards with their lives, like Roman standard-bearers and medieval bearers of the oriflamme. "The loss of an eagle is an affront to regimental honour for which neither victory nor the glory acquired on a hundred battlefields can make amends," wrote Napoleon.[21]

In 1804, Denon commissioned a commemorative medal of Pius and Notre Dame from his protégé, engraver Jean-Pierre Droz. Shown in right profile, Pius wears the three-tier papal tiara and ecclesiastical garments. The reverse featured the façade and north side of Notre Dame with Percier and Fontaine's decorations. The double date of the ceremony in Gregorian and revolutionary calendars and the inscription *imperator sacratus* invoked Napoleon. Romain-Vincent Jeuffroy also designed a commemorative medal series including the Coronation at Paris, Coronation festivities, Standards presented to the Army, and Napoleon's planned Invasion of England.

In one of the medallions, Jeuffroy depicted Napoleon in Caesar-like profile. On the reverse, the emperor stands on a shield carried by a senator and a soldier beneath the inscription "le senat et le peuple." A similar medallion minted in 1643 shows four-year-old Louis XIV sitting on a shield held high by figures of France and Providence.[22]

The custom of acknowledging a new leader by raising him on a shield can be traced back to 360 C.E. when Flavius Claudius Julianus, known as Julian the Apostate, was proclaimed Roman emperor by his soldiers in Paris. As Roman historian Ammianus Marcellinus writes: "he [Julian] was placed upon an infantryman's shield, raised on high and was hailed by all as Augustus."[23] The tradition was continued by the Franks who replaced the rectangular shield of the Romans with a circular shield. In Jeuffroy's medallion, Napoleon I is shown standing on the round Frankish shield, which also appears to be the model for one of his many thrones.[24]

In his studio in the former chapel of the College of Cluny near the Sorbonne, Jacques-Louis David went to work. In October, the fifty-six-year-old artist received a commission from Napoleon for a four-painting series to commemorate the coronation. The emperor's personal involvement was unusual. Since his appointment as director of the Louvre, Dominique-Vivant Denon handled most official dealings with artists. To David, Napoleon's participation underscored the commission's importance. He was about to immortalize the most important moment of Napoleon's extraordinary career.

David's own path to the position of "First Painter of the Emperor" began three decades earlier. In 1774, after four tries, he won the prestigious Prix de Rome. He spent the next five years studying ancient sculpture and Renaissance painting. Like his fellow neoclassicists, David most valued the ancient monuments of Rome. Back in Paris, he enjoyed great success with his historical, classicizing scenes including the *Oath of the Horatii* commissioned by the king of France. David soon became an influential leader of the French Revolution. As head of the Revolutionary Committee for General Security, he signed death warrants for several hundred people, including his patron Louis XVI.

By the time David met Napoleon Bonaparte at an official reception in 1797, he was France's most celebrated painter. Having failed to enlist Antonio Canova, the ambitious young general began wooing David. Though the painter declined Napoleon's invitation to join the Egyptian campaign on the grounds that he was too old for the adventure, he persuaded the general to sit for a portrait. "At last my friends," he told his students after the session, "this is a man to whom one would have raised altars in antiquity; yes, my friends; yes my dear friends; Bonaparte is my hero!" About Napoleon's head, the David declared: "It is pure, it is great, it is beautiful as antiquity."[25]

After the second Italian campaign and coup, the first consul summonsed David to execute another portrait. When David shared that he was currently working on *The Battle of Thermopylae*, Napoleon told him, "you are wrong, David, to waste your time depicting losers."

David defended the subject, explaining that the three hundred heroes died keeping the Persians out of Greece.

"No matter," replied Napoleon. "Only the name of Leonidas has reached us. All the rest is lost to history."

In response to David's request for a sitting, Napoleon replied, "Sit? What for? Do you think that the great men of antiquity whose images have come down to us ever sat?"

Walking the artist out, Napoleon's brother Lucien explained: "You see, my dear David, he loves only the subjects of national history, because he can play a part in them. It's his weakness: he's rather fond of being talked about."[26]

Now with the monumental *Napoleon Crowning Joséphine*, also known as the *Sacre*, David hoped to show his superiority to both the Venetian Renaissance master Paolo Veronese, whose recently confiscated *Wedding at Cana* was the Musée Napoléon's largest painting, and Peter Paul Rubens's *Coronation of Marie de Medici* cycle then at the Luxembourg Gallery.[27] Marie de Medici was the last French queen to be anointed nearly two hundred years earlier in 1610.

To lend his canvas authenticity, David had plans of Notre Dame delivered to his studio and borrowed Biennais's "Charlemagne" crown. Using cardboard models and wax figures, David reconstructed the interior of Notre Dame. Several of the coronation's participants came to his studio to pose. Thanks to Joachim Murat, David wangled private sittings with his wife Caroline (Napoleon's sister) and Joséphine, and Pius VII. "I shall have painted an emperor, and finally a pope!" "I will slip into posterity in the shadow of my heroes," David famously declared.[28]

Like Rubens in the *Coronation of Marie de Medici*, David used a rich palette to recreate Notre Dame's lavish décor and the colorful costumes of the imperial couple, family members, and courtiers. An initial preparatory sketch showed the shocking moment when Napoleon crowned himself and pressed his sword to his heart. But believing that image sent an overly authoritarian message, Napoleon may have instructed David to change the scene, to show him in a more chivalrous light. David re-sketched the composition, with Napoleon raising the crown in the air, about to anoint Joséphine.[29] Napoleon would compare himself to a "French knight."

David made other changes to the canvas in deference to his powerful patron. Napoleon had banned his brothers Lucien and Jérôme from the service; his mother refused to attend. With Napoleon insisting on an image of family unity, David added the absent relatives. Wearing a diadem, Madame Mère is shown in the center of the canvas, looking down on her son's coronation from a front row seat in the first level of the VIP gallery. In his propagandistic use of imperial family imagery, Napoleon was invoking Rome's emperors. The same kind of historical revision appears in Roman reliefs. For example, Augustus's son-in-law Agrippa, dead at the time of the procession, appears on the relief at Augustus's *Ara Pacis*.[30]

Originally, David painted Pius VII seated to Napoleon's right by other ecclesiastics with his hands folded in his lap. Explaining that he hadn't brought the pope all the way from the Vatican to sit and do nothing, Napoleon had David portray the pontiff blessing the coronation with his right hand. To give Napoleon and Joséphine more importance, David also downsized Notre Dame. In addition to Napoleon's changes, David himself took artistic license. Behind Napoleon, he inserted another military general who seized power with a coup—Julius Caesar in ecclesiastic robes.

David spent much of 1806 painting the participants' portraits and opulent costumes. Like Rubens in the Medici cycle, David organized some 230 figures into groups. Napoleon's siblings appear on the left. The dignitaries of the Empire are shown in the right foreground in three-quarter back view, holding the eagle-topped scepter, globe, and hand of Justice. Joséphine, painted to look younger than her forty years, kneels by Joachim Murat who holds the coronation cushion.[31] The crossbearer's cross reaches up to the second level of the tribune where David stands sketching with his wife, twin daughters, and several friends.

Three years after the coronation, on January 4, 1808, Napoleon visited David's studio, spending an hour studying the *Sacre*. Measuring nearly thirty-three feet wide and just over twenty feet tall, the giant canvas entranced the emperor who drew his hat in salute to David.[32] "How grand! How all the objects project! It is so beautiful! What truth! This is not a painting; one walks in this picture!"[33]

In February and March, the *Sacre* was the hit of the Musée Napoléon's annual Salon. Despite its acclaim, David's relationship with Napoleon and his courtiers remained prickly. In 1806, Denon gave David, along with other painters, their marching orders. They had twenty-four hours to pack up their studios in the Musée Napoléon's Cour Carrée. Due to a rift over money, the remaining two paintings in the coronation cycle were never completed.

David's second canvas, *The Distribution of the Eagle Standards at Champs de Mars*, proved far less of a critical success than the *Sacre*. David captured the impressive military event in an enormous canvas for the Tuileries throne room. He portrayed Napoleon like a Roman emperor distributing eagles to his soldiers. The Grande Armée's military signs and symbols were directly modeled on Roman models.[34]

David also painted Pius VII's portrait. But the December sitting at the Tuileries almost didn't happen. The sixty-three-year-old was hesitant to pose for a man "who had killed his King and who would make short work of a poor papier-mâché Pope."[35] David portrayed the pontiff seated in a three-quarter-length pose, wearing an ermine-trimmed red velvet cape over a white tunic, and a red stole with gold embroidery. In his right hand, the sitter holds a piece of paper with the Latin *Pio VII bonarum artrium patrono,* Pius VII Patron of the Fine Arts.

"He was beautiful to see;" wrote David. "He reminded me of Julius II, whom Raphael painted in the Heliodorus of the Vatican."[36] To this he added, in February 1805: "This good old man, what a venerable figure! How simple he is . . . and what a fine head he has! A truly Italian head; the large eyes set so well, very pronounced! . . . He's a true Pope, that one! Poor, humble; he's only a priest."[37]

FOUR
KING OF ITALY

In agreeing to officiate at Napoleon's coronation in Paris, Pope Pius VII hoped to reset their relationship. His goal was to secure the return of Romagna, Ferrara, and Bologna, formerly part of the Papal States. He also wanted the Catholic Church to be named France's state religion. But the pope returned to Rome on May 17, 1805, empty-handed, still smarting from the symbolic insult of Napoleon placing the crown on his own head.

Not only were the three territories not returned, France's new emperor was about to turn the former Cisalpine and Italian Republics into the Kingdom of Italy, with himself as king.[1] So when Napoleon asked Pius to accompany him to Milan for the royal coronation, he passed, delegating the role to his Paris legate, Cardinal Caprara, archbishop of Milan.

Originally, Napoleon tapped his brother Joseph Bonaparte for the job. By late January 1805, Joseph reneged on the agreement, choosing instead to retain his succession rights to the French imperial throne. On March 31, Napoleon's entourage left Paris for a week of receptions in Lyon. From there, they crossed the Mont Cenis Pass on mules, arriving in Turin by April 24 where they ran into Pius on his way back to Rome.

By early May, a bust of Napoleon was ordered for the façade of the Malatestiana Library in Cesena, along with an Egyptian pyramid and a triumphal arch based on the Arch of Septimius Severus for Mantua. A new road outside Verona was to be named Strada Bonaparte. On May 8, Napoleon made a triumphal entry into Milan through the city's medieval gate, Porta Ticinese, renamed Marengo after his victory in 1800. The welcome included French and Italian troops, spectators, and cannon fire. As general of the Army of Italy, Napoleon had addressed his victorious troops from the very same spot on May 15, 1796:

"Soldiers, You have rushed like a torrent from the top of the Apennines; you have overthrown and scattered all that opposed your march. Piedmont, delivered from Austrian tyranny, indulges her natural sentiments of peace and friendship toward France. Milan is yours, and the Republican flag waves throughout Lombardy . . . we are the friends of the people everywhere, and those great men whom we have taken for our models. To restore the capitol, to replace the statues of the heroes who rendered it illustrious, to rouse the Roman people, stupefied by several ages of slavery—such will be the fruit of our victories; they will form an era for posterity, you will have the immortal glory of changing the face of the finest part of Europe. . . . The French people, free and respected by the whole world, will give to Europe a glorious peace, which will indemnify them for the sacrifices of every kind which for last six years they have been making. You will then return to your homes and your country. Men will say, as they point you out, "*He belonged to the army of Italy.*"[2]

Now as emperor, Napoleon and his retinue checked into Monza Palace, conveniently located across from his coronation venue, the pink-hued marble Duomo. Accommodating some forty thousand, the monumental cathedral competed in scale with Rome's St. Peter's Basilica and Seville's Cathedral. But its two thousand exterior statues and 135 delicately carved towers were unrivaled. Since 1762, the highest spire had been topped with *Madonnina*, a towering copper and gold leaf statue of the Virgin Mary by Giuseppe Perego.

Begun in the fourteenth century, Milan's Duomo was built by thousands of European artists, sculptors, and artisans. Canals were dredged and a new road built to haul marble for the cathedral from quarries near Lake

Maggiore. But after its consecration in 1418, the Duomo remained unfinished for centuries due to a shortage of funds and stylistic disagreements. As a young general in 1797, Napoleon tried to win over the Milanese by completing the façade. Now one week before his coronation, Napoleon again ordered the façade to be completed in the neoclassical style by Carlo Pellicani. The centuries-old project was finally realized in 1813 with Napoleon's statue capping one of the spires.

On May 25, French and Italian gendarmes under General Duroc assumed their posts outside the Duomo. The next morning, cheering crowds lined the streets as Napoleon's stepson Eugène de Beauharnais commanded the processional troops. A covered walkway running from the grand stairs of the Palazzo Reale to the entrance of the Duomo had been left open on both sides to give spectators a view of the corteges. Above the cathedral's main doors hung the coat of arms of the Kingdom of Italy.

Sunlight filtered through the soaring stained-glass windows as the deputations began taking their seats inside the storied cathedral. Silk and gold-fringed gauze draped the vaults, walls, and columns. At eleven, Caprara left the archbishop's palace with cardinals, archbishops, and other ecclesiastics. Around noon, he escorted Joséphine to her seat in the tribune. France's first lady wore a classical dress and diadem; her gold necklace featured cameos depicting the labors of Hercules. Preceding Joséphine was her sister-in-law Elisa accompanied by her equerry and chamberlains. Matrons of honor and ladies-in-waiting followed.

To a salvo of artillery, Napoleon left the Royal Palace at midday in a magnificent green velvet costume with gold and silver embroidery. Like his Paris coronation six months earlier, Napoleon chose to surround himself with symbols of Charlemagne. The most important was the Iron Crown of the Kingdom of Italy. Several days earlier, the treasured Byzantine crown had been retrieved from nearby Monza Cathedral by the coronation's master of ceremonies and fifty cavalry.

En route to being crowned Holy Roman Emperors in Rome, Roman-German kings would stop in Lombardy to be crowned King of Italy with the Iron Crown. Starting with Conrad II in 1026, Milan replaced Pavia as the host city for the coronations. Similar in form to Otto I's Crown of

Charlemagne with six hinged gold plates, the bejeweled and enameled Iron Crown was both regalia and relic, writes W. Augustus Steward.[3]

The Iron Crown got its name from its narrow inner ring, said to have been forged with nails used in the crucifixion (twenty-eight other places in Europe also claim a holy nail, including Paris).[4] According to Milan's patron saint Ambrose, Constantine's mother Helen found the True Cross and the nails that had crucified Christ, one of which she placed in her son's diadem and the other in his horse's bridle.

Pope Gregory gave one of Constantine's nails to the Frankish princess Theodolina. It was Theodolina who incorporated the nail into her Iron Crown, donated to the church in Monza in 628.[5] A second nail, given to Ambrose by Emperor Theodosius, had been venerated in a reliquary kept high up in the vault of the choir of Milan's Duomo since the fifteenth century.

Besides the Iron Crown from Monza, three more crowns featured in the Milan coronation. Napoleon entered the Duomo wearing two—the new crown of the King of Italy by Parisian jeweler Marguerite and Biennais's gold imperial laurel crown. Biennais's imperial crown of Charlemagne was carried in the corteges and placed on the altar, but not worn. The "honors of Charlemagne" transported from Paris were also carried into the Duomo with Napoleon.

Seated on a throne, Napoleon was invested with the insignia of royalty by Caprara. After the archbishop blessed the Iron Crown, Napoleon took it from the altar and placed it briefly on his own head. Apparently the crown was too small for his head.[6] Then, channeling the Lombard kings, Napoleon proclaimed: "God has given it to me; Let him who touches it beware!"[7]

Applause filled the sanctuary and bells pealed as Eugène de Beauharnais directed an escort of thirteen imperial carriages. Accompanied by French and Italian grenadiers, the cortege traveled from the Duomo to the red brick basilica of Sant'Ambrogio for more prayers and a Te Deum. One of Milan's oldest churches, the basilica was founded by Ambrose in the fourth century and rebuilt in the eleventh century in Romanesque style. During the Napoleonic suppression in 1797, its monastery had been converted to a military hospital.

Coronation festivities continued over the next several days with fireworks, ancient-style games, and a fête at the La Scala opera house.

Napoleon and Joséphine watched as the wife of celebrated balloonist André-Jacques Garnerin ascended in a balloon, showering them with flowers. "In one day and in a single spectacle," reported the *Moniteur*, "the Italians combined what to the ancients was most spectacular and what to modern science was most daring, in the presence of a hero who surpasses both the ancients and the moderns."[8]

On June 5, Napoleon created the Order of the Iron Crown, featuring grand cross knights (twenty), commander knights (one hundred), and ordinary knights (five hundred). The order's badge featured an imperial eagle above the Iron Crown on a green and gold ribbon. On his second day in Milan, Napoleon issued a decree creating an Italian version of the French Council of State. Now he introduced Eugène de Beauharnais as the viceroy of the Kingdom of Italy. The twenty-four-year-old, who didn't speak Italian, suddenly found himself responsible for nearly four million people across today's Lombardy, Venetia, and Romagna.[9]

For his official coronation portrait, Napoleon turned to Andrea Appiani. When Napoleon first arrived in Milan in 1796, he sat for a charcoal and chalk portrait drawing by the Milan-born artist. The twenty-seven-year-old general was so pleased with his likeness, he named Appiani "senior commissioner" responsible for selecting Lombard and Venetian art for Paris. Thanks to Napoleon, Appiani had become one of northern Italy's best known painters. A visit to Paris in 1801 had introduced him to the austere Neoclassicism of Jacques-Louis David. He painted Napoleon as first consul in 1803 and several more times as Emperor and King of Italy.

Appiani portrayed the new King of Italy in three-quarter pose, wearing a green velvet version of the purple petit habillement he wore en route to the sacre at Notre Dame. In one of some twenty versions of the portrait, Napoleon rests a gloved hand on the crown of the King of Italy and wears the new Order of the Iron Crown.[10]

In 1800, Appiani began a Napoleonic cycle for the Caryatid Hall at Milan's Royal Palace. *The Glories of Napoleon* (*I Fasti di Napoleone*) would grow to thirty-five episodes from Napoleon's life. Other propaganda works include the *Apotheosis of Napoleon* for the Caryatid, and the *Triumphs of Napoleon* for the Throne Room, in which the artist divinized Napoleon as Jupiter Olympic.

⚜

In his memoirs, Cardinal Ercole Consalvi recounted the insults Pius VII experienced at the hands of Napoleon. "I do not want to speak of what he had to suffer in Paris. Nor to tell in detail of the encounter between Napoleon and the Pope at Fontainebleau when Napoleon appeared disguised as a huntsman with fifty hounds . . . nor of his having kept the Pope waiting an hour and a half at the altar, dressed in sacred garb, on the morning of the ceremony."[11]

Though Napoleon made no concessions, he ordered Pius an expensive papal tiara. Parisian jeweler Marie-Étienne Nitot and goldsmith Henri Auguste collaborated on the sumptuous gift, possibly designed by Charles Percier. To the traditional hive-shaped tiara covered with beige silk velvet, the jewelers added three crowns of chiseled gold with bas-reliefs depicting the Concordat, the restitution of the Church, and Napoleon's sacre. Diamonds, rubies, sapphires, emeralds, and pearls covered each crown; the largest of the stones was set in vine leaves.[12]

On May 21, 1805, Auguste wrote Talleyrand that his colleague Nitot had been dispatched "to go to Milan [. . .] present the tiara enriched with diamonds destined for His Holiness [. . .] I dare flatter myself that this work will have the approval of S. Maj. The Emperor and your (. . .) Artists who have seen in Rome The seven tiaras which adorned the treasury of St. Peter, have decided that the Popes had never worn crowns of so remarkable a taste and wealth."[13]

Nitot delivered the tiara to the Vatican in May. The diamond cross at the top was supported by a spectacular emerald—the gem Pius VI surrendered to pay the indemnity imposed by Napoleon's Treaty of Tolentino. Pope Gregory XIII had originally placed the emerald on Pope Julius II's tiara around 1580; Pius VI repurposed the gem for his own tiara in 1789. The famous stone had been deposited at Paris's Museum of Natural History. In a symbol of reconciliation, Napoleon now returned the emerald to Rome.[14]

Napoleon had another request for Pius. Two days before his Milan coronation, Napoleon wrote to Rome, demanding an annulment of his younger brother Jérôme's marriage to American Protestant Elizabeth Patterson. Pius refused. A year later, with the help of the Archbishop of Paris, Napoleon would dissolve Jérôme's marriage and marry him off to the Protestant daughter of the king of Westphalia. In addition to the annulment issue, Napoleon was angry with Pius for welcoming his estranged brother Lucien and his family to Rome.

But Napoleon got his way on another religious matter. August 15, his birthday, had been declared a national feast day—just as Augustus's birthday along with anniversaries of his victories had been celebrated in ancient Rome. To create an anniversary for his new Empire, Napoleon forced Pius to canonize a Roman warrior-martyr, Neopolis. This probably fictitious figure was believed to have been martyred for refusing allegiance to Emperor Maximilian.[15]

By inventing Saint Napoleon and elevating himself to saintly or demigod status, Napoleon was drawing on the Caesarian tradition. "As Julius Caesar counted divine members among his ancestry and the Caesars at times demanded, and received, worship as gods, the propagandistic value and the meaning of comparing Napoleon to Julius Caesar, Trajan, or a Roman-style demi-god were indistinguishable . . ." writes Oliver Benjamin Hemmerle.[16]

Starting in 1806, the Church had to share one of its holiest days, the feast of the Assumption, with Napoleon's new patron saint of warriors. For the inaugural festivities, a religious ceremony at Notre Dame was accompanied by hoisting an illuminated star thirty feet in diameter over the cathedral's towers. Saint-Napoleon day effectively became a national holiday honoring the emperor. When Napoleon introduced a new imperial catechism that positioned his rule as anointed by God, Pius refused his approval.[17]

After his Milan coronation, while Joséphine took the waters in the Lake District, Napoleon stopped in Brescia. "I have received your letter, my good little Joséphine, and I learn with pleasure that bathing is doing you good," he wrote from Brescia. "I advised you to do this a week ago. Lake Como will be good for you. The weather here is very warm. . . . Tomorrow I shall have 40,000 troops on the battlefield of Castiglione. I shall be at Verona on Saturday and at Mantua on Monday. Adieu, my dear. Be sensible, gay, and happy. Such is my will."[18]

At the end of June, the couple reunited in Genoa, newly annexed to France. Napoleon justified the annexation on the grounds he was protecting the city from English attacks. Napoleon's own ancestors were minor Italian nobility from the area near Genoa. Until Genoa ceded its rights to his native Corsica to the king of France in May 1768, a year before Napoleon's birth, the Mediterranean island had been part of the Republic of Genoa.

In 1797, Napoleon replaced the nearly eight-century-old Republic with the Ligurian Republic under the protection of France. In a foreshadowing of things to come, the young general wrote the provisional government that June after learning that the statue of Genoa's great naval hero Andrea Doria had been toppled. Through a series of naval victories, Doria had liberated Genoa from the French. Calling him a "great sailor and statesman," Napoleon suggested that a new statue be erected. "Aristocracy was liberty in his day. The whole of Europe envies your city the honour of having produced that celebrated man. You will, I doubt not, take pains to rear his statue again: I pray you to let me bear a part of the expense which that will entail."[19]

Napoleon admired the larger-than-life, self-made hero who, like himself, came from an aristocratic family that had fallen on hard times. Orphaned young, Doria rose from *condottiero,* or mercenary, to admiral of Charles V's Habsburg fleet and ruler of the city-state of Genoa. And like Napoleon, he had gained power and wealth through his stunning military victories, seizing spoils from his enemies along the way. Andrea Doria served France's François I in the 1520s before switching allegiance to Holy Roman Emperor Charles V.

In 1528, Andrea began building the Palazzo del Principe west of Genoa's ancient walls, in a strategic location overlooking the harbor's western entrance. At this combination stronghold and country retreat, the admiral moored his six-ship fleet in a small harbor at the end of the garden. Perino del Vaga was hired to decorate the grand new home that resembled a Hellenistic-Roman porticoed villa. The Florentine-born artist, who had worked under Raphael in Rome, proceeded to adorn the palazzo with tapestries, furniture, flags, and embroideries of his own design.[20]

It was Perino who introduced a comparison of his patron with Neptune, Roman god of the sea, explains Ilaria Bernocchi. In a series of tapestries, now lost, Perino created an allegorical program around Doria's rule of the sea. The same heroic guise was adopted by other artists—medals by engraver Leoni, a painting by Agnolo Bronzino (Pinacoteca di Brera), and an unfinished Carrara marble sculpture by Baccio Bandinelli (Piazza del Duomo, Carrara).[21]

Thanks to Andrea's interest in tapestries and the strong relationship between Genoa and the tapestry center of Flanders, his villa boasted a collection of some two hundred pieces.[22] Charles V gave Andrea two of the best—the *Stories of Alexander the Great*. Woven in the mid-fifteenth century in Tournai, Burgundy, of gold and silver yarns with silk and wool, the large detailed panels depicted historical and legendary events in the life of the Macedonian king.

In 1529, Andrea ordered temporary triumphal arches for Charles V's entry into Genoa. Four years later, on his way back to Barcelona following his defense of Vienna against the Turks, Charles V made another triumphal entry into Genoa. As part of the celebrations, Charles proceeded from a temporary arch to the just finished Villa Doria where he was a guest. It was during such official visits that Doria persuaded Charles V to grant Genoa its independence. Andrea's heir, Giovanni Andrea I, continued embellishing the villa with art, including a tapestry series of the 1571 Battle of Lepanto where he commanded a fleet.

For Napoleon's stay at Palazzo del Principe, restorations had quickly been made to some of Perino's antiquity-inspired décor.[23] According to Bourrienne, Napoleon made sure to sleep "in the Doria Palace, in the bed where Charles V had lain."[24] As Matthew Zarzeczny explains, Napoleon admired Charles V's handling of the papacy, which included Clement VII's incarceration after the 1527 sack of Rome.[25]

In 1806, Napoleon invoked the Holy Roman emperor in a letter to Joseph. "The court of Rome . . . think[s] that I cannot reconcile a great respect for the spiritual authority of the Pope with the repression of his pretensions to temporal dominion. . . . They forget that St. Louis, whose piety was undoubted, was almost always at war with the Pope, and that Charles V, who was an eminently Christian prince, long besieged Rome, and ended by taking possession of both the city and the States of the Church."[26] Napoleon would soon use Charles V's action to justify his own treatment of Pius VII.

Obsessed with his self-made dynasty, Napoleon could not help but be impressed with the Doria Villa's Loggia of the Heroes. Originally open to the sea, the five arches of the Loggia were now enclosed by sheet glass. The frescoes depicted a dozen members of the Doria family as ancient Roman warriors. The Latin inscription on the shields read: "The great men of the illustrious family, supreme leaders, performed excellent deeds for their homeland."[27]

From the Villa's terraced garden facing the sea, Napoleon and Joséphine descended the same steps where Andrea Doria returned from his numerous voyages. Before an enormous crowd at the harbor, the imperial couple embarked a barge decorated like a floating temple. In the middle of the bay, four huge rafts, covered with trees, flowers, statuary, and fountains flanked their barge. Fireworks over the flotilla of boats illuminated the city.

After a week in Genoa, Napoleon left for Turin. It's there he received word of an impending military threat. To stop Napoleon from further land grabs, Great Britain, Russia, and Austria had formed a new coalition. Traveling incognito, the new Emperor of the French and King of Italy crossed the Mont Cenis Pass and rushed back to Fontainebleau.

When the Treaty of Amiens fell apart, Napoleon began training his forces for an invasion of England. He organized his army at a large military camp at the port of Boulogne on the Channel. Docks, roads, and barracks were built for some two hundred thousand soldiers, the heart of the future Grande Armée. In early August 1805, Napoleon left Paris for Boulogne, poised to lead his forces across the English Channel. He told Joséphine: "I will take you to London. I intend the wife of the modern Caesar to be crowned in Westminster."

In 56 B.C.E., Julius Caesar launched back-to-back expeditions to Britain. For the first reconnaissance mission, he took just two of his eight legions. He thought it would be valuable "if he simply visited the island and observed the kind of people and investigated the localities, the harbors and the approaches." When Caesar returned to Britain the following year with five legions, his ambition was conquest. But the results were mixed, with Caesar securing only the promise of a tribute payment.[28]

To drum up support for the offensive, Napoleon organized a public relations campaign around a more successful invader. William the Conqueror, Duke of Normandy, had vanquished England in the eleventh century. About a decade after his 1066 invasion, the Bayeux Tapestry was produced to glorify the Norman Conquest. Handstitched with wool threads, 224 feet in length, and nearly twenty inches tall, the embroidered linen scroll depicts the decisive battle of Hastings in southern England. Thousands died in the hilltop conflict, including the newly crowned King Harold II from a French arrow to the eye. After six hundred years of Anglo-Saxon rule, William became England's first Norman king. The Norman Conquest transformed England's laws, customs, and architecture. French became the language of the court; Norman nobility became the new English aristocracy.

Denon arranged to borrow the extraordinary tapestry from Bayeux in Normandy for a two-month exhibition of the work at the Musée Napoléon. To make room for the medieval masterpiece, Denon removed several hundred framed Old Master drawings from the Apollo Gallery. On December 5, 1804, escorted by Denon and antiquities curator Visconti, the newly crowned Napoleon I attended the opening. Visconti penned a guide to the epic embroidery; excerpts were reprinted by the influential Paris newspaper, *Le Moniteur*.

The tapestry's patron is thought to be Bishop Odo of Bayeux, William the Conqueror's half-brother, named Earl of Kent after the conquest. Though there's no agreement on whether the work was stitched in England or France, Odo probably intended it for his bishopric of Bayeux in northwest France. The first written reference to the tapestry appears four centuries later, in 1476; it seems to have been displayed in various churches and castles throughout England and Normandy, including the nave of Bayeux Cathedral. Confiscated during the French Revolution, the tapestry was covering military wagons when a local lawyer rescued it and sent it to city administrators for safekeeping.

Napoleon and his advisers were aware of the connection between various scenes of the Bayeux Tapestry and Trajan's Column in Rome. Early eighteenth-century French scholar Abbé Bernard de Montfaucon had identified the famous column as a reference for the tapestry creators. Like the ancient carved marble friezes of the Roman column, many of the tapestry's fifty-plus embroidered scenes center on war preparations, shipbuilding, and battle scenes. Like the Bayeux Tapestry, Trajan's Column presents both sides in the conflict as worthy opponents.

"Both the Column of Trajan and the Bayeux Tapestry show wars that are methodically prepared, carefully directed, and strategically executed," writes Otto Werckmeister ". . . they unfold the visual record of a campaign in stages, including the technical and logistical preparations . . ."[29] The ancient carved marble column and the medieval embroidered linen also have a shared purpose. As masterful propaganda vehicles, both works helped justify brutal military campaigns and glorify the commanders.

Now Napoleon put the celebrated tapestry to work again. By resurrecting France's successful invasion of its ancient enemy, the Bayeux Tapestry helped justify his planned assault on Britain. When Denon returned the tapestry a year later, he wrote Bayeux's sub-prefect: "The First Consul has seen with interest this precious monument of our history, he has applauded the care that the habitants of the city of Bayeux have brought for seven centuries and a half to its conservation. He has charged me to testify to them all his satisfaction and to entrust them with the deposit. Invite them to bring new care to the conservation of this fragile monument, which retraces one of the most memorable actions of the French Nation."[30]

Among the matching scenes are the Dacians crossing the marsh and sinking, like the Normans crossing the quicksands of the river Cuesnon; a meeting of William and his scout like one between Trajan and two scouts on horseback; and woodcutters building Norman ships, a recurring motif on the column.[31] As Carola Hicks explains, boat-building was the first step in the invasion conceived by William, who quickly assembled an eight-hundred-ship fleet. Napoleon ordered seven hundred transport barges built.[32]

But Napoleon's dream of being a new William the Conqueror was dashed. The threat of a French invasion led to a new government in Britain, which strengthened the coastal defenses. From his chief admiral, Napoleon learned that only one hundred transport ships could leave the harbor on any one tide; their stability depended on good weather.[33] The superiority of the Royal Navy and the memory of the French fleet's destruction at Alexandria, Egypt, six years earlier consumed Napoleon. In August, he called off the invasion. Unlike Julius Caesar and William the Conqueror, Napoleon never crossed the English Channel.

Instead, Napoleon pivoted to continental Europe. By the end of September, he was leading his Grande Armée across the Rhine. Marching some thirty miles a day, foraging as they went, his soldiers were devoted to their commander. Wearing a simple coat and bicorn hat, Napoleon rode for ten hours at a stretch. When the army did stop to rest, he studied reports and issued orders.

Pius VII, who insisted on maintaining neutrality in the ongoing conflicts, had allowed the British to use ports on the Tyrrhenian and Adriatic. In October, French General Lamarois seized the papal port of Ancona, along with the Adriatic coast from Rimini to the border with Naples. In Ancona, French troops would have admired a well-preserved triumphal arch dedicated to Roman emperor Trajan. It was from Ancona that Trajan set off for war against Dacia (today's Romania) in the early second century. Trajan enlarged the port at his own expense, making improvements to the wharfs and fortifications. In his honor, the Roman Senate erected the elegant arch made with marble from the storied Marmara quarries.

Pius considered the port's seizure another instance of Napoleon's complete disregard for papal rights. He demanded that the French evacuate. Not surprisingly, Napoleon dismissed his letter. "For the Pope's purposes I am Charlemagne," he wrote his uncle, Cardinal Fesch. "Like Charlemagne, I join the crown of France with the crown of the Lombards . . . I expect the Pope to accommodate his conduct to my requirements. If he behaves well, I shall make no outward changes; if not, I shall reduce him to the status of bishop of Rome . . ."[34]

Russia entered the fray, joining the Third Coalition against France. With his forces about to be outnumbered almost two to one, Napoleon decided to strike at the Austrians before the Russians arrived. On October 19, Napoleon forced the Austrians to surrender at Ulm. But the victory was quickly eclipsed. French Vice-Admiral Pierre-Charles Villeneuve had positioned the fleet at Cadiz, a threat to British trading ships and Britain. On October 21, Admiral Lord Nelson caught a combined French and Spanish fleet at Trafalgar. Nelson divided his twenty-seven ships into two divisions. In the ensuing battle, some 1,700 British sailors were killed, including Nelson. After five hours, Villeneuve surrendered. Nineteen of his thirty-three ships were destroyed.

Napoleon continued the ground assault. By November 14, he paraded through the streets of Vienna in triumph. Beethoven, who had dedicated his Third Symphony to the first consul, now denounced him as a tyrant. By month's end, Napoleon learned that the Russian and Austrian armies had combined into a fighting force of ninety thousand; Prussia was threatening to declare war on France. Nearly one thousand miles from Paris, the 75,000-man Grande Armée was running dangerously low on supplies. Studying the battles of Prussia's Frederick the Great, poring over maps, Napoleon decided to make a stand at the village of Austerlitz (today's Slavkov, Czech Republic).

The Battle of Austerlitz came to be known as the Battle of the Three Emperors because of the presence of Napoleon I, Francis II, and Alexander I. The night before the battle, Napoleon enjoyed his favorite campaign dish, potatoes fried with onions. Waving flaming torches, his adoring soldiers shouted "Long live the emperor!" In a moment of reflection, Napoleon recalled the Egyptian campaign. Likening himself to sixth-century B.C.E. King Cyrus who created the Persian royal guard known as the immortals, and Alexander the Great who defeated the elite fighters at Issus (modern Turkey), Napoleon told his staff:

"If I had been able to take Acre, I would have put on a turban, I would have made my soldiers wear big Turkish trousers, and I would have exposed them to battle only in case of extreme necessity. I would have made them into a sacred battalion—my immortals. I would have finished the war against the Turks with Arabic, Greek, and Armenian troops. Instead of a battle in Moravia, I would have won a battle at Issus, I would have made myself emperor of the East, and I would have returned to Paris by way of Constantinople."[35]

As day broke, fog blanketed the gently sloping hill. Hidden in the haze were Napoleon's two divisions, some 17,000 soldiers. Napoleon ordered his men to advance and attack the Allies from behind. As the sun rose, French forces appeared out of nowhere, surprising the inexperienced twenty-eight-year-old Alexander I. An estimated 16,000 Austrian and Russian soldiers were killed and wounded; France lost nearly 1,300 men that day.[36] After the battle, the first anniversary of his coronation, Napoleon told an aide, "This is the finest evening of my life." The victory over Europe's two imperial dynasties was his proudest moment, an answer to the naval disaster at Trafalgar. "Soldiers I am pleased with you," he told his men. "You have decorated your eagles with an immortal glory."

Alexander and his surviving soldiers retreated to Russia. With Austria's morale shattered, Francis sued for peace. In addition to paying France an indemnity of forty million francs, the Austrian emperor lost some four million subjects and roughly a sixth of his empire, including territories in Italy and central and Eastern Europe. By year-end, Napoleon was in Munich, awaiting Austria's ratification of the Treaty of Pressburg.

Tensions between France and the Kingdom of Naples were reaching a boiling point. Though Bourbon King Ferdinand IV and Queen Maria Carolina (Marie Antoinette's sister) had pledged neutrality in the Napoleonic wars, the Neapolitan rulers allowed an Anglo-Russian force to land in the Bay of Naples.

The betrayal was the perfect excuse for Napoleon. He wrote to his brother Joseph, dispatching him to assume command of the Army of Naples.

FIG. 1 (RIGHT): Vase depicting Napoleon in front of Italian works of art being delivered to Louvre, 1810–13, porcelain, Sèvres manufacture, Ile-de-France. France, nineteenth century. FIG. 2 (BELOW): *Laocoön and his sons*, marble, early first century B.C.E., copy after a Hellenistic original from ca. 200 B.C.E. Vatican Museums.

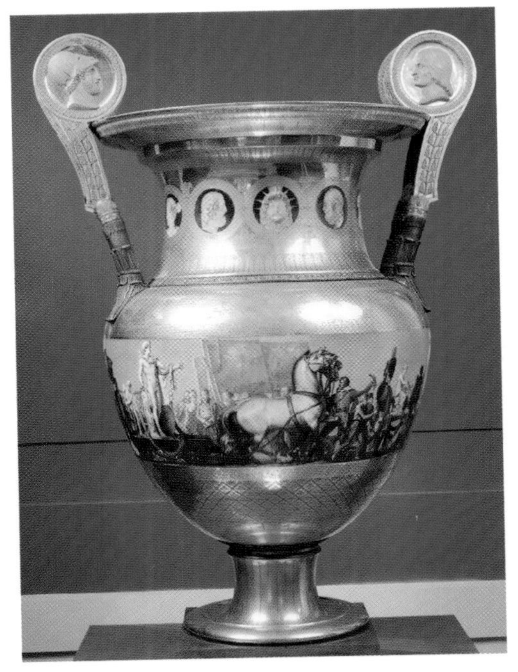

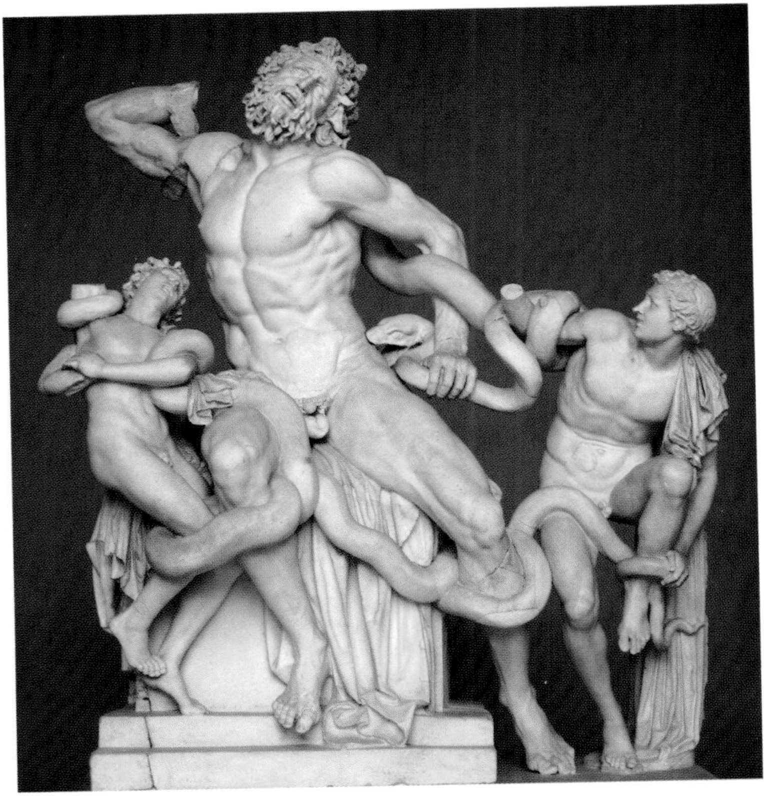

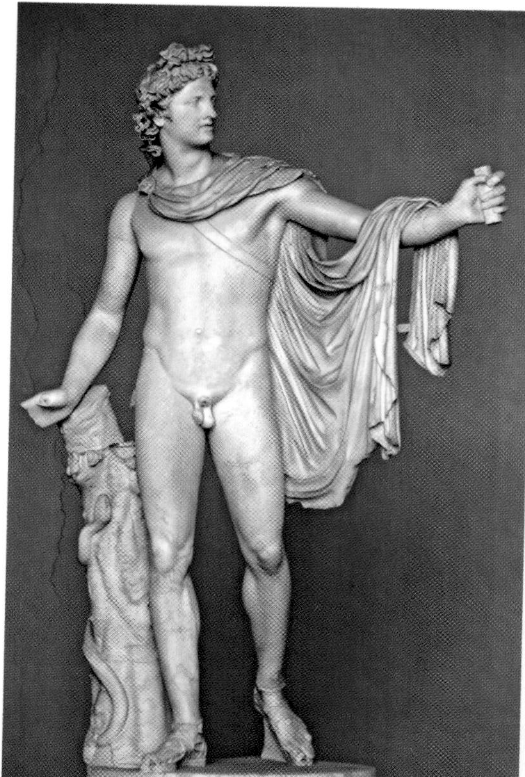

FIG. 3 (LEFT): *Apollo Belvedere*, second century C.E., marble, Vatican Museums.

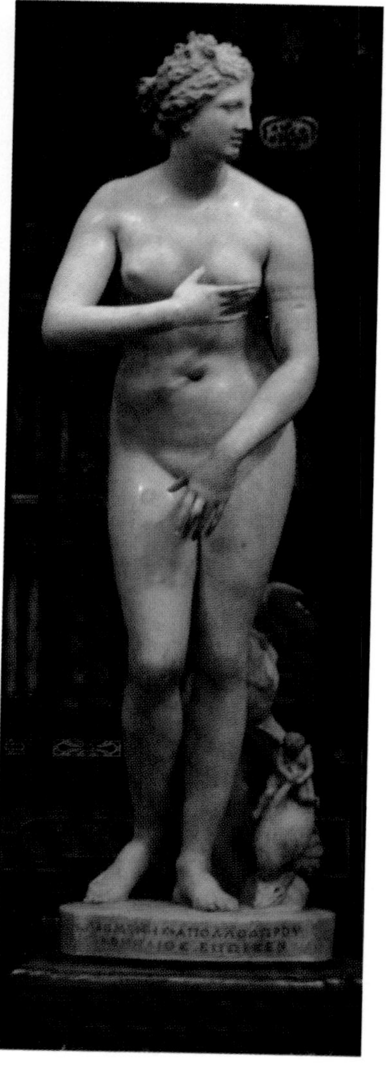

FIG. 4 (RIGHT): *Venus de' Medici*, first century C.E., marble, Uffizi, Florence.

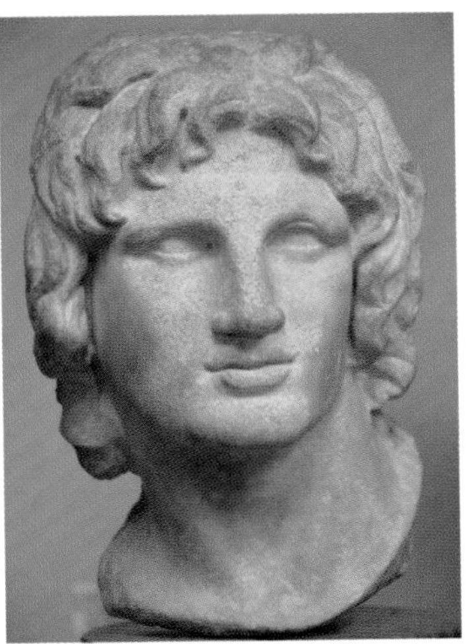

FIG. 5 (LEFT): *Alexander the Great*, marble, Hellenistic Greek, second to first century B.C.E., said to be from Alexandria, Egypt, British Museum. FIG. 6 (BELOW): Frontispiece to Volume 1 of the "Description of Egypt," engraved by Girardet and Sellier, and published under the orders of Napoleon, 1822 (aquatint), Cecile.

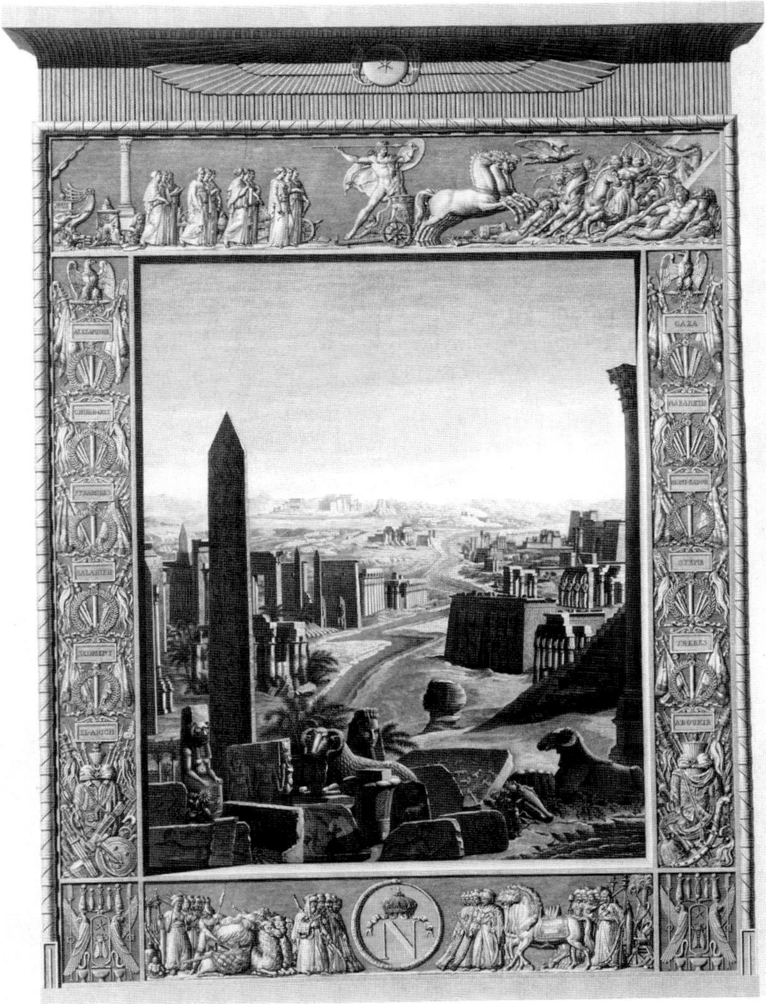

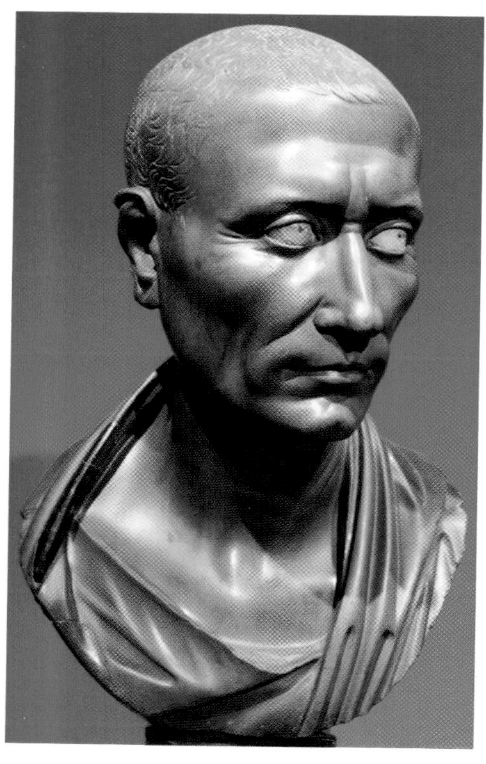

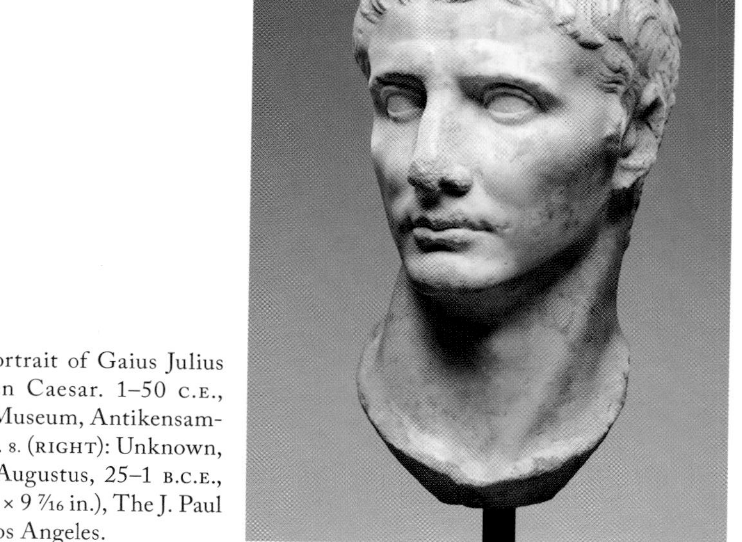

FIG. 7 (ABOVE): Portrait of Gaius Julius Caesar, the Green Caesar. 1–50 C.E., greywacke, Altes Museum, Antikensammlung, Berlin. FIG. 8. (RIGHT): Unknown, Portrait Head of Augustus, 25–1 B.C.E., marble (15 ⅜ × 8 ¼ × 9 7⁄16 in.), The J. Paul Getty Museum, Los Angeles.

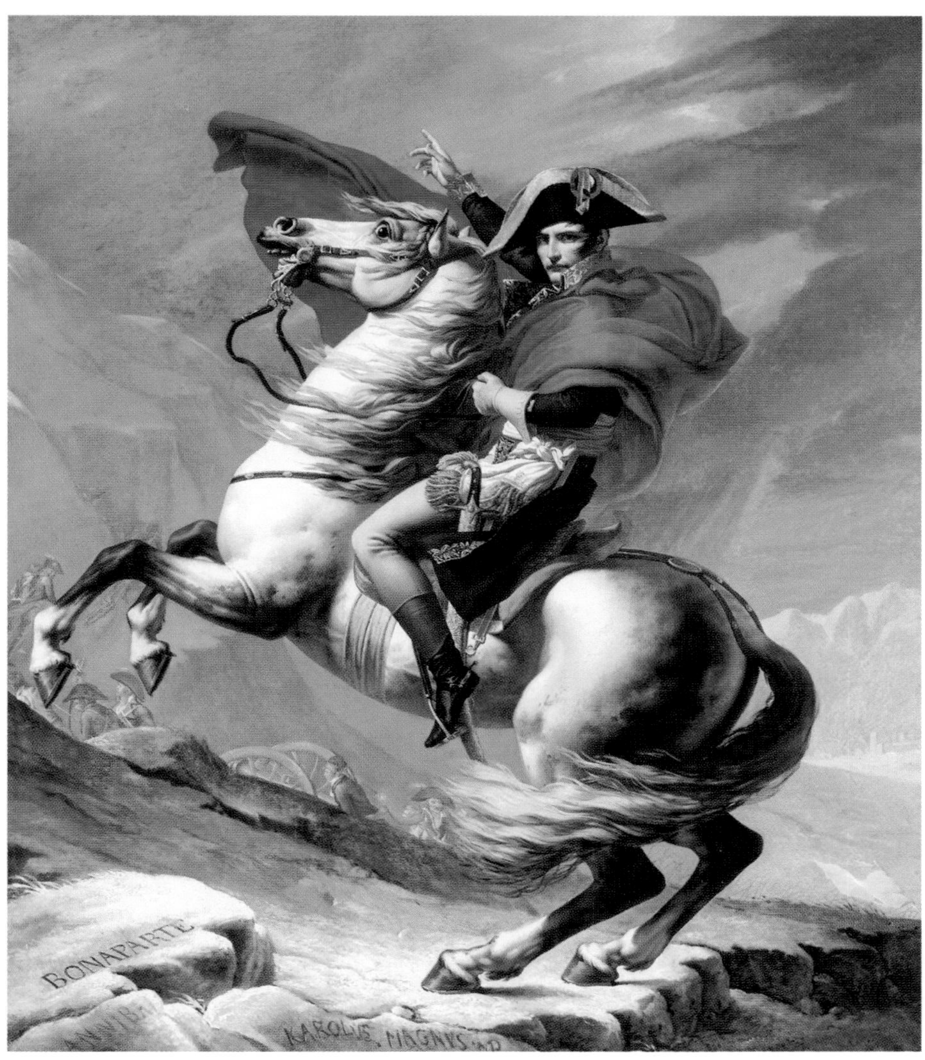

FIG. 9: Jacques-Louis David (1748–1825), *Napoleon Crossing the Grand Saint-Bernard Pass, 20 May 1800*, 1802 (oil on canvas), Château de Versailles, France.

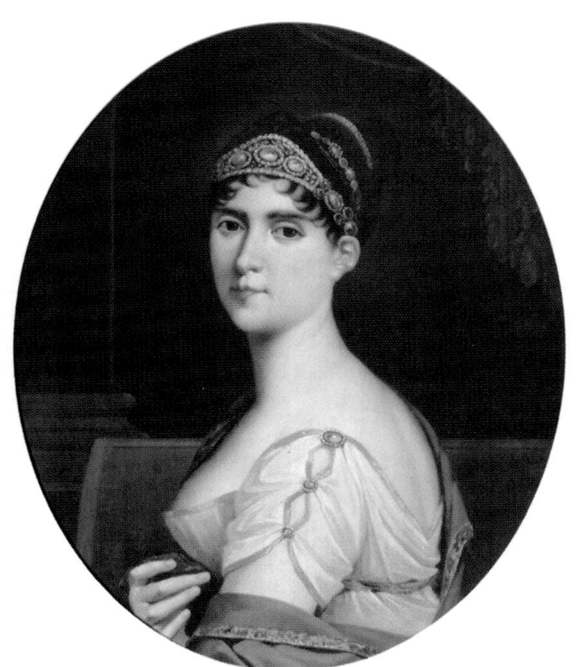

FIG. 10 (LEFT): Robert Lefèvre, *Portrait of Josephine*, 1806, Wellington Collection, Apsley House, London.

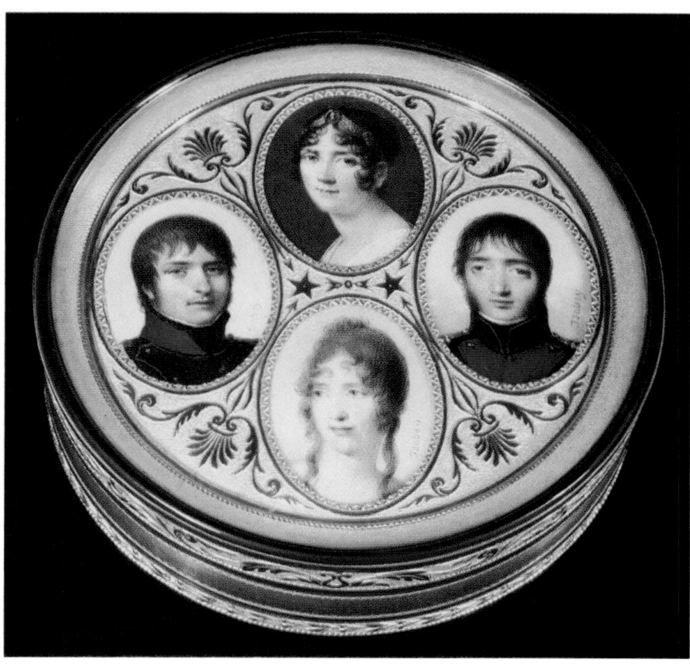

FIG. 11 (BOTTOM): Bonbonniere with portraits of Eugene (1781–1824), Hortense (1783–1837), Joséphine Beauharnais (1763–1814), and Louis Bonaparte (1778–1846); (gold, ivory & enamel), Isabey, Jean-Baptiste (1767–1855) given to Napoleon I (1769–1821) by Joséphine, Empress of France; Eugene, Viceroy of Italy and stepson of Napoleon, Malmaison, France.

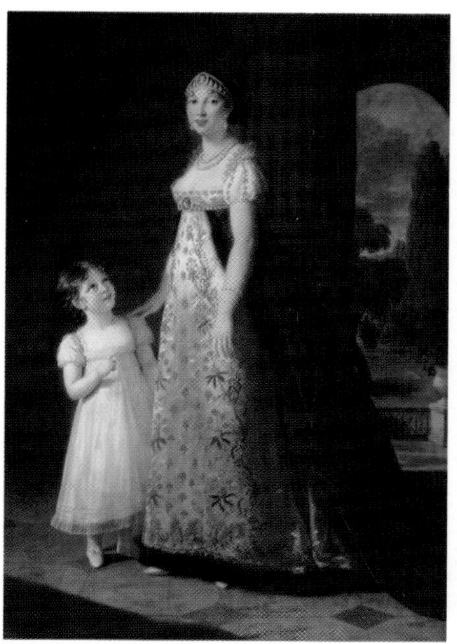

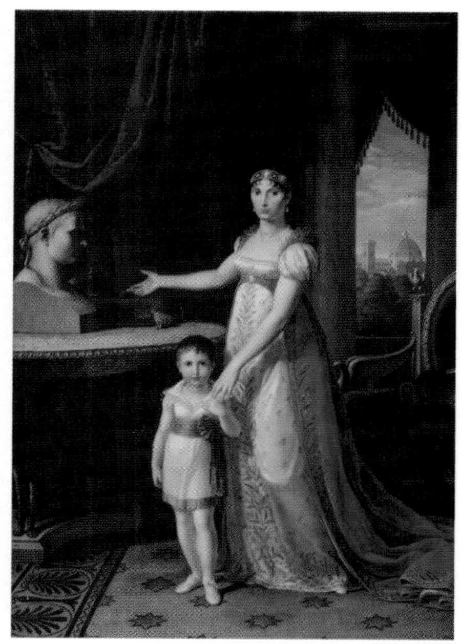

FIG. 12 (ABOVE LEFT): *Marie-Annuciade-Caroline Bonaparte, Queen of Naples with her daughter Laetitia-Joséphine Murat*, 1807, Louise Élisabeth Vigée Le Brun. Musée National des Châteaux de Versailles et de Trianon. *Public domain.* FIG. 13 (ABOVE RIGHT): *Elisa Bonaparte (1777–1820) Grand Duchess of Tuscany and her Daughter Napoleone-Elisa* (oil on canvas) Benvenuti, Pietro (1796–1844) / Chateau de Fontainebleau, Seine-et-Marne, France. FIG. 14 (BELOW): *Bust of Joachim Murat*, 1813, Antonio Canova, marble, private collection.

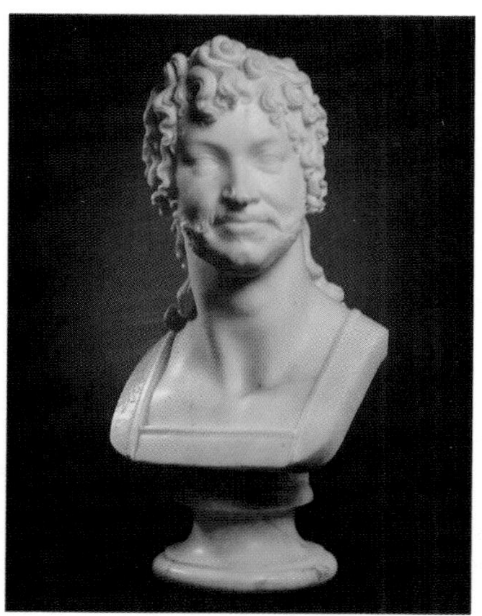

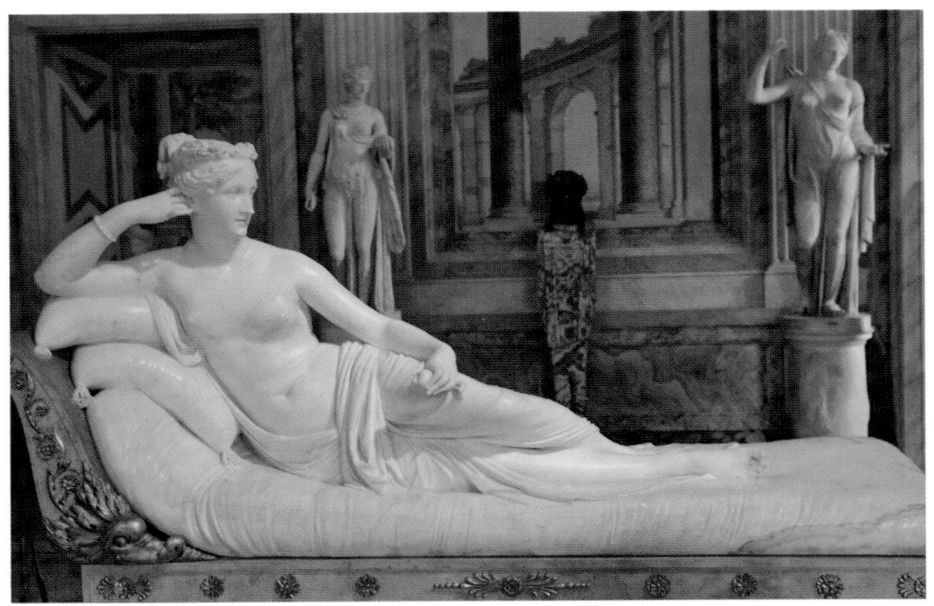

FIG. 15 (ABOVE): *Pauline Borghese as Venus Victrix*, 1805–1808, marble, Antonio Canova, Borghese Gallery, Rome. FIG. 16 (BELOW): *Letitia Ramolino Bonaparte*, ca. 1804–07, marble, Antonio Canova (1757–1822), Collection of the Duke of Devonshire, Chatsworth House, United Kingdom.

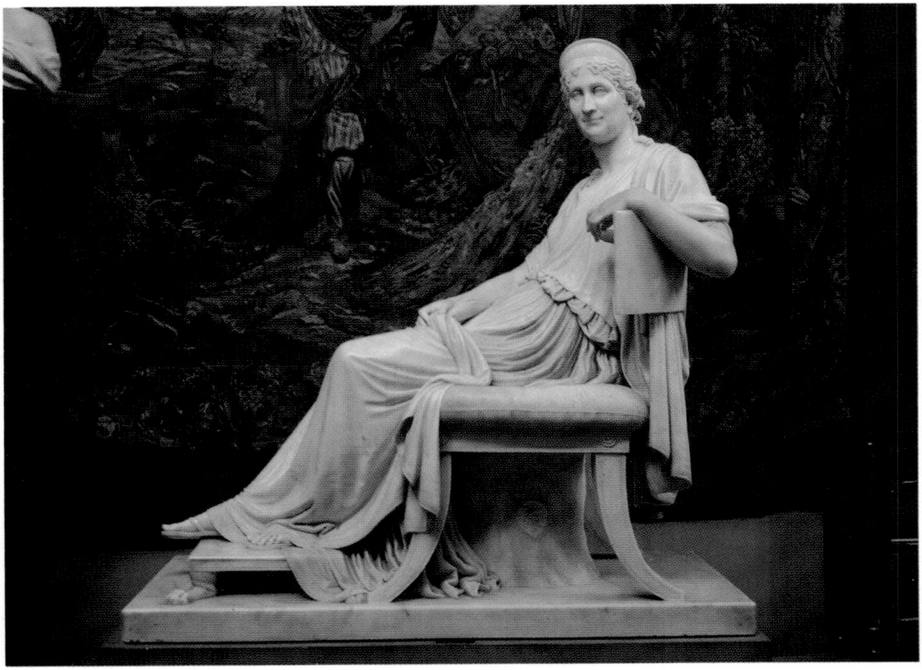

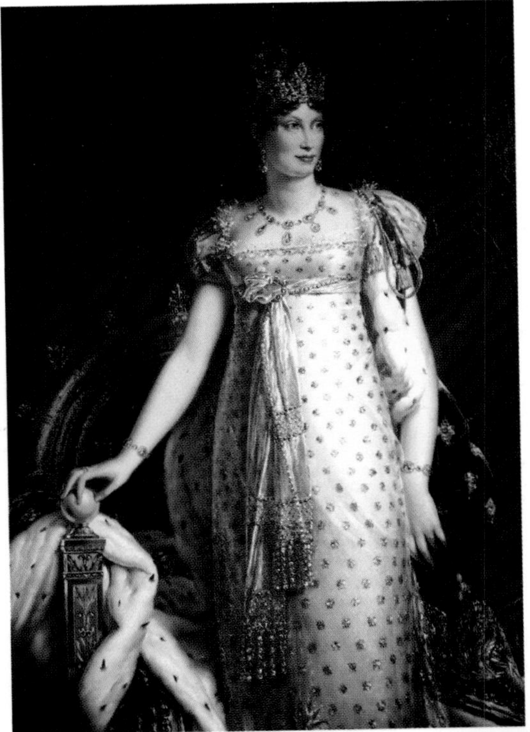

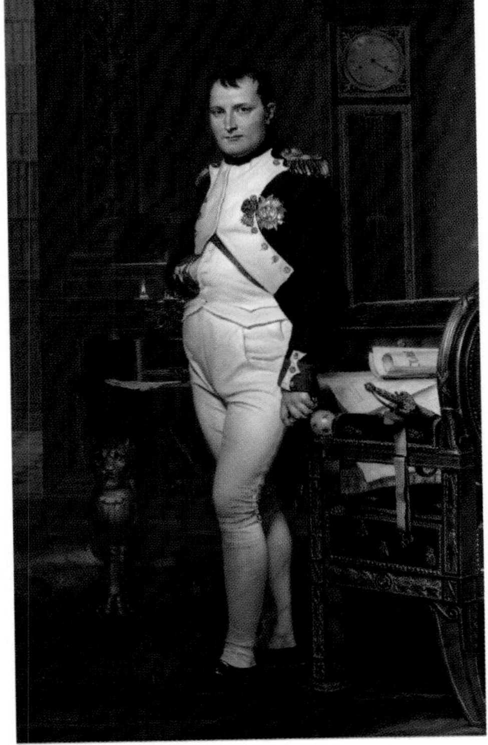

FIG. 17 (ABOVE): François Pascal Simone Gérard, *Marie Louise, Empress of the French*, 1811, Kunsthistorisches Museum. FIG. 18 (RIGHT): Jacques-Louis David, *The Emperor Napoleon in His Study at the Tuileries*, 1812, oil on canvas (80 ¼ × 49 ¼ in.), Samuel H. Kress Collection, National Gallery of Art, Washington, D.C.

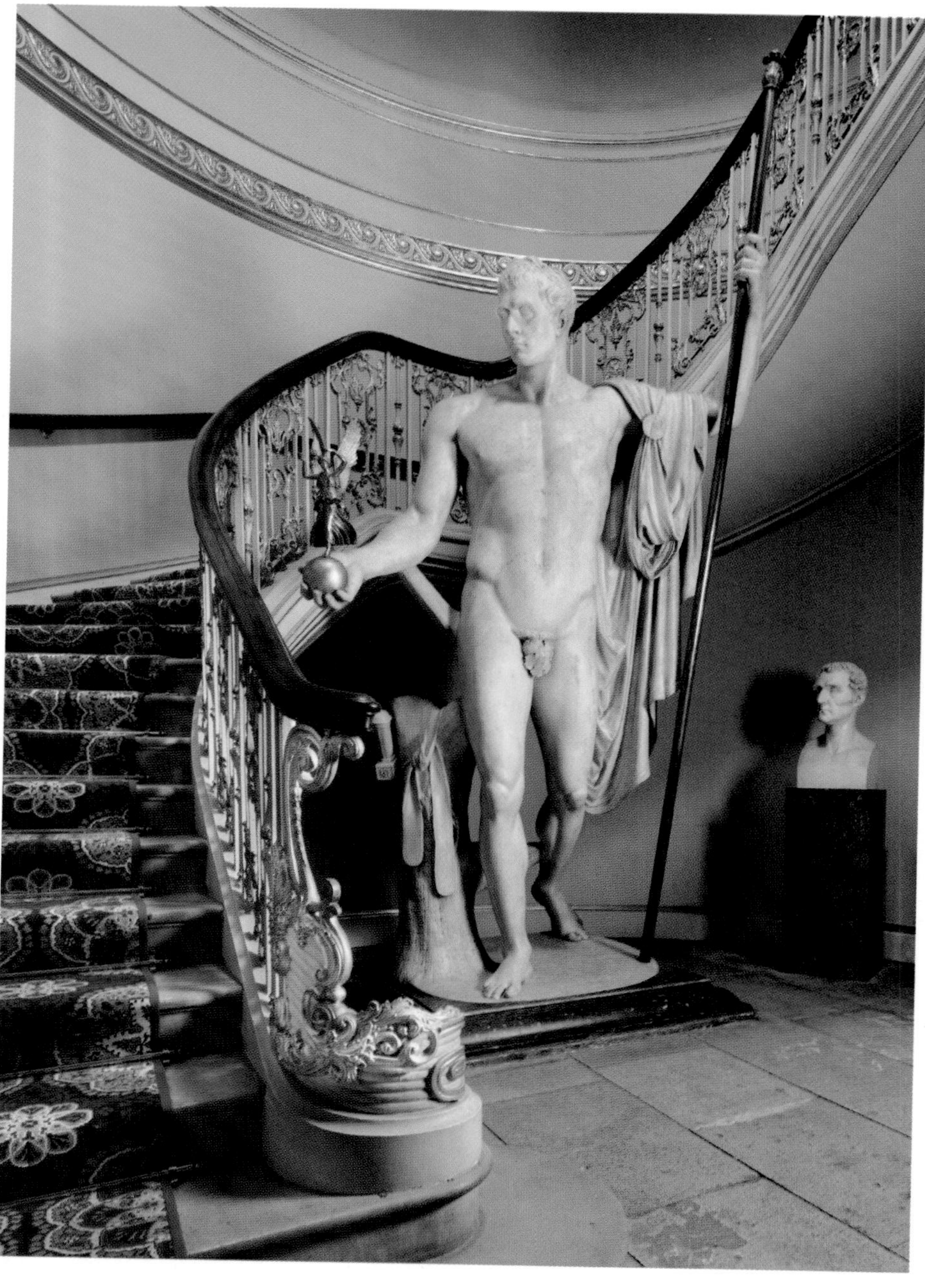

FIG. 19: *Napoleon as Mars the Peacekeeper*, 1806, Antonio Canova, marble, Wellington Collection, Apsley House, London.

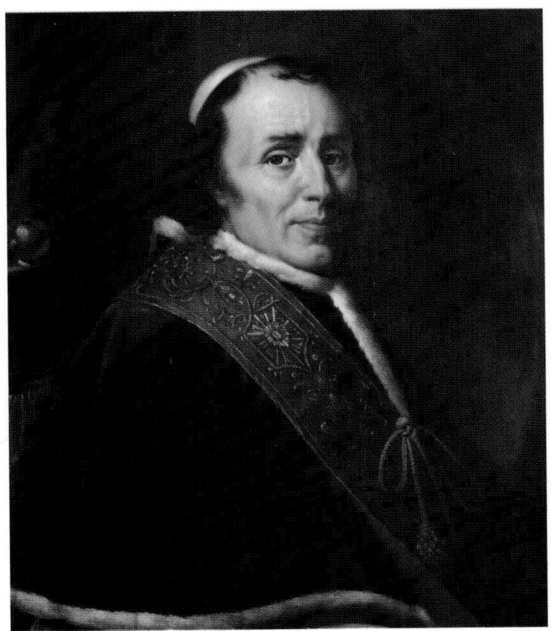

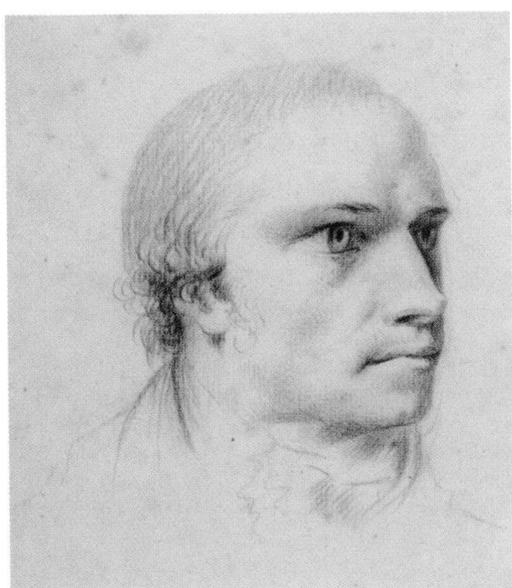

FIG. 20 (ABOVE): Robert Lefèvre, *Portrait of Pope Pius VII*, 1805, Wellington Collection, Apsley House, London. FIG. 21 (LEFT): Johann Heinrich Wilhelm Tischbein, *Portrait of Antonio Canova*, 1787, Black chalk (9 ¼ × 7 ½ in.), The J. Paul Getty Museum, Los Angeles. FIG. 22 (BELOW): Louis Léopold Boilly, *Portraits of Charles Percier, Pierre-Francois Leotard Fontaine, and Claude-Louis Bernier*, before 1807, black-and-white chalk on buff paper, the Clark Art Institute, Williamstown, Massachusetts.

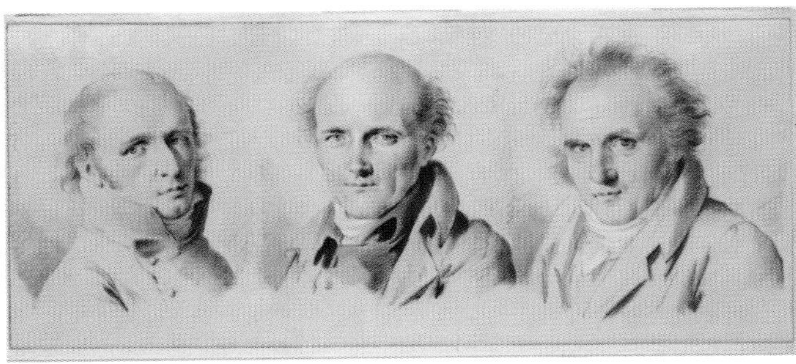

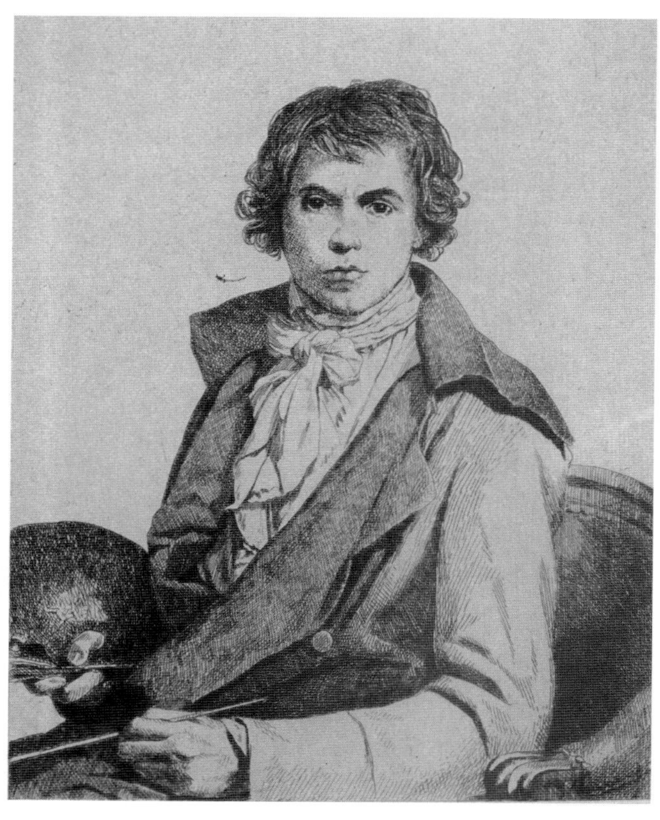

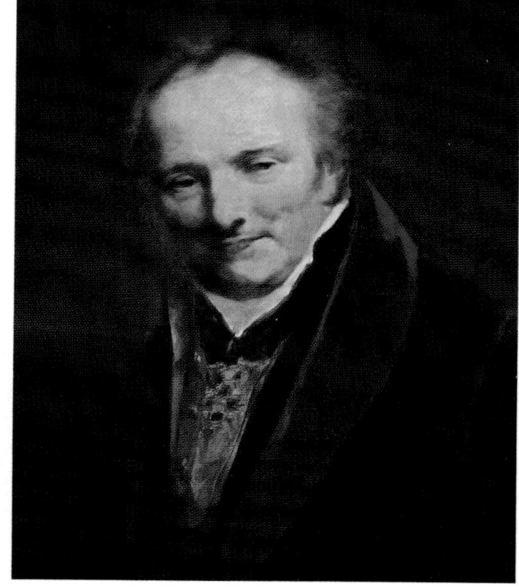

FIG. 23 (ABOVE): *David par lui-même* (1794), David, Jacques-Louis, engraving, 1880–82, The J. Paul Getty Museum, Los Angeles. FIG. 24 (RIGHT): *Portrait of Baron Dominique Vivant Denon* (1747–1825), French writer, engraver, art historian, and Egyptologist. Painting by Pierre Paul Prudhon (1758–1823).

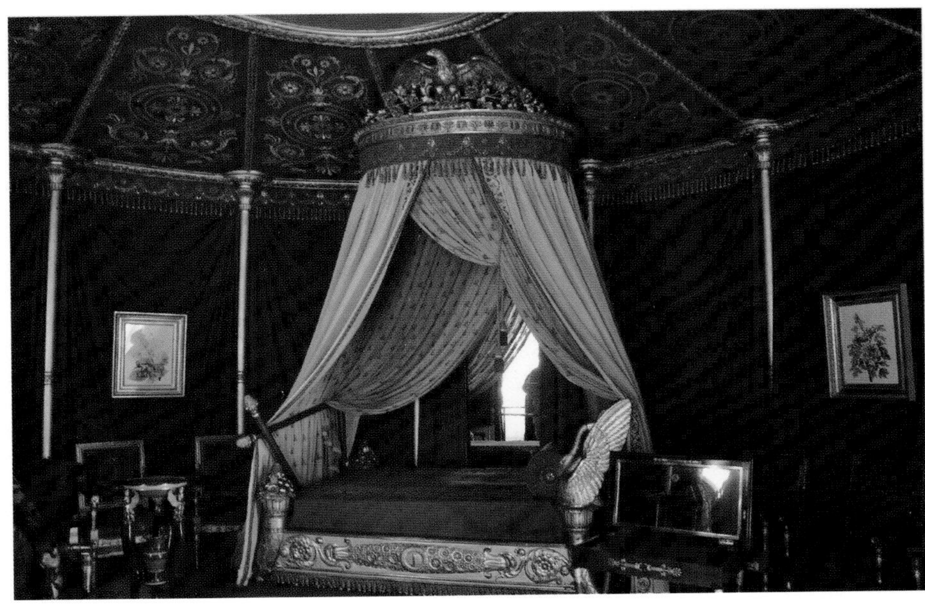

FIG. 25 (ABOVE): Joséphine's Bedroom at Malmaison. FIG. 26 (BELOW): François-Honoré-Georges Jacob-Desmalter after a design by Charles Percier, Gondola Chair from Château de Saint-Cloud, ca. 1804, Château de Malmaison.

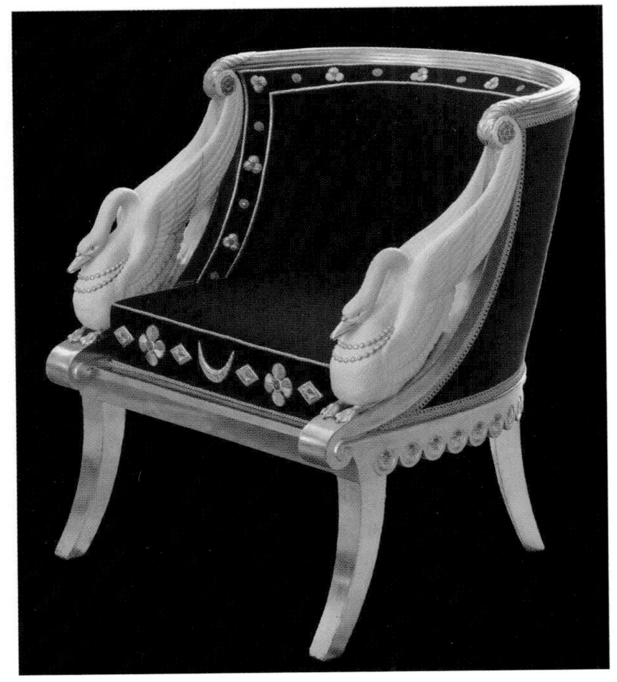

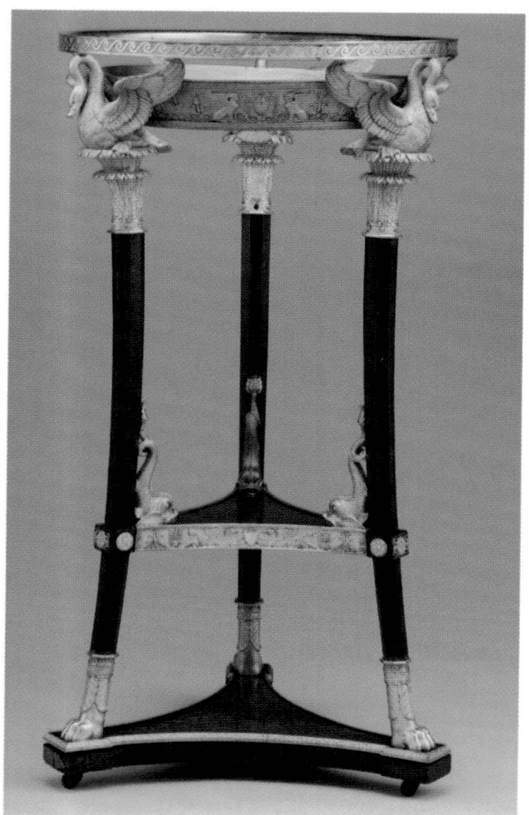

FIG. 27 (LEFT): Athénienne. Design attributed to Charles Percier, gilt bronze mounts by Martin-Guillaume Biennais (1800–14) (36 ⅜ in. x 19 ½ in.), Metropolitan Museum of Art, New York.

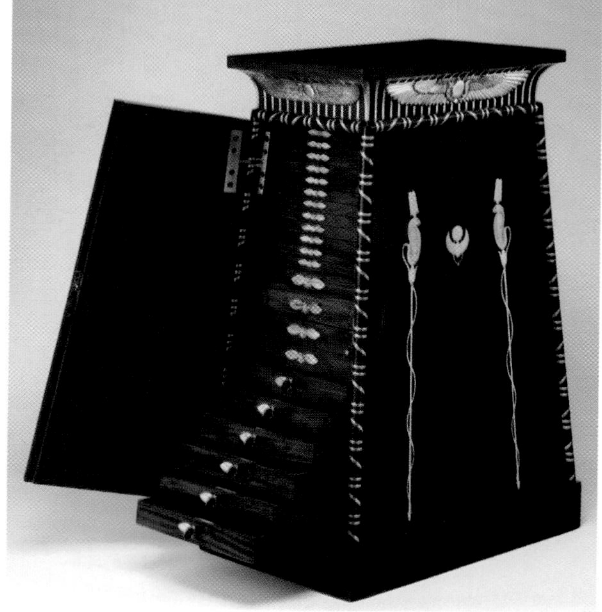

FIG. 28 (RIGHT): Coin cabinet, designed by Charles Percier, probably made by François-Honoré-Georges Jacob-Desmalter. Silver mounts by Martin-Guillaume Biennais. Decoration after drawings by baron Dominique-Vivant Denon ca. 1809–19, mahogany and inlaid silver (35 ½ × 19 ¾ × 14 ¾ in.), Metropolitan Museum of Art, New York.

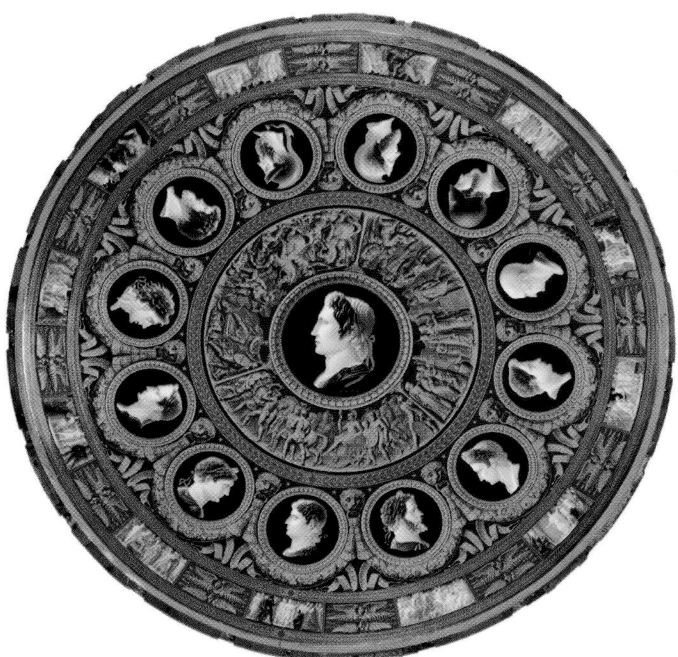

FIG. 29 (ABOVE): Table of the Great Commanders, 1806–12, hard-paste porcelain and gilt bronze over wood, French School, nineteenth century, Buckingham Palace, London. FIG. 30 (BELOW): The Austerlitz Table, inlaid with Sèvres plaques commemorating Napoleon's victory at Austerlitz, 1808–10, gold and porcelain, French School, nineteenth century, Musée National du Château de Malmaison.

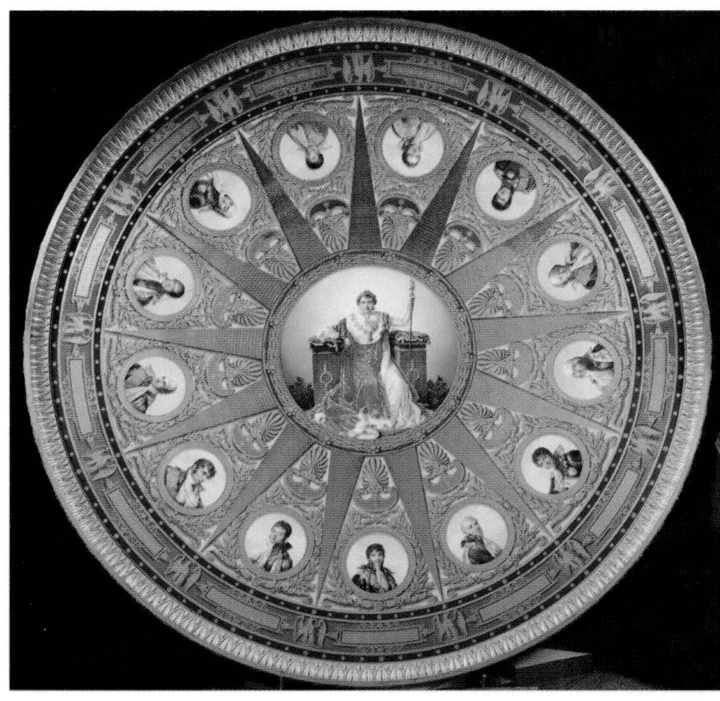

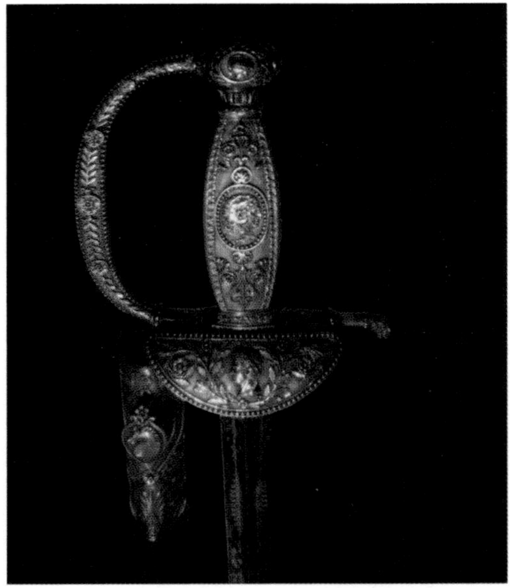

FIG. 31 (ABOVE): Martin-Guillaume Biennais, Sword worn by Napoleon I at the Battle of Austerlitz, steel, gold, bronze, leather (34.2 in. x 4.2 in.), ca. 1803. Put on Napoleon's coffin at the Retour des cendres on December 15, 1840, by General Bertrand. Musée de l'Armée, Paris. FIG. 32 (BELOW): Bayeux Tapestry, scene 57, Harold's death, Bayeux Museum, France.

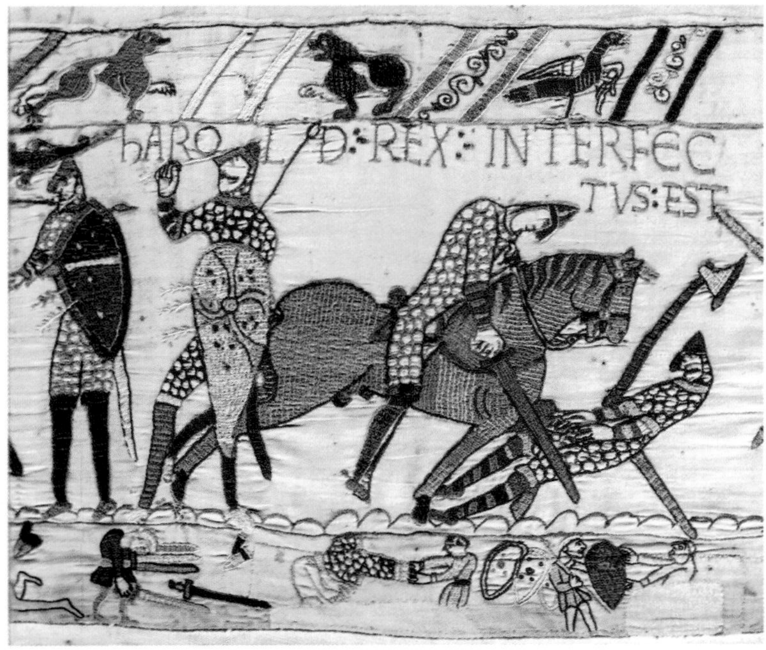

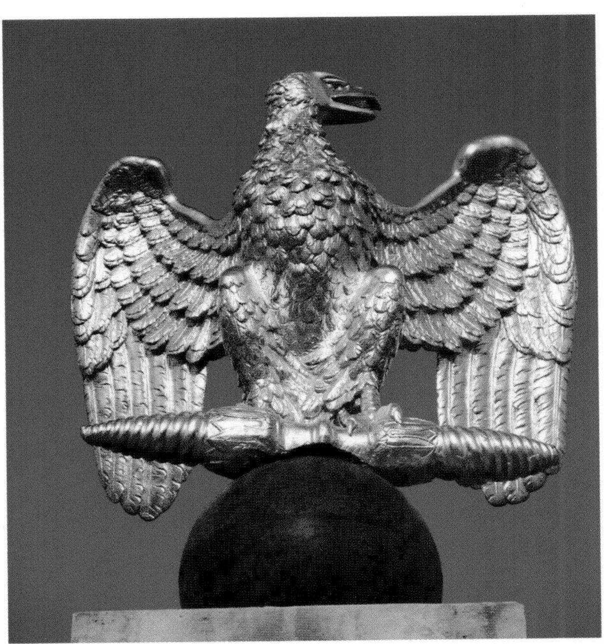

FIG. 33 (ABOVE): Imperial Eagle on main portal of Fontainebleau. FIG. 34 (BELOW): Unknown, Eagle, C.E. 100–200, Bronze (41 × 31 × 30 in.), The J. Paul Getty Museum, Los Angeles.

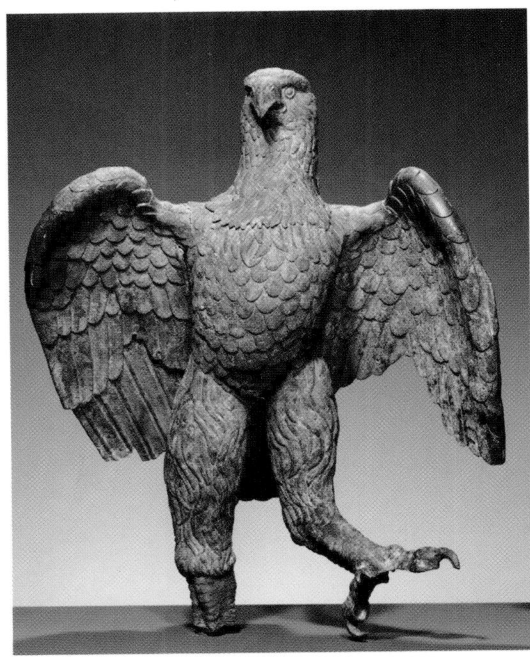

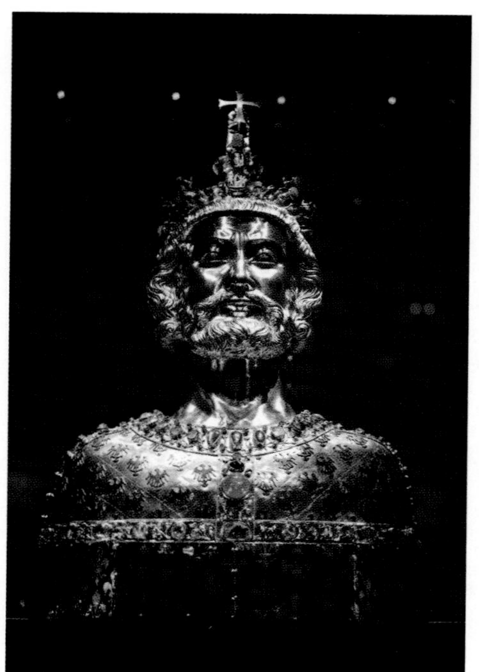

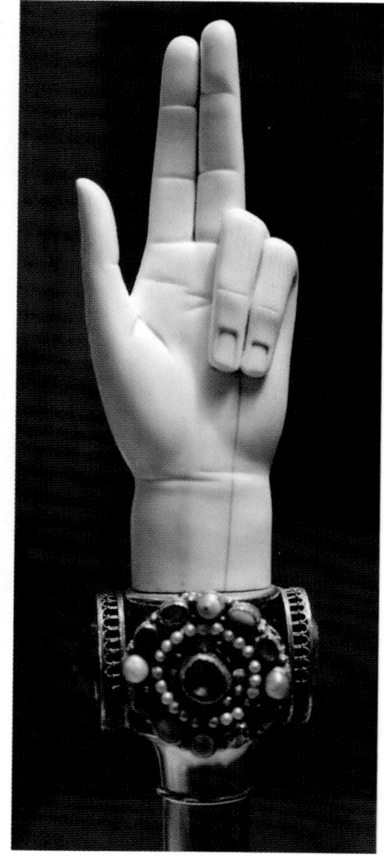

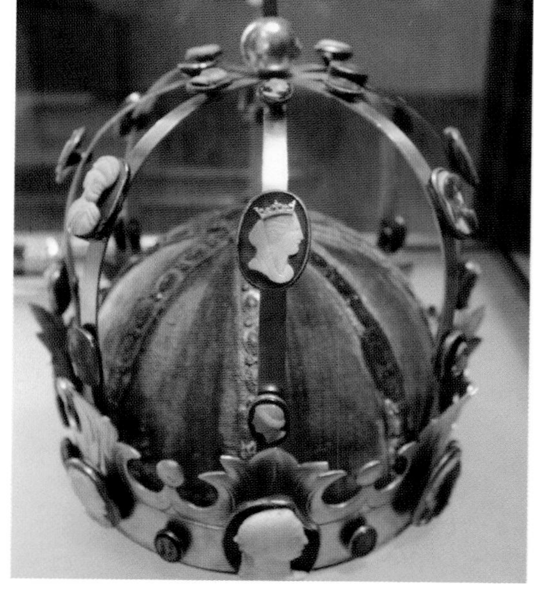

FIG. 35 (TOP LEFT): Reliquary *Bust of Charlemagne* (742–814), gold inlaid with gems, the Treasury of Aachen Cathedral, 1350. FIG. 36 (TOP RIGHT): Martin-Guillaume Biennais (1764–1843), *Hand of Justice*, made for the crowning of Napoleon I, including the so-called ring of St. Denis from the Treasure of Saint-Denis. Ivory, copper, gold and cameos, 1804, Louvre, Paris. FIG. 37 (BOTTOM RIGHT): Martin-Guillaume Biennais, *Crown of Charlemagne*, Louvre, Paris.

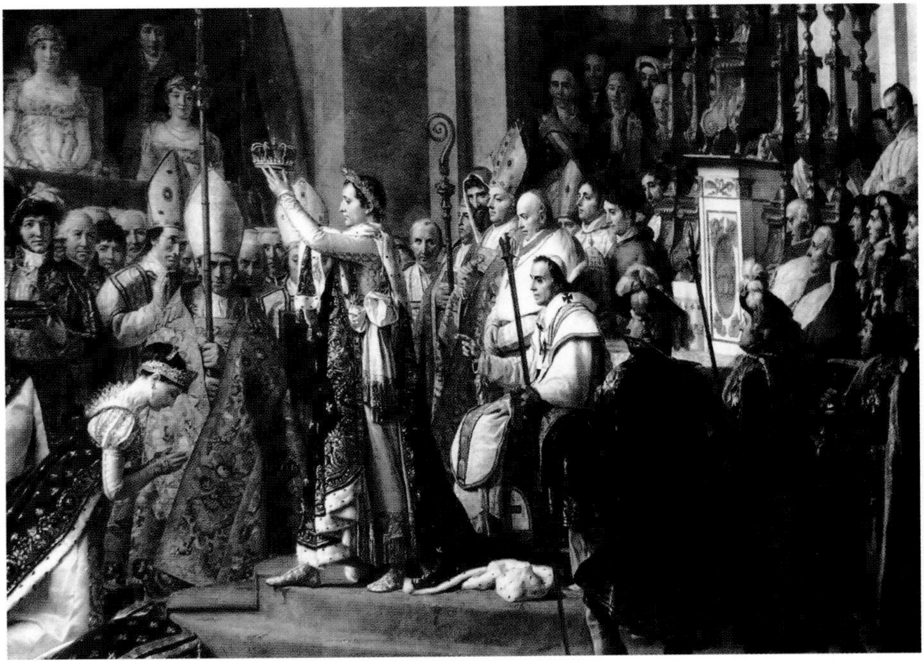

FIG. 38 (ABOVE): Jacques-Louis David, *The Coronation of Napoleon*, detail, 1808, Louvre, Paris.
FIG. 39 (BELOW): Silver medallion of Napoleon and Charlemagne, 1806, by Bertrand Andrieu (1761–1822) and Dominique Vivant baron Denon (1747–1825), 37g, 40mm diameter. The obverse with jugate busts of Napoleon and Charlemagne, with the legend NAPOLEON. EMP., CHARLEMAGNE. EMP. The reverse with jugate busts of Vitikind and Frederick Augustus, with the legend VITIKIND. R. S., FREDERIC. AUG. R. S.

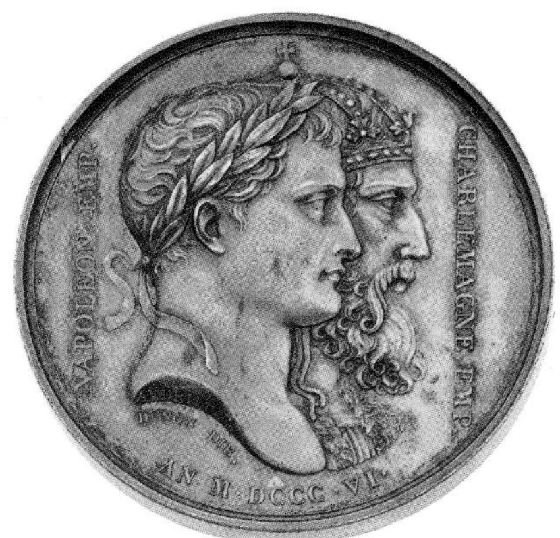

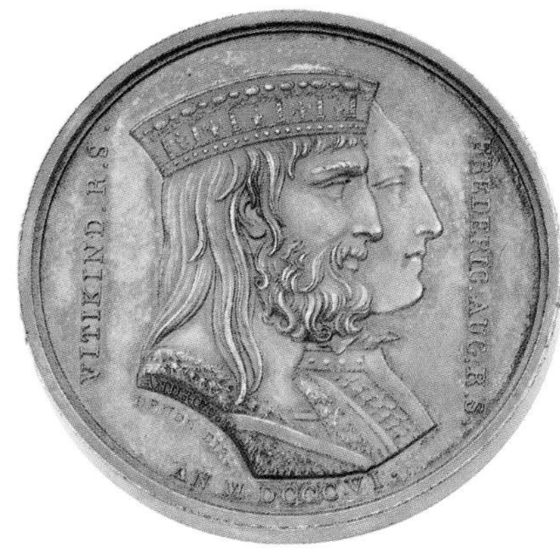

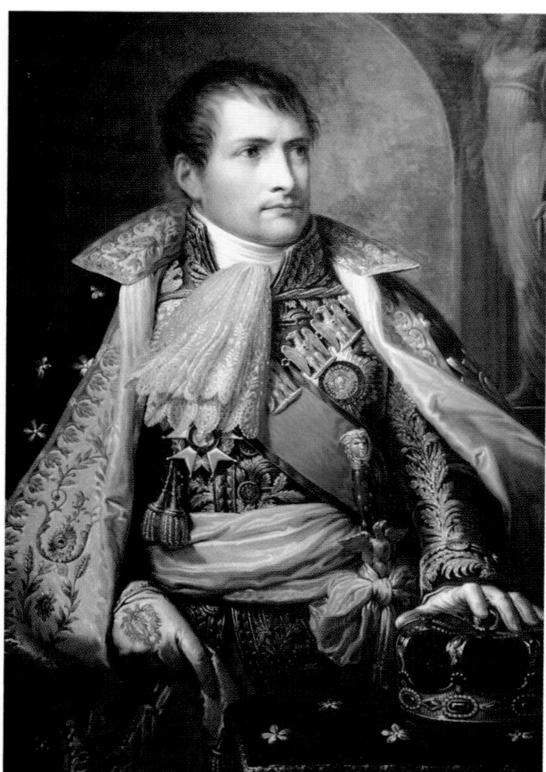

FIG. 40 (LEFT): Andrea Appiani, *Portrait of Napoleon I as King of Italy*, 1805, Kunsthistorisches Museum, Vienna.

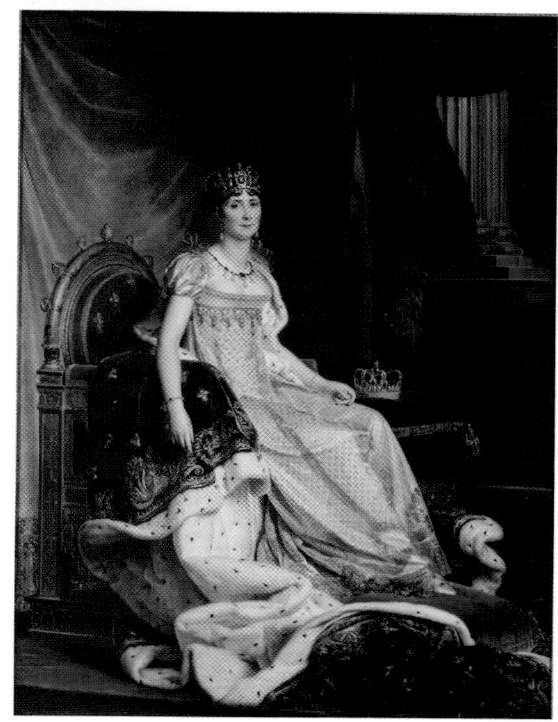

FIG. 41 (RIGHT): François Gérard, *Josephine in Coronation Costume*, Musée National du Château de Fontainebleau, Paris.

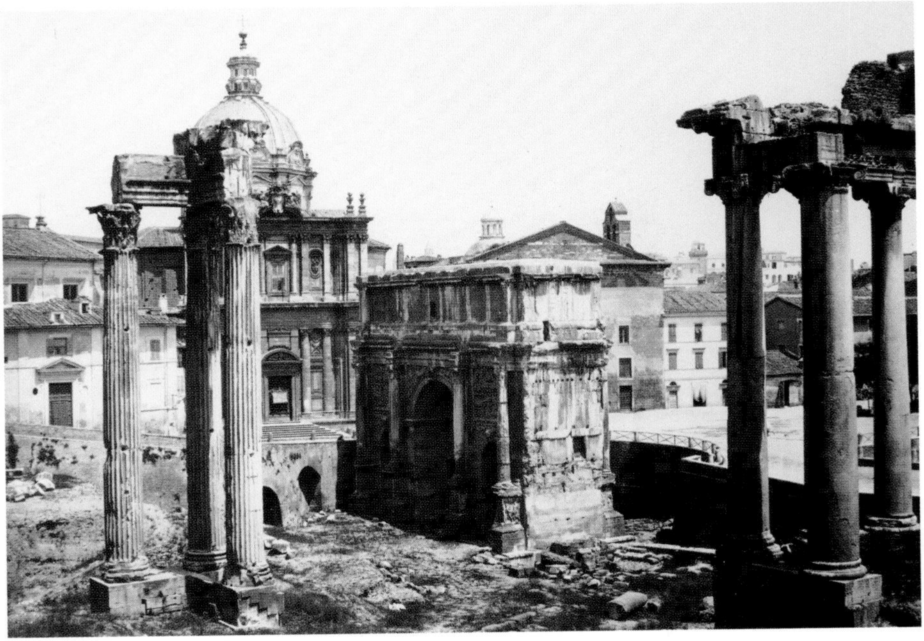

FIG. 42 (ABOVE): Giorgio Sommer (1834–1914), The Arch of Septimus and Temple of Vespasian, Rome, about 1860–70, albumen silver print (6 ¾ × 9 5⁄16 in.), The J. Paul Getty Museum, Los Angeles. FIG. 43 (BELOW): Robert Macpherson (1811–72), Arch of Constantine, 1850s, albumen silver print (11 7⁄8 × 15 5⁄8 in.), The J. Paul Getty Museum, Los Angeles.

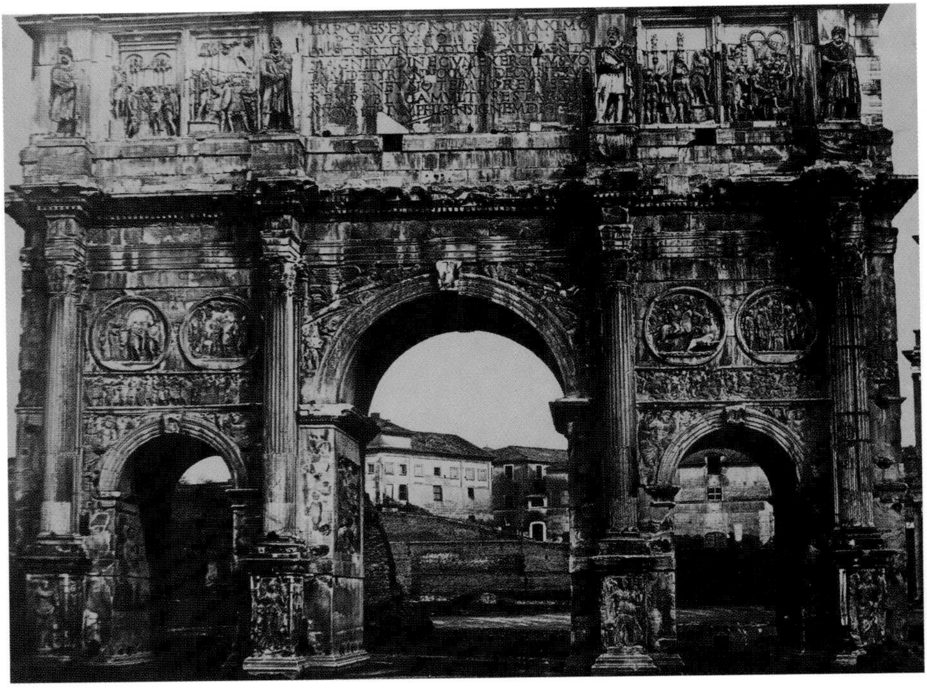

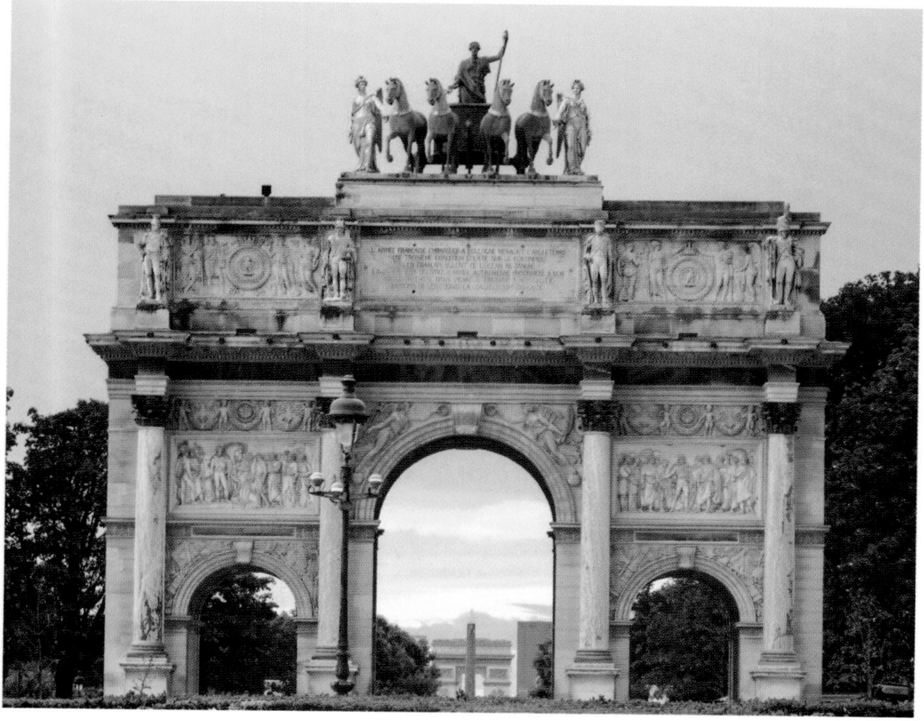

FIG. 44 (ABOVE): Arc de Triomphe du Carrousel, Paris. FIG. 45 (BELOW): The Horses of St. Mark's Basilica, Venice.

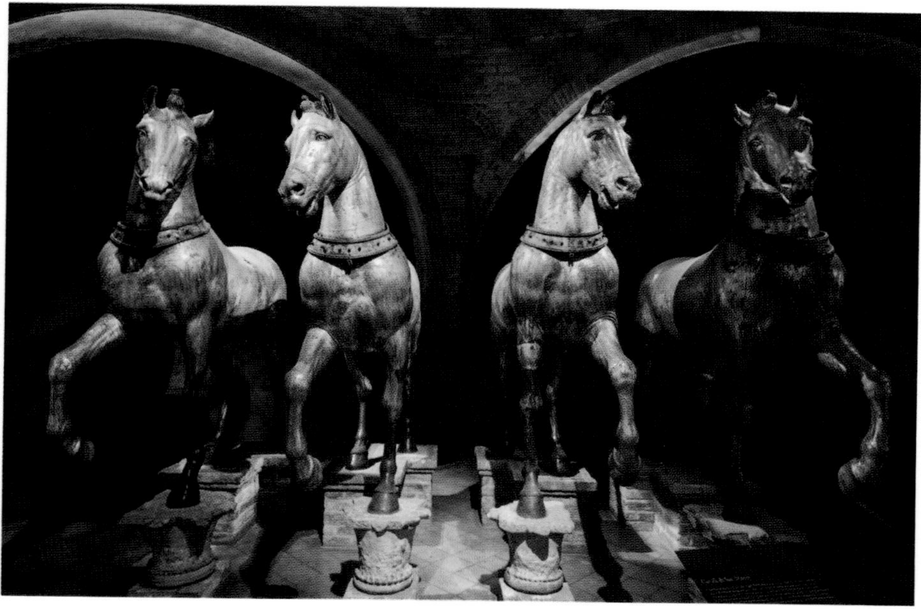

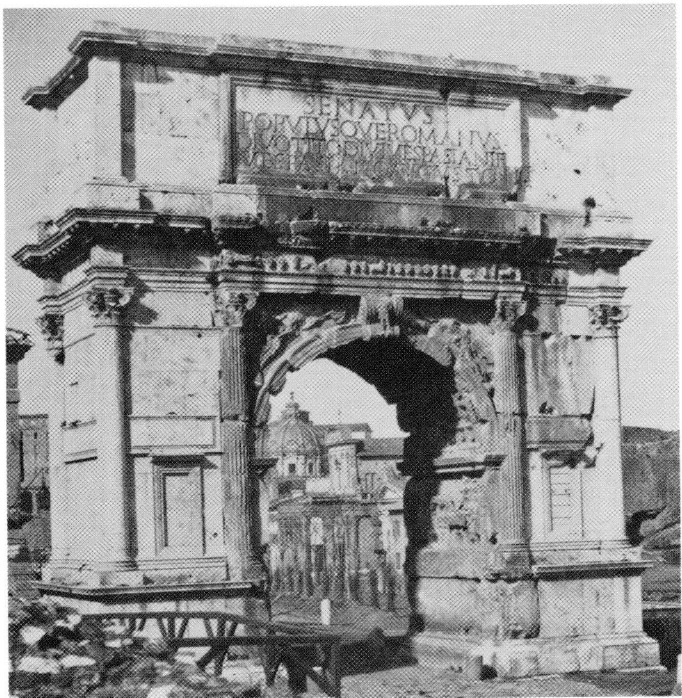

FIG. 46 (ABOVE): Jane St. John (1801–1882), Arch of Titus, Rome, 1856–59, albumen silver print from a paper negative (7 ⅜ × 9 ¾ in.), The J. Paul Getty Museum, Los Angeles.

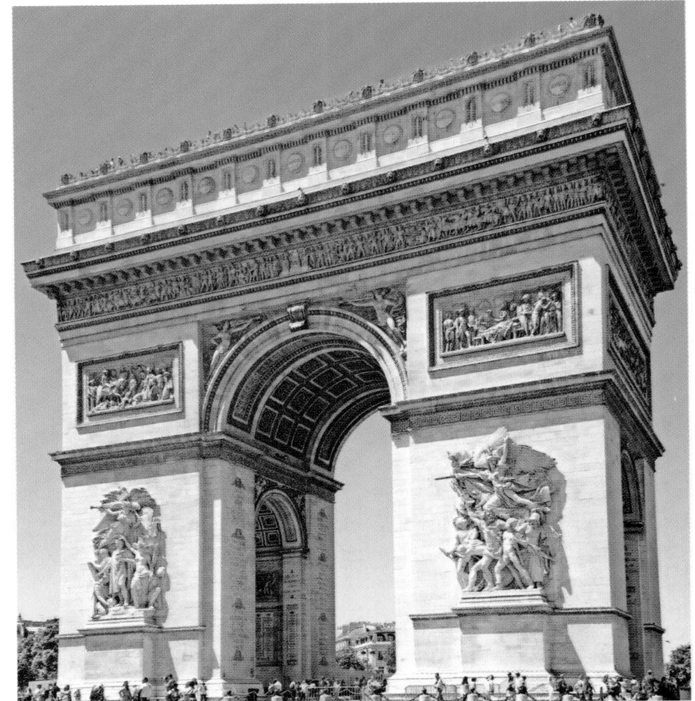

FIG. 47 (RIGHT): Arc de Triomphe de l'Étoile, Paris, from the east.

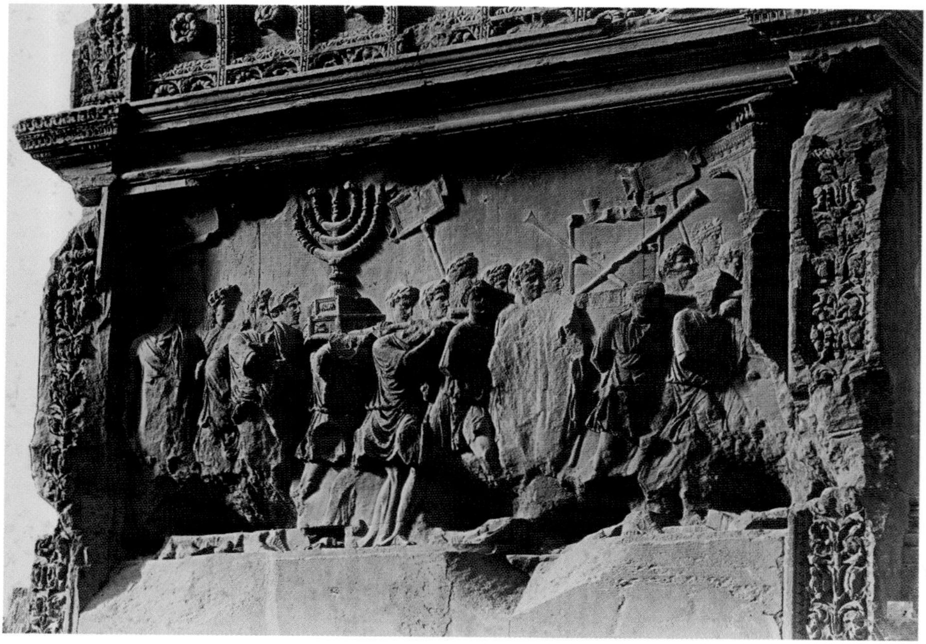

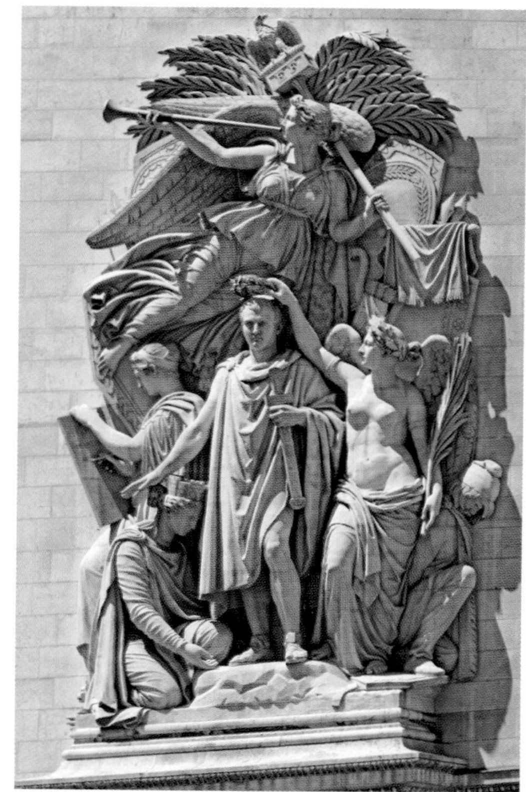

FIG. 48 (ABOVE): Tommaso Cuccioni (1790–1864), Interior of the Arch of Titus, Rome, 1850–59, albumen silver print (13 ¼ × 18 ⅜ in.), The J. Paul Getty Museum, Los Angeles. FIG. 49 (RIGHT): Triumph of 1810, Arc de Triomphe.

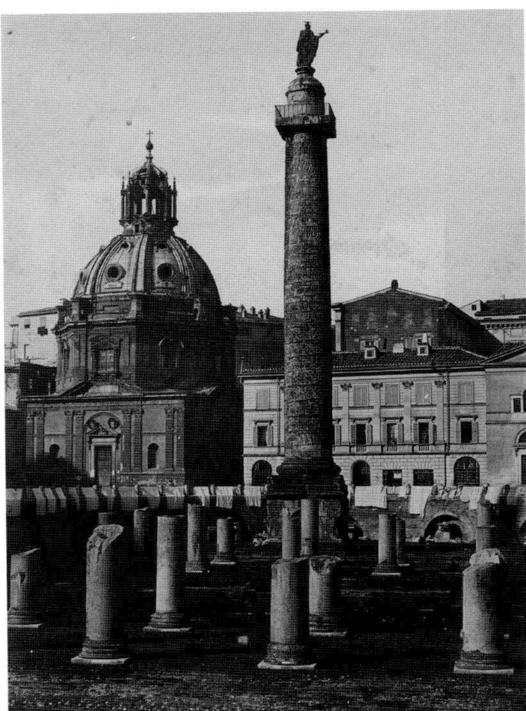

FIG. 50 (LEFT): Tommaso Cuccioni (1790–1864), Column of Trajan, 1850–59, albumen silver print (17 ⅞ × 12 ⅞ in.), The J. Paul Getty Museum, Los Angeles.

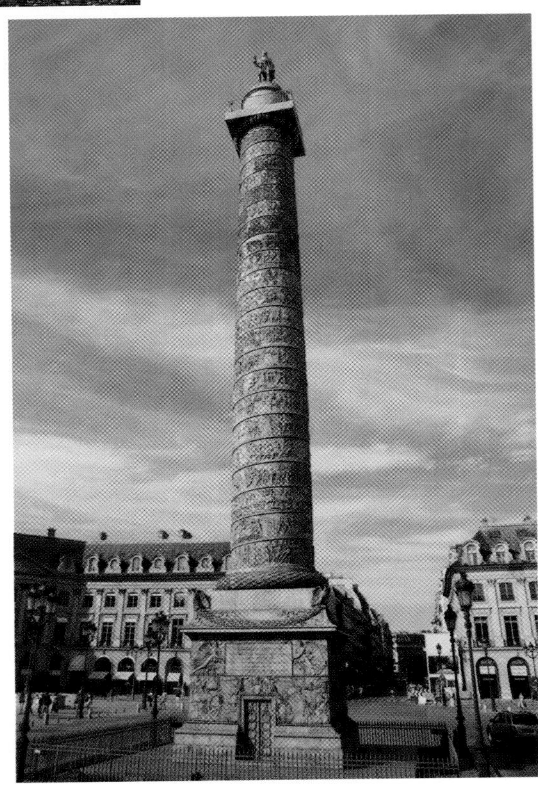

FIG. 51 (RIGHT): Vendome Column, Paris.

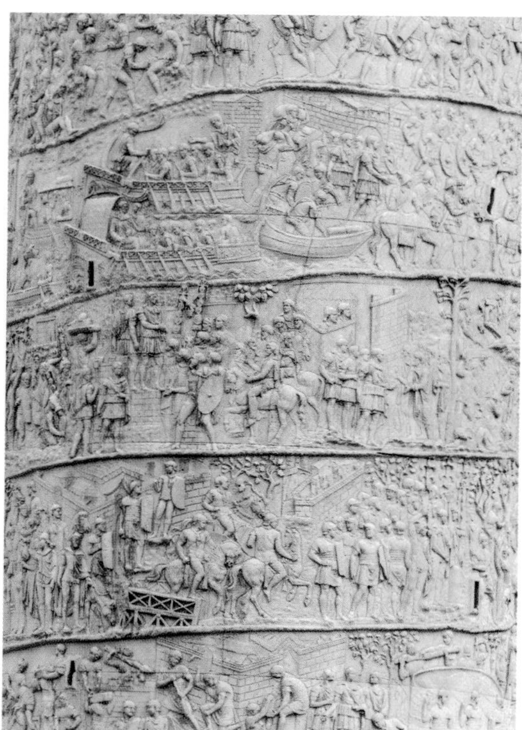

FIG. 52 (LEFT): Trajan's Column, detail, Rome.

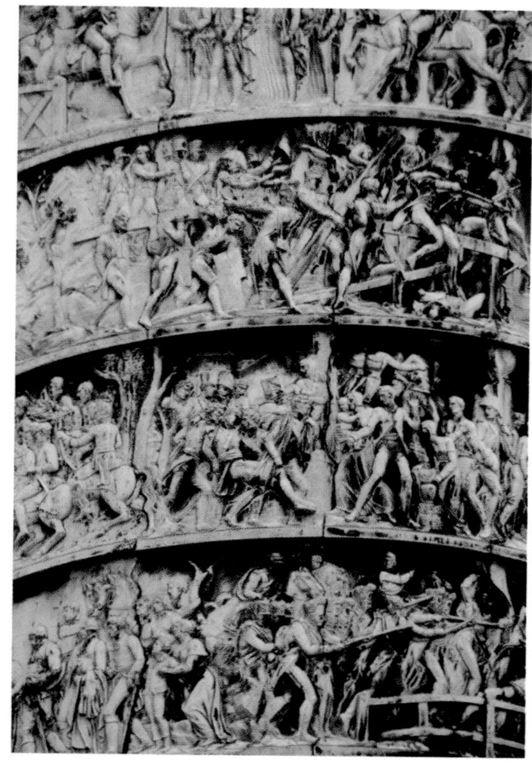

FIG. 53 (RIGHT): Vendome Column, detail, Paris.

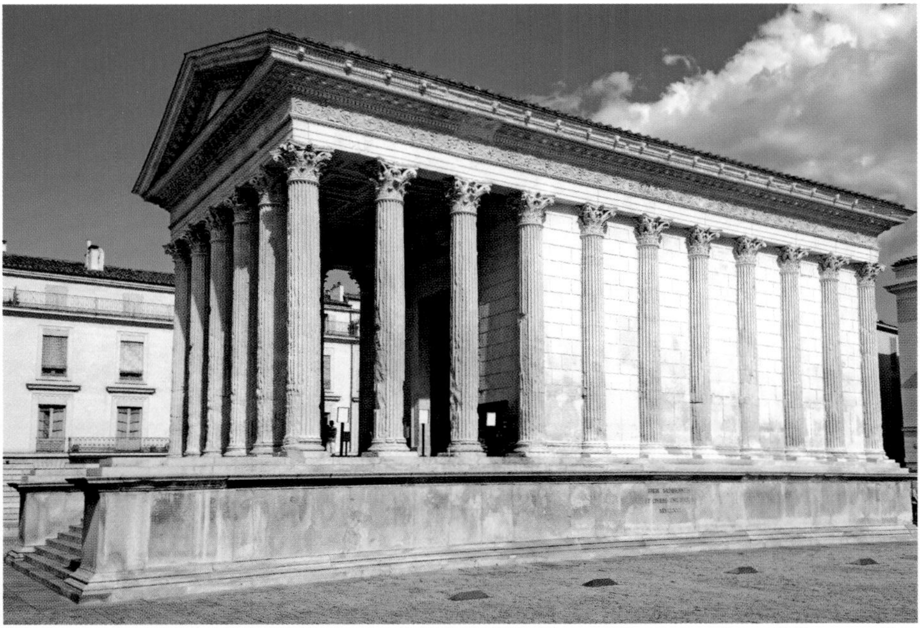

FIG. 54 (ABOVE): Maison Carrée, Nîmes. FIG. 55 (BELOW): The Madeleine Church, Paris.

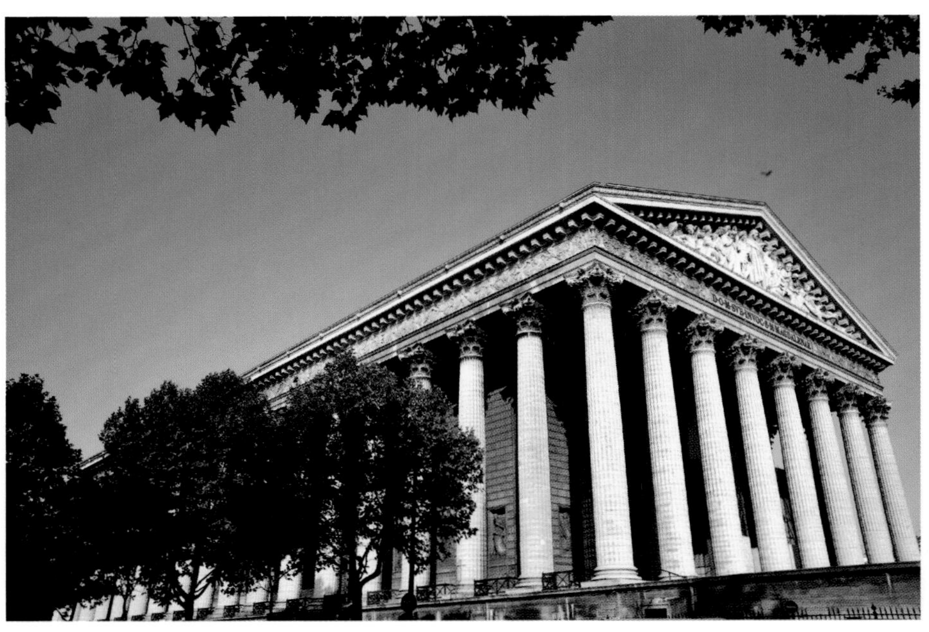

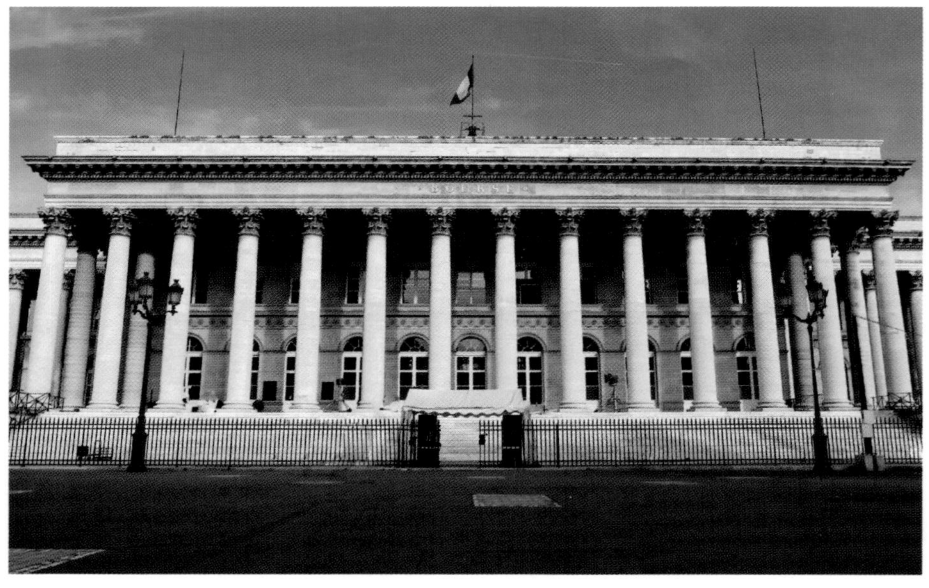

FIG. 56 (ABOVE): The Bourse of Paris (Palais Brongniart). FIG. 57 (BELOW): View of the Elephant Fountain at the Place de la Bastille, Paris, ca. 1805–10, watercolor on paper, Alavoine, Jean Antoine (1776–1834), Musée Carnavalet, Paris.

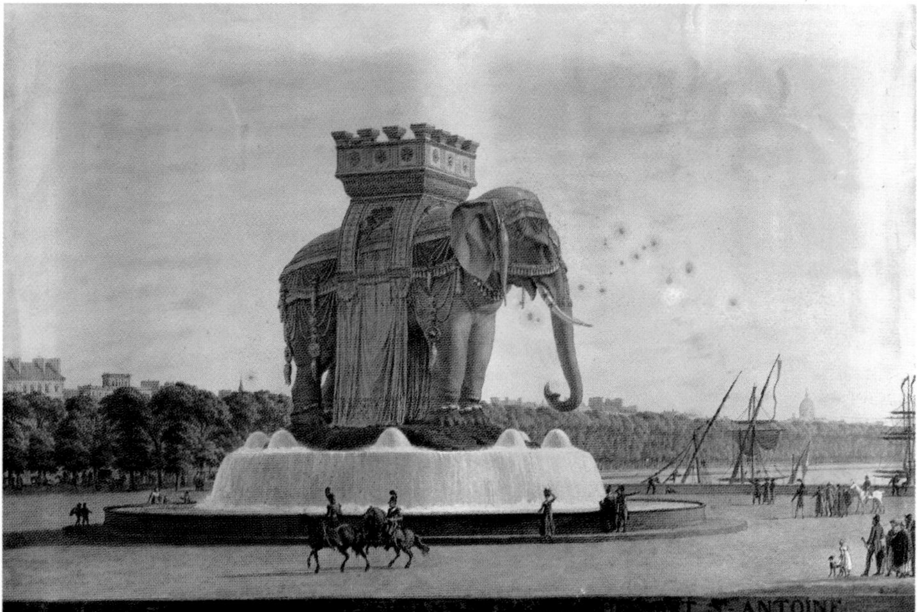

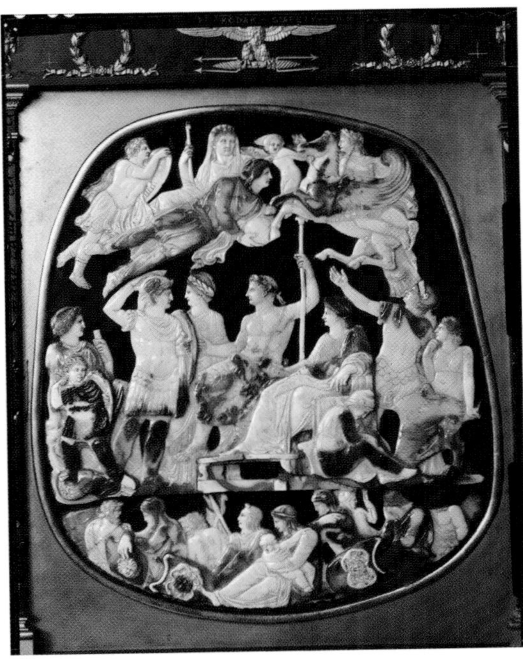

FIG. 58 (ABOVE): The Great Cameo of France (agate), Roman, first century C.E., Bibliothèque Nationale, Paris. FIG. 59 (BELOW): Marie Louise of Austria (1791–1847) guiding her son, with the ribbon of a medal of the Legion of Honour, towards a bust of Napoleon Bonaparte (1769–1821), 1813, oil on porcelain, Louis-Bertin Parant (1768–1851), Musée National de la Légion d'Honneur, Paris.

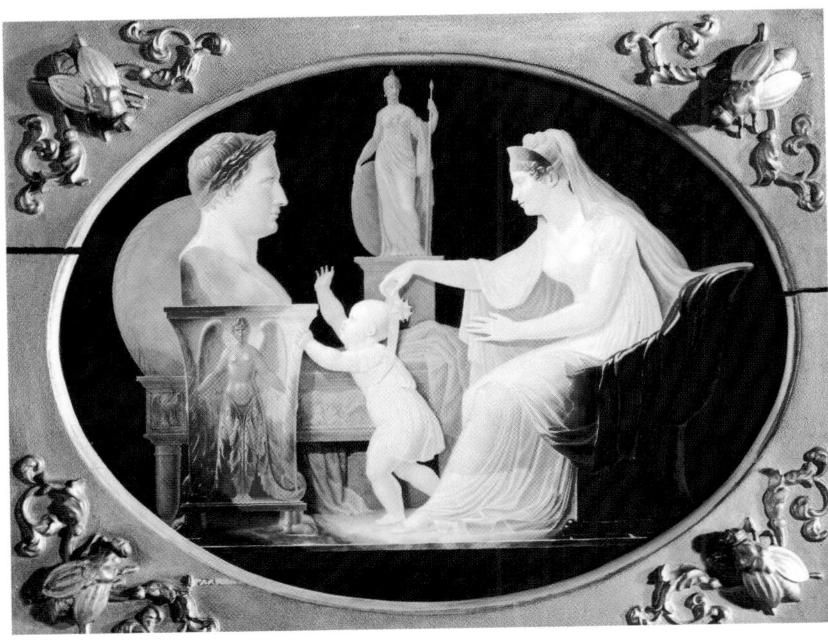

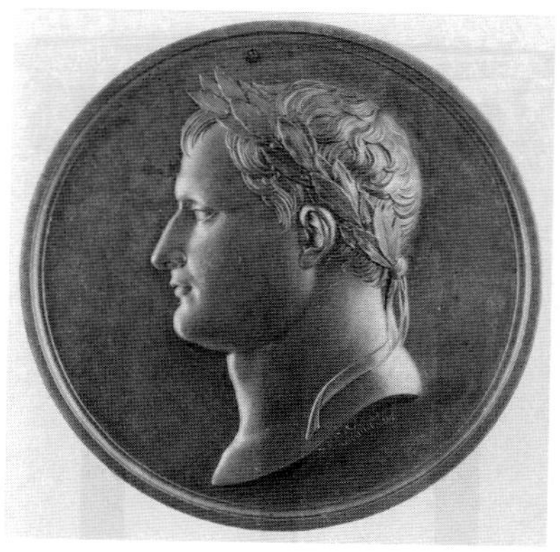

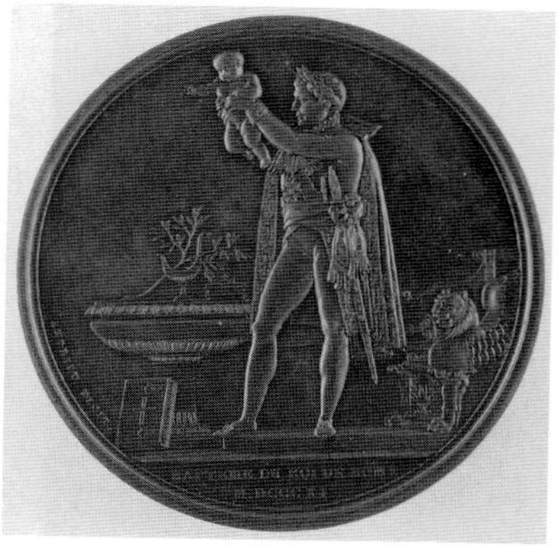

FIG. 60 AND 61 (ABOVE LEFT AND RIGHT): Bertrand Andrieu, 1811, Napoleon, *Baptism of the King of Rome*, bronze, struck (diameter: 2 11⁄16 in.), Metropolitan Museum of Art, New York. FIG. 62 (BELOW): *Cradle of the King of Rome*, Pierre-Paul Prudhon (1758–1813), Henri-Victor Roguier (1758–after 1830), Jean-Baptiste-Claude Odiot (1763–1850), and Pierre-Philippe Thomire (1751–1843), Paris, 1811, silver-gilt, gold, mother-of-pearl, copper plates covered with velvet, silk, and tulle with gold and silver embroidery. Hofburg Palace, Vienna.

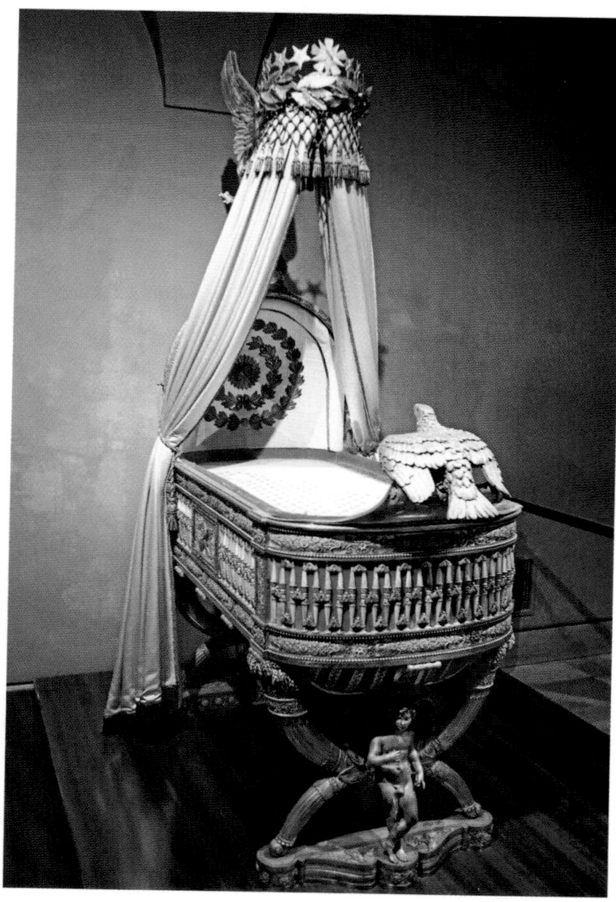

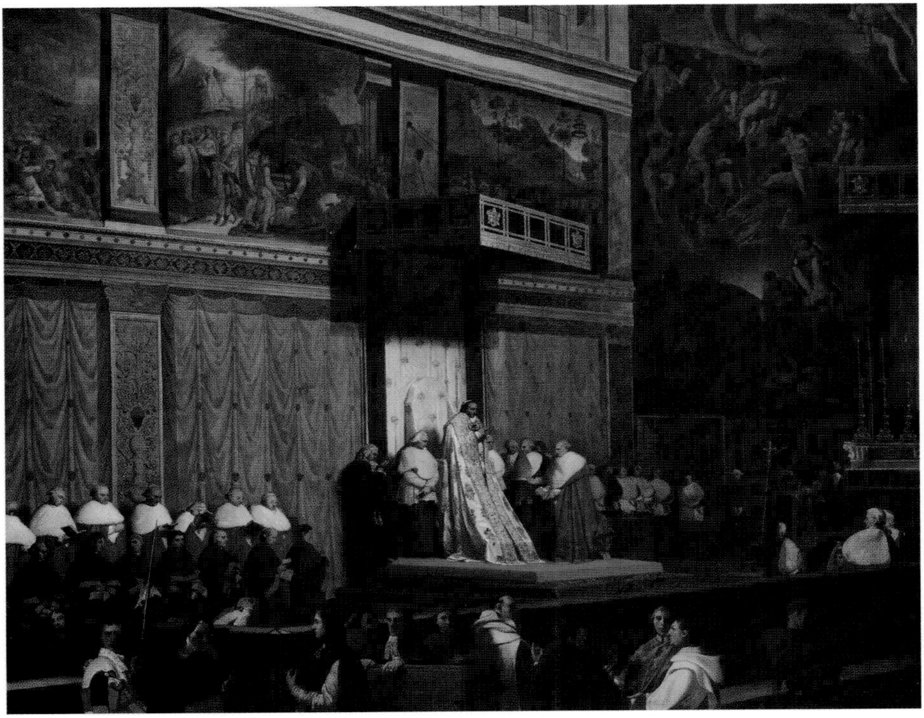

FIG. 63 (ABOVE): Jean-Auguste-Dominique Ingres, *Pope Pius VII in the Sistine Chapel*, 1814, oil on canvas (29 5⁄16 x 36 ½ in.), National Gallery of Art, Washington, D.C. FIG. 64 (BELOW): Tempio Canoviano, Possagno, Italy.

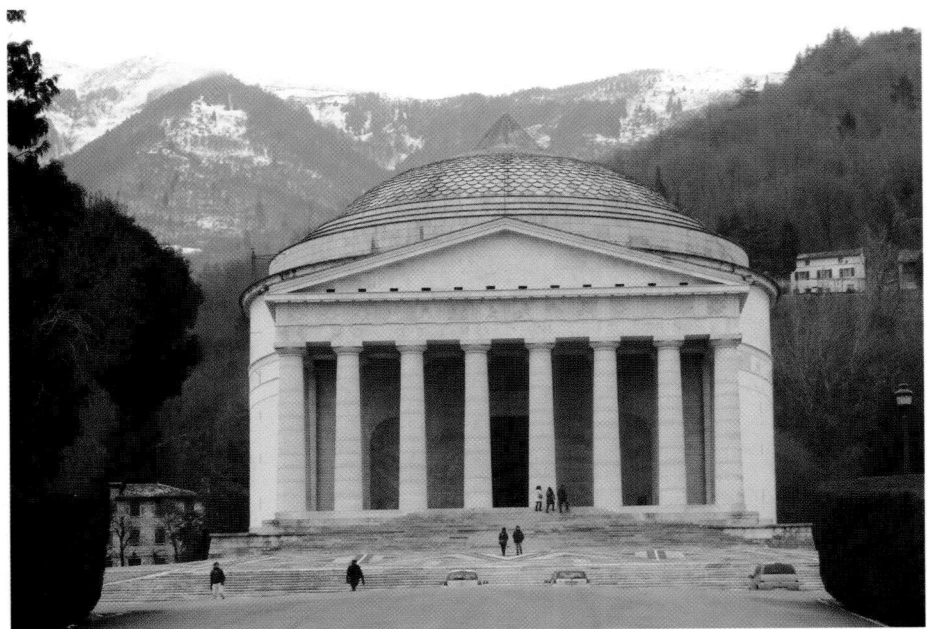

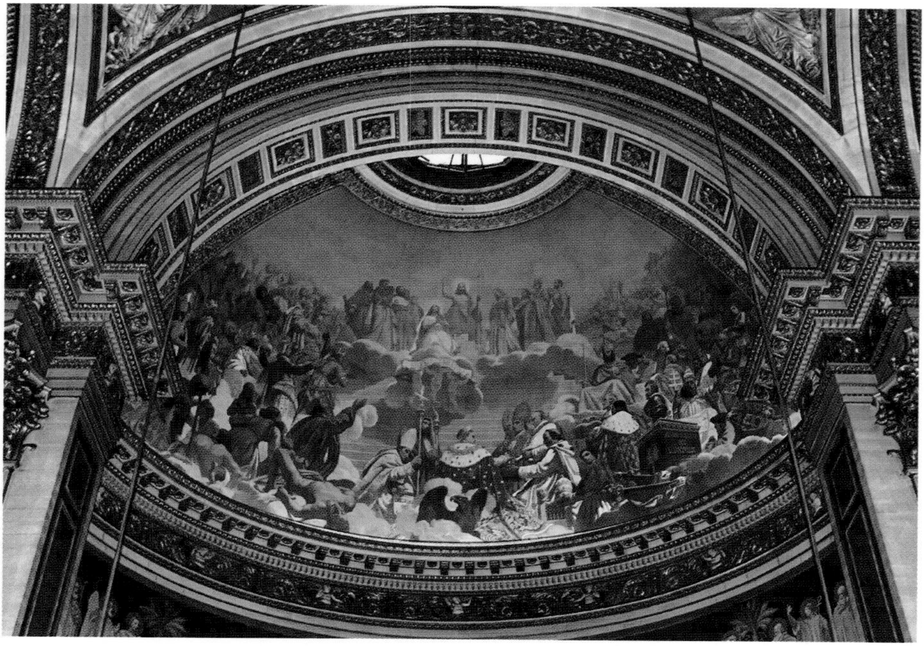

FIG. 65 (ABOVE): Jules-Claude Ziegler, *The History of Christianity,* 1835–38, mural, Madeleine Church. FIG. 66 (BELOW): Tomb of Napoleon, Les Invalides.

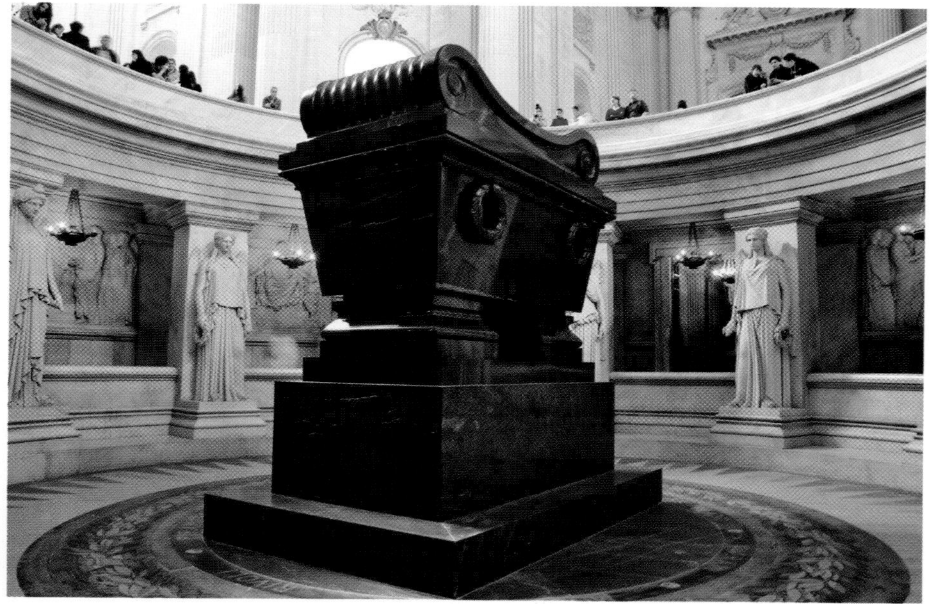

PART FOUR

A NEW ROME

"Men are only as great as the monuments they leave behind."

—Napoleon Bonaparte, 1804

ONE

COLUMNS OF CONQUEST

In 97 C.E., to garner the support of Rome's army, the uncharismatic Emperor Nerva adopted the military hero Trajan as his heir. When Nerva died after just sixteen months in power, he was succeeded by the popular forty-five-year-old. Hailing from the Roman province of Hispania (today's Spain), Trajan was the first Roman emperor born outside of Italy. Perhaps because of this, Trajan went out of his way to tie himself to Rome's first emperor, even wearing Augustus's distinctive forked hairdo.

To protect Rome's forty-five provinces, Trajan dispatched his army across the Empire. As Lino Rossi notes, it was the world's greatest professional army until World War I. Trajan's war machine numbered around 400,000 land forces—180,000 legionaries, 5,000 praetorians (guards), 6,000 police, and 200,000-plus auxiliaries.[1]

From north of the Danube (today's Romania), the Dacians regularly raided the Roman Empire. In 101, Trajan pushed back, fortifying the border and invading with tens of thousands of troops. After nearly two years of battle, Dacian King Decebalus negotiated a treaty with Trajan, then promptly broke it. In 105, Trajan returned to finish the job. The back-to-back wars were the defining episode of Trajan's nearly twenty-year reign. Trajan colonized his new province with Roman war veterans, leading to the country's current name of Romania.[2]

Accompanying the Roman legions was a talented engineer named Apollodorus who had been summoned to Rome at age twenty from Damascus, Roman Syria. In addition to forts and camps, Apollodorus built an extraordinary bridge that enabled Trajan's soldiers to cross the Danube and reinvade Dacia. Fortresses on both ends prevented the Dacians from using the bridge.

Roman historian Dio Cassius raved about the engineering feat: ". . . it has twenty piers of squared stone one hundred and fifty feet in height above the foundations and sixty in width, and these, standing at a distance of one hundred and seventy feet from one another, are connected by arches. How, then, could one fail to be astonished at the expenditure made upon them, or at the way in which each of them was placed in a river so deep, in water so full of eddies, and on a bottom so muddy?"[3]

When Trajan returned to Rome, it's thought that he appointed Apollodorus his *praefectus fabrum,* or minister of works, supervising the capital's *fabri*, engineers and artisans. The position was formerly held by Rabirius, starchitect under Domitian. In addition to Apollodorus's innovative military projects, Trajan may have been aware of his earlier buildings in Syria.[4]

In contrast to the lavish private building projects of Nero and Domitian, Trajan focused on public architecture. He reworked the Circus Maximus to accommodate 250,000 spectators, fortifying the wood structure with concrete and brick. On top of Nero's Golden House (razed by Vespasian), Trajan built his Baths. Fed by the Aqua Traiana, Trajan's Baths were four times as large as the Baths of Titus. Apollodorus located the bathing block in the center and arranged the main rooms in axial relationships to one another. In addition to a swimming pool, the frigadorium, Apollodorus constructed a library, meeting hall, and a hemicycle with seating for performances.

In 108 C.E., rich with looted gold and silver from Dacia, Trajan decided to commemorate his victory with a vast complex linking the Republican Forum and the Campus Martius. To make room, Apollodorus removed

125 feet of the Quirinal Hill. Almost as large as Rome's other imperial fora combined, Trajan's Forum boasted a shopping mall, plaza, two libraries, and the immense white marble Basilica Ulpia (after Trajan's family name, Ulpius). In a great rectangular courtyard lined with Carrara marble stood a heroic bronze equestrian statue of Trajan surrounded by Dacian captives.

Apollodorus saved the best for last. In the northernmost part of the Forum he built the soaring Trajan's Column. Wrapping around the column in an upward spiral was a marble frieze carved with 155 scenes from Trajan's Dacian campaigns. Twenty-nine blocks of solid marble were quarried at Carrara, shipped down the Tyrrhenian coast to Portus, and then taken by riverboat up the Tiber to Rome.[5] It's thought that these massive marble drums, roughly ten feet in diameter, were hollowed out to make room for a spiral staircase inside the column (185 stairs, lit by over forty slit windows).

As Lynne Lancaster explains, each drum was rolled by cart or sledge onto the base of a sophisticated lifting device featuring scaffolding and a pulley system, and lifted into the air with a series of capstans, each pushed by teams of men and horses. The highest drum had to be lifted 125 feet. To prevent damage from the blocks, Apollodorus reinforced the vault of the courtyard portico substructure with brick ribbing.[6] The column rested on a pedestal made of eight marble blocks seventeen feet square, decorated with Dacian arms and armor held up by eagles. Above, between the pedestal and shaft, the base was formed by an oak wreath.

Apollodorus entrusted the carving of the marble drums to a frieze designer, or maestro. Though it is not known how many sculptors helped carve the nearly seven-hundred-foot frieze, the Hellenistic figures have led experts to conclude that Greek slaves worked alongside Roman craftsmen. There are a number of theories about the technique used and whether the carving was done in place or at a workshop. Some experts believe that after smoothing the marble surfaces, the sculptors copied art onto the marble drums using pointing instruments and *puntelli*. Alternatively, artisans may have transferred ideas directly to the stone with the help of chalk or painted guidelines. It's also possible that masons used a cartoon design attached to a wooden drum wrapped around the marble.[7]

Casualties from the Dacian wars numbered in the tens of thousands. In addition, Trajan took an estimated ten thousand Dacians back to Rome as slaves—many fought in gladiatorial games; others were sent to work quarries and gold mines throughout the Empire. According to historian Dio Cassius, the head of Dacian king Decebalus was brought back to Rome, along with silver and gold that he had buried.[8] Despite the carnage, less than a quarter of the column's marble frieze depicts battle scenes.

Amidst hundreds of fallen Dacians, only two injured Romans are depicted. In Trajan's fifty-eight appearances, he is never shown fighting. Instead, the emperor is portrayed on foot and on horseback, addressing his troops, performing sacrifices, and receiving prisoners of war. In a scene of *adlocutio*, the traditional military oration before a campaign or after a victory, Trajan is portrayed with his right hand raised, thanking his troops for their bravery and distributing awards.

According to Giuliana Calcani, episodes for Trajan's Column were chosen to give the war a positive spin, rather than show its brutality. "The scenes sculpted on the Column repeatedly play on the theme that it was not a matter of Rome subduing Dacia, but of civilization triumphing over non-civilization," writes Calcani.[9] In the propagandistic war monument, Dacians are portrayed as a worthy but barbaric opponent. In one scene for example, Dacian women are shown torturing Roman soldiers.

Running chronologically from bottom to top, the tableaux feature over 2,600 Romans and Dacians in two-thirds life size. The Dacians are identified by their long hair and caps. To make the scenes easier to read, the height of the figures was increased at the top. Halfway up the column, a winged image of Victory marks the end of the first Dacian War and the start of the second. The epic drama opens at a staging area on the Roman banks of the Danube (today's Bulgaria), with soldiers unloading provisions from ships. As the troops cross a pontoon bridge, a huge half-length bearded river god, personification of the Danube, blesses them. One of the other three personifications of gods on the column is Jupiter who hurls a thunderbolt at the enemy.[10]

The second campaign depicts the Roman army's hunt for Decebalus. In the final battle, after the Dacians set fire to their capital and abandon it, a group commits mass suicide by drinking poison. Legionnaires pay tribute to Trajan while Dacians surrender, Roman soldiers carry off booty, and Trajan receives the acclamation of his troops. In the final episode, javelin-throwing Romans chase Decabulus. Rather than be captured, the king kneels under an oak tree, poised to cut his throat with a curved knife.

Six years in the making, Trajan's Column was dedicated by the Roman Senate in May 113 C.E. Four years after the dedication, an ailing Trajan left Syria and headed back to Rome. But too sick to continue, the sixty-three-year-old emperor stopped at Selinus in Cilicia (today's southern Turkey) where he died.

Before announcing Trajan's death, his childless widow Plotina adopted her beloved Hadrian as heir. Trajan's Column became a tomb. A small door on the entrance side of the column's base led to a chamber where Trajan's cremated ashes were deposited in a golden urn. In 121, Emperor Hadrian added a second urn with Plotina's ashes to the *cella*, or burial chamber. Debate continues over whether Trajan's Column was originally intended as an honorary or a funerary monument.

The sculpted surface of Trajan's Column was probably painted in bright colors and the soldiers armed with small metal spears and swords. As part of the propaganda to deify Trajan, a colossal gilded bronze statue of the emperor was installed on top. This wasn't a new practice. According to Filippo Coarelli, the use of freestanding columns as the bases for divine or honorary statues was an ancient tradition, probably originating in Greece.[11] A century before, Pliny wrote that this tradition elevated mortals to an exulted status.

Apollodorus flanked the column with Greek and Latin libraries. Square-shaped with vaulted roofs, the two buildings sported second story balconies for bird's-eye views of the marble reliefs. Furnished with statuary and reading tables, the libraries' holdings included Latin and Greek versions of Trajan's military dispatches, recorded on illustrated scrolls. Trajan's own written commentaries may have inspired the scenes for his unprecedented marble frieze. "The two hundred meter long spiral frieze can be seen as a scroll unfurled from bottom to top," writes Diana Kleiner.[12]

Numerous images of Trajan turned his Forum into what James Packer calls "a biography in stone which successively revealed the various stages in the life of its hero as he progressed from mortality to deification."[13] As Packer writes, "The expensive imported marbles and the standards and statues of gilded bronze that crowned the surrounding buildings were the unmistakable signs of an overwhelming imperial prosperity and achievement."[14]

Apollodorus's novel idea of a column decorated with a spiral frieze was copied by Marcus Aurelius in Rome and Theodosius and Arcadius in Constantinople. Around 608, a forty-five-foot-tall Corinthian column dedicated to Byzantine Emperor Phocas was erected in the Roman Forum, the last such column. Almost 250 years after its debut, Trajan's Forum was still inspiring awe among visitors to Rome, including Emperor Constantius II, son of Constantine the Great. ". . . when Constantius II reached the Forum of Trajan [357 C.E.], a complex unique in the world, and in our judgment, worthy the admiration of the gods, he stopped amazed, considering all around him those gigantic structures, which words cannot describe or mortal hands again build," wrote Ammianus Marcellinus.[15]

After Trajan's death, in the early years of Hadrian's reign, Apollodorus continued as master architect, possibly designing the Pantheon. The brilliant engineer is credited with many projects in and around Rome, including the harbor at Portus, Ostia, the port at Civitavecchia, and the arches at Ancona and Benevento. Built between 114 and 118, the Arch at Benevento between Rome and Naples honored Trajan with relief panels covering his greatest achievements. Hadrian would finish the arch, adding himself to scenes with Trajan.

Apollodorus was working on a statue to the moon for Hadrian, intended to match Nero's one-hundred-foot-tall Colossus. But he never finished the project. Apollodorus made the fatal mistake of insulting Hadrian's own dome design for Tivoli. "Be off, and draw your gourds [vaults]," he told Hadrian condescendingly. "You don't understand anything of these matters."[16] In 117 C.E., Hadrian banished Apollodorus from Rome and proceeded to fill his villa with the maligned vaults. According to Dio Cassius, the exiled Apollodorus was charged with trumped-up crimes and executed in 130. The renowned engineer was somewhere between sixty and seventy years old at his death.

The statue of Trajan atop his column was melted down in Christian times. From surviving coins, it seems possible that the figure may have been a heroic nude topped by an eagle.[17] The gold urns containing the ashes of Trajan and Plotina were looted in the Middle Ages. In 1588, Pope Sixtus V replaced the missing statue of Trajan with one of St. Peter by Bastiano Torrigiano. (Sixtus also topped the Marcus Aurelius column with a statue of St. Paul). The pope explained that a monument like Trajan's could become worthy to bear the effigy of Christ's Vicar on Earth only if it was rededicated in the cause of the Catholic Church. Sixtus also removed marble from the façade of Septimius Severus's Septizodium for his own building projects.[18]

The richly decorated Trajan's Column continued to be a source of artistic inspiration. In the early eleventh century, Saint Bernard, bishop of Hildesheim, copied Trajan's Column with a bronze column for the Church of St. Michael's featuring a spiral frieze of Christ's life crowned with a triumphal cross. Starting in the 1500s, plaster casts of the column's extraordinary friezes were commissioned by France's François I followed by Louis XIV. In 1595, Henri IV built a replica of Trajan's Column by the Petit Palais. Ten scrolled bands were engraved with key events from his own rule. The column, writes Margaret McGowan, helped Henri IV strengthen his authority and foster acceptance for his new Bourbon dynasty.[19] In the eighteenth century, Vienna's Church of St. Charles Borromeo added two Trajan-like columns to its façade depicting the life of St. Charles, a sixteenth-century Italian bishop who ministered to plague victims.

Michelangelo reportedly said that if the Lombards could draw, no one would pay attention to his or anyone else's work; only in Rome was there a Trajan's Column. While visiting Paris in 1665, his famous successor Gian Lorenzo Bernini noted that Trajan's Column was the training school for Renaissance greats Raphael and Giulio Romano.[20] Throughout the centuries, the column remained a powerful symbol of military victory. As other iconic Roman monuments crumbled, Trajan's Column survived. As Robert Hughes puts it, Trajan's Column is "bar none, the greatest piece of narrative sculpture from the ancient world."[21]

⚜

Napoleon was wrapping up his victory over Russia and Austria when the Gregorian calendar went into effect on January 1, 1806, throughout the French Empire. The Republican calendar implemented in 1792 had started over with Year I, giving poetic names to the months. Napoleon's coup d'état on November 9, 1799, for example was known as the coup of 18 Brumaire, Year VIII from the French word *brume,* or mist. Days were divided into ten hours of one hundred minutes each; months into three ten-day weeks with five days (six in a leap year) added at year end.

Napoleon's Concordat with Pius restored the Gregorian calendar days of the week and made Sunday the official day of rest, but left the months and years of the Republican calendar. With its three ten-day weeks per month, the calendar was unsustainable. It was also getting increasingly difficult to synch the calendar with Napoleon's growing Empire. In ordering the replacement of the Republican calendar, Napoleon further disassociated himself from the Revolution.

Ancient Rome also changed the way time was measured. After being named *Pontifex Maximus* in 63 B.C.E., Julius Caesar introduced major calendar reforms with the help of the Greek astronomer Sosigenes of Alexandria. Among the changes aimed at synching the monthly and yearly calendars was the first leap year, created by adding an extra day to February every fourth year.[22]

Augustus continued to manipulate Rome's calendar. These included the introduction of numerals to the *fasti consulares* (lists indicating the year) to indicate the number of years elapsed since Rome's founding. To the religious calendar, Augustus added festival days commemorating imperial events.[23] "After centuries in which no human being was named on the calendar," writes Denis Feeney, "the imperial family is now everywhere, with specific year dates often attached to their various doings."[24]

By late January, Napoleon was back in Paris, eager to give his capital a fitting monument to the Grande Armée's victory at Austerlitz. As his private secretary Bourrienne observed, Napoleon's "passion for monuments almost equaled his passion for war. The destruction of men and the construction of monuments were two things perfectly in unison in the mind of Bonaparte."[25]

Napoleon actually considered dismantling and moving Trajan's Column to Paris, all 1,100 tons of it. Fortunately his advisors dissuaded him, arguing against the spoliation of one of ancient Rome's greatest architectural achievements. Instead, Vivant Denon suggested a new column for the Vendôme Square dedicated to the Grande Armée's recent victories, modeled after the celebrated Trajan's Column.

For Napoleon, Trajan was a worthy role model. During his nearly two-decade rule, from 98 until 117 C.E., the skilled general and emperor expanded the Roman Empire to its greatest size; his military exploits equaled or exceeded those of Alexander the Great. Modeling his own column after that of Trajan underscored the parallels between the victories of his Grande Armée and the Roman legions. "Such a noble and classical the monument would attest to a French Empire equal to that of the ancient Romans under the leadership of an emperor equal to the greatest of Rome's rulers," writes Charles Mack. It would be "symbolic of Paris's position as the new Rome of Europe and point to the fulfillment of the nation's dreams of achieving a continental hegemony . . . an ambition which extended back . . . to Charlemagne himself."[26]

In a bulletin to his soldiers, Napoleon described Trajan's famous bridge built by Apollodorus during the second Dacian war. "In Hungary it diminishes a great deal; and at the place where Trajan raised a bridge it is almost unnoticeable. There, the Danube is 450 toises broad; here it is only 400. The bridge of Trajan was a stone bridge, the work of several years. Caesar's bridge over the Rhine was raised, it is true, in eight days, but no loaded carriage could pass over it."[27]

In addition to disbursing spoils of war to their officers, troops, and themselves, Roman generals felt a moral obligation to spend a large part of booty on the public for temples, basilicas, and aqueducts. "The decision to build something spectacular carried the greatest prestige and won the most acclaim," writes W. Jeffrey Tatum. ". . . Roman public building was dynastic."[28]

As first consul, Napoleon wanted to build Roman-style triumphal columns. At his direction in 1800, the French Assembly issued two decrees for a "column dedicated to the [Revolutionary] heroes" of each administrative department in France to be installed in each major city. Two were to be built in Paris. One of these, dedicated to revolutionary heroes, was earmarked for the Place de la Concorde; the second, honoring heroes of the Department de la Seine, was to be erected in the Place Vendôme north of the Tuileries Gardens. Jacques-Louis David, Charles Percier, and Pierre Fontaine judged the submissions for the Place Vendôme column.

Built in the late seventeenth century by Jules Hardouin-Mansart to honor Louis XIV, the Place Vendôme took its name from the residence of Henri IV's son, the Duc of Vendôme. Mansart razed the residence to make room for his new square. For over a century, the Place Vendôme was dominated by François Girardon's monumental equestrian statue of Louis XIV wearing the cloak of a Roman emperor and a large curly wig. The statue was toppled by revolutionaries in 1792.

The statue's thirty-foot-deep foundation was still intact on Bastille Day, 1800, when Lucien Bonaparte, then interior minister, laid the foundation stone for the new column. But the ambitious plan was never realized, probably due to budget constraints. Three years later, Napoleon tried again, this time scaling back the project. On October 1803, he proposed building one national column in the Place Vendôme "equaling that in Rome set up in honor of Trajan."[29] Like its ancient prototype, the proposed column was to be decorated with frieze panels in an upward spiral containing over one hundred figures symbolic of the various departmental units in France. Napoleon also proposed that this column be capped with a statue of Charlemagne.

According to Valérie Huet, Napoleon chose Trajan's Column as his model because of his "fascination for Rome, its power and its strategies of display in art . . ."[30] "Napoleon was the true reincaration of a Roman emperor," adds Huet. The column in the Place Vendôme "expressed Napoleon's triumph, celebrating his *Grande Armée* just as Trajan's column had commemorated the victories of Trajan and of his Roman soldiers . . ."[31]

After the National Assembly ratified the proposal, Denon tapped architects Jacques Gondouin and Jean-Baptiste Lepère for the high-profile commission. Gondouin, the son of a royal gardener and student of Jacques-François Blondel, had studied at the French Academy of Rome as a recipient of the second Grand Prix. After his position as Louis XV's Furniture Designer to the Crown, Gondouin survived the Revolution by posing as a gardener at his country house. Lepère, who Denon knew from the Egyptian campaign, designed propagandistic medals for Napoleon. In 1802, he succeeded Percier and Fontaine at Malmaison.

Gondouin and Lepère conceived a core cylinder twelve feet in diameter made of ninety-eight hollow stone drums. This stone column was to be covered by 425 spiraling plaques depicting France's recent military victories. While the frieze of Trajan's Column was carved from marble, the Vendôme Column reliefs were to be made of plates of cast bronze, fixed by hooks to the column. Three-feet-eight-inches high and 722-feet long, the frieze would cover the column's shaft in twenty-two upward spirals.[32]

In a highly symbolic gesture, the bronze for the plates was to come from melting down some 130 Austrian and Russian cannons captured at Austerlitz and other battles in 1805.[33] Two years later, this practice would be repeated for a bronze statue of General Desaix, whom Napoleon called his Hephaestion, best friend of Alexander the Great. For Hephaestion's cremation in Babylon in 323 B.C.E., Alexander heaped gold, jewels, ivory, and spices onto the pyre. To supply the bronze for Desaix's statue in the Place des Victoires, captured mortars were melted down from the Prussian campaign.[34] According to Frances Steiner, Napoleon was fascinated with the idea of incorporating the spoils of war into his buildings, part of his desire to "associate symbolically his new public monuments with his military exploits."[35]

Napoleon's use of enemy weapons for sculpture revived a tradition dating back to antiquity. In his encyclopedic bestseller *Natural History*, Pliny the Elder wrote that the Greeks cast bronze statues of both gods and mortal heroes. Roman quaestor Spurius Carvilius made a devotional bronze statue using the breastplates, greaves, and helmets of the defeated Samnites. After Octavian's admiral Agrippa defeated Sextus in 36 B.C.E., the future emperor had a column erected in the Forum decorated with prows from enemy ships.[36] Repurposing enemy weapons continued in the Renaissance. In the sixteenth century for example, Giambologna cast his Equestrian Monument to Henri IV with enemy artillery from Livorno.[37]

To design the column's reliefs, Denon hired Bordeaux-born painter and lithographer Pierre-Nolasque Bergeret, a student of David, along with two assistants, François Mazois and Benjamin Zix. Trained as an architect,

Mazois was an expert on the monuments of Roman Gaul. As official artist of the Napoleonic campaigns, Strasbourg-born Benjamin Zix would travel with Denon to Prussia, Poland, Spain, and Italy.

Napoleon personally selected the events to be represented. Like Roman emperor Trajan, Napoleon plays a starring role in the reliefs. Bergeret, Mazois, and Zix produced drawings for seventy-six episodes from the Grande Armée's recent campaign in southern Germany and Austria. Starting from the military camp at Boulogne, the vignettes continued with the army's departure, various battle scenes, and finally the Treaty of Pressburg and Napoleon's triumphant return to Paris on January 26, 1806.

A team of sculptors executed Bergeret's designs in bronze at the foundry of Jean-Baptiste Launay and Bonon. Among them were François Joseph Bosio, François Rude, Jean-Joseph Foucou, Louis-Simon Boizot, Lorenzo Bartolini, Claude Ramey, Charles-Louis Corbet, Clodion, and Henri-Joseph Ruxthiel. Julie Charpentier was the only woman on the project.[38]

The Vendôme Column rests on a twenty-two-foot-tall pedestal made of Corsican granite blocks covered in cast bronze. Like Trajan's Column, the pedestal was decorated with war motifs, in this case enemy cannons, uniforms, helmets, and flags after drawings by Mazois and Dix. On the south side of the pedestal above the doorway, a panel supported by winged Victories bore a Latin inscription: "The august Emperor Napoleon set up this monument of the German War and dedicated it to the glory of his greatest army; it is made out of bronze captured from the Germans routed by his leadership in the space of three months in 1805."[39]

Like Trajan's Column, an inside staircase of 176 steps winds up the hollow interior to a square viewing platform, the abacus of the Doric capital.[40] Also like Trajan's Column, the Vendôme Column was topped with a bronze statue of the emperor. Antoine-Denis Chaudet's elegant Hellenistic style was influenced by Antonio Canova whose works he had admired as a pensioner at the French Academy in Rome in the mid-1780s. A decorative sculptor, Chaudet had also designed reliefs for Joséphine's jewelry cabinet and the eagle on top of the standards of the imperial army. After the proclamation of the Empire, Chaudet received exclusive rights to reproduce in plaster his portrait bust of Napoleon. In January 1805, Chaudet's statue *Napoleon the Legislator* was installed in the rooms of the Legislative Corps.

Chaudet portrayed Napoleon as a Caesar, wearing a toga, his bare head crowned with a laurel wreath. In his left hand, the emperor held an orb topped by a winged Victory; his right hand rested on the pommel of a *spatha*, the three-foot long battle sword used by the Romans.

Napoleon carried his own favorite sword at Austerlitz. Created by Biennais, the solid gold hilt was chased and embossed with scrolling foliage and featured the emperor's portrait in profile. After applying a blend of mercury and gold paste, Biennais drove the mercury away, creating highly toxic fumes along with the spectacular gold decoration. By heating the blade to between 545 and 563 degrees Fahrenheit, Biennais imparted a spectacular blue finish to the metal. Napoleon dubbed the weapon "my sword." Like the *spatha*-wielding Romans, Napoleon must have felt invincible.

TWO

ARCHES OF TRIUMPH

After his 1800 victory at Marengo, France's first consul told his brother Lucien: "I will arrive at Paris unexpectedly. My intention is to have neither triumphal arches nor any kind of ceremony. I have too good an opinion of myself to estimate such baubles, trinkets. I know of no other triumph than public satisfaction." As Thomas Gaehtgens describes, Napoleon soon prohibited Lyon from erecting a triumphal arch in his honor and rejected a suggestion for a similar arch at the Place du Châtelet in Paris.[1]

Five years later after his stunning victory at Austerlitz, Emperor Napoleon I made a complete about-face. "You will march home through arches of triumph," he promised his soldiers.

Napoleon proposed a series of monumental arches for Paris. "One of the first two must be a Marengo arch and the other an arch of Austerlitz. I shall have another erected somewhere in Paris, to be the arch of Peace, and a fourth to be the arch of Religion," he wrote in spring 1806. "With these four arches I am confident that I can finance French sculpture for twenty years. . . . Generally speaking, no opportunity should be missed to humiliate the Russians and the English."[2]

Napoleon would scale back his grandiose plan to a pair of arches—the Arc de Triomphe du Carrousel and the Arc de Triomphe de l'Étoile based on Rome's most celebrated ancient models. As Diana Rowell explains, ". . . the Napoleonic regime mixed, manipulated and reinvented the language of Rome's various arch forms to create a particularly forceful instrument of contemporary propaganda."[3]

Like the Forum and Capitol of ancient Rome, the Louvre-Tuileries complex became France's cultural and political nerve center under Napoleon. He ordered a triumphal arch erected for the Place du Carrousel, located between the Louvre and Tuileries. In 1662, to celebrate the birth of his first child, Louis XIV turned the area into a parade ground. The cavalry performed an Italian-style pageant here known as a carrousel, giving the interior court its name.[4]

Napoleon's Arc de Triomphe du Carrousel would do double duty—creating an elegant entry for the Tuileries Palace and uniting the Louvre and Tuileries (an unrealized ambition of the Bourbon kings). Before the Battle of Austerlitz, Charles Percier and Pierre Fontaine planned to top the masonry guardhouses at the gate of the Place du Carrousel with two enormous lanterns. Now they tabled that idea and began designing a triumphant arch. The result was a sophisticated take on the Arches of Septimius Severus and Constantine, two of antiquity's most notable surviving arches.

The arch, which first appeared in the second millennium B.C.E., became hugely popular in ancient Rome. The architectural form featured in some of Rome's greatest engineering feats—including the Colosseum (70 to 80 C.E.) and the aqueducts that supplied fresh water to the city and its provinces. Commemorative or triumphal arches make their debut in the Roman Republic in the early second century B.C.E.; Scipio Africanus's triumph over the Carthaginians was among the earliest.

From Augustus on, the triumphal arch commemorated the victories of emperors in permanent, lasting form and celebrated the apotheosis of imperial power. As Christopher Tadgell explains, Augustus instituted the eastern inspired "cult of the emperor" in which divine rulers achieved apotheosis, joining the gods after their deaths.[5]

Triumphal arches were erected in the Forum, the heart of Rome's political and ceremonial life. Among the earliest of these was built by Augustus in 19 B.C.E. to celebrate a diplomatic coup—the surrender of standards captured by the Parthians. On top, Augustus is shown as a conqueror in a chariot drawn by four horses. To celebrate another victory over the Parthians, Nero built a triumphal arch in 62 C.E. on the sacred Capitoline Hill. Featuring sculpture and statues focusing on war and victory, the arch was topped with a quadriga driven by Nero, flanked by personifications of Peace and Victory.

The history of the Arch of Septimius Severus goes back to 192 C.E. when the elite Praetorian Guard murdered Roman emperor Commodus and confirmed Pertinax as his successor. When Pertinax tried to enforce new disciplinary measures, the Guard killed him too. Lifting Pertinax's head on a lance, they announced that the throne was available to the highest bidder—in this case Didius Julianus. Meanwhile, Septimius Severus, governor of the province of Pannonia was declared emperor by his own legions. Severus marched on Rome to avenge Pertinax. After a nine-week rule, Didius Julianus was also killed by the Praetorian Guard and forty-eight-year-old Severus was proclaimed emperor. One of Severus's first actions was to fire the Praetorians and recruit his own bodyguards.

Born into a wealthy family in Leptis Magna (today's Libya), Severus became a senator and rose through the ranks with posts in Sardinia, Spain, Gaul, Sicily, and Pannonia (today's western Hungary and parts of eastern Austria and several Balkan states). He grew up speaking Punic (Carthaginian), and learned Greek and Latin. As a widower, Severus married Syrian Julia Domna. Descended from a priestly caste, her family was preeminent in the cult of the sun god Elagabalus. The couple established a new dynasty with their sons Caracalla and Geta.

Having seized control by force after a bloody four-year civil war, Severus badly needed to legitimize his shaky new dynasty. "Physically strong but small" according to Cassius Dio, Severus had himself represented in portraits to resemble Marcus Aurelius and had himself and his family adopted into the Antonine family.[6] Toward this same end, the autocratic emperor glorified his victory over the Parthians with a spectacular triumphal arch.

For maximum impact, Severus chose the northwest corner of the Roman Forum, possibly where Severus's triumphal procession in 202 began its ascent to the Temple of Jupiter on the Capitoline Hill. The location was also diagonally across from Augustus's three bay Parthian arch, which may have been the model. The prestigious site reflected Severus's ambition for immortality. "By building the arch in the Forum," writes Susann Lusnia, "Severus forever enshrined himself and his family in one of Rome's most sacred and history-drenched locales. He put himself in the company of Vesta, Castor and Pollux, Saturn, and Concord, among the memories of great Romans and great events in Roman history."[7]

Dedicated in 203 C.E., the Arch of Septimius Severus featured a central passageway with a coffered semicircular vault and two smaller arches. The triumphal route ran through the central arch; steps led to the side passageways.[8] On the attic, an enormous gilded bronze dedicatory inscription praised Severus, his two sons, and their two victories over Parthia (modern Iran). Constructed of concrete, travertine, and marble, the arch measured over sixty-eight feet tall, seventy-six feet wide, and nearly thirty-seven feet deep. The eight freestanding columns and exterior facing were made of banded gray and white Proconnesian marble (from today's Marmara Island, Turkey). Travertine was used for much of the core of the arch.[9]

Instead of traditional half-columns, the Arch of Septimius Severus featured detached or freestanding fluted columns on tall pedestals. The bases of these columns featured reliefs of Roman soldiers and Parthian prisoners. Inside the south pier, a staircase led to the roof topped with a gilded bronze statue of Severus and his sons driving a two-wheeled chariot drawn by six horses. Facing the Arch was the *Equus Severi*, a colossal gilded bronze equestrian statue of the emperor.[10]

While military scenes had been used in the columns of Trajan and Marcus Aurelius and in complexes for specific emperors and dynasties, the Arch of Septimius Severus was Rome's first known triumphal arch with battle imagery as its central decoration.[11] Above each of the side arches are four enormous, richly decorated relief panels, possibly in Carrara marble, portraying major battles from the two Parthian wars. Battle imagery served a political and dynastic purpose. "The battle scenes were important elements of the propaganda message of Severus's Arch in the Forum," writes Susann

Lusnia. "The panels of the arch not only glorified the military exploits of the emperor and his sons, but also bore witness to the legitimacy of his sons' succession and the continuation of Severan rule at Rome."[12]

Though similar to the Columns of Trajan and Marcus Aurelius, the decoration of the arch may have been inspired by the brightly painted battle scenes commissioned by Severus and sent back to Rome for his triumphal procession, posits Maggie Popkin.[13] Such large scale panels were part of a tradition started during the Roman Republic. According to Richard Brilliant, the variety of styles in the relief panels indicates the hand of different sculptors or workshops, perhaps to help expedite completion of the monument.[14] Unlike his cookie-cutter soldiers, Severus is portrayed with physical accuracy.[15]

Weakened by gout and arthritis, Septimius Severus died in February 211 after an eighteen-year rule in the Roman town of Eboracum (today's York, Great Britain). Caracalla and Geta ignored their father's deathbed wish for them to rule as co-emperors. In December 211, Caracalla used his mother to lure Geta to a meeting where he was ambushed and killed. Five years later, an officer in the imperial bodyguard murdered the unpopular twenty-nine-year-old Caracalla. The mastermind of the assassination, Praetorian Guard commander Marcus Opellius Macrinus, succeeded him.

Though Septimius Severus's dynasty was short-lived, his arch had a lasting impact. A century later, Constantine adorned his own larger triumphal arch with similar war scenes. Like Severus, Constantine chose a highly visible location—the Triumphal Way next to the Colosseum, just before a turn into the Roman Forum and ascent to the Temple of Jupiter Optimus Maximus. Adding to the drama, the central passageway of Constantine's Arch framed a view of a colossal bronze statue of the sun god Sol by the sculptor Zenodorus.

It was Hadrian who moved the Colossus of Nero from the entrance of Nero's Golden House to make room for his Temple of Venus and Roma. According to Elizabeth Marlowe, Romans could not miss the gleaming sun god perfectly aligned with a figure of Constantine driving the quadriga on top of his Arch. The positioning advertised Constantine's worship of Sol, who appears several times in the Arch's sculptures and reliefs. "Like all Roman emperors before him," writes Marlowe, "Constantine . . . saw no contradiction between his worship of Christ and the worship of himself and his family in the traditional rites and practices of the Roman imperial cult."[16]

Begun in 312 and dedicated on July 25, 315 C.E., the Arch of Constantine celebrated the tenth anniversary of the emperor's reign. Carved on the attic or top section on both sides of the arch, the inscription read: "To the emperor Flavius Constantine the Great, pious and fortunate, who by divine inspiration and his own great spirit with his army avenged the state in rightful battle against the tyrant and all his faction, the Senate and the People of Rome dedicate this arch adorned with Triumphs."[17] The "tyrant" was Emperor Maxentius, whose six-year reign ended at the Battle of the Milvian Bridge in 312.

Like the Arch of Septimius Severus, the Arch of Constantine featured a triple bay—a large central passage flanked by two smaller passageways. Each façade has four freestanding Corinthian columns on tall pedestals. The carved decoration combines an assortment of Constantinian decoration and *spolia*, art removed from earlier monuments. The fourth-century reliefs include spandrels with victories and river gods, column pedestals, two roundels on the short sides, and a frieze depicting Constantine's defeat of Maxentius and his entry into Rome on a quadriga.

From the second century came four statues of Dacians and the Great Trajanic Frieze, likely removed from Trajan's Forum. Measuring ten feet high and over fifty-eight feet long, the continuous bas-relief of carved battle scenes was cut into four panels and recycled for the main passageway and the attic of the short sides of the Arch of Constantine. Flanking the inscription are four reliefs from the age of Commodus featuring scenes from the life of Marcus Aurelius. Eight circular marble reliefs depicting hunting and sacrificial scenes were removed from a Hadrianic monument that did not survive. Portraits of second-century emperors were replaced with likenesses of Constantine.

The purpose of the spolia appears to be political. As Emidio De Albentiis explains, having seized power after a bloody civil war, Constantine sought legitimacy through association with illustrious predecessors like Trajan, Hadrian, Domitian, and Marcus Aurelius.[18] Constantine's power grab goes back to Diocletian who formed the Tetrarchy in 293, naming Maximian as co-Augustus, and Galerius and his father Constantius as subordinate

Caesars. The arrangement lasted a short time. The ambitious Constantine defeated his rivals and reunited the Eastern and Western halves of the Roman Empire in 324. Symbolizing the end of the Tetrarchy, Constantine's Arch was "the first state monument to depict civil war explicitly in its sculptural decoration," writes Maggie Popkin.[19]

The Arch of Constantine was one of Rome's last official works. In 330, after Constantine transferred his court to Constantinople, Rome was abandoned. Roman architecture continued to be a model for Constantinople's building program which included the Hippodrome, aqueducts, and the Hagia Sophia. Under Constantine, Christianity replaced paganism as the main religion of the Roman Empire. During the early Christian period, the triumphal arch's military and political symbolism was replaced with religious associations. Roman architects added arches between the nave and apse of churches, alluding to Christian triumph over death. During the Middle Ages, the Arch of Septimius Severus was incorporated into a church and fortress by the Frangipani family, with towers added to the top. Parts of the monument were lost in the process, including the original crowning equestrian statuary.

The Roman arch continued to be a popular for Renaissance churches. Leon Battista Alberti used the single arch for the nave and façade of the Church of Sant'Andrea in Mantua; Andrea Palladio added arches to the façades of San Giorgio Maggiore and the Redentore in Venice.[20] From the early sixteenth century, temporary arches made of wooden frames and banners or canvases became a feature of royal entries into cities. Albrecht Dürer supervised a huge triumphal arch woodcut for Holy Roman Emperor Maximilian I who gave hundreds of copies away as gifts. Palladio designed an arch for a visit to Venice by France's Henri III in 1574. Temporary arches were erected for the coronation processions of the popes through Rome.

Rome's Arch of Septimius Severus had long been a favorite of artists. From the Renaissance on, attempts had been made to excavate the half-buried monument, including a request by Percier and Fontaine. In 1803, Pius VII commissioned Carlo Fea to excavate and build a retaining wall. Now Percier and Fontaine turned to the arch for their most impressive work, the Arc de Triomphe du Carrousel.[21] With their help, Napoleon revived Rome's triumphal arch, long associated with imperial power.

The first stone for the Arc de Triomphe du Carrousel was laid on July 7, 1806. Leaving the passage free on its four faces, the arch offered a triumphal entrance to the Tuileries. Percier and Fontaine used the three arch format of the Arches of Septimius Severus and Constantine. From the Arch of Septimius Severus, the designers borrowed rectangular reliefs over the lateral arches. Like the Arch of Constantine, Percier and Fontaine used colored marble. "With red marble columns and bronze capitals and bases, the Arch was the first work of 19th-century French architecture to break with the classical tradition of monochrome masonry," writes Jean-Philippe Garric.[22]

Much to Fontaine's annoyance, Dominique-Vivant Denon participated in the Arc de Triomphe du Carrousel project. In his *Journal*, Fontaine had this to say about his rival: "The director of the painting museum, M. Denon, whose taste and pretensions in art are not in agreement with ours, is one of those unwelcome flies which cannot be caught, and against which one must have patience."[23]

According to Pierre Rosenberg, former director of the Louvre, his predecessor Denon played a role for Napoleon similar to that of culture minister André Malraux for French president Charles de Gaulle. Like Malraux, Denon understood the political power of cultural display. He was "a man of action, a practical man, an organizer."[24]

For the Arc de Triomphe du Carrousel, Denon took a page from the playbook of Septimius Severus. In the third century, the Roman emperor ordered that his victories be painted and exhibited. According to Clifford Ando, Severus "understood the need to inform Rome about his activities in spite of his inability to be in Rome himself."[25] Similarly, Denon saw that Napoleon's military achievements were lauded in Paris where he spent little time. The Arc de Triomphe du Carrousel functioned in a similar way as the Arch of Septimius Severus.

The Arc de Triomphe du Carrousel was decorated with bas-reliefs, with subjects chosen by Denon and designed by Charles Meynier. A team of neoclassical artists executed Meynier's sculptural program, including Clodion, Claude Ramey, Pierre Cartellier, Jean-Joseph Espercieux, Louis-Pierre Deseine, and Jacques-Philippe Le Sueur.[26] Resting on pilasters, the eight rose marble columns (four to each façade) were topped with statues of French soldiers in full dress uniform—reminiscent of the Dacian prisoners above the columns of the Arch of Constantine taken from Trajan's Forum.

Denon also oversaw the decoration for the top of the arch, commissioning a gilded lead sculptural group from François-Frédéric Lemot. Napoleon, dressed as a Roman triumphator, drove a chariot of Victory drawn by four horses, flanked by two figures of Fame. In modeling Napoleon's face, writes Thierry Sarmant, Lemot may have been inspired by his pupil Lorenzo Bartolini's massive bronze bust for the Musée Napoléon.[27] The work was to be made of gilded lead—a material as solid as bronze, but three times less expensive.[28]

The horses were extraordinary. The arch would be capped by the antique gilded bronze horses nabbed in 1798 by Napoleon from St. Mark's Basilica in Venice. Scholars suggest they were made in the Roman imperial period between the second half of the second century or early third century C.E. Around 330 C.E., Constantine transported them to Constantinople (today's Istanbul) where he had them installed atop the triumphal gate leading into the Hippodrome, symbol of Byzantine grandeur.

During the Fourth Crusade in 1204, Western European armies led by Venice sacked Constantinople, bringing about the fall of the Byzantine Empire. During the pillage, many of the Hippodrome's bronze statues were melted down and turned into coins. Other treasures were taken to Venice, including the ancient horses. After fifty years in the Venice Arsenale, the expressive horses with their flaring nostrils and green patina caught the eye of Florentine ambassadors and were placed in pairs in the loggia over the central portal of St. Mark's Basilica. Through the centuries, the horses hadn't lost their association with triumph and imperial power.

For the drapery of Napoleon's statue, Lemot combined the paludamentum, a cloak worn by Roman dignitaries, and the full-length ceremonial costume of an emperor. Lemot referred to the emperor's official iconography from François Gérard's painting of Napoleon I in his coronation robes. Napoleon grasps the pommel of his sheathed sword, part of the "honors of Charlemagne" restored for his coronation. In his right hand, he holds the imperial scepter topped by the eagle. Together with the laurel wreath crown, they symbolized Victory in ancient Rome. The emperor also wears the chain of the Legion of Honor, composed of eagles linked with rings.

To affirm his image as a modern ruler, Napoleon ordered that the inscription for the Arc de Triomphe du Carrousel be in French, not Latin: "At the Voice of the Victor of Austerlitz/The German Empire Falls/The Confederation of the Rhine Begins/The Kingdoms of Bavaria and Wuerttemberg Are Created/Venice is Reunited to the Iron Crown/Entire Italy Ranges Herself/Under the Laws of Her Liberator."

In the end, Napoleon was disappointed in the Arc de Triomphe du Carrousel's lack of monumentality. The pink marble columns, Carrara marble, and bronze bases and capitals gave it a more delicate appearance than its ancient models in Rome. The emperor described the elegant Arc de Triomphe du Carrousel as a "pavilion" rather than a triumphal arch. A second more grandiose arch would not disappoint.

⚜

Napoleon originally wanted to locate his second triumphal arch near the former Bastille in the eastern part of Paris. The prison had been demolished and the area was in need of a makeover. But his interior minister Jean-Baptiste de Champagny appointed a committee of architects and sculptors to come up with a recommendation. In April 1806, Champagny wrote Napoleon, proposing the tollgate at Étoile at the end of the Champs-Élysées:

"This place is, in a way, part of the most beautiful district of Paris . . . It will leave the person going away from the capital a profound souvenir of its incomparable beauty. Although a long way away, he will always be in front of the Triumphant General. Your Majesty will cross it when going to Malmaison, Saint-Germain, Saint-Cloud, and even Versailles."[29]

The site had been laid out in the seventeenth century by Louis XIV's landscape architect André Le Nôtre. At that time, the Grand Cours was renamed the Champs-Élysées, French for "Elysian Fields," the paradise for dead heroes in Greek mythology. At the top of the hill, Le Nôtre added an octagonal square planted with rows of trees, called the *butte de l'Étoile*.[30]

With its west-east orientation, the monument would be the start of a triumphal way, like Rome's Via Sacra, replacing the royal medieval north-south axis along the rue Saint Denis (in 1671, French architect Nicolas-François Blondel created a permanent triumphal arch at Porte St.-Denis, Paris's city gates). In direct line with the future Arc de Triomphe du Carrousel, its elevated location at the west end of Paris offered a spectacular perspective along with sunset views. Napoleon personally approved the location on May 9.[31]

But there was disagreement over what form the monument should take. Some of Napoleon's advisers argued for a triumphal column; others favored an obelisk. Both Champagny and his successor Crétet lobbied for an arch, as did Pierre Fontaine, provided it was monumental in scale. "In such an elevated place, it is absolutely necessary that this monument be of colossal size," Fontaine declared.[32]

After initially favoring an obelisk, Napoleon changed his mind a few days later in favor of an arch. After an open contest, the submissions of Jean-François-Thérèse Chalgrin and Jean-Arnaud Raymond were shortlisted.[33] However, the designers did not see eye to eye and wound up submitting two rival proposals to Napoleon.[34] Rome-trained Chalgrin was inspired by classical antiquity; Raymond by the Italian Renaissance.

Chalgrin's Church of Saint-Philippe-du-Roule was one of Paris's first sacred buildings in the neoclassical style. The architect's ties to aristocratic patrons led to his imprisonment during the Revolution. In 1795, Chalgrin was appointed to the Conseil des Bâtiments; three years later he succeeded Charles de Wailly at the Institut de France. Between 1803 and 1807, Chalgrin renovated his former prison in the Palais de Luxembourg, adding a semicircular Senate Room toward the rear of the palace. Until he was succeeded by Percier and Fontaine in 1805, Jean-Arnaud Raymond had been architect to the Louvre.

Ultimately, Chalgrin prevailed. By imperial decree in the fall of 1808, the Paris-born, Grand Prix–winning architect became sole designer of the Arc de Triomphe.[35] Fontaine, who Napoleon consulted on the project, believed that columns would be lost in the distant view of the Arch. Of the nearly forty surviving ancient Roman arches, Fontaine suggested the column-less fourth-century Janus Arch as a model. Janus, the Roman god of gates and passages, carried protective associations. Chalgrin instead chose the Arch of Titus, one of Rome's best known landmarks. Chalgrin's plan was adopted by imperial decree on March 27, 1809.

In contrast with Percier and Fontaine's Arc de Triomphe du Carrousel, Chalgrin emphasized monumentality. Keeping the Arch of Titus's exact proportions, he supersized the ancient monument and abandoned columns for smooth pillar surfaces. Measuring 167 feet high and 148 feet wide, the Arc de Triumphe would nearly double the Arch of Titus. Like the view from the Arch of Septimius Severus at the lower end of the Forum to the Arch of Titus, the Arc de Triomphe du Carrousel would offer a magnificent view to the Arc de Triumphe.

During the Middle Ages, the Arch of Titus had been incorporated into the Frangipani stronghold in the Forum; its single passage used as a gate. Thanks to this, the arch was not dismantled as spolia. But the ancient decoration was damaged by the gate brackets; the arch itself suffered during fighting in the tweflth and thirteenth centuries. In the early nineteenth century, architects Raffaele Stern and Giuseppe Valadier restored the famous monument, demolishing the flanking houses, dismantling and reassembling the arch, and restoring missing pieces in travertine.[36]

The eldest son of Flavian emperor Vespasian, Titus seized power following civil chaos in 69 C.E., the bloody "Year of the Four Emperors." After the civil war, the Flavians needed a foreign victory to gain legitimacy. In the summer of 71, Vespasian and Titus crushed a revolt in Judea and the honor of the triumph was conferred jointly. The procession of spoils from the Second Temple of Jerusalem rivaled anything Rome had ever seen.

Jerusalem-born historian Josephus who served as Titus's translator during the Roman siege of the city, described the Temple sanctuary: "This structure was ninety feet high, ninety feet long, and thirty feet wide. Its length, however, was divided into two parts. The first hall was sixty feet long, and contained three of the world's most incredible and famous works of art: the lampstand, the table, and the incense altar. The lampstand, which branched into seven lamps, symbolized the seven planets; the twelve loaves of bread on the table represented the circle of the Zodiac and the year; the altar of incense is kept replenished with thirteen aromatic incenses collected from both land and sea, and from places both inhabited and deserted, thus symbolizing that all creation is of God and for God."[37] In 71, Josephus traveled to Rome where he became a citizen and wrote his works under the name Flavius Titus Josephus, after his patrons.

Following the sack of Jerusalem, Titus began an affair with Berenice, daughter of Herod Agrippa I, whose family ruled Rome's Judaea Province. When Berenice and her brother Agrippa traveled to Rome in 75, she and Titus lived together. But four years later, when Titus succeeded his father Vespasian as emperor, public pressure forced him to break up with his unpopular lover, some eleven years his senior. Titus rebuilt cities in Campania destroyed by the eruption of Vesuvius in 79 and opened the Coliseum with one hundred days of festivities. In 81 C.E., after just two years in power, Titus died of the plague.

Too young to take part in the Judean war, Domitian exploited his older brother's popularity with a posthumous triumphal arch. Located at the highest point of the Sacred Way, the Arch of Titus symbolically linked the Flavian's monumental Colosseum with the Roman Forum. Rabirius, Emperor Domitian's talented architect, may have helped design the fifty-one-foot-tall arch constructed of marble from Greece's Penteliko Mountains.

The top panel featured a Latin inscription in large capital letters gilded with bronze: "The Senate and the Roman people to the deified Titus Vespasian Augustus the son of the deified Vespasian." To placate members of the Senate unhappy with his attempt to divinize the Flavians, Domitian placed the word "senatus" first in even larger letters. Flanking each side of the arch on square pedestals are engaged and fluted columns with rare Composite style capitals.

Inside its barrel vault are two deeply carved reliefs, among Rome's most famous. On one panel, Romans soldiers are shown in the triumphal procession of 71 C.E. carrying the treasures taken from the Temple in Jerusalem on wooden stretchers. The booty includes a seven-branched Menorah, silver trumpets, and the gold shewbread table that held twelves loaves of bread representing the twelve tribes of Israel. The actual treasures were placed in the new Temple of Peace in Vespasian's Forum.

The opposite panel depicts Titus driving a triumphal quadriga as the helmeted goddess Roma leads the horses and Victory crowns the emperor with laurels. A young man, representing the Roman people, and an older man, symbolizing the Senate, follow. The coffered vaulting, or soffit, features sculptured rosettes; a central relief depicts the apotheosis, or divinization, of Titus with the emperor carried to heaven on the back of an eagle. The arch possibly served as Titus's tomb. Inside the attic is a spiral staircase and chamber that may have contained an urn with his remains.

Domitian went on a building spree, replacing the public buildings of Vespasian and Titus with palatial architecture. Rabirius's masterpiece was the Domus Augustana, a palace for his patron on top of the Palatine Hill. He also designed the Alban Villa on the shore of Lake Albanus (now enclosed in the papal gardens at Castel Gandolfo), renovated the temple of Jupiter Optimus Maximus on the Capitoline, and rebuilt the temple of Venus Genetrix in the Forum of Julius Caesar, damaged in a fire during Titus's reign.

Megalomaniacal, Domitian insisted on being addressed as lord and god and dramatically reduced the power of the Senate. After fifteen years in power, he was assassinated in 96 C.E., bringing an end to the Flavian dynasty. The Flavians were succeeded briefly by the elderly Nerva followed by Trajan.

Unlike Domitian's Arch of Titus, Napoleon's Arc de Triomphe was plagued by setbacks. After the first stone was laid on the emperor's birthday, August 15, 1806, another two years went by just to lay the foundation because of the site's highly porous, chalky soil. To support the weight of the colossal monument, a large underground platform had to be constructed. In a symbolic move, Napoleon insisted that the structure honoring his Grande Armée be made of French stone. Work slowed when the original white stone of L'Isle-Adam was replaced with a harder stone from Château-Landon near Nemours where a new quarry had to be opened. Political and financial problems, along with Chalgrin's death in 1811, further slowed progress.

Napoleon would not live to see the Arc de Triomphe. After three decades and a succession of regimes and architects, his arch was finally finished in 1836 under King Louis Philippe. Dedicated to the military victories of the French Revolution and the First Empire, the Arc de Triomphe surpassed its ancient model in both scale and splendor. Like Titus, Napoleon was glorified along with dozens of his greatest battles and hundreds of his generals.

Soon after its completion, Victor Hugo wrote a poem about the new monument, "À l'Arc de Triomphe": Three thousand years from now, when people will talk about Napoleon in the same way as they now do of Cyrus, when the Seine will be choked with stones, and all Paris except Notre Dame, the Vendôme column, and the Arc de Triomphe has fallen into ruin, a man resting on a hill at dusk when the mists have begun to fall will be lost in wonder at the scene and then the monument will truly at last have what it now lacks."[38]

THREE

TEMPLE TO THE GRANDE ARMÉE

In the summer of 1806, Napoleon organized a group of sixteen south and west German states into a defensive buffer known as the Confederation of the Rhine. As a signing bonus to would-be members, Napoleon promoted the electors of Württemberg and Bavaria to kings and the electors of the smaller Baden to grand dukes. For added insurance, Napoleon married off his brother Jérôme to Catherine de Württemberg, daughter of the new king Frederick I of Württemberg. Similarly, Napoleon arranged for his stepson Eugène de Beauharnais to wed Princess Amalia of Bavaria, eldest daughter of Maximilian I, the first king of Bavaria.

On August 1, the new Confederation of the Rhine declared it was no longer part of the Holy Roman Empire. Austria's Francis II had no choice but abandon his title of Holy Roman Emperor and settle for a diminished role as Francis I, Emperor of Austria. After a millennium, Charlemagne's Holy Roman Empire ceased to exist. At a Diet in Erfurt in 1808, four kings and thirty-four princes of the Confederation of the Rhine paid tribute to Napoleon as Europe's de facto ruler.

Refusing to participate, Francis received a threatening letter from Napoleon: "It was in my power to destroy the Austrian monarchy. What your Majesty is, is by virtue of our will."[1] Prussia's Frederick William III considered the Confederation a threat and joined a renewed coalition against Napoleon. "The idea that Prussia could take the field against me by herself seems so ridiculous that it does not merit discussion," declared Napoleon.

At Saint-Cloud, Napoleon planned his next move—defeating Prussia before Russian reinforcements arrived. On September 25, 1806, he left Paris to join the Grande Armée, arriving in Mainz three days later. Within a week, Frederick William delivered an ultimatum to Talleyrand to dissolve the Confederation and withdraw the Grande Armée.

It took Napoleon just three weeks to crush the Prussian army. On October 14, the twin battles of Jena and Auerstädt west of the Saale River left an estimated 38,000 Prussians and 12,000 French dead or wounded. A week later, Napoleon confiscated the Prussians territories in between the Rhine and the Elbe, the states belonging to the Duke of Brunswick, Hanover, and the territory around Osnabrück.

Napoleon and the Grande Armée reached Potsdam on October 25. Despite his easy defeat of Prussia, Napoleon appears to have been moved by the memory of Frederick William's great uncle, Frederick the Great. Just before becoming emperor, Napoleon stated that Frederick was the man whose history he most wanted to read because he understood his "business in every sort of way." A "great statesman . . . is a completely eccentric personage, who stands always alone . . ." wrote Napoleon.[2]

The eccentric Frederick II put Prussia on the map, taking on the rest of Europe in the Seven Years' War. Like Napoleon, Prussia's king was an avid reader of history, adopting military strategies from ancient battles. An ardent Francophile, Frederick spoke French and collected eighteenth-century French art.[3]

When Julius Caesar visited Alexandria, he famously paid his respects to the tomb of Alexander the Great. The Roman poet Lucan derided Caesar's visit as a stunt, "one demented despot paying homage to another." Now on the night of his arrival in Potsdam, Napoleon visited Frederick the

Great's tomb in the large, dimly lit crypt of the Garrison Church. After the seventy-four-year-old's death in 1786, Frederick William II ignored his uncle's wish to be buried near the terraced vineyards of his Potsdam retreat Sanssouci by his beloved greyhounds. Instead, the new king had his uncle entombed in the same church as his ruthless father, Frederick William I.

On entering the crypt, Napoleon reportedly told his generals: "Hats off, gentlemen! If he were alive, we would not be here." Napoleon then stood silently before Frederick's tomb. About the visit, a member of his entourage recalled: "He [Napoleon] walked rather hurriedly at first, but as he drew near the church, he moderated his pace, which became slower still and more measured as he approached the remains of the great king to whom he had come to pay homage. The door of the monument was open; and he stopped at the entrance in a grave and meditative attitude. His glances seemed to penetrate the gloom which reigned around these august ashes, and he remained there nearly ten minutes, motionless and silent, as if absorbed in profound thought."[4]

About Frederick, Napoleon later wrote: "The battle of Leuthen is a masterpiece of operations, maneuvers, and resolution. By itself it would be enough to immortalize Frederick and place him among the greatest generals." To this he added, "What distinguishes Frederick most is not the cleverness of his moves but his boldness."[5] Napoleon's esteem for the Prussian king did not prevent him from turning two of Potsdam's churches into horse stables.

On the afternoon of October 28, to the strains of "The Marseillaise," Napoleon paraded through Berlin's Brandenburg Gate. Following Napoleon were twenty thousand grenadiers, an honor guard of cuirassiers (cavalrymen wearing a breastplate called a cuirass), and foot and horse-guards. Though some curious Berliners turned out to witness the triumphal entry, the streets of the Prussian capital were largely empty. Thousands had fled, including Frederick William and his court, which retreated to the Baltic seaport of Memel.

Napoleon's army was dressed to kill, so to speak. Embroidery and lace, plumes, towering helmets, breastplates, dolmans, and bear and tiger skins adorned the military uniforms.[6] The Grande Armée's impressive costumes had an ancient precedent. Julius Caesar reportedly equipped his soldiers richly, including weapons inlaid with silver and gold. "Roman soldiers, like most of their kind before and since, undoubtedly found pleasure in parade and display," writes H. Russell Robinson, "and both legionaries and auxiliaries would have strutted around in their glistening finery . . . their gilded, silvered and tinned belt fittings, inlaid daggers, decorated swords and shield bosses, and tinned and enameled helmet fittings all add up to a very brilliant ensemble."[7]

In contrast to Marshals Berthier, Davout, and Augereau in their splendid gold-embroidered uniforms and ornate hats, Napoleon wore a plain gray overcoat and black felt bicorn hat that day. "Not everyone has the right to dress simply," he said. Rather than wear his bicorn with the corners pointing forward and back, Napoleon turned his hat sideways. Unlike his generals whose bicorns sported elaborate braiding and feathers, the emperor ordered eight plain bicorns annually from the Parisian hat maker Poupard, and had them broken in by his valets.[8]

About the Grande Armée's entry into Berlin, imperial guard Captain Jean-Roch Coignet wrote: ". . . it was a curious sight to see the worst-dressed man the master of such a splendid army. The people were gazing out of the windows as the Parisians did on the day we came back from Austerlitz. . . . We drew up in line of battle in front of the [Charlottenburg] palace, which is isolated by beautiful squares in front and at the back of it, and a handsome square filled with trees, where the great Frederick stands on a pedestal with his little gaiters on."[9]

Napoleon was "the worst-dressed man" by careful calculation, choosing to stand out from his officers and generals on the battlefield. From Berlin, Denon wrote François Gérard about a new commission, instructing the painter to ". . . put a great deal of magnificence in the costume of the officers who surround the Emperor, since this contrasts with the simplicity which he affects, which makes him suddenly distinguished among them."[10] Napoleon's unique sartorial style became a potent symbol and led his enemies to call him "The Bat." For the upcoming 1807 campaign, Napoleon donned a bicorn lined in olive-brown silk with an interior circumference over twenty-three inches—relatively large for his five-foot-six-inch stature.[11]

Napoleon did own an ornate ceremonial breastplate, a gift from the arms makers of Paris. Designed by Denon, the chiseled brass and steel cuirass likened Napoleon to Mars, the Roman god of war. Wearing a breastplate, boots, and a helmet, the figure of Mars holds a shield with two winged griffins in his left hand and adjusts his helmet with his right. His skirt is carved with various animal heads including lions, rams, and eagles. As Anne Forray-Carlier notes, the two nude spirits around Mars evoke depictions of angels surrounding Christ in the Ascension.[12]

Over six hundred fragments of cuirassed statues survive from the Greco-Roman world.[13] Arguably the most famous example is the *Prima Porta Augustus* (circa 15 C.E.), a six-foot-tall Parian marble sculpture of Rome's first emperor discovered in 1863 at an imperial villa north of Rome. Made to imitate the bronze battle costume, Augustus's elaborately decorated cuirass combined mythological and contemporary events.

The afternoon that Napoleon occupied Berlin, he directed Denon to remove the quadriga on top of the Brandenburg Gate and ship it to Paris. Commissioned by Frederick William II and modeled on the Propylaia or gate of the Acropolis in Athens, the Brandenburg Gate was inaugurated in 1791 to celebrate the Prussian army's victories. Denon visited the quadriga designer, sculptor Johann Gottfried Schadow, to discuss logistics for its removal. "Denon is most certainly one of the most lively phenomenons [sic] of our era, and it will be a mistake to let him go without seeing him," the sculptor wrote. The chased copper statue of Victory and her four-horse chariot were disassembled and packed into a dozen enormous crates. By December, the sculpture was on its way to Paris.

Frederick William left Berlin's royal palace Charlottenburg empty. For almost a month, Napoleon occupied Frederick the Great's former office. Just as he had done with Charlemagne in Aachen, Napoleon collected memorabilia relating to Frederick the Great. In November, he ordered a marble bust of the Prussian king transferred from Berlin to Paris, adding an inscription regarding its capture. At the same time, he pilfered a bronze model of a statue of Frederick's ancestor, the Great Elector. From Sanssouci, Napoleon took Frederick's large silver watch.[14]

Corresponding with his arch-chancellor Cambacérès, Napoleon directed that Frederick the Great's flags, sword, and decorations be installed in a May 1807 ceremony in Paris at Les Invalides, a retirement home for veterans.[15]

Napoleon dedicated Frederick's sword to the resident veterans—some nine hundred of whom had fought in the Seven Years' War.[16]

Like his military heroes, Napoleon understood that his power and authority depended on the support of his army. He went to great lengths to cement a lasting bond with his soldiers. In this regard, he was following the lead of Julius Caesar, whose soldiers trusted him unconditionally.[17] On his deathbed in 211 in York, Roman emperor Septimius Severus reportedly told his feuding sons: "Be harmonious, enrich the soldiers, and scorn all other men." France's own hero General Turenne was also beloved by his soldiers as was Frederick the Great.

"Bonaparte's reception by the troops was nothing short of rapturous," recalled Claire de Rémusat. "It was well worth seeing how he talked to the soldiers—how he questioned them one after the other respecting their campaigns or their wounds, taking particular interest in the men who had accompanied him to Egypt. I have heard Madame Bonaparte say that her husband was in the constant habit of poring over the list of what are called the cadres of the army at night before he slept. He would go to sleep repeating the names of the corps, and even those of some of the individuals who composed them; he kept these names in a corner of his memory, and this habit came to his aid when he wanted to recognize a soldier and to give him the pleasure of a cheering word from his general. He spoke to the subalterns in a tone of good fellowship, which delighted them all, as he reminded them of their common feats of arms.

"Afterwards when his armies became so numerous and his battles so deadly, he disdained to exercise this kind of fascination. Besides, death had extinguished so many remembrances that in a few years it became difficult for him to find any great number of the companies of his early exploits; and when he addressed his soldiers before leading them into battle, it was as a perpetually renewed posterity to which the preceding and destroyed army had bequeathed its glory. But even this somber style of encouragement availed for a long time with a nation which believed itself to be fulfilling its destiny while sending its sons year after year to die for Bonaparte."[18]

The Grande Armée's latest round of victories in northern Germany supplied more treasures for the Musée Napoléon. Between November 1806 and June 1807, Denon scoured the palaces, galleries, and museums of Cassel,

Brunswick, Schwerin, Berlin, Potsdam, Danzig, and Warsaw. In the hunt, he was assisted by artist Benjamin Zix who often acted as his translator. Ultimately, Denon filled 250 cases with several thousand paintings, sculptures, and drawings. Unlike in Italy, there were no treaties including art.

From art-loving Frederick the Great's prized gallery at Sanssouci, Vivant Denon hand-picked 123 pictures and fifty-six antique busts and reliefs, along with a treasure chest of antique medals from the king's coin cabinet.[19] Among the painted masterworks was Correggio's *Leda and the Swan*, part of the artist's series for the Duke of Mantua. Before its arrival at Sanssouci, the picture had belonged to many renowned collections, including that of France's Duke of Orléans.

After the victory at Jena, Napoleon deposed the Elector of Hesse-Cassel, William I (who had declared himself neutral in the conflict), adding the domain to the Kingdom of Westphalia. At William I's residence in Cassel, Denon discovered 1,600 paintings. He reportedly told the gallery keeper, painter J. H. Tischbein, that he had never had such a difficult choice "because these are all pearls and jewels."[20]

The quality of the art surprised the discerning Denon. "I have just come from Cassel, where I have made an ample harvest of superb things," he wrote. "In all, I shall have gathered a crop that cannot be compared to that of Italy, but which is far above what I had hoped for from Germany."[21] Among Denon's "crop" of 299 paintings were eight Rembrandts, three Rubenses, five Claude Lorrains, and one Titian. Four dozen of the pictures wound up at Malmaison after being discovered packed and hidden in a vault (these would later be acquired from Joséphine's son by Russia's Alexander I).[22]

Nearby in Brunswick, Denon grabbed another forty-two sculptures, eighty-five paintings, and 174 enameled Limoges objects. From the cathedral in Danzig, Denon plucked Hans Memling's early altarpiece, the *Last Judgement*. Painted between 1467 and 1471 for Angelo Tani, the Medici's representative in Bruge, the triptych measured over seven feet tall and nearly ten feet wide.[23]

On December 11, 1806, the Treaty of Posen brought Saxony into the Confederation of the Rhine. Napoleon named the Saxon elector Frederick Augustus I king of Saxony, enlarging the realm with territory seized from

Prussia, his former ally. In Berlin, Denon tried to persuade Napoleon to include an article in the treaty for masterpieces from the Dresden gallery, considered the greatest German art museum. After learning about Denon's scheme, Frederick Augustus insisted on meeting Denon in Berlin. Saxony's quick alliance with Napoleon spared the gallery.

Austria and Prussia had surrendered, but Russia remained a threat. Before leaving the Prussian capital on November 21, Napoleon issued the Berlin Decree, forbidding the import of British goods into European countries allied with France. From Berlin, Napoleon marched his army into Poland. In Warsaw, Napoleon issued an imperial decree for a bridge in Paris overlooking the military school to be named the Pont d'Iéna or Jena Bridge after his recent victory (today the bridge links the Eiffel Tower and Trocadéro). The tympana along the sides of the five arch bridge would be adorned with imperial eagles designed by François-Frédéric Lemot and sculpted by Jean-François Mouret.

While in Warsaw, Napoleon learned of a surprise Russian attack. On February 7 in a blinding snowstorm at Eylau, 130 miles from the Russian border, he struck back. On June 14, the Grande Armée fought the Russian army in Friedland (today's Kaliningrad). The carnage on both sides was terrible—seventy thousand French and Russian soldiers killed or wounded. On June 25, Alexander I traveled to Tilsit on the western border of Russia to negotiate peace. To symbolize their equal status, Alexander met Napoleon on a raft in the center of the Niemen River, the boundary between Russia and Europe. Alexander told Napoleon in French: "Sir, I hate the English as much as you do." To which Napoleon replied, "So we have made peace."[24]

Napoleon did not demand territory. In return, Russia became France's ally and joined the Continental System, Napoleon's blockade against Britain. The Grand Duchy of Warsaw was created from Prussia's Polish provinces. French troops would occupy Prussia until it paid a war indemnity of 140 million francs. Over the next two weeks, Alexander and Napoleon enjoyed a bromance, inspecting each other's armies and awarding medals to soldiers on both sides. Charmed by Catherine the Great's beloved grandson, Napoleon described him as "especially handsome, like a hero with all the graces of an amiable Parisian."

In December 1807, Napoleon named his brother Jérôme King of Westphalia, a new kingdom created in northern Germany from Prussian real estate and land seized from Hesse-Cassel, Brunswick, and southern Hanover. Mecklenburg and several other small principalities also joined the Confederation of the Rhine. By 1808, Napoleon's buffer state boasted thirty-nine members.

⚜

Napoleon's obsession with monumental architecture continued. After his 1804 coronation, suggestions had been made to turn Paris's unfinished Church of the Madeleine into either a parish church or one dedicated to Pius VII.

The history of the Place de la Madeleine dated back seven centuries. The site was consecrated to the biblical figure Mary Magdalene in the tweflth century, when a cult linked to her relics emerged. According to tradition, after the crucifixion, Mary Magdalene traveled from the Holy Land to Provence where she converted the French to Christianity.

Louis XV decided to replace the old parish Church of Sainte-Marie-Madeleine de la Ville l'Évêque with a more stately building. The goal was to close the view along the rue Royale looking north from the Place Louis XV, the largest of Paris's three royal squares (today's Place de la Concorde).[25] Plagued by criticism, architect Pierre Constant d'Ivry made numerous changes to his design, modeled after the domed Baroque church at Les Invalides. After d'Ivry's death in 1777, his successor Guillaume-Martin Couture le Jeune demolished the unfinished building and started a new church based on the Panthéon. Couture's plan also proved unpopular.

After the Revolution, there were a number of ideas for secularizing the unfinished church, including a festival hall, national assembly, and national library. More proposals followed during the Consulate, among them a tribunal and a Temple of Concord.[26] In February 1806, Napoleon announced a plan for a business district at the site, consisting of the Stock Exchange, Bank of France, and the Court of Commerce.

But Paris's bankers pushed back on the idea, disliking the less than central location (in 1808, the Bank acquired the count of Toulouse's former mansion in the rue de la Vrillière for its headquarters). Pierre Fontaine also weighed in, suggesting a national assembly or opera house.[27]

On December 2, 1806, from his military camp in Posen, Poland, Napoleon ended the long-running debate. An imperial decree turned the Church of the Madeleine into a "Temple to the Glory of the Great Army" after the Athenian Acropolis. "I have in mind a monument like many were in Athens and of which there is none in Paris."[28]

Napoleon provided detailed instructions. In addition to displaying enemy flags and trophies, the temple was to have marble tablets inscribed with the names of soldiers from the battles of Ulm, Austerlitz, and Jena, and bas-reliefs and marble statues of his colonels and marshals. Between preparations for the battle of Friedland, Napoleon wrote Interior Minister Champagny instructing him to organize a contest for the design of the temple.

From some eighty anonymous submissions, a jury of judges awarded first prize to architect Claude-Etienne de Beaumont in spring 1807. Beaumont's design featured a vast commemorative program composed of ornaments and sculpture that met Napoleon's requirements including statues of marshals and the names of war casualties engraved on silver or gold tables. But after receiving the top four entries at his camp in Finkelstein, Napoleon replied to Champagny that Beaumont's plan had been the first he rejected.

As he often did, Napoleon overruled the jury's decision, awarding the commission to Pierre-Alexandre Vignon, protégé of neoclassical architect Claude-Nicolas Ledoux. Vignon's proposal most closely resembled Napoleon's vision for a monumental neoclassical temple. "It is the only one that fulfills my intention," wrote Napoleon. "It is a temple that I asked for and not a church. What could be done in the style of the churches which was in the case of fighting with St. Genevieve, even with Notre Dame and especially with St. Peter's in Rome?"[29]

Napoleon ordered that the quadriga from Berlin's Brandenburg Gate be placed outside the new temple. But the quadriga arrived in Paris in June 1807 damaged from the journey. Vivant Denon wrote his rival Fontaine asking for permission to use the Orangery at the Musée Napoléon for three months to make the necessary repairs. Believing the quadriga would be dwarfed by the monumental temple, Denon suggested it be placed instead on a fountain or statue on the Pont Neuf facing the Place Dauphine (where a statue of Henri IV stands today). The fountain was never built; the quadriga was forgotten at Versailles's Dépôt des Menus Plaisirs.

Following ten months of war, Napoleon returned to France in August 1807, regrouping for two weeks at Saint-Cloud. On his birthday, Napoleon staged a triumphal entry into the capital worthy of the Caesars. With ten thousand soldiers of the Imperial Guard, the procession passed through a temporary Arc de Triomphe, before proceeding down the Champs-Élysées to the Tuileries and the new Arc de Triomphe du Carrousel. Along the Champs-Élysées, tables were set for a banquet in honor of the Imperial Guard; a tent was installed at the Rond Point for the general staff. Toasts were raised to Napoleon, Paris, and the Grande Armée.

Marshal Bessières led the rest of the Grande Armée into the city through the Porte de la Villette, beneath an unfinished triumphal arch. The day's festivities ended with balloon flights and fireworks displays. Poems compared members of France's Imperial Guard to the "ten thousand immortals"—the elite infantry unit of Persia's Achaemenid Empire. As Matthew Zarzeczny writes, ". . . if his [Napoleon's] soldiers were the great warriors, modern immortals, then he was their great commander, a modern Trajan or Caesar."[30]

Meanwhile, little progress had been made on Napoleon's "Temple to the Glory of the Grande Armée." In July 1808, over a year behind schedule, Pierre Vignon razed what remained of the 1790 church and began work. Though Napoleon wanted a temple like the Acropolis, Vignon found his inspiration closer to home. Along with the temple of Augustus and Livia in Vienne, the Maison Carrée in Nîmes (today's Provence) remains one of the world's best preserved Roman temples.

After Caesar's decade-long conquest of Gaul, the Romans organized the region into four provinces, including Gallia Narbonensis in the south in 122 B.C.E. During the Celtic era, the Narbonne region had been occupied by the Volcae tribe, which founded Nîmes and made it their capital. They called it Nemausus, after the god of the nearby sacred spring. Around 120 B.C.E., the Romans established control of Nemausus, founding a colony here sometime in the late first century B.C.E., one of many in Provence.

Under Augustus, the city developed into an important center of Gaul, along with Marseille and Lyons. In 16–15 B.C.E., as part of a major urban program across Gaul and Spain, Augustus funded gates and walls for Nemausus. A forum was constructed at the intersection of the north to south road known as the *cardo* and the east to west road, the *decumanus*. On the forum's south side, in the middle of a flat, colonnaded court stood the elegant temple, later known as the Maison Carrée or Square House.

Built of local limestone by architects from Rome, the graceful edifice is a textbook example of the Tuscan-style temple Vitruvius described in the first century B.C.E. Elevated on a nine-foot-tall podium, the temple was originally approached by a monumental flight of stairs on the west end. Despite its name, the Maison Carrée is not a square but a rectangle, twice as long (eighty-two feet) as it is wide (forty feet). The building features a deep pronaos or vestibule leading to the cella, a windowless room that originally housed a cult image.

The façade is executed in the Roman Corinthian order with six free-standing columns topped by capitals decorated with acanthus leaves. The twenty columns along the sides and back are engaged—attached to the exterior walls of the cella. The workmanship and details recall Augustus's Temple of Mars Ultor in Rome; the frieze of deeply carved acanthus garlands evokes Augustus's Ara Pacis (Altar of Peace) on the Campus Martius dedicated in 9 B.C.E.[31] Above the columns, the architrave is divided into three zones, carved with reliefs of rosettes and acanthus leaves.[32]

It's thought that the Maison Carrée was originally a gift to Nemausus from Augustus, rebuilt during the reigns of Trajan, Hadrian, or Antoninus Pius. James Anderson suggests that the rebuilding may have been inspired by the increasing importance of Nîmes, as the likely birthplace of Trajan's wife, Empress Plotina.[33] Hadrian would dedicate a basilica to Plotina in Nîmes. The Maison Carrée's purpose was not just religious. As Sheila Bonde writes, "In the colonies, in particular, these cult sites often served the purpose of demonstrating corporate identity with, and allegiance to, Rome."[34]

Thanks to the Maison Carrée's continuous use over the centuries—as a town hall, private home, Christian church, granary, seat of town prefecture, and horse stable—it managed to avoid despoliation and major changes. Lost in the Middle Ages, the original inscription was reconstructed in 1758. The dedication honors Augustus's grandsons and presumptive heirs Gaius and Lucius Caesar, who both died suspiciously young, two years apart:

"To Gaius Caesar, son of Augustus Consul [and] to Lucius Caesar son of Augustus Consul Designate; to [them], First Citizens of the Young."[35]

Even the renowned Italian Renaissance architect Andrea Palladio, who drew his ancient and Renaissance models from Italy, looked to the spectacular Maison Carrée. ". . . the local inhabitants say that it used to be a basilica. But as the composition of the edifice is unrelated to that of basilicas, I tend to think that it was a temple," wrote Palladio. The harmonious Maison Carrée also became a model for French architects. Louis XIV considered moving it to Versailles.[36]

France's classical monuments were rediscovered in the latter third of the eighteenth century. In 1778, architect Charles-Louis Clérisseau published *Antiquités de la France,* an assortment of architectural plates of Nîmes's Roman monuments. Thomas Jefferson visited and was so impressed with the Maison Carrée, he had a stucco model made, which he used as a model for Virginia's statehouse in Richmond, co-designed with Clérisseau.

After the French Revolution, Nîmes's iconic temple became the headquarters for the first prefecture of the Gard region and later an archive. Stendhal was also a fan. "The overall effect is admirable," he wrote. "I have seen more imposing monuments in Italy itself but nothing as pretty as this pretty antique, even though rather overcharged with ornamental detail, which however doesn't exclude the beautiful. It's the smile of someone who is habitually serious."[37]

Vignon's neoclassical temple was a larger version of the Maison Carrée, combining the grandeur of Rome with the new symbols of the French Empire. An exterior frontispiece contained the dedication pediment: "The Emperor Napoleon to the soldiers of the Grande Armée." As Annie Jourdan puts it, in his temple to heroism, Napoleon distinguished himself from France's kings by sharing glory with his soldiers.[38]

Twenty-eight steps led up to the Madeleine's porch and a majestic view down the rue Royale across the Place de la Concorde to the Palais Bourbon across the Seine. Fifty-two fluted Corinthian columns sixty-six feet tall surrounded the entire building, with eight along the portico (versus six in Nîmes). Vignon embellished the entablature with an architrave topped by a frieze adorned with garlands and putti—less ornate than the Maison Carrée. The dentils adorning the cornice gave the façade an austere look.

Like the Maison Carrée, the interior of the Madeleine featured a cella, or inner room. The windowless building was lit from above, with three cupolas over the nave resting on pendentives and Corinthian columns. Each year, on the anniversaries of the battles of Austerlitz and Jena, the monument was to be illuminated, and a preliminary concert given on the virtues needed for a soldier, and praise of those who perished in battle.[39] Per Napoleon's order, marble tablets were inscribed with the names of the fallen soldiers from the battles of Ulm, Austerlitz, and Jena (organized by army corps and regiment). There were to be bas-reliefs featuring the Grande Armée's regiments, statues of marshals, along with the "flags, standards and drums" taken from the enemy.

As counterparts to his Army's Temple of Glory, Napoleon ordered two additional "temples." The riverfront Palais-Bourbon on the Quai d'Orsay occupied a strategic position in the axis of the Vendôme Column and Place de la Concorde. In 1750, Louis XV acquired the palace, originally owned by the daughter of Louis XIV and his official mistress Madame de Montespan. Confiscated from the Prince du Condé during the Revolution, the mansion was adapted for use by the Council of the Five Hundred and later by the Legislative Body during the Consulate and Empire.

In 1806, Napoleon hired Bernard Poyet to replace the palace's original 1722 façade with one that would complement the Madeleine. To the existing mansion, Poyet attached a peristyle of one dozen Corinthian columns perpendicular to the axis of the Concord bridge, creating a temple portico. Part of the plan went unrealized, included statues of legislators for the foot of the staircase leading to the peristyle. The first sculpture by Chaudet in 1810 depicted Napoleon returning from Austerlitz and followed by the flags, which he dedicated to the Legislative Body. Napoleon reportedly disliked the result, declaring that he regretted "no longer being an artillery lieutenant to fire a cannon on this portico of bad effect."[40] Today the building houses the French National Assembly.

After the Revolution, Notre-Dame-des-Victoires had housed the Bourse, or stock exchange. Now Napoleon returned the building to the Church and ordered a new Roman style temple—a "temple de l'argent." In 1807, Napoleon Bonaparte hired Alexandre-Théodore Brongniart to design the new stock exchange. A friend of sculptor Jean-Antoine Houdon and member of the Academy of Architecture, the Paris-born architect had sheltered portraitist Élisabeth Vigée Lebrun in his home before she fled Paris during the Reign of Terror. Brongniart was among those who stayed and was ruined by the Revolution.

As Renée Davray-Piekolek writes, the architect regarded the Bourse commission as a consecration.[41] Responding to Napoleon's wish to have his stock exchange look like a temple of commerce, Brongniart may have looked to Rome's imperial cult Temple of Vespasian and Titus for inspiration. Located at the westernmost area of the Roman Forum near the Arch of Septimius Severus, the temple was begun by Titus in 79 and finished by his brother Domitian around 87. Measuring 108 feet long by 72 feet wide, with six freestanding columns across the front, the temple was dedicated to the deified father and son. Three of its Corinthian columns still stand at the southeast corner of the podium (a section of the entablature featuring a carved frieze with cult objects and sacrificial implements is housed at the Capitoline Museum).[42]

The site chosen for the new stock exchange was a former convent, the Filles Saint-Thomas d'Aquin, confiscated during the Revolution. After numerous sketches by Brongniart, the first stone was laid in 1808. Roughly twice as big as the Temple of Vespasian and Titus at 226 by 135 feet, the building was accessed by steps leading to a gallery. Adorning the main and lateral façades were twenty-four and forty Corinthian columns, respectively. Each corner featured an allegorical statue; Justice by Duret, Commerce by Dumont, Agriculture by Seurre, and Industry by Pradier. Brongniart died in 1813; his monumental temple de l'argent was finished twelve years later by Éloi Labarre. The Palais de la Bourse was called "Palais Brongniart" in honor of its designer.

FOUR

COINING AN EMPIRE

While campaigning in Egypt, Napoleon reportedly found a medallion of Julius Caesar at the ruins of Pelusium on the easternmost bank of the Nile. He considered it a lucky omen.[1]

In 44 B.C.E., to mark his proclamation as perpetual dictator, Caesar ordered his portrait struck in silver. Distributed throughout the Empire, the coin featured his unique profile—receding hairline covered up with a laurel wreath, prominent nose and chin, protruding cheekbones, and long neck with an Adam's apple.[2] On the coin's flip side were the initials of the triumvir of the mint, Lucius Aemilius Buca, along with the symbolic caduceus (staff), fasces (bundle of rods and a single axe), orb, and axe.

Caesar was the first to have his portrait on a Roman coin.[3] Because portraits were associated with the ousted kings of the sixth century B.C.E., Rome's early coins had been decorated instead with symbols of the city. With the formation of the Republic in 509 B.C.E., coins frequently featured images of divinities on the obverse (front) and symbols of power on the reverse (back). For example, the head of Mars was paired with an eagle holding a thunderbolt; Jupiter matched with Victory placing a wreath on a trophy.

With the Republic, wealthy, illustrious Romans were allowed to glorify their ancestors and families by minting coins. As Daniele Leoni explains, ". . . coins began to take on a cultural expression with ever-more obvious political implications quite apart from the economic function for which they had been conceived. They thus became a "*monumentum*", or rather they provided new evidence testifying to what it meant to actually be a part of ancient Rome . . ."[4]

In 44 B.C.E., the same year that his commemorative coin was issued, Julius Caesar's dictatorship ended with his assassination on the Ides of March. Caesar's adopted son and heir, Caius Julius Caesar Octavian, who would rule as Emperor Augustus, perfected the propagandistic use of portraiture. Augustus had more portraits made than any other emperor—in cameos, sculptured portraits, relief sculptures, and coins. A fan of Hellenistic art, Augustus introduced a new iconographic style for his portraits modeled after the image of the god Apollo, whom he considered his protector.

According to Diana Kleiner, coins were an especially effective vehicle for imperial propaganda because they were handled daily by citizens both in Rome and the Empire's provinces.[5] Without an information system to communicate, the widely circulated coins helped preserve loyalty and disseminate news throughout the growing Roman Empire, explains C.H.V. Sutherland.[6]

In 37 B.C.E., Octavian used a sestarius to legitimize his claim to power by highlighting his adoption by Caesar. The obverse shows Octavian wearing a beard of mourning with the label *Divi filius*, the son of a god. The flip side features *Divus Julius*, the deified Julius Caesar (the Senate proclaimed Caesar a god in 42 B.C.E.).[7] In 28 B.C.E., Octavian starred on a silver cistophorus as the harbinger of peace, crowned with a laurel wreath with the text: "Protector of the freedom of the Roman people."[8]

The next year, Octavian took the name Augustus and minted a gold coin to celebrate Rome's conquest of Egypt. His image was paired with the text: "Augustus, consul for the seventh time . . . Imperator, son of the divine Caesar." A hippopotamus representing Egypt with the words "Egypt conquered" decorated the reverse.[9] To commemorate the honor bestowed on him by Rome's Senate, Augustus minted another coin that year with Jupiter's eagle clutching a garland of oak leaves.

As part of Augustus's reform of Rome's monetary system, various base metal denominations were introduced including the gold aureus.[10] Powerful symbols appeared in coinage to evoke Augustus's main propaganda themes—military victory, peace, and prosperity (*pax romana*), and his divine descent from Aeneas, son of Venus.

Like during the Roman Republic, buildings were reproduced on imperial coins. Augustus minted images of public monuments including the Altars of Peace and the Lion, Temples of Jupiter Tonans, Jupiter Olympus, and Mars Ultor, and the Triumphal Arch after the Parthian Victory. An aureus minted in Spain around 18 B.C.E. featured the three-vaulted Parthian Arch topped by a quadriga from the Roman Forum.[11]

According to Suetonias, the aging Augustus "had only partial vision. His teeth were small, few and decayed; his hair, yellowish and rather curly; his eyebrows met over his nose. . . . His body said to have been marred by blemishes of various sorts . . . and a number of dry patches suggesting ringworm."[12] Still, Augustus was always portrayed as youthful and athletic—even at his death at 76 in 14 C.E.

Rome's future emperors continued to incorporate prestigious architecture into their imperial coinage. Nero featured his Golden House, the Triumphal Arch, Gate of Ostia, and Temple of Janus. Titus depicted the Colossus; Trajan the Basilica Ulpia, Trajan Forum, the Trajan Aqueduct Way and Column, and Trajan Gate.[13]

As Daniele Leoni details, the Imperial Roman Mint produced coins in gold, silver, and bronze/brass using the time-honored proportions of twenty-five denarrii to the aureus, four sestertii to one denarius, and four asses to the sestertius. A quinarius was worth half an aureus. Sestertii and dupondii were minted in brass, an alloy of copper and zinc regarded as more valuable than bronze. Provincial mints were also active. Among them, Alexandria produced bronze drachmas; Pergamon and Ephesus turned out silver sistoforii (equivalent to three dinari); and Tyre created silver tetradams.[14]

Rome's emperors followed Augustus's lead, using coins to spread their images and proclaim their military victories throughout the Empire. As they did in sculpture and cameos, emperors starting with Augustus often minted coins bearing the names and images of their wives, parents, children, grandchildren, and siblings. Special consecration coins with the words *consecratio* or *aeternitas* were minted to spread word of the divinization of emperors and family members.

Starting with Augustus and continuing until the end of the Roman Empire, the emperor's image took the place of the sacred figure on the obverse of coins. Imperial appellatives were also inscribed in abbreviated form on the obverse; if space ran out, the list of titles and honors continued on the reverse. For example, imperator (emperor) appeared as IMP; Pontifex Maximus (Rome's highest religious appointment) as P M or Pont Max; and Caesar as CAE, CAES or CAESAR. Of his many ranks, *Pater Patriae* or P P (Father of the Fatherland) is the title Augustus most wanted on his coins.[15] Of all his titles, Trajan most prized *Optimus Principi*, the best of the emperors.

The Senate hailed new emperors with the slogan "may you be as lucky as Augustus and better than Trajan." Trajan was the first Roman emperor to regularly issue bronze medallions. Generally heavier than sestertii, these dramatic medallions were commemorative and not part of the monetary system. It was during the reign of Trajan's successor Hadrian, explains Jocelyn Toynbee, that continuous series of bronze medallions debuted, including "framed" medallions with a broad rim or circle around the central design.[16] According to Toynbee, medallions marked key events in the personal and political lives of the emperors. These included everything from adoptions, marriages, births, and deaths to religious celebrations and imperial *adlocutios* (allocutions) to the Praetorian Guard or imperial armies.[17]

Commodus was especially a fan. His medalists produced exceptional medallions in high relief to commemorate imperial events and honor the gods. After Commodus's assassination in 192, successive emperors like Septimius Severus continued to commission medallions. The largest and most striking were probably presented as gifts by Rome's emperors.[18]

"From the middle of the 1st century onwards," writes Toynbee, "the imperial government had appreciated, as few governments have done before or since, not only the function of coinage as a mirror of contemporary life, of the political, social, spiritual, and artistic aspirations of the age, but also its immense and unique possibilities as a far-reaching instrument of propaganda."[19] For example, to mark Rome's nine-hundredth anniversary in 147, Antoninus Pius issued a propagandistic nine medallion series including the story of Hercules and Cacus, and Aeneas's flight from Troy.[20]

Allegory was central to Roman coinage, with the reverses featuring personifications like Victoria, Abundance, and Peace. Thanks to their clothing and attributes, these representations were easy to recognize. Victoria was usually represented by a seminude, winged female figure in various poses. Often she crowns or offers a crown to the emperor, or leads his triumphal quadriga. Abundance, also a female figure, was typically depicted holding a cornucopia and ears of corn. Though Rome was founded and maintained by war, writes Francesco Gnecchi, peace was considered a gift from the gods. In numerous coins, Pax was celebrated as a female figure, commonly carrying a long scepter, olive branch, palm, or crown.[21]

Like Rome's emperors, Charlemagne used coins to help unify his growing empire and enforce his authority. As part of a series of monetary reforms, the Frankish king consolidated minting authority and deleted the names of moneyers from coinage. Like today's euro, silver coins bearing Charlemagne's name or initial and title were accepted throughout his realm. Around 794, Charlemagne launched a thinner, larger, heavier version of the denier, introduced by his father Pepin the Short. The new design featured a cross and royal title on the obverse, and Karolus (Charlemagne in Latin) monogram and mint name on the reverse.[22]

The Roman medallion also inspired the creation of a new genre in Renaissance Italy. Starting in the fourteenth century, as part of the interest in classical civilizations, Italian humanists began collecting ancient Greek and Roman coins. In 1439, the northern Italian court painter Pisanello invented a prototype of the modern medal. It featured a portrait on the obverse of visiting Byzantine emperor John VIII Palaeologus with a symbolic image on the reverse. As in ancient Roman coinage, inscriptions often reflected the subject's titles, qualities, or motto. Pisanello's format—the antiquity-inspired subject in profile—caught on and became the standard for portrait medals.

Initially, Renaissance medals were cast using methods similar to those for bronze sculpture—a process in which molten metal was poured into a carved mold. Striking, a technique used in antiquity to produce coins, required special tools and physical force to shape a heated metal disk between two engraved dies. Thanks to a new screw press, striking made a resurgence in the early sixteenth century.[23] Rome's long history with medals continued with the popes who began minting medals in the 1470s to commemorate events like the opening of the Porta Sacra, jubilee years, and various stages of St. Peter's.

Unlike coins, which were struck at mints using specific materials and specific weights, medals were commemorative, produced in various sizes, weights, and materials.[24] Often designed by famous painters and sculptors, beautifully crafted in lead, bronze, silver, or gold, or combinations of these precious metals, medals were lasting works of art, writes Aimee Ng.[25]

Starting in the sixteenth century with Henri IV, French medals conveyed a similar propaganda message to that of Rome's emperors. Henri IV's sculptor Guillaume Dupré began using casting for medals and larger medallions, elevating the technique to a sophisticated level that approached striking.[26] In 1662, Louis XIV's minister Colbert began an ambitious "Metallic History" to glorify the Sun King's reign. Responding to Colbert about the project, the critic Chapelain wrote: "As for . . . Medals . . . they are an invention which the Greeks and Romans used to immortalize the memory of the heroic actions of their princes, of their captains, and their emperors, because of the incorruptibility of the metals of which they were comprised . . . I strongly approve of your using them . . . to perpetuate those of the King, as it is a method which has been used at all times for a similar purpose and is very suitable to the royal dignity."[27]

Colbert enlisted painters, historians, poets, engravers, and medalists to design and produce the medals. In addition to a Roman emperor and a general, Louis XIV was portrayed as Apollo driving the chariot of the sun and even the sun itself with his motto *Nec Pluribus Impar*, "not unequal to many." A luxurious illustrated volume (*Médailles sur les principaux événements du règne de Louis le Grand*) featured some 286 medals highlighting the king's life and achievements.

Medalists continued to use ancient historical and mythological figures throughout the seventeenth and eighteenth centuries. For example, to celebrate his recapture of Padua in 1690, Francesco II of Carrara had medals struck to imitate Roman sestertii, comparing himself and his father to Roman emperors.[28] The Grand Dukes of Tuscany commissioned a series of cast medals depicting political and cultural figures of the day. Members of the ruling Medici dynasty, foreign dignitaries, and scientists appeared on the obverse; their lives or characters featured on the reverse. By the Enlightenment, medals, also known as commemorative coins, became prized collector's items.

In the second half of the eighteenth century, Habsburg Empress Maria Theresa also fashioned her image with an ambitious medal program. As her State Chancellor Wenzel Anton (prince of Kaunitz-Rietberg) wrote her in 1770: "Of all the engravings, that of medals in art is the most important: it is intended to preserve for posterity the memory of festive events, [and] the monarchs' remarkable deeds and orders . . ."[29] The medal was a handy way to promote the Habsburg's connection with Rome. Maria Theresa was portrayed in the guise of a helmeted Athena and Minerva. In her final death medal, she is shown in profile wearing a widow's veil after the empresses of Rome.

Augustus and successive Roman emperors minted coins to market their heroic image and position their military campaigns in a positive light. Napoleon did the same. "He [Napoleon] looked like an antique medallion," observed Comtesse de Rémusat at his Paris coronation.[30] Napoleon fully exploited the medium, commissioning more medals than Louis XV and Louis XVI combined.[31]

From the start of his meteoric career, Napoleon used commemorative medals to fashion a heroic reputation. To publicize his stunning victories in the Italian campaign, the young Corsican general ordered the "Five Battles" series struck at the Milan Mint. Four of the five propaganda medals were designed by Andrea Appiani. In a decorative practice started in Renaissance Italy, Appiani would incorporate larger versions of these medals into the frieze of his Napoleonic fresco at Milan's Royal Palace.[32]

The Po-Adda-Mincio medal marked the crossing of three rivers by the Army of Italy, leading to the French occupation of Lombardy. Napoleon is featured on horseback, leading his troops across the Adda Bridge at Lodi. According to John L. Connolly, the image of the bridge evoked well-known Roman legends, including Horatius Cocles's defense of the Sublician Bridge, Constantine crossing the Milvian Bridge, and Trajan defeating the Dacians by crossing the Danube on Appolodorus's bridge.[33] The series was duplicated with small changes at mints in Lyon and Paris, helping spread Napoleon's fame.

Medals also commemorated Napoleon's founding of various Italian republics between 1797 and 1799, including the short-lived democratic republic in Venice, the Ligurian Republic in Genoa and Pisa, Cisalpine Republic in Milan and Lombardy, Roman Republic, and Parthenopean Republic of Naples. Napoleon borrowed the name "Cisalpine" from a province governed by Julius Caesar. Napoleon also marked the Treaty of Campo Formio with Austria, the Egypt campaign, and Battle of Marengo with medals.

As first consul, Napoleon continued to choose medal subjects—from the Battle of the Pyramids to his failed assassination attempt in December 1800. That year, Bertrand Andrieu designed a dramatic medal based on Jacques-Louis David's famous painting of Napoleon at the Saint-Bernard Pass. Like David, Andrieu set his miniature version against a dramatic setting with Napoleon on a rearing horse. But as Stephen Scher describes, the medal version depicts Napoleon clutching lightning bolts in his raised hand like Jupiter, blasting passage for his army through the dangerous pass.[34]

Napoleon's medals teemed with classical allusions. One example by engraver Benjamin Duvivier (Louis XVI's Engraver at the Mint), depicted Napoleon as peacemaker, triumphant general, and patron of the arts. The obverse shows a portrait profile of Napoleon circled by "Bonaparte gen al. en chef de l'armée Franc SE. en Italie." On the reverse, Napoleon rides a rearing horse led by Prudence and Valor, while Victory extends a laurel crown over him—like a Roman triumph. In her other hand, Victory holds a statue of *Apollo Belvedere*, representing the antiquities seized as war booty. In Napoleon's right hand is an olive branch, representing the Treaty of Campo Formio.[35]

In 1799, a veritable treasure chest of medals from the Vatican Medagliere arrived in Paris. A year earlier, French troops under General Berthier filled hemp bags with rare coins and medals from the papal numismatic cabinet. The exceptional collection (today totaling over three hundred thousand Greek, Roman, and Papal coins and medals) got its start in the mid-sixteenth century when the Cardinal librarian, the future Pope Marcellus I, donated his collection to the Vatican Library.

Clement XII (Corsini, 1730–40) established the Library's Medagliere, acquiring over three hundred Greek and Roman medals from Cardinal Alessandro Albani (Clement is also the pope who famously placed fig leaves on the Vatican's classical nude sculptures). Popes Benedict XIV and Clement XIV expanded the papal coin and medal collection through prestigious acquisitions. In addition to donating part of his personal coin collection to the Medagliere, Pius VI bought the collection of Queen Christina of Sweden in 1794. After the French cleaned out the Medagliere, Pius started over, acquiring the collection of P. M. Vitali, featuring mainly Roman coins.

Medal production was a highly bureaucratic process. Case in point was a medal to mark Napoleon's return from Egypt. Before gaining Napoleon's approval, the medal went through some twenty revisions.[36] The most popular subject was Napoleon himself. Produced in large numbers, mainly *jetons*, these medals usually featured Napoleon in profile and an inscription or legend on the face and a representative inscription on the reverse, celebrating the young general's stunning victories. The self-promoting medals contributed to Napoleon's tremendous popularity, which allowed him to depose the Directory regime.

As first consul, Napoleon turned over his public relations effort to Dominique-Vivant Denon, naming him director of the Monnaie des Médailles, the medals Mint. As part of a major reorganization, Denon relocated the Mint from the Musée Napoléon to rue Guénégaud. The Mint became a state-controlled monopoly with a March 1804 decree prohibiting the striking of medals or jetons anywhere except the Monnaie. During the first four years of his post, Denon ordered the minting of nineteen medals. The first of Denon's medals, *Aux arts la victoire,* was struck to mark Napoleon's August 1803 visit to the Louvre to admire the newly arrived treasure, Florence's *Medici Venus.* The medal featured Napoleon's profile on the obverse and the renowned antique marble on the reverse.

Another effective propaganda tool was the new germinal franc, created in 1803 to address a coin shortage and the circulation of counterfeit money. Named after the month in the Republican calendar, the first coins featured the first consul's profile and later Napoleon I in the guise of a Roman emperor with the inscription "Emperor Napoleon" writes Karine Huguenaud. Half and quarter Francs, as well as two and five Franc pieces were minted using the same metal; twenty and forty Franc pieces were made of gold.[37]

In 1806, after Napoleon's victory at Austerlitz, Denon conceived a far-reaching medal series in the tradition of Louis XIV. As Napoleon described, the "Histoire métallique de Sa Majesté" was created "for the perpetuation of the memory of the most important actions." Among the best-preserved objects from antiquity, medals helped immortalize emperors and military leaders. Now Napoleon would seal his rule for posterity, using medals as a historical record of his achievements.

Denon elevated medallic art by adding it to the prestigious Prix de Rome competition founded by Louis XIV. Medalists were given two seats at the French Academy in Rome alongside painters, sculptors, and architects. One of the few medalists who made the transition from the ancien régime was Bordeaux-born Jean-Bertrand Andrieu. In 1789, he engraved a famous medal of the Storming of the Bastille. According to Mark Jones, Andrieu's portrait of Napoleon as an emotionless Roman hero became the standard obverse of Denon's Medallic History.[38] After the coronations in Paris and Milan, the standard observe also included "Napoleon Emp. et Roi."

One early work in the series records Napoleon's arrival at Frejus in October 1799. On one side, his ship is shown arriving, with the British ships he's avoided in the distance; the flip side depicts the Roman god of good fortune. As Jones explains, these early medals evoked Classicism—from Dumarest's medal with the head of Athena and Jean-Pierre Droz's *Peace of Amiens and return of Astraea* medal of 1802 to Brenet's *A la Fortune Conservatrice* struck in commemoration of the preparation for an invasion of England.[39]

The analogy between the Napoleonic and Roman Empires was made very clear. For example, a medal depicting the resumption of the flags at Innsbruck was modeled after a Roman medal representing Germanicus retaking an eagle from the Germanic tribe of Marses removed from the

Roman legions commanded by Varus.[40] Coins and medals featured the laurel wreath-toting Napoleon in profile, often the spitting image of Augustus.

Napoleon's coronation inspired several medals. Among them was a medal commemorating the pope's attendance. Denon's protégé Droz created an obverse featuring Pius in profile, wearing the traditional tiara and ecclesiastical orfrois; the reverse depicts Notre Dame. Napoleon is suggested by the Gregorian and revolutionary dating of the ceremony and the inscription *imperator sacratus*.[41]

In February 1806, Denon announced a medal series relating to the Austria campaign, starting with the camp of Boulogne. Multiple copies of the sixteen-medal series were struck and given to French dignitaries, ambassadors, and foreign princes. A copy of the series was also placed inside the base of the Vendôme Column as a record for posterity.

For medals of the Battle of Austerlitz, Denon decided on "Charlemagne's scepter with a thunderbolt." The battle was symbolized by an imperial scepter armed with the wings and flashes of lightning. "This medal represents an empty throne," explained Denon. "The eagle that is in the air, and which comes out from under the royal mantle, is the emblem of the watch. The hand of justice, which is on the throne, expresses that justice has remained. And the lightning that is above the throne indicates the power that threatens the guilty."[42]

Denon also oversaw production of a medal by Bertrand Andrieu with the double profiles of Napoleon and Charlemagne. To celebrate France's alliance with Saxony, Andrieu designed a silver version of the medal with a bearded Charlemagne overlapping with Napoleon in a laurel wreath, and the legend "Napoleon. emp., Charlemagne. emp." The obverse featured the paired portraits of Saxon Prince Vitikind, created the first Duke of Saxony by Charlemagne, and Frederick Augustus, named king of Saxony by Napoleon.

Denon kept close tabs on medal production—from the subjects, iconography, and compositions to the hiring of die engravers and instructions. Napoleon was also involved, reviewing medal designs during his military campaigns. Denon usually first submitted his idea and description for a medal, then a finished drawing, and finally a completed proof. At each stage, Napoleon weighed in, ordering changes or requiring substitution of other subjects or designs.

Napoleon was brutally frank. On one occasion at Saint-Cloud, after Denon showed him several medal prototypes, he hurled one of the gold medals to the back of the room. Denon explained that the medal showed the French eagle strangling a leopard, representing England. "Cheap flatterer," Napoleon reportedly replied, "how dare you say that the French eagle is strangling the English leopard? I can't put even a fishing boat to sea without the English seizing it. It's rather this leopard that is strangling the French eagle."[43]

Subject matter for medals was never in short supply with Napoleon's continued campaigns. To prevent medals from wearing out too fast, Denon saw they were done in strong relief, not low relief. Small, strong, and mass-produced, medals were a cost-effective propaganda tool. But the medals' small size required compressed, highly symbolic images; the circular format of the propagandistic reverses presented a design challenge. Following an iconography of ancient Roman coins, using ancient allegories and symbols, the medals reflected the most important events in Napoleon's personal and public life—from his birthday, second marriage, and birth of his son to his coronation, military victories, and treaties. An assassination attempt on Napoleon's life and his introduction of a smallpox vaccination also inspired medals.

Since the Italian Renaissance, the design and production of medals had been a collaborative, multi-phased process. Napoleonic medals continued this tradition. Among the hand-picked painters, illustrators, sculptors, and architects were Pierre-Nolasque Bergeret (of Vendôme Column fame), Charles Percier, Antoine-Denis Chaudet, Auguste Boucher Desnoyers, Alexandre-Évariste Fragonard (son of the celebrated painter), Pierre Lafitte, Jean-Baptiste Lepère, Charles Meynier (Arc du Carrousel), Pierre-Paul Prud'hon, and Benjamin Zix. To produce the medals, Denon assembled a team of designers and engravers, matching their skills to the various subjects. Images were adapted into designs by professional draftsmen and then executed for die engraving by higher paid craftsmen.

Some of the medals conceived by Denon are engraved with "Denon direxit." According to Antony Griffiths, Denon may have felt justified because of his high level of involvement in the design and production process. In addition to hiring designers and engravers, Denon thought up compositions and issued detailed instructions based on his classical knowledge. For some projects, writes Griffiths, Denon bypassed a designer altogether, supplying the composition to the engraver directly from a coin in his own collection.[44]

Napoleon presented medals on state occasions, as awards and diplomatic gifts and as signs of his favor. Special editions struck in precious metals were sent to foreign allies. Many were struck in copper covered with a patina to prevent erosion and to add a bronze-like appearance. A single copy of most medals was also struck in gold for Napoleon's personal collection. The ratio of silver to bronze medals was nearly eight to one. In parallel with the Paris Mint, Napoleonic medals continued to be struck in Milan until 1810, mainly after designs by Appiani.

During the Napoleonic era, Denon oversaw the production of some 130 medals. Though rulers such as Louis XIV and Maria Theresa used medals extensively, often incorporating classical mythology, Napoleon's medal program was completely unique. Ushering in a more sophisticated neoclassical style with iconography resembling the frieze compositions of ancient coins, Napoleonic medals became a permanent reference to antiquity. To this, Denon added the new symbols of the Empire, the *N* and the eagle. The strict classical style modeled on Roman coinage and medals powerfully tied Napoleon to the Caesars.

PART FIVE
PRINCIPATE

"Power and pageantry go hand in hand. I had to project an image, to appear grave, to establish rules of etiquette. Otherwise, people would have slapped me on the shoulder daily."

—Napoleon Bonaparte

ONE
CURIA REGIS

After being proclaimed emperor on May 18, 1804, Napoleon established an imperial household consisting of six departments or services, each run by a Grand Officer. By mid-August, Napoleon's architect Pierre Fontaine wrote:

"The interior of the Household now presents the shape and appearance of a sovereign's residence. The Emperor is surrounded by civil and military Grand Officers who take his orders, administer the various departments at his service, and represent him on his behalf . . . He ordered the creation of a great number of chamberlains, equerries, ladies of the robes, attendants and others under the orders of the Grand Officers in each department, both for the Emperor and the Empress. There is talk of a coronation ceremony."[1]

The Emperor's household ballooned to 3,500 employees, whose purpose was to attend to the imperial family's daily lives and official ceremonies. Joséphine enjoyed her own household, consisting of a First Almoner, a lord-in-waiting who escorted her on public occasions, and a First Equerry in charge of her stables. For Joséphine's principal lady-in-waiting, Napoleon recruited aristocrat Claire Elisabeth de Rémusat who had lost her family fortune during the Revolution. By 1809, the Empress's ladies-in-waiting numbered twenty, compared to Marie Antoinette's sixteen.[2]

From uniforms and etiquette to sumptuous palace décor, Napoleon revived the pageantry and heraldry of the French court, the *curia regis*. As he explained, "My power is dependent on my glory, and my glory on my victories. . . . A newly established government must dazzle and astonish. The moment it ceases to glitter, it falls."[3]

For his Grand Officers, Napoleon appropriated many titles from the Holy Roman Empire. Grand Dignitaries of the Empire included Arch-Chancellor Cambaceres, Arch-Treasurer Lebrun, and Vice-Grand Elector Talleyrand, who was also minister of foreign affairs. As Grand Marshal of the Palace, Napoleon's longtime aide-de-camp Duroc held the most influential position. With a staff of seven hundred, Duroc oversaw security, furnishings, procurement, and meals and banquets at dozens of imperial palaces. Duroc would sign the treaties of Fontainebleau and Bayonne, and negotiate the treaty in Spain after Charles IV's abdication.

The urbane, flattering Grand Master of Ceremonies, Louis-Philippe de Ségur, organized Napoleon's back-to-back coronations in Paris and Milan, and choreographed other state ceremonies. The son of a war minister, Ségur had been ambassador to the court of Russia's Catherine the Great under Louis XVI. During Napoleon's frequent absences, he required Joséphine to follow the rules outlined in Ségur's sixty-page *Etiquette du Palais Imperial*. Stendhal called Ségur "a dwarf . . . one of the Emperor's weaknesses . . . consumed with chagrin at not being a duke."[4]

As Grand Chaplain, Napoleon's uncle Cardinal Fesch served as ambassador to the Holy See. He directed religious services at the palace, administered Church sacraments to the imperial family, and officiated at imperial marriages and baptisms. He was also a noted art collector. For his participation in the Concordat negotiations, Napoleon appointed him archbishop of Lyon; in 1803 he was named cardinal.

Napoleon created the new post of Intendant-General, filled by Charles de Fleurieu, Pierre-Antoine-Noël Daru, and former minister Jean-Baptiste de Champagny. The office's purview included "first painter" Jacques-Louis David, palace architects like Percier and Fontaine, palace furnishings, court physicians, and the Emperor's notary. Treasurer-generals

Martin-Roch-Xavier Estève and his successor François-Marie-Pierre de La Bouillerie oversaw finances.

The Grand Chamberlain, held first by foreign secretary Charles-Maurice de Talleyrand followed by the comte Pierre de Montesquiou-Fezensac, was Napoleon's gatekeeper and chief of staff, overseeing audiences and the running of his daily calendar. Grand Equerry Armand de Caulaincourt, the youngest of the Grand Officers, supervised the imperial stables, with responsibility for horses, carriages, messengers, and Napoleon's weapons.

Napoleon named his minister of war, Marshal Alexandre Berthier, Grand Master of the Hunt and revived the sport. Though Roman society was agricultural, some Hadrianic emperors associated themselves with hunting. Domitian for example is shown slaying beasts in reliefs and carvings. According to Suetonius, the emperor hunted in the game park on his estate outside Rome.

Napoleon hunted in the forests of Compiègne, Versailles, and Fontainebleau, sometimes with hounds descended from those of Louis XIV. Though Napoleon used hunting parties to fashion himself as heir to a long tradition, his skills were not impressive. On one outing in 1803, the first consul was injured by a wild boar, nearly losing a finger. As Sylvain Cordier writes, the myopic emperor was "a poor huntsman and a notoriously bad shot" often missing his target. On a hunt in September 1808, Napoleon nearly blinded his marshal André Masséna, blaming his Grand Master of the Hunt for the accident.[5]

Napoleon also reinstated the royal *grand couvert.* The public meal was associated with Louis XIV, whose courtiers watched him dine most evenings at Versailles. Now Napoleon's guests stood watching while he and the imperial family ate. In this culinary drama, Napoleon's grand officers played highly scripted roles. Fesch blessed the table, Talleyrand gave Napoleon a moist cloth for his hands and served him coffee. Caulaincourt offered him armchair; Duroc brought his napkin and poured water and wine. Meanwhile officers of Joséphine's household performed the same tasks.[6] In the end, Napoleon was not a fan of the ritual and only hosted eight of these banquets.

Ségur's *Livre du Sacre* detailed the required ceremonial apparel for princes and princesses, grand dignitaries, and grand officers of the Napoleonic court, with artist Jean-Baptiste Isabey providing illustrations.

Specific colors were established for various members of the imperial household (red for the palace, scarlet for the chamber, blue for the stables, green for the hunt, and violet for the ceremonies.[7] Symbolic gold and silver embroideries were assigned to various titles and functions—reminiscent of the decorative embellishments instituted for soldiers and non-military officials in the late imperial period by Roman emperor Diocletian. The palm tree was embroidered onto the uniforms of the various civil uniforms—perhaps a nod to Napoleon's fond memories of the Egyptian campaign.[8]

". . . the costumes worn at the Napoleonic court transformed the styles of ancient republicanism into the aesthetic of classical imperialism," write Sylvain Cordier and Chantelle Lepine-Cercone. "Such associations with ancient Rome were further exemplified in the grand habillements [coronation costumes] of the imperial couple . . . Their mantles were of the deep crimson that historically defined imperial Rome. These associations anchored the Empire in the memory of antiquity."[9]

Milliner Louis Hippolyte LeRoy dressed the trendsetting Joséphine, Napoleon's female relatives, and the wives of his marshals. "I counted amongst my clientele two empresses and all the crowned heads of Europe. . . . The coronation started my fortune," wrote the well-dressed designer.[10] In addition to court dress, Joséphine wore the couturier's masquerade dress, daywear, hats, and accessories. According to Madame de Rémusat, Joséphine often picked her outfit to coordinate with specific palace interiors. She was not a fashion repeater, and avoided wearing the same gown twice in public.[11]

Joséphine's substantial wardrobe budget was just one line item that helped make Napoleon's court as costly as that of Louis XIV at Versailles. The court's initial budget of twenty million francs a year was roughly three percent of the government's annual expenses. On top of this, the emperor received another three million francs annually, revenue from the Crown lands near Paris. Toward the end of Napoleon's rule, that income ballooned to over thirty-six million francs as he added the confiscated properties of defeated monarchs, popes, and aristocrats to his portfolio.[12]

Distinct from the civil household, Napoleon operated a military household overseen by thirteen aides-de-camp and thirteen ordonnance officers. The staff of over eight hundred accompanied Napoleon on all his campaigns. As a student of ancient history, Napoleon understood the dangers of the Imperial Guard. Alexander the Great's father, Philip II of Macedonia, was fatally stabbed by his own bodyguard at a banquet. Rome's Augustus had relied on the Praetorian Guard, nine thousand strong, for his personal safety. After Augustus, the powerful Praetorian Guard routinely eliminated emperors.

Napoleon later acknowledged that under another emperor, "my Imperial Guard could also have become fatal."[13] To prevent any of his commanders from becoming too powerful, Napoleon divvied up control of his guard between four marshals. Mameluke horsemen from Egypt became part of the Consular Guard in 1802; in 1804 the squadron was made part of the Mounted Chasseurs of the Imperial Guard. Napoleon's personal Mameluke guard, Raza Roustam, slept at the foot of his bed, and accompanied him on hunts and military campaigns. Named First Mameluke to the Emperor in 1813, Roustam would remain Napoleon's bodyguard until 1814. Napoleon did not completely trust his police minister Joseph Fouché and instituted checks to his power.[14]

In an address to the Senate in 1807, Napoleon proposed a new hereditary nobility for his marshals in the form of imperial duchies. According to Rafe Blaufarb, Napoleon did not consider recipients of his Legion of Honor, with their modest wealth and social background, sufficient to protect the imperial succession. "For the stability of our throne and brilliance of our crown," declared Napoleon, "for the greatest benefit of our peoples, it is necessary to grant titles to the most distinguished citizens to whom we owe a debt of gratitude for the homeland's prosperity . . ."[15]

Géraud-Christophe-Michel Duroc (Grand Marshal of the Palace) and Armand de Caulaincourt (Grand Equerry) became Dukes of Friuli and Vicenza respectively. Louis-Alexandre Berthier (Grand Huntsman) was made Prince of Neufchâtel, Valengin and Wagram; Charles-Maurice de Talleyrand-Périgord (Grand Chamberlain) gained the title Prince of Benevento. Recreating France's court culture was no small feat for a country that had fought a bloody revolution to get rid of hereditary titles.

The term "palace" comes from the Palatine, one of ancient Rome's Seven Hills where Augustus and Tiberius resided in the first century. ". . . since the days of Charlemagne," writes Sylvain Cordier, "giving the principal residence of a ruler that name was linking his authority to the memory of Roman sovereignty."[16] Napoleon was the first ruler of France since Charlemagne to own palaces outside the Île-de-France and the Loire valley, including the archbishop's palace at Strasbourg, and palaces in Bologna, Brescia, Mantua, Modena, Stra, and Venice, writes Philip Mansel.[17] By 1812, Napoleon had amassed a real estate empire of forty-four imperial palaces.

Napoleon also made himself at home in the palaces of his enemies. He stayed twice at the Habsburg palace of Schönbrunn, near Vienna, first in late 1805 before and after Austerlitz, and again in May and June 1809, before the Battles of Essling and Wagram. After defeating Prussia at Jena in October 1806, Napoleon moved into Sanssouci, Frederick the Great's Potsdam retreat.

Many of Napoleon's palaces were redecorated in the fashionable Empire style launched by his Rome-trained designers Charles Percier and Pierre Fontaine. Antique forms were combined with Napoleonic symbols like the Carolingian-inspired bee and the letter *N* surrounded by a laurel wreath, stars, and the eagle. Cabinetmakers, goldsmiths, silversmiths, porcelain makers, and bronze smiths all helped create a luxe setting for the court. Napoleon's monogram was ubiquitous, adorning everything from palace door bolts and keys to regimental colors and public monuments.

In July 1804, Napoleon replaced the Bourbons' Garde-Meuble de la Couronne with the Garde-Meuble Impérial, a government department of some thirty employees responsible for palace furnishings. Pierre Daru, Intendant-General of the Imperial Household (and first cousin of the novelist Stendhal), and Alexander Desmazis, administeur du mobilier, were often at odds with the spendthrift Joséphine. The redecoration of the Empress's state apartment on the ground floor of the Tuileries started in 1805. "For a long time, she [Joséphine] had been asking for changes and embellishments to her apartments . . . desiring above all that we create a beautiful bedroom," wrote Fontaine.[18]

Percier and Fontaine also transformed Louis XIV's first-floor bedroom at the Tuileries into Napoleon's throne room. The designers supplied Jacob-Desmalter with life-size drawings for two thrones and ceremonial chairs. The thrones may have been inspired by Bacchus's Throne, created in 1792 by Roman sculptor Francesco Antonio Franzoni. Pilfered from the Vatican in 1797 along with the Ceres Throne, the Bacchus Throne was displayed in the antiquities gallery at the Musée Napoléon. Between late August and early September 1804, Jacob-Desmalter produced the carved and gilded frames; Garde-Meuble upholsterers covered them in silk woven by Camille Pernon of Lyon.

The new seating was installed in the east-facing throne room overlooking the Carousel on December 1—just in the nick of time for Napoleon's coronation the next day. Featuring a rounded back and globes on the arms, the throne's heraldic decoration included an *N*, an imperial eagle, the chain of the Legion of Honor, and bees. Napoleon liked the throne so much, he had it replicated for the throne rooms at Fontainebleau and Saint-Cloud.

The court at Tuileries ". . . became the most brilliant and numerous ever seen," wrote Emmanuel-Auguste de Las Cases. "It had social circles, ballets, performances; an extraordinary magnificence and splendor was deployed. . . . This luxury, the pomp he encouraged around him, reflected his plans, but not his tastes. [They] were calculated to stimulate our national productions and industry . . ."[19]

Napoleon's obsession with splendor has its roots in antiquity when craftsmen produced exquisite furniture, gold and silver plate, hard stone vessels, carved gems, and jewelry for the ruling class. With war spoils and other sources of wealth streaming into Rome during the late Republic, generals and other elite Romans formed libraries and furnished their villas with lavish artworks. Decorated with divinities, heroic narratives, and portraits, luxury objects bestowed "status, prestige, and cultural as well as economic capital on those who possessed and appreciated them," writes Kenneth Lapatin.[20]

But the word *luxuria* also carried negative associations, deriving from *luxor*—to sprain or dislocate—and *luxurio*—to flourish immoderately. Philosophers like Cicero and Pliny the Elder blamed the moral decline of Roman society on extravagant foreign objects. Though they denounced luxury, Cicero and Seneca enjoyed beautiful things. Cicero spent millions on his villas; Seneca owned some five hundred tables with ivory legs and citrus wood tops.[21] Augustus tried putting the kibosh on such ostentation, but well-heeled Romans continued to covet luxury.

Across the Roman Empire, private contractors used slaves to mine silver and gold, which was turned into coins, jewelry, and vessels. Cicero reported that Verres, Sicily's greedy governor, opened a workshop to remove ancient reliefs from bowls he appropriated and reset them in new gold vessels. Along with their aesthetic function, luxury objects conveyed political, religious, and social meaning. Decorative tableware was a conversation starter at Roman banquets, one that advertised the host's taste and wealth.

Precious stone was also hollowed out for drinking and carved in cameo. One of the most beautiful, the double handled agate *Cup of the Ptolemies*, is thought to have been produced in Alexandria, Egypt during the mid-first century B.C.E. Dionysiac symbols are carved in high relief—masks, animals, garlands, along with tables filled with luxe vessels and statuettes. Repurposed as a Christian chalice, the cup was gifted to the treasury of Saint Denis, possibly by King Charles the Bald. During the French Revolution, the basilica's treasury was deposited in the former Cabinet des Medailles, renamed the Musée des Antiques. Stolen in a heist in 1804 along with the Grand Camée de France, the cup was recovered from Holland and returned to Paris.

Eighteenth-century France had been the world's preeminent luxury goods producer, with high-end brands like Sèvres porcelain, Roettiers silver, and Lyon silk coveted by Europe's monarchs and aristocrats. Luxury goods went out of style with the French Revolution. Under the Directory and Consulate regimes, a wealthy new French bourgeoisie developed with a taste for fine craftsmanship. Napoleon and Joséphine helped make luxury acceptable again, reviving France's top position in the luxury trades.

To encourage production of luxury goods, Napoleon visited textile, porcelain, and furniture workshops. He also gave large loans to struggling entrepreneurs like furniture maker Jacob Desmalter and bronzier Pierre Philippe Thomire. In 1809, Napoleon named Thomire "Engraver to the Emperor." Two years later, his firm of some eight hundred craftsmen became Furniture Suppliers to their Majesties. The ongoing Napoleonic wars and the Continental blockade hurt French exports. Despite the turmoil, Paris reclaimed its position as the center of style and taste.

Among Napoleon's most extraordinary commissions were table services and furnishings from the Sèvres porcelain factory. Founded in Vincennes in 1740 and relocated to Sèvres in 1756, the factory became the preeminent porcelain manufacturer in Europe. Louis XV, an early investor, became sole owner in 1759. After the French Revolution, the factory nearly went bankrupt. In 1800, Lucien Bonaparte appointed Alexandre Brongniart director. Namesake of his father Alexandre Theodore Brongniart, architect of the Bourse, he was trained as an engineer and scientist and had taught mineralogy at Paris's Museum of Natural History.

For the next nearly five decades, Brongniart transformed Sèvres's organization and production. The former engineer oversaw the development of a more cost effective two-story kiln and a lathe to produce intricate guilloche decoration. Brongniart recruited top designers including his father and Charles Percier to create new neoclassical style models and forms. Empire-style gilding, rich border designs, and elaborate figural scenes were introduced. A new enamel color palette enabled the factory to create faux marble and hardstone surfaces. In 1804, soft-paste porcelain was abandoned for a more durable hard-paste porcelain.

Also that year, Brongniart began reporting to Vivant Denon, newly named head of imperial factories. In addition to keeping Napoleon posted on progress at Sèvres, Denon made suggestions about production and the selection of his favorite Etruscan and Egyptian forms. Denon also ordered busts of himself and medallions with his own portrait. Among his projects were the Egyptian breakfast service with images based on his bestseller *Travels*.

For his personal dinner service, also known as the Headquarters service, Napoleon supplied a list of twenty-eight palace views, city images, and landscapes to which Brongniart and Denon added images of artworks, museums and monuments in Paris. ". . . his wish is that of these designs, there be not one battle scene or named individual, but that, on the contrary, the subjects offer only vague allusions which will provoke pleasant memories," Daru wrote Brongniart.[22] Many of these "pleasant memories" happened to be in Italy, Egypt, Austria, Prussia, and Poland where he had won battles.

Napoleon visited Sèvres once a year, often showing up unannounced with Joséphine and several ladies of her court. Sometimes Joséphine visited by herself, appropriating objects. Napoleon enjoyed showing off the factory to visiting sovereigns and dignitaries. On January 4, 1805, Brongniart sent the mayor of Sèvres a list of invitees for a visit by Pius VII. Napoleon instituted New Year's gifts, a chance to show off the artistry of Sèvres. The presents were given to foreign sovereigns and members of the imperial family, along with senior officials. Sèvres produced a wide variety of decorated dishes, toilet articles, and inkwells for the numerous imperial residences. Table services, clocks, plaques, and candelabra required the collaboration of different craftsmen.

Napoleon continued to offer suggestions. In 1806, he instructed Sèvres to: "Place on the services . . . views of the Adige, of Venice, of Genoa, and of the realm of Italy, more interesting and more historical than those to be found elsewhere."[23] For diplomatic gifts, the Emperor directed Sèvres to "use portraits, views of Paris and of different imperial palaces," and "finally, replace all the figures of nude women and insignificant landscapes . . . with things that are known and historical." But Napoleon could be a demanding, impatient patron. On August 18, 1807, after someone in the imperial entourage complained about color flaws in the porcelain, he threatened to close the factory. The following year, when Brongniart was away from Sèvres, he was told that as a result of delays, Denon feared "that the Emperor might become angry and the results might be very unpleasant for everyone."

Paris was still celebrating the victory of Austerlitz in April 1806 when Napoleon ordered a series of four *guéridons* or circular tables. Sèvres had produced some circular tables during Louis XVI's reign, adorned with porcelain plaques. The recent development of hard-paste porcelain allowed the factory to produce larger plaques—over three feet in diameter. Napoleon's admiration for Alexander the Great was expressed in the Table of the Great Commanders. The table combines some of the finest and most technically challenging work achieved by Sèvres in the early nineteenth century, writes Joanna Gwilt.[24]

The heads and scenes on the circular porcelain table top are painted to resemble antique cameos in sardonyx on a dark brown ground. The central medallion is a profile of Alexander the Great, with an unmistakable resemblance to Napoleon. Around Alexander's head is a frieze in simulated relief painted in matte gold washed with brown, depicting three major events: his entry into Babylon; his reception by the Egyptian priests in the temple of Jupiter-Ammon; and his defeat of the Persians under Darius.

Surrounding Alexander are one dozen smaller profile heads of other commanders and philosophers from antiquity, along with scenes recalling key events from their lives. Clockwise from the top, the figures are: Pericles, Scipio Africanus, Pompey, Augustus, Septimus Severus, Constantine, Trajan, Caesar, Mithridates, Hannibal, Themistocles, and Miltiades. The table took six years to finish at a cost of thirty thousand francs, a hefty increase from the original ten-month, nineteen-thousand-franc estimate.[25]

Napoleon also thought up the companion Table of the Marshals, also known as the Table of Austerlitz, with himself taking Alexander the Great's place. Charles Percier provided drawings for the portrait of Napoleon standing in ceremonial costume surrounded by medallions of a dozen of his leading marshals and generals, along with martial virtues for the pedestal.

Though Brongniart warned Daru in July 1807 that Jean-Baptiste Isabey had never painted on porcelain before, the miniaturist was summonsed to Sèvres. Isabey painted Napoleon encircled by thirteen gold rays, each with the name of a victory. Between the rays are thirteen polychrome medallions with portraits of eleven marshals of the Empire and of two great court dignitaries. The gilded porcelain cylindrical pedestal featured biscuit relief figures representing the martial virtues. Thomire supplied the table's rich bronze mounts.

Four years and 35,000 francs later, the Marshal's Table was delivered to Napoleon at the Tuileries Palace where it was installed in the Empress's apartment (November 18, 1810). The classically inspired table perfectly expressed Napoleon's taste for the monumental and grandiose. "The epic of Napoleonic France represented with striking simplicity in the portraits of her most famous leaders. Another new and spectacular success for artists of Sèvres," wrote Grandjean.[26] Two years later, Napoleon loaned the Marshal's Table to the Salon of 1812, where Isabey exhibited it under his own name.

Imperial glamour rubbed off on Napoleon's family members whose Paris residences featured lavish décor. Caroline and Joachim Murat commissioned a shimmering silver salon at the Élysée Palace. Pauline Bonaparte's boudoir at the Hôtel de Charost boasted a canopied bed framed by four Egyptian caryatids. Eugène de Beauharnais and his mother Joséphine spent vast sums transforming the Hôtel de Torcy into the luxurious Hôtel de Beauharnais (today's German embassy) complete with a Turkish fantasy boudoir. The Hôtel de Beauharnais was irreconcilable with Napoleon's frugal Corsican upbringing. Exasperated by the bills, he appropriated the property.

In a court noted for extravagance, Napoleon surprisingly kept a close eye on the purse strings. After reviewing a furnishings budget, he wrote: "I am returning approval of the budget for 1807. I have verified the figures myself and eliminated unnecessary expenditure. No money should be spent before I have approved the estimate either for decoration or for furnishing. Everything must be of the best, as if it were to last 100 years."[27]

In addition to refurbishing the former royal châteaux, Napoleon continued to beautify Paris. From Saint-Cloud, he commissioned fifteen monumental fountains on May 2, 1806. Announcing that it was his wish "to do something grand and useful for Paris," he decreed that the city's new fountains would run twenty-four seven. "Starting next July 1, the water will flow in all the fountains of Paris day and night, so as to provide not only for the particular services and needs of the public, but also to refresh the atmosphere and wash the streets."[28]

As Katia Frey notes, "The utilitarian aspect of the act was essential, for if the fountains contribute to the beautification of the city, they also made it possible to palliate a cruel shortage that its population had always suffered."[29] In the end, Napoleonic fountains totaled nearly thirty. Napoleon's engineers built new fountains in the city's major outdoor markets, and installed several hundred simple stone blocks with water taps. In 1812, Napoleon would make water from Paris's fountains free.

Once again, Napoleon looked to Rome for his water program. According to Pliny, before leaving to defeat Antony and Cleopatra in Actium, Agrippa added hundreds of pools, water jets, and fountains. Inspired by Hellenistic fountains, Rome's new fountains were often lavishly decorated with bronze and marble statues and marble columns.[30] Houses and villas of wealthy Romans also featured small fountains. After visiting Rome around 164 C.E., the Greek doctor Galen wrote: "The beauty and number of Rome's fountains is wonderful. None emits water that is foul, mineralized, turbid, hard, or cold."[31]

Fed by its aqueduct network, Roman fountains came in many forms, including large flat vases of various sizes made from a single piece of hard stone like porphyry, granite, alabaster, and marble. "More than isolated monuments, they [fountains] are integral elements of Roman identity, linked together by hidden, subterranean conduits of metal, stone, and terra-cotta," writes Katherine Rinne. "Each fountain is part of a hydrological system that includes the Tiber River, springs, streams, swamps, sewers, aqueducts, wells, conduits, cisterns, floors, and rainwater, all linked through topography."[32] Where an aqueduct entered the city, it was the ancient custom to build a nympheum, a large splendid fountain inscribed with the name of the sponsoring emperor. Many fountains were decorated with bronze or marble statues of divinities and marble columns. Often the water flowed out of bronze statues of boys, tritons, Nereids, and satyrs, and into basins.

The popes continued the fountain tradition, placing their names and insignia below the miter and crossed keys on the six great papal terminal fountains—Trevi, Moses, Paul V, Naiads, Pincian Hill, and Piazzale degli Eroi. For added prestige, the popes also incorporated a half-dozen ancient Egyptian obelisks transported to Rome by a series of emperors. Sixtus V started the trend in the late sixteenth century with the Vatican obelisk (in front of St. Peter's), the Lateran obelisk, and the obelisk of the Piazza del Popolo—on top of which he placed crosses. Relocating obelisks continued in the seventeenth and eighteenth centuries with the Piazza Navona (Bernini's Four Rivers Fountain, 1651) and Piazza del Pantheon (1711), along with the obelisk of Monte Cavallo placed between the statues of the Dioscuri by the Palazzo Quirinale (1786).[33] Pius VII embellished his predecessor's monument at the Quirinale, substituting an ancient basin for the Renaissance fountain.

Rome's spectacular fountains distinguished the city from other European capitals. As the poet Percy Bysshe Shelley wrote: "The fountains of Rome are in themselves magnificent combinations of art, such as alone, it were worth coming to see."[34] Fountains with spectacular sculpture moved beyond their original functional purpose. During the summer, the drains of the Palazza Navona were plugged, filling the square with water as a refuge from the heat.

Napoleon's early fountains were relatively modest in size, fed by a limited amount of water that poured through traditional spouts. One of the first to be completed, the Fontaine des Invalides at the esplanade of the Hôtel des Invalides, displayed one of Napoleon's war trophies—Venice's famous winged lion taken from St. Mark's in 1797. Bearing inscriptions in Latin and French, a simple stone pedestal supporting the lion rose from a large circular basin. On each of the pedestal's four sides, water spouted from small bronze lion heads modeled by Chaudet.

Many of the city's fountains were designed by François-Jean Bralle, chief engineer of the water service for the City of Paris, who had worked on water pumps at Chaillot, Gros Caillou, and La Samaritaine. Among Bralle's fountains were the Palm, Censier Street, Fellah, Pointe Saint-Eustache, Mars, and Leda. Two of the most dramatic were the Fellah Fountain on the rue de Sèvres and the Palm Fountain in the Place du Châtelet (both circa 1806).

With sculptor Pierre-Nicolas Beauvallet, Bralle created the Fellah Fountain to commemorate Napoleon's Egyptian campaign. *Fellah* is Arabic for peasant or worker, associated with carrying water. Reflecting France's craze for Egypt, the fountain evokes a portico from an Egyptian temple. In the trapezoidal niche stood a stone statue of Emperor Hadrian's young lover Antinous, who was considered a model of antique male beauty. Wearing an Egyptian headdress and loincloth, the figure pours water from two pitchers into a basin. From there, the water flows to the grid from a lion's mouth.

Beauvallet modeled Antinous after a famous statue at the Louvre, part of the art confiscated from Italy by Napoleon, originally at Hadrian's Villa at Tivoli. Bralle and Beauvallet may have also been inspired by artist Hubert Robert's depiction of Rome's Villa Albani where two statues of Antinous in niches frame the main pool. At the top of the monument, Bralle replaced the winged globe that usually adorned the tympanum of Egyptian temples with the symbol of the Empire—an imperial eagle with spread wings.

In 1806, Bralle and Beauvallet collaborated again on the Mars Fontaine on rue Saint-Dominique, inspired by the nearby L'Hôpital de la Garde du Gros-Caillou and Champs de Mars. One side of the fountain features a sculpture of Mars, Roman god of war, and Hygeia, goddess of health and daughter of the god of medicine. Beauvallet depicts Mars in antique style—helmeted, naked, and leaning on a large shield, though he did give the god of war a moustache. Beside him, Hygeia offers Mars a drink. The fountain's other sides are decorated in high relief with large urns featuring Bacchic scenes. Below, allegorical marine animals adorn the corners of the pedestal.

In 1802, to improve traffic and access to the Île de la Cité, Napoleon ordered the demolition of the Grand Châtelet on the Seine. Gridlock in early nineteenth-century Paris was nothing new. The narrow streets of ancient Rome were effectively one-way, allowing just one wagon or chariot to pass at a time. Drivers sent a runner to hold up traffic at the other end of the street until the chariot had passed by. In 45 B.C.E., Julius Caesar tried to improve congestion in the city by banning carts, wagons, and chariots between sunrise and mid-afternoon. Goods could only be delivered to the shops of Trajan's Market by wagon at night. As Kenneth D. Matthews writes: ". . . the late Republican and imperial governments considered the safety and unimpeded flow of pedestrian traffic a primary requirement in the effective protection of private and public life during the daytime."[35]

Over the centuries the Grand Châtelet, a tweflth-century stone stronghold, had been repurposed as a prison and headquarters for Paris's military police. Now the structure was replaced with the small square, the Place du Châtelet. Following proposals for an arch or column dedicated to Napoleon, the decision was made to construct a large fountain in the center of the new square. Modeled after a Roman triumphal column, the 1808 Fontaine du Palmier, or Palm Tree Fountain, took its name from its palm leaf/stalk decoration of its column and capital. The top of the seventy-foot-tall column was crowned with Louis-Simon Boizot's gilt bronze figure of Victory holding a laurel wreath in each hand. A proxy for the emperor, she symbolized a dozen of Napoleon's victories inscribed on bands in gold letters on the column—Arcole, Austerlitz, Danzig, Eylau, Friedland, Jena, Lodi, Morengo, Mont-Thabor, Pyramides, Rivoli, and Ulm.

Simon Boizot ringed the column's square base with four female allegorical stone figures representing the cardinal virtues of Prudence, Temperance, Justice, and Strength. Boizot also adorned the pedestal with bronze imperial eagles and dolphin heads, and water-spouting cornucopia.[36] The dramatic monument ended up costing four times the estimate of fifteen thousand francs.[37] After the Palm Fountain was moved some fifty feet in 1858 to accommodate changes to the place du Châtelet, architect Gabriel Davioud added the circular basins adorned with Henri Jacquemart's four dramatic water-spewing sphinxes.[38]

The Leda Fountain, built in 1808, was originally built against the wall of a private garden at the corner of the rue de Vaugirard and rue du Regard (in 1864, it was moved to the back side of the Medici Fountain). Inspired by Renaissance sculpture, Achille Valois created an elegant bas-relief panel of Leda and the swan. While Cupid draws an arrow from his quiver, Leda plays with the swan spewing water from its beak into a basin. The bas-relief is raised on a pedestal, between two pilasters decorated with intertwined dolphins. The pediment originally featured a large eagle holding a laurel crown—symbol of the Napoleonic Empire.

Later fountains, including those designed by Girard, featured water as the main decorative element, shooting dramatically into the air and cascading into the basins. The Château-d'Eau (located in what was later renamed the Place de la Republique) was Paris's first monumental fountain to feature two circular stone basins, one above the other on a column, with water overflowing the basins and falling into a larger circular basin below (this design had appeared on a smaller scale in Roman gardens and in Aix-en-Provence). In a nod to Egypt, eight Nubian lions spouted water into the lower basin.

Napoleon, like Julius Caesar, was consumed by warfare and spent little time in his capital. Despite this, the two energetic leaders succeeded in executing numerous civic improvements for Rome and Paris. Nearly two millennia later, Napoleon took his cues from the great Roman general and his successors—improving Paris's water supply, beautifying the capital with fountains, and glorifying his Empire with monumental architecture and luxurious imperial palaces.

Like Julius Caesar, Napoleon would also grapple with governing his growing realm.

TWO

A FAMILY OF KINGS

Through continued military conquests, Rome's emperors expanded the network of provinces. By the reign of Marcus Aurelius, the Roman Empire was a global superpower, with a population of some fifty million. In 212, Caracalla, the eldest son of Septimius Severus, extended Roman citizenship to all freeborn inhabitants of the Empire. A cynical Cassius Dio remarked that rather than being honorable, Caracalla's edict was intended to increase the number of taxpayers.

United by Roman rule and administration, the provinces were cash cows and food baskets supplying wheat, oil, and wine. Local industries also helped feed the Empire's war machine. The iron works in Gaul and the Danubian basin, for example, produced weapons for Rome's legions.

Local artistic traditions were encouraged—from glassmaking and mosaics to ceramics and textiles. In the third century, Rome-based writer Philostratus raved about the refined champlevé enamel of "barbarian" artists living in Gaul and Britain. Though each area retained its traditions, shared Roman art and architecture created a cultural unity across the Empire. As Jean Sorabella writes, early third-century Roman tourists would have felt right at home in the provinces whose cities boasted statues of the emperor and Roman baths, basilicas, and amphitheaters.[1]

The Roman Forum in the city center was the Republic's political hub. In 46 B.C.E., Julius Caesar dedicated the Julian Forum nearby, financed with spoils from the Gallic wars (Caesar's rival Pompey, meanwhile, built in the Campus Martius). Its temple was dedicated to Venus Genetrix, alluding to Caesar's descent from the goddess. Four more imperial forums followed: the Forums of Augustus, Vespasian, Nerva, and Trajan. These *Fora Imperatorum* assumed cultural, administrative, legal, and cultural functions, and served as powerful propaganda for their eponymous emperors.[2] The Forums were "the setting for the most important rite of legitimisation of the power of the emperors, with their deification after their death . . ." writes Marta Chiara Guerrieri.[3]

Nepotism was alive and well in the Roman Empire. In fact, the word came from the Latin word *nepos,* meaning grandson or descendant, evolving over time to signify nephew. In the Renaissance and Baroque periods, the term nepotism described the standard practice of popes and the French nobility naming their "nephews" (often their illegitimate children) as cardinal nephews, prelates, and other elite positions.

To guarantee themselves allies, France's Bourbon kings placed members of their family on the thrones of Spain and Naples. Napoleon extended this tactic beyond Spain and Naples, establishing what he called a "system" of family appointments. In 1805, after launching the Kingdom of Italy with his stepson Eugène de Beauharnais as viceroy, Napoleon told diplomat François Miot de Mélito, "I am making a family of Kings or rather of Viceroys." In addition to his stepson, Napoleon elevated five of his seven siblings: Joseph as king of Naples and later Spain, Louis as king of Holland, Jérôme as king of Westphalia, Elisa as grand duchess of Tuscany, and Caroline and Joachim Murat as queen and king of Naples.

Though Napoleon brought his clan great wealth and prestige, his largesse came with strings attached. The Bonaparte siblings were expected to be puppet rulers. Napoleon's demand that his family members be extensions of him weakened their effectiveness, explains Philip Dwyer.[4] Independent thinking was not tolerated, as Elisa soon learned. After complaining about an order by French officials, she received this alarming letter from her brother:

"You have the right to appeal to me against my Minister's decisions, but you have no right to hinder their execution in any way. The Ministers speak in my name. No one has any right to paralyse, or stop the execution, of the orders they transmit. . . . You are a subject, and, like every other French subject, you are obliged to obey the orders of the Ministers—for a writ of Habeas Corpus, issued by the Minister of Police, would fully suffice to arrest you."[5]

Napoleon shared power until he was challenged. About Joseph's ambition to be named heir to the throne in 1804, Napoleon told civil servant Pierre Louis Roederer: "Nothing can wipe this from my memory. It was as if he [Joseph] had told a passionate lover that he had slept with his mistress, or at least that he had hopes of doing so. . . . Power is my mistress. I have worked too hard at her conquest to allow anyone to take her away from me or even covet her."[6] When Louis Bonaparte tried to create Dutch marshals, Napoleon overruled him, arguing that satellite kingdoms could not have this prerogative.[7]

The purpose of Napoleon's family-run satellites was to achieve, like the Romans, a pan-European empire. As he explained: "One of my first grand ideas was the consolidation, the concentration of the same geographic peoples who were dispersed and fragmented by revolutions and politics. In Europe there are thirty million French, fifteen million Spaniards, fifteen million Italians, thirty million Germans, and twenty million Poles; I want to make of each one nation."[8] Toward this end, satellite kingdoms across continental Europe were governed under the Napoleonic Code.

In Napoleon's quest for European hegemony, matchmaking continued to be a tactic, helping strengthen France's strategic positions across the continent. Roman generals and emperors almost exclusively arranged marriages for strategic dynastic and political purposes. The strategy had mixed results. In 59 B.C.E. for example, Julius Caesar married off his beloved teenage daughter Julia to forty-four-year-old Pompey, thirty years her senior, to seal a political alliance, the First Triumvirate. Five years later, while her father was in Britain, Julia died in childbirth along with her baby (Julia's mother had also died in childbirth). The alliance fell apart after Julia's death, leading to civil war.

In 178, Marcus Aurelius arranged for his sixteen-year-old son and co-ruler Commodus to marry Crispina. Hailing from a wealthy, illustrious family, the new empress was the daughter of a consul and granddaughter of an heiress and a consul/senator. A decade into their marriage when Crispina hadn't produced an heir, Commodus accused her of adultery and exiled her to Capri where she was executed. Several years later, Commodus was strangled in his bath, ending the Nerva-Antonine dynasty.

As in imperial Rome, Napoleon's political unions were largely failures. In 1802, his brother Louis, who suffered from poor mental health, wed Joséphine's daughter Hortense. After a miserable marriage, they separated in 1810. In August 1803, less than a year after his sister Pauline's first husband General Victor-Emmanuel Leclerc died of yellow fever in Saint-Domingue (today's Haiti), Napoleon married off the twenty-three-year-old widow. The groom was Camillo Borghese, uber-wealthy scion of the aristocratic Roman family. Napoleon saw the union as a way to legitimize his claim to the Kingdom of Italy. About the unhappy match, Pauline said that she would have preferred to remain a widow than "be married to a eunuch."[9]

In January 1806, two days after being adopted by Napoleon, Joséphine's son Eugène married Princess Amalia of Bavaria, eldest daughter of his stepfather's ally in the Confederation of the Rhine, King Maximilian I. In April 1806, Napoleon further secured the alliance by arranging for Joséphine's niece, Stéphanie de Beauharnais to wed the crown prince of Baden, another Confederation member. Jérôme succumbed to pressure from his brother, divorcing his pregnant American wife and marrying Catherine of Wurttemberg. In 1807, he became king of newly created Westphalia.

The Bonaparte siblings brought their own households with them, and added preeminent local nobles to their satellite courts. They refurnished the interiors of their numerous palaces in the Empire style, helping spread the aesthetics and symbols of Napoleonic France throughout Europe. In addition, they copied the etiquette and lavish costumes of their brother's court for their own.[10]

In Milan, Eugène de Beauharnais, Viceroy of the Kingdom of Italy, established a household administered by French and Italian grand officers and an intendant. Among the duties of his household was running and decorating palaces in Milan, Parma, and Venice with French- and Italian-made furnishings.[11] The vice-regal couple first moved into the Royal Palace. They would soon occupy the Villa Belgiojoso Bonaparte, along with the Villa Pisani at Stra, and the Villa Reale in Monza.

In January 1807, Napoleon bought the Villa Pisani near Padua for Eugène. Ridden with gambling debts, the Venetian patrician family sold their beautiful gardens and villa to the emperor for 1,901,000 Venetian liras. Built by Alvise Pisani, former ambassador to the court of Louis XIV, the late baroque villa boasted a beautiful garden and 114 rooms in honor of its owner who became Venice's 114th doge in 1735. Eugène made a series of improvements, adding Empire-style rooms at the end of the façade facing the Brenta River.

Over the next five years, the Kingdom of Italy grew to include Venice, Dalmatia, the Papal territories of Macerata, Fermo, Urbino, Ancona, and the South Tyrol. Napoleon's loyal stepson established a centralized state government with new legislative and administrative institutions. Eugène also undertook an ambitious plan to turn Milan into what Hugh Honour calls "the cynosure of Empire taste."[12] Handsome neoclassical gateways were erected around the city.

The area surrounding the Castello Sforzesco, used by the Austrians as a barracks, was transformed into an enormous circular piazza—home to the future Bonaparte Forum. Like the fora of ancient Rome, the Bonaparte Forum was to feature baths, a museum, Pantheon, theater, and customs house. Work began to the north on a triumphal arch, the Arco del Sempione, intended as the Forum's entrance. A nearby arena was built in 1806 and 1807 with neoclassical gateways designed by Luigi Canonica. The largest arena since Roman times, it was used for chariot racing, mock sea battles, and other neoclassical entertainments.

Like ancient Rome, Napoleon "wanted the capital of his thirty departements to contain the richest store of treasures in the Empire," writes Germain Bazin.[13] In addition to a network of provincial museums created in France, galleries were established in several satellites including Milan. Eugène de Beauharnais dispatched commissioners to Venice, Bologna, Emilia, and the Veneto to select works from various depots containing art confiscated from suppressed churches and convents.[14] The Pinacoteca di Brera became home to northern Italy's most important works of art, including many altarpieces and other religious paintings. The gallery opened on Napoleon's birthday, August 15, 1809. Andrea Appiani, a professor at the Brera Fine Arts academy established by Austrian empress Maria Theresa, was named curator.

Masterpieces of the Brera include Raphael's *Sposalizio* or *The Marriage of the Virgin* (1504), acquired by the government of Milan for the museum. Originally from the Church of San Francesco in Città di Castello, the painting was inspired by an altarpiece of the same subject by Raphael's teacher Pietro Perugino. Raphael placed his figures in a semicircle before a precisely painted temple, connecting all the elements by mathematical relations of proportion. The picture perfectly expresses Raphael's view that artists had the duty of "making things not as Nature makes them, but as Nature should."[15]

The Brera was also enriched with Eugène's gift of two paintings. Piero della Francesca's *Madonna of Montefeltro* (1472–74) originally graced Urbino's Church of San Bernardino, built by Federico da Montefeltro for his tomb. Montefeltro is in fact part of Piero's altarpiece, dressed as a military commander, kneeling in front of the sacred group. In 1811, Eugène donated Giovanni Bellini's *Pietà* (1467–70), formerly in Bologna's Sampieri collection.

⚜

In March 1806, Napoleon replaced Ferdinand and Maria Carolina with his brother Joseph as king of the Two Sicilies. Also that year, in recognition for Joachim Murat's role in the German campaign, Napoleon rewarded his sister and brother-in-law with the Duchy of Berg and Cleves, created with territory seized from Prussia and Bavaria.

The seventh of the Bonaparte siblings, Caroline Murat was born in Ajaccio, Corsica, and schooled in Saint-Germain-en-Laye where she was classmates with her future sister-in-law, Hortense de Beauharnais. In Paris, she fell head over heels for dashing cavalry officer Joachim Murat who was recovering from an injury suffered during the Egypt campaign.

In early 1800, the eighteen-year-old married Murat, fourteen years her senior.

The son of an innkeeper from the Lot region, Murat entered the army after a brief stint at the seminary in Toulouse. He earned a reputation as one of revolutionary France's most daring soldiers. Impressed by Murat's abilities during the 1795 royalist insurrection in Paris, Napoleon promoted him to aide-de-camp. During the battles at Austerlitz, Jena, Stettin, and Eylau, Murat became famous for his daring maneuvers and equestrian skills, along with his splendid uniforms. From Egypt to Russia, Murat participated in all of Napoleon's major campaigns.

About his youngest sister, Napoleon remarked: "Of all my family, she's the one that resembles me the most." French foreign minister Talleyrand echoed this when he wrote: "Madame Murat had the head of Cromwell upon the shoulders of a well-shaped woman. Born with much grandeur of character, strong mind, and sublime ideas; possessing a subtle and delicate wit, together with amiability and grace, seductive beyond expression; she was deficient in nothing but in the art of concealing her desire to rule . . ."[16]

The Murats expressed their sophisticated taste at various residences: the Hôtel de Thélusson in Paris with its impressive rotunda by Ledoux, the Château de Villiers with Antonio Canova's two statues of *Cupid and Psyche*, and the Élysée palace, which they bought in 1805. After renovating the palace with Empire-style furnishings, the Murats hosted balls, receptions, and parties, showing off their art collection featuring Italian Renaissance paintings by Fra Bartolomeo, Guido Reni, and Veronese. After the Murats' departure for Naples, Joséphine had many of the pictures transferred to Malmaison.

While Murat had a series of affairs, Caroline took as lovers General Junot, her husband's successor as governor of Paris, and Clemens von Metternich, Austria's ambassador to France.[17] In her memoirs, Madame de Rémusat summed up Caroline's ambition and charm. "Her beauty was set off by the most exquisite dress; her pretensions were great; her manners affable when she thought it prudent, and more than affable to men whom she wished to fascinate. . . . [S]he endeavored to make friends among the influential members of the Government who might be useful to her. . . . She wanted to secure her present position, and especially to elevate her husband in spite of himself."[18]

In 1808, the Murats succeeded Joseph Bonaparte in Naples when he was promoted to king of Spain. Like Joseph, the couple and their four children made Caserta their main residence. During his tenure, Bourbon Charles VII (future Charles III of Spain) had renovated the Royal Palace which had fallen into disrepair during the rule of the Habsburg's viceroys. He preferred the country palaces and hunting grounds at Portici, Persano, and the Astroni.

As a symbol of his court, Charles decided to outdo Versailles with a spectacular new palace. Rome-trained architect Luigi Vanvitelli designed and supervised construction of the Reggia at Caserta. With the help of Luigi's son Carlo Vanvitelli, Charles's son Ferdinand continued the ambitious project (the palace was finally finished after the return of the Bourbons in 1815). The Reggia's state apartments boasted "one of the most splendid flights of rooms in any royal palace in Europe," writes Anthony Blunt, filled with classically inspired sculpture, paintings, and furnishings.[19]

Now it was the Murats' turn. The fashionable power couple tried to out-dazzle the deposed Bourbons, recreating their posh Paris interiors with some of the state treasures from the Elysée Palace. For the royal palaces of Caserta, Capodimonte, and Portici, Caroline ordered Empire-style furniture—bronzes from Thomire, clocks from Breguet, and furnishings from Jacob-Desmalter. To redecorate her favorite residence, Portici, near Herculaneum, Caroline hired architect Étienne-Chérubin Leconte.[20]

A savvy collector, Caroline acquired a pair of Correggio paintings, the *Ecce Homo* and the *Education of Love.* Caroline also cultivated relationships with contemporary painters, notably Jean-Auguste-Dominique Ingres. Commissions from Ingres included the *Betrothal of Raphael* and *Paolo and Francesca*, along with the famous *Grande Odalisque* and its lost companion, the *Sleeper of Naples.* The lost picture was a pendant for a female nude that Joachim Murat had bought in 1808. Unable to complete the order on time, Ingres later sold the *Grande Odalisque.* Ingres would stay at the court of Naples from February to May 1814, when he visited Pompeii and painted Caroline's portrait.

Caroline also tapped one of her brother's favorite portraitists, François-Pascal-Simon Gérard, to portray her family in numerous portraits, including her two sons and two daughters. She also commissioned works from landscape painters Alexandre-Hyacinthe Dunouy, Jean-Joseph-Xavier Bidauld, and Benjamin Rolland. Caroline recruited two Parisian artists to be her court painters—David student Élie-Honoré Montagny and Louis Nicolas Lemasle, who painted events of her reign and scenes of Naples.

The Murats also collected engraved gems, including those of Filippo Rega. After a decade in Rome where he studied with the celebrated engraver Giovanni Pichler, Rega returned to his native Naples where his clients included the Bourbons and Joseph Bonaparte (who made him a knight of Napoleon's Legion of Honor). From 1804, Rega worked for the Naples Mint, which he would later direct. Like Pichler, Rega liked to sign his cameo portraits and engraved gemstones in Greek letters, adding to their aura of antiquity.[21]

The Murats' ambitious urban renewal projects included construction of the Piazza del Plebiscito and the Corso Napoleone, restoration of the Academy of Drawing, and creation of a museum of natural history. But their most important accomplishment was resuming archaeological excavations at Pompeii begun by Charles and Ferdinand. For the first time, the archeological sites were open to the public, attracting foreign artists and architects.[22]

Among the frequent visitors to Pompeii was French architect François Mazois, recruited by Joachim Murat. Like his teacher Charles Percier, Mazois traveled to Rome to study the city's ancient monuments in 1808. During his restoration of the palace of Portici, Mazois became smitten with Pompeii. Caroline Murat gave him access to the site, closely guarded by the Naples Academy, and an allowance of one thousand francs a month. The result was Mazois's *Les Ruines de Pompéi dessinées et mesurées pendant les années 1809, 1810, 1811*, featuring measurements, descriptions, and drawings.[23]

New discoveries continued attracting artists. French antiquary Aubin-Louis Millin described the human tragedy along the Street of Tombs outside Pompeii: "A mother fled, dragging after her a part of her family: two daughters, and an infant whom she clutched in vain at her breast. There was no longer any hope; still gasping for breath in the midst of swirling clouds of burning cinders, and pressing against the walls of the portico, they fell exhausted by fatigue and suffering. The ash covered them, burying them all in the same tomb . . ." The finds were displayed at a public exhibition. In 1807, to protect Naple's cultural patrimony, the Murats passed a law prohibiting the export of antiquities and fine arts.[24] Louis Nicolas Lemasle would paint Joachim Murat's portrait by the Villa of Diamedes in Pompeii.

Caroline, who had owned a collection of Etruscan vases at the Château de Villiers, became increasingly passionate about antiquities. "She [Caroline] took a great interest in the excavations going on there and the number of workmen doubled and trebled during her stay in Naples," wrote Hortense de Beauharnais. "Many of the interesting objects dug up were used to form her own small museum" (the Queen's Museum at the Royal Palace of Naples).[25]

Caroline often found herself caught in the middle between her uncompromising brother and her husband. But she proved more adept at ruling than her husband. Having secured the authority to succeed Joachim as regent, the clever Caroline ruled Naples ably when he left for the Russian campaign in 1812. For a short, fleeting moment, her vast ambition was realized. In *Chariot of Aurora*, one of the last works by the porcelain factory Real fabbrica della porcellana di Napoli, Aurora leads a dozen dancers, the Hours, and two small putti. Caroline Murat sits on a chariot of the sun in place of Apollo.[26]

⚜

In June 1806, Napoleon transformed the two-hundred-year-old Dutch republic into a monarchy and installed his brother Louis as king. Louis chose the prosperous city of Amsterdam instead of The Hague, Holland's former administrative center, as his seat of power. For his palace, he appropriated the imposing Town Hall, centrally located in Dam Square by the Gothic Nieuwe Kerk (New Church). After ordering Amsterdam's city council to vacate the seventeenth-century building, Louis hired architect Jean-Thomas Thibault, a friend of Percier and Fontaine, to supervise a complete makeover.

Money was no object for the one-million-plus-guilder project (roughly equivalent to seven million euros today).[27] The finest decorators, cabinetmakers, and upholsterers from Amsterdam and The Hague went to work. The décor featured thousands of yards of sumptuous silk and satin and hundreds of chairs and tables in mahogany in the fashionable Empire style. The most expensive of the palace's thirteen clocks sported a figurine of Napoleon as Julius Caesar.[28]

On April 20, 1808, Holland's twenty-nine-year-old king traveled south from Utrecht to Amsterdam, where he received the keys to the city and passed through temporary triumphant arches. His state coach arrived at the new Dam Square Palace to a thirty-three-gun salute. Missing from the celebration were his estranged wife and son. In addition to the sumptuous Empire-style surroundings, Louis tried emulating the protocol of his brother's court in Paris. A copy of Ségur's detailed *Etiquette* was found in the palace library. Throughout the book, Louis had crossed out the words "imperial" and replaced them with "royal."[29]

Toward the back of the palace on the second floor, Louis formed a Royal Museum with works previously owned by the House of Orange, the city of Amsterdam, private collectors, and the National Gallery in The Hague (since 1800). (During the Directory in 1795, stadtholder William V's art collection was taken from The Hague to Paris.) Now the city of Amsterdam was forced to relinquish seven large paintings to Louis including Rembrandt's *Night Watch* and *Syndics of the Drapers' Guild* and Bartholomeus van der Helst's *Celebration of the Peace of Munster*. The Royal Museum opened on September 15, 1808, with an exhibition of Living Masters, largely historical paintings of the Netherlands. The museum's first catalogue appeared the next year with some 459 paintings. The collection would form the nucleus of the Rijksmuseum in 1885.

Louis's imperial household consisted of several hundred people, many of whom lived in the palace. Along with the impressive Grand Salon (the former Citizen's Hall) and Throne Room on the first floor, the king's apartment and queen's apartment were located in diagonal opposite corners. When Hortense finally arrived in 1810, she could not have been more unhappy with her dark northwest suite. "My salon was once a courtroom in which criminals were brought to justice," Hortense wrote. "It had a frieze of death's heads in black and white marble. . . . The corridors were gloomy; the air was foul and the suffocating sulphorous vapours rising from the canal came wafting through my windows."[30] After a four-week stay, Hortense and Crown Prince Napoleon-Louis left and never returned.

Not satisfied with three former palaces of the House of Orange, Louis Bonaparte acquired Het Loo, several properties in Utrecht, and a pavilion in Haarlem. But he would not get to enjoy them much. Displeased by his brother's reforms, Napoleon forced him out. In the summer of 1810, Louis abdicated in favor of his son. Napoleon overruled the succession and annexed Holland to the Empire. A month later, the royal palace at Dam Square officially became an imperial palace. Napoleon would stay there only once, in October 1811.

⚜

Frustrated by Portugal's defiance of his European blockade against British trade, Napoleon ordered General Jerot to cross the Pyrenees and invade the country. The Portuguese offered no resistance; Prince Regent John of Braganza left for Brazil aboard the Portuguese fleet. By the end of November 1807, the French army closed Lisbon's ports to English ships, bringing Britain into the Peninsular Wars.

The following March, Spain's ineffective Charles IV abdicated in favor of his son Ferdinand VII. Two months later, at a conference in Bayonne, Napoleon forced both father and son to abdicate. He installed his reluctant brother Joseph Bonaparte to the Spanish throne. After an uprising that month in Madrid and the French defeat at Bailén in July, Joseph fled his new capital.

Spanish opposition to French rule surprised Napoleon. Rather than being seen as a liberator, he was staunchly opposed with revolts and guerilla warfare. By the fall 1808, Napoleon crossed the Pyrenees to deal personally with "the Spanish ulcer" and reestablish Joseph on the throne. By December, Napoleon entered Madrid and began reorganizing its administration. Napoleon was impressed with the Royal Palace, Palacio Nuevo. Built on the site of the Alcázar Royal, the Habsburg palace destroyed by fire in 1734, the vast royal residence had taken three decades to erect. Napoleon would return to Paris determined to update Versailles.

In addition to forming an art museum, Joseph built and refurbished Madrid's public squares and boulevards, nicknamed "*plazuelas*," or little plazas.[31] In mid-1810, architect Silvestre Pérez, former pensionaire of the Saint Ferdinand Academy of Rome, proposed a transformative urban-development project. Several houses opposite the Royal Palace were razed to create a large space for a Forum Bonaparte, like the proposed forum in Milan.

A series of monumental plazas with columns and triumphal arches would link the palace to the Basilica of Saint Francis, repurposed as the National Assembly's Chamber. With these plazas, writes Adrián Almoguera, Pérez intended to create "an architecturally symbolic union" between executive power represented by the palace and the legislative power of the people of Spain, represented by the former church. The ambitious plan also featured access routes to the Forum, including a triumphal arch as a grand entrance for the Avenue de Segovia.[32]

Denon accompanied Napoleon to Spain in 1808, looking for the finest art for the Musée Napoléon. Though the museum was now filled with pilfered masterworks from the Renaissance and Dutch and Flemish Baroque, Spain was not well represented. Long isolated from France, Spain's art represented an exciting new school for the museum director. But Denon's excitement quickly faded when he discovered that Joseph Bonaparte had beaten him to it.

In just months as Spain's new king, Joseph consolidated some 1,500 artworks at the Prado from various royal castles and suppressed religious houses to form a national museum. Built by Charles VII in 1785 to house the Natural History Cabinet, the building was repurposed by his grandson Ferdinand VII as the Royal Museum of Paintings and Sculptures. On January 18, 1809, the disappointed Denon wrote a friend from Valladolid: ". . . twenty paintings of the Spanish school absolutely needed by the Musée . . . [which] would have been a trophy in perpetuity of this last campaign."[33]

Denon urged Napoleon to suggest to Joseph that he donate a selection of paintings to the Musée Napoléon. To identify potential canvases, Denon formed a committee whose members included Charles's IV's former court painters Francisco Goya and Mariano Salvador Maella. The committee earmarked masterworks by Velazquez, Ribera, and Murillo, mainly from the Spanish royal collection.

But the Spaniards stalled. When the art finally arrived in Paris in 1813, Denon deemed just half a dozen of the fifty paintings museum worthy.[34] In 1819, the restored Ferdinand VII opened the Museo del Prado to the public. Decades later, Francisco Goya's powerful commemoration of Spanish resistance to Napoleon, *The Third of May 1808*, was taken out of storage.

THREE

VENUS VICTRIX

On April 24, 1808, Prince Camillo Borghese was welcomed to Turin by the city's mayor and other officials. The crowds also turned out—not to see Piedmont's new governor general, but to catch a glimpse of his glamorous spouse. A celebrity in her own right, Napoleon's favorite sister Pauline Bonaparte Borghese was considered one of Europe's most beautiful women.

When Napoleon dispatched the couple to Turin, Pauline was living in Nice apart from her husband. She initially refused to go, declaring the city ugly and boring. Pauline reportedly didn't say a word to Camillo throughout the trip. As their convoy entered Turin, Pauline looked out from her sedan. Her worst fears were confirmed—the former capital of Savoy and the kingdom of Sardinia reminded her of a military camp.[1]

By installing his sister and wealthy Italian brother-in-law in Turin, Napoleon hoped to win over Piedmont's nobility and reduce tensions with the locals. Under French control since 1799 and annexed in 1802, Piedmont had been plagued by revolts and economic woes. The couple moved into the Palazzo Chiablese, part of the Royal Palace and former residence of Maurice and Luisa Cristina of Savoy. Like Napoleon's other relatives, the Bogheses organized their own court, mainly consisting of the old Piedmont nobility.

For a short time, Pauline played along, attending parties, banquets, receptions, and horse races. But soon after their arrival in Turin, Pauline left Camillo and the Palazzo Chiablese for the Palazzina di Caccia, confiscated from the former king of Piedmont-Sardinia. Built in the early eighteenth century as a royal hunting lodge for Victor Amadeus II, king of Sardinia, the Palazzina was located at Stupinigi, about six miles southwest of Turin. The House of Savoy had used the residence for dynastic weddings, like that of Maria Teresa, princess of Savoy, to Louis XVI's brother Charles Philippe, the future Charles X of France. In April 1805, before his coronation as king of Italy in Milan, Napoleon went hunting in the park.

Pauline and Camillo Borghese had been living separate lives for some time. Pauline was only happy in Paris and spent much of her time at her chic Paris residence, the Hôtel de Charost in rue du Faubourg Saint-Honoré (today's Hôtel Borghese). Though Pauline was not fond of her sister-in-law Joséphine, the two women shared a sophisticated sense of style and luxurious taste.

For her wedding, Pauline received three hundred thousand francs worth of jewelry. Among her most prized items was a spectacular diadem with Roman cameos set in a diamond frieze.[2] In addition to a five hundred thousand-franc dowry, Napoleon gave Camillo the title prince of France and a 1,600-piece vermeil service by Parisian goldsmiths Odiot and Biennais with the Borghese family arms.[3]

A year into the marriage, tragedy struck. For an extended vacation in Tuscany, Camillo persuaded Pauline to leave Dermide, her six-year-old son with her first husband, in the care of his brother in Frascati. Napoleon had named his nephew after a hero in the epic poem, *Ossian*. During the vacation, Dermide fell ill with a fever and convulsions and died at the Villa Mondragone. Pauline never forgave Camillo and their shaky marriage fell apart.[4]

In 1806, Napoleon named Pauline the Princess and Duchess of Guastalla (Italy). Pauline proceeded to sell the duchy off to Parma for six million francs, retaining the princess title. Pauline's eccentric behavior and love life became legendary. According to Anthony Majanlahti, she used her ladies-in-waiting as footstools and had her African footman carry her to her bath.[5] Extramarital affairs with celebrities like violinist Niccolò Paganini, actor François-Joseph Talma, and writer Alexandre Dumas caused a scandal. In contrast to her infidelity, Pauline remained fiercely loyal to Napoleon.

After just forty days in Turin, Pauline left to take the waters at the spa at Val d'Aosta in the Italian Alps. The area was part of the former royal hunting ground of the House of Savoy. Pauline would not see Camillo again for nearly a decade.[6]

After Pauline's departure, an enormous crate arrived at Chiablese from Rome. Before shipping the life-size statue of Pauline Borghese to Turin, Antonio Canova unveiled the work in his studio on Via Giacomo. Canova's studio manager Antonio D'Este described the public's reaction to the marble: "It aroused such desire in the illustrious foreigners, who crowded to admire her, and who were not satisfied to worship her by the day, but also in the evening by candlelight they yearned to see her to better appreciate her beauty and the varying hues of her skin, that it was necessary to limit access."[7]

Pauline Borghese as Venus Victrix represented a dramatic shift for Canova, away from his austere funerary and religious marbles. About the work, art historian Giuseppe Antonio Guattani observed at the time: "She does not elude, she does not deceive. The statue of which it is, and a very real imitation of that beautiful nature, which when fortunately finds in a woman, makes her rightly deserve the name of Venus."[8]

Originally, Canova intended to sculpt Pauline Borghese as Diana, chaste goddess of the hunt. But Napoleon's sister insisted on being portrayed as Venus, goddess of beauty and love. The choice suited both the sitter and the Borgheses who considered themselves descendants of Rome's founder, Aeneas, son of Venus. Because of this connection, explains art historian Paola Mangia, Venus was a favorite decorative theme in the eighteenth-century renovation of the Borghese Villa. Over ten statues of Venus adorned the Villa's ground-floor statue gallery.[9]

Depicting women with attributes of goddesses was part of an ancient Roman tradition that bestowed divine qualities to imperial family members. Rome's empresses were often portrayed in statues and coins in the guises of divinities and heroines. Livia, wife of Augustus and mother of Tiberius, was frequently depicted as Ceres with a cornucopia. Nearly two centuries later, Julia Domna, wife of Septimius Severus, was also portrayed as Ceres along with the personification of Abundance.

Venus was a leitmotif in Canova's career, from his *Venus Italica* to replace the Uffizi's *Medici Venus* to his 1820 *Hope Venus*. With *Venus Victrix*, Canova externalized "the fascination of the goddess through the human guise of Pauline," writes Paola Mangia, creating a work that represents "an unparalleled stage in the Veneto artist's sculptural evolution . . ."[10]

Venus Victrix refers to the fateful beauty contest known as the Judgment of Paris. After judging Venus more beautiful than rival goddesses Minerva and Juno (Hera and Athena), the Trojan prince gave Venus the golden apple of discord from the garden of the Hesperides. Venus then introduced Paris to the beautiful Helen, wife of Sparta's king Menelaus. Paris's abduction of Helen caused the Trojan War and the flight of Aeneas to Italy. Out of jealousy, the runner-up goddesses allied themselves with the Greeks against Paris and the Trojans.

Art historians generally agree that Canova's reclining *Venus Victrix* was inspired by Titian's *Venus Urbino* and Giorgione's *Sleeping Venus*. As Fernando Mazzocca notes, Canova felt a deep connection to Titian, reflected in his design of a funerary monument for the painter at the Frari in Venice.[11] Canova would certainly have also known the Borghese's *Danaë* (1531), a late work by the Italian Mannerist Correggio. In Correggio's take on the story, Eros pulls a sheet off the half-naked, reclining Danaë, with Jupiter hovering over in the form of a golden cloud. Canova, who often painted as a preparatory tool, began experimenting with the reclining pose in the 1780s. His voluptuous nude paintings from this period include *Venus with Cupid in Fasce*, *Venus with Mirror*, and *Venus with Faun*.

Canova may also have been influenced by a more recent addition at the Villa Borghese. For the central canvas in the ceiling of the Stanza del David (named for Bernini's famous sculpture), Domenico de Angelis chose the Judgement of Paris. De Angelis depicted the victorious Venus holding the apple from Paris while her competitors return to Olympus, where they are met by Jupiter. A well-known bas-relief from a Roman sarcophagus at the nearby Villa Medici provided the model for de Angelis's work.[12]

Pauline posed for Canova both in the grand saloon at the Palazzo Borghese and the sculptor's nearby studio. Canova finished the plaster model by July 1804. From a block of white Carrara marble, he sculpted Pauline reclining on her side on an embroidered marble mattress, draped in a sheet from the waist down. Resting her right arm on two pillows, Pauline seductively touches the nape of her neck with the fingers of her right hand. In her left hand, she holds the famous apple of discord. Canova added ribbons to her Psyche knot, a fashionable take on an ancient Greek coiffure.

Using his signature technique, known as "the last hand," Canova polished the surface of the finished marble, giving it a deep luster and the lifelike texture of skin. The Italian art historian Leopoldo Cicognara observed that this step not only imparted softness to Canova's sculptures, but also "sweetness of contours, that subtlety of expression, which is unnecessarily sought and difficult to find in the works of its contemporaries . . . the slightest differences are those that cost more sweat, and lead to higher results . . ."[13]

Canova also heightened the work's sensuality by covering Pauline's skin with a light layer of molten pink wax. The discovery of marble statues with remnants of color, gilding, and glass had sparked a debate in artistic circles about the use of polychromy in antiquity. Canova's friend Quatremère de Quincy claimed that color was an essential element in the finest Greek sculptures—the gigantic cult figures of Zeus at Olympia and Athena in the Parthenon. Masserini, Canova's secretary and biographer, commented that the sculptor had noticed a preparation on antique works; Pliny cited Praxiteles as having been admired for similar method. Canova, like his fellow neoclassical sculptors, added subtle color to some of his works. Neoclassical purists criticized the sculptor for adding colored wax to *Venus Victrix*.[14]

Pauline's marble mattress rested on a plaster and wooden Empire-style bed. The mattress resembled a triclinium—an ancient Roman couch used for reclining at meals. Canova covered the base in flowing drapery like on a catafalque—a raised platform used to support coffins. In Greek and Roman art, reclining female figures were often depicted on the lids of sarcophagi. The bed hid a revolving mechanism allowing viewers to experience the work in the round.

Venus Victrix coincided with a busy period for Canova. At the same time that he undertook the sculpture, he was at work on two colossal statues—*Napoleon as Mars the Peacemaker* and *Ferdinand of Bourbon with Minerva*. In addition to exhibiting finished works in his studio, Canova displayed his terra-cotta and plaster models to show prospective clients. European aristocrats and heads of states queued up for portraits and statues for their own palaces.

In Germaine de Staël's 1807 autobiographical novel, *Corinne, Or Italy* written during her exile by Napoleon, her heroine and Lord Nelvil visit Canova's studio to view his sculptures by torchlight. "By the light of the torches, the shade more pronounced dampens the brilliant uniformity of the marble, and the statues appear pale figures, which have a more touching effect of grace and life."

Painter Francesco Hayez's firsthand account of Canova's workshop offers further insights into his creative process: "The studio consisted of a number of rooms, all full of models and statues, and here all could enter," he wrote. "Canova had a secluded chamber, closed to visitors, to which only those with special permission were admitted. He wore a kind of robe with a paper hat on his head; a hammer and chisel were always in his hands even when receiving visitors; he would talk and work at the same time, then suddenly stop working and turn to the person he was talking to."[15]

To keep up with demand, Canova hired studio assistants. Their presence may have also been necessary because of an injury he suffered while producing a funerary monument for Pope Clement XIV. While drilling the marble he had personally selected in Carrara, Canova repeatedly pressed a borer into his body, damaging his right rib cage. For the rest of his life, the sculptor suffered painful stomach problems.

As Canova chiseled away at a rough-hewn block of marble, his assistants often read classical literature out loud to him; he frequently drew upon the same literary sources for sculptural subjects.[16] Canova seems to have been self-conscious about his lack of formal education. "If I write badly in Latin and in Italian, remember the statues," he wrote his friend Giannantonio Selva in 1794.[17]

Perhaps to compensate, Canova became a bibliophile. The sculptor began assembling a large library in fall 1779 when he bought guides to Rome's churches, palaces, and monuments. Lining his bookshelves were rare ancient and modern folios, engravings of famous antiquities, and illustrated catalogues of museum collections. Titles ranged from Plato, Plutarch, and Homer to Dante, Locke, Alfieri, and Byron. He read eighteenth-century history, art criticism, and texts by philosopher Francesco Algarotti, art historian Johann Joachim Winckelmann, and neoclassical painter Anton Raphael Mengs.[18]

Canova's *Venus Victrix* became known in Rome as *La Paolina*. Pauline Borghese's love life added to the marble's fame, as did its nudity and sensuality. Napoleon's sister seems to have reveled in the attention. When asked if she minded posing nude, Pauline replied: "Why should I? The studio was heated."[19] In 1808, Pauline wrote to Camillo in Turin, urging him to allow *Venus Victrix* to travel to Paris. Four of Canova's works, including his statue of her mother, *Madame Mère Seated*, were to be displayed for the prestigious Salon at the Musée Napoléon.

Canova began the full-length seated portrait of Maria-Letizia Ramolino shortly before accepting the commission for Pauline Borghese's sculpture. He based the portrait of the formidable Bonaparte matriarch on the Capitoline's famous antique statue of Agrippina (second or fourth century C.E.). Canova portrayed Letizia like the ancient female figure, sitting on a curved leg chair, her sandaled feet on a footstool, wearing the fashionable classically inspired garb. Madame Mère apparently liked this type of classical dress. For a ball celebrating Napoleon's promotion to first consul for life, she came dressed as the tragic bacchant Erigone.

But which Agrippina was Canova comparing Letizia Bonaparte to? The loyal, principled Agrippina the Elder or her conniving, murderous daughter Agrippina the Younger? The two were often confused through the centuries. As direct descendants of Augustus through his first wife Scribonia, both Agrippinas were key to Rome's dynastic succession.[20]

Agrippina the Elder married Germanicus, nephew of Tiberius, who died abroad under suspicious circumstances. The jealous Tiberius was rumored to have done in his charismatic nephew. Forced into exile by Tiberius, the widowed Agrippina starved herself to death. Agrippina the Younger reportedly had incestuous relationships with two future emperors, her brother Caligula and her son Nero. After poisoning her second husband Claudius in 54 C.E., she finagled Nero onto the throne, in lieu of Claudius's own son with Messalina. But Agrippina soon became the victim of matricide. After a failed poisoning and several drowning attempts, Nero hired thugs to stab his mother.

In either case, argues Mary Beard, Canova's *Madame Mère Seated* was an insult to Napoleon. "If there was an honorable option for Madame Mère herself here in the model of Agrippina the Elder, there certainly wasn't one for Napoleon. One thing that both these Agrippinas good and bad had in common were their truly terrible sons. Agrippina the Elder gave birth to the mad Caligula and Agrippina the Younger gave birth to the equally mad Nero. There were not a few critics and commentators who felt that had been Canova's point and that through the imperial mother, Canova's target was actually Napoleon."[21]

Letizia Ramolina Bonaparte had a complex relationship with her powerful son, the second of her eight surviving children. Napoleon was reportedly embarrassed by his pious, barely literate mother who spoke Corsican-Italian, not French. Despite Napoleon's increasing power, Letizia did not hesitate to express her opinions, including her displeasure with his treatment of Lucien and his marriage to Joséphine. About his position as emperor, Letizia presciently declared "Let us hope it will last!"

Napoleon gave Letizia the title Her Imperial Highness, Mother of the Emperor, or Madame Mère. Along with an annual pension of three hundred thousand francs and a jewelry collection, she had her own household. This included a chamberlain, the Comte de Cossé-Brissac, an equerry, General de Beaumont (a former page of Louis XVI), several chaplains, a lady of honor, ladies-in-waiting, a secretary, and an intendant.[22] Napoleon gave his mother the keys to the Grand Trianon, built by Louis XIV at Versailles for Madame de Montespan, but she hated it and considered it uncomfortable.[23] In 1805, Napoleon bought his mother the Château de Pont-sur-Seine in the Aube in the northeast of France. Despite her son's generosity, Madame Mère remained notoriously stingy.[24]

Canova's portrait of Pauline Bonaparte never joined that of her mother in Paris. The seminude marble resembled his wife so strongly, an embarrassed Camillo Borghese kept it hidden from public view inside the Palazzo Chiablese. Along with Gros's *Napoleon on the Battlefield of Eylau*, Canova's

Madame Mère Seated proved a hit at the Salon, but not with her son who may have understood that the underlying subject was himself. Rather than install the marble opposite his throne at the Tuileries as his mother had requested, Napoleon packed it away to the palace storeroom.

Despite his resentment toward Napoleon's policies in Italy, Canova accepted a number of commissions to sculpt his female family members after classical and mythological figures, a Roman tradition. In addition to *Pauline Borghese as Venus Victrix* and Letizia Bonaparte as Agrippina, Canova portrayed Napoleon's sister-in-law Alexandrine de Bleschamp as Terpsichore, second wife Marie-Louise as Concordia, and sister Elisa Bonaparte as the Greek muse Polyhymnia. Canova produced an extraordinary gallery of the Bonaparte women, writes Mario Guderzo, "placing the characters in timeless, heroic and poetic dimensions, ensured by instruments of classical sculpture, the nude and ancient drapery."[25]

Of all these marble portraits, the masterpiece remained *Venus Victrix*. The work's erotic Classicism proved influential for other artists. As Stefano Grandesso notes, Jean-Auguste-Dominique Ingres's *Grande Odalisque* (painted in 1814 for Pauline's sister Caroline Murat) recalls *Venus Victrix* in its composition and naked back.[26] With the work, Canova also immortalized Pauline Borghese. "It is one of the absolutely iconic images of woman in Western art," writes Robert Hughes, "as justly celebrated in its way as the *Mona Lisa*, and not without a parallel mystery of expression."[27]

In the summer of 1808, while Romans were ogling *Venus Victrix* at Canova's studio, the first of two huge convoys of wagons left the city. The cargo was so heavy, specially built carts drawn by a dozen oxen each were required.[28]

Inside were hundreds of statues, busts, and bas-reliefs from the famed Borghese collection, considered one of the most important private collections of Roman antiquities. In addition to works from the Borgheses' Museo di Gabbii and Villa, the trove included antiquities stripped from the Villa's façade.

In May 1806, Napoleon directed Dominique-Vivant Denon and antiquities curator Ennio Quirino Visconti to secretly evaluate the antique masterpieces belonging to his brother-in-law. "Three days ago, all of a sudden, three French commissioners appeared," wrote Pius VII's secretary of state Cardinal Ercole Consalvi. "They went to the Villa Borghese and very carefully looked over all the ancient statues and bas-reliefs . . . "[29]

The knowledgeable Visconti, part of a dynasty of Roman antiquarians responsible for the papal collections, estimated every piece. Visconti was familiar with the Borgheses' archeological finds at family-owned land at Gabii, south of Rome, having written a book about them in 1797. Visconti took into account each object's archeological context or provenance in his appraisal. He recommended to Napoleon that he acquire the Borgheses' entire antiquities collection, but the emperor believed there wasn't enough space in the Musée Napoléon.

The extraordinary trove of antiquities got its start in 1605 when Camillo Borghese's namesake was elected pope. Paul V continued his predecessor Sixtus V's building spree, constructing the Acqua Paola aqueduct, completing the façade of St. Peter's Basilica, and decorating the Palazzo del Quirinale, the papal summer palace.[30] In another fateful move, the pope named his sister's twenty-six-year-old son, Scipione Caffarella, his cardinal-nephew.

The Borghese family's wealth allowed Scipione to indulge his passion for art. Assuming the name Borghese and purple robes of a cardinal, Scipione set about amassing a world-class art collection featuring antique sculpture and contemporary painting and sculpture. Scipione proved an adept talent scout. In addition to assembling one of the largest collection of Caravaggio paintings, he cultivated a young sculpture prodigy, Gian Lorenzo Bernini.

Nothing stood in Scipione Borghese's way. In 1607, he had his powerful uncle confiscate over one hundred pictures from Mannerist painter Giuseppe Cesari when he didn't pay his taxes.[31] The loot included Caravaggio's *Boy with a Basket of Fruit* and *Sick Bacchus*. On another occasion, Scipione hired a gang to rip Raphael's *Deposition* from the Baglioni Altarpiece in Perugia's Church of San Francesco. After refusing to sell Scipione *Diana and the Hunt* commissioned by Cardinal Pietro Aldobrandini, artist Domenichino was hauled off to jail. Scipione got his painting.[32]

As showplaces for his art treasures, Scipione accumulated multiple properties, including a palace in the Borgo near the Vatican, a family seat near Ripetta port in the Campus Martius, a palace on the Quirinal, and a country villa at Frascati.[33] To display his growing antiquities collection, Scipione also built the Villa Borghese and garden on the family's vast suburban property outside the city walls by the porta Pinciana. As Carole Paul writes, Scipione used the villa to "fashion a link between the ancient past and the Borghese family."[34] Antiquities adorned the façade of the Villa Borghese—some seventy busts, forty-three statues, and 144 bas-reliefs. Inside, sculpture was the main attraction. Unlike many of his paintings that he seized, Scipione bought antiquities, many from Lelio Coeli and scholar Giovanni Battista della Porta.

In 1619, Scipione hired Bernini to carve a mattress for one of his masterpieces, the *Sleeping Hermaphrodite*. Discovered near the Baths of Diocletian about a decade earlier, the marble is considered a Roman copy of a Greek original from the second century B.C.E. An excavation sponsored by Scipione unearthed another treasure. Found among the ruins of Nero's seaside palace in ancient Antium south of Rome was the *Borghese Gladiator*. Carved around 100 B.C.E., the life-size, muscle-bound fighter is shown raising his arm to fend off a blow. The tree trunk bears the rare signature of its creator, Agasias of Ephesus (today's Turkey) who revived the athletic heroism of Lysippos, the famed bronze sculptor of the fourth century B.C.E.[35]

Another prize, the *Borghese Vase*, was discovered in the sixteenth century in the gardens of Sallust, Rome. Standing nearly six feet, the vase represents the Roman taste for lavish garden decoration. Adorning the vase in low relief are satyrs and maenads in a Bacchic procession presided over by a half-naked Dionysus and his wife Ariadne. At the time, the vase was valued at two hundred thousand francs (roughly 1.1 million dollars today).[36] Much reproduced, the renowned vase inspired the decoration of the Fountain of Leto at Versailles.

During Scipione's lifetime, the Villa Borghese was hailed as a showplace. When the collector died in 1633, his cousin Marcantonio II inherited the art and real estate, becoming one of the wealthiest men in Italy. A century and a half later, art-loving Marcantonio IV picked up where Scipione left off. Around 1775, he began an ambitious two-decade-long neoclassical renovation of the villa. Each room was named for the most coveted ancient statue on display. Masterpieces of the sculpture collection were reinstalled, with decorative themes designed to complement these works. Ovid's *Metamorphoses* and Virgil's *Aeneid* inspired marble reliefs and painted ceilings and walls by a team of international painters and sculptors.[37]

The refurbished Villa became one of Rome's most important museums, alongside the antiquities collections at the Villa Albani and papal museums. In parallel with the Villa renovation, the Museo Gabbino in the Villa's clock pavilion displayed ancient finds from Gabii. Marcantonio also added an English-style park at the Villa decorated with ancient statues, including the Temple of Aesculapius and the faux ruins of the Temple of Antoninus and Faustina. The publication of two illustrated volumes increased the collection's renown among European cognoscenti.

In 1800, Marcantonio IV's eldest son Camillo succeeded him as head of the Borghese family. Three years later, he married into the Bonaparte family. Despite considerable pressure from his powerful brother-in-law, Camillo was reluctant to sell the family's prized antiquities. Denon suggested to Napoleon that he double Visconti's estimate of five million francs. At Fontainebleau in September 1807, Napoleon signed a contract for thirteen million francs (about $71.5 million dollars today). To sweeten the deal, Napoleon named Camillo governor general of Piedmont and Genoa.

Of the hundreds of antiquities, Napoleon was most taken with the portrait busts. As Souren Melikian writes, these constituted a gallery of celebrities of the Roman Empire to which Napoleon saw himself as heir.[38] The images included Marcus Aurelius and a bearded Lucius Verus unearthed near Rome at Acqua Traversa, along with a bust of Augustus's son-in-law, Marcus Vipsanius Agrippa, dug up in 1792 in Gabii. Praetor, governor, consul, and edile, responsible for the renovation and construction of Rome's aqueducts, baths, and sewers, Agrippa is depicted with his hair combed forward, steely and resolute. The marble copy may have been modeled after a large bronze in the Pantheon.

The further loss of Rome's cultural patrimony to France caused an uproar. On visits to the Borghese Villa starting in 1779, Antonio Canova had admired the antiquities, studying masterworks like the *Gladiator* and *Centaur with the Young Jupiter* along with a number of Venuses. Now Canova and Cardinal Filippo Casoni, Pius's secretary of state at the time, appealed to the pope to stop the sale. But since the deal had been executed legally, Pius's hands were tied. Canova would denounce the sale of "the most beautiful private collection in the world," declaring "That family [Borghese] will be dishonored as long as history is written!"[39]

With maritime routes cut off by England, the Borghese collection had to travel across the Alps. Napoleon originally planned to display the prize at a summer house in the countryside, at a residence similar to the Borghese Villa in Rome. But the decision was made instead to exhibit the antiquities at the Musée Napoléon.

The Borghese antiquities were a tremendous addition to the museum's antiquities department, formed in 1793 with the former royal collections and other objects seized during the Revolution, as well as Napoleon's treasures from the Vatican. The Hall of the Caryatids debuted in 1811 with an exhibition of some of the Borghese treasures. But by the following summer, 180 packing boxes, half the total, remained unopened.[40] In the end, Camillo Borghese was only paid 8.3 million of the agreed upon 13 million francs.[41]

FOUR

CARRARA

After a real estate swap with Spain's Bourbons, Napoleon awarded Piombino to his eldest sister Elisa and brother-in-law Felice Pasquale Baciocchi in March 1805. With its proximity to Corsica and Elba, the small principality on Italy's west coast was of strategic importance. In June, Napoleon added the nearby Republic of Lucca to the couple's purview, confiding that the promotion was "not from fraternal tenderness but out of political prudence."[1]

That July, on the anniversary of the storming of the Bastille, the princess made a grand entrance in a carriage drawn by four horses, a gift from Napoleon. Elisa and Felice were accompanied by their household—twenty-five equerries, chamberlains, ladies-in-waiting, a majordomo, a doctor, butlers, soldiers, and officials.

Elisa's sisters were extremely jealous of her appointment. Hortense recalled Caroline's reaction. "Well! So Elisa is now a sovereign princess. She is going to have an army of four men and a corporal. It really is a fine thing!" Pauline, who disliked her older sister, also weighed in. "My brother only cared for Elisa and is not interested in the rest of us," she said.[2]

The ambitious and capable Elisa ran both principalities. As Austrian Foreign Minister Clemens von Metternich put it, her husband Felice had an "entire want of intellectual faculties." The best educated of the Bonaparte sisters, Elisa spent ten years at the college of Saint-Cyr near Paris, and returned to Ajaccio just in time for her family to flee to Marseilles. In June 1797, Elisa married Felice, a Corsican captain fifteen years her senior, in a double ceremony near Milan with her sister Pauline and Victor-Emmanuel Leclerc.

Though Elisa made some public improvements, most of her efforts were focused on her own palaces. Like her siblings, she imposed the French Empire style, seeking design advice from its creators Charles Percier and Pierre Fontaine, and importing Parisian furniture, Sevres porcelain, and silver by Biennais. She also recruited Parisian ébéniste Jean Baptiste Youf who set up a furniture workshop in Lucca.

To make room for the new Piazza Napoleone in front of her palace in Lucca, Elisa leveled an entire block, including the medieval Church of San Paolo, a move that not surprisingly proved very unpopular. For her court's summer residence, Elisa acquired the eighteenth-century Villa Marlia outside Lucca. In addition to the Empire-style interiors, the Villa sported a new animal park.[3] Elisa also restored Lucca's popular thermal baths.

At her art-filled Paris residence, Hôtel de Maurepas, Elisa had hosted a salon frequented by her brother Lucien and noted academicians. She resumed this role at Piombino and Lucca. Her new court also became known for music. As Christopher Hibbert describes, Elisa hired members of the Puccini family as *maestri di cappella* and organists at Lucca's San Martino cathedral. Giovanni Paisiello, one of Napoleon's favorite composers, dedicated the opera *Proserpina* to her.[4] French architect Pierre-Théodore Bienaimé, who had worked for Elisa in Paris, designed an opera house near the redecorated palace.

Genoese musician Niccolò Paganini, who had performed at Lucca's annual music festival in 1801, returned to give violin lessons to Felice. At some point, Paganini and Elisa became lovers. In 1807, she appointed the handsome twenty-four-year-old court violinist, conductor, and captain of the gendarmes, an honorary title giving him the right to wear a uniform.[5] Paganini wrote a sonata for solo violin in Elisa's honor and a military sonata for violin and orchestra, "the Napoleon." According to Sante Bargellini, despite a decade of lessons from the virtuoso, Felice "remained a wretchedly bad player."[6]

In March 1806, Napoleon expanded his sister's realm to include Massa and Carrara. Located just north of Pisa along Tuscany's west coast, Carrara was one of Europe's biggest suppliers of white marble. It had taken an eon or two of erosion and tectonic movement to raise the marble up to the surface of the towering Apuan Alps. Northern Tuscany once lay at the bottom of a deep primordial sea brimming with shellfish and tiny calciferous creatures. As Joel Leivick explains, over tens of millions of years, the animals' skeletal remains formed a limestone sediment on the sea floor. Some twelve million years ago, a continental collision occurred, subjecting the limestone seabed to heat and pressure. About a million years later, the base limestone petrified into white crystals known as marble.[7]

Renaissance artist and inventor Leonardo da Vinci recognized the geologic forces at work. "Shells that appear on mountain tops and fish bones in caves must be the remains of animals that long ago swam in these places when they were covered in sea," he wrote. "The claim they were swept there by the biblical flood is a completely inadequate explanation. So the surface of the earth has changed over time, with land where once there was sea."[8] Leonardo would invent a marble-cutting machine for Carrara.

Each quarry boasted marble with distinct color, luminosity, and hardness.[9] The most prized *bianchi* marble ranged from dazzling white, bluish, and flesh color. Like wood, marble has knots and grains called *peli*, fine lines that crisscross the blocks at irregular intervals. Hidden faults, invisible or created after a block is cut, are known as *peli nemici*, or enemy faults.

The Romans discovered the exceptional white marble after founding Luni just north of Carrara. Slaves were sent to the colony to extract the stone. Wagons hauled the large slabs to the port of Luni, where they were loaded onto ships for the roughly two-hundred-mile voyage to Rome. To avoid taxes, the marble was engraved A.U.PH., short for *ad usum phori*—for use in the Forums.[10] The first villages in Carrara were settlements established for extracting marble. When the Apuans attacked Roman settlements and quarries, they were deported. For three centuries Luni flourished as a center for shipping wood, cheese, wine, and marble. A small version of the Roman forum and amphitheater were built.

In his *Res Gestae*, Augustus famously bragged that he had inherited a city of bricks and left Rome a city of marble. Augustus's reign marked the first time marble was used on a large scale in Roman architecture. To work the Carrara marble, Augustus and his minister Agrippa imported craftsmen from Greece, which had a long history of building with marble from Mount Hymettus and Mount Pentelicus near Athens, along with white marble from Naxos and Paros in the Cyclades. The Greek sculptors brought a classicizing, Hellenic look to Rome's new buildings. Augustus continued Caesar's building projects around the Roman Forum along with the area around the Campus Martius west of the Capitoline.[11] Augustus built numerous grandiose buildings from Carrara marble—including the Temple of Mars Ultor in his eponymous Forum.

In his famous first-century work *Geography,* Strabo mentions a "wall of white marble around Augustus's place of cremation."[12] Strabo also describes Luna's quarries that supplied the luxe building material for Rome and its provinces: "The harbor [of Luna] is shut in all around by high mountains, from which the high seas are to be seen, as also Sardo [Sardinia] . . . And the quarries of marble, both white and mottled blueish-gray marble, are so numerous, and of such quality (for they yield monolithic slabs and columns), that the material for most of the superior works of art in Rome and the rest of the cities is supplied therefrom; and indeed the marble is easy to export, since the quarries lie above the sea and near it, and since the Tiber in its turn takes up the cargo from the sea and conveys it to Rome."[13] Napoleon had Strabo's *Geography* translated into French.

Rome's successive emperors turned marble into a symbol of wealth and power. As the Empire grew, the coveted marble became a big business; organization and control of the quarries increasingly structured. According to Suetonius, the Luna quarries (and many others) were made imperial property under Tiberius, Augustus's stepson and successor.[14] From Tiberius's reign on, Luna's marble quarries were controlled by Rome's imperial family and administered by the Empire's accounting office. In addition, colored marble was imported to Rome from quarries in its provinces in Africa, Asia Minor, and the Mediterranean.[15]

In addition to Carrara, the Romans exploited other marbles for their buildings and sculptures. With its mixture of white and blue-gray layers, Aphrodiasian marble from ancient Aphrodisias (today's southwest Turkey) was popular from Hellenistic to the late Roman period. From the mid-first to the mid-third century C.E., Romans used dark gray, white veined Bigio Antico marble for building and for large figurative sculptures, and gray Bigio Morato marble for statuary. Both stones were quarried in Teos and islands on the coast of Asia Minor. The green and white-banded Cipollino marble from the island of Euboea in Greece was an especially popular for columns.[16]

Lustrous Parian type I marble was quarried on Paros in the Cyclades. Because of its remote location, the white to pale yellow Phrygian marble from Docimium in Asia Minor was among the most expensive, prized by Emperors Augustus and Hadrian. Pentelic marble from Mt. Pentelikon near Athens was used widely for sculpture and architecture. Frequently veined, the white marble often turned golden brown after sculpting. White with blue-gray bands, Proconnesian marble was often used for sarcophagi.[17]

Ranging from light red to dark purple, marmor Taenareum (Rosso Antico) was prized for its similarity to porphyry. Quarried in small blocks on Cape Tainaron (today's Matapan, Peloponnese), Crete, and Asia Minor's Iasos, it was mainly used by the Romans for small architectural elements. Romans used the white Thasian dolomitic marble from the Aegean island of Thasos for sculpture, architecture, and sarcophagi.[18]

Still, Carrara marble enjoyed a greater reputation among ancient sculptors than even the prized Pentelic, Hymetian, and Parian marbles. Many of the greatest monuments of antiquity, including the Pantheon, Trajan's Column, and the Column of Marcus Aurelius, were carved from Carrara marble. Trajan's Forum alone required an estimated 34,000 cubic yards of marble.[19]

With Rome's fall, Luna's storied quarries were abandoned. Around 1000 C.E., Carrara passed to the bishops of Luni who reopened the quarries. From the 1300s to the 1450s, the quarries were controlled by eight different powers, including the Florentines, Lucchese, Milanese, Dukes of Carrara, and the duchy of Modenas. Fourteenth-century methods had not improved much since the Roman era and extracting the prized marble was a risky occupation.

Teams of *lizzatori*, or stonecutters, climbed the mountain peaks, drilling holes in the rock into which they drove wooden stakes. Wetting the wood expanded the stone, allowing blocks to be split off. The blocks were then slid down the steep slopes on wooden *lizzas*, or sleds, pulled by oxen. The only thing controlling the multi-ton marble blocks were ropes. Many miners lost their lives in the process. In 1442, the area came under the control of the Marquis Malaspina of Massa. Gunpowder was introduced to the quarries in 1570, but proved too destructive, reducing much of the prized marble to dust.

Carrara marble enjoyed renewed popularity during the Renaissance. Marble that broke easily was considered to be more alive; sometimes described as containing a soul or anima.[20] The Florentines, referred to sculptors as "masters of la pietra viva" or live stone.[21]Renaissance sculptors traveled to the Apuan Alps to personally choose the finest marble for their works. Michelangelo was among the first to recognize the quality of Carrara's beds, carving his masterpieces *David* (Florence) and the *Pietà* (St. Peter's Basilica) from its marble. The renowned artist worked in the Serra gorge, favoring the whitest, most finely veined marble. At one point, Michelangelo dreamed of carving a giant out of the five-thousand-foot Monte Sagro. "If I could have been sure of living four times longer than I have lived, I would have taken it on," he declared.[22]

Michelangelo would eventually open up rival quarries for the Medici, including Pietrasanta. Still, Carrara remained a favorite. "He loved the very quarries of Carrara," writes Walter Pater, "those strange gray peaks which even at mid-day convey into any scene from which they are visible something of the solemnity and stillness of evening, sometimes wandering among them month after month . . ."[23]

During one visit to Carrara, Michelangelo carved his initials "MB" onto a surviving ancient *aedicule.* In the first century C.E., a Roman slave named Scarpellino carved a relief on a rock face overlooking the quarry at the middle of the Miseglia basin. The bas-relief featured three divinities—Hercules, Jupiter, and Bacchus—standing between incised columns, possibly a temple. These votive reliefs known as *aediculae* were common in the quarries. Slaves prayed to them on their way to work. Michelangelo signed his initials between Hercules's club and leg. Successive sculptors like Bernini and Giombologna continued the tradition, leaving their signatures below and to the side of the ancient bas-relief.

The quarry that produced the marble for Michelangelo's *David* was named "Fantiscritti" after *fanti*, the three small gods, and *scritti*, the sculptors' signatures. Toward the end of 1784, Antonio Canova traveled to Carrara to select marbles for his monument to Clement XIV. During another visit to the Del Medico family, Canova carved "Canova 1800" in a rough sprawling scrawl. According to Mario Guderzo, Canova probably returned to the fabled quarry on other occasions, but usually entrusted the selection of marbles to Antonio D'Este, director of his studio in Rome. Canova even designed his business card with the image of his signature on the marble.[24]

The striking quarries of Carrara had a spiritual resonance for sculptors. "They had carried out an act of association by carving their names into the rock of this ancient site," writes Alison Yarrington, "leaving their imprint on this source of some of the most beautiful sculptures of antiquity and more modern times . . ."[25] In 1863, the famous autographed aedicule of Fantiscritti was detached from the summit of the quarry and moved to the courtyard of Carrara's Academy of Fine Arts. Today it is on display inside Palazzo del Principe, a building that houses the Academy.

During the seventeenth and eighteenth centuries, the marble quarries were controlled by the Cybo and Malaspina families who ruled over Massa and Carrara. The family created the Office of Marble in 1564 to regulate the marble mining industry. Massa was completely redesigned with new roads and plazas. The Basilica of Massa that housed the famous Iron Crown was built exclusively with Carrara marble; the old Ducal Palace also showcased the precious stone. By the eighteenth century, explosives were used to dislodge huge quantities of rock quickly; large irregular blocks were squared by hand.

The quarries languished until Napoleon swept across northern Italy. As a builder of monuments, Napoleon was an even greater marble consumer than the French kings, writes Eric Scigliano.[26] It was Napoleon's sister Elisa who turned the factory around, glorifying her powerful brother with mass production of his portrait bust. During her eight years as head of the quarries, Carrara enjoyed a revival, regaining its near monopoly over the marble market.

The energetic grand duchess immediately instituted changes at the storied quarry, modernizing operations. In October 1807, Elisa convinced Lorenzo Bartolini to return to his native Tuscany to direct the Academy of Carrara. Bartolini had produced the monumental herm-like bronze *Napoléon Empereur* for the entrance to the Musée Napoléon. A fervent Francophile and staunch Bonapartist, Bartolini named his eldest sons Girolamo-Napoleone and Paolo Napoleone.

In January 1808, Bartolini succeeded Milanese sculptor Angelo Pizzi as head of the Carrara Academy, and became chief of Carrara's highly profitable workshops. Bartolini's main responsibility was producing and directing production of large quantities of Bonaparte family portraiture. All satellite states were expected to have portraits of the emperor and his family, and busts were reproduced *en masse* and shipped to Europe's various courts. Carrara enjoyed a veritable monopoly on official portraits of the imperial family.[27]

To provide the factory with new financial resources and provide support for sculptors and workers, Elisa created a credit institution, the Banca Elisiana. Favorable new customs tariffs helped Tuscan sculpture spread throughout the Empire. The neoclassical craze made Carrara's white marble highly fashionable. In addition to portraits, the factory turned out fireplaces, tombs, altars, clocks, and statues.

Bartolini also oversaw the execution of the most prestigious commissions. In early May 1807, Elisa began issuing authorized copies of Antoine-Denis Chaudet's portrait bust of her brother in Carrara. The copies were slightly altered from the original, without the crown, belt, or mantle. The austere marble busts proved so popular with Bonapartists and for public buildings in France that Bartoloni produced copies of Chaudet's "crowned" versions. For the hundreds of copies, Bartolini made small modifications to the originals, including the addition of crowns or laurels, or both. Elisa opened a shop in Paris to sell her brother's popular portrait busts after plasters by Chaudet and Canova; forty sold in the summer of 1808.[28]

The Malaspina family had established Carrara's Academy of Fine Arts in 1769. Now to enhance its prestige and improve the training of students, Elisa enlarged the collection of plaster casts. Among the donations from well-known neoclassical sculptors were some thirty casts by Lorenzo Bartolini, Antonio Canova, and Bertel Thorvaldsen. Canova's donations include casts for such works as the fighters *Creugas* and *Damoxenos*, the *Penitent Maddalena*, and *Letizia Ramolino Bonaparte as Agrippina*.

Bartolini trained a new generation of marble sculptors. Like his mentor Jacques-Louis David, the sculptor emphasized drawing and the use of live models. Besides Bartolini, the Academy's teachers included French painter Desmarais, the poet Giovanni Fantoni, and Lorenzo Papi. In 1810, Elisa relocated the Academy to an expanded palace. She created a prize for a three-year study program in Rome for students to apprentice at the studios of famous artists.

⚜

On November 28, 1807, Elisa Baciocchi accompanied her brother on his official visit to Venice. Napoleon made a brief stop in Milan where he tried unsuccessfully to convince his brother Lucien to divorce his wife and become king of Spain. The entourage also included Eugène de Beauharnais, the sovereigns of Bavaria and their children, the grand duke of Berg, the prince of Neuchâtel, ministers Champagny and Decrès, and Duroc, Marshal of the Palace. Several days later, Lucien and Joseph, king of Naples, joined the entourage.

As a general, Napoleon had regarded the Venetian Republic as a symbol of excess. Napoleon turned Venice over to the Austrians, reducing the once powerful maritime Republic to a lowly province. In 1805, after defeating Austria a second time, Napoleon took Venice back, incorporating it into his new Kingdom of Italy. In another setback for Venice, Napoleon chose Milan as its capital. The following July, by vice regal decree, nine Venetian churches, fifteen monasteries, and nineteen nunneries were closed, an anti-monastic policy that would continue. These religious buildings were stripped of their art; many of the finest works were displayed at Milan's

Brera gallery. Napoleon's ongoing war with England led to the collapse of Venice's maritime commerce.

Still, the Venetians did their best to make a good impression for Napoleon's visit. During the grand entry, Mayor Daniele Renier gave Napoleon two keys to the city in silver and gold. At the north entrance to the Grand Canal near the Church of Santa Lucia, a floating triumphal arch was erected, part of a long Venetian tradition that began with Andrea Palladio's ephemeral arch for France's Henri III. Giuseppe Borsato created the decoration for the arch that was topped with statues of Victory and Genius and sported Victories between the Doric columns.

With soldiers of the Italian Royal Guard lining the shore, Napoleon and the imperial procession passed under the triumphant arch and traversed the Grand Canal in the ceremonial vessel, the *peata* (largest of the traditional Venetian cargo boats) accompanied by five bissone, a dozen rowers, and twenty-one private bissone.[29] After disembarking at the Piazzetta, Napoleon and his entourage proceeded to their lodgings at the Palazzo Reale in the Procuratie Nuove.

Soon after his arrival, Napoleon conducted a private inspection of the Arsenal. The previous August, Eugène de Beauharnais unveiled a bust of his stepfather in the shipyard where twenty new cannon ships were scheduled to be built. On Wednesday December 2, 1807, the third anniversary of his coronation, Napoleon returned to the Arsenal along with the Lido, launching two corvettes for the French Navy. On both visits, he praised the efforts of the shipbuilders and workers. Refusing to give up on challenging England at sea, Napoleon allocated 8.1 million francs to rebuilding the French fleet. He told workers that their efforts were important to give the English "the lesson they deserved."[30]

Among the planned festivities was a regatta hosted in Napoleon's honor. Spectators clamored in windows and carpet-festooned balconies for a glimpse of the emperor. At the turn of the canal alongside Ca'Foscari, Giuseppe Borsato constructed and decorated a "macchina" with statues. The entertainment featured carnival feats like the human pyramid known as the Force of Hercules. Napoleon assisted in the boat race with his family by a loggia set up on the façade of the nearby Palazzo Balbi. The regatta was followed by a banquet and ball at the

Ridotto, and a Te Deum at St. Mark's. The city was lit by over four thousand torches.

Napoleon was reportedly pleased with a visit to the Marciana Library where he was shown papers suggesting that the Bonapartes descended from an ancient Roman family, the Bona Pars. Napoleon, an opera fan, also attended performances at the Gran Teatro La Fenice, The Phoenix. Rebuilt after a fire in the classical Italian style by Giannantonio Selva in 1792, the theater featured a number of sealed logge, or balconies, reminiscent of the Italian piazza. More changes followed during the French occupation to turn it into a state theater. For Napoleon's reception, Selva decorated the theater in blue and silver, and built a temporary loggia in lieu of a royal box. On December 1, 1807, Napoleon took his seat in the loggia to watch a performance of the cantata *Il Giudizio di Giove*, The Judgment of Jupiter by Lauro Corniani Algarotti. Jupiter resembled Napoleon, who was lauded as a quasi-divinity.

The previous year, work had been carried out at La Scala in Milan, capital of the Kingdom of Italy. Now Milan contributed 150,000 Italian lire for a permanent imperial box and new décor for La Fenice.[31] Giuseppe Borsato designed the Empire-style box with a triumphant Apollo in a coach surrounded by a chorus of the muses, evoking Napoleon's victories. Borsato would become La Fenice's official stage designer for over a decade.

On December 3, Napoleon traveled to Murano to inspect the island's glass factories. Since the eighth century, Venice had been a center for glassmaking, refining techniques from the Roman and Byzantine empires. Napoleon's elimination in 1797 of the Venetian guild system, including glassmakers, had hurt the already declining industry. Over the next two days, Napoleon made stops at San Giorgio Maggiore (where Pius VII had been elected pope), Torcello, Burano, and S. Erasmo.

On December 7, shortly after Napoleon's departure, a grand urban plan was announced with Giannantonio Selva as official architect. As in Paris, Napoleon hoped to improve traffic and aesthetics by straightening and widening streets. To prevent contagion, a new cemetery was to be built away from the city center on San Cristoforo in the northern lagoon. Other projects included an extension of the Riva degli Schiavoni, a new public garden, and a large piazza on Guidecca opposite San Giorgio Maggiore for military displays. Napoleon also removed the gates of the Ghetto, ending restrictions on Jewish residents. It was said that Napoleon made more changes in Venice in four days than Austria had in four years.[32]

Shortly after his state visit, the emperor ordered the Ala Napoleonica or Napoleonic Wing constructed in Venice's famed Piazza San Marco. Dubbed "the finest drawing room in Europe," the Piazza had been the Venetian Republic's political and religious center. Eugène de Beauharnais initially awarded the prestigious project to Milanese architect Giovanni Antonio Antolini. But Antolini's plan to demolish the beloved ensemble proved highly controversial. After many changes and Antolini's replacement by architect Giuseppe Maria Soli, work finally began in 1810.

The Ala Napoleonica was located between the Procuratie Vecchie and Nuove, two long arcades running the length of St. Mark's Square that formerly housed offices and residences of the Republic's political VIPs. With a façade facing St. Mark's Basilica, the wing featured a monumental neoclassical staircase and an opulent ballroom. At Antonio Canova's recommendation, Lorenzo Santi was hired to supervise the interiors. The multifaceted artist Giuseppe Borsato went to work, applying a sophisticated take on Percier and Fontaine's Empire style.

Borsato dressed the elegant grand staircase with balusters, Ionic pilasters, facings in stone and pink marble, bas-reliefs of winged Victories and garlands, military trophies, and scenes from ancient history. The staircase led to a salon (today's Museo Correr bookshop) that served as a vestibule to the ballroom. The walls and the ceiling are decorated with frescoes and paintings in cameo executed by Borsato and his workshop. Napoleon never got to enjoy his new abode. Finished when Venice was under Austrian rule, the Ala Napoleonica became the official Venice residence of the Habsburgs and the king of Italy.

A month before the state visit, Napoleon and Spain's monarchs signed the Treaty of Fontainebleau, transferring the Kingdom of Etruria (Tuscany) to the French Empire. Called Etruria after the region's ancient Roman name, the kingdom was established in 1801. As part of the Third Treaty of San Ildefonso, Spain returned Louisiana to France, along with Elba. Initially, Etruria was ruled by the Spanish princess Maria Louisa and her sickly husband and first cousin Louis, great grandson of Louis XV, and son of Ferdinand, grand duke of Parma and Maria Amalia of Austria.

Since the death of thirty-year-old Louis in 1803, Maria Louisa had ruled Etruria as regent for their son, Charles Louis. Now she and her children left for Spain. In recognition of Elisa's accomplishments and organizational skills, Napoleon named his sister Grand Duchess of Tuscany. Elisa moved her court to Florence, taking along Niccolò Paganini. Felice was made a general in charge of a local military division and given his own less formal court in the Via Della Pergola.[33] While the couple appeared together publicly, they led separate lives.

Elisa replaced many of her old courtiers in Lucca, establishing a grander court style modeled after the Tuileries Palace.[34] Elisa was also trying to compete with Caroline's splendid court in Naples. Deeming Pitti Palace completely unsatisfactory, she hired her cabinetmaker Youf to produce consoles, toilettes, psyches, dejeuners, and beds for Florence.[35] Elisa also hired a team of Italian cabinetmakers to supply Parisian-style furniture. In 1810, when the Pitti Palace became an imperial residence for her brother, Elisa ordered more furniture.

As she did near Lucca, Elisa acquired and redecorated houses around Florence, including the Villa of Poggio Imperiale that Medici Cosimo I confiscated from the Salviati.[36] During the summer, Elisa moved her grand ducal court to the Villa Reale at Marlia, which she had rebuilt and redecorated in neoclassical style by Bienaimè and Lazzarini. Youf created the furniture for Elisa's palatial villa at Massa.

In addition to her design team, Elisa assembled artists like Lucchese painter Stefano Torelli and Florentine Pietro Benvenuti. In 1809, Elisa met with Antonio Canova. The sculptor had traveled to Florence to supervise construction of the tomb of poet Vittorio Alfieri in Santa Croce Basilica. Elisa hosted a banquet in Canova's honor at the Pitti Palace and commissioned Benvenuti to paint a canvas of her entire court with the celebrated sculptor. During the visit, she also commissioned Canova to sculpt her portrait.

Among Elisa's court artists was Giovanni Santarelli, a Rome-trained engraver. Santarelli executed relief portraits in wax as models for medals and cameos.[37] Elisa also brought French porcelain techniques and styles to Florence's Ginori porcelain factory. Founded in 1735 by Florentine marquis Carlo Ginori, the factory developed a new style featuring cameo decoration based on a model from Sèvres. In addition to Carrara, Elisa supported Florence's hardstone workshops. The Opificio delle Pietre Dure, which began as grand ducal workshops under the Medici, started producing Empire-style table tops.

From time to time, Elisa stood up to her brother, a risky proposition. In 1810 for example, when Napoleon demanded she fork over some two hundred thousand lira in grants he had made to Massa and Carrara, she refused, arguing the areas lacked the resources. Napoleon threatened to take back Carrara, her success story. Elisa signed her letters to Napoleon "Your most devoted and submissive sister," and signed official documents with an *E* like her brother's *N*.[38]

One of Elisa's pet projects was to send her brother a complete set of the family's portrait busts—Madame Mère *and her eight children*.[39] For the series, Lorenzo Bartolini sculpted Madame Mère in antique drapery with a wreath of laurels. The graceful busts of Caroline and Pauline were based on prototypes by Canova; those of Jérôme, Louis, and Joseph were after French and Italian models. Thanks to a prototype by Bartolini, Elisa, like her brother, bears an uncanny resemblance to Julius Caesar.[40]

PART SIX

CAPITAL OF THE UNIVERSE

"I am Charlemagne, the sword of the Church and their emperor."

—Napoleon Bonaparte

ONE
ABDUCTION

On the balmy night of July 5, 1809, a gentle breeze stirred at the Quirinale Palace, the summer residence of the popes. The palace took its name from its location on the northwestern slope of the Quirinale, highest of Rome's seven ancient hills on the east bank of the Tiber. The hill itself was named for a third-century B.C.E. temple dedicated to the cult of Quirinus, rebuilt after a fire by Augustus in 16 B.C.E. In the early third-century C.E., Caracalla added the Baths of Constantine and Temple of Serapis.

Like the ancient Romans, the city's cardinals and patricians appreciated the prime hilltop real estate and built summer retreats here. In addition to splendid views of Rome, the Quirinal offered an oasis from the summer heat and the foul smell of the Tiber. In 1583, Pope Gregory XIII began building a summer palace on a view property originally owned by the Neapolitan cardinal Oliviero Carafa. For the next century and a half, architects including Ottaviano Mascherino, Carlo Maderno, and Gian Lorenzo Bernini would enlarge and embellish the residence on behalf of their papal patrons.

In 1585, Gregory's dragon emblem was replaced atop the Quirinal Tower by Sixtus V's cartouche of mountains and a star. The new pope loved the quietude of the summer palace at night—a dramatic change from the Vatican where he was often awakened by bells, drums, dogs, and roosters. In frustration, the sleep-deprived pontiff ordered the bells of the Vatican silenced.[1]

Two years into his short five-year pontificate, Sixtus bought the property from the Carafa family and revived Gregory's ambitious building plan. Architect Domenico Fontana created an elegant inner courtyard by adding a long wing and a second larger palace. A two-story barracks was built for the pope's Swiss guards. To improve the piazza in front of the palace, Sixtus repositioned the famous marble horses and their tamers around a fountain fed by water from the newly finished Felice aqueduct.

The ancient sculptural group known as the *Dioscuri* had been partially restored by Paul II over a century earlier. Once adorning the Baths of Constantine, the works depicted the twin demigods Castor and Pollux taming their horses. The famous duo had stood here for so long, the Quirinal Hill was also called Monte Cavallo, or Hill of the Horse.

Aldobrandi Pope Clement VIII embellished the palace gardens, astonishing guests with a series of baroque fountains built on top of the ancient temple of Quirinus. These include the Fountain of the Dwarf, Fountain of Mirrors, and Fountain of the Dog. A flight of marble steps led to a special apse-like building housing the extant Organ Fountain where water powered a musical mechanism inside a tall niche. A pair of seated cupids flanking the pipes blew trumpets to the music; decorative panels depicted the creation, the story of Moses, and the mythology of water.[2]

In the early seventeenth century, Borghese Pope Paul V completed the palace, adding an east wing adjacent to the garden, a large hall of the consistory, papal apartments, staircase of honor, and a private Chapel of the Annunciation featuring an altarpiece by Guido Reni. With its high ceiling, the Pauline Chapel was intended to rival St. Peter's Sistine Chapel, but Paul V ran out of money and struggled to find artists willing to compete with Michelangelo's spectacular new ceiling.

Thanks to his predecessors' additions, Urban VIII moved into an impressive, imposing residence. But embroiled in dangerous alliances, he began fortifying the palace in 1625. The gardens were enclosed with high walls and a garden entrance on Via Pia was demolished; the Swiss Guards wing was secured along with the round tower at the entrance. Urban also increased the papal property by purchasing the adjoining D'Este estate.

In 1638, Urban commissioned Gian Lorenzo Bernini to add a benediction loggia above the main portal. From here, Urban and his successors blessed worshipers gathered in the piazza below. Bernini encased the tall round arched opening with an aedicule, fronted by a balcony. Leading to the balcony was the small Precordium Room where the bodies of popes who died at the Quirinale were prepared for public display. As Louis Godart describes, part of the embalming process included removal of the precordium (the area over the heart), which was divided and placed in two metal containers and housed in the Cistercian Church of St. Vincent and St. Anastasio in Piazza di Trevi.[3]

In 1656, Bernini also redesigned the long Swiss Guard wing for Alexander VII's court officials. Known as the *manica lunga,* it was completed in the first half of the eighteenth century by Innocent XIII and Clement XII. Benedict XIV added a coffee house for informal garden entertaining in 1741. After the Vatican became a museum in the eighteenth century, the popes retreated more to the Quirinale. The palace's magnificent art collection was displayed under a gilded ceiling in the Salone dei Corazzieri.

It was onto the grounds of this historic compound that General Radet quietly entered. Urban VIII's fortifications did not faze the French general, whose men came with ropes, ladders, and axes. All it took was a bribe to a former servant, fired for stealing, for the intruders to wind their way through the palace. Radet and his men waited until two A.M., when Pius VII turned out the light in his bed chamber and his guard stood down.

A month earlier, on June 10, cannons in Rome had announced the transfer of the Eternal City to French imperial rule. That day, Pius ordered the Bull of Excommunication against Napoleon posted on the doors of the city's major basilicas. Napoleon wrote an angry letter to his brother Joseph, newly installed as king of Naples, calling Pius a "raving madman" who should be punished. "Philip the Fair arrested Boniface VIII, and Charles V kept Clement VII in prison; and they had done much less to deserve it," he wrote.[4]

After overwhelming the fleeing Swiss guards, Radet arrested the frail sixty-seven-year-old pope and his closest adviser, Cardinal Bartolomeo Pacca. Still, the break in did not go smoothly. In the course of entering through a window, some of the ladders fell, waking the Swiss Guards. As one of Pius's servants rang an alarm bell, the French soldiers let their colleagues into the palace. The Swiss Guard abandoned the papal chambers and the troops ransacked the residence.[5]

Awakened by Cardinal Pacca, Pius quickly dressed in his white robes. With Cardinals Pacca and Antonio Despuig, he made his way to the public audience room and waited until the doors were broken down with an axe. Radet found Pius seated under a canopy. Just before being hauled off, Pius wrote a note: "When you are old you have to hold out your hands and let people take you where you do not want to go . . ."[6]

After a short conversation, Radet led Pius and Pacca out of the palace to a closed carriage outside. Given just minutes to pack, they quickly put breviaries, rosaries, and the Sacrament inside a ciborium. Pius must certainly have been struck by déjà vu. Eleven years earlier in February 1798, the French had kidnapped his predecessor from the Quirinale. Humiliated, moved from place to place, eighty-one-year-old Pius VI died in France in 1799 after a twenty-four-year pontificate. Pius VII had attended his funeral in February 1802 when Napoleon finally allowed the pontiff's body to be returned from Valence.

As he passed the Dioscuri group, Pius thought about his relative. Pius VI had repositioned the giant sculptures, turning them slightly inward. Between the works, he installed a fifty-foot-tall Egyptian obelisk discovered in the ruins of the Mausoleum of Augustus. As his carriage pulled away from the Quirinale, the pope focused on the view of the dome of St. Peter's Basilica in the distance below. He'd been forced to move from the Vatican to the Quirinale in February 1808 when Napoleon's General Miollis occupied Rome. Now he wondered if he would ever see St. Peter's again.

When General Radet was asked how he felt arresting Pius, he recalled that it had been business as usual until he actually saw the pope. "At that moment," he recalled, "my first communion flashed before my eyes!"[7] Eighteen years earlier, in June 1791, Radet had tried to rescue Louis XVI when the king and his family were captured at Varennes.

The honeymoon between Napoleon and Pius VII was short. Their relationship had steadily deteriorated after the Concordat. The Organic Articles added after the fact left the Curia reeling. In addition to allowing divorce, the revisions gave Protestantism and Judaism equal status as Catholicism, and France's new Consulate wound up with almost complete control over the Church in France. Rome never accepted decrees giving other religions equal standing. The feast of Saint Napoleon and the 1806 imperial catechism were never ratified.

In 1805, Napoleon gave Pius eight sumptuous New Testament tapestries woven at Gobelins in the mid-1700s, including The Tapestry of Christ Driving the Merchants from the Temple and the Washing of the Feet. But later that year, the gift was forgotten.

To prevent a British landing during the Austerlitz campaign, French troops occupied the strategic port of Ancona on Italy's east coast. From the start of his pontificate, Pius tried to remain neutral in the continent's ongoing wars. In mid-November 1805, Pius wrote a strongly worded protest to Napoleon, demanding the evacuation of French troops from Ancona and complaining about Napoleon's failure to offer a quid pro quo for his attending the coronation.

Busy defeating Austria at Austerlitz, Napoleon responded to Pius from Munich on January 7, 1806. Calling the pope's letter a stab in the back, Napoleon berated Pius for his unaccommodating attitude to France. The same day, Napoleon wrote Cardinal Fesch, describing Pius's letter as "ridiculous and senseless." In his polite reply, Pius did not renounce his call for the French evacuation of Ancona.

In February, Napoleon upped the ante, firing off another angry letter to Pius, emphasizing that political matters were under his control. "Your Holiness is sovereign in Rome, his relations with me are the same as those your predecessors with Charlemagne. You are sovereign in Rome, but I am its emperor." He pressed the pope to cease working with "heretical" Britain and "extra-ecclesial" Russia and demanded he expel Sardinian, British, Russian, or Swedish agents living in the Papal States.

Napoleon sent an urgent letter to his uncle, Cardinal Fesch, "As far as the pope is concerned, I am Charlemagne, for like Charlemagne I have united the crowns of France and Lombardy, and my Empire extends to the borders of the Orient." He soon sent his uncle a follow-up letter: "Tell them that I have my eyes open. That I am only fooled inasmuch as I let myself be fooled. I am Charlemagne, the sword of the Church and their [the clergy's] Emperor . . . I am informing the pope of my plans in a few words. If he does not acquiesce, I shall reduce him to the same status that he held before Charlemagne."[8]

Pius responded to Napoleon's threat on March 21: "I reply with apostolic frankness that the Holy Father [. . .] does not recognize and has never recognized, in his states, any power superior to his own, and that no emperor has any rights over Rome." Napoleon still needed the Catholic Church politically. "Catholic priests are a great help; they were the reason why conscription this year worked much better than in previous years. . . . No other state body speaks as well as they do regarding the government," remarked Napoleon in 1806.

In 1807, Napoleon continued to dominate the continent with victories in Jena and Friedland. A series of decrees effected the Continental System, aimed at reducing the power of Britain by closing French-controlled territory to its trade. In addition to keeping the main papal port open to British shipping, Pius began refusing to invest Napoleon's nominees for bishop.

While fighting Austria, Napoleon decided that he could no longer tolerate the noncooperative pope. On February 2, 1808, French troops occupied Rome. Two months later, he decreed the papal territories Urbino, Ancona, Macerata, and Camerino "irrevocably" part of "my kingdom in Italy." By the following May, France formally annexed Rome to the Empire, proclaiming it a free imperial city.

Napoleon had long dreamed of annexing Rome. The Eternal City held a particular fascination for him, evoking the splendor of the Roman imperial tradition. The pretexts for his seizure of Rome were numerous. Pius had refused to annul the marriage of his brother Jérôme, support the Continental blockade, and accept the occupation of Ancona. By 1809, Napoleon's struggle with Pius reached a climax.

That May, he annexed the Papal States. Pius's temporal powers were revoked; his realm was reduced to the spiritual domain along with the Quirinale and pontifical palaces. In protest, Pius issued a bull memoranda on June 10, 1809, excommunicating all those who "usurp, encourage, advise or perform" violation of the temporal sovereignty of the Holy See. The immunity Pius enjoyed was now over. He and his advisers withdrew to the Quirinale.

In an irate letter to his brother-in-law Joachim Murat, king of Naples, Napoleon wrote: "This instant I have received the news that the pope has excommunicated all of us. By this he has excommunicated himself. No more regard for him! He is a raving madman and must be locked up!"[9] On June 19, Napoleon wrote again: "If the pope preaches revolt . . . then you must arrest him."[10] He ordered Rome's military governor, General Miollis, to lock up anyone who infringed on public law and order—including members of Pius's household. Despite this, after learning of the pope's abduction, Napoleon called the arrest "utter folly" in a letter to police minister Joseph Fouché. Yet he did not order the pontiff released. "Now there is no remedy: what is done is done," he wrote.[11]

After his arrest in Rome in early July 1809, Pius was transferred to Tuscany, where he was joined by his private chaplain, doctor, cook, and servant. An envoy from Elisa Bonaparte's court paid his respects but the pope was too tired from the journey to receive him. The grand duchess quickly decided that the sympathetic figure was too big a political liability to remain in Tuscany. He was whisked off toward Grenoble, France.

Napoleon, who did not want to be associated with the pope's arrest, ordered that he stay in Italy. "If he stops being so foolish, I should even have no objection to his being brought back to Rome," Napoleon wrote Fouché.[12] But Pius was dragged back over the Alps, passing through Valence where his predecessor Pius VI had died, then the former papal city of Avignon, continuing to Marseilles and Nice. After two weeks, he arrived in Savona (between Nice and Genoa) on August 10. The same month, Cardinal Pacca was imprisoned at the infamous Fenestrelle Fortress in Piedmont, one of Europe's largest prisons.

After several days at the mayor's residence, Pius was moved to the more secure Bishop's Palace, a former Franciscan monastery. A week later, 150 infantry and another one hundred artillery soldiers arrived, along with a squadron of dragoons and gendarmes as his "guard of honor." Pius was allowed a visit to the nearby Shrine of Our Lady of Mercy where the Virgin was believed to have appeared in 1536. Cut off from his advisers, Pius had no ability to govern the Church. But he refused to cave in to the demands of Cardinals Fesch, Maury, and Caprara that he confirm Napoleon's nominees for bishops. Nor would he approve the French Empire's incorporation of Rome or accept a position in France as Napoleon's chaplain-in-chief.

In response to his letter to the emperor, Pius was read this letter aloud: "His Majesty does not judge it fitting to reply to the pope's personal letter. He will write when he is satisfied with him. . . . The emperor was pleased to scorn the said criminal and ridiculous document [Bull of Excommunication]. . . . His Majesty pities the pope's ignorance. . . . As the pope is not sufficiently enlightened by the Holy Spirit, why does he not resign? For he is evidently incapable of distinguishing dogma from the essentials of religion. . . . If [he] is unable to understand this fairly obvious distinction, easy enough for a young seminarian, let him come down from the Pontifical Chair and make way for a man of better sense and comprehension."[13]

Napoleon wrote Camillo Borghese in 1811: "Since nothing induces the pope to behave reasonably, he will see that I am powerful enough to do what my predecessors have done—to depose a pope."[14] In another letter that year, Napoleon justified the imprisonment of Pius by invoking Charlemagne: "I know that I must render unto God that which is God's, but the pope is not God . . . the present epoch takes us back to the age of Charlemagne. All the kingdoms, principalities, and duchies which after the breaking up of his empire set themselves up as republics have now been restored under our laws. The Church of my Empire is the Church of the Occident and of nearly the universality of Christendom. I am resolved to convoke a council of the Western Church, to which I shall summon the bishops of Italy and of Germany, in order to draw up, as has been suggested by many bishops, a general discipline. Thus the Church of my Empire shall be one in its discipline as well as in its creed."[15]

Napoleon's true goal was to nationalize the French Church. His precedent was fourth-century Emperor Constantine, who Christianized pagan Rome and dominated the popes and the Church.[16] Napoleon later explained his intentions:

"Thus I had at last achieved the long-desired separation between temporal and spiritual power. . . . Thenceforth, I was in a position to exalt the pope beyond all bounds and to surround him with such pomp and ceremony that he would have ceased to regret the loss of his temporal power. I would have made an idol of him. He would have resided near me; Paris would have become the capital of Christendom, and I would have become the master of the religious as well as of the political world . . . I would have called religious as well as legislative bodies into session; my church councils would have been representative of all Christendom, and the popes would have been mere chairmen. I would have opened and closed these assemblies, approved and made public their decisions, as did Constantine and Charlemagne."[17]

In addition to gathering the world's finest art, Napoleon planned to place all European learning in a world library in Paris. His unrealized plan was to move the Bibliothèque Impériale to the Musée Napoléon, bringing added prestige to both.[18] Toward this end, Napoleon sent his chief archivist Daunou to Rome.

In 1804, Napoleon had created a new home for the National Archives in the Marais district. The building was the Louis XIV–era Palace of the Dukes of Guise and Soubise, known as the Hôtel de Soubise. Six years later, Berthier received a letter from the emperor about "collecting in Paris a single body the archives of the German Empire, those of the Vatican, of France, and of the United Provinces, it may be interesting to search what has become of the archives of Charles V and of Philip II, which would so nicely complete this vast European collection."[19]

That year, much of the Vatican archives, the Sacred College, was shipped to Paris in hundreds of wagonloads. Fearing the P. M. Vitali collection would also be taken, Pius had entrusted Antonio Canova to safeguard it in his home before his abduction.[20] Marino Marini, nephew of Gaetano Marini, secret chamberlain of the prefect of the archives, was sent to Paris with the Vatican archives, over three thousand cases of material, to assist in their arrangement. Unofficially, he was there to keep an eye on them.[21] French officials also traveled to Simanca, Spain, Piedmont, and Holland to select and remove valuable archives.

Two years earlier, in 1808, Napoleon requested that a librarian and geographer collect "memoirs about the campaigns which have taken place on the

Euphrates and against the Parthians, beginning with that of Crassus up to the 8th century and including those of Antonius, Trajan, Julian, etc.; he is to mark upon maps of suitable size the route which each army followed, together with the ancient and modern names of the countries and principal towns, and add notes on the geographical features and historical descriptions of each enterprise, taking these from the original authors."

With his library of the world, Napoleon may have been inspired by the great libraries of antiquity. It's thought that around 295 B.C.E., scholar and orator Demetrius of Phalerum, an exiled governor of Athens, persuaded Ptolemy I to form a library in Alexandria, Egypt, to house a copy of every book in the world. It was under Ptolemy II that the idea of a universal library arose. Part of a complex that included a cult center called the Temple of the Muses or *musaeum*, the library may have housed as many as half a million papyrus scrolls. Strabo, Euclid, and Archimedes were among the brain trust of some one hundred resident scholars.

The destruction of Alexandria's famous library remains a mystery. Julius Caesar is among the prime suspects. In 48 B.C.E., Caesar found himself in the city's Royal Palace with the Egyptian fleet threatening in the harbor. He reportedly ordered his soldiers to set the ships on fire, which spread out of control.[22] Some scholars believe the harbor fire damaged the library whose destruction came later in the thirrd or fourth centuries.

Julius Caesar's father-in-law is thought to have assembled another extraordinary library, the Villa of the Papyri, in his Herculaneum home. When nearby Mount Vesuvius erupted in 79 C.E., some 1,800 scrolls were buried under ninety feet of volcanic material. Among the blackened scrolls uncovered in the eighteenth century were writings of the Epicurean philosopher and poet Philodemus.[23]

Imperial Rome boasted some two dozen major libraries. One of the most prestigious was located at Emperor Trajan's mega-forum, flanked by the soaring Trajan's Column. The concrete, marble, and granite libraries featured central reading chambers and two levels of alcoves lined with an estimated twenty thousand scrolls. The libraries were still being mentioned as late as the fifth century C.E.[24] Soon after Trajan's library debuted, the son of Roman consul Tiberius Julius Celsus Polemaeanus unveiled an elegant library/mausoleum for his father in Ephesus (Turkey). Celsus was buried in an ornamental sarcophagus surrounded by an estimated 12,000 scrolls. The façade featured a marble stairway and columns, along with statues of Wisdom, Virtue, Intelligence, and Knowledge.

In the fourth century, Constantine the Great formed an imperial library in Constantinople. A century later, its collection mushroomed to some 120,000 scrolls and codices. The renowned library was never the same after the Crusades in 1204. But by making parchment copies of the aging papyrus scrolls, the library's scribes helped preserve classical literature.[25]

⚜

Inspired by the Spaniards' success against the French, Austria's Francis I launched a campaign to liberate neighboring countries from French rule. Hoping to trigger an insurrection in the Confederation of the Rhine, Francis invaded Bavaria on April 8, 1809, proclaiming a War of German Liberation. But having benefited by Napoleon's 1805 defeat of Austria, Bavaria remained allied with the French emperor.

Sensing their marriage was on the rocks, Joséphine insisted on going along with her husband. Napoleon left her in Strasbourg while he saw his Polish mistress Maria Walewska, before embarking on another campaign. After the victory at Ratisbon, Napoleon addressed his troops: "Soldiers: You have justified my anticipation. You have supplied by bravery the want of numbers, and have shown the difference which exists between the soldiers of Caesar and the armed rabble of Xerxes. Within the space of a few days we have triumphed in the battles of Thaun, Abersberg, and Eckmuhl, and in the combats of Peissing, Landshut, and Ratisbon. One hundred pieces of cannon, forty standards, fifty thousand prisoners, three bridge equipages, three thousand baggage-wagons with their horses, and all the money chests of the regiments, are the fruits of the rapidity of your marches, and of your courage. . . . In one month we will be in Vienna."

Francis I and his family fled to Hungary, leaving Vienna's defense to Archduke Maximilian Joseph of Austria-Este. From a base camp at Linz, Napoleon assaulted the capital. Unable to keep the French at bay until reinforcements arrived, the inexperienced archduke also fled. By May 13, Vienna surrendered. In a speech to his victorious soldiers, Napoleon compared the Habsburgs to Medea: "The princes of that house have abandoned their capital, not like the soldiers of honor, who yield to circumstance and the reverses of war, but as perjurers haunted by the sense of their crime. In flying from Vienna, their adieus to its inhabitants have been murder and conflagration. Like Medea, they have with their own hands massacred their own offspring . . ."[26]

In an echo of Roman emperor Trajan, Napoleon ordered a bridge built over the Danube with a bridgehead of thirty thousand soldiers. On May 21 and 22, Archduke Charles launched a surprise attack, defeating the Grande Armée at Aspern and Essling, with each side suffering around twenty thousand casualties. The Austrian victory was short-lived. Napoleon quickly rebuilt the bridge, led his army across the Danube, and defeated Charles at Wagram.

Four years earlier after the victory at Austerlitz, Napoleon and his army stayed in Vienna. About the Hofburg, Francis's palace in Vienna, he had commented, "How can the descendant of so many Emperors live in this garret?"[27] For the two-week stay, the emperor chose instead Schönbrunn Palace, the Habsburg summer residence west of Vienna's city walls. Now, Napoleon returned for several months.

According to legend, the name Schönbrunn came from Emperor Matthias's discovery of a beautiful spring (schöner Brunnen) on the property while hunting. In the mid-seventeenth century, Eleanora Gonzaga, the cultured wife of Emperor Ferdinand II, expanded the old manor house in Italian baroque style. Damaged during the Turkish siege soon after, the palace was extensively rebuilt by Empress Maria Theresa. During her reign, six-year-old Mozart played in the palace's mirrored hall.

Napoleon now used the Hall of Ceremonies for an audience chamber. Franz Stephan's council chamber, the Blue Chinese Salon featuring Chinese floral wall-hangings and walnut paneling, and the Vieux Laque Room, Franz Stephan's private study, became Napoleon's drawing rooms. For his bedroom, Napoleon occupied the bedroom shared by Franz Stephan and Maria Theresa with a view of the Gloriette—an elegant, colonnaded neoclassical building with a long row of arches and topped with an imperial eagle. Marie Theresa ordered the elegant structure in 1775 as a "temple of glory" for the palace garden.

Napoleon turned Maria Theresa's chinoiserie Porcelain Room into his study; its painted wood paneling and carved blue and white framing were made to look like porcelain. On the way to Wagram, Napoleon packed several boxes of his portable library organized by Antoine-Alexandre Barbier. The emperor's library included forty volumes on religion, forty epic poems, forty tragedies, a hundred novels, and titles in philosophy and history.[28] From Schönbrunn, Napoleon ordered an updated traveling library to include three thousand volumes, mainly classics and reference works. To decrease the weight, he wanted them printed on thin paper without margins. Barbier drew up a catalogue, requesting half a million francs and six years for the project.[29]

Despite the emperor's complaints that Schönbrunn was poorly furnished, he was impressed by the palace. At either side of the entrance leading to a huge courtyard, Napoleon erected a pair of obelisks crowned by eagles. Napoleon restored the palace theater where he attended German opera performances from his box.[30]

That summer, Dominique-Vivant Denon supervised the plunder of the court library and the imperial art collection housed at the Belvedere Palace. The picture gallery got its start in the sixteenth and seventeenth centuries thanks to Archduke Ferdinand II, Emperor Rudolf II, and Archduke Leopold Wilhelm. In the eighteenth century, the holdings were brought together at Vienna's Stallburg, where they were displayed in the late baroque style.

In the mid-eighteenth century, Maria Theresa acquired the Belvedere summer palace from the heirs of Prince Eugene of Savoy. Some twenty-five years later, she and her son and coruler Joseph II transferred the imperial picture gallery from the Stallburg to the Upper Belvedere. They added to the collection by confiscating large Flemish and Italian altarpieces from disbanded cloisters and churches in the Low Countries. In 1781, the gallery opened its doors to the public.

In late 1805, with Napoleon's army nearing Vienna, many masterworks of the Habsburg imperial gallery had been hurriedly packed up. Heinrich Füger, director of the Viennese painting gallery, supervised the evacuation of roughly half the displayed works—some 625 paintings in fifty-four crates. In mid-1809, Denon managed to pilfer over four hundred paintings from the Belvedere.[31] For the journey to Paris, smaller unframed works were stacked one on top of the other; larger canvasses were rolled up. Rubens's *Assumption of the Virgin* was so large, it was cut into three pieces. The newest loot included fifteen of the Belvedere's three dozen Titians.[32]

From Schönbrunn, Napoleon founded a new imperial order. The Order of the Golden Fleece had arisen during the Middle Ages, inspired by the heroic story of Jason and the Argonauts. "My eagles have conquered the Golden Fleece of the kings of Spain and the Golden Fleece of the emperors of Germany," Napoleon wrote Baron Lejeune. "I want to create for the French Empire an imperial Order of the Three Golden Fleeces. It will be my eagle, with wings outstretched; in each of its talons it will grasp one of the ancient fleeces that it has taken, and in its beak it will proudly brandish in the air the fleece that I am instituting." Napoleon reportedly wanted to use fragments of burned grenades for the chain. A number of goldsmiths including Biennais presented designs for the new insignia. By 1813, the order joined the Legion of Honor.[33]

Napoleon considered dethroning the Habsburgs, but decided instead to demand real estate. Despite losing his capital, Francis I held out, refusing to sign a peace treaty. On October 12, with negotiations dragging on, Napoleon was inspecting his troops on the steps of Schönbrunn's parade court when a young Austrian approached him with a dagger. After admitting he had intended to kill the emperor, the seventeen-year-old was quickly tried and executed.

The foiled attack spooked Napoleon. Two days later, he signed the Treaty of Vienna. Austria ceded Salzburg and parts of Upper Austria to Bavaria. Trieste, Carniola, and Croatia were incorporated into the French Empire as the Illyrian Provinces. Napoleon gained three million subjects (out of Austria's sixteen million). In addition, the Austrian army was limited to fifty thousand men until a peace treaty with Britain was signed. Napoleon instructed Eugène de Beauharnais to invade the Tyrol region in the south and end a long-running insurrection.

Napoleon arrived back in Paris in late October, around the same time as sixty-plus wooden crates of Belvedere paintings. Most of the art went to the Musée Napoléon; Denon dispersed some fifty of the pictures to provincial museums (Caen, Dijon, Lyon, Toulouse, Grenoble, and Brussels), the palaces of Strasbourg and Compiègne, and a handful of Parisian churches.

Napoleon's return coincided with what turned out to be the publishing event of the century. In 1802, the same year Denon published his best-selling Egyptian travelogue, Napoleon authorized the publication of the findings of the French Commission on the Sciences and Arts of Egypt, founded in Alexandria in 1798. The commission's members, some 150 civilian savants, had been recruited to build Napoleon's military infrastructure including roads, canals, and bridges.

During the ensuing three years, the civilian army of scientists and artists crisscrossed the country, sketching and measuring the monuments, flora and fauna, and the people of Egypt. One of the most prolific artists was Nicolas-Jacques Conté, a portrait painter and inventor of the graphite and clay Conté crayon. With supplies cut off by Nelson's destruction of the French fleet, Conté came up with tools and machines to manufacture arms, surveying devices, and surgical instruments.[34]

In Cairo, Napoleon also founded the Institut d'Égypte, after the prestigious Institut de France. Back in Paris, a team of researchers directed by Institut members and top military authorities translated the expedition findings into the sumptuous imperial edition of the *Description de l'Égypte*. Some four hundred engravers and two thousand artists collaborated on 855 engraved plates, a forty-seven sheet topographic map, and a three-sheet geographic map. Eleven volumes of text covered everything from archeology and botany to urban mapping and zoology.[35]

Many of the engravings of Egypt's temples were populated with figures of ancient Egyptians, Romans, and Greeks. "The reader, imagining him or herself to be gazing upon the ruins of ancient Egypt, is suddenly catapulted back in time to witness a procession or to gaze upon ancient scholars in Thebes . . ." writes Anne Godlewska.[36] The connection between contemporary France and ancient Egypt was also expressed by the *Description*'s frontispiece, made to look like a monumental Egyptian doorway. Designed by Cecile and engraved by Girardet and Sellier, the frontispiece is a masterpiece of triumphant propaganda, describing a French conquest of Egypt that never occurred.

In the foreground, famous monuments like Pompey's Column, Cleopatra's Needle, and the Sphinx at Giza are shown alongside seized treasures like the Rosetta Stone and zodiac of Dendera. A river winds its way back through a fantasy landscape, flanked by Egypt's major monuments. At the top of the doorway, below an Egyptian sun disk, Napoleon or a Roman general is shown riding a quadriga, following the imperial eagle and fleeing Mamelukes. At the bottom, Egyptians admire an *N* topped with the imperial crown encircled with a snake eating its tail. The vertical borders are decorated with trophies and insignia inscribed with the names of the campaign's victories and defeats. Adorning the border's two lower corners is Napoleon's personal symbol, the bee, in a pharaonic cartouche.[37]

Like Diderot's eighteenth-century *Encyclopédie,* the *Description de l'Égypte* had a profound impact, helping fuel the Egyptian revival in decorative arts and architecture. In 1828, nineteen years after Napoleon received his imperial edition, the *Description de l'Égypte* was finally finished. Six years earlier, savant Jean-François Champollion deciphered the mystery of hieroglyphics. Champollion made the groundbreaking linguistic discovery using a copy of the Rosetta Stone's royal decree, inscribed with two forms of Egyptian language and Greek. Along with sculptures, steles, and sarcophagi, the Rosetta Stone was among the Egyptian booty ceded by the French to Britain.

One of the main goals of the Napoleonic expedition and *Description de l'Égypte* was to associate France with the extraordinary civilization of ancient Egypt. But the stakes were even bigger. "Behind this association," writes Anne Godlewska, "was the suggestion that cultural superiority, which gave France the rights of conquest, was derived from a sort of passage of reason and science . . . from its birthplace in Egypt, to the Greco-Romans, to its full realization in Europe and it return to its birthplace by France."[38]

With the annexation of Rome and abduction of the pope, Napoleon's dream of turning Paris into Europe's cultural and political capital was coming closer to reality. Stripped of its leader and artistic treasures, Rome was reduced to the second imperial city of the French Empire. The relative status of the two cities was clear. "I wanted this capital to be splendid that it would dwarf all the capitals in the universe," Napoleon would later declare. "I did everything, and wanted to do everything, for Paris."

TWO

TROPHY WIFE

Napoleon's thirteen-year marriage to Joséphine had weathered a number of storms, from his family's hostility and long separations to numerous extramarital affairs on both sides. But there was one deal breaker. Napoleon was desperate for a male heir and Joséphine had been unable to conceive. Her childbearing years appeared over.

Napoleon had been contemplating divorce for some time. When he left Paris in 1806 for the Prussian campaign, his young mistress Eléonore Denuelle de la Plaigne was pregnant. Intensely jealous of her sister-in-law Joséphine, Caroline Murat had introduced her brother to Denuelle, who gave birth to his first child in December. Charles Léon's birth convinced Napoleon that Joséphine's failure to conceive was her fault. In May 1807, four-year-old imperial heir Napoleon Charles, eldest son of Joséphine's daughter Hortense and Napoleon's brother Louis, died suddenly of croup at The Hague. Napoleon refused to name the boy's younger brother, Louis-Napoleon (the future Napoleon III) as his new heir.

In September 1808, Napoleon left for Erfurt, Germany, to discuss an alliance with Russian tsar Alexander I. Before sending reinforcements to

Spain, he wanted Russia's help shoring up France's eastern frontier against Austria. Napoleon also wanted something else from Alexander—his teenage sister Anna Pavlovna's hand in marriage. From Erfurt, Napoleon raised the issue of divorce with foreign minister Talleyrand:

"My destiny demands it and France's tranquility demands it also," he wrote. "I have no successor. Joseph is nothing, and he has only daughters. It is I who must found a dynasty; I cannot found one except by allying myself to a princess who belongs to one of the great ruling houses of Europe. The Emperor Alexander has sisters; there is one whose age suits me. Speak of it to Romanzoff: tell him that once the affair in Spain is finished, I shall consider his views regarding the partition of Turkey. Nor will you lack for other arguments; I know that you are in favour of divorce, and, I should warn you, the Empress knows it too."[1] Napoleon did not know at the time that the sly Talleyrand favored his marriage to a Habsburg, and leaked information about Napoleon to Alexander's court.

Napoleon also took up the subject with his grand equerry Caulaincourt. "It is to be seen whether Alexander is really a friend of mine, if he is really interested in France's happiness; for I love Joséphine, and never shall I be happier. But we shall know, through this, the feelings of the rulers regarding this act, which will be for me a sacrifice. My family, Talleyrand, Fouché, all my ministers, demand this of me in France's name. A son would offer you far more stability than my brothers, who are disliked and incapable. Perhaps you would prefer Eugène [de Beauharnais]? It is the wish of certain people, because he is a made-man, he has married a Bavarian princess and he has children. But that does not serve your argument. Adoptions do not found new dynasties. I have other projects for him."[2]

"All being said," Napoleon later wrote, "I like only those people who are useful to me, and only so long as they are useful." On November 30, after dinner at the Tuileries Palace, Napoleon let Joséphine know that she was no longer useful. The next day, Napoleon broke the news to his step-daughter and sister-in-law Hortense: "My decision is made. It is irreversible. The whole of France wants the divorce: they cry out for it. I cannot ignore their wishes. Nothing will bring me back, not tears, not prayers." When Hortense replied that she and her brother would leave Paris with their mother, Napoleon replied angrily:

"What! You will all leave me, you will abandon me! You no longer love me, is that it? If it were simply for my happiness, I would sacrifice it, but it is for France. You should be consoling me for being forced to give up the dearest of my affections. . . . After me, anarchy will return and the prize for so much effort will be lost for France. Instead, in leaving a son raised in my image, a son which France will be prepared to regard as my successor, [France] will profit from the good that I have left her as the very least of the fruits of my labour. I will have suffered, but others will profit from it."[3]

Joséphine's days as France's empress were numbered. At Fontainebleau, Napoleon walled off the passageway between his topographical office and the Joséphine's study in their private apartments.[4] On December 4, Jérôme Bonaparte, not Joséphine, accompanied Napoleon to Notre Dame Cathedral to mark the fifth anniversary of his coronation. There was no place of honor for her at the lavish reception thrown by the City of Paris to mark both the anniversary and the peace treaty with Austria.

A week and a half later, on December 15, the imperial couple announced the dissolution of their civil marriage in the Tuileries throne room. Members of the Bonaparte and Beauharnais families were present, along with Napoleon's aides. Among them was the person who had helped orchestrate the divorce, Napoleon's éminence grise Michel Regnaud de Saint-Jean d'Angély. A lawyer by training who had followed Napoleon from Italy to Egypt, Regnaud was entrusted with the imperial family's private matters and government relations with the Senate. For Regnaud's loyalty, Napoleon named him count of the Empire in 1808.

Now Napoleon told those gathered: "God knows what such a decision has cost to my heart! But there is no sacrifice that is beyond my courage if it is shown to be for the good of France. I must add that, far from having any reason for reproach, I have nothing but praise for the attachment and the affection of my beloved wife: she has graced fifteen years of my life; the memory of them will remain engraved in my heart. She was crowned by my hand; I desire that she retain the rank and title of crowned empress, but more than this, that she never doubt my feelings and that she value me as her best and dearest friend."

Joséphine had difficulty getting through her prepared speech. "With our most august and dear husband's permission, I must declare that no longer holding out any hope for a child that could satisfy both his political needs and the good of France, I give to him the greatest proof of attachment and devotion that has ever been given on this earth. Everything I have comes from his greatness; it is his hand that crowned me, and up on this throne, I have received evidence of nothing but affection and love from the French people.

"I acknowledge these feelings in agreeing to the dissolution of this marriage, which from this moment on is an obstruction to the well-being of France, depriving it from the joy of one day being governed by the descendants of a great man clearly chosen by Providence to eradicate the evils of a terrible revolution and re-establish the altar, the throne and social order. Nevertheless, the dissolution of my marriage will change nothing of the feelings in my heart: the Emperor will have in me always his greatest friend. I know how much this act, called for by politics and greater interests, has pained his heart; but glorious is the sacrifice that he and I make for the good of our nation."[5]

Joséphine and Napoleon signed a record of the proceedings formally annulling their civil marriage. The next day, Joséphine left Tuileries for Malmaison in the pouring rain with Hortense, her ladies-in-waiting, parrot, dogs, and multiple pieces of luggage. As a reward for going quietly, her settlement included Malmaison, a generous allowance, and the title Empress Dowager. Napoleon was apparently not too broken up. He departed for a rendezvous at Versailles with Pauline's Piedmontese lady-in-waiting, Madame de Mathis.[6] In early January 1810, in front of the court, Joséphine and Napoleon signed the official documents annulling their 1804 religious marriage on the grounds that the civil marriage had been conducted illegally.

In his dynastic obsession, Napoleon recalled Augustus. In bad health, the emperor's concern for his own mortality led to a fixation about an heir. In order to shape Rome's future, Augustus chose his successor. He married his only daughter Julia to his sister's promising son Marcellus, but he died after just two years of marriage. Next, Augustus made his boyhood friend Marcus Agrippa divorce his wife of ten years to marry Julia. They had two sons, Gaius and Lucius Caesar. But the deaths of all three dashed his plan, leading Augustus to adopt Tiberius, son of his wife Livia by her first husband.[7] Interestingly, Augustus supported the institution of marriage by making adultery a crime punishable by exile and confiscation of property.

The Romans were more liberal in their divorce practices than was Napoleonic Paris. One or both parties to a Roman marriage simply had to consider themselves no longer married. At first, Roman husbands could divorce their wives for adultery or drinking wine. Later, men could divorce if their wives failed to produce children. Since the wife was not regarded as being at fault, the husband was required to return her dowry. By the first century B.C.E., either spouse could divorce the other or they could mutually agree to divorce. As Susan Treggiari writes, Roman society looked at divorce as a sad necessity.[8]

In 62 B.C.E., Julius Caesar divorced Pompeia for a scandal she had nothing to do with. With the Vestal Virgins, Pompeia co-hosted a women-only party for a religious festival. Plotting to seduce Pompeia, a young politician Publius Clodius Pulcher crashed the party dressed as a woman. Though Publius did not succeed, Caesar divorced Pompeia, famously pronouncing "Caesar's wife must be above suspicion."

In his search for a new spouse, Napoleon drew up a list of seventeen candidates. Besides Alexander I's sister, Napoleon considered Maria Augusta of Saxony. But with fertility the main criteria, the twenty-seven-year-old princess was thought to be past her prime. Emerging as a top contender was eighteen-year-old Habsburg archduchess Marie Louise, eldest daughter of Napoleon's nemesis Francis II.

As the great-granddaughter of Empress Maria Theresa and great-niece of Marie Antoinette (through both her father and her late mother Maria Teresa of Naples), Marie Louise was considered outstanding bride material. A union with Europe's oldest reigning imperial family greatly appealed to Napoleon, along with Austria's ambitious chancellor Clemens von Metternich. Not only would the match head off a dangerous alliance between France and Russia, Marie Louise could subdue the "Corsican usurper" and soften the punishing treaty he had just imposed on Austria.

Metternich's plan was missing just one thing—the buy-in of the archduchess. Born in Vienna in December 1791, Marie Louise had grown up at war with France. When Napoleon defeated Austrian and

Russian forces at Austerlitz, Austria was reduced to a quarter of its size and forced to pay a forty-million-franc indemnity. A year later, the mass exodus of princes from the German Imperial Confederation led to her father's abdication as Holy Roman emperor. Austria's latest rout at the hands of Napoleon forced Marie Louise and her family to flee Vienna for a second time.

Marie Louise had just returned home when rumors of Napoleon's marriage proposal began circulating. "Napoleon is too afraid of being refused and too intent on hurting us further to make such a demand, and father is too good to insist on something of such importance," she wrote naively. Around this time, Marie Louise told her father that she was in love with a relative, Archduke Franz of Modena-Este.

Meanwhile, Russia's Alexander I was stalling. His mother, Dowager Empress Maria Feodorovna, strongly opposed the marriage of her daughter to Napoleon. "As a mother, I cannot wish nor desire this union," she wrote Alexander on January 19. "However, as it should not be considered from a mother's perspective, but as a matter of State of the highest importance, it should be discussed and judged as such. [. . .] All that the State can wish of me is the total abnegation of my maternal rights; in this (unique) case I must make this sacrifice to you and to [the State]: [the decision] on your sister's fate belongs to no-one but you, my dear Alexander."[9]

By early February, Napoleon was expressing concerns about Anna Pavlovna's age. "[It has been] observed that Princess Anne [is] not yet mature; occasionally it takes a couple of years for some girls to attain maturity having reached the marriageable age and the idea of waiting three years with no hope of conceiving a child goes against the intentions of the Emperor," he wrote Champagny. There was also a religious complication. Sweden's Gustav IV had jilted Alexander's sister Marie after her grandmother Catherine the Great insisted that her granddaughter would not convert. Marriage to Marie's young sister would require adding Russian Orthodox chapels to Napoleon's many palaces.

By the end of January, Napoleon began negotiating for Austria's archduchess. Marie Louise seems to have come to terms with the political reality of her situation. "Since Napoleon's divorce, I continue to open the *Gazette de Francfort* in the hope of finding an announcement of his new bride," she confided to a friend. "I must admit that this delay has given me much cause for worry. [. . .] I am placing my fate in the hands of divine Providence. [. . .] If misfortune so wishes it, I am prepared to sacrifice my own happiness for the good of the State, convinced as I am that true happiness comes only from the accomplishment of one's duties, even at the expense of one's wishes."[10]

Francis couldn't bring himself to tell his favorite child that she was about to be married off to his archenemy. Instead, he delegated the task to Metternich who broke the news to Marie Louise in mid-February. Marshal Berthier, who made the official request for Marie Louise's hand in Vienna, wrote Napoleon that "without being a pretty woman," Marie Louise had "everything needed to make Your Majesty happy."

On March 9, Metternich and Berthier signed the marriage contract, modeled after that of Louis XVI and Marie Antoinette. Berthier accepted the five hundred thousand-franc dowry in rolls of gold ducats. Marie Louise formally renounced her claim to the Austrian crown, along with her two hundred thousand florin jewelry collection.[11]

Three months after his divorce, Napoleon married Marie Louise by proxy. Archduke Charles, the bride's uncle and staunch opponent of Napoleon, stood in for the groom. On March 11, the procession made its way through the Hofburg Palace past a double line of grenadiers to the Augustinian Church, the Habsburg's traditional wedding venue. Since no one knew Napoleon's ring size, the archbishop consecrated eleven rings of various sizes for the actual Paris ceremony.[12]

A few days later, Marie Louise climbed into a carriage with her canary in a cage and her spaniel Zozo in her lap. As the teenager left Vienna, she tried not to think about her great aunt. Just fourteen when she set off from Vienna to marry the future Louis XVI, Marie Antoinette was despised by the French. Relatives were powerless to save the thirty-seven-year-old from the guillotine.

Meanwhile Napoleon wrote his siblings, demanding they return to Paris for the wedding of the century. About the upcoming event, he remarked, "I am marrying a belly."

⚜

An Austrian entourage accompanied Marie Louise to the border with Bavaria near Braunau in St. Peter am Hart. A special pavilion was erected with a central hall flanked by matching rooms for the Austrian and French delegations. Wearing a gold brocade dress and a miniature of Napoleon framed by diamonds, Marie Louise took a seat on a canopied throne in the central hall.[13]

Prince Trauttmansdorff, the Habsburg chief chamberlain, formally delivered Marie Louise to Berthier. After the marriage contract was signed and read aloud, the Austrian entourage kissed the archduchess's hand one last time. "I assure you, dearest Papa, that I am truly unhappy and cannot console myself," she wrote her father.[14]

Marie Louise made a good first impression on her future sister-in-law Caroline Murat, who greeted her in the French pavilion. Though the archduchess wasn't beautiful, Caroline found the tall young woman to have "charming blond hair, hands, and feet, a cultivated mind and dignified bearing; all in all she was very amiable and sweet."[15] But the choice of Caroline as official greeter was tactless on Napoleon's part.

Two years earlier, Napoleon named Caroline and her husband Joachim Murat queen and king of Naples, the throne belonging to Marie Louise's grandparents. Driven from Naples, Maria Carolina and Ferdinand IV fled to Palermo, Sicily, in 1805. About Marie Louise's engagement, the deposed queen and daughter of Maria Theresa wrote angrily: "The Emperor dares to give his daughter as an adulterous concubine to a man besmirched with all crimes and abominations!" She called herself the "Devil's grandmother."[16]

Like her great aunt Marie-Antoinette, Marie Louise changed into French-style clothing the next morning. Before the three-dozen-coach fleet embarked for France, Caroline required her sister-in-law to give up her spaniel and canary.

For his marriage to the Habsburg archduchess, Napoleon decided to recreate the nuptials of Maria Carolina's ill-fated sister. In May 1770, Marie Antoinette was greeted at Château de Compiègne by Louis XV and her fiancé, the future Louis XVI. Four decades later, Napoleon met Marie Antoinette's grandniece in the same place.

Located some seventy miles northeast of Paris on the road to Flanders, surrounded by forest and the Oise and Aisne rivers, Compiègne had long charmed France's kings. Louis XIV reportedly said, "At Versailles I am the King; at Fontainebleau a Prince, at Compiègne a country man." Begun by Charles V in the fourteenth century, the château was altered by successive royals. In the mid-eighteenth century, Louis XV demolished the medieval-style residence and replaced it with a fashionable neoclassical limestone palace. Louis XVI continued to expand and decorate. Compiègne was finished just in time to be looted during the French Revolution.

In 1807, Joséphine's favorite architect Louis-Martin Berthault began a major makeover of the château. Berthault turned the apartments of Louis XVI's family into spectacular apartments for Napoleon and Joséphine. Cabinetmakers Jacob-Desmalter and Pierre-Benoit Marcion supplied elegant Empire-style furniture, and Sèvres produced special porcelain. Berthault asked Vivant Denon for paintings and sculpture from the Musée Napoléon to decorate the apartments with a focus on themes of love and fertility. Canova's sensual *Cupid and Psyche* was installed by the entrance to the imperial apartments. Large portraits of the Empire's great figures by Prud'hon, Fabre, and Lefèvre lined the new Gallery of Minsters; paintings by Le Dominiquin, Patel, and Flinck hung in the empress's Galerie des Tableaux.

Napoleon took up residence in Louis XVI's former gunpowder room and converted the garden-view bedchamber into a large reception room. His bedroom's red and gold wall coverings, curtains, bed covers, and chairs were adorned with symbols of the Empire—oak leaves, stars, and bees. Napoleon personally chose a landscape by Jean-Joseph Bidault to hang between the windows. Dubois, Redouté, and Girodet produced the painted décor; the gilt wood furniture and cabinetry was by Jacob-Desmalter, who also produced a mechanical desk for the adjoining library, accessible only to Napoleon's most senior court officials.

Past the library were the empress's apartments. Built in 1755, the north wing of the terrace had been home to the Dauphin Louis and Dauphine Maria Josepha of Saxony, along with Marie Antoinette before she relocated to the newer south wing of the terrace. Jacob-Desmalter's ethereal gilded bed featured symbols of fertility, cornucopias, along with two standing winged figures. "Compiègne speaks of Napoleon as Versailles does of Louis XIV," observed the nineteenth-century French writer Auguste Luchet.[17]

Joséphine never saw her finished apartments by Berthault. Ironically, her replacement Marie Louise got to enjoy the sumptuous remodel. On the eve of Marie Louise's arrival at the château, Napoleon said goodbye to his mistress, Christine de Mathis, the Piedmontese lady-in-waiting of his sister Pauline. On March 27, Napoleon rode to meet Marie Louise and her retinue with his brother-in-law, Joachim Murat, king of Naples.

Climbing into her carriage, Napoleon kissed his bride on both cheeks, saying "Madam, I feel great pleasure to see you."

"Sire, you are much better than on your portraits," she replied.

Canceling the welcome ceremony, Napoleon went straight to Compiègne. Taking his arm, Marie Louise climbed the palace's grand staircase. To her delight, Zozo and her pet parrot were waiting in her apartments, along with a tapestry she left behind at the Hofburg palace. That evening, Caroline Murat joined the couple for dinner in the empress's antiquity-inspired dining room. Above them, the ceiling painting featured two winged lovers holding a bunch of grapes and sharing a cup. Rather than wait for the civil or religious ceremonies, Napoleon spent the night with Marie Louise.

On Sunday, April 1, arch-chancellor Cambacérès presided over the couple's civil wedding at the Château de Saint-Cloud. The turnout was so large that guests spilled over from the Apollo Gallery into the Salon du Mars. Marie Louise entered the gallery alongside Napoleon in full court dress and a diamond crown. At the end of the gallery, the couple sat at a dais below a canopy.

After the exchange of vows, Cambacérès declared: "In the name of the Emperor and the Law, I declare that his Imperial and Royal Majesty Napoleon, Emperor of the French, King of Italy, and her Imperial and Royal Highness the Archduchess Marie Louise are united in marriage." Salvos of artillery at Saint-Cloud and the Invalides in Paris announced the marriage.

The next morning, Parisians began gathering along the avenues of the Bois de Boulogne to the Tuileries Palace. Their main objective was to catch a glimpse of the new teenage empress. The newlyweds meanwhile were en route to the capital in a gilded coronation coach drawn by eight horses. The retinue was led by the cavalry of the Imperial Guard, followed by other horsemen, heralds of arms, and numerous carriages. The impressive procession numbered fifty carriages and 240 horsemen.

Entering Paris from the west, the newlyweds paused for speeches at the Arc de Triomphe. With the arch still under construction, they passed through a full-size model in wood and painted cloth. Napoleon declared the arch to be the capital's official gateway. From there, the procession proceeded past cheering crowds along the Champs-Élysées to the Tuileries Palace.

The gate at the Tuileries Garden sported a special veneered decoration courtesy of Percier and Fontaine—a triumphal arch adorned with bas-reliefs in the middle of a colonnade. As an expression of the dynastic union, the top of the arch featured two kneeling female figures holding out their arms to a crown resting on a cushion, supporting a sculpted altar with the arms of the French and Austrian Empires.

A few weeks before the wedding, Napoleon informed Denon that he had decided to transform the Louvre's Salon Carré into a chapel. To make room for two levels of seating, all of the paintings had to be moved out, including Veronese's monumental *Wedding at Cana.* To get to the Salon Carré, the large wedding party would have to pass through the Grand Gallery, representing a risk to the masterpieces lining the walls. Denon expressed his concern for the precious canvases.

"Well, there is nothing to do but burn them!" Napoleon replied.

Denon rolled up and stored the canvases. Percier and Fontaine covered the empty walls of the Salon with Gobelins tapestries and gold embroidered textiles.

The wedding cortege made its way from the Tuileries to the Grand Gallery, with the imperial couple following behind the great dignitaries of the Empire. After five years and numerous delays, Percier and Fontaine's renovations to the gallery were finally finished.

Skylights bathed the long corridor with natural light. Large arches supported on double columns divided the gallery into bays, providing wall space for hundreds of stolen masterpieces. The first bay displayed French paintings by Poussin, Le Sueur, and Vouet; Dutch, Flemish, and German pictures made up the next four bays, with Rubens's *Descent from the Cross* from Antwerp enjoying a central location. The last four bays were dedicated to the Italian schools and starred Leonardo, Tintoretto, Veronese, Titian, and Raphael.[18]

Marie Louise entered the gallery wearing a new gown designed by Joséphine's favorite dressmaker, Leroy. The 12,000-franc, form-fitting dress in silver tulle netting, embroidered with pearls and lamé, featured a high waist and long, flowing skirt. A diadem held an Alençon lace veil in place over her blond hair. But no one had bothered to find out the bride's shoe size and her white satin slippers with silver embroidery were painfully small.

Over her gown, Marie Louise donned Joséphine's eighty-pound crimson velvet and gold embroidered coronation mantle. Four of her sisters-in-law—Caroline Murat, Joseph's wife Julie Clary, Hortense de Beauharnais, and Catharine of Württemberg—reluctantly carried the weighty ermine-lined train. In another awkward move, Napoleon named Hortense Mistress of the Robes for her mother's successor.

Napoleon's wedding attire was equally elaborate. Trading his signature bicorn for a plumed hat, Napoleon wore a dress coat of embroidered purple velvet—similar to those designed by Isabey for his coronations in Paris and Milan. Embellished in point couché embroidery with sequins and gold and silver thread by Augustin François-Andre Picot, the coat's decoration was highly symbolic. "For the heir to Augustus and Charlemagne," writes Yves Carlier, "the ceremonial garment conveyed a powerful message through its ornaments: the stars of glory, the oak and olive trees of Jupiter, the laurels and radiant glory of Apollo, the grapes and wheat of abundance, the emblematic bee and the imperial flower."[19] A diamond-studded sword completed the ensemble.

The choice of purple was also symbolic. Purple, antiquity's most enduring status symbol, took hold in Rome, the ancient world's "most status symbol-conscious culture," writes Meyer Reinhold.[20] During antiquity, the red-violet hue was reserved for authority figures. Senators and members of the equestrian order wore tunics with a vertical purple stripe; priests and magistrates donned togas with a purple border. During the early Roman Empire, empresses went to a "purple palace" chamber or Porphyra to give birth.[21]

The highly prized purple dye was made from a secretion of mollusks from the Mediterranean; one gram required eight thousand mollusks.[22] With Constantinople's fall to the Turks in 1453, manufacture of sea purple ended, creating something of a wardrobe emergency for the Church. In 1464, Pope Paul II decreed that vivid scarlet dye derived from the New World cochineal insect would be used to produce clerical robes and hats.[23] The female cochineal was dried and crushed to extract a red acid; additives produced a range of shades from light pink to a deep purple. Cochineal became second to silver as Spain's most profitable export. The introduction of synthetic dyes in the nineteenth century led to the decline of cochineal.[24]

Four hundred wedding guests had been waiting hours for the bride and groom. Finally at one o'clock in the afternoon, the imperial couple ascended the grand stairway and entered the white and gold Salon Carré. Surrounded by family members and dignitaries, Napoleon and Marie Louise stood facing the silver gilt altar crowned with a large cross with a tabernacle cabinet at its base and six chased vermeil candlesticks.

Napoleon originally intended to give Henri Auguste's cross and candlesticks to Pius VII, but redirected the gift to the Basilica of St. Denis when their relationship soured. The financially strapped Auguste was forced to hand over his completed pieces to goldsmith Martin-Guillaume Biennais who completed the commission.[25] Auguste combined antique motifs like acanthus leaves, leaf-and-dart moldings, gadroons, tortoiseshell, quatrefoil, and lion's paw feet with symbols of the Eucharist, including sheaves of wheat, vine branches, and reeds.

Cardinal Fesch officiated the wedding, pronouncing the nuptial blessing, blessing of the rings, and the exchange of gold coins. Placing the ring on Marie Louise's finger, Napoleon repeated: "I give you this ring in token of our marriage." Jean-Roch Coignet, a member of Napoleon's Imperial Guard, described the ceremony:

"The whole assembly remained standing, and the most solemn silence prevailed. The procession moved slowly. As soon as it had passed by General Dorsenne called us together, marched us into the chapel, and formed us into a circle. We saw the Emperor on the right, kneeling upon a cushion decorated with bees, and his wife kneeling beside him to receive the benediction. After having placed the crown on his own head and on that of his wife, he rose, and sat down with her on a settee. Then the celebration of mass was begun . . ."[26]

Napoleon and Marie Louise proceeded back through the Grand Gallery to the Tuileries with their courtiers and the imperial family to the cheers of thousands of spectators. Napoleon insisted on the formal banquet of the ancien régime, known as the *grand couvert*. In the theater of the Tuileries, courtiers stood in the galleries watching Napoleon and his family eat at a horseshoe-shaped table. Guests were arranged according to rank on either side of the couple.

Among them was Vivant Denon, standing in a box at the left. One of the guests invited to welcome Marie Louise to Compiègne, Denon had played a major role in the wedding preparations. In addition to Auguste's Grand Vermeil Service, the table was set with an Egyptian service designed by Denon and Sèvres director Alexandre Brongniart. Finished just days before the wedding, the service featured some seventy-two plates, a cabaret or coffee service, and a centerpiece in biscuit. The coffee service and a number of plates were decorated with images from Denon's popular *Travels in Lower and Upper Egypt*. The centerpiece included miniature reproductions of famous antiquities in the Musée Napoléon.[27]

While Napoleon and his guests dined at the Tuileries, Parisians enjoyed an alfresco meal. Like the post-triumph feasts of ancient Rome, Napoleon provided poultry, meat, and barrels of wine. To bolster public support for his Austrian bride, the emperor also showered the crowd with a commemorative wedding medallion.[28] Vivant Denon conceived the medal's design with the double portraits of the imperial couple, but was surprised by the enormous quantity ordered by Daru—forty thousand pieces.

To meet the demand, writes Marie-Anne Dupuy, Denon hired extra workers at the Mint. To each copy, the director added his own signature, *Denon direxit*.[29] From Milan, Andrea Appiani and Luigi Manfredini collaborated on a highly symbolic commemorative medal. The obverse featured a double portrait in profile—Napoleon wearing the iron crown of Italy, alongside Marie Louise. On the reverse, Hymenaeus, god of weddings, held a wedding veil in his left hand and a torch in the other, driving away Mars, god of war.

With the awarding of medals, Napoleon was also following a Roman tradition. Roman imperial weddings were commemorated with coins. In fifteenth-century Rome, art-loving Pope Paul II tossed coins to the crowd from his new Palazzo San Marco (today's Palazzo Venezia). During the Possesso, the inaugural Mass for the popes in the late seventeenth century, coins were also thrown from the Lateran Basilica's Loggia delle Benedizioni and given to dignitaries inside the church.[30]

The *Moniteur Universel* described the lavish setting: "Rearranged for the imperial banquet, the splendid theatre had been transformed into a hall of celebration. This had been achieved by redecorating the stage to merge with the rest of the space, so that instead of an audience area and a stage, one saw only a single room, forming a perfectly ordered whole. The décor comprised two cupolas supported by double arches, together with two pendentives ornamented with columns. One of the sections, placed beside the other, was occupied by the imperial banqueting table, set on a platform beneath a magnificent canopy. . . . The emperor and empress were surrounded by the kings, queens, princes, and princesses of their families."[31] Throughout the twenty-minute meal, "nobody uttered a word," recalled Captain Coignet. "One was only allowed to speak when addressed by the sovereign master. Imposing it may be, but cheerful it ain't."[32]

Following the banquet, the newlyweds made an appearance on the palace balcony for an homage of the troops below. Heralds distributed gold and silver coins to the crowds in the gardens. A concert was held beneath the windows of the palace. This was followed by fireworks that extended the length of the Champs-Élysées. Throughout the day, music, games, acrobatics, and other entertainments were offered in the public squares, along with barrels of wine. Festivities continued until late in the night.

Napoleon was pleased with the wedding—except for one important exception. Thirteen of twenty-seven cardinals, including Pius VII's secretary of state Cardinal Consalvi, boycotted the religious ceremony. Since Pius had not recognized the annulment of his marriage to Joséphine, the absence of nearly half the invited cardinals at Napoleon's wedding raised questions about his future heir's right of inheritance. Napoleon met their passive resistance harshly, stripping them of their red robes, offices, and estates. Made to wear the simple black robes of priests, the "black cardinals" were exiled to various French provinces until Pius secured their release in January 1813.

The couple spent April at Compiègne, with Napoleon remaining by Marie Louise's side. The charm offensive was a success. "I assure you, dear papa, that people have done great injustice to the Emperor," Marie Louise wrote her father. "The better one knows him, the better one appreciates and loves him."[33]

Napoleon wooed his bride, twenty-two years his junior, with lavish gifts. LeRoy created items for Marie Louise's elegant trousseau—linen and silk, hats, capes, fichus (triangular scarves), shoes, gold-leaf fans, embroidered shawls, ball gowns, day dresses, hunting outfits, and overcoats.

As a wedding gift for Marie Louise, Napoleon commissioned a twenty-eight-piece tea service from Biennais (shared today by the Louvre and the National Museum of Scotland). Percier designed many of the main pieces including the double salts, sugar bowl, and punch bowl. The tea caddy features a bas-relief copy of the ancient Roman fresco, the *Aldobrandini Wedding* (named for its owners, the Aldobrandini family, until it was acquired for the Vatican in 1818). The service brimmed with Napoleonic references—from Jupiter's eagle on the sugar bowl to the emperor's portrait on the knife handles. The figures of lovers Cupid and Psyche on the sugar bowl were meant to celebrate the marriage of Napoleon and Marie Louise.[34]

As part of her marriage contract, Marie Louise had to give up her jewelry collection. Now her husband more than compensated her for that loss, placing a large order with François-Regnault Nitot, who had succeeded his father Marie-Etienne as official jeweler to the emperor. As part of the Crown Jewels, Nitot created a spectacular diamond parure including a crown, diadem, necklace, comb, pair of three-drop earrings, bracelets, a belt, ten dress jewels, and eight rows of gold collets. Nitot set the diadem with the most beautiful of the French crown diamonds, including the Grand Mazarin bequeathed to Louis XIV by Cardinal Jules Mazarin. The light pink, nineteen-carat square-cut diamond was first worn by a relative of Marie Louise—Louis XIV's wife Maria Theresa of Austria. After Maria Theresa's death, Louis added the Grand Mazarin to his own chain of diamonds.[35]

Napoleon placed another order for Mare Louise's private jewelry collection that fall. Nitot delivered two parures, one of emeralds and diamonds, the other of opals and diamonds, to the emperor in mid-January 1811.

Nitot set thirty-two emeralds in the necklace with the center gem weighing a whopping 13.75 metric carats. Ten alternating oval and lozenge-shaped emeralds surrounded by diamonds were separated by palmettes, each of which enclosed a small round emerald. A pear-shaped emerald surrounded by diamonds hung from each large emerald. Two beautiful pear-shaped emeralds were used for the earrings, embellished with brilliants and two smaller emeralds (the emeralds were replaced by turquoise in the diadem, today at the Smithsonian in Washington, D.C.).

In 1811, Napoleon also ordered 150 diamond ears of wheat for Marie-Louise's dress and hair, with over eight thousand white brilliant diamonds. Marie-Louise appears to have approved of the motif, symbol of fertility and attribute of Ceres, Roman goddess of the harvest. In 1812, she received an aigrette of ears of wheat in emeralds and diamonds for her personal jewelry collection.[36]

Expensive jewelry in the form of earrings, bracelets, necklaces, and rings were Roman status symbols. Roman jewelers used amber, amethysts, sapphires, uncut diamonds, and emeralds. It was Pompey the Great who introduced pearls to Rome. Pompey celebrated his victory over Mithradates VI by parading thirty-three pearl crowns and his portrait in pearls in his triumphal procession.[37] As Kenneth Lapatin notes, Pliny considered the general's pearl infatuation outrageous and effeminate. Nor did he care for Caligula's pearl slippers, Nero's pearl scepters and couches, and women's high-priced pearl earrings. Julius Caesar dedicated a pearl-encrusted breastplate in the temple he built for Venus Genetrix in the Forum Julium. The short-reigned Vitellius reportedly sold one of his mother's pearl earrings to fund a military campaign.[38]

Shortly before her divorce from Napoleon, Joséphine received a delivery at her Tuileries apartment, a spectacular cabinet to house her legendary jewelry collection. In his invoice for 55,000 francs, François-Honoré-Georges Jacob-Desmalter wrote: "All of the ornaments relate to the principal subject, the birth of the queen of the earth [Venus, goddess of love] to whom cupids and goddesses hurry to present their offerings."[39] With Marie Louise now occupying Joséphine's bedchamber, Napoleon changed the locks for the cabinet's thirty drawers and secret compartments. For extra storage room, he ordered two smaller cabinets for the sides.

A collaboration between Charles Percier, Antoine-Denis Chaudet, and Jacob-Desmalter, the Grand Écrin recalls the beautiful jewelry cabinet of Marie Antoinette, a gift from the city of Paris in 1787 (moved to Saint-Cloud during the Empire). Designed by Percier to evoke a Greek temple, the Grand Écrin's locks were concealed by mother-of-pearl jewelry motifs—diadems, strands of pearls, engraved rings, and butterfly hairpins. The entablature was decorated with a frieze of bronze and mother-of-pearl tiaras. In Chaudet's gilded central motif of Venus Anadyomene (Venus Rising from the Sea), the goddess is flanked by handmaidens and cupids playing with swans. Topping the cabinet are Venus's doves, constant in love.

THREE

BREAKFAST WITH NAPOLEON

Two weeks after the imperial wedding, on April 15, the Austerlitz Column was unveiled. But out of respect for Marie Louise, Napoleon did not attend the dedication ceremony. Made with bronze from seized Austrian cannons, the column celebrated her father's catastrophic defeat five years earlier.

The soaring column was inscribed "Monument élevé à la gloire de la Grande Armée"—"Monument erected to the glory of the Grande Armée." Also known as the Column of the Grand Army and the Vendôme Column, the project took four years to finish at a cost of one million francs. It stood nearly twenty-five feet taller than its ancient Roman model, Trajan's Column.

Just as Romans interpreted Trajan's column as their emperor's *res gestae*, writes Valérie Huet, so too would Parisians experience the Vendôme Column as a testament to the military accomplishments of Napoleon I.[1] With the column, Napoleon equated himself and the Grande Armée to Trajan and his Roman legions.

Topping the statue was a figure of Napoleon in a Roman toga with an immense sword and a winged Victory on a globe in his hand. According to Caulaincourt, Napoleon was not pleased. "I don't want any idols, not even statues outdoors," he reportedly told him. "It is to my great discontent and without consulting me that Denon made mine for the column in the Place Vendôme." Some of Napoleon's advisers were jealous of Denon's growing authority. "The Emperor commanded, but he was indifferent to the mode of execution, because he lacked the taste to judge by himself (. . .)," wrote Interior Minister Chaptal. "Denon wanted to sign the Emperor through all. Full of himself, of simple amateur, he placed himself in the rank of painters and architects."[2]

Several weeks after the column's debut, Napoleon's mistress Marie Waleska gave birth to his son, Alexandre-Florian-Joseph, Comte Colonna Walewski. On the evening of June 10, some four thousand guests awaited the imperial couple's arrival at the Hôtel de Ville, Paris's City Hall. Nicolas Frochot, prefect of the Seine and de facto mayor of Paris, hired fellow Burgundian Pierre Prud'hon to transform the civic building into Mount Olympus. From a throne outside, Napoleon and Marie Louise enjoyed a mock sea battle on the Seine followed by fireworks and the debut of a choral work.[3]

As part of the extravagant décor, Prud'hon created an allegory for the imperial marriage, *The Wedding Celebration of Hercules and Hebe.* After the Greek hero ascended to Mount Olympus, he married Hera's daughter Hebe, goddess of youth. "The French emperor often fashioned himself as a modern reincarnation of an ancient hero. Napoleon's young bride . . . could have been seen as a latter-day Hebe," writes Elizabeth Guffey.[4]

At the end of the evening, Marie Louise was presented with a spectacular Empire-style toilette set for her apartment at the Tuileries Palace. For the prestigious gift, Prud'hon called on a number of talented colleagues including imperial gold and silversmith Jean-Baptiste-Claude Odiot, bronze caster Pierre-Philippe Thomire, and sculptor Henri Victor Roguier. Filled with antique symbols and mythological references, the five hundred thousand-franc set was "remarkable even by the standards of the French court," writes Guffey.[5]

Meanwhile Vivant Denon reported to Napoleon that sixty paintings were exhibited at the 1810 Salon, recording the "severity, simplicity and truth of history." Among them was Louis-Philippe Crépin's *The Arrival of the Imperial Couple in Antwerp*. To avoid hurting Marie Louise's feelings, Joséphine was removed from Jacques-Louis David's monumental *Distribution of the Eagles*.[6]

After returning from their honeymoon in the Low Countries, Napoleon kept Marie Louise out of the public eye. To fight homesickness, Marie Louise filled her days with activities. Since returning from her honeymoon, she kept busy reading, doing needlework, and taking music and drawing lessons. For her art teacher, Denon selected Pierre-Paul Prud'hon, who he called ". . . the man who draws the best with both pencils and whose talent is the most graceful."[7]

Napoleon kept his young wife hidden from public view, possibly because she reminded Parisians of her unpopular relative Marie-Antoinette, or possibly to avoid negative comparisons between the shy teenager and her charming predecessor Joséphine. But the tactic backfired. Marie Louise did not receive a warm welcome by the French, who nicknamed her "the Austrian."

Napoleon's consort was also not well accepted at court, or by his favorite sister Pauline. Marie Louise's cloistered court life was governed by formal etiquette and protocol. Jealous and doting, Napoleon made sure that men were kept safely out of range. In an effort to improve his wife's popularity, Napoleon had her depicted by the day's great artists.[8]

On August 12, 1810, Marshal of the Palace Duroc wrote from Saint-Cloud to Pierre-Antoine Daru, Napoleon's Intendant-General: "It's the intention of his majesty to have in Paris Mr. Canova, who, in regard to the arts of painting, sculpture, and architecture, and for all that matters in decorating, can be of great service to His Majesty's service, whether for his palaces or for all the public establishments, No one has more taste than he has and no one can give better advice."[9]

Two days later, Daru fired a letter off to Antonio Canova who was in Florence installing the Monument to Vittorio Alfieri. The sculptor had also been in Florence several months earlier (late April) to oversee the installation of *Venus Italica* in the Uffizi, his replacement for the *Medici Venus*, Napoleon's "bride" for *Apollo Belvedere*.

"I am authorized by the Emperor, Sir, to invite you on his behalf to return to Paris to make the statue of her Majesty the Empress" wrote

Daru.[10] A week later, Daru penned another letter to Canova: "The particular case which he makes of your superior talents, and your extended knowledge in all the arts which depend on drawing, has led him to think that your opinions could contribute powerfully to the perfection of works of art which must perpetuate the splendor of his reign." The letter went on to convey Napoleon's desire to have the sculptor move to Paris.[11]

Declining the invitation was not an option. Since their last meeting in 1802, Napoleon had crowned himself Emperor of France and King of Italy, annexed Venice and Rome, and kidnapped the pope. On September 1, Canova wrote Daru from Florence, confirming that he would return to Paris. But he politely declined to move to France, making it clear that Marie Louise's full-length portrait would be executed in his Rome studio:

"And here I implore Your Excellency to consider the invincible reasons that link me to Italy, and to Rome. It is true to say that this city, mother and ancient seat of the arts, is the only refuge for a sculptor, especially one who has fixed his residence there . . . for very many years. I have given many of these years, however, in service either to His Majesty or to the imperial family, in preference to other very advantageous and honorific commissions, for the dear ambition of ensuring the immortality of my name."[12]

⚜

On Thursday, October 11, Canova and his stepbrother Giovanni Battista Sartori Canova arrived at the historic Château de Fontainebleau. Though Canova had met Napoleon eight years earlier, this occasion assumed a heightened importance. His patron Pius VII was still under house arrest in Savona. Rome was in dire straits.

As instructed, Canova returned to Fontainebleau two days later. At mid-morning on Saturday, Duroc presented him to the imperial couple. He entered the elegantly furnished room to find the maître d'hôtel serving Marie Louise and Napoleon a morning meal of fricassee of chicken with green beans and rice (the dish was renamed Chicken Marengo after his victory in Italy).[13] The head waiter was pouring a glass of the emperor's favorite white burgundy, Chambertin, when Napoleon looked up.

"You have grown rather thinner, Monsieur Canova."

Canova thought the emperor had grown older and paunchier.

Napoleon considered meals a waste of time. He usually rushed through breakfast and dinner, spending just ten or fifteen minutes with Marie Louise. But today was an exception. He lingered over his coffee.

"Paris is the capital of the world—you must remain here: we shall make much of you," he told Canova.

"Sire, you may command me, but if it please your Majesty that my life should be devoted to your service, permit me, Sire to return to Rome, after having completed the object of my visit here."

Napoleon smiled. "In Paris you will be in your element; for here are all the chef-d'oeuvres of art, the *Farnese Hercules* alone excepted; but we shall soon have that too."

"May it please your Majesty to leave Italy, at least, something. These monuments of antiquity are inseparably connected with many others, which it would be impossible to remove, either from Rome or Naples."

"Italy can indemnify herself by excavations. I shall order some to be commenced at Rome. Pray has the Pope been at much expense in excavations?" Napoleon asked.

Canova replied that Pius had spent little due to a lack of funds, but he had managed to form a new museum. Interrupting, Napoleon asked if the Borghese family had spent much on excavations, to which the sculptor replied that they had not, as they generally undertook them with others, whose shares they later bought.

The subject of Rome's excavations was of special importance to the sculptor. Canova told Napoleon that the Romans possessed "a sacred right" over its buried antiquities: ". . . neither the noble families of Rome, nor even the Pope himself, had a right to remove these precious remains from Rome, to which city they belonged, as the inheritance of their ancestors, and the reward of their victories."

Napoleon continued to press on the pope's patronage. "The Borghese marbles cost me fourteen millions. How much does the Pope annually expend on the fine arts? A hundred thousand crowns?"

"Not so much; for he is extremely poor."

"Great things, then, may be done with much less?"

"Certainly."

The conversation turned to Canova's colossal statue of the emperor awaiting shipment to Paris. When Napoleon expressed disappointment that he was not depicted in contemporary dress, Canova defended his choice of the heroic nude. "Omnipotence itself would have failed, had it attempted to represent your Majesty as I now see you, with small clothes, boots . . . in short, in the French costume. In statuary, as in all the other arts, we have our sublime style; the sculptor's sublimity is nakedness, and a kind of drapery peculiar to our art."

Canova was also scheduled to start an equestrian statue of Napoleon for the Place Vendôme. ". . . for Napoleon the way of representing the protagonists of history's events was crucial, his references were the equestrian monuments, Donatello's *Gattamelata*, Verrocchio's *Colleoni*, but above all the Marcus Aurelius of the Campidoglio," writes Mario Guderzo.[14] Now Canova drew a distinction between the colossal nude *Napoleon as Mars the Peacemaker* and the future equestrian statue.

"I could not represent your figure undraped, since my intention is to represent you in the act of commanding an army. This was customary with the ancient sculptors . . ."

"Have you seen the bronze statue of General Dessaix?" Napoleon asked. "It appears to be very ill executed; his sash is ridiculous." Canova knew that the nude statue of France's fallen general had just been unveiled to widespread derision. Before he could respond, Napoleon asked "Is my statue a full length?"

"It is, Sire, and is already cast very successfully, an engraving has also been executed from it."

"I wish to visit Rome."

"That country well deserves to be seen by your Majesty, who will find in it many objects capable of warming your imagination such as the Capitol, the Forum of Trajan, the Sacred Way, the columns, triumphal arches . . ." Canova proceeded to describe some of the finest monuments, including the Appian Way, from Rome to Brindisi, bordered with tombs on both sides.

"What is there astonishing in this, the Romans were masters of the world?" Napoleon asked.

Canova seized the opportunity to laud his compatriots. "It was not only the power, but Italian genius and our love of the sublime, which produced so many magnificent works," the sculptor replied. "Let your Majesty be pleased to reflect upon what the Florentines alone have done, who possessed but a very straitened territory, what also the Venetians. The Florentines had the courage to raise their wonderful cathedral by an additional tax of one penny in the pound upon the manufacture of woolen stuffs; and this alone was found sufficient for the erection of an edifice, the expenses of which would be too much for the treasury of any modern power. They also cased the gates of St. John to be executed in bronze, by Ghiberti, at the expense of forty thousand sequins, equivalent in the present day to several millions of francs. Let your Majesty also consider their industry and at the same time their public spirit."

Napoleon ended the meeting, giving Canova his marching orders to start the statue of Marie Louise.[15]

Two days later, Canova returned to Fontainebleau to begin the commission. Marie Louise had just sat down to breakfast with her husband when the sculptor arrived. Though the empress knew she was in excellent hands, she felt self-conscious about sitting for the celebrated artist. She had recently learned that she was pregnant and her elated husband was acting clingier than usual.

When she was a girl, Canova had sculpted her father's portrait bust for the Marciana Library in Venice. The imperial government wanted him portrayed in contemporary court dress; Canova insisted on an ancient cuirass and military cloak, or chlamys.[16] In 1805, Canova visited Vienna to oversee the installation of his large funerary monument for her great aunt Maria Christina in the family's Augustinian Church. Canova and her great uncle Albert had gone head to head on a number of issues relating to the monument.[17]

Like her husband, her father had courted Canova, trying to convince him to move to Vienna. When that failed, Francis offered to build him a large studio in Venice if he would live there half the year.[18] Before Canova left for Vienna in 1805, the pope awarded Canova a 400–silver scudo annuity and promised him a new studio and house near Piazza del Popolo, to be designed by Raffaele Stern. Canova politely declined the pope's offer, donating his annuity to the Academy of St. Luke.[19]

Now, her husband broke the ice. "Is the air of Rome as bad and unhealthy in the time of the ancients as in our days?" he asked Canova.

"It appears to have been so, according to the historians," Canova replied. "The ancients, it is clear, took precautions against the unwholesome air by means of woods and forests, which they called sacred; besides, the immense population which covered the country diminished the fatal effects of this scourge. I remember to have read in Tacitus that upon the return of the troops of Vitellius from Germany, they fell ill, from having slept on the Vatican Mount."

On hearing this, Napoleon immediately rang for his librarian to bring him a copy of the *Annals* by Tacitus. When they could not find the passage, Napoleon resumed the conversation, describing how soldiers arriving in Rome from distant countries always fell ill the first year, but then recovered.

Sensing Napoleon's interest in Rome, Canova brought up the city's desperate situation without the pope. ". . . Rome is in want of everything and your Majesty's protection is all that is now left it."

"We will make it the capital of Italy, Napoleon said smiling, "and we will also join Naples with it. Well, what do you say? Will that please you?"

Canova paused. "The arts would also be productive of great prosperity to Rome, but the arts at present languish; and, with the exception of your Majesty and the imperial family, who have given some commissions, artists are now without employment . . ." Then citing examples from the Egyptians, Greeks, and Romans, Canova argued that religion alone had caused the arts to flourish; the Romans had impressed the seal of religion upon all their works. He concluded that every religion has been favorable to the arts, and the Roman Catholic much more than any other; "a chapel and a simple cross suffice for the Protestant and consequently afford no encouragement to the arts."

Turning to Marie Louise, Napoleon said, "He is right, religion always promotes the arts, and the Protestants can produce nothing great."[20]

At the next sitting, Canova was surprised to find Napoleon again by his young wife's side. In fact, the emperor would never leave the sculptor alone with Marie Louise. Canova was struck by the contrast between the doting husband and the first consul of eight years before who was too impatient to sit for his own portrait. With Napoleon completely unoccupied, Canova decided to raise the touchy subject of Pius.

"Why does not your Majesty become reconciled, in some degree, with the Pope?"

"Because priests wish to command everywhere, because they wish to meddle with everything, and be masters of everything, like Gregory VII," replied Napoleon.

"It seems to me that, at present, there is no reason to apprehend this, since your Majesty's power is everywhere supreme."

"The Popes have always hindered the resuscitation of the Italian nation, even when they were not the absolute masters of Rome; and this they effected by means of the factions of the Colonnas and the Orsini."

"Truly, if the Popes had had your Majesty's courage, they might have found many favourable opportunities of making themselves masters of all Italy."

"As to that," said Napoleon, placing his hand on his sword, "this is the one thing needful."

"That is true, we have seen, that if Alexander VI had lived, Duke Valentino would have commenced the conquests of Italy. The attempts of this kind made by Julian II and Leo X were, likewise, not unsuccessful; but in general the Popes were elected at too advanced an age, and if one of them was enterprising, the succeeding one, perhaps, was mild and pacific."

"It is the sword that is wanted," Napoleon repeated.

"Not the sword only, but also the pastoral staff. Machiavelli himself dared not to decide which of the two had more contributed to the aggrandisement of Rome, the arms of Romulus or the religion of Numa. So true it is, that these two means should be employed simultaneously. If the pontiffs did not always signalize themselves by military exploits, they, however, performed such brilliant actions, as always to excite the admiration of the world."

After disparaging the popes, Napoleon expressed admiration for the ancient Romans. "What a great people were the Romans!" he declared.

"So they were, undoubtedly, till the second Punic War."

"Caesar, Caesar, was the great man, not Caesar only, but some of the succeeding Emperors, such as Titus, Trajan, Marcus Aurelius . . . the Romans were always great till the time of Constantine. The Popes were wrong in fomenting discord in Italy; and in always being the first to call in the French and Germans. They were not capable of being soldiers themselves, and they have lost much."

"Since it is so, your Majesty will not permit our evils to increase; but I can assure your Majesty, that unless you come to Rome's assistance, this city will become what it was when the Popes transferred the Papal seat to Avignon. Before that time, it had immense supplies of water and many fountains; but the aqueducts fell into ruins, and the water of the Tiber was sold in the streets: the city was a desert."

Napoleon seemed affected by this. "Obstacles are thrown in my way: and this, too, when I am master of France, Italy, and three-fourths of Germany; I am the successor of Charlemagne. If the present Pope were like his predecessor of that day, all might be arranged. And have not your Venetians also quarrelled with him?"

"Not in the same manner as your Majesty. You are so great, Sire, that you could easily grant the Pontiff some spot in which his independence might be conspicuous, and in which he could have the free exercise of his ministry."

Canova's comment triggered an angry reaction. "What! Do I not allow him to do everything he pleases, so long as he does not interfere in temporal concerns?"

"Yes, but your ministers do not follow your example. As soon as the Pope publishes any order which is displeasing to the French Government it is immediately annulled."

"How, do I not permit the bishops to govern the church as they think fit? Is there no religion here? Who restored the Altars? Who protected the clergy?"

"If your Majesty had pious subjects, they would be still more attached and submissive to your person."

"This is what I desire, but the Pope is German all over," Napoleon said, looking at Marie Louise.

"I can assure you, that when I was in Germany the Pope was said to be wholly French," she said.

"He would not drive either the Russians or the English from his dominions. That is the cause of our misunderstanding." At this moment, Marshal Duroc entered the room. "He has even pretended to excommunicate me.

Is he not aware that we might become the same as the English and the Russians?"

"I humbly crave your Majesty's pardon; but the zeal which animates me inspires me with confidence to speak with freedom; you must allow, Sire, such a schism is contrary to your interests. I sincerely pray, that heaven may grant you a long life; but when misfortune arrives, it is to be feared that some ambitious person might suddenly appear, who, for his own views, embracing those of the Pope, might occasion great disturbances in the state. In a short time, Sire, you will be a father; you should think of fixing things upon a solid basis. I earnestly entreat your Majesty to effect, in some shape or other, a reconciliation with the Pope."

"You are then anxious to see us reconciled—so am I too; but recollect what the Romans were before they had Popes."

"Let your Majesty also reflect, how religious the Romans were when they were great," Canova replied. "That Caesar who is so much celebrated, ascended on his knees the steps of the Capitol to approach the Temple of Jupiter. Armies never engaged unless the religious auspices were favourable; and if a battle were fought, or even gained without them, the general was punished. Marcellus's zeal for sacred things is well known; also how a consul was condemned for having taken off the tiles from the temple of Jupiter, in Greece. In God's name, I entreat your Majesty to protect religion and its chief, and to preserve the beautiful temples of Italy and Rome. It is far more delightful to be the object of affection that that of fear."

"That is what I wish," Napoleon said, ending the conversation.[21]

In the course of their sessions, Canova found Marie Louise to be warm with her husband, who she affectionately called "Nana" and "Popo." During the next sitting, the discussion focused on the art and architecture of Canova's beloved Venice. "I assure your Majesty that the Venetians are a worthy people," said Canova, his eyes brimming with tears.

"You speak the truth, I believe them to be so."

"But they are not happy Sire; commerce is proscribed—the taxes are heavy; in some departments people cannot sustain life, this is the case with Passereano, in favor of which a celebrated pamphlet has been published, which perhaps your majesty has seen."

Canova gave Napoleon a copy of the pamphlet from his portfolio.

"I will speak to Aldini about it," said Napoleon, who took the pamphlet with him when he left the room.

During the next sitting, the discussion centered on Florence and the Church of Santa Croce where Canova had just installed Alfieri's funerary monument, alongside those of Machiavelli and Galileo.

"The Church of Santa Croce is in a wretched condition; the rain penetrates through the roof and a thorough repair is necessary," explained Canova. "Your Majesty's glory is interested in the preservation of these fine monuments; if the government takes the revenues, it is but just to leave the donations for the necessary repairs of the building. It is the same with the cathedral of Florence; dilapidations have already commenced, for want of funds to keep it in order. As we are upon the subject of churches, the repositories of interesting works of art I beg to say, that I am charged to supplicate your Majesty, that you will not permit the monuments of art to be sold to the Jews."

"How sold? All that is worth anything shall be brought here."

"May it graciously please your Majesty to leave Florence in possession of all its monuments, which are a necessary accompaniment to the works in fresco, which it is impossible to remove. It would even be advisable, that the president of the academy of Florence might be at liberty to take the necessary measures for the preservation of these beautiful specimens, both of architecture and of fresco."

"I am very willing."

"It will be very glorious for your Majesty; the more so, as I have heart it reported, that your Majesty's family is Florentine."

At this, Marie Louise turned around and said to her husband, "You are not a Corsican then?"

"Yes, but of Florentine origin."

Canova added: "The president of the academy of Florence, who interested himself with so much zeal in the preservation of the monuments, was the senator Alessandri, descended from one of the most illustrious families of Florence, one of whose daughters had formerly been married to a branch of the Bonaparte family. Thus you are an Italian, Sire, and we pride ourselves upon it."

"I am so, certainly."[22]

Since his effort on behalf of Pius had not gone well, Canova changed his approach. During their next encounter, the sculptor made an appeal for Rome's Academy of St. Luke. Lacking a school, revenues, or resources, the Academy, he suggested, needed to be organized like that of Milan.

Speaking of the Academy and the Roman artists, Napoleon said, "Italy is ill provided with painters; we have much better ones in France." He added that the French were deficient in coloring; but they surpassed the Italians in design.

Canova defended Italy's painters, adding that ". . . French artists received far greater encouragement; that they were far more numerous; and that if reckoned, their number would be found to exceed that of all the artists in the rest of Europe."

Napoleon questioned Canova about the architectural works in Paris. "Have you seen the bronze column?" [the Austerlitz Column]

"It strikes me as very fine, Sire."

"I do not like those eagles at the corners."

"The same ornament, however, is found on the Trajan column, of which this is an imitation."

"Will the arch constructing in the Wood de Boulogne be a fine one?"

"Particularly so. There are so many of your Majesty's works which are truly worthy of the ancient Romans, especially the magnificent roads."

"Next year, the Cornice road will be completed, by which you may travel from Paris to Genoa without crossing the snow. I shall make another from Parma to the Gulf of La Spezia, where I intend forming a large harbour."

"These are grand projects worthy of your Majesty's vast genius; but the preservation of the fine productions of the ancients should not be forgotten," said Canova.[23]

On the evening of November 4, Canova returned to Fontainebleau with the clay bust of the empress. For the first time, Napoleon was not present. Canova had modeled the portrait without formal sittings. He observed Marie Louise in her daily routine and playing billiards with her ladies-in-waiting. After finishing the model, Canova wrote to Quatremère de Quincy, "I wanted to pick a fairly cheerful moment."[24]

Marie Louise told Canova that she would show her husband the bust the next morning at breakfast. "Is it, indeed, true, Monsieur Canova that you will not remain here?"

"I wish to return immediately to Rome in order that your Majesty upon your arrival, which I hope will not be long, may find the model of your full-length statue complete."

Marie Louise asked questions about the making of the cast and the marble carving process. About Canova's statue of the Princess Leopoldina Esterhazy Liechtenstein, she observed, "It was, indeed there, that ideal beauty was to be found."[25]

A few days later, Canova returned to Fontainebleau. Napoleon placed his wife in the same pose as the plaster bust and instructed her to smile. Canova said the cheerful expression was consistent with Concordia, the Roman goddess of agreement in marriage and society, which he had chosen for the empress. Napoleon seem pleased and approved the theme.

Marie Louise had a cold, and Canova told her that she needed to take better care of herself, going out in an open carriage was dangerous for someone in the "family way."

At this, Napoleon interjected: "You see what she is, everyone is astonished at it; but women (striking his forehead with the end of his finger), women will have their own way. Listen, she now insists upon going to Cherbourg, which is at so great a distance; for my part, I am always telling her to take care of herself. Are you married?"

"No, Sire, I have been often on the point of marriage, but several circumstances have preserved me my freedom; add to which, the fear of not meeting with a woman who would love as I should have loved, deterred me from altering my condition, that I might be more at liberty to devote myself completely to my art."

"Ah! Woman, woman!" said Napoleon, smiling and continuing to eat.

On several occasions, Canova had expressed his desire to return to Rome. Now with the portrait bust finished, he mentioned his imminent departure.

This seemed to irritate Napoleon who dismissed him, saying "Go then, since you will have it so."[26]

A week later, on November 12, the court announced Marie Louise's pregnancy.

⚜

Before returning to Rome, Antonio Canova spent time in Paris as the guest of Italian diplomat and politician Ferdinando Marescalchi. On November 10, the sculptor traveled to Malmaison to see Joséphine. The visit was not without its risks. Marie Louise was extremely jealous of her stylish predecessor.

Post-divorce, Joséphine retained her imperial title and continued to enjoy her own household.[27] Thanks to Napoleon keeping her on the *liste civile*, Joséphine could still afford ladies-in-waiting, chambermaids, and laundresses. She also maintained her position as Paris's fashionista, continuing to dress stylishly in Leroy's designs.[28]

While waiting for Joséphine in the elegant black-and-white tiled reception area, Canova thought back to their first meeting at Saint-Cloud in October 1802. Against his wishes, he had traveled to Paris to sculpt the first consul's portrait bust. Joséphine seemed to sense his nervousness and had put him at ease with her charming demeanor. That summer, while attending a party in her husband's honor at the Murats' Château Villiers-la-Garenne, Joséphine admired Canova's reclining and standing *Cupid and Psyche*. By late September, Canova agreed to sculpt a second standing version of *Cupid and Psyche* for her, along with a second version of his ethereal *Hebe*.[29]

Canova couldn't help but be moved when a teary Joséphine greeted him and began to cry.[30] He was struck by Joséphine's appearance. Though she wore a luxurious satin dress and beautiful jewelry, she looked older and heavier.

It was an emotional moment for Canova as Joséphine led him into the Grand Gallery. Two of his works had arrived here two years earlier. Through the glazed ceiling, filtered sunlight bathed his *Cupid and Psyche* and *Hebe* in a soft glow. Though he used the same model for *Cupid and Psyche* as the Murats' version, Joséphine's sculpture was more affectionate than erotic. In addition to subtle changes to the figures' hair and drapery, Canova depicted the adolescents more as brother and sister than lovers.[31]

For *Hebe*, Canova portrayed the cupbearer to the gods descending from Mount Olympus on a marble cloud. Though Quatremère considered the work one of the finest of the day, other critics disagreed. Exhibited by

Denon at the 1808 Salon, *Hebe* was criticized for the addition of a gilt bronze pitcher and cup, along with the pale yellow and pink hues Canova applied to her breasts and torso. But it's these qualities, writes Christopher Johns, which would have appealed to Joséphine, "because the general idea was to heighten the abstracted erotic element while creating a nubile deity of considerable chic."[32]

From the Grand Galerie, Joséphine led Canova under a white-and-blue canopy outside to show him her English-style garden. Louis Berthault had transformed the property, planting groves of trees on the lawns and installing decorative ruins and windmills. Joséphine's passion for exotic flowers and plants had begun as a child on Martinique in the West Indies. Malmaison's gardens were celebrated, boasting over two hundred rose varieties.[33] In the hothouse designed by Berthault, Joséphine cultivated rare species from Australia, New Zealand, and South Africa. Flanking colorful hibiscus and other flowering plants were two green tunnels leading to marble copies of the *Medici Venus* and *Callipygian Venus*.[34]

The park's meandering river became a waterfall before forming a lake dotted with floating rhododendrons and graceful black swans. Joséphine was so smitten with the swans, she chose the motif for her garden-view bedroom furnishings and bathroom sconces. Considered an allegory of love, the elegant bird was also incorporated into Malmaison's chair arms, curtains, carpets, and porcelain.

According to Johns, Canova welcomed the opportunity to work for Joséphine, whose refined taste aligned with his. Their warm relationship may also have been a function of gender. Generally more sympathetic toward women than men, Canova "responded positively to their flattery, which invariably tickled his fancy," writes Johns.[35] Unlike the other Bonaparte women, Joséphine did not commission Canova to sculpt her own portrait.

Back in Rome, Canova began executing a plaster cast for *Marie Louise as Concordia*. Canova portrayed Marie Louise seated on a throne, wearing ancient drapery and a tiara and veil, holding the attributes of Concordia—a *patera*, or sacrificial bowl, in her left hand and a scepter in her right. The Romans built several temples in Concordia's honor. The oldest on the Capitol was dedicated in the fouth century B.C.E. by Camillus, and later restored by

Augustus's wife Livia. Offerings were made to the goddess on the birthdays of the emperors. Concordia Augusta was worshipped as the promoter of harmony in the imperial household.

Canova would remark that in annulling his marriage to Joséphine and marrying the Habsburg teenager, Napoleon had "divorced his Good Fortune."[36] *Marie Louise as Concordia* remained in Canova's studio until 1817, when it was delivered to the sitter under far different circumstances.

PART SEVEN
DYNASTY

"I have only one passion, only one mistress, and that is France. I sleep with her. She has never failed me, she has lavished her blood and her treasures on me. If I need five hundred thousand men, she gives them to me."

—Napoleon Bonaparte

ONE
THE EAGLET

At ten o'clock in the morning on March 20, 1811, guns began firing from the courtyard of the Invalides, bringing traffic to a grinding halt. A twenty-one gun salute signified the birth of a girl; a boy commanded 101 rounds. As the twenty-second boom rang out, Parisians filled the streets and headed to the Tuileries where troops had gathered in the Carrousel. To the delight of the cheering crowd, Napoleon stepped onto the balcony holding his newborn son.

After a difficult night of labor, Marie Louise gave birth that morning to an eight pound, thirteen ounce baby boy. The infant was baptized Napoleon François Joseph Charles after his father, maternal grandfather, eldest uncle and godfather, and paternal grandfather.[1] In France, he was affectionately called l'Aiglon, the Eaglet.

Over a year earlier, while confirming the annexation of Rome, the Senate had named Napoleon's future son the "King of Rome." As Magnus Olausson writes, the title suited Napoleon's claim to be heir to the Roman Empire and underscored the fact that Rome was now part of his own Empire.[2]

The day he was born, the king of Rome was wrapped in a tulle blanket embroidered with bees and tucked into a sumptuous cradle below a canopy. Designed by Prud'hon, founded and chased in gilt silver by Thomire and Odiot, and modeled by sculptor Henri-Victor Roguier, the cradle was presented to the imperial couple by the city of Paris. Made with over six hundred pounds of silver, the gift set the city back over 150,000 francs. Mother-of-pearl balusters were set against red-orange satin velvet embroidered with bees. The back of the cradle sported a golden *N* surrounded by palm, laurel, and olive branches.

Bas-reliefs on the sides featured mythological representations of Paris and Rome, the Empire's two main cities. In one relief, Mercury placed the newborn in the arms of the personification of the Seine (symbol of Paris). On the other, a figure of the Tiber (symbol of Rome) accompanied by the twins Romulus and Remus watched the new star of the young king rise over Rome.[3] According to legend, Romulus founded Rome on the Palatine Hill in 753 B.C.E.

At the head of a cradle, a winged Victory held a double crown of stars and laurels. The largest star bore a shield with Napoleon's cypher *N* surrounded by palms and laurels. Perched at the foot of the cradle was a gold eaglet.[4]

The king of Rome motif appeared throughout the Eaglet's apartment at the Tuileries. For example, a clock in his grand salon sported a figure of Pallas, goddess of war, sitting between the Tiber, represented by a bearded old man holding a horn of abundance, and Romulus and Remus suckling the she-wolf. Below this group surrounding the clock face, trophies of war evoked those on Trajan's Column.[5]

The Eaglet's elaborate furnishings were part of a barrage of decorative objects and paintings promoting imperial dynasty. Like the empresses of first- and second-century Rome, Marie Louise was portrayed as a symbol of fertility. To Augustus, women and children "were symbols of his dynastic ambitions," writes Diana Kleiner.[6] They appear for the first time in the friezes of Augustus's Altar of Peace, the Ara Pacis. Though Augustus's wife Livia had not conceived, she was shown as a symbol of fertility and regeneration. Despite being childless, Hadrian's wife Sabina was also portrayed as youthful and capable of childbirth.[7]

Even before Marie Louise delivered a male heir, she enjoyed favorable press. Four days before the birth, the *Journal de l'Empire* wrote: ". . . All of France, represented by the habitants of Paris, awaits her at Notre Dame . . . holding in her arms a child, the hope of the Empire . . . this day, as the empress herself has said, will be the happiest of her life."[8]

Numerous works celebrated the birth of Napoleon's heir, with frequent comparisons made between the Eaglet and ancient Rome. In Prud'hon's *The King of Rome asleep*, the infant is shown sleeping surrounded by exotic red fritillary blooms known as "imperial crowns" along with laurel, myrtle, and palm leaves. The imperial mantle, white sheets, and a blue drape represent France's tricolor. The sleeping infant conjures up both Romulus and Jesus, writes Marco Fabio Apolloni.[9] Bartolomeo Pinelli portrayed the goddess Roma holding Napoleon's infant son guarded by the imperial eagle, all watched by the she-wolf and Romulus and Remus.

Two weeks after his son's birth, a proud Napoleon commissioned a watercolor portrait from Jean-Baptiste Isabey. Against a background of triumphal altars and olive branches, Isabey depicted the baby lying in the helmet of Mars, Roman god of war. The infant is shown holding the ancient iron crown of the kings of Lombardy, worn for centuries by Holy Roman Emperors and by Napoleon during his coronation in Milan. Napoleon sent Isabey's watercolor to his father-in-law Francis, the last Holy Roman emperor.[10]

In the early evening on Sunday June 9, the imperial couple left the Tuileries Palace in a coronation coach. Napoleon was dressed in his lavish *petit costume*; Marie Louise wore a diamond-studded white dress. Meanwhile governess Madame de Montesquiou held the baby on her lap in a special carriage. Guests and foreign diplomats (except for England) were seated when the clergy, headed by Cardinal Fesch, entered Notre Dame Cathedral. It was a watershed moment for an Empire founded without a hereditary pedigree.

Before entering the cathedral, the imperial cortege proceeded through a spectacular tent. The ceiling sported over 2,500 gold stars against a blue background and an *N* in the center surrounded by a laurel wreath and topped with an imperial crown. Thirty-two rented chandeliers along with some 225 pounds of candles lit the interior.[11]

The baby's ermine-lined silver cloak was borne by Marshal Kellerman, Duke of Valmy.[12] For the luxurious cloak, embroiderer Picot spun thirty-one bees and two dozen roses of Italy.[13] Godmother Caroline Murat and godfather Joseph Bonaparte presented their newborn nephew at each stage of the sacrament: the baptismal request, the exorcism and the renunciation of Satan, the anointing, the profession of faith, the giving of the candle, and the reading of the Gospel. Afterward, Madame de Montesquieu handed the baby back to his mother.

At this moment, Napoleon went off script. Taking his son in his arms, Napoleon raised the baby up into the air triumphantly. Some seven thousand congregants burst into spontaneous cries of "Vive l'Empereur! Vive l'Imperatrice! Vive le Roi de Rome!"[14] After the musicians of the imperial chapel performed the *Vivat* (Long live the emperor), the infant returned to the Tuileries with his governess; his parents left for civic celebrations at City Hall. These included four official receptions, a banquet, and a concert featuring Méhul's *Chant d'Ossian*.[15] Parisians celebrated the baptism with wine fountains, fireworks on the Seine, and other festivities.

But the lasting impression from the evening was that of Napoleon lifting his son into the air. As Elisabeth Caude writes, "He demonstrated the originality of his power, knowing how to use the traditions of the ancien régime and drawing references from the Roman world. . . . There were in the Emperor's gesture some reminiscences of both the Roman *imperator*—still acknowledged during the Principat—and the Carolingian Emperor [Charlemagne] who had legitimized his power with the coronation. . . . The acclamation was reminiscent of the ancient custom, before the evolution of the *imperium* in its essence, from the salute of the legions to the *imperator*."[16]

A month before the baptism, Napoleon's grand chamberlain, the Count of Montesquieu, wrote his boss. "Your majesty has indicated the intention to have medals awarded to the mayors and deputies of the good towns of France and Italy who will travel to Paris for the baptism of the King of Rome. These have the double advantage of flattering to those who receive them, and of incurring a small expense . . ." Two days later, Napoleon approved the expense of 35,000 francs.[17]

Napoleon's large-scale coin distribution had a precedent in Rome. The triumphal Arch of Constantine near the Colosseum sports two reliefs depicting the offering of coins by emperors. The upper relief shows Marcus Aurelius; the lower Constantine, who distributed money on an extensive scale to his troops and subjects. A solidus of Constantine's son Constantius II from around 350 to 361 C.E. shows the co-emperor riding a quadriga and throwing coins.[18] The word *largitio*, or bountiful largesse, appears on a brass medallion of Constantius II's older brother and co-emperor Constantine II.

Napoleon's commemorative medal was executed by Jean-Bertrand Andrieu after a drawing by Louis Lafitte. It featured an image of Napoleon crowned with a laurel wreath on the obverse. On the reverse, Napoleon in imperial dress stood before his throne holding his son in the air over the baptismal font. A second version of the medal was engraved with the same scene, with forty-nine cities of the Empire arranged in crowns in two circles around the inscription: "A l'empereur/les bonnes villes/de l'empire" (To the Emperor/the Good Cities/of the Empire).

Napoleon lifting his son became a powerful image for the imperial propaganda machine, repeated in different genres including porcelain. Sèvres created a dramatic Etruscan-style dark blue vase featuring Andrieu's composition as the central motif surrounded by the crenelated walls of the good cities. As Christophe Beyeler describes, the Eaglet's head was cleverly positioned right below the walls of "Rome"—creating a symbolic crown. Dihl also produced porcelain cups with the image of Napoleon lifting his newborn son aloft.[19]

In *The Baptism of the King of Rome in Notre Dame*, Innocent-Louis Goubaud depicted the infant playing with a necklace of imperial eagles, surrounded by an ermine-trimmed cloak, a crown, and other emblems of imperial authority. In addition to the medals and artworks, poems extoled the birth, comparing Napoleon and his son to Caesar and the Caesars.[20]

Napoleon appointed an imperial governess for life, Anne Elisabeth Pierre de Montesquiou-Fezensac, wife of his grand chamberlain. Reporting directly to the emperor, with a staff of several wet nurses, a doctor, and two under-governesses, Madame de Montesquiou looked after the Eaglet. "Such was the responsibility, with such great honours bestowed upon it, that the governess became almost the second lady of state and, in some respects, even took precedence over the empress," writes Frédéric Masson. ". . . unable to leave the child's side even for a moment, she became the official mother; she continually served as the intermediary between the child and its natural mother, who had absolutely no control or supervision over it."[21]

Despite being left out of her son's care, Marie Louise felt closer to Napoleon. "Never could I believe I could be so happy," she wrote home. "My love for my husband grows all the time, and when I remember his tenderness I can hardly help crying. Even had I not loved him before, nothing could stop me from loving him now."[22] Napoleon meanwhile wrote his ex-wife Joséphine: "My son is plump and in good health. I hope he will make out well. He has my chest, my mouth, and my eyes. I hope he will fulfill his destiny."[23]

Carved gemstones, intaglios, and cameos were the ultimate status symbol in Rome, valued more than silver and gold. By the first century, Rome's most sought-after carvers were Greeks who created intricate designs with a variety of stones, from cornelian and onyx to amethyst and sapphire. Among the renowned engravers were Dioskourides, his sons Hyllos, Solon, and Aulos.[24]

With multi-layered, multi-hued sardonyx, artists created depth by carving figures in the lighter layers and the background in the darker shades. Roman emperors and empresses had themselves depicted in double portraits of sardonyx.

Like Napoleon and Joséphine, Trajan and Plotina married shortly before he became emperor. A carved cameo in white and dark purple sardonyx shows them side by side in profile, with Trajan crowned with a laurel wreath and his wife elegantly coiffed (circa 105–115 C.E., now in the British Museum). The realistic portrait of the middle-aged couple includes crow's feet and sagging necks.[25] Also like Napoleon and Joséphine, Trajan and Plotina did not have children. In 100, Trajan's great-niece Sabina married Hadrian, the son of his cousin. On his deathbed, Trajan adopted Hadrian as his heir. Because the adoption letter was signed by Plotina, there is speculation that she may have manipulated the succession.

About a century later, a deeply cut sardonyx portrait cameo of Septimius Severus and Julia Domna shows the couple in three-quarter frontal pose (circa 207–211, Kansas City, The Ferrell Collection). The emperor is depicted in the guise of his patron god Serapis—with a long beard divided in the middle and corkscrew hair on his forehead. He also wears a laurel wreath and a military cloak or paludamentum at his shoulder. Julia, who wielded great power as a widow, sports long wavy hair and a beaded necklace.[26]

Augustan dynastic propaganda reached its height with cameos created in state workshops.[27] Among surviving imperial cameos, the largest and finest are the *Gemma Augustea* and the *Grand Camée de France*. Decorated with members of the imperial family, the elaborate group scenes are tour de forces of gem cutting. Both cameos are thought to have been gifts from ambitious Empresses Livia and Agrippina the Elder to Augustus and Tiberius. Both women are notorious for doing whatever it took to promote their sons, Tiberius and Nero.

The cameos feature two very different images of Augustus. The first seen on the *Gemma Augustea* is that of the father of his country, Pater Patriae, a title Augustus received in 2 B.C.E. Jupiter, who Virgil called "the father of gods and men," represented the all-encompassing authority of father.[28] Poets promoted the Jupiter/Augustus connection. "You reign, (Jupiter), with Augustus second in power!" wrote Horace.[29] In the second image used in the *Grand Camée de France* and the Ara Pacis, Augustus wears a veil and toga, the garment of peace.

Carved in low relief during the last decade of Augustus's reign, the *Gemma Augustea* is white above dark bluish-brown sardonyx. The elaborate carving marks the victories of Livia's sons Tiberius and Drusus and their service to Augustus, their stepfather. Augustus sits on a bisellium, the seat of honor, holding a scepter of Jupiter and augur's staff while a veiled woman, a personification of the civilized world, crowns him with an oak wreath.[30] As Martin Henig describes, the goddess Roma hints at Augustus's quasi-divinity; the eagle perched by his feet suggests he is a sort of earthly Jupiter.[31] Wearing the toga *picta*, the embroidered toga for triumphant generals, Tiberius, his adopted son and heir, disembarks a triumphal chariot. Germanicus, Tiberius's adopted son and nephew, stands in front of Augustus in a military uniform. The lower tier depicts conquered barbarians and soldiers.

Another imperial portrait group, the *Grand Camée de France* is the largest known cameo from antiquity (circa 23 C.E., 31 x 26.5 cm, Cabinet des Médailles, Bibliothèque Nationale de France). Against a background of dark layers of sardonyx, the artist carved some two dozen figures, many recognizable, in three tiers. The goal of the gem was to assert the dynastic continuity and legitimacy of the five Julio-Claudian emperors (Augustus, Tiberius, Caligula, Claudius, and Nero). The top section features the deified Augustus surrounded by other deceased family members including Germanicus, husband of Agrippina the Elder and father of Drusus Caesar, Nero Caesar, and Caligula, along with Drusus the Younger (son of Tiberius), and Drusus the Elder (brother of Tiberius).

The veiled Augustus looks down upon his successor, the enthroned Tiberius. Tiberius is surrounded by his living family members, with his mother and Augustus's wife Livia enthroned to his right and Agrippina the Younger and her brother Nero Caesar to his left. Holding sheaves and poppies, Livia is portrayed as the unifier of the Julian and Claudian houses. As Julia Fischer puts it, the cameo was an advertisement for *domus Augusta*, a phrase coined at end of Augustus's reign in reference to his dynasty. Livia was now celebrated as the wife of emperor and the mother of his successors.[32] In front of Tiberius are Germanicus, his designated heir, with his wife Agrippina the Elder. Behind are Nero and the figure of Providentia (Foresight); behind Livia and Tiberius are Claudius and his wife Agrippina the Younger.

Wearing a laurel crown and the aegis of Jupiter as a hip mantle, Tiberius holds the lituus and scepter. Tiberius presides over a solemn ceremony, possibly the appointment of armed Nero. From the Augustan period on, notes Christopher Hallett, Roman emperors were depicted wearing Jupiter's aegis like a chlamys or hip-mantle, holding the scepter and thunderbolt of Jupiter.[33] Like the *Gemma Augustea*, Rome's conquests are illustrated by barbarian Parthian and Germanic captives at the bottom.

It's thought that Agrippina the Elder gave her stepfather Tiberius the cameo after the death of his son and heir to persuade him to choose one of Germanicus's three sons (Caligula, Nero Caesar, and Drusus Caesar) as his successor. The strategy did not go as planned. In 29 C.E., Tiberius had Agrippina arrested, along with the two elder sons, Nero Caesar and

Drusus Caesar. Tried and exiled, Agrippina died in 33; Nero Caesar and Drusus Caesar died in 31 and 33, respectively. Caligula eventually succeeded Tiberius, but not thanks to Agrippina's efforts.

After the end of the Roman Empire, the *Grand Camée* was taken to Constantinople where it became part of the treasury of the Byzantine Empire. Gradually, it lost its original meaning and became an object of Christian worship. Enclosed in a holy mount, it came to be known as the Triumph of Joseph at the Court of the Pharaoh. The extraordinary gem was among the relics acquired by Saint Louis. By 1279, it was part of the treasury of the Sainte Chapelle in Paris. In 1791, France's National Assembly ordered the chapel's treasures sold. After Louis XVI intervened, the famed cameo was deposited at the Cabinet of Medals.

Napoleon was familiar with the famous *Grand Camée.* On February 16, 1804, the Cabinet of Medals was robbed; the ancient cameo (along with the future Hope diamond and other objects) was taken to Amsterdam. According to Millin, the Cabinet conservator, the thief was trying to sell the cameo when the consul at Amsterdam recognized it and alerted authorities. The *Grand Camée* was returned to Paris in 1805, minus its original gold Byzantine setting. Millin hired David's pupil Auguste Delafontaine and his son Pierre-Maximilien Delafontaine to design a new gilded bronze frame.

The Delafontaines replaced the old mount with one in the fashionable neoclassical style. "This mount must have been expensive," writes Jean-Baptiste Giard, "but it no doubt answered the need to enhance the brilliance of the stone whose representation particularly interested the strong man of the moment, Napoleon, and his close collaborators . . . the *Great Camée* again evoked the gloriousness of the day, and it was important that it be worthily presented, even sanctified in a new monstrance."[34]

For the rectangular frame, the Delafontaines combined the legendary story of Rome's founding with the Apotheosis of Augustus, depicted in an esteemed ancient cameo in the Louvre. As Chantal Bouchon writes: "The choice of the Apotheosis of Augustus embellished by the mythical scene of the foundation of Rome, confirms at the highest symbolic level Napoleon's desire to assert his direct descent from the reign of Augustus, which was regarded as the beginning of European civilization."[35]

The center of the upper band features a Roman eagle grasping a thunderbolt in its claws, flanked by laurel wreaths inscribed with the names of Horace, Ovid, Virgil, and Maecenas. On the lower band below, the Wolf suckles the twin infants Romulus and Remus, flanked by laurel wreaths containing their names. On the right, a half pediment shows Fame bearing a bust of Augustus within a laurel wreath. Pilasters decorated with trophies support a frieze, horns of abundance, two crowns, and the Roman eagle; above the frieze, a pediment adorned with a bust of Rome in a crown worn by two Victories. The pedestal features seated griffins and golden ornaments.[36]

Napoleon recognized the political value of gem engraving, patronized millennia ago by the rulers of ancient Greece and Rome. With their ancient provenance, carved gems became a popular art form for imperial dynastic propaganda. Keen to associate the ancient art form with his own regime, he instituted a biannual prize for medalists and gem engravers in 1803; the Prix de Rome began two years later.

As a result of Napoleon's 1796 Italian campaign, many ancient Greek and Roman cameos and intaglios had been seized and brought to France. As emperor, Napoleon claimed the national collection of engraved gems housed at the Cabinet des Medailles. In 1808, eighty-two cameos and intaglios were removed by imperial decree; the jeweler Nitot mounted them with pearls into a parure of tiara, necklace, bracelets, and belt. State property, these were returned after the divorce and used by Marie Louise.[37]

With the birth of the Eaglet, members of the imperial family exchanged gifts featuring dynastic themes. Thanks to a wider color palette, artist Louis-Bertin Parant refined a technique for painting porcelain that simulated the sardonyx, agate, carnelian of antique cameos.[38] Parant became renowned for the technique after creating the antique cameos for the Sèvres *Table of the Grand Commanders.* With his colleague Jean-Marie Degault, Parant specialized in these *trompe l'oeil* cameos. Napoleon ordered two *iconographique grec* services painted by Degault with figures from antiquity; one was delivered to his uncle Cardinal Fesch in 1811.

In 1812, Napoleon gave his wife a Sèvres oval plate, *Empress Marie Louise guiding the first steps of the King of Rome.* Painted against a brown background to imitate sardonyx, Minerva and the infant march toward

Napoleon represented by a bust. The insignia of the Legion of Honor is already pinned to the baby's chest. Parant exhibited the faux-cameo plate at the Salon of 1812, along with his *Table of the Grand Commanders.* "The most important piece, in terms of composition, is a bas-relief representing the Empress guiding the steps of the King of Rome," observed art writer Charles Paul Landon. "This work is full of grace, finesse, correction, and a complete illusion."[39]

Napoleon ordered a number of Sèvres porcelain services to mark his son's birth. As a New Year's present, Napoleon gave his sister-in-law Queen Julie of Spain *The great legislators of antiquity.* The cameo-like tray featured Minerva instructing the King of Rome. As Tamara Préaud writes, "Augustus shows a remarkable similarity to Napoleon, which cannot have been a coincidence."[40] The covered bowl, for example, sported a pair of Parant's painted cameo-style medallions—Minerva bringing the newborn king of Rome by boat to the Roman river god Tiber, and Minerva handing over the king of Rome in the shape of Hercules to his father, Napoleon I.

Shortly after his marriage to Marie Louise, Napoleon decided to build a "Palace for the King of Rome." "Napoleon convinced himself of the need to build an entirely new palace in Paris which would free him from the impression of being a guest in the old residences designed for other monarchs . . ." writes Sylvain Cordier.[41]

Before the Eaglet was even born, work began on his gilded nest. Napoleon purchased land on the hill of Chaillot in the western part of Paris near the Bois de Boulogne, on the right bank of the Seine opposite the Champ-de-Mars. As the symbol of Napoleon's dynasty, the palace was to be Europe's largest, outdoing Versailles. Napoleon carefully examined alternative plans drawn up by Charles Percier and Pierre Fontaine. The range of ideas writes Jean-Philippe Garric, illustrates the complexity of representing Napoleon's new dynasty.[42]

By this point, Napoleon had stayed in a number of famous palaces throughout Europe, including Andrea Doria's Villa del Principe in Genoa, Frederick the Great's Sanssouci in Potsdam, the Habsburg's Schönbrunn

Palace in Vienna, and Madrid's Royal Palace. These grand residences, highly personal expressions of their celebrated owners, provided a point of comparison for the emperor as he considered his own new palace.

"Napoleon himself almost always designated the residences whose plans seemed fitting, and which he wanted to compare with the one he intended to build," recalled Percier and Fontaine in their final book, *Résidences de souverains.*[43] According to Garric, "Critical discussion of the principal palaces of modern Europe was one way for the emperor to imagine his own place in the gallery of great men; the latter were represented by their residences, and it was his intention, with his architect's help, to fashion an analogous monumental self-portrait."[44]

Pierre Fontaine describes one planning meeting on the future palace with members of Napoleon's court. With the exception of Duroc, the courtiers simply repeated whatever the emperor said. Finally Napoleon turned to Marie Louise, five months pregnant, for her opinion.

"I do not know anything," she responded.

"Do not be afraid," replied the Emperor. "Speak, they know even less than you and I have not committed to do or to believe anything they say. Your opinion is necessary to me; it concerns the palace where our son will live."

According to Fontaine, "the Empress examined the plans and made some judicious observations, which everyone hastened to applaud . . ."[45]

One of Percier and Fontaine's concepts was an Italianate-style palace rising directly from a quay on the Seine. Another imagined a series of stepped terraces leading up from the river to a rectangular five-floor hilltop palace.[46] The main façade alone, not counting the wings, was to span over 325 feet. A vast park and gardens would encompass the Bois de Boulogne. According to Fontaine, the palace was to be "the most extensive and extraordinary creation of our century."[47]

As Sylvain Cordier explains, the hilltop Palace of the King of Rome was intended to dominate Paris—much like the legendary palaces of the Roman emperors had dominated Rome. "The elevated position recalled in principal the legendary memory of the residences of the Caesars on the Palatine Hill in Rome, dominating the Forum," writes Cordier.[48] Symbolically, the palace would face the Champ des Mars and Napoleon's alma mater, the École Militaire.

In January 1811, a budget of twenty million francs was approved for the palace, and Percier and Fontaine started work on a series of neo-baroque Italianate-style ramps and terraces. Their original plan called for three terrace levels, a courtyard, and a five-hundred-meter-long colonnade. The main body of the palace formed a parallelogram, with a large central salon. As a model for the imperial apartments, Percier and Fontaine looked to Versailles, designing parallel apartments for the emperor and empress on the first, or "noble," floor. Two small courtyards with fountains flanked the salon. There were plans for a chapel, theater, and galleries, and room for four hundred horses and eighty carriages.

In March 1812, Napoleon extended the project to include an administrative complex below the Chaillot hill opposite the palace on the left bank of the Seine. The complex was to encompass institutional palaces for the Archives Impériales, the Arts, the University, and the Grand Master.[49]

Fontaine continued to upstage his talented partner, receiving the Legion of Honor award in 1811. A few years before, painter Théophile Vauchelet described the retiring Percier: "Percier resided at the Louvre; he lived like a philosopher, in extreme simplicity; the walls of his cabinet were of neutral gray plaster, completely covered with precious old master drawings and painted sketches by his friends, who were then the likes of David, Gérard, Girodet, etc. Percier always wore a long gray frock coat, buttoned all the way up; his health was delicate and he almost never went out; it was Fontaine who took care of external business. . . . He was a good man and had exquisite manners but was very sparing with his time; he dreaded the distraction of visitors."[50]

In addition to Percier and Fontaine's grandiose Paris palace for his son, Napoleon added the Château de Meudon to the Eaglet's real estate portfolio. Located between Paris and Versailles, the château was one of the last projects of Jules Hardouin-Mansart, designer of Versailles. Louis XIV commissioned Meudon for his eldest son and namesake. But the Grand Dauphin didn't get much time to enjoy his new castle. Louis died of smallpox at Meudon shortly after its completion. Before the French Revolution, artist Hubert Robert relandscaped the gardens for Louis XVI.

In 1807, Napoleon added the château to his list of imperial palaces, ordering renovations by architect Jean-Baptiste Lepère. Among the changes was a wing to replace one destroyed by fire, along with new Empire-style furnishings. Further refurbishments were undertaken at Meudon between 1810 and 1811, part of Napoleon's plan to turn the château into the residence of the Children of France. This "Institute of Meudon" would educate the children of his siblings, rulers of the satellite kingdoms, along with the sons of the "first families" of those states. The plan was to have youngsters live in the princely apartments organized around the king of Rome's state apartment.[51]

Napoleon visited Meudon in April 1811. Two months later, the residence was offered to his mother, Madame Mère. The following spring, the toddler king of Rome moved in with his devoted governess who he affectionately called "Maman Quiou," two under-governesses, and his own medical team consisting of a physician, surgeon, and vaccinator.[52]

One year later, in March 1812, Napoleon declared another estate the official "palace of the King of Rome." Located some thirty miles southwest of Paris, the Château de Rambouillet was built in 1784 by Louis XVI as a government meeting place. An avid hunter, Louis had admired the estate with its game-rich grounds and beautiful gardens. In late 1783, he bought the medieval château from his cousin, the duke of Penthièvre, for sixteen million French livres. When his wife Marie Antoinette first saw the new royal residence, she reportedly called it a "gothic swamp." Louis redid a luxe apartment for her, richly furnished and decorated with the latest styles.[53]

Deserted after the Revolution, Rambouillet fell into disrepair. In 1804, Napoleon visited for the first time and added the estate to the civil imperial list. Napoleon loved Rambouillet's informality; he would spend about sixty days here during his reign, ranging from a few hours to several days per visit. In August 1806, Napoleon hired architect Auguste Famin to renovate the building. A winner of the Prix de Rome, Famin had studied the Academie Française in Rome from 1801 to 1806.

Famin knocked down one wing of the main building, giving the château a unique appearance. He redesigned the entrance with a new staircase leading to the empress's apartments on one side and the emperor's on the other. The rooms were redecorated in sumptuous Empire style, including Marie Antoinette's small courtyard-side apartment. A luxurious bathroom was installed in Napoleon's apartment. Godard's neoclassical décor featured ancient motifs like Glories, Apollo's lyre, a frieze of triglyphs and metopes, cornucopias, and various mythological creatures. Symbols of the Empire were also thrown in, from an *N* and an eagle surrounded by a laurel wreath to bees and the cross of the Legion of Honor.[54]

Originally the bathroom sported medallions with portraits of the imperial family. Deeming this inappropriate, Napoleon had Jean Vasserot change the design. The artist replaced the portrait medallions with painted views of places, châteaux, and monuments associated with particular family members.[55]

TWO

IN MEMORIUM

The Eaglet's birth heightened the importance of a dynastic imperial crypt. Five years earlier, in February 1806, Napoleon had decreed that France's former royal necropolis, Saint Denis, would be the final resting place for himself and his descendants.

According to nineteenth-century architect Eugène Viollet-le-Duc, Napoleon chose Saint Denis for its royal pedigree. "At Saint Denis he intended to restore the representations of the principal personages of the dynasties before his own. His orders were in accordance with this desire; in the curious archives of Saint Denis, there are still plans dating from 1811 on which are marked indications such as these: Chapel of the Merovingians, Pillar of Charlemagne, Altar of the Dynasties, Chapels of the Valois Charles, etc."[1]

Napoleon's concern for an imperial crypt was very much in the tradition of Rome's first- and second-century emperors. Between 28 B.C.E. and 193 C.E., seven of Rome's eighteen emperors built funerary monuments while others were interred in dynastic sepulchers. Others had their bodies mutilated and thrown into the Tiber by decree of the Senate. According to

Penelope Davies, the stakes were high for Rome's imperial families. "For the ruling family . . . the future of the living was dependent, to a large degree, upon the honors (or lack thereof) bestowed upon the dead."[2]

In choosing the locations for their mausoleums, Rome's emperors sought high-impact real estate, explains David Rollason. For his final resting place, Augustus selected the Field of Mars, the city's high-traffic entry where triumphs began and military exercises took place.[3] Augustus broke ground on his mausoleum early in his reign, completing it over two decades before his death in 14 C.E. A "great mound near the river on a lofty foundation of white marble" is how Greek geographer Strabo described the structure that featured five concentric walls surrounding a soaring rectangular travertine pillar. Augustus's nephew Marcellus was the first to be buried in the vast mausoleum in 23 B.C.E. Other relatives who predeceased Augustus were also buried in the mausoleum, along with his Julio-Claudian successors Tiberius and Claudius (probably), and the first Flavian emperor, Vespasian.[4]

Inscribed on pillars outside the entrance to the mausoleum was a copy of Augustus's *Res Gestae* (Things Achieved) listing his honors, victories, and personal spending for the public good. Flanking the pillars was a pair of small red granite obelisks.[5] The mausoleum was part of a complex in the Campus Martius that also included the Ara Pacis Augustae and Solarium. Augustus's message, writes Rollason, ". . . was first and foremost that of the majesty and grandeur of the emperor—and also of his family, members of which were also to be buried there. . . ."[6]

A century later, during a building spree that included the Pantheon and his villa at Tivoli, Hadrian began constructing his mausoleum on the west bank of the Tiber. The enviable location was made even more striking by the addition of its own bridge.[7] Dedicated in 139, a year after Hadrian's death, the massive mausoleum was crowned with a bronze statue of the triumphant Hadrian driving a quadriga. Known as the Antinoeion, it became the resting place for Antonines and Severans.[8] By the sixth century, Hadrian's mausoleum was incorporated into the city's defenses. In the thirteenth century, the popes turned the funerary monument into a fortress, Castel Sant'Angelo, connecting it to the Vatican with a corridor.

Napoleon's mausoleum choice, Saint Denis, had roots going back to Roman Paris. Located some ten miles north of the city, the abbey was named for France's patron saint, the first bishop of Lutetia. Saint Denis became a royal necropolis under the Capetians. During the ensuing Merovingian dynasty, it was designated a basilica—an early Christian church with a three-nave floor plan like those of the civic buildings of ancient Rome. For three centuries starting with early tweflth-century Louis VI, "the Fat," France's kings carried the abbey's sacred red oriflamme banner into battle. Named for *aurea flamma*, the banner (*flamma*) and the color of the lance, the oriflamme was destroyed during the Revolution.[9]

In the tweflth century, Abbot Suger, adviser to Louis VI and Louis VII, rebuilt the abbey in "three years, three months, three days." With its light-flooded apse displaying the relics of saints and spectacular stained glass windows, the early Gothic-style church became a favorite pilgrimage site. Among the stained glass designs was the South Rose window, over forty-five feet in diameter, depicting God surrounded by angels, signs of the Zodiac, and agricultural tasks carried out during the year.

Thanks to Suger, the Saint Denis treasury was one of the finest of medieval Europe. A cross nearly twenty-three feet tall bearing a gilded silver Christ stood at the entrance of today's choir. Relics and liturgical objects bequeathed by abbots and kings adorned the chapels. Among these was the pear-shaped rock crystal "Eleanor" vase, carved in the type of honeycombed pattern used in Roman glassware, gold, and silverware. A gift to Suger from Louis VII, the vase had been passed down from his wife Eleanor's grandfather, William IX of Aquitaine. Suger also had an antique porphyry vase placed in a vermeil setting in the shape of an eagle. These along with many of Saint Denis's other treasures, including Charlemagne's sword used for Napoleon's coronation, landed at the Musée Napoléon after the Revolution.

Napoleon's plan to transform historic Saint Denis into an imperial crypt presented a major challenge. In mid-1792, to celebrate the anniversary of the overthrow of the Bourbons, France's National Convention ordered the "tombs and mausoleums of the former kings destroyed." Along with the trials and executions of Louis XVI and Marie Antoinette, the government conducted official exhumations.

Workers opened the royal coffins at Saint Denis with pickaxes and crowbars, took out the bodies, and dumped them in two large pits in a cemetery north of the basilica. Metal objects and lead coffins were repurposed to make military arms. Henri IV's open coffin was propped up against a pillar in the ambulatory of the crypt for two days, displaying his well-preserved remains. Louis XIV's features were black, probably due to the gangrene that killed him at age seventy-six. Louis XV's linen-wrapped body reportedly dissolved in "liquid putrefaction" when lifted out of the coffin.[10]

Severely damaged with only the basilica left standing, the prestigious Gothic structure was turned into a warehouse. "Saint Denis is deserted," wrote French politician and historian François-René de Chateaubriand. "Birds fly in and out, grass grows on its smashed altars and all one can hear is the dripping of water through its open roof."[11] Thanks to the Commission of Monuments, many of Saint Denis's tombs and monuments escaped destruction. In 1795, Alexandre Lenoir displayed the funerary sculptures at the new Musée national des Monuments Français located in the nationalized convent of the Petits-Augustins in Paris.

On Napoleon's orders, the Ministry of Interior made emergency repairs to the basilica in 1806. These included a roof repair, new floor, and clearing the crypts and vaults. Following these renovations, religious service was reestablished. The following June, while meeting Russia's Alexander I in Tilsit, Napoleon learned that his four-year-old nephew Napoleon Charles Bonaparte had died of croup at The Hague. The eldest son of Holland's Louis I and Hortense de Beauharnais, the young boy was his putative heir. The emperor wrote to arch-chancellor Jean-Jacques Régis de Cambacérès to speed up work at Saint Denis. Until the imperial vault could be finished, his nephew's body was placed in a chapel in Notre Dame.

Napoleon's restoration of Saint Denis required an understanding of the Gothic architecture and a revival of forgotten techniques in sculpture, mural painting, stained glass, and ceramics.[12] Jacques Legrand was the first in a series of architects to work on the restoration. After Legrand's death in 1807, neoclassical architect Jacques Cellerier took over. Cellerier, whose prior experience including work on the gothic Saint-Médard Church in Tremblay-en-France, installed a series of pillars, raised the floor of the structure, and tiled the sanctuary and choir with colored marble. Cellerier also changed the crypt entrance, making the vaults accessible through the transept. He started building a small neoclassical chapel, or sacristy, on the southern side of the nave known as the canons' choir.

To decorate Cellerier's sacristy, Vivant Denon commissioned a series of ten paintings by ten artists. Napoleon now found it politically advantageous to tie himself to two of France's greatest kings, François I and Henri IV. The subjects in the series celebrated the early history of Saint Denis and great moments of the French monarchy since Dagobert, the first king of France buried at Saint Denis.[13] By focusing on France's early dynasties, the goal was to erase the memory of the recent vandalism and the deposed Bourbons.[14]

For the prestigious commission, Denon chose several of Jacques-Louis David's favorite students—Antoine-Jean Gros, Rome-born François Gérard, and Anne-Louis Girodet. Gros's *Francis I Receiving Charles V at Saint Denis* (1810, now in the Louvre) depicts Charles V and the French king inside Saint Denis flanked by the Dauphin Henri and his younger brother Charles d'Orleans, along with courtiers dressed in grand style like that of Napoleon's court. In late 1539, François made peace with the Habsburg emperor by inviting him into his kingdom to crush an uprising in Ghent. Gros's painting, explains David O'Brien, was a clear allusion to Napoleon's reconciliation with his father-in-law, Habsburg emperor Francis II, and likened him to the founder of France's Valois dynasty.[15] The detailed painting was exhibited at the Salon of 1812 before being hung at Saint Denis.

To mark Saint Denis' rededication, Napoleon had the names of France's kings engraved on bronze tables at the abbey in 1811. But he did not reinstall their funerary monuments or move their remains from the mass graves.

During the desecration of the royal necropolis at Saint Denis, only one corpse escaped the mass graves. Marshal General Henri de La Tour d'Auvergne, vicomte de Turenne, served Louis XIV for five decades. In line with his motto "Few sieges and many combats," Turenne defeated a series of enemies, including the prince of Condé, the Spanish, Dutch, and Holy Roman Empire. Fatally wounded by a cannonball in 1675, the beloved commander was buried in a small crypt at Saint Denis near the Bourbon kings.

"It is very rare under a monarchy where men pursue only their selfish interest," wrote Voltaire, "that those who served the fatherland die mourned by the public; nonetheless, soldiers and the people mourned Turenne."[16] A

British biographer compared Turenne's modest comportment to "a hero of antient [sic] Rome who never distinguished himself by outward pomp."[17]

Rather than dumped with the French royals into the mass grave at Saint Denis in 1793, Turenne's well-preserved body was displayed in the small sacristy before being moved to the Jardin des Plantes's Museum of Natural History. But the setting was widely seen as disrespectful for the body of a French national hero. In 1799, Turenne's remains were moved to Alexandre Lenoir's Musée des Monuments Français. One of Napoleon's early acts as first consul in 1800 was to reunite the military hero's remains with his monumental tomb beneath the dome of the Church of Invalides, renamed the Temple of Mars.

In acknowledgement of Turenne's heroism and service, Louis XIV had ordered his general buried at Saint Denis among France's kings. Louis also commissioned a grandiose funerary monument for Turenne in the Church of Invalides, part of his vast Hôtel des Invalides built to house and care for France's wounded war veterans. Like the façades of its buildings, the domed soldier's church had a military appearance. The three-nave, nine-bay baroque chapel was decorated to glorify the Sun King and his army.

Designed by Charles Le Brun and sculpted by Jean-Baptiste Tuby and Gaspard Marsy, Turenne's monument took four years to complete. In the central scene, the general's antique-style effigy lies in the arms of Glory, with a pyramid of immortality behind. Female personifications of Religion/Liberality and Valor/Wisdom flank the sarcophagus decorated with a bronze relief of the general's victory at the battle of Turckheim in Alsace.[18]

Napoleon staged an elaborate funeral for Turenne, turning the Invalides into a military pantheon. Turenne's sarcophagus was topped by his sword and fatal cannonball. The monument would be the touchstone for warriors of all generations, declared War Minister Lazare Carnot. In his speech, Lucien Bonaparte focused on France's destiny: "Might one say that the two centuries meet at the moment and join hands over this august tomb? . . . He who was great then is so today, the living heroes and illustrious dead unite in the same place to celebrate the great day when France changed laws without interrupting the course of its great destiny."[19]

Also scattered during the Revolution were the remains of another marshal of France. The foremost military engineer during Louis XIV's reign,

Vauban designed fortifications and made France's borders more defensible. When Vauban's heart was discovered in 1808, Napoleon ordered it moved to a mausoleum opposite Turenne's monument at Invalides.

Throughout his career, Napoleon sought to fashion his image after Turenne—that of a commander beloved by his soldiers. Declaring that Turenne's genius grew bolder as it grew older, Napoleon recommended his soldiers "read and reread" the general's campaigns. Like Augustus, Napoleon had to tread carefully between republicanism and monarchy. Having just fought a revolution to overthrow its monarchs, the French did not want another king. As self-proclaimed emperor, Napoleon needed to keep up the appearance of continuing France's hard-won republican ideals. Much like the Roman emperors, Napoleon exploited his image as France's great military leader, entrusting command to men of bravery.

In an echo of Louis XIV's tribute to Turenne, Napoleon honored his loyal commander Desaix with a tomb and commemorative monuments. Napoleon referred to Desaix as his Hephaestion, Alexander the Great's best friend. In 323 B.C.E., Alexander honored Hephaestion with a costly cremation, adding gold ingots, jewels, rare spices, and ivory to the pyre. On June 14, 1800, thirty-one-year-old Desaix was leading a counterattack against the Austrians at Marengo when he was shot in the heart.

Vivant Denon had followed Desaix and his troops as they chased Mameluke leader Mourad Bey through Upper Egypt. Now Napoleon put Denon in charge of identifying Desaix's corpse in the sacristy of the convent San-Angelo in Milan and arranging his funeral. Desaix was buried in 1805 in the presence of Berthier. Napoleon ordered a tomb for the Church of the Hospice of the Great Saint Bernard Pass. Designed by Jean-Guillaume Moitte and installed in 1806, the memorial featured Desaix's heroic death scene and allegories. As Suzanne Glover Lindsay observes, Napoleon directed the tomb from start to finish, marking the "first consul as the fledgling sovereign that he was becoming, intent on extending and advertising his powers."[20]

After a juried competition, a Paris fountain in Desaix's honor was sculpted by Augustin Félix Fortin after a design by Charles Percier. Erected in 1801 on Place Dauphine, the fountain featured a circular basin below a bust of the general being handed a sword and crowned with a laurel wreath by an allegorical warrior (in 1872, the square was enlarged and the fountain later transferred to the Place Desaix in Riom, near his birthplace).

A few months after Desaix's death, Napoleon also laid the foundation stone at the Place des Victoires in Paris for an Egyptian temple to honor Desaix, known as the "Just Sultan" from the Egyptian campaign, and General Jean-Baptiste Kléber who was killed around the same time in Cairo. The monument replaced a bronze statue of Louis XIV by Martin Desjardins, destroyed during the Revolution. But the proposed monument overwhelmed the square and was never executed.

As first consul, Napoleon decided to build a monument in the same location, but this time dedicated only to Desaix. In June 1806, Napoleon greenlighted the statue, approving the following year twenty thousand kilograms of bronze melted down from mortars captured during the recent Prussian campaign.[21] Denon chose Claude Dejoux for the commission that debuted on August 15, 1810, the feast day of Saint Napoleon.

Because of Desaix's role in the Egyptian campaign, the monument featured a number of Egyptian motifs. Installed on a twenty-foot-tall pedestal by Jean-Baptiste Lepère and decorated with Egyptian symbols, the towering sixteen-foot monument depicted Desaix in the nude, his left arm outstretched toward a small red granite obelisk from Rome's Villa Albani. By Desaix's foot was a sculpted head wearing a *nemes*, the head cloth worn by Egypt's pharaohs.

The work was a rare miss for Denon. After an overwhelmingly negative response to the nude general, a wooden palisade was quickly added to cover the figure. Denon proposed replacing the unpopular work and small obelisk with the obelisk from Rome's Piazza del Popolo. This was never done. Removed from the Place des Victoires in 1814, the offending bronze was repurposed during the Restoration for an equestrian statue of Henri IV at the Pont Neuf. Denon kept a thumb from the Desaix statue. In 1822, Louis XIV would return to the Place des Victoires with an equestrian statue by François Joseph Bosio.

⚜

Napoleon's immortalizing of France's fallen marshals evoked the *elogia* of the great men of ancient Rome. With their legitimacy and rule closely connected to their military victories, emperors depended on the heroism of their legions and commanders.

A new ideology developed during the Augustan era, explains Ida Östenberg, transforming funerals into triumphal expressions of world-wide hegemony. The fates of young soldiers were celebrated as heroic acts, performed for the good of the Empire.[22] At the funerals of Roman VIPs, family members gave speeches commemorating the achievements of the deceased. Inscriptions permanently recorded the deeds of great men.

Roman emperors tightly controlled the installation of monuments. Leading senators were honored with statues in prestigious civic spaces. During the Principate (the first two and a half centuries C.E.), about eighty honorific public monuments of senators were raised. The majority were *uiri triumphales*—men who had won military victories. Most were exhibited in the Forum of Augustus and Forum of Trajan.

The Forum of Augustus celebrated the regime's military victories. The vast complex was organized around the massive temple of Mars Ultor with a large statue of the emperor on a quadriga. Situating his reign in the context of Roman history, Augustus set up an *elogia* of Rome's great men, including a tribute to the consul and praetor Marius.[23]

In his biography of Augustus, Suetonius explains the emperor's edict about the Forum: "In addition to the immortal gods, he [Augustus] honored the memory of the generals who had raised the power of the Roman people from small beginnings to greatness. Accordingly, he restored buildings of these men with their original inscriptions, and in the two colonnades of his forum dedicated statues of all of them in triumphal dress, declaring in an edict that he had built this so that citizens would require him, as long as he lived, and leaders of later ages as well, to attain the standard set by these men."[24]

Galleries of honorific statues adorned the square. The western side was devoted to ancestors of the Julio-Claudian dynasty, from Caesar to Augustus and his heirs. The eastern side featured statues of great generals and officeholders of the republic next to contemporary senators who had won victories.[25] "The Forum of Augustus was a machine for making Romans into followers of Mars," writes Greg Woolf, "and it kept running long after Augustus."[26]

Trajan elaborated on the same themes in his even larger forum. Dedicated in 112 C.E. to celebrate his conquest of Dacia, Trajan's Forum replaced the Forum of Augustus as the primary site for honorific statues of senators. The site was dominated by a massive equestrian statue of Trajan in military dress, and its famous spiraling column frieze narrating the Dacian conquests. As John Weisweiler writes, the message was that "after a century and a half of monarchical rule, the Empire still retained its ability to defeat, humiliate, and exterminate its enemies."[27]

By advertising heroic deeds and glorifying fallen commanders, both the Forum of Augustus and the Forum of Trajan were meant to inspire future generations. ". . . memory was a tool of statecraft, which made a crucial contribution to Roman political success," writes Weisweiler.[28] Interestingly, demonstrating respect for enemy commanders was regarded as a sign of leadership and morality. In the first Punic War, Consul Lucius Cornelius buried Carthaginian Hanno with a lavish funeral. Mark Antony treated Brutus's body respectfully, wrapping it in his own scarlet cape and sending the cremated remains to the deceased's mother. Caesar famously did not accept the head of his rival and former son-in-law Pompey.

⚜

At his December 1804 coronation at Notre Dame, Napoleon remarked: "The candles that are lit in full daylight today once lit up the catacombs."[29] From the Latin *catacumbas* for recesses or holes, catacombs were built by early Roman Jews and Christians. With burial within the city walls forbidden, catacombs were dug in the soft volcanic tufa bedrock beneath Rome's outskirts. During religious persecutions of the second century, the subterranean burials were conducted secretly. There are forty known underground catacombs in Rome, six of which are Jewish.[30] Reaching up to sixty-five feet deep, these structures contain frescoes, inscriptions, and murals on the architectural supports.

As Christianity grew in popularity, catacombs expanded with areas of the tunnels turned into shrines for martyrs. There may have originally been sixty to ninety miles of these underground passages with some three quarters of a million bodies housed in niched chambers.[31] After Constantine legalized Christianity in 313 C.E., funerals moved above ground. By the fifth century, catacombs had become sacred sites for pilgrims.

In the early ninth century, Rome's catacombs were pillaged by Germanic invaders. As a result, relics of Christian martyrs and saints were moved from the catacombs to churches in the city center. Eventually, the underground burial tunnels were abandoned to be rediscovered during excavations in the seventeenth century. In 1634, antiquarian Antonio Bosio wrote about the ancient structures in *Roma Sotterranea,* or Underground Rome.

In the time of Augustus, Romans developed an efficient tomb. There were large communal burial chambers for the freedmen of large households and of the imperial house. Usually subterranean rooms built in series, their walls featured hundreds of semicircular niches housing cinerary urns, sometimes portrait busts. Many were decorated with precious materials and a short inscription with the deceased's name. Communal sepulchers became common, usually as tombs for a whole family or members of collegia. A Roman patronus was morally obligated to provide a burial space for his slaves and often for his freedmen. A burial chamber was reserved for his family; freedmen and slaves had simple graves in the antechamber or garden surrounding the mausoleum.[32]

Around the second century, inhumation replaced cremation in Rome, leading to the creation of miles of underground cemeteries. Early Christians called these burial places *coemeteria,* or places of repose. Luxurious marble sarcophagi with carved reliefs often featured mythical scenes to evoke the virtues of the dead. Biographical sarcophagi depicted battles and important stages of a military commander's life. Burial chamber walls were lavishly painted, ceilings stuccoed, and floors laid with mosaics. Reflecting the wealth of deceased, mausolea were adorned with statues and large tomb gardens. In contrast, the graves of the poor were marked with plain stele. The very poor were buried without markers or in mass graves in ground between the mausolea of the wealthy.[33]

As Anthony Grafton describes, the term catacomb first appeared in 354 C.E. in reference to a *coemeterium ad catacumbas*, identified as the cemetery of St. Sebastian on the Via Appia Antica, two miles outside Rome's Aurelian Wall. From this site, associated with the worship of saints Peter and Paul since the mid-third century, catacomb gradually came to refer to all underground cemeteries since the ninth century. Even after Constantine officially recognized Christianity, catacombs continued to be used. Their use declined in the fifth century; by the eighth century they had achieved cult status. Barbarian invaders of Rome raided the catacombs; their entrances became overgrown with vegetation during the Middle Ages[34] (today, Rome's catacombs are under Vatican control).

Like Rome, Paris experienced dramatic changes in burial practice. In the late eighteenth century, a dangerous public health issue arose. Parisians had been buried inside parish churches and adjacent or nearby burial grounds. At Paris's largest cemetery, Saints Innocents (today's Forum Les Halles), decomposing human remains had pushed through the basement wall of a local restaurant. During the plague of 1418, some fifty thousand bodies were added to the cemetery. The risk of contagion and disease forced Louis XVI to close Saints Innocents.

In 1786, bones from the city's overcrowded cemeteries were transferred to the old Tombe-Issoire quarries on the left bank, and deposited in a new three-acre ossuary. In the first century C.E., the Gallo-Romans had built Lutetia with high quality limestone, known as "pierre de Paris" or Parisian stone. From the thirteenth century, open quarries along the Bièvre river were replaced by underground workings to supply vast quantities of stone for Notre Dame, the Louvre, and the city ramparts.[35]

The quarry was named for Saracen giant Isouard who had threatened Paris during the Crusades. Now by torchlight, nightly processions of priests chanting the service for the dead accompanied the horse-drawn carts filled with bones, and covered with black veils. The remains included residents of ancient Lutetia, nuns from convent graves, lepers, and Protestant victims of the Saint Bartholomew's Day massacre and their Catholic assailants.

The number of transferred skeletons was estimated to be ten times greater than the population of Paris.[36] In memory of ancient Rome, supervisor Charles-Axel Guillaumot called his Paris ossuary the Catacombs. During the French Revolution, victims were buried directly in the Catacombs—from the Swiss Guards killed in the storming of the Tuileries and guillotined aristocrats to Robespierre, mastermind of the Terror. After being released from prison in 1794, Guillaumot continued as inspector of quarries and director of the Gobelins tapestry factory until his death in 1807. His own bones were later moved to his ossuary.[37]

Quarries Inspector Louis-Étienne Héricart de Thury succeeded Guillaumot. In addition to structural and ventilation improvements, the engineer dreamed up an imposing setting inspired by antiquity and the English Gothic novel. He carefully arranged long bones and skulls to form a back wall behind which other bones were piled.[38] Bones were arranged in columns and courses, with walls of tibias, femurs, and skulls. In the middle of the area called the Crypt of the Passion, or the tibia rotunda, a supporting pillar was hidden by skulls and tibias sculpted into the shape of a barrel.[39]

The Catacombs opened to the public on July 1, 1809. After descending a staircase some sixty-five feet, visitors were met at the tomb's entrance with the Alexandrine verse: "Stop, this is death's empire!" Grave inscriptions indicated the geographical origin of the remains; others featured moral maxims. Reminiscent of antiquity, white geometric shapes on a black background adorned stone masonry pillars.

"I believed it was necessary to take special care in the conservation of this monument, considering the intimate rapport that will surely exist between the Catacombs and the events of the French Revolution; as a result of this work [the Catacombs] were repaired, their interior was restored, the ventilation system was improved, [and] bones were arranged with as much art as skill. Nothing was spared to make this monument worthy of public veneration," wrote Héricart de Thury.[40]

In 1810, to give the ossuary a more hopeful ambiance, de Thury added inspirational maxims. A devout Catholic, he flanked ancient texts with inscriptions confirming a Christian afterlife. The result, writes Erin-Marie Legacey, was a collection of reflections on death taken from the Bible, Marcus Aurelius, and Seneca, and various French poets.[41] That year, Alexis-François Artaud de Montor's *Voyage dans les catacombes de Rome* created great enthusiasm for the Roman Catacombs in France.[42] In 1815, Héricart de Thury published his own *Description of the Paris catacombs*. In addition to engravings, his book included "a historical record of the catacombs of all peoples of the old and new continents."

Early on, Napoleon looked to Roman precedents for a hygienic city. In June 1804, a month after being named emperor, he prohibited burial in churches, convents, and cemeteries within the walls of Paris. Like the Greeks and Romans, he ordered four necropolises on the outer edges of

Paris: one to the north (Montmartre), one to the south (Montparnasse), one to the east on the Charonne hill (Père Lachaise), and one to the west (Passy). Construction of the small Passy Cemetery (in today's 16th arrondissement near the Eiffel Tower) came later.

Seine prefect Nicolas Frochot hired architect Alexandre-Theodore Brongniart to design the park-like Père Lachaise Cemetery. The chosen site, some thirty-four acres, was a former Jesuit property, the refuge of Louis XIV's confessor Père François d'Aix de La Chaise.[43] Brongniart's plan included two long alleys of lime trees on the hillside and access to the realm of the dead symbolized by an Egyptian-style pyramid, an architectural form Napoleon especially liked.

Père Lachaise Cemetery was a dramatic contrast to the macabre Paris Catacombs. Following the site's natural contours, Brongniart added plantings and created paved walkways between graves. To protect the graves, he conceived an ambitious plan for a covered gallery preceded by a courtyard. The proposal was so impressive, the government reserved space for France's national heroes. But the uniformity imposed for the tomb design was deemed unsuitable, and the administration returned to concessions.

The first burial at Père Lachaise took place in May 1804, for a five-year-old girl. But Parisians were skeptical at first about being buried on a hill outside Paris. To build acceptance for the new cemetery, Napoleon had the remains of two prestigious figures transferred to Père Lachaise—Louise de Lorraine, widow of Henri III in 1806, followed by his naval commander Admiral Eustache Bruix, a recipient of the Grand Eagle of the Legion of Honor. Frochot convinced authorities to rebury Molière, La Fontaine, and the famous tweflth-century lovers Abélard and Héloïse at the cemetery in 1817.

Alexandre Brongniart died in 1813 before he could finish the pyramid; fittingly he was buried at Père Lachaise. The cemetery soon became the final resting place for the Empire's generals and marshals, politicians, scientists, artists, architects, and musicians. Not to mention Napoleon's mistresses—Mesdemoiselles Bourgoin, Duchesnois, Georges, Mars, Madame Saqui (the tightrope walker), Pauline Fourès, Eléonore de la Plaigne, mother of his son the Comte Léon, and Marie Walewska, and mother of his second son Alexandre Walewski.[44]

THREE
MARS THE PEACEMAKER

In April 1811, Napoleon hurried to the Musée Napoléon. After nine years, his highly anticipated sculpture had finally arrived from Rome. During his recent visit to Paris, Canova had chosen a spot for the statue alongside the museum's most famous antiquities.[1]

Art theorist Quatremère de Quincy commented on the dramatic shift in Napoleon's attitude toward public monuments. "It is indeed curious to see the same man who, a few years before, had refused the honor of an honorary monument (because, he said, men owed it only to men after their death) to be sculpted in Rome as a colossal statue for Paris."[2]

The marble's shipment unfolded like a covert military operation. To avoid being spotted by British spies in Rome, the crate containing the thirteen-ton statue was removed from Canova's studio late at night the previous July. After traveling by barge along the Tiber to Ostia, the cargo continued by ship to Genoa, then on to Toulon, Lyon, and Paris. The sea route had its own risks. As a precaution against the statue being captured by the British fleet, Napoleon ordered the large crate positioned on the ship for easy jettison.[3]

Napoleon had discussed the commission with Canova during his sittings at Saint-Cloud in 1802. While the sculptor molded his terra-cotta bust, the first consul had expressed his strong preference to be portrayed in his military uniform. But Canova insisted the figure be nude, believing it elevated the work from portraiture to what he considered the nobler genres of history and mythology.

To neoclassicists like Canova the ideal body also represented spiritual perfection.[4] Nudity, "when it is pure and adorned with exquisite beauty," could appear "like a spiritual and intellectual thing" and raise "the spirit to the contemplation of the divine," Canova wrote.[5] He would also have been familiar with the many nude marbles of Roman emperors, including one of Augustus holding an orb and scepter.[6]

Both Dominique-Vivant Denon and Ennio Quirinio Visconti had agreed with Canova, arguing that both the Greeks and Romans had produced timeless marbles of their heroes in the nude.[7] A generation earlier, in the name of artistic freedom, an elderly Voltaire deferred to sculptor Jean-Baptiste Pigalle, who portrayed him in the nude. The resulting sculpture caused a scandal and great embarrassment for the philosopher. Despite his better judgment, Napoleon respected the renowned sculptor and his art advisors, reportedly saying: "No rule can be imposed on Genius."[8]

On January 1, 1803, Canova signed the contract for sixty thousand francs. At the time of the commission, Quatremère de Quincy weighed in, suggesting that his friend depict Napoleon as an equestrian Roman emperor in bronze—after Rome's renowned *Marcus Aurelius*. But after exchanging ideas, Canova chose the mythological guise of Mars the peacemaker. It seemed an appropriate allegory at the time. After nine years of fighting, France and Britain had negotiated the Treaty of Amiens in March 1802. Napoleon and Pius had finally come to terms on the Concordat.

There were many precedents for presenting Napoleon as Mars. In Roman antiquity, it was common to represent humans in the guise of divinities. The tradition continued during the Renaissance when, for example, Bronzino painted Andrea Doria as Neptune and Cosimo I de Medici as Orpheus, both in the nude.[9] During Louis XIV's reign, the same held true in paintings of the king and the French aristocracy.[10]

According to Christopher Johns, "disguising" controversial subjects like Napoleon in mythological guises appealed to Canova both personally and professionally. It allowed him to avoid becoming "the cultural propagandist for any particular ideology."[11] Canova's idea of depicting Napoleon in the guise of Mars may in fact go back to 1801 when Count Giovanni Battista Sommariva, art collector and president of the Cisalpine Republic, spoke with him about a sculpture of the "Man of Destiny" for a Bonaparte Forum in Milan.[12] Shortly after, Napoleon invited Canova to Paris to sculpt his portrait bust.

Before leaving Paris in late November 1802, Canova made preliminary sketches for the statue and modeled a larger-than-life-size clay bust of Napoleon that he used to create the plaster cast for the finished marble. To "improve" the bust of Napoleon, writes David O'Brien, Canova straightened the nose, heightened the cheekbones, and strengthened the brow and chin. He also slightly rearranged the sitter's signature hairstyle to evoke the Roman emperor Augustus.[13] For the body, Canova combined elements of two famous classical masterpieces—the muscular *Farnese Hercules* and the Vatican's elegant *Apollo Belvedere*, which had been taken to Paris.[14] Toward the end of 1803, Canova took delivery of a large block of Carrara marble.

From early on, buzz surrounded the commission. A year into the project, François Cacault, France's ambassador in Rome, declared: "The statue must become the most perfect work of this century. It is not a figure to be placed on a public square; it must be placed in the museum in the midst of the ancient masterpieces we owe to the first consul."[15]

Denon agreed. In a letter to Napoleon in December 1806 he wrote: "The whiteness and the purity of the material do not permit that this statue be exposed to the inclemencies of our climate; its nudity has made me think of placing it in the museum among the emperors and in the niche where the Laocoön is, in such a manner that it would be the first object that one sees on entering."[16]

By late 1806, the finished marble was inspiring superlatives from visitors to Canova's studio. Tuscan painter Pietro Benvenuti reported that Canova had surpassed himself, producing "a truly sublime and noble figure."[17] The *Mercure de France* announced that Canova had created a "masterpiece of modern sculpture."

In 1807, Eugène de Beauharnais, viceroy of the Kingdom of Italy, commissioned a bronze replica of Canova's marble for the Napoleon Forum in Milan. With this outdoor version, writes Valérie Huet, Napoleon's stepson was following the tradition of Roman senators who commissioned and displayed statues of their emperors throughout the Empire.[18] After being cast by founders Francesco and Luigi Righetti, the statue was installed in 1812 on a plinth in the court of the Milan Senate (today the statue is housed at the Brera Art Gallery).

In Rome, Napoleon's estranged brother Lucien Bonaparte expressed his surprise that Canova had agreed to immortalize someone who had destroyed his homeland. Canova replied that he had portrayed Napoleon as a bringer of peace, adding that "Everything is in my signature Canova da Venezia."[19] Despite the accolades for *Napoleon as Mars the peacemaker*, Canova feared the worst. In November 1806, he wrote Quatremère de Quincy: "The statue of the Emperor will one day come to Paris; it will be criticized without pity, and I know it will certainly have its defects, above all the others it will have the disgrace of being modern and by an Italian."[20]

After years of delays, Napoleon now stood in his museum's *Salles des Hommes Illustres,* dwarfed by the eleven-foot marble. Though the head was recognizable, the physique was completely unbelievable. Napoleon's short, portly body bore no resemblance to the buff, six-packed nude figure of Mars.

Canova sculpted him striding forward, looking at a small cast copper Victory on an orb in his right hand, holding a long scepter topped by an eagle in his left. Behind his right leg, an abandoned sword and belt rested against a tree trunk. With the exception of a chlamys flung over the left shoulder and a vine-leaf covering the genitals, the figure was stark naked.

Napoleon rejected the work on the spot and ordered the statue removed to a niche in the museum. It was hidden from view by a screen of planks and a curtain with access restricted to a handful of artists.[21]

Nudity wasn't the statue's only problem. Canova applied his signature surface polish to the muscle-bound figure, giving Napoleon's imperial state portrait a sensual appearance.[22] In addition, the public mood in France had shifted. When Napoleon ordered the statue in 1802, he seemed invincible. He had made peace with Britain and the Church and had just issued a sweeping new legal code. By 1811, the French army was embroiled in a grueling guerrilla war in Spain and Napoleon was considering an invasion of Russia.[23] In this far less optimistic environment, Napoleon needed to change his image to that of a statesman.[24]

Canova's loyalty to the abducted pope and his Italian patriotism have led some historians to conclude that he purposely chose the guise of a nude Roman god for Napoleon to undermine the statue's propaganda potential.[25] "Surely such a monument," writes Christopher Johns, "with its pretensions to deified status and its connections to august artistic lineage, must have been recognized as a rejection, in cultural terms, of the achievements of the Revolution."[26]

Denon delivered the bad news to Canova. On April 15, the museum director wrote: "I have the honor of informing you, Sir and Dear Colleague, that the emperor has come to see your statue. His Majesty has seen with interest the beautiful execution of this work and its imposing aspect, but he thinks that the forms of it are too athletic and that you may be a bit mistaken about the character that eminently distinguishes him, that is to say the calmness of his movements . . ." Denon tried to cushion the blow by adding: "His Majesty, my dear colleague, has not yet decided on its destination."[27]

Denon indicated that he thought the work would go to the Senate and he would have it installed as soon as Napoleon informed him of his orders.[28] Ironically, notes David O'Brien, calmness of movement was not at all how observers saw Napoleon. "With his impetuous nature," wrote François-René de Chateaubriand, "instead of having a straightforward and continuous way of walking, he advanced by jumps, and he threw himself on the universe and jerked it along."[29]

In early May, Quatremère de Quincy wrote a reassuring letter to Canova, expressing that Napoleon's negative reaction was based on politics, not artistry. A month later, Jacques-Louis David also penned a supportive note. "You have made a beautiful figure representing the Emperor Napoleon," David wrote. "You have made for posterity all that a mortal can make; the calumny that clings to it disregard, allow to mediocrity its little habitual consolation. The work is there, it represents the Emperor Napoleon, and it is Canova who has made it. That is all there is to be said." Canova responded to David's support with a letter of thanks.[30]

In addition to Napoleon's rejection, 1811 was a difficult year for Canova personally. In January, the sculptor's beloved housekeeper Luigia Giuli died. For twenty-seven years, his "*madre morale*" had cared for him and looked after his homes in Rome and Possagno. Later that year, Canova also lost his mother, Angela Zardo. After his father died, she had remarried, leaving him at age three in the care of his grandfather. Despite this abandonment, he had reconciled with his mother. He dedicated a funerary stele to both women.

Napoleon as Mars the peacemaker joined another banished portrait. After a brief meeting with the emperor, twenty-six-year-old Jean-Auguste-Dominique Ingres painted *Napoleon on His Imperial Throne* in 1806. The hieratic frontal pose was inspired by the central image of God in Van Eyck's famous *Ghent Altarpiece*, stolen for the Louvre. Dressed in his coronation garb, Napoleon sits on a throne atop a carpet with the imperial eagle, holding the scepter of Charlemagne and the hand of justice. His head is crowned with laurel wreaths, beside him is the sword of Charlemagne.

As Andrew Graham-Dixon posits, with its over-the-top references to Roman emperors, Holy Roman emperors, and the Christian God, the disturbing portrait may have been too close to the truth, revealing Napoleon's monstrous ego.[31] Napoleon had the portrait hidden away in the Musée de l'Armée, where it hangs today.

⚜

Canova's heroic nude was a sculptural genre with ancient roots, going back to at least the sixth century B.C.E. The Greeks depicted athletes, gods, and heroes in the nude. In his *Natural History*, Pliny the Elder explains that "heroic nudity" was a Greek element incorporated into Roman art. "In old days the statues dedicated were simply clad in the toga," writes Pliny. "Also, naked figures holding spears, made from models of Greek young men from gymnasiums . . . became popular. The Greek practice is to leave the figure entirely nude, whereas Roman and military statuary adds a breastplate."[32]

Nudity had different meanings for the ancient Greeks and Romans. According to Michael Squire, nudity was an essential part of honorific portraiture for the Greeks, while Romans seemed more worried about its political, social, and cultural ramifications.[33] "In Greece the ancient pre-Homeric sense of male nudity was overturned," writes Larissa Bonfante. "In Italy, Greek civilization brought with it its "modern" ways, without, however changing customs and attitude deeply rooted in the religion and traditions of the peoples living in Etruria and other regions of ancient Italy."[34]

Napoleon's shock at his nude statue by Canova was not unlike the response of Roman republicans eighteen centuries earlier.[35] ". . . nudity itself was more of a cultural taboo in Rome than it had been in the Greek cultural world," explains Squire. "The few times that we do hear of Roman generals stripping off their clothes, it is not to show off their bodies, but rather to parade their military scars—to display the corporeal disfigurements which embody military prowess."[36]

Given the Roman aversion to public nudity, Octavian's decision to be represented naked was a daring one, explains Christopher Hallett. To mark his victory over Sextus Pompey at Naulochos in 36 B.C.E., Octavian permitted his depiction in a colossal nude gilded bronze statue set on a column near the speaker's platform (rostra) in the Roman Forum.[37] In celebration of his naval victory at Actium, Octavian was portrayed in an *agate intaglio*, naked, and holding a trident in the guise of Neptune, riding in a chariot drawn by hippocamps. In another engraved gem, Octavian again appears nude, wearing the aegis of Jupiter over his shoulders.[38]

While nudity in art was acceptable, Octavian drew a line at public exposure. Suetonias reported the rare occasion when Octavian exposed his chest: "When the people did their best to force the dictatorship upon him, he knelt down, threw off his toga from his shoulders, and with bare breast begged them to desist." When Octavian hosted Greek games (at Nicopolis) to mark the victory at Actium, women were not allowed, presumably because of the nudity of the athletes.[39]

After the Senate awarded Octavian the name Augustus, for august, the sacred one, he launched an image makeover. The fully nude portraits from his days as *triumvir* disappear, replaced by clothed images with a toga and veiled head. Augustus writes in his *Res Gestae*: "There stood in the city about eighty statues of myself, standing, on horseback, or in chariots, all of silver; these I arranged to have removed, and with the money so obtained,

I dedicated golden offerings in the temple of Apollo, in my own name, and in the name of those who had honoured me these statues."[40]

Augustus began his imperial career with an image of Alexander the Great on his seal. Images of Alexander also appear in his Forum. As Shelley Hales describes, the famous *Prima Porta Augustus* "flirts with Alexander's look through a Roman filter. . . . Divine nudity is implied despite heavy cuirass on which Augustus literally bears the cosmos."[41]

After Augustus, Roman emperors returned to nude depictions in the guise of powerful gods. "Statues of emperors show them as Mars and Jupiter, full-blooded Olympian males who know how to fight, rule, and love like men. This virility was often flaunted in the guise of divine nudity . . ." adds Hales.[42] Roman emperors are depicted wearing Jupiter's aegis like a chlamys or hip-mantle, holding the scepter and thunderbolt of Jupiter.[43] After she is deified by Claudius, Livia appears as Venus alongside Augustus as Mars.

In attitude and attributes, writes Benjamin Hemmerle, *Napoleon as Mars the Peacemaker* resembles a Roman copy of a Greek statue. The tree trunk suggests the ancient translation of a statue cast in bronze into a version carved in marble. Canova depicts Napoleon as a demi-god, surpassing comparison with the Roman emperors.[44]

In defense of Canova's controversial statue, his biographer Melchior Missirini wrote: "Art chose the nude as its language. Moreover, the portraits and statues of living men were nudes, so that Pompey, Marcus Vipsanius Agrippa, Augustus, Tiberius, Germanicus, Claudius, Domiziano, Nerva, Hadrian, Marcus Aurelius, Lucius Verus, Septimius Severus, and Macrinus are all represented in the nude. [. . .] the nude is the poetry of art, it is eternal just as art is eternal [. . .] and invests physical man with this universal existence that brings renown to moral man."[45]

⚜

During their breakfasts together, Canova tried to convince Napoleon to reconcile with Pius VII. When this failed badly, he switched strategies, flattering the emperor into becoming a patron of excavations and artists in Rome. In this effort, the sculptor was far more successful. In Canova's diary, he notes that Napoleon told him of his desire to emulate the great

Roman patrons who had preceded him. Canova came away with edicts that included support of the Accademia di San Luca, part of the Roman academy system.

Founded in the late sixteenth century under the directorship of Federico Zuccari, the Accademia di San Luca sought to elevate the work of painters, sculptors, and architects above that of craftsmen. Members considered drawing to be the unifying principle of painting, sculpture, and architecture. The association of artists took its name from Saint Luke the evangelist, patron saint of the painter's guild. According to legend, Luke created a portrait of the Virgin Mary. Artists of all nationalities were welcome.

In contrast, France's academies were created by the state to train artists who would work on government projects. The Académie Royale de Peinture et Sculpture was founded in 1648, and the Académie Royale d'Architecture in 1671. In addition to the Paris schools, in 1666 a Rome branch was also opened where pensioners would study masterworks of antiquity, the Renaissance, and the baroque.[46]

A decade later, thanks to an agreement by Pope Innocent XI and Louis XIV, an attempt was made to combine the Accademia di San Luca with the Académie de France. But the plan for one arts institution in Rome was never realized. Now Napoleon resurrected the idea, proposing to merge the storied institutions into one arts school in Rome. By a decree in November 1810 engineered by Canova, the new institution was to be located in the suppressed convent of the Aracoeli housed in the former medieval monastery and Church of Ara Coeli above the Capitol near the Villa Medici, home of the French Academy since 1804.

Napoleon's plan was to install Canova as director of the new imperial academy, which would include departments of painting, drawing, sculpture, architecture, mythology, anatomy, and geometry, along with schools for music and mosaics. A member of the Accademia di San Luca since 1800 and a staunch supporter, Canova had been involved in reorganizing its curriculum and classrooms in Via Vonella into several rooms next to the Church of Saints Luca and Martina. Now Canova was nominated "Direttore Perpetuo" of the schools dependent on the Accademia; other members elected him "Principe."[47] As Susan Nicassio puts it, Canova "returned to Rome virtual director of the arts."[48]

In the November decree, Napoleon pledged two hundred thousand francs for excavations in Rome, along with one hundred thousand francs for the Accademia di San Luca, three quarters of which was for maintenance and repair of monuments.[49] By July, the Accademia had begun repairs to the Colosseum and Pantheon and the reconstruction of the Temple of Vespasian. But as Ronald Ridley writes, requests for repairs to the vast Colosseum were constant and the Accademia became insolvent.[50]

Canova found himself at loggerheads over finances and red tape with Baron Martial Daru, Intendant of the Crown Assets. The younger brother of Pierre Daru, former intendant general of the imperial household, Martial Daru was posted to Rome in March to supervise excavations. Finally in frustration, Canova wrote to Napoleon later that year, begging him to honor his commitment, conveying how circumstances were "much more wretched than what I have already described to you."[51]

By 1812, Napoleon's political fortune and imperial treasury were seriously reduced, making support for Rome a low priority. The new arts academy under Canova was officially decreed in May 1812, but never realized. According to Philippe Durey, Napoleon's rejection of Canova's statue combined with Canova's refusal of any official position in Paris marked a turning point in the relationship of the two men.[52]

Napoleon's Consulta, established in June 1809, was charged with modernizing Rome. From a police report the previous May, the emperor was aware that the Eternal City was deteriorating. "The population has already lost 30,000 inhabitants; if the emperor does not turn his eyes and hand to it, those who know the place well are certain that in less than ten years the city of the popes will be almost as ruined as that of the Caesars. . . . The gardens of the Quirinal are dry; the palace is nothing more than a deserted and crumbling monastery. The great families close their houses, either from distress or from greed; the streets are empty except for beggars . . ."[53]

By imperial decree in July 1811, Napoleon committed one million francs a year for sweeping renovations.[54] The ambitious program featured creation of the Villa Napoleon—a large public complex with gardens between the Milvian Bridge and the city walls. Other projects included a pair of cemeteries outside the city, new markets, slaughterhouses and stockyards, piazzas around Trajan's column, the Pantheon, and the Trevi

Fountain, and a bigger square outside the Quirinal Palace. Two connecting boulevards were also proposed—one from St. Peter's Basilica to the Castel Sant'Angelo and another from the Quirinal to the Coliseum.[55]

In late August 1811, Rome's young new prefect Camille de Tournon enclosed an urban plan with his letter to Napoleon: "On arriving from France, your Majesty will enter through the Porta del Popolo and proceed along the fine street of the Corso, which will be extended to the Forum, passing under the arches of Septimus and Titus, enter the capital and the temple of Antoninus, and by this proceed to Your palace by a great street cut through one of the most densely populated quarters."[56]

Until the emperor banished Canova's *Napoleon as Mars the peacemaker* to the storeroom, the plan had been to install an exact replica in the middle of the Roman Forum between the arches of Titus and Septimius Severus.[57] To celebrate the birth of Napoleon's son, the newly cleared ancient sites of the Forum, the Colosseum, and the area around the Capitol were illuminated.

In the summer of 1811, while Nero's Golden House was being excavated in Rome, architect and engineer Scipione Perosini submitted a plan for an even larger palace for Napoleon, one of several ambitious proposals. Occupying prime real estate, the imperial compound called for demolition of the city's ancient monuments. In the end, Napoleon decided to enlarge and redecorate the Quirinal palace where Pius had recently been kidnapped.[58]

Napoleon had assured Canova that the art confiscations in Italy were over. Despite this, Denon arrived in August 1811, lured by the suppression of monasteries the previous fall. After closing down convents and monasteries, Napoleon demanded a loyalty oath that required signers to swear hatred to all monarchs other than the emperor. As Susan Nicassio explains, this meant clerics had to swear hatred to the pope. Those refusing to sign were deported or imprisoned. By decree of France's Council of State in May 1812, anyone who did not sign the oath of loyalty was declared a felon and arrested, their possessions confiscated.[59]

Meanwhile, Canova could do nothing to stop Denon's latest looting. Assisted by Benjamin Zix, Denon spent five months scouring the monasteries of Pisa, Siena, Genoa, Perugia, and Florence, all departments of France. Specifically, Denon was looking to fill a gap at his encyclopedic Musée Napoléon—the so-called "primitives" of Tuscany. This little-known, underappreciated school of the tweflth through the fifteenth centuries is considered the precursor to high Renaissance art. The paintings were created with egg tempera—pigment mixed with beaten egg and water—on a smooth white ground of gesso—whiting, glue, and water applied in thin coats to a wooden panel.

Among the masterworks Denon negotiated for was Cimabue's enormous altarpiece, *Madonna with Angels*, from Pisa's Church of San Francesco, along with works by Giotto, Pisano, Fra' Filippo Lippi, Lorenzo di Credi, Domenico Ghirlandaio, and Perugino, Raphael's teacher. From Venice's new Accademia, Denon plucked Fra Angelico's *Coronation of the Virgin*. Originally from the Church of San Domenico a Fiesole, the six-part predella included scenes from the legend of St. Dominic, grouped around a painting of the dead Christ with the Virgin and Saint John.

The *Coronation* inspired Renaissance art critic Giorgio Vasari to write: "Above all the things that he did, fra Giovanni surpassed himself and demonstrated his greatest excellence . . . indeed it seems that those blessed souls could not appear otherwise in heaven, or rather, would appear so if they had bodies, because all the male and female saints there are not only full of life with gentle and charming expressions, but all the coloring of the works seems as though by a saint or an angel . . . I never see this work without something new appearing to me, nor do I ever have my fill of it."[60]

PART EIGHT

THE FALL

"You who know history so well, are you not struck by the similarities of my government with that of Diocletian—that tight-knit web of government that I am spreading over such distances, those all-seeing eyes of the Emperor, that civil authority which I have been obliged to keep all-powerful in the midst of an entirely military empire?"
—Napoleon Bonaparte to aide-de-camp Narbonne, 1812

ONE

THE GOLDEN PRISON

By mid-1812, Napoleon was at the height of his power, ruling over Europe's largest empire since ancient Rome. He was preparing to invade Russia when he learned that Pius's declining health was alarming supporters, including his father-in-law, the Austrian emperor.

Much to Napoleon's consternation, the pope's two and a half years of captivity in Savona had not produced any political concessions. Throughout his confinement, Pius resisted pressure from several delegations to sign a new concordat and affirm bishops nominated by Napoleon—a move that threatened the Church with schism.

Pius further enraged Napoleon by refusing to acknowledge the dissolution of his marriage to Joséphine (Pius had performed their religious union before the coronation in December 1804). This position threw the legitimacy of Napoleon's newborn son and heir into question. In early June 1812, Napoleon decided to move "the obstinate old man" to France where he would personally deal with him when he returned from Russia.

To minimize the risk of a public relations disaster, Napoleon wrote his brother-in-law, Prince Camillo Borghese, at Turin with meticulously detailed instructions to ensure that the pope's transfer remain a secret. "Precautions will be taken to see that [Pius VII] passes through Turin at night . . . that he passes through Chambery and Lyon at night. . . . The Pope must not travel in his Pontifical robes . . . (but) in such a way that nowhere . . . can he be recognized."[1]

At midnight, the seventy-year-old pontiff was hustled out a side door into a carriage. Per Napoleon's order, his white vestments and pectoral cross were replaced by a priest's black cassock. The pope's white satin shoes were smeared with ink, the gold embroidered crosses ripped off.

By the time Pius reached the Alps, his bowels were blocked and he could not urinate. In agony, delirious with fever, he was helped into the Benedictine hospice at Mount Cenis, where an abbot administered the Last Sacraments.[2] Captain Lagorse, who Pius had chosen to travel with him, sent for a surgeon.

When Dr. Balthazar Claraz arrived at the hospice, Lagorse told him, "You are going to see a sick man, I do not tell you who he is, you will know him; but if you come to publish it, tremble . . . it's all about your freedom, and maybe your life."

In his account two years later, the doctor would write of the pope: ". . . he was as pale as a dying man, he had a fever and suffered continual pains without being able to sleep; his urine, which flowed only in drops, was red, showing great inflammation . . ."[3]

According to the surgeon, he urged rest for the ill pontiff, but Lagorse insisted on setting off Monday night, June 15. He ordered Claraz to attend to the pope during the journey. The monks provided cushions, sheets, a blanket, and a quilt. To ease the pain, Claraz gave the pontiff drugs and had him lie on a makeshift cot in the coach, which he called a "bed of misery and pain."[4]

The passage through Lyon was especially painful, with its unequal pavement and the speed of the horses, recalled Claraz. "I was obliged to hold with one hand, the head of the SP [Pius VII] to avoid the counter-blows of the car, and I put the other on the stomach. When we had crossed Lyon, and when the horses stopped, SP [Pius] asked me if this path was finished, I answered him affirmatively, and then he pronounced these remarkable words which will remain engraved, forever, in my memory: 'May God forgive him [Napoleon]. I already have.'"[5]

After a grueling four and a half days, Pius arrived at Fontainebleau at noon on Friday June 19. The château's imposing gates were now adorned with Napoleon's monogram *N* topped with an imperial crown and surrounded by laurel leaves. According to Claraz, the gatekeeper was not expecting the pope and would not allow the coaches to enter. Pius spent the first night in the Palace of the Senate, before being transferred to the château.[6]

Though Pius was exhausted, memories came flooding back as he was carried through the château into his apartment. It was the same suite he had stayed in eight years earlier when he had traveled to France to officiate at Napoleon's coronation. In honor of his stay, the apartment of the former Queen Mother (the widowed Anne of Austria) had been redecorated in a record nineteen days.

This time, Pius was not an honored guest, but a prisoner. As Christophe Beyeler writes, "Rome, the 'Eternal City,' became the second capital of the French Empire, while Pius VII was relegated to Fontainebleau, the 'golden prison.'"[7] For the first two weeks after his arrival, Pius was too sick to speak or move.

As the favorite palace of François I and his Valois successors followed by the Bourbon kings, Fontainebleau's guestbook included such notables as Holy Roman Emperor Charles V and Sweden's Queen Christina. During the queen's stay, she ordered her master of the horse murdered in the Stags Gallery.[8] Through the centuries, Italian, Flemish, and French artists had decorated the sumptuous château.

During the Revolution, Fontainebleau's furnishings were sold off in the Fountain Courtyard. The splendid tapestries, chandeliers, and mirrors were all gone. Despite the ransacking, the French court's décor survived, leading Napoleon to describe it as having "the shape and color of time." On June 29, 1804, Napoleon visited the château with Pierre Fontaine. He instructed the architect to transform the storied palace into his fall country residence. Money was no object. In one decade, Napoleon spent twelve million francs on construction and furniture for the palace, which he called "the true home of kings."[9]

To create a stately entrance and facilitate the review of his troops, Napoleon's architects razed the historic western wing and opened up the courtyard. The magnificent upper chapel of Saint-Saturnin, built by Henri

II and Henri IV, was repurposed as a library. The François I Gallery became the Emperor's Gallery, adorned with many of the military portrait busts from Tuileries Palace's Gallery of Consuls.[10]

Percier and Fontaine turned the Bourbon bedchamber into Napoleon's Throne Room, filled with military motifs including laurel and oak wreaths, eagles clutching thunderbolts, the emperor's monogram, and lion's maws and paws. Flanked by two imperial standards, his throne was installed in 1808 in the alcove formerly housing the king's bed. Produced by Jacob-Desmalter after a design by Percier and Fontaine, the dark blue velvet throne with gold bees sat on a raised dais beneath a soaring canopy.

Pierre-Philippe Thomire carried the military theme into his candelabra for the Throne Room's fireplace and console tables. Ancient helmets and victory wreaths were joined at the base by swords and a shield adorned with figures of Temperance, Prudence, and Fortitude. The Savonnerie carpet, woven after a design by the architect Sainte-Ange, sported the inscription SPQR, acronym for *Senatus Populusque Romanus*, or The Senate and People of Rome. The Roman Senate adopted the official slogan at the start of the Republic. The carpet's panoply of Roman symbols include lictors' fasces, a sword with an eagle hilt, a crested helmet, an ancient breastplate adorned with an eagle, and a standard topped by a she-wolf.

Fontainebleau's game-rich forests had long attracted France's royals. In the tweflth and thirteenth centuries, France's Capetian kings traveled to Fontainebleau to hunt. François I hosted hunting parties here, and the Bourbons continued the tradition, decorating some of the rooms with hunting themes.[11] Napoleon revived the tradition of fall hunting trips. He would spend some fifty days hunting here during three imperial court visits.

In the fall 1807, the château hosted one thousand courtiers, guests, and foreign dignitaries; with another four thousand in the town itself. Theater companies from Paris entertained guests. Napoleon's sisters Caroline and Pauline organized dances in the ballroom featuring an extraordinary coffered octagonal ceiling and Renaissance frescoes.[12] At the close of the second imperial court stay in 1808, Napoleon informed Joséphine of his decision to divorce.

The last imperial court visit had taken place in the fall of 1810. With the octagonal Pond Pavilion restored, newlyweds Napoleon and Marie Louise floated across the Carp Pond in a decorated gondola, like Louis XIV and his courtiers.[13] In November, Napoleon's nephew Prince Charles Louis Napoleon Bonaparte, son of King Louis and Queen Hortense of Holland, was baptized in the château's Trinity Chapel by Cardinal Fesch. In 1850, the prince became president of France's Second Republic, then Emperor Napoleon III two years later.

Pius did not enjoy the spectacular château that his adviser Cardinal Bartolomeo Pacca dubbed "another state prison." The former Benedictine monk lived simply, writes Christophe Beyeler, confining himself to his apartments where he found strength in prayer and study.[14]

To add insult to injury, Napoleon selected the Palazzo del Quirinale, the papal residence where Pius had been kidnapped, as his imperial palace in Rome. The Eternal City's second largest palace after the Vatican, the Quirinale had its start in the 1580s during the pontificate of Gregory XIII. Over two centuries of popes had commissioned the most celebrated architects and artists of their day to design and decorate the palace.

Napoleon did not consider the Quirinale sufficiently grand. According to the emperor's architect, "it lacks everything: the apartments are very small and it is merely a skeleton." At the start of 1811, Napoleon ordered an extensive redo of the palace, which was renamed Monte Cavallo. In February, Raffaele Stern, Pius VII's architect since 1805, was named "Architect to the Imperial Palace." He joined Antonio Canova, Martial Daru, and Denon on a special planning commission.

Stern submitted three plans for the renovation. The first focused on making the palace immediately habitable. The second included demolition of the semi-cylindrical stronghold in the façade, the Dataria, Panetteria, and the ex-monastery of San Felice in order to enlarge the piazza with its famed Dioscuri statues. The third proposal involved moving the main palace entrance to the Strada Pia and razing buildings on the other side of the road to create a large garden.[15]

Given Napoleon's planned trip to Rome in 1812, the first option was chosen with the focus on reorganizing and redecorating the palace interiors. Monte Cavallo turned out to be one of the Empire's most costly projects, with a budget of over half a million francs. In addition to refurbishing the gilding, stucco, and woodwork, many of the palace's physical spaces were reconfigured. A throne room, a hall of the marshals, and antechambers were created. Apartments for the emperor and empress were configured from a papal audience hall and gallery. The corner papal summer apartment (with a wood balcony offering panoramic views of Rome) was turned into Napoleon's dining room with a new mythological-themed frieze and ceiling decoration. Tapestries, silver, furniture, and china were ordered from Paris.

To create ceiling paintings and friezes for the palace's new iconographic program, Stern quickly assembled a dozens of Rome-based neoclassical artists. They included painters Felice Giani, Francesco Hayez, Palagio Palagi, and Jean-Auguste-Dominique Ingres. Among the sculptors were Bertel Thorvaldsen, Carlo Finelli, Giuseppe Pacetti, Carlo Albacini, and Francesco Massimiliano. The artistic program was designed to glorify the Empire by explicitly comparing Napoleon to his ancient predecessors.

History painter Vincenzo Camuccini, named head of the Accademia di San Luca in 1805, applied his formal academic style to two paintings for the emperor's apartment. Both works related to state patronage of the arts throughout history—*Charlemagne Summoning Italian and German Scholars to Found the University of Paris* and *Ptolemy III Philadelphus Among Scholars Brought to the Library of Alexander.* (Camuccini would paint Pius's portrait in 1814 after Raphael's famous Pope Julius II.)[16]

With its papal throne, the Carlo Marotta Hall had been used by the popes for audiences and consistory meetings. Stern divided the large space to create Napoleon's bedroom and bath. Carlo Albacini produced the bedroom's porphyry fireplace. Next door in the bathroom, Pelagio Palagi alluded to Napoleon's accession with images of mythological investiture and weaponry, including five canvases inspired by the *Iliad* and the *Aeneid.*

In 1806, the year Ingres arrived in Rome, his portrait *Napoleon on the Imperial Throne* was an abject failure in Paris. Now he was hired to execute the ceiling painting for Napoleon's bedroom, along with two works for Marie Louise's second salon. Knowing Napoleon's passion for the poem *Ossian,* Baron Martial Daru, Intendant of the Crown Assets, suggested the subject for the oval ceiling painting. In a letter to Napoleon in 1797, Jean-Pierre-Louis de Fontanes, future Grand Master of the Imperial

University, wrote: "It is said that you always have *Ossian* tucked away in your pocket, even in battle, like some sort of bard of valour."[17]

Billed as a translation of an epic cycle of Scottish poems from the early dark ages, *Ossian* turned out to be written in the eighteenth century by Scot James Macpherson from fragments of ancient sagas. Like Homer's *Odyssey*, the blind bard Ossian sings about the life of the Scottish warrior Fingal, with subjects taken from ancient Roman history. Ingres would buy back *Ossian's Dream* from an art dealer in 1835 when he returned to Rome as director of the French Academy. Back in France, Ingres restored the canvas and continued adding touch-ups until his death (today in the Musée Ingres, Montauban).[18]

In the Emperor's Great Study, created by joining two symmetrical rooms, the décor united Napoleon and Julius Caesar. Adorning the ceiling were groups of *Winged Victories* in white and gold faux mosaic style, and six colorful medallions by Felice Giani of the protecting gods of the Roman Empire against a Wedgwood blue background. The center of the ceiling sported Palagi's large *Julius Caesar Dictating Commentaries,* based on an episode from Plutarch's biography of Caesar. Palagi subbed Napoleon's face for that of Caesar.[19] Napoleon's First Study celebrated victory and war. Giani filled his ceiling battle scene with references to classical art. A frieze by Giuseppe Pacetti and plasterwork expert Pietro Trefogli depicted pairs of *Victories* holding helmets over medallion portraits of the twelve Caesars, Rome's emperors until Diocletian.[20]

The Room of Peace glorified peace as a necessary condition for the arts. Giani created a sacrificial scene for the ceiling, with two altars dedicated to Peace and Janus. Giani also painted the inside panels of the coffers with four tablets depicting personifications of the arts. Canova's student Alessandro D'Este continued the theme with a stuccoed frieze of twenty-six dancing winged figures of *Fame* alternating with twenty-two portrait medallions of Italian and French artists, architects, and musicians. Among the notables are Leonardo, Raphael, Titian, Palladio, and Michelangelo.[21]

A large space in the north wing had functioned as another papal audience hall. Now it was repurposed as the Emperor's Third Salon with decoration comparing Napoleon's achievements with those of antiquity's great commanders. Octagonal ceiling sections by Giani featured allegorical representations of four Virtues—*Strength*, *Justice*, *Abundance*, and *Prudence.*

These alternated with *en grisaille* circular paintings of winged *Victories riding chariots*. Paul Duqueylar replaced the ceiling's central papal coat of arms with an enormous painting, *Trajan distributing the Scepters of Asia*, an allegory for Napoleon distributing wreaths to his family members in Europe.

Below, Danish neoclassical sculptor Bertel Thorvaldsen produced the remarkable *Alexander Frieze*. Three feet tall and nearly 115 feet long, the frieze depicted Alexander the Great's triumphal entry into Babylon—an allusion to Napoleon's upcoming triumphal entry into Rome. Thorvaldsen completed the frieze, considered among his masterpieces, in a record three months for the imperial couple's planned visit.

Two rooms of Pope Paul V's apartment became the Hall of the Emperor. Above the walls dedicated to Charlemagne, Ptolemy Philadelphus, and Pericles was Luigi Agricola's ceiling painting *Justinian Decrees the Pandects*. A bas-relief stucco frieze, Carlo Finelli's *Triumph of Julius Caesar* features carts filled with war booty, soldiers, and elephants. The frieze ended over the entrance with a sacrifice on ancient Rome's sacred Capitoline Hill.[22]

The addition of two walled partitions in the Alexander VII Gallery formed three halls for Marie Louise's apartment. Stern also bricked up thirteen courtyard-facing windows to create continuous wall space. A biblical cycle directed by Pietro da Cortona during Alexander's pontificate was covered over by classical-themed works by Ingres and other artists.[23] Marie Louise's sitting room also boasted a series of ancient battles that included *The Fight of the Thermopylae* by Giacomo Conca, the *Battle of the Trojans for the Body of Patroclus* by David student José Madrazo, *Horatius Cocles on the Bridge* by Luigi Agricola, and Ingres's frieze-like *Romulus' Victory over Acron*.[24]

Ingres's subject was drawn from Plutarch's *Life of Romulus*. After the rape of the Sabines, several neighboring peoples attacked the Romans. Romulus killed Acron, King of the Caeninenses, and went to offer to Jupiter the arms of his enemy. In contrast to the controversial nude classical heroes of his teacher Jacques-Louis David, Ingres "turned the painting into a costume piece," writes Susan Siegfried.[25] To simulate fresco, Ingres executed the huge mythological scene in tempera. (In 1814, Ingres would paint a portrait of the Quirinale's returning resident, *Pope Pius VII in the Sistine Chapel*.)

As Louis Godart describes, among the most beautiful paintings for Monte Cavallo are scenes in the empress's apartment inspired by imagery from imperial iconography and Ovid's *Metamorphosis* thought to be by Livorno artist Giuseppe Sforzi. The latter feature episodes with Mercury, Argus, Io, and Daedalus and Icarus.[26] Also for the apartment, Albacini sculpted a white marble and green porphyry mantel piece with small black marble columns, and designed a floor incorporating fifteen mosaic panels with images of birds removed from Hadrian's Villa in Tivoli.[27]

Work proceeded at a feverish pace in anticipation of the imperial couple's visit, rescheduled for summer 1813 when Napoleon was to stage a spectacular third coronation at St. Peter's.[28] On March 1812, lightning struck the entrance to the Quirinale. Many Romans considered this one of many omens of the impending apocalypse.[29]

Around this time, Antonio Canova left Rome to supervise the installation of his *Venus Italica* at the Uffizi Tribune in Florence. It had been nine years since he received the commission to replace the famous *Medici Venus,* purloined by Napoleon in 1802 from Palermo where it had been moved for safekeeping.

From the start, the project had been mired in politics. In June 1803, Louis I, king of Etruria, died. Four years later, his widow was forced to abdicate when France annexed Tuscany and Napoleon installed his sister Elisa Baciocchi as grand duchess. Not excited about paying for a public work commissioned by her predecessor, Elisa persuaded her brother to compensate Canova in 1812.

When *Venus Italica* arrived in Florence on April 29, it was displayed on the plinth of the *Medici Venus.* Canova arrived a few days later, insisting that another pedestal be found. In a May 9 letter to Cicognara, President of Venice's Accademia, Canova wrote that the newly installed Venus had received a reception he would never have dared to expect.[30]

For the Florentines and the rest of Italy, it was worth the wait. "When I saw this divine work of Canova," wrote poet Ugo Foscolo, "I sighed with a thousand desires, for really, if the *Medici Venus* is a most beautiful goddess, this is a most beautiful woman."[31]

⚜

Napoleon's ambition was to fold the various territories and countries of Europe into the First Empire, like Rome did with its extensive network of provinces. "One of my first grand ideas was the consolidation, the concentration of the same geographic peoples who were dispersed and fragmented by revolutions and politics. In Europe there are thirty million French, fifteen million Spaniards, fifteen million Italians, thirty million Germans, and twenty million Poles; I want to make of each one nation," he declared.[32]

A month after the Grande Armée's June 1807 victory at Friedland, Napoleon and Alexander I signed the Treaty of Tilsit. Though Russia escaped land concessions and reparations, under the terms of the treaty it was prohibited from trading with Britain. Russia did not comply, allowing English ships in its ports. This was all the excuse Napoleon needed to begin preparing for an invasion of Russia.

This time, Napoleon's sycophantic courtiers spoke up, voicing serious concerns. Among them were his most loyal aides Berthier and Duroc, along with Caulaincourt, Dorosnel, Turenne, and Narbonne.[33] But determined to enforce his Continental blockade and crush France's global rival, Napoleon rejected their warning.

He had already defeated the Russians twice. The Grande Armée was twice as large as the Russian army. It was to be another quick campaign. In 1812 "some thought Napoleon would not stop with Russia," writes David Markham. They believed the emperor would follow Alexander the Great's footsteps and continue from Russia to India.[34]

In late May 1812, Napoleon hosted a magnificent "court of kings" in Dresden attended by the kings of Saxony, Prussia, and Westphalia, along with Austria's Francis I. Throughout the dinners, plays, and concerts, Napoleon's court upstaged the others. "The ladies of the Empress of Austria felt like Cinderellas compared to the glittering duchesses attending the Empress of the French," writes Philip Mansel.[35] A minor rivalry developed between Marie Louise and her stepmother, the Austrian empress. It was here in Dresden that Marie Louise met the charming Count Adam Albert von Neipperg, her future lover and husband.

On May 29, Napoleon left Dresden to take charge of Grande Armée. By June, the army was assembled in eastern Germany. Like the Roman legions that included conscripts from its vanquished enemies, the Grande Armée's half-million-plus soldiers included conscripts from Prussia, Austria, and other defeated territories. With magnificent fanfare, Napoleon reviewed his troops on the west bank of the Niemen River on June 22. Reminiscent of Apollodorus's bridge over the Danube for Trajan, Napoleon's engineers built a pontoon bridge over the Niemen.

On June 24, while the ailing Pius VII was being secretly transferred to Fontainebleau, Napoleon led the Grande Armée across the river into Russian-controlled Poland. Four days later, his forces reached Vilnius, meeting no opposition from Russian troops. Around this time, Napoleon got word that Arthur Wellesley, Marquess of Wellington, and his Anglo-Portuguese army had advanced to Madrid.

Napoleon's economic war on Britain was intended to force the nation to sue for peace. But the European blockade had drastic consequences on Britain's trading partners like Portugal. After Napoleon occupied the Iberian Peninsula, Spain and Portugal revolted, giving Wellesley, the future Duke of Wellington, an entrée. In late July, Wellesley defeated French troops near Salamanca, Spain, a major supply depot. Now Napoleon sent reinforcements to trap the Anglo-Portuguese. Though Wellesley's army would retreat to Portugal, the invasion of Spain's capital did irreparable harm to Joseph Bonaparte's shaky rule.

With Napoleon in Russia, Marie Louise had withdrawn to the privacy of Saint-Cloud. Napoleon instructed her to reassure the public by taking their young son for public strolls in his carriage. The empress celebrated August 15, her husband's birthday and feast day of Saint Napoleon, by receiving the diplomatic corps at the Tuileries and attending a Te Deum at Notre Dame.[36]

On September 6, the day before the Battle of Borodino, Napoleon received a letter from his wife along with François Gérard's new portrait of their son, *The King of Rome* sitting in his cradle. The proud emperor displayed the picture on a chair in front of his tent. As Leo Tolstoy describes in *War and Peace*, "He was a very pretty child with curly hair and eyes like those of Christ in the Sistine Madonna, and he had been portrayed playing cup and ball. The ball represented the earth and the stick in his other hand was meant as a sceptre."[37]

The next day, the Grande Armée fought the Russians at Borodino, a village seventy miles west of Moscow. The bloodbath claimed seventy thousand lives and did not produce the decisive result Napoleon had sought. It was a Pyrrhic victory—named for Pyrrhus of Epirus whose army suffered irreplaceable losses while defeating the Romans at the Battles of Heraclea and Asculum in 280 and 279 B.C.E. Though the Russian army retreated, Napoleon's forces like those of Pyrrhus were depleted and exhausted.

On September 14, French troops entered Moscow. Napoleon moved into the Kremlin, waiting for the civil authorities to present him with the keys to the city and Alexander to surrender. But the capital was eerily empty. By early October, Napoleon was still waiting for the tsar to sue for peace.

Pierre Duroc arranged to have a crate of artworks shipped to Paris and penned a letter to Vivant Denon, who had recently been named a Baron of the Empire. "Your presence would certainly have been necessary in Moscow to choose the historical monuments and treasures which should complete the numerous collections we possess in Paris," wrote Duroc.[38]

A week later, all hell broke loose. A fire started in the Bazaar. There was no means to fight the flames, no pumps or hoses. Later that night, more fires erupted in the suburbs, believed to be the result of carelessness by soldiers. The following night fires raged across the north part of the city, spreading over the next few days. The Russians had set their capital on fire intentionally. With its numerous wood buildings, three-quarters of Moscow was destroyed.

Napoleon had placed Gérard's portrait of his young son in his bedroom at the Kremlin. Now from the window, he watched his plans go up in flames.

Still hoping for the Russians to surrender, Napoleon wrote to Alexander. "My lord Brother. Beautiful, magical Moscow exists no more. How could you consign to destruction the loveliest city in the world, a city that has taken hundreds of years to build?" Alexander refused to negotiate, declaring that the burning of Moscow "illuminated his soul."[39]

TWO

RETRENCHMENT

In mid-October, after thirty-five days at the Kremlin, Napoleon ordered his army to retreat from the capital. But the devastation continued. With winter approaching, food and supplies were running out. Freezing temperatures led to massive deaths from hypothermia and starvation. An outbreak of typhus killed 140,000 of his soldiers.

Napoleon's adviser Armand de Caulaincourt described the epic human tragedy: "The cold was so intense that bivouacking was no longer supportable. One constantly found men who, overcome by the cold, had been forced to drop out and had fallen to the ground, too weak or too numb to stand. . . . Sleep comes inevitably, and to sleep is to die. I tried in vain to save a number of these unfortunates. The only words they uttered were to beg me, for the love of God, to go away and let them sleep.

"To hear them, one would have thought sleep was their salvation. Unhappily, it was a poor wretch's last wish. But at least he ceased to suffer, without pain or agony. Gratitude, and even a smile, was imprinted on his discoloured lips. What I have related about the effects of extreme cold, and of this kind of death by freezing, is based on what I saw happen to thousands of individuals. The road was covered with their corpses."[1]

When Napoleon reached Poland, he learned of an attempted coup d'état in his absence on October 23. After Napoleon's accession to emperor, Brigadier General Claude François de Malet had resigned, becoming governor of Pavia, then Rome. An accusation of conspiracy by Eugène de Beauharnais led to his imprisonment. Now Malet and four other generals published a proclamation announcing Napoleon's death in Russia and establishment of a provisional government:

"Citizens, Bonaparte is no more! The avengers of humanity have dealt a blow to the tyrant. . . . Let us work together on public regeneration, let us become imbued with this great endeavor . . . which in the eyes of Europe will cleanse the nation of the infamies committed by the tyrant." The plot was thwarted by Paris's military governor General Hulin. Malet and thirteen coconspirators were quickly arrested and court-martialed. By month's end, they were executed by firing squad.[2]

Napoleon abandoned his dwindling army and rushed back to France, arriving in Paris on December 18. His first order of business was to rebuild his forces, decimated from battle, starvation, desertion, typhus, and suicide. The combat force had been reduced to less than ten thousand men. New conscripts included the elderly, the young, and semi-invalids, along with more soldiers from the Rhine Confederation and Italy. At the beginning of January, the Senate voted to allow sedentary troops to serve abroad, freeing up some 350,000 men.

On January 19, 1813, the issue of Pius VII came to a head. On their way back from hunting at Grosbois, Napoleon and Marie Louise stopped at Fontainebleau. Since the previous June, Pius had been held in the former Queen Mother's apartment at the château. Napoleon saw an opportunity to break the isolated pontiff who had been without his advisers since his abduction on July 1809.

For six days, Napoleon coaxed and pressured the pope. On January 25, an exhausted Pius finally relented, signing a concordat entirely favorable to France. Pius ceded his temporal powers and condemned cardinals who had refused to acknowledge Napoleon's marriage to Marie Louise. Napoleon also gained the authority to name all bishops in the empire except in

Rome's immediate vicinity.[3] Pius thought the agreement was a draft for future discussion, but it was presented to the public as the "concordat of Fontainebleau" and published by the *Moniteur officiel* as the "law of the Empire."[4]

Shortly after the signing of the agreement, Pius's adviser Cardinal Bartolomeo Pacca was released from the Fenestrelle fortress. In his memoirs, Pacca describes how he arrived at Fontainebleau to discover Pius seriously ill and so upset that he thought the pontiff would lose his mind. According to Pacca, Napoleon had grabbed the buttons on the pope's soutane, like he did with officers who annoyed him. Pius told Pacca that the negotiations with Napoleon had begun as a comedy and would end as a tragedy.

"I knew the modest and easy character of the pope, who was brought down by the sufferings of a long captivity;" wrote Pacca. "I knew he was surrounded by people beholden to the Emperor, timid people and courtiers; I understood then that the fight between Gregoire Barnabé Chiaramonti and Napoleon Bonaparte would be unequal, and I foresaw which side would be the victor."[5]

The concordat of Fontainebleau proved short-lived. On March 24, Pius, still in captivity, revoked his approval, repudiating the agreement.[6]

In addition to rebuilding the army, Napoleon busied himself with other projects—mining iron deposits, extracting salt from marshes, and road building. But frustration soon set in. Like Rome's emperors, Napoleon paid for his public works from the spoils of war. As Tom Stammers writes, "The beautification of his capital was to be paid for not from state coffers, but from the indemnities extracted from defeated foreign powers, and so construction happened in fits and starts."[7] Of course, the calamitous invasion of Russia did not produce the anticipated spoils. Napoleon found himself with no alternative but to abandon several pet projects.

Work stopped at his mega-palace for the king of Rome. Conceived as Napoleon's most grandiose statement, the palace's final proposal by Percier and Fontaine never went beyond sketches. By 1815, the palatial complex had shrunk to a garden pavilion.[8] Like the Arc de Triomphe, work on

Napoleon's Temple to the Glory of the Grande Armée was also proceeding at a snail's pace. In 1813, with only the foundations visible, Napoleon gave up on his original idea and downscaled the project to a church.

Despite his financial straits, Napoleon asked Fontaine and engineer Louis Bruyère to survey the public projects across Paris. Their 1813 status report, "Rapports sur les édifices publics de Paris faits par l'ordre de l'Empereur," was divided by type: "abattoirs," "barrières," "bibliothèques," and "boulevards" to "rues," "théâtres," and "temples."[9]

Napoleon clung to one last monument. By imperial decree on February 9, 1810, he had ordered construction of a colossal fountain for eastern Paris at the Place de la Bastille, formerly occupied by the demolished fortress. The fountain was to take ". . . the form of an elephant in bronze from the melted canons of the Spanish insurgents; this elephant will carry a tower like those of the ancients; water will spring from its trunk. Measures will be taken so that this elephant will be finished and opened by December 2, 1811 at the latest," (the anniversary of Napoleon's coronation).[10]

Napoleon was not in Paris for the historic storming of the Bastille on July 14, 1789. Though the ensuing Revolution and its aftermath would lead to his meteoric rise to power, Napoleon remained wary of mass protests and mobs. Simon Schama writes that the colossal elephant fountain on the historic site represented "the superiority of imperial conquest over chaotic insurrection."[11]

Not surprisingly, rivals Dominique-Vivant Denon and Pierre Fontaine took opposing sides on the exotic-themed fountain. Denon embraced the idea. In a July 1810 letter to the new interior minister Joseph Fouché, he wrote: "Believe, I beg you, my lord, that in this operation, as in all those which His Majesty has deigned to entrust to me, I will bring the most severe economy of public money and that my care will equal my zeal so that this monument is worthy of the time."[12]

Fontaine expressed his strong disapproval directly to Napoleon: "Sir, I've already been consulted on this project. And I've already criticized the idea of elevating on the pedestal a monstrous image of an elephant and to make it the subject of a fountain. I could never really visualize what effect this enormous mass will produce. A monument of an elephant will always be for the intellectuals a grand subject of criticism to which reason will have a hard time rationalizing."[13] In the end, Napoleon ignored Fontaine and proceeded with the grandiose project.

The idea for an elephant fountain first surfaced in an October 1808 note from Napoleon to his former interior minister Emmanuel Crétet requesting drawings and a cost estimate. A symbol of wisdom, strength, and longevity, the elephant was among the potential emblems proposed for the new French Empire in 1804. Napoleon's choice of an elephant fountain was a conscious effort to further associate his rule with antiquity when elephants were "status symbols of ancient warfare."[14]

In a nod to antiquity, Alexander VII commissioned Bernini's *Elephant and Obelisk* for Rome's Piazza della Minerva by the Pantheon. Unveiled shortly after the pope's death in 1667, the monument features an elephant carrying an Egyptian obelisk from Sais (discovered in 1655). Bernini grudgingly added a support beneath the elephant, causing it to be nicknamed "Procino della Minerva," or Minerva's Piggy, due to its heavy appearance. As William Heckscher describes, Bernini was inspired by Francesco Colonna's popular 1499 novel *Poliphilo's Strife of Love in a Dream* in which the protagonist meets a stone elephant carrying an obelisk.[15]

During his 1806 occupation of Berlin, Napoleon saw an elephant motif on a clock in Frederick the Great's cabinet. He would also have been familiar with elephant depictions at Fontainebleau. *The Royal Elephant* by Rosso Fiorentino is part of a fresco cycle in the François I Gallery (renamed the Emperor's Gallery in 1805). An allegorical portrait of François, the white elephant wears a shield on its forehead adorned with the king's emblem, a salamander. An elephant also appears woven in the *Triumph of Mars* tapestry in the château's Great Salon.[16]

For Napoleon, who considered himself successor of Alexander the Great, Caesar, and Hannibal, the image of an elephant was especially appealing. In addition to hauling military supplies, pachyderms were the army tanks of antiquity, causing terror on the battlefield. Pliny the Elder, who penned thirteen chapters on elephants in *Natural History*, wrote that "male elephants when broken in serve in battle and carry castles manned with armed warriors on their backs; they are the most important factor in eastern warfare, scattering the ranks before them and trampling armed soldiers underfoot."[17]

Alexander the Great assembled his own elephant corps and installed a group of elephants to guard his palace in Babylon.[18] Commemorative silver decadrachms minted in Babylon portray the warrior-king in his final battle, attacking Indian king Poros on an elephant. After Alexander's premature death, the vehicle carrying his body sported a painting featuring elephants. Ptolemy Philadelphus minted gold and silver coins depicting Alexander wearing an "elephant-scalp" headdress along with gold staters depicting a deified Alexander driving a chariot drawn by four elephants.[19] Elephants were taken from India until Ptolemy discovered the smaller forest species from northern Africa. After training, the captured animals were shipped up the Red Sea to Egypt on a new fleet of "elephant carriers."[20]

Around 218 B.C.E., Carthaginian general Hannibal led some three dozen elephants (along with one hundred thousand men) across the Alps into Italy where he used the animals with little success against the Romans.[21] Pachyderms could be unreliable. In 202 B.C.E., when Hannibal tried breaking the Roman's diamond-shaped formation with eighty elephants at Zama, Carthage (modern Tunisia), Scipio ordered trumpets sounded to confuse the animals. The animals abruptly turned on the Carthaginians; Scipio returned to Rome with many of his enemy's elephants.[22]

During Rome's civil war, Metellus Scipio assembled elephants to face Julius Caesar in 46 B.C.E. at Thapsus (modern Tunisia). Before the animals could charge, Caesar ordered his infantry to attack the elephants, causing them to panic and retreat through their own lines.[23] Among the coins Julius Caesar issued was the silver "elephant denarius" produced in huge numbers to reward his legions. The obverse featured images of priestly symbols related to Caesar's religious title *pontifex maximus;* the reverse pictured an elephant trampling a snake with the legend "Caesar."[24] According to Debra Nousek, Caesar's choice of an elephant for his coinage may have been a politically motivated attack on his rivals who had also used this iconography.[25]

Because Alexander the Great was associated with the elephant, many of his successors used the animal's image to assert their connection to the illustrious commander. Elephants decorated Hellenistic coins in a number of forms—driving a quadriga, a head in profile, and standing or walking. The elephant headdress was worn by the personification of "Africa" on the coins of some Roman emperors, including Hadrian and Septimius Severus.[26]

In addition to their combat role, elephants participated in Rome's triumphal processions. Pompey even tried to ride into Rome on an elephant quadriga. This proved less than heroic when the pachyderms got stuck in the city gate. Romans made the long-lived elephant a symbol of eternity.[27]

To design Napoleon's elephant fountain, Denon chose architect Jacques Cellerier. The first stone was laid on December 2, 1808, the fourth anniversary of Napoleon's coronation. By 1810, work was proceeding on the ground works, with the vaults and underground pipes and main pool completed by 1812. But busy with the restoration of Saint Denis, Cellerier delegated the fountain project to Jean-Antoine Alavoine with whom he had worked on a new Théâtre des Variétés in 1807.

Napoleon did not like Alavoine's early plans, deeming them too simple. He was after something grander, a monument to evoke the exoticism of Asia and the Orient. Napoleon wrote his interior minister reminding him that the elephant for the Bastille fountain should resemble the war elephants of antiquity. He also wanted the bronze elephant to bear a tower, like the elephants of antiquity who carried soldiers inside towers strapped to their backs.

Alavoine went back to the drawing board, producing a series of variations for the three-story bronze elephant. To please Napoleon, he adorned the elephant with drapery and ornaments. He experimented by topping the elephant with a tower, or howdah, and a throne. In one drawing, a Greek warrior stood atop the elephant, holding a round shield in one hand, aiming a spear with the other. Another sketch featured a turbaned dignitary offering a sword as a gift, perhaps a reference to the 1807 visit of the Shah of Persia's ambassador who offered Napoleon the sabers of Tamerlane and Shah Thamas Kuli-Khan.[28] Alavoine also sketched various mythological gods for the base, along with multiple water effects.

In Alavoine's final model from 1812, the fountain measured about fifty-two feet in length and forty-nine feet in height (seventy-eight feet including the pedestal). The medieval crenelated tower atop the elephant's back and the animals' folds of drapery and harness were all to be made of gilded bronze. On its forehead, the elephant sported an ornament with a sun, symbol of the east. This detail may have been a reference to Alexander the Great, who after defeating Poror at Hydaspe, consecrated the elephant he rode to the sun.[29] A stairway inside the elephant led up to an observation platform on its back.

On his return from the Russian campaign, Napoleon visited the construction site at the Place de Bastille in 1813. An estimated 177 tons of bronze was needed to cast the enormous elephant. With insufficient Spanish cannon, it would be necessary to supplement the material with cannons from Friedland. Almost two years behind schedule, with only the water basin finished, the project's slow progress angered Napoleon. When the emperor complained that there were not enough workers at the site, the contractor replied that workers had all been conscripted to the army. Napoleon ordered that all available workers be hired for the project, declaring, "It is precisely the old workers who are most in need of work."[30]

Alavoine recruited Pierre-Charles Bridan to create a full-size model using plaster over a wooden frame. Installed in 1814, the seventy-eight-foot-tall model was watched by a guard named Levasseur who lived in one of the elephant's legs.

⚜

Napoleon's defeat in Russia damaged his invincible reputation and weakened French hegemony across Europe. Emboldened by the disastrous Russia campaign, Prussia and Austria broke their tense alliances with France, joining Russia, England, Sweden, Spain, Portugal, and a number of German states to form the Sixth Coalition.

By the end of March, Napoleon ordered the movement of some two hundred thousand troops toward the Elbe. By April, the force was concentrated in the angle formed by the Elbe and Saale, threatening Berlin and Dresden. In April, the Senate agreed to mobilize the half-trained members of the National Guard, which Napoleon had created for home defense.

In May 1813, Napoleon was visiting the 1632 battlefield at Lützen in Saxony. Part of the Thirty Years' War, the battle was a victory for the Protestants, but took the life of Sweden's Protestant king Gustav II Adolph. Standing near the Gustav Adolphus Monument, Napoleon was pointing out the various sites to his staff and describing the events when he heard the sound of cannon. Rallying his troops, he led his own Battle of Lützen. Leaving the leading troops to fight the combined Russian and Prussian forces, Napoleon organized a reserve force. When both sides were exhausted, he sent some one hundred guns forward and marched his reserve through the gap.

During the battle Napoleon reportedly told his troops: "Remember, gentlemen, what a Roman emperor said: 'The corpse of an enemy always smells sweet.'" This was probably not the most propitious emperor to be quoting. The author, Vitellius, was one of Rome's most cruel emperors, the last of Nero's three successors. Declared emperor by his legions in Germany at the start of 69 C.E., Vitellius went on to defeat Galba and Otho before marching into Rome in April. In *Lives of the Twelve Caesars*, Suetonias reports: "When he [Vitellius] came to the plains where the battle was fought and some shuddered with horror at the mouldering corpses, he had the audacity to encourage them by the abominable saying, that the odour of a dead enemy was sweet and that of a fellow-citizen sweeter still."[31]

According to Suetonias, the gluttonous Vitellius gouged on four feasts a day and drank so much that his cheeks were always red. On one large platter "he mingled the livers of pike, the brains of pheasants and peacocks, the tongues of flamingoes and the milt of lampreys, brought by his captains and triremes from the whole empire, from Parthia to the Spanish strait."[32] After eight months, Vitellius was murdered in especially gruesome fashion by Vespasian's forces. With his arms tied behind back, Vitellius was dragged to the Forum, tortured and pelted with dung, dragged off with a hook, and tossed into the Tiber. In the nineteenth century, the French Academy sponsored a contest for the Prix de Rome with submissions on Vitellius's grisly death scene.

The Peninsular War in Spain raged on. In June 1813, the armies of Great Britain, Portugal, and Spain defeated the French force led by Joseph Bonaparte at the Battle of Vitoria, south of Bilbao. With Wellington advancing toward the Pyrenees and the Franco-Spanish border, the French were forced to abandon Andalusia. By early July, Napoleon was in Dresden to negotiate for peace, with Austria mediating. When none of the parties would negotiate, Napoleon became convinced of Metternich's duplicity.

"I saw Metternich and he seemed to me to be running many intrigues, much misrepresenting Papa Franz," he wrote Marie Louise. "The Emperor has been deceived by Metternich, who had sold his soul to the Russians; furthermore, he is a man who thinks that politics is a question of lying."[33]

Against his nature, Napoleon had to wait for the Allies' next moves. That summer, he wrote detailed instructions to ready the Grande Armée. In addition to arms, clothing, and food, the army had an urgent need for some thirty thousand horses, saddles, and harnesses. On August 9, Austria declared war. In anticipation of large battles, the October 9 sénatus-consulte signed by the empress called up 280,000 new recruits, known as "Marie Louise men."

Just as this was happening, the Allied armies with a combined 325,000 soldiers were converging on Leipzig, Saxony, where they hoped to trap Napoleon's force of two hundred thousand men.[34] On the eve of the Battle of Leipzig, also known as the Battle of the Nations, Napoleon said: "Between a battle lost and a battle won, the distance is immense and there stand empires."[35] The following day, Napoleon distributed eagles and colors to three battalions. As each standard was unfurled and given to the officers, Napoleon addressed the troops:

"Soldiers of the 26th regiment of light infantry, I entrust you with the French eagle. It will be your rallying point. You swear to abandon it but with life? You swear never to suffer an insult to France. You swear to prefer death to dishonor. You swear!" With their swords raised, soldiers and officers responded "We swear!"[36]

Napoleon's rousing speech echoed that in Paris nine years earlier. As France's newly crowned emperor, he had distributed eagle standards to regiments of various departments based on the Aquila of the Roman legions. There, too, his men swore to defend the standards with their lives. In *The Distribution of the Eagle Standards* (1810), Jacques-Louis David depicted Napoleon blessing the standards. Like the *adlocutio* of Rome's emperors portrayed in ancient sculpture and coins, Napoleon is shown with his right arm raised, about to address his troops. Because of his impending divorce, Napoleon instructed David to remove Joséphine from the canvas.

During Rome's battles, it was sometimes necessary to conceal the eagle standards. A standard-bearer in Julius Caesar's legions recorded that in times of danger, he pulled off the eagle and hid it in the folds of his girdle. A wounded or dying standard-bearer was supposed to get the standard to his general. Rome went to great lengths to reclaim its standards. The central relief on the cuirass of the famous statue of *Augustus of Prima Porta* shows the return of the eagles lost to the Parthians decades earlier. Securing their return was among Augustus's greatest diplomatic feats.

After three days of combat, Napoleon gave the order to retreat on October 19. Some 47,000 men were lost and another 38,000 captured, making Leipzig statistically the worst defeat of Napoleon's career.[37] During the 1813 campaign, thirty-three generals, as well as Marshals Bessières and Poniatowski, were also killed.[38]

Between September 27 and October 14, Napoleon hosted a summit with Alexander I and various German sovereigns at Erfurt in central Germany. Intense negotiations took place during daily meetings between Napoleon and Alexander. Arriving a day before Napoleon, Talleyrand told the tsar, "Sire, what have you come to do here? It is up to you to save Europe and you will only succeed by standing up to Napoleon. The French people is civilised, its ruler is not; the ruler of Russia is civilised, his people is not. It is thus up to the Russian ruler to be the ally of the French people."[39] At Erfurt, Joachim Murat also betrayed his brother-in-law, making a secret deal with the Allies in exchange for a guarantee of his Naples throne.

Back in Paris, Napoleon issued an emergency levy to muster 120,000 recruits. With the treasury depleted, there was a real concern about the war ministry continuing to function. Toward this end, Napoleon doubled the taxes on tobacco, postage, and salt, and suspended payment of pensions and salaries.[40] Without sufficient forces in Spain, Napoleon was forced to release Ferdinand VII and restore him to the Spanish throne. He held Joseph responsible. "All the nonsense that takes place in Spain comes from my misguided complacency for the King who is not only incapable of commanding an army, but does not even know how to deliver justice and leave the command to the military," he wrote General Henri Jacques Guillaume Clarke on July 1, 1813.

Along with his exiled court and sister-in-law Catherine of Westphalia, Joseph was now under house arrest at Mortefontaine in Oise, northern France. In happier days, the castle had hosted the weddings of Caroline and Joachim Murat and Camillo Borghese and Pauline Bonaparte. Ever the matchmaker, Napoleon proposed that Ferdinand VII marry Joseph's thirteen-year-old daughter Zénaïde to repair French and Spanish relations. Zénaïde instead would marry her ornithologist cousin, Lucien's son Charles Lucien Bonaparte.

Napoleon also denounced Jérôme for abandoning Westphalia. "In general, I feel humiliated by the ridiculous role played by this prince who has neither administrative qualities nor common sense," Napoleon wrote Cambacérès. "If he had remained in Cassel, his troops would not have been overwhelmed and he would have retained control of his kingdom. If he had had the first notions of common sense, he would have had around 8 to 10 thousand French, Swiss, and Italians around him . . ."

Already deposed from the throne of Holland, Louis volunteered his services after the evacuation of Amsterdam. Napoleon responded by threatening to have him arrested. In a letter to Cambacérès, Napoleon wrote:

"It is my destiny to see myself constantly betrayed by the dreadful ingratitude of men to whom I have shown the most generosity, especially by this one, for whose own education I deprived myself of everything, even necessities, at the age of twenty. You know that the libelous words he published against me were printed with emphasis by Austria, after the declaration of war, as if to blacken my character and increase the animosity that was erupting on all sides."

THREE

FUNERAL OF THE EMPIRE

After the defeat at Leipzig, Prussian, Russian, and Austro-Hungarian troops threatened France from the north and east, and Wellington's forces were approaching from the south over the Pyrenees. On New Year's 1814, Allied forces crossed the French border and headed for Paris.

Napoleon did not want to give the Allies the public relations coup of freeing the pope. After five years of captivity, Pius VII was released on January 23. The next day, Napoleon embraced twenty-three-year-old Marie Louise and their three-year-old son and left to lead the campaign for France. He would never see them again.

With the Allies closing in on the capital, Marie Louise was persuaded to leave Paris by Henri Clarke, who had received the order from Napoleon. On March 29, she and her toddler son, along with other members of the Bonaparte family, left the Tuileries Palace for Rambouillet, then Blois. As their carriages departed, a crowd gathered in silence, "watching the funeral of the Empire," wrote Napoleon's longtime private secretary

Claude-François Méneval who would later accompany the empress and king of Rome to Vienna.[1] Two days later, the Allies entered Paris.

From Fontainebleau, Napoleon learned that his brother Joseph had fled to Rambouillet. On April 3, the Senate voted to depose Napoleon. With his generals deserting, Napoleon decided to abdicate in favor of his son. But the Senate, headed by Talleyrand, had other plans. The cunning foreign minister succeeded in restoring Louis XVI's exiled brother to the throne as Louis XVIII.

On April 6, Napoleon penned his abdication at a mahogany table in his drawing room at Fontainebleau. "The allied powers having proclaimed that the emperor Napoleon was the sole obstacle to the re-establishment of peace in Europe, the emperor Napoleon, faithful to his oath, declares that he renounces, for himself and his children, the throne of France and Italy, and that there is no sacrifice, even of life itself, that he is not willing to make in the interests of France."[2]

On the night of April 12, in his bedroom at Fontainebleau, Napoleon swallowed a vial of poison that he had carried around his neck during the Russian campaign. For the generals of antiquity like Hannibal and Mark Antony, suicide was an honorable alternative to capture by the enemy. But over the year and a half, the mix had lost its potency. A doctor managed to save Napoleon's life. Five days later, he wrote his ex-wife Joséphine: "My fall is great, but . . . I shall substitute the pen for the sword [to write] the history of my reign. . . . Remember him who has never forgotten you and never will. Goodbye, Joséphine."

At noon on April 20, Napoleon descended Fontainebleau's monumental horseshoe staircase to the White Horse courtyard where members of the Imperial Guard stood waiting. Napoleon ordered the two ranks of *grognards* to form a circle around him. Then he delivered his famous last speech, described by Chateaubriand: "Soldiers of my Old Guard, for twenty years I've always found you on the path of honor and glory. Do not abandon France—love her always, love her well. I bid you farewell, and I kiss your flags."[3] Napoleon embraced a flag belonging to the first regiment of the infantrymen of the Imperial Guard. After half a minute, he held up his left hand and said, "Farewell! Preserve me in your memories! Adieu, my children!" As Andrew Robert writes, ". . . officers and men wept . . . while others were prostrated with grief, and all the others cried 'Vive l'Empereur!'"[4]

The Treaty of Fontainebleau exiled Napoleon to the tiny Mediterranean island of Elba off the coast of Italy with the imperial title Emperor of Elba, four hundred troops, and an annual income of two million francs. Marie Louise was given the duchies of Parma, Piacenza, and Guastalla, with her son as heir. En route Napoleon was initially welcomed by locals, but an angry mob confronted his entourage in Provence. On April 29, Napoleon left Fréjus on the British frigate HMS *Undaunted*, ironically from the same jetty that he had arrived at fifteen years earlier after the Egypt campaign.[5] When Napoleon disembarked at Elba on May 3, he was greeted by a welcome committee and cries of "Vive l'Empereur!" and "Vive Napoleon!" The same day, after twenty-three years in exile, the restored Bourbon king Louis XVIII returned to Paris.

In the middle of the crisis, Vivant Denon continued Napoleon's propaganda campaign. He arranged the production and distribution of a print showing Napoleon's son praying "for my father and for France."[6] In late July, the museum director organized the Salon at the Musée Napoléon. In February, the Italian "primitives" he had stolen in 1811 arrived in Paris. Now he displayed some eighty-two of these, two-thirds of the 124 pictures on view.[7] Though Fra Angelico was celebrated in his day as Italy's most famous painter, he and his compatriots were largely unknown in early nineteenth-century France. Two hundred thousand visitors descended on the Musée Napoléon's Salon Carré to see these beautiful pictures for the first time.[8] Around the same time, the Musée Napoléon became the Musée Royal.

Louis XVIII refused to pay Napoleon's pension; by December, he ordered Napoleon's personal property confiscated. Rather than joining Napoleon in exile, Marie Louise returned to Vienna with their young son. On July 3, Napoleon wrote his wife: "The news you give me about your health and my son gives me great pleasure. I think that you should as much as possible go to Tuscany where there are waters as good and of the same nature as those of Aix in Savoy. . . . My health is good, my feelings for you the same, and my desire to see you and prove it to you very great."

Six weeks later, his positive tone changed dramatically. "I often write to you, I hope you did the same, yet I have not received any of your letters since a few days of your departure from Vienna, I have received no news of my son, this conduct is beastly."[9]

Joséphine appeared more concerned about Napoleon's welfare than Marie Louise. From Malmaison she wrote her ex-husband: "Why can I not fly to you? I have been on the point of quitting France to follow in your footsteps. . . . Say but the word and I depart. It is no longer by words that my sentiments for you are to be proved, and for actions your consent is necessary. Malmaison has been much respected, and I am surrounded by foreign sovereigns but would rather leave."[10]

Among the "foreign sovereigns" who paid their respects to Joséphine was Russia's Alexander I, impressed by Joséphine's four statues by Antonio Canova. According to Christopher Johns, her Canova collection was "for too brief a time, the best in existence, and Malmaison became a pilgrimage site for the sculptor's admirers, including Stendhal and Quatremère."[11]

In February 1813, Joséphine had written Canova: "Your two beautiful statues have arrived without any incident in all their splendor. Because the *Dancer* arrived in time for the public exhibition, it was sent right away, and I'm delighted to tell you that everyone admired the statue. A lot of people came to see it and agreed that it is perfect. I regret that the statue of *Paris* came too late for the public to see at the Salon but some of the art connoisseurs who saw it really enjoyed it. If I was allowed to judge, I like *Paris* better, even though I find the *Dancer* charming. They are now located at opposite ends of my gallery. I never tire of seeing them.

"I think you are doing better than Pygmalion because his masterpieces were made for him, while yours are made for us. My gallery will be complete if I could have the statue of *The Three Graces* between *Paris* and the *Dancer*. I would love to know if you're working on this composition and which sculpture you are working on right now. Everything that comes from your chisel has the potential to be interesting before it's even finished. I take advantage with pleasure of this circumstance to communicate the high value with which I regard you."[12]

It was Joséphine who suggested the subject for *The Three Graces* to Canova. The sculptor depicted Venus's handmaidens sharing a rose. To the left behind them, Canova added a garland of roses to an antique altar, suggesting that the rose-loving Joséphine was Venus, posits Christopher Johns.[13]

During Alexander's first visit to Malmaison on April 16, he met Joséphine's daughter Hortense and her grandchildren. At a subsequent visit, the tsar suggested the family move to Russia, offering them financial assistance and a palace. In an effort to seal the deal, Joséphine presented the tsar with the famous *Gonzaga Cameo*. Fittingly, the ancient sardonyx was thought at the time to be a double portrait of Olympius and her son Alexander the Great who had shown great generosity to the wife of his enemy, Persian king Darius (it was later identified as Ptolemy II Philadelphus and his wife Arsinoe II). The gem's impressive provenance included the Gonzaga Dukes of Mantua, Sweden's Queen Christina, and the Vatican. After French troops removed the stunning cameo from the Vatican, Napoleon gave it to Joséphine.[14]

Joséphine had been allowed to keep the title of empress after the divorce. With a generous allowance, she maintained a luxe lifestyle and her court. On May 24, Joséphine led the tsar and his brothers Nicholas and Michael on a tour of her renowned gardens. It was a rainy day and Joséphine caught a chill that quickly developed into pneumonia. At Hortense's invitation, Alexander visited the ailing Joséphine four days later. On May 29, days before her fifty-first birthday, Joséphine died in the arms of her son Eugène in her swan-shaped bed. Even at the end, she was ". . . entirely covered with ribbons and rose-colored satin."[15]

Two days later, the Treaty of Paris was signed. Some twenty thousand people passed through the vestibule at Malmaison, lit by hundreds of candles. On June 2, Joséphine was buried to the right of the altar inside the sixteenth-century Church of Saint Pierre and Saint Paul in Rueil, near Malmaison. For the tomb, Eugène and his sister Hortense ordered from Pierre Cartellier a marble sculpture of their mother kneeling in her famous pose from Jacques-Louis David's *Coronation*.

Antonio Canova was working on an ambitious group marble for Joséphine in early June when he learned of his patron's death. Two years earlier, Joséphine had commissioned *The Three Graces,* a popular artistic subject since antiquity. She intended to install the famed female trio at Malmaison between his *Paris* and *Dancer.* Canova shipped the marble to Eugène in 1816. From Eugène, Alexander bought all of her Canovas, many French objects, and over one hundred of her best paintings for the Hermitage in St. Petersburg.[16]

Months later on Elba, Napoleon received word of Joséphine death. He shut himself in his rooms for days.

⚜

Madame Mère, long critical of her son, now told him on Elba: "Fulfil your destiny . . . you were not meant to die on this island."[17] In late February 1815, Napoleon heeded her advice, pulling off a daring escape with his guards.

On March 1, Napoleon landed with a small flotilla at the small fishing port of Golfe-Juan near Cannes. Stepping on French soil for the first time in ten months, he addressed the gathered group: "Land of France! Fifteen years ago I adorned you with the title of *Fatherland of the Great Nation*. I salute you again and in the same circumstances, one of your children, the most deserving of this beautiful title, comes once again to save you from anarchy."[18] Napoleon called on the army to shape the nation's future. "Victory shall march in double quick time; the eagle bearing the colors of the nation will fly from steeple to steeple until it reaches the towers of Notre-Dame Cathedral." Troops sent to arrest Napoleon wound up joining him instead.

To avoid a royalist crowd in Provence, Napoleon headed north on an icy mountain path, reaching Grenoble on March 7. Stendhal, who was born in Grenoble, described the enthusiastic reception. The gates had been closed, but locals and troops disobeyed royalist orders and tore them down for Napoleon. He also received a hero's welcome in Lyon where he issued several proclamations—including restoring the tricolor as France's national flag and dissolving royalist assemblies.[19] Another turning point came at Auxerre where Marshal Michel Ney backed the former emperor, describing the Bourbons as unfit to reign, and advising his troops to join Napoleon (that December, Ney would be tried and executed for treason in Paris).

After a stop at Fontainebleau, Napoleon and his entourage entered Paris on the evening of March 20 with three carriages, each drawn by six horses. It was his son's fourth birthday. At the Tuileries Palace, a friendly crowd of several thousand gathered to see the dramatic return. Many of his former ministers greeted him at the top of the stairs, along with his stepdaughter Hortense. At ten the next morning, Napoleon appeared at the window of the palace; by noon he reviewed the troops on the Place du Carrousel.

Napoleon addressed his troops: "Soldiers! In my exile, I heard your voice; your General . . . is restored to you; come and join him. Tear down those colours which the nation has proscribed, and which for twenty-five years served as a rallying signal to all the enemies of France: mount the cockade tricolor: you bore it in the days of our greatness."[20]

By the time Napoleon arrived at Fontainebleau, Louis XVIII had fled to Ghent, Belgium, with the French crown jewels. "Without firing a single shot," as General Marchand described, Napoleon managed to overthrow the Bourbons once again. On March 20, at the courtyard of Fontainebleau, grenadiers shouted, "Vive l'Empereur!" and tossed their caps into the air. After reviewing his troops, Napoleon set off for Paris.[21]

Writing about what he called the "flight of the eagle," Napoleon would later say that he began the escape from Elba as an "adventurer" and became a "Prince." Napoleon's return to power "was perhaps the most audacious scheme ever conceived by his fertile mind," writes Sudhir Hazareesingh.[22] But the triumphant comeback did not last.

From Vienna, the Allies reaffirmed their support for Louis XVIII. It was the equivalent of declaring war against Napoleon. On April 10, Napoleon told politician Benjamin Constant: "I wanted to rule the world, and in order to do this I needed unlimited power . . . I wanted to rule the world—who wouldn't have in my place? The world begged me to govern it; sovereigns and nations vied with one another in throwing themselves under my scepter."

Two days later, on the morning of April 12, Napoleon arrived at Malmaison with his stepdaughter Hortense. "Nowhere, except on the field of battle, did I ever see Bonaparte happier than in the gardens of Malmaison," wrote Bourienne. Now he spent hours alone in the magnificent red tented bedroom where Joséphine had died the previous May.

With Prussian soldiers approaching Malmaison, Napoleon considered leaving for the United States. By June, he changed his mind, dictating a plan to the provisional government for defeating the British and Prussians. He proposed that the government give him temporary command of the army to defend Paris. "I promise on my word as a citizen and soldier to leave the country the very day I save the capital," he wrote. The government refused his offer.

To broaden support, Napoleon made liberal reforms to the constitution. On June 1, he staged the proclamation of the revised constitution on the Champs de Mars. A covered room with benches for fifteen thousand people housed deputations from the regions, the electoral colleges, and representatives of the people. It was open at the center to allow the throne to be seen from the Pont de Iéna. Thirty thousand members of the Imperial Guard and Parisian National Guard lined the route from the Tuileries Palace to the Pont de Iéna and the Champ de Mars; over one hundred thousand people watched.

Napoleon ordered his brothers to wear their lavish *petits costumes.*[23] Napoleon took a seat on a throne against the façade of the École Militaire in an antique-inspired purple outfit. The ensemble did not have the desired effect, according to English observer John Cam Hobhouse. Napoleon appeared "very ungainly and squat" in "his Spanish black bonnet, shaded with plumes, and looped with a large diamond in front. His mantle was of purple velvet edged with broad embroidery of gold on the outside, and lined with white ermine, scarce descending to his ankles, and tied round his throat without any arm-holes."[24]

The acceptance of the new constitution was announced, a Te Deum was sung, and a choral Mass celebrated. The eagles were blessed and the emperor took his place on a second, raised throne two hundred paces into the Champ de Mars. The colonels of the regiments gathered with the officers of the Imperial and National Guard, and they swore their oaths to defend their eagles. General Claude-Étienne Guyot, commander of the Horse Grenadiers of the Guard and an ardent supporter of the emperor, was impressed by the order and calmness in this gathering of people from every part of France and thought that "it must prove to our external enemies and might teach our internal ones that they should despair of again changing the form that the Government wishes to adopt and the chief that France has just chosen once more."

That same day in Bamberg, Bavaria, Napoleon's former chief-of-staff Marshal Berthier fell to his death from an upper-story window. The next day French troops began to concentrate on the border and spies were sent to check the locations of Allied troops. The newly elected chambers took their oath of loyalty to the emperor and the following evening there was a huge fireworks display in the Place de la Concorde. The first units of the Guard left Paris on June 5, and Napoleon sent his chief of staff Marshal Soult to the northern border on June 7, the day of the opening of the Corps

Législatif. On June 9, the Allies signed the Treaty of Vienna reaffirming their intention of defeating Napoleon.

Rather than wait for an attack at home, Napoleon marched his army of 125,000 across the northeast border. In June, he invaded Belgium, hoping to capture Brussels. His strategy was to separate the British and Dutch forces led by Wellington from the Prussian troops led by Blücher and defeat them separately.[25] Though Napoleon did surprise the Allies, the plan backfired. On the evening of June 18, 1815, some twelve miles south of Brussels, combined British, Dutch, and Prussian forces defeated Napoleon's army at the battle of Waterloo. One quarter of the French army died in the carnage.[26]

On June 21, an exhausted Napoleon returned to Paris and the Élysée Palace on rue du Faubourg Saint-Honorè (since 1848, the official residence of the President of France). After their promotion to the throne of Naples in 1808, the Murats sold the mansion to the state. Napoleon gave the residence to Joséphine as part of the divorce settlement, and had stayed here in 1809, 1812, and 1813. Now under pressure from France's legislators, Napoleon signed his abdication in the palace's Salon d'Argent. The One Hundred Days were officially over.

Napoleon spent a final night at the Château de Rambouillet on June 29. Hortense opened Malmaison one last time for her stepfather. Having decided to start over in America, Napoleon spent hours flipping through Alexander von Humboldt's monumental book about the New World. Madame Mère arrived to say goodbye. Before leaving, Napoleon handed his stepdaughter a valuable diamond necklace and told her: "How beautiful Malmaison is, isn't it, Hortense? It would be wonderful if I could stay here."[27] Hortense later wrote: "I feel sad to think how this place, which he visited at the height of his success and fame, now received him reduced to the last stage of wretchedness."[28]

From Malmaison, Napoleon traveled to Rochefort on the Atlantic Coast where he surrendered to the British and made an appeal to the Prince Regent for asylum in England. "I come like Themistocles to sit at the hearth of the British people," he wrote the future George IV, associating himself with the ancient Greek general who served a democracy and then a Persian monarch.[29] But clemency was not what the British had in mind.

One week after Louis XVIII's July 8 return to Paris, Napoleon left France on the English frigate HMS *Bellerophon* across the Channel. At Plymouth, he learned that England was not his final destination. Seventy-one days later, on October 17, the deposed emperor stood on the deck of the *Northumberland* at St. Helena, an island in the South Atlantic over four thousand miles from Paris. "It's not an attractive place," he remarked.[30]

Charles Darwin described the bleak volcanic island as "rising abruptly like a huge black castle from the ocean."[31] "The island of St. Helena is the ideal place to lock away such a character. In such a place, so far away, no scheming of any kind will be possible and, far from Europe, he will be quickly forgotten," declared British prime minister Lord Liverpool.[32]

By December, Napoleon and a small staff had settled into Longwood House. The adjoining outbuildings accommodated his inner circle, including his secretary Emmanuel de Las Cases, Generals Gourgaud, Montholon, and Bertrand (Napoleon's chief of staff), and their wives. Once the owner of some four dozen palaces, Napoleon had packed fifty boxes. Before leaving France for St. Helena, Napoleon asked Vivant Denon to compile a list of books, medals, and engravings to take with him into exile. Among the items were Denon's own *Journey in Lower and Upper Egypt* and engravings of Napoleon's battles. The furnishings included Biennais's campaign kit and bed, along with Percier's athénienne, the yew and silver washbasin, and ewer designed after an ancient Greek tripod. Six dozen dessert plates from the Sèvres Service des Quartiers Généraux provided a travelogue of Napoleon's military campaigns. Isabey's ivory miniatures were among the family portraits.

As Matthew Zarzeczny reports, Napoleon also surrounded himself with souvenirs of his many military heroes—Roman, monarchial, and imperial.[33] Las Cases describes an "Augustus and a Livia, both exceedingly rare; a Continence of Scipio and another antique of immense value given to him by the Pope; a Peter the Great, on a box; another box with Charles V; another with a Turenne; and some, which were in daily use, covered with a collection of medallions of Alexander, Sylla, Mithridates, &c."[34] Beyond the portraits to the left of the fireplace, Napoleon hung Frederick the Great's large silver watch, "which is sort of a morning bell," wrote Las Cases.[35]

Six weeks into the exile, Napoleon swapped his military uniform for a green hunting outfit. But he retained formal court dress, requiring his servants to wear green and gold livery.[36] A British officer supervised his walks. Remarking "I do not have too much of anything but time," Napoleon passed time dictating to Las Cases.[37] On a billiards table that arrived in July 1816, Napoleon spread the maps he had used in battle to dictate an account of his campaigns. A little over a year into their arrival, Las Cases was expelled from the island by the British.

Napoleon weighed in on his ancient heroes, starting with Alexander the Great. He admired the Macedonian's skill in combining Greek and Persian cultures and armies, an achievement he had tried to emulate in Europe. "What I like in Alexander the Great is not his campaigns, which we cannot understand, but his political methods," wrote Napoleon. "At thirty-three he left an immense and firmly established empire, which his generals partitioned among themselves. He possessed the art of winning the love of the nations he defeated. . . . It was most politic of him to go to Amon [to be proclaimed a god]: it was thus he conquered Egypt."[38]

Napoleon also dictated an examination of Julius Caesar to his valet Count Marchand. At the end of each chapter of *Caesar's Wars*, Napoleon added personal observations and details, at times describing where Caesar could have done better. For example, he writes that Caesar's two campaigns in Britain were poorly planned and understaffed; his victories in Gaul were achieved thanks to a better trained army and superior technology, not superior military skills. Napoleon also criticized Caesar's cruelty toward his enemies.

But Napoleon concluded with a defense of Caesar's dictatorship—by extension a defense of his own regime. "Caesar . . . had to fight courageous enemies," wrote Napoleon. "He took great risks in the adventures into which he was pushed by his boldness; his genius got him out of his difficulties. His battles in the Civil War—that's what I call real battles, taking into account the enemies he had to fight as well as the qualities of their generals. He was a man whose genius and boldness were equally great."[39]

Winston Churchill said that Napoleon was the greatest man of action since Caesar. Comparisons between the two strongmen were made by both Napoleon's supporters and detractors. Both rose to power as charismatic young military leaders and secured the loyalty of their soldiers with rewards. Both were decisive leaders who ruled during turbulent times. Like Caesar, Napoleon was absent from his capital for long periods of time. Both were multitaskers.

Marcus Cornelius Fronto reported that Caesar worked on his linguistic treatise *On Analogy*, "writing about the declensions of nouns in the midst of flying weapons and about the aspiration and systems of words amidst the call of the military trumpets." According to Plutarch, Caesar could dictate letters on horseback, to more than one secretary.[40] Madame de Rémusat records that Napoleon's secretaries had to devise short hands to keep up with his dictation. Napoleon's own handwriting was illegible both to himself and others. According to Goethe, Napoleon's mind was the greatest the world had ever produced.[41]

During his exile on St. Helena, Napoleon also reflected on his own life. He recalled his childhood on Corsica fondly. "Happy times! The native earth has invisible charms. Memory embellishes it in all its aspects; the very smell of its soil is so present to my senses that with my eyes closed I could recognize the earth I trod as a small child."[42] He seems to have come to terms with his longtime rival, telling an aide in 1816: "Pius is a real lamb, a wholly good man, a truly upright man whom I esteem, of whom I am very fond, and who, for his part, reciprocates my feeling to some extend I am sure."[43] But there was no reconciliation with his estranged family, most of whom had remained loyal. From St. Helena, he wrote Marie Louise: "Take pity on me for having such a bad family, I who showered them with riches."

Napoleon continued to blame his demise on the failures of his family. "My strength of character has often been praised, but I have been a soft touch, especially for my family, and they knew it well. If . . . they had each imparted a common impetus to the various masses I had entrusted them with, we would have marched to the stars. Everything would have bowed down before us, we would have changed the face of the world . . . I did not have the luck of Genghis Khan with his four sons, who were rivals only when it came to serving well."[44]

PART NINE
LEGACY

"Despite all the attempts made to belittle me, get rid of me or reduce me to silence, it will be difficult to make me disappear completely from public memory."

—Napoleon Bonaparte

ONE

A MORAL LESSON

The Musée Napoléon was the crown jewel in Napoleon's glittering capital. Ascending the grand stairway to the second floor, the Salon Carré opened into the1,200-foot-long Grand Gallery. With nine bays and over 1,100 paintings, the Gallery was an embarrassment of riches. The first bay displayed 107 French paintings, including two dozen Poussins. Six hundred and six Dutch, Flemish, and German pictures filled the next four bays, among them fourteen Van Dycks, fifteen Holbeins, thirty-three Rembrandts, and fifty-four works by Rubens. Denon devoted the last four bays to the Italian schools. Among the 463 paintings were a staggering seven Leonardos, ten Tintorettos, fifteen Veroneses, two dozen Titians, and twenty-five Raphaels.

On the ground floor, a dozen high-ceilinged rooms lined with dark-colored marble housed over four hundred antique statues. Flanked by red granite sphinxes, the *Apollo Belvedere* stood in a niche with ornamental rails in front. *Venus de Medici* had her own room to the left of the *Laocoön*. The *Dying Gladiator* faced the *Torso*; the *Borghese Gladiator* stood near the *Meleager.*[1]

The 1814 Treaty of Paris left in place the looted riches at the Musée Napoléon, now renamed the Musée Royale. The goal was to restore the Bourbon monarchy and not humiliate France. But as Katherine Eustace writes, Napoleon's escape from Elba and the Battle of Waterloo left the Allies in a far less generous mood.[2]

Declaring Napoleon "an Enemy and Disturber of the Tranquility of the World" at the Congress of Vienna, the Allies reduced France to its 1789 pre-Revolution boundaries under the Second Treaty of Paris.[3] Napoleon's young son was sent to live with his Habsburg relatives in Vienna. The Congress of Vienna also addressed the political issue of art repatriation from Paris. As Jonah Siegel writes, "The allies were keenly aware of the cultural force of the museum."[4]

Leading the repatriation drive was the Duke of Wellington. In a letter penned in Paris to Lord Castlereagh on September 23, 1815, Wellington wrote about France's war trophies: "The Allies then, having the contents of the museum justly in their power, could not do otherwise than restore them to the countries from which, contrary to the practice of civilized warfare, they had been torn during the disastrous period of the French revolution and the tyranny of Bonaparte."

"The same feelings which induce the people of France to wish to retain the pictures and statues of other nations would naturally induce other nations to wish, now that success is on their side, that the property should be returned to their rightful owners, and the Allied Sovereigns must feel a desire to gratify them . . ." Wellington concluded. "Not only, then, would it, in my opinion, be unjust in the Sovereigns to gratify the people of France on this matter, at the expense of their own people, but the sacrifice they would make would be impolitic, as it would deprive them of the opportunity of giving the people of France a great moral lesson."[5]

The French resisted repatriation, holding up Napoleon's various treaties as legal proof of permanent ownership. Despite his fierce opposition to Napoleon, Louis XVIII maintained that France was legally entitled to retain the confiscated art and would not cede works now housed at the Louvre or the Tuileries Palace. In his first official speech in 1814, the restored Bourbon king declared: "The masterpieces of the arts belong to us forevermore, by rights more stable and sacred than those of conquest."[6]

On July 10, 1815, Prussian troops arrived at the Musée Royale to retrieve the country's art, including Correggio's *Leda and the Swan*, one of Frederick the Great's favorites. In August, the Austrians formally requested that the French government return their art as well. With the art restitution underway in Paris, Pius VII dispatched Antonio Canova to recover the paintings and antiquities seized in Rome nearly two decades earlier. For the mild-mannered sculptor, the diplomatic mission represented the challenge of a lifetime—pitting him against Louis XVIII, the wily Talleyrand, and Tsar Alexander I. The day after Canova accepted the assignment from the pope at the Quirinale Palace, he made out his will.

On Monday, August 28, Canova arrived in Paris with his stepbrother and personal secretary Giovanni Battista Sartori, armed with little more than letters from the pope. After settling into 23 rue Basse du Remparts, the sculptor delivered a letter from Pius to Prussia's minister Baron Wilhelm von Humboldt.[7] Canova's hope was that Prussia, having already removed its pictures from the Louvre, would be sympathetic to the Italian mission.

Two days later, Canova delivered a similar letter to British foreign secretary Robert Stewart, Lord Castlereagh. It was Castlereagh's undersecretary of state William Richard Hamilton who proved instrumental, helping the sculptor frame the case for the return of Rome's art. Their central argument was that the Treaty of Tolentino should be annulled on the grounds that Pius VI had signed it under extreme duress. "To respect the treaty," Canova argued, "would be to respect that which the wolf dictated to the lamb."

Denon already disliked "this viper Hamilton" for seizing the famous Rosetta Stone and sarcophagus of Nectanebo II from the French at the port of Alexandria during the Egyptian campaign. Now the passionate museum director continued to dig in, penning letters to foreign diplomats and to Louis XVIII's intendant la maison du Roi, the comte de Pradel. "What is most certain is that Mon. Hamilton has behaved in this matter like a maniac, that he has set on the entire destruction of the Museum and that he has got the support of Lord Wellington in the execution of his project."[8]

Canova's effort was hurt by a rumor that the papacy and the British were colluding in a sale of Roman antiquities. In exchange for helping

Rome, the Prince Regent and Lord Liverpool had discussed acquiring some of the repatriated works. Castlereagh put the kibosh on the suggestion, announcing that the Prince Regent would pay the cost of returning artworks to Italy.

But the French held firm. In a dramatic face-off between Canova and Denon, the museum director drew on the Treaty of Tolentino and claimed that France had rescued the masterworks from adverse conditions. Talleyrand invoked "a right of conquest . . . [that] has been admitted by all nations in all times" and argued the French couldn't be liable for the misdeeds of the Napoleonic government. When Canova tried visiting the Halle d'Etudes of the Academie Française, he was pelted with bread pellets by the students. He overhead one of the artists say that he would like to stick a dagger into him.

In September, when Dutch representatives arrived in the museum's galleries to take down the stadtholder's pilfered pictures, they discovered that all the museum's ladders had been removed.[9] Not surprisingly, there was no French staff available to help de-install the works. Denon may have choreographed the disappearing ladders, but that is conjecture.

The Duke of Wellington, general-in-chief of the army of the Netherlands, called on Talleyrand to intervene. Wellington declared that if the French prime minister and Denon continued to impede the restitution efforts, he would have armed escorts remove paintings belonging to the king of the Netherlands on September 20 at noon. As Judith Nowinski writes, it was only when a regiment of Grenadiers showed up at the museum pointing bayonets at Denon that he told his twenty-five museum guards to step aside.[10]

The dismantling of the galleries caused a conflict of authority between Wellington and Paris's Prussian governor, Friedrich Karl Ferdinand von Müffling. After being closed, the museum reopened with a British regiment stationed along the galleries. As a reminder of Allied strength, Wellington staged a review of the army on September 22.

"Thanks to the personal intervention of the Duke of Wellington, a large part of the property of the House of Orange was returned to the Netherlands in the autumn of 1815," writes Quentin Buvelot. "Some 120 paintings were returned, which now constitute the nucleus of the collection of the Mauritshuis. But sixty-eight works remained in France, some of which now hang in the Louvre. These include Hendrick Pot's *Portrait of Charles I*, paintings of lute-players, and a music ensemble by Gerrit van Honthorst, and a landscape by Peter Paul Rubens. A masterpiece by Jan Davidsz de Heem, the *Portrait of William III in a garland of flowers*, is in the collection of the Musée des Beaux-Arts in Lyon."[11] After William I (son of stadtholder William V) gifted the returned paintings to the state, they were incorporated into the Netherlands' public collections in 1816. Six years later, the paintings were transferred to the Mauritshuis where they remain today.[12]

Over the next six weeks, Canova worked to gain the support of Austria, Prussia, and an uncompromising Russia. The sculptor finally achieved a diplomatic breakthrough on Sunday, September 10, when Louis XVIII received him. Speaking in Italian, the king commissioned his portrait. His hard line position appeared to be softening. The following day, Louis submitted an address to the Allies' diplomatic agents questioning the validity of Tolentino and asking that the works be returned to the people of Rome for "the usefulness and advantage of all civilized nations in Europe."[13]

At the invitation of Austrian chancellor Metternich, Canova visited the Louvre on September 28. He came prepared with a list of looted artworks delivered to him by Alessandro D'Este. Denon gave the celebrated Italian sculptor a rude reception. When Canova pointed out that this was no way to treat an ambassador, Denon replied, "Ambassador! Come on, you mean packer, surely."[14] Ironically, Denon himself had been dubbed "the packer" for his talent at confiscating art.

Metternich sent an ultimatum to Richelieu threatening the use of force if works of the Holy See were not handed over within twenty-four hours.[15] Sensing that the momentum had shifted, Italian cities like Perugia and Bologna asked Canova for help getting their own treasures back. On September 30, France formally recognized the papal claim for restitution. Canova returned to the museum the next day, escorted by a platoon of Prussian and Austrian soldiers, and began removing works.

A week later, Denon resigned as museum director, citing his advancing age (sixty-eight) and failing health.[16] Still he remained defiant: "Let them take them then, but they have no eyes to see them with: France will always prove her superiority in the arts that the masterpieces were better here than elsewhere."[17]

Canova secured the restitution of 294 statues taken from Rome's Villa Albani. But Cardinal Giuseppe Albani considered the cost of transporting his family's antiquities back to Rome prohibitive. He sold several objects to Crown Prince Ludwig of Bavaria, including the *Laughing Faun* (today at the Glyptothek, Munich). The Antinous bas-relief from Hadrian's Villa was returned to the Villa Albani, reinstalled in the salon to the left of the main gallery.[18]

After being taken to Paris in 1807, Rome's storied Giustiniani collection was dispersed. Now Prussia's Frederick William III bought about one hundred sixty of the paintings (today in various museums in Berlin and Potsdam). The Carpegna collection stayed in France. The Braschis had been already compensated in 1802 for their art. Napoleon's brother-in-law Camillo Borghese was unsuccessful in annulling the sale of his family's antiquities. Several hundred Borghese pieces stayed in Paris, including the *Gladiator*, the *Hermaphrodite*, and a group of outstanding Roman sarcophagi.

Outside the Louvre, Parisians could only watch. Canova drew up detailed notes of all the objects taken from the museum, including the day of their collection. Works were divided by their final destination in Rome or the Papal States. Canova spent his last weeks in Paris organizing logistics for the art convoys. England provided two convoys, a British frigate, and 35,000 pounds to pay for packing and transporting art from Paris to Italy.[19] Canova hired the firm Larcher Becquemis to handle the transport. Canova's tenacity led one contemporary to call the modest sculptor the "greediest of claimants."[20]

Ultimately Canova managed to get back seventy-seven of the original hundred papal works taken under the Treaty of Tolentino.[21] On October 16, Canova wrote: "The cause of the Fine Arts is at length safe in port . . . we are at last beginning to drag forth from this great cavern of stolen goods the precious objects of art stolen from Rome . . . yesterday the *Dying Gladiator* left his French abode and the [Belvedere] *Torso*. We removed today the two first statues of the world, the *Apollo* [Belvedere] and the *Laocoön* . . . the most valuable of the statues are to go off by land, accompanied by the celebrated Venetian horses."

The first convoy left Paris by land on October 25 with Raphael's *Transfiguration*, and *Madonna of Foligno*, *Caravaggio's Deposition*, *Apollo Belvedere*, *Belvedere Torso*, and the *Laocoön*. The convoy was escorted by Austrian soldiers as far as the frontier of the Papal States. On the afternoon of November 23, while crossing the Mont Cenis Pass, a heavy sledge skidded on icy snow. The crate carrying the *Laocoön* fell from the wagon and crashed on the ice, damaging the famous marble group. The convoy of masterpieces finally reached Rome on January 4, 1816, entering the city through the Porta Angelica.[22]

Alessandro D'Este supervised the shipment of the remaining art. Sculptures, including the colossal *Nile,* went by sea. In mid-November, crates of art were loaded onto fifteen wagons and left for Antwerp. The following May, the British naval vessel *Abundance* lent by the Prince Regent left for Civitavecchia. Works were transferred to Rome in July and August. In thanks for his support, Pius sent a gift for the future king on the ship—a circular *tempietto* of rosso antico topped by a statue of peace with plaster casts of works returned to Rome.[23]

The world's most prestigious museum was dismantled, with nearly five thousand objects returned. Denon wrote pessimistically: "Such an assembly—this comparison of the achievements of the human mind through the centuries, this tribunal where talent was constantly being judged by talent—in a word, this light which sprang perpetually from the inter-reaction of merits of all kinds has just been extinguished, and will never shine again."[24]

Yet France's network of twenty-two provincial museums made it nearly impossible to track the location of hundreds of other paintings dispersed by Denon. Thanks to Denon, paintings like Veronese's *Marriage of Saint Catherine* and Rubens's *Adoration of the Magi* from Munich stayed in the cities of Rouen and Lyon, respectively. Looted art also hung at the Brera in Milan, the Accademia in Venice, and Napoleon's imperial palaces, including the Tuileries, Saint-Cloud, Fontainebleau, the Trianon, and Meudon.[25]

Some of the Musée Royale's pictures escaped repatriation because they were supposedly being restored; others were said to be inaccessible or lost.[26] Prussia's Frederick William III caved in after Denon argued that removing the ancient marble columns from Charlemagne's Aachen Cathedral would cause the roof of the Louvre to collapse.

In the end, writes Andrew McLellan, roughly half of the stolen art remained in France due to "a combination of diplomacy, bureaucratic obstruction, and the inability of weak nations to reclaim what was theirs."[27] Along with these works, the museum retained its royal collections, confiscated Church treasures, and artworks left behind by those fleeing revolutionary France. Denon managed to keep two masterpieces—Tintoretto's *Paradise* from Verona and Veronese's *Wedding at Cana* from San Giorgio Maggiore.

As a result of the Congress of Vienna, Venice reverted to Austria, rendering its confiscated art in Paris Austrian property. Denon sent the *Wedding at Cana* off to a workshop in the provinces for restoration, delaying compliance with Austria's restoration order. After Denon argued that the painting was too big and fragile to travel to Venice, Austrian commissioners agreed to trade the Veronese for Charles Le Brun's lesser work, *Feast in the House of Simon*. Over the strong protests of Canova, this exchange was executed. One of the largest paintings at the Louvre, the *Wedding at Cana* hangs today across from Leonardo's *Mona Lisa*.

Another loss was Titian's *The Crowning with Thorns* (1542–43), commissioned as an altarpiece by Milan's Church of Santa Maria delle Grazie (the refectory is home to Leonardo's *Last Supper*). The violent scene, the first of the artist's two versions, was taken to Paris after Napoleon's 1797 conquest of Milan. The canvas evokes two famed antiquities also taken to Paris. The figure of Christ appears to be modeled after the *Laocoön*; the upper body of Christ's torturer on the left by the *Belvedere Torso*. The bust of Tiberius Caesar in the background refers to the Roman authorities who condemned Christ.

The Italian "primitives" were so little understood, they were not returned and became part of the Louvre's Italian art collection. Among the works that remained in France were paintings by Pietro Perugino. Considered a less significant artist at the time than he is now, many were deemed unsuitable for the Louvre and sent to various provincial museums. Perugino's *Marriage of the Virgin*, considered one of his most important works, remains on view at the Museum of Fine Arts in Caen, northwestern France.

When Canova returned to Rome, doubts arose about his effort. Of 506 pictures taken to France, only 249 were recovered, 248 stayed in France, and nine were declared missing.[28] But in Canova's defense, Pius allowed many paintings to stay in Paris and gave Louis XVIII a number of sculptures. He did not want to antagonize the restored Bourbons who seemed to be reversing two decades of anticlericalism. The sculptures included *Seated Demosthenes*, *Curule Chair*, *Seated Trajan*, *Sphinx of red granite*, *white marble Altar*, *Tripod of Apollo*, *Tiberius in a toga*, three candelabra, *colossal figure of Melpomene* (from the courtyard of the Palazzo della Cancelleria), a *chair of rosso antico*, and *Caesar Augustus in consular dress*.[29] The *Nile* was returned despite French efforts to retain it, but the colossal *Tiber* also remained in Paris, along with the *Sarcophagus of the Muses*.

In parallel with Canova, Abbot Marino Marini was sent to Paris to retrieve material seized from the Vatican Library in 1798 and 1799, including the archives and contents of the Medalgliere, or Medal Cabinet. When the archives of the Roman Curia were toted off to Paris by Napoleon, Marini's uncle Luigi Gaetano Marini accompanied them, reaching Paris on April 11, 1810.[30] In 1800, newly elected Pius VII had appointed Gaetano Marini primus custos of the Vatican Library and prefect of the archives. In 1805, he was made a *cameriere d'onore* to the pope.

After Napoleon's fall, the count of Artois, vice-regent and the king's brother, issued a decree directing the restitution to the Holy See of the archives, of all documents and manuscripts, and of several other collections. On April 28, the papal commissioners, Mgr. de Gregorio, Mgr. Gaetano Marini, and his nephew Marino Marini took charge of this property. Before it reached Rome, Gaetano Marini died in Paris in May 1815. Without a complete inventory of the numismatic collections, Marino Marini disappointedly accepted the same number of coins, but not the same objects. Manuscripts were returned, including the celebrated Codex B, the Virgil, and Terence codices. France kept medals and cameos from the Vatican Medalgliere.

Marini filled sixteen cases with the treasures of the pontifical chapel, including miters the queen of Etruria gave the pope when he passed through Florence, and the tiara Napoleon gave Pius after his coronation. But the archives proved more difficult. According to Maria Luisa Ambrosini, documents had been stolen, sold, and removed. A large quantity of papers deemed unimportant were sold by weight in Paris in 1816 for wrapping paper and making cardboard. Marini found several hundred volumes of the registers of the bulls of the Apostolic Datary in the butcher shops of Paris.[31] The journey back to Rome also proved challenging. The first wagons, loaded with priceless objects, were left standing unguarded throughout the night in Turin. During the crossing of the Taro River, Marini had to act fast to prevent the archival material from suffering water damage. He saved some seven hundred cases of papers by having them removed from the wagons and taken across the river by boat.[32]

Back in Rome, the recovered objects along with the Vitali collection and the small "Roman" nucleus from excavations was arranged in the Chapel of St. Pius V, next to the library, in old cabinets. An inventory was prepared by Giuseppe Baldi, son of Elia, and Bartolomeo Borghesi. Baldi rebuilt the Vatican's medal collection with the support of Pius VII's art acquisition commission whose members included Canova, Filippo Aurelio Visconti, Carlo Fea, and Bertel Thorvaldsen.[33]

While Canova worked for the pope, the Austrians managed the return of stolen works from Milan, Venice, Parma, Piacenza, and Florence. Parma's art recovery was supervised by diplomat Giuseppe Poggi, under the protection of Austria's emperor, father of Marie Louise, the duchy's new ruler. Only a fraction of the fifty-three paintings were returned, but the masterly Correggios including *La Madonna di San Gerolamo* were recovered for Venice's reorganized Galleria dell'Accademia. Paintings taken from Piacenza and from churches of Parma were not returned to their original locations.[34]

One big convoy was organized for works intended for Italy.[35] On October 24, 1815, forty-one wagons pulled by two hundred horses left Paris escorted by two squadrons of German Uhlans for Milan through Mont Cenis. In Milan, the cargo was sorted and sent to other destinations.[36] The Russians under diplomat Karl Robert Nesselrode refused to budge over art repatriation. Alexander I had a vested interest in the situation. In October 1815, just as Napoleon was arriving at St. Helena, the frigate *Archipelago* arrived in Russia with thirty-eight paintings and four Canova sculptures from Malmaison. Alexander had bought the artworks from Joséphine's children for 940,000 francs. He hung the paintings in the new Malmaison Hall of the Hermitage in St. Petersburg.

Twenty-one of the paintings came from the 1806 French confiscation of the landgrave of Hesse-Kassel's collection including four Claudes and Rembrandt's *Descent from the Cross.* (In 1829, Alexander's youngest brother Nicholas I would buy another thirty of Joséphine's paintings from Hortense.[37]) Since 1918, when the Bolshevik government signed a peace treaty with Germany and Austria, German negotiators have demanded the return of the stolen paintings. The pictures remain in the Hermitage.

On September 25, the aide-de-camp of the prince of Schwarzenberg, commander of the Austrian troops, informed Denon that the Arc du Carrousel was to be dismantled. The bronze horses of St. Mark's had starred in the July 1798 Fête de la Liberté. Denon argued that as a public monument, the arch fell outside the restitution agreements.

Two days later, Austrian troops closed off all the streets leading to the Arc du Carrousel and the Tuileries, dispersing protesters. To the indignation of the French, the Prussians climbed Percier and Fontaine's marble arch and took down the famous bronze horses. Louis XVIII reportedly observed the scene from a window at the Tuileries Palace.

The *London Courier* published this eyewitness account: "I just now find that the Austrians are taking down the bronze horses from the Arch. The whole court of the Tuileries, and the Place du Carrousel are filled with Austrian infantry and cavalry under arms; no person is allowed to approach; the troops on guard amount to several thousands; there are crowds of French in all the avenues leading to it who give vent to their feelings by shouts and execrations . . . the number of cannons of the bridges has been increased."

It took an entire day to get two of the horses down from the top of the arch. English engineers were seen cavorting in the chariot. Rumors spread that English soldiers had scraped the gilding off the horses (in fact, the scoring was purposefully done in antiquity). By October 1, all four steeds were removed; Victory, Peace, and the chariot lay on the ground in pieces. Four gray horse replicas would replace the originals.

The day after the bronze horses were removed, a writer for the *London Courier* reported that "The public mind of Paris still continues in a state of extreme agitation; the public appear every day more and more exasperated against the Allies. . . . The stripping of the Louvre is the chief cause of public irritation at present . . . the Grand Galerie of the Museum presents the strongest possible image of desolation; here and there a few pictures giving greater effect to the disfigured nakedness of the walls.

"I have seen several French ladies in passing along the galleries suddenly break into extravagant fits of rage and lamentation; they gather round the Apollo [Belvedere] to take their last farewell with the most romantic enthusiasm; there is so much passion in their looks, their language and their sighs, in the presence of this monument of human genius that a person unacquainted with their character or accustomed to study the character of the fair sex in England, where feeling is controlled by perpetual discipline, would be disposed to pronounce them literally mad . . ."[38]

On October 12, artist Andrew Robertson reported from Paris: "The Louvre is truly doleful to look at now, all the best statues are gone, and half the rest; the place full of dust, ropes, triangles, and pulleys." His colleague Thomas Lawrence lamented "the breaking up of a collection in a place so central to Europe, where everything was laid open to the public with a degree of liberality unknown elsewhere."[39]

Stendhal summed up his compatriots' bitterness. "The allies have taken from us 1,150 pictures. I hope that I am allowed to note that we acquired the best of them *by a treaty*, that of *Tolentino*. . . . The allies, on the other hand, took our pictures from us *without a treaty*."[40]

Before Venice's bronze horses left Paris on October 17, Austria's Francis I asked Canova where they should be installed. The sculptor suggested that pairs of the horses could flank the main entrance to the doge's Palace, directly across from Palladio's San Giorgio Maggiore. But Count Leopoldo Cicognara, president of Venetian Academy, disagreed. Cicognara insisted the icon be returned to its original home, the façade of St. Mark's Basilica (to protect the ancient horses after a restoration, they were reinstalled inside the Basilica in 1982, replaced by replicas outside).

After arriving in Venice on December 7, the bronze horses crossed the lagoon by raft and were taken to the Arsenale for repair. At some point, the decoration on their collars was lost. The bronze lion from the column on the Piazzetta was also returned, but required extensive repairs after being smashed into dozens of pieces during its removal in Paris. The following April, the lion was reinstalled atop its column.[41]

On December 13, the eighteenth anniversary of the horses' confiscation, a raft with Austrian and Venetian standards came around the eastern end of Venice carrying the famous bronzes. With Francis I in attendance, Academy president Cicognara addressed the crowd. To musket shots and cannon fire, the horses were lifted and repositioned at their place on the Basilica's loggia.[42]

TWO

EXILES AND HEROES

With the Allies in France, Napoleon ordered Pius moved back to the northern Italian port town of Savona where he was released two months later. Resistance to Napoleon turned the aging pontiff into a heroic figure. Parallels were made between the end of his captivity and Saint Peter's freedom from a Jerusalem prison.[1] From St. Helena, Napoleon would write of his adversary, "Alexander the Great declared himself the son of Jupiter, and in my time I have met a priest more powerful than I."

For centuries, the papal coronation ceremony known as the *possesso* had followed the imperial Roman triumphal route through the Forum to the Capitol in reverse. Temporary arches were erected on the Campidoglio and in the Forum near the Arch of Titus and the Farnese Gardens. But with Pius VII's election in Venice, the tradition had ended. On May 24, 1814, nearly halfway into his fifteenth year as pope, Pius finally enjoyed a triumphal entry into Rome. The celebration lasted two days.

From the Via Flaminia, the papal procession continued to the Piazza del Popolo and Church of Santa Maria where a large, emotional crowd gathered. Ephemeral monuments inspired by ancient Rome and the Renaissance celebrated Pius's return. Among the structures designed by Giuseppe Valadier was an arch for the Piazza Venezia. A neoclassical commemorative column on the Ponte S. Angelo depicting the Triumph of Constancy featured a figure carved by Bertel Thorvaldsen.

To help the crowds navigate from the Piazza del Popolo to St. Peter's, a bridge supported by boats was erected over the Tiber after the Renaissance invention of the triumphal bridge, or *Pons Triumphalis.*[2] The pope's coach was unhitched from the horses. Some five dozen young men in powdered wigs pulled his coach through a series of laurel arches to St. Peter's and then up to the Palazzo Quirinale where he'd been abducted.[3]

With his return, Pius VII began the process of restoring the Church and the city of Rome. A rift arose between Cardinal Bartolomeo Pacca (secretary of state, 1814–15), who favored going back to conservative eighteenth-century ideals, and Cardinal Ercole Consalvi, who wanted to maintain some of the more liberal reforms of the French.

Pius retained much of the Napoleonic code, along with improvements like street lighting and house numbering.[4] At the same time, he reestablished the conservative Jesuit order banned by Clement XIV in 1773 and made Rome's Jews return to the ghetto that had been abolished by Napoleon.[5] Somewhat ironically, Pius became a hero for the Risorgimento, Italy's nationalist movement.[6] In 1821, members of the Carbonari, a secret society calling for constitutional reforms and Italian unity, were arrested across Italy. That year, Pius published a bull condemning the Carbonari and the Masons, and their objectives.

Pius resumed his earlier art patronage including archaeological excavations, the restoration of monuments, and expansion of the Vatican museums. Projects included the restoration of the Arch of Titus and an excavation of Constantine's basilica, the precursor of St. Peter's. He also continued the work of the French at the Forum, temples, and the Via Sacra.[7] Valadier was rehired to reconfigure the Piazza del Popolo, scene of his triumphal entry, and the ramps and terraces on the adjacent Pincio. For the Piazza del Popolo, Valadier designed four identical buildings at the corners, relocated the existing fountain, and designed a new fountain around the obelisk.

Pius also removed Napoleon's lavish refurbishments at the Quirinale. In the piazza, he added a basin to the Dioscuri fountain and the inscription "pivs. vii. pom" on the base of the obelisk between the figures of Castor and Pollux. The message was subtle but symbolic, writes Roberta Olson. "Since antiquity, Castor and Pollux, the Dioscuri, were viewed as guardian figures of Rome, and Pius VII was the ottocento guardian of Rome and its heritage."[8]

A February 1816 visit to see the restored art from Paris inspired Pius to reorganize the Vatican galleries. To the Museo Chiaramonti, established in 1807 with Antonio Canova's help, he added an elegant sculpture gallery, the Braccio Nuovo, or New Wing. Begun in 1817 by Raffaele Stern and finished after his death in 1820 by Pasquale Belli, the nearly 230-foot-long gallery is considered one of the finest examples of neoclassical architecture in Rome.

To create an authentic setting, Stern and Belli used colored marble repurposed from Roman buildings. For the floor, large marble slabs framed original Roman mosaics illustrating the *Odyssey*. Adorning the walls were Francesco Massimiliano Laboureur's stucco friezes inspired by antique reliefs. On either end of the gallery, Egyptian granite columns decorated the doors. Canova, president of the Committee for the Fine Arts whose members included Filippo Aurelio Visconti and Antonio D'Este, curated the display of the gallery which opened in February 1822. (After an extensive restoration, the Braccio Nuovo reopened in January 2017.)

Below a coffered barrel-vault ceiling with skylights, twenty-eight niches housed larger-than-life statues of emperors and Roman replicas of famous Greek statues. In between, busts of antiquity's superstars were placed on corbels, half columns, and consoles. One of the masterworks of the gallery was the recently returned *Nile*, a Roman copy of a first-century Hellenistic statue of the great Egyptian river and its tributaries.

Among the treasures was a new acquisition—the *Minerva Giustiniani* (late-fifth to early-fourth century B.C.E.) Discovered in the early seventeenth century on the Esquiline Hill, the Roman copy of a Greek original depicts the goddess of wisdom and warfare wearing a helmet. Bought in 1805 by Napoleon's brother Lucien Bonaparte for his Rome residence, the Palazzo Nunez, the Parian marble escaped export to Paris with the rest of the Giustiniani collection two years later.

Meanwhile, Canova financed a series of fifteen allegorical lunettes for the long, narrow Galleria Chiaramonti. Cardinal Consalvi chose the subjects—historical events and arts-related projects sponsored by Pius VII. Canova hired his protégé Francesco Hayez to paint five of the lunettes. The central fresco, *The Issue of Laws Protecting Antiquities* by Vincenzo Ferreri is the only scene featuring Pius.[9]

The Allies decided that the paintings from Paris should be displayed together rather than going back to their original locations. With his predecessor's picture gallery now housing the Raphael tapestries, Pius created a new Pinacoteca Vaticana in the former Borgia apartments, named for Spanish-born Pope Alexander VI, Rodrigo de Borja. Among the chosen masterworks were twenty-six canvases returned from Paris. These included Raphael's celebrated *Transfiguration,* Giovanni Bellini's *Pietà* or *Lament over the Dead Christ*, Poussin's *Martyrdom of St. Erasmus*, and a pair of predella panels by Fra Angelico.

Hung alongside these were selected pictures from the Quirinale, Capitoline, and Papal apartments, along with Titian's *Madonna in Glory* from Venice and two Veroneses—*Vision of St. Helena* and an *Allegory.* Also installed in the new Pinacoteca was another acquisition, the *Aldobrandini Wedding*. Named for its owner, Cardinal Pietro Aldobrandini, the wealthy art-loving nephew of Pope Clement VIII, the Roman fresco was bought in 1818 at the recommendation of Canova's acquisitions commission.[10]

Also added permanently to the Vatican collections were paintings by Fra Angelico, Raphael, and Perugino previously in Perugia and Foligno. Some had belonged to churches and convents in the Papal States. Among these were Raphael's *Transfiguration*, Caravaggio's *Deposition* from Santa Maria in Vallicella, *The Communion of St. Jerome* by Domenichino, Andrea Sacchi's *Saint Romuald*, and Barocci's *Annunciation* and *Blessed Michelina*. When the original owners protested, Cardinal Consalvi responded that the returned canvases had been reconsigned to Pius by the Allies for public display.[11]

With thousands of repatriated paintings and sculptures, Italy was confronted with the question of what to do with art removed from its suppressed churches and convents. According to Valter Curzio, the return of the Napoleonic plunder played a key role in the formation of a handful of important museums, including the Pinoteca in Bologna, the Galleria Nazionale dell' Umbria in Perugina, Milan's Pinacoteca Brera, and the Gallerie dell'Accademia in Venice.[12]

When Napoleon's soldiers took Pius VI prisoner, the papal tiaras were looted. For his papal coronation in Venice, Pius VII wore a papier-mâché tiara decorated with silver cloth and jewels donated by aristocratic Venetian women. In 1805, Napoleon gave Pius a new tiara, ironically made with objects from the looted ones. But considering it too heavy and not liking the glowing inscriptions to Napoleon, Pius kept wearing the papier-mâché tiara. In 1820, Pius received a new silver tiara, but seemed to prefer wearing the paper one.[13]

Pius had refurbished and then stayed at the papal palace at Castel Gandolfo in 1804 and 1805 after Napoleonic troops invaded the Papal States. Now he returned to the retreat above Lake Albano, some twenty miles south of Rome. Urban VIII built the palace in the early seventeenth century on the ruins of the favorite villa of Roman emperor Domitian. Designed by imperial architect Rabirius, the three-story villa featured a small theater, a terrace overlooking the Tyrrhenian Sea, and a covered passageway or cryptoporticus that still survives.

With the art restitution from Paris came a sense that Rome was reborn. "Rome is yet the capital of the world. It is a city of palaces and temples, more glorious than those which any other city contains, and of ruins more glorious than they," wrote Percy Bysshe Shelley in 1819. After being inaccessible for years, the city again attracted tourists. Its antique art had become even more famous as a result of the pillage. In 1819, the Prince Regent commissioned Thomas Lawrence to paint the pope's portrait in Rome. In the background, to the left of the seated Pius, Lawrence added the Chiaramonti Gallery with three of its recently returned treasures—the *Apollo Belvedere,* the *Belvedere Torso,* and the *Laocoön.*

In July 1823, Pius VII fell in the papal apartments and fractured his hip. The news of a devastating July 16 fire that destroyed much of S. Paolo fuori le Mura and its artworks was kept from the bedridden pontiff.[14] With Cardinal Consalvi at his side, the eighty-one-year-old died on August 20, bringing an end to his stormy twenty-three-year pontificate.

After a funeral on August 25, Pius VII was buried in Saint Peter's Clementine Chapel. Danish sculptor Bertel Thorvaldsen sculpted his marble tomb monument.

⚜

After two challenging months in Paris and with the bronze horses en route to Venice, Antonio Canova left for London. As a gesture of thanks for their support, Canova presented female Ideal Heads to the Prince Regent, the Duke of Wellington, and Lord Castlereagh. The sculptor inscribed a fourth bust to his ally Hamilton: "Antonio Canova made this gladly for William Hamilton a man of distinction and a friend in acknowledgement of his exceptional goodwill to himself and of his patronage in the recovery of artistic monuments from France."[15]

Ironically, the person who had just recovered part of Rome's cultural patrimony became involved with the Elgin Marbles. In 1802, in a move worthy of Denon, Britain's ambassador to Constantinople, the seventh Earl of Elgin, detached nearly half of the Parthenon frieze along with seventeen sculptures from the pediments and fifteen marble panels. As Lord Elgin's secretary at the time, William Hamilton supervised the removal of the frieze. Its arrival in London sparked a national debate. Byron attacked Elgin for exporting the marbles from the Acropolis in Athens, then under Ottoman control.

Though Canova never traveled to Athens, he was considered an authority on classical Greek sculpture. During his early training in Venice, he had copied plaster casts of Greek statues at the Palazzo Farsetti; he had also seen Greek sculpture in Italy. In 1803, Lord Elgin visited Canova's studios in Rome with drawings, molds, and a few fragments of the Elgin Marbles, asking him to undertake a restoration. Canova told him it would be a sacrilege to touch the masterpiece. Now the sculptor was asked to examine the looted Parthenon frieze and weigh in on whether it was a Greek original or a Roman copy.

Canova declared the "stupendous and unforgettable" works to be original, perhaps by the hand of the most celebrated Greek sculptor of antiquity. As Athens's state artist in the fifth century B.C.E., Phidias participated in the design and supervision of the Parthenon's sculptural program. Among his other masterworks were monumental gold and ivory statues of Zeus (Rome's Jupiter) and Athena (Rome's Minerva) for their temples at Olympia and Athens.[16]

Canova raved about the pilfered marbles in a letter to Quatremère. "I saw the Greek marbles, nothing artificial, exaggerated, nor harsh. The works of Fidias are real flesh, beautiful Nature. I must confess dear friend that seeing such beautiful things has heightened my self-esteem because I have always been convinced that the great maestros had to work in this way and in no other way."[17] As the "Phidias of Europe," Canova's opinion carried tremendous weight. His conclusion helped persuade the British government to acquire the Elgin Marbles for the nation for 35,000 pounds. Greece continues to demand their return from the British Museum.

Canova received a warm reception in London, where he secured several important commissions. In the wake of the Allies' victory over Napoleon, the Prince Regent ordered *Mars and Venus*, an allegory of war and peace for Carlton House. Distracted by the seductive Venus, Mars no longer has much use for his shield, spear, and sword. Canova adorned Mars's plumed Roman helmet with a British lion, but ignored the Prince Regent's request to have his profile carved on the shield. Before Canova left London, the Prince Regent gave him a diamond snuffbox with his portrait and a five hundred-pound note tucked inside.

The British government also commissioned a cenotaph for the exiled Stuarts, to join Canova's funerary monument for Clement XIII in St. Peter's Basilica. Commemorating the last three members of the Royal House of Stuart, the truncated pyramid-shaped monument features a trio of bas-relief portraits of the Stuart princes—James III and his sons Bonnie Prince Charlie and Henry. Two weeping angels flank the monument's closed doors, symbolizing the passage from life to death (the Stuarts are buried in the crypt below).

On December 1, Canova and his stepbrother dined at the Royal Academy. Four days later, Hamilton hosted a farewell dinner for Canova who was to leave London the next morning. The mild-mannered sculptor made a favorable impression. According to one of the guests, R. Smirke, ". . . what English He [Canova] does speak is remarkably pure and correct." Royal portraitist Thomas Lawrence "said He thought the manners of Canova a *pattern* for an Artist; that he had modest but manly comportment."[18] Earlier in his stay, Canova sat for his portrait by Lawrence.

Though only about half of the paintings taken to France were returned to Rome, Canova was welcomed as a hero for his efforts in the restitution when he arrived back on January 3, 1816.[19] The next day, a grateful Pius VII awarded Canova the title marquis of Ischia di Castro. Canova donated the annual three thousand scudi among various art academies. For his marquisate, he chose the lyre and the snake, emblems of Orpheus and Eurydice.[20] Pius also inscribed Canova's name in the Libro d'oro or Golden Book on the Campidoglio, and bestowed him with the highest pontifical honor—the Order of Christ.[21]

Later that year, Canova received another commission, his first from America. The North Carolina Senate ordered a full-length posthumous statue of George Washington for the State House in Raleigh. Virginia's State Capitol in Richmond already boasted a Carrara marble statue of Washington in his military uniform by Jean-Antoine Houdon. The renowned French sculptor had traveled to Mount Vernon in 1785 to take measurements and model a life mask of Washington. Two decades later, consulted again on what sculptor to hire for the Raleigh statue, Thomas Jefferson replied: "There can be but one answer to this. Old Canove of Rome."[22]

Canova had little to work with for the portrait of the six-foot-two-inch president.[23] Relying on a bust of Washington supplied by an American diplomat, Canova produced a series of preparatory sketches, a nude plaster model, and a full-sized clothed plaster model. According to Xavier Salomon, naked models were part of Canova's artistic process. "He always did a nude model of his sculptures so he could understand how the body worked under the drapery. . . . He would start with rough drawings and then move to three-dimensional plaster models such as this one."[24]

But Canova did not repeat the mistake of the nude *Napoleon as Mars the Peacemaker.* Though two decades earlier Jefferson had recommended a military uniform for Houdon's sculpture of Washington, he now expressed a different opinion. "as to the style or costume, I am sure the artist, and every person of taste in Europe would be for the Roman, the effect of which is undoubtedly of a different order. our boots & regimentals have a very puny effect," wrote Jefferson in 1816.[25]

Following Jefferson's instruction, Canova sculpted the president in Roman attire. Canova found references for the commission among the depictions of Roman generals and emperors, particularly a *Seated Claudius* uncovered in Herculaneum.[26] He sculpted Washington seated on a throne-like chair, holding a quill while drafting his farewell address on a stone tablet perched on his left leg. A sword lay at his feet. In anticipation of the statue, the *Raleigh Register* reported: "Even the celebrated Statues of the Apollo of Belvedere and the Venus of Medici have their blemishes, but the Statue of Washington, like Washington himself, is without a stain or spot."[27] When the marble arrived in Raleigh in December 1821, it attracted crowds of tourists, and Canova was likened to Phidias and Praxiteles. Sadly a decade later, a fire in the State House completely destroyed the portrait (a replica was placed in the center of the rotunda in 1970).

Also in 1816, Canova finished the statue of Elisa Baciocchi as Polyhymnia, muse of history. With Napoleon's sister off the Tuscan throne, Canova sold the work to Count Cesare Bianchetti of Bologna. After being displayed at the Accademia in Venice, the marble left for Vienna where it was exhibited by Titian's *Assumption*. Canova also finished *Marie Louise as Concordia*. In Spring 1817, he sent the portrait to Parma where Marie Louise had been installed as ruler by the Congress of Vienna after her husband's exile. Canova depicted her seated, holding the sacrificial patera, with cornucopia decorating the reliefs of her throne (today in the Galleria Nazionale, Parma).

Another of Canova's projects during this time was an equestrian statue of Charles III of Naples. After becoming king of Naples, Joseph Bonaparte commissioned Canova to produce an equestrian statue of his brother. The bronze monument was to stand in a semicircular piazza to be created in front of the royal palace (today's Piazza del Plebiscito). Canova's portrayal of Napoleon looking over his shoulder and encouraging his troops was criticized as overly dramatic. With the Bourbons' return to Naples, Charles III, father of the new king, replaced Napoleon. Canova, who was not a fan of the Neapolitan Bourbons, changed his original composition with Charles holding a baton.[28]

In mid-1819, Canova received an enthusiastic welcome in his hometown of Possagno. He supervised the quarrying of a local stone for a new church as a "beautiful memory to his homeland . . . more solid, more permanent and more visible" than the town's old church. Financed by Canova, designed by several architects, the imposing domed and columned temple combined elements of Athens's Parthenon and Rome's Pantheon with an early Christian apse. Wearing the uniform of the Order of the Knights of Christ, Canova laid the cornerstone of his temple on July 11.

But Canova would not see his church completed. In October 1822, the sculptor took ill while staying in Venice at Casa Francesconi in the Orseolo basin not far from Piazza San Marco, where he was a guest of his friend Florian (owner of the famous Caffé Florian). Canova died on St. Anthony's Day, October 13, two weeks shy of his sixty-fifth birthday. Starting as a young man in the 1780s, Canova had suffered from severe stomach pains, the likely result of continuous pressure of a drill on his ribs during the sculpting of Pope Clement XIV's tomb. According to the doctor who performed the autopsy, Canova died from bowel disease (*male ai visceri*), thought to be related to the earlier injury to his digestive tract.[29] At the time, Canova was working on a series of biblical scenes for the façade of his church in Possagno. Seven were completed.

Concerned that the funeral of the famous Italian hero would spark unrest, Austrian officials imposed strict rules. Black, the color associated with the revolutionary Carbonari (literally the charcoal burners) was prohibited. Instead, Count Leopoldo Cigognara, president of the Venetian Academy, and his fellow mourners wore green, the color of the house of Savoy that had become a symbol for Italian unification.

On October 16, following a religious ceremony in St. Mark's Basilica, the funeral procession moved to the Academy of Fine Arts. Draped with a black veil, Canova's coffin was placed on a bier in the main hall before Titian's massive altarpiece, *The Assumption of the Virgin* (1516–18). Canova called the twenty-three-foot-tall canvas from the high altar of the Frari the greatest painting in the world.[30] While the apostles reach up toward Mary, she looks up toward God, her arms outstretched and supported by angels. Leopoldo Cigognara gave the moving funerary oration before Canova's coffin.

On October 25, Canova was buried at Possagno's old church. Funeral rites were also held in late January in Rome at the Church of the Holy Apostles, home to Canova's funerary monument for Clement XIV and funeral stele for engraver Giovanni Volpato.

A decade later, Canova's remains were moved to the west side of his neoclassical temple. Canova's own painting *The Deposition* hung behind the main altar. Below the domed ceiling of carved and gilded rosettes was a floor made with red and white marble from the nearby Piave River. The sculptor's sarcophagus was adorned with his coat of arms, the lyre of Orpheus and the snake of Eurydice chosen "in memory of his first statues." As a teenager, Canova sculpted the famous mythological couple for the Asolo villa of his first patron, Senator Giovanni Falier.

Napoleon had expressed to Canova the prevailing notion that Italy's artistic genius was over, with Canova a lone exception. Stendhal echoed this sentiment, writing that Canova "had emerged quite by chance out of the sheer inertia which this warm climate imposed, but he is a freak. Nobody else [in Italy] is the least like him."[31] But for Italians, Canova represented Italy's enduring cultural supremacy.

Shortly after Canova's death, his friend Antonio D'Este began a memoir, a counter to Missirini's 1824 biography, *Della vita di Antonio Canova*. Published posthumously in Florence in 1864, *Memorie di Antonio Canova* was a portrait of the master and his studio practice.[32] Quatremère de Quincy also wrote a biography of his lifelong friend. Tellingly he wrote this passage about Napoleon:

"Time, however has revealed to us that in him [Napoleon] there was still something other than the desire to entrust the portrait of himself to the most renowned talent of that time. This kind of ambition, since Alexander, has not been lacking in any celebrated man. But with Bonaparte, there was already the expectation of that universal conquest that was the object of his whole life. Hence his covetousness of everything there was in each country, whether masterpieces or precious objects, or men of talent and famous subjects. What follows will make better known, in regard to Canova, the extraordinary desire that he had to appropriate him, his works even less than his person."[33]

In life, Canova achieved extraordinary fame as the greatest artist of the day. In death, he became a hero for Italian nationalism. Keats, Coleridge,

Thomas Moore, the Brownings, and Byron were all fans. "Italy has great names," wrote Byron in his preface to Canto IV of *Childe Harold's Pilgrimage* (1818), "Canova, Monti, Ugo Foscolo . . . will secure to the present generation an honourable place . . . and in some the very highest: Europe—the World—has but one Canova."[34]

Canova's students modeled his Carrara marble cenotaph in the Frari after the sculptor's own unrealized funerary monument for Titian (1795). In front of a pyramid, symbol of eternity, Sculpture leads the weeping figures of Painting and Architecture to the open tomb door. A youthful nude Genius reclines and the lion of St. Mark grieves (decades later, the Habsburgs ordered a pyramidal funerary monument for Titian, across the nave from Canova's cenotaph).

A competition arose between Venice and Possagno over Canova's body. In the end, Canova's heart was placed in a porphyry vase inside the Frari cenotaph; his right hand was kept at the Academy of Fine Arts in Venice in the Palladian Tablino in an urn designed by Giuseppe Borsato. In 2008, when the Academy school changed its headquarters, the sculptor's hand was transferred to the Canova Temple of Possagno. It is now in a gold and crystal sphere by his tomb. Canova's stepbrother Giovanni Battista Sartori shares the tomb; their marble portrait busts flank the sarcophagi.

In the first volume of his history of sculpture dedicated to Napoleon in 1813, Cicognara wrote that Canova "had led modern art along the way of Greek sculpture."[35] Cicognara dedicated the final volume to Canova. About *The Three Graces* he wrote: "If statues could be made by stroking marble rather than by roughly cutting and chipping, I would say that this one had been formed by wearing down the surrounding marble by dint of kisses and caresses."[36]

After seeing the marble version of *Helen*, Byron wrote *On the bust of Helen by Canova* in 1816. "In this beloved marble view/Above the works and thoughts of Man/What Nature could but would not, do/And Beauty and Canova can!/Beyond Imagination's power/Beyond the Bard's defeated art/With Immortality her dower/Behold the Helen of the heart."[37]

After Canova's death, European collectors continued to covet his cool, polished marbles. But starting with British critic John Ruskin, his distinctive neoclassical style fell out of favor. Italian art historian Roberto Longhi wrote about the "funereal blunders of Antonio Canova, the stillborn sculptor whose heart is buried in the church of the Frari, whose hand is in the Accademia and the rest of him buried I know not where."[38] Today, Canova's superstar reputation has been reestablished. Plaster casts of his masterworks, including *Napoleon as Mars the Peacemaker* and *The Three Graces* are assembled in his Gipsoteca in Possagno.

⚜

France's art plunder catapulted the Louvre from a "national museum to an encyclopedic sensation," writes Noah Charney. Throughout, Dominique-Vivant Denon had been Napoleon's "mastermind art hunter" and "architect of the art looting and assembly at the Louvre . . ."[39]

After his forced retirement as museum director, Denon turned his elegant apartment at 7 quai Voltaire into a private museum. His eclectic collection included Egyptian, Persian, and Roman antiquities, medieval, Renaissance, and Chinese works, medals, costumes, and furniture. Fittingly, the man responsible for Napoleon's "reinvention of relics" assembled his own reliquary.[40]

In a fifteenth-century gilded copper reliquary shaped like a Gothic cathedral, Denon enshrined dozens of his own secular relics. Among them were a lock of Napoleon's hair, a strip of the blood-stained shirt he wore when he died, and a leaf from the willow tree by his grave on St. Helena.[41]

One of the first artists to draw the temples and ruins of ancient Egypt, Denon now started an ambitious art history book. His goal was to link the ancient Egyptians to the Greeks, Romans, Byzantium, Michelangelo, Titian, and finally to France's contemporary painters.

Denon's first job at Louis XV's court was conservator of engraved gems. He returned from the Egyptian campaign with a large number of Roman copper medals, which he acquired from locals who had discovered them tending their fields and building houses near ancient ruins.[42] After being made a knight of the empire by Napoleon in 1808, Denon picked a medal scale for his coat of arms that he kept when he was named a baron four years later.[43] By the end of his life, Denon had amassed some three thousand medals.

Honoré de Balzac called Denon's early erotic short story, *Le Point de lendemain* (*No Tomorrow*), a primer for married men. Denon himself never married. He met the love of his life, Isabella Teotochi, in Venice. The portrait he commissioned of her in Venice still hung his salon. A few days before his death, Denon wrote his former lover: "Your last letter was of a youth so graceful, that I believed on reading it that I was only twenty. I assure you that I was worthy of it, and I thank you for it with all my heart. Good-bye, dear friend, I embrace you with all my heart."[44]

After attending an auction in April 1825, the seventy-eight-year-old fell ill and died. Joining his funeral cortege at Père Lachaise Cemetery was painter Jean-Auguste-Dominique Ingres, who called the powerful art figure "my anti-moi." Peering into Denon's grave, Ingres reportedly said "Good, and there he'll stay."[45] Ingres soon replaced Denon at the Académie des Beaux-Arts (over four decades later in 1867, Ingres would also be buried in the Père Lachaise Cemetery). To mark his tomb, Denon's nephews commissioned a naturalistic, seated statue of their uncle in bronze from sculptor Pierre Cartellier. Denon's beloved art collection was dispersed in a series of sales.

In 1803, Isabella Teotochi received a note from her former lover, expressing his emotional attachment to Napoleon: "It is rare to love much the grandest men but I assure you that the more I see this there, the more I love him. I feel happy that my final epoch of my life could be devoted to existence so distinguished. It is the burning star who revives my soul."[46]

⚜

After the First Empire, the successful decades-long collaboration of Charles Percier and Pierre Fontaine ended. Percier turned his attention to teaching at the École des Beaux-Arts. Among his students were sixteen Prix de Rome winners and seven members of the Institut de France. Percier also pursued his graphic work, organizing his voluminous drawings and producing ornamental compositions for books. Percier's deep attachment to Italy continued. In a letter to Antonio Canova in Italian, probably from 1811, the architect wrote:

"The little free time I have left I want to devote to the study of the fine arts that I love so much and [I] will tell myself by way of encouragement: 'work, you are almost Roman.'" Adding that he "brought back from Rome a number of drawings made after monuments and buildings there," Percier confided that "Every night before going to bed I spent two hours finishing them and in doing so forgot all my other tasks, thinking only of the sweet memories of my happy days."[47]

When Percier died in Paris on September 5, 1838, he left his drawing albums to his students and one hundred thousand francs to the École gratuite de dessin. Successors to Percier's chair at the Institut de France continued to hand down his gold ring featuring an oval Carnelian intaglio created in the late first century or early second century. According to Jean-Philippe Garric, the portrait profile most likely represents Marciana, sister of Roman emperor Trajan. As a token of friendship, Julien-David Le Roy, member of the Royal Academy of Architecture, bequeathed the antique ring to the promising young Percier when he died in 1803.[48]

Beyond an expression of imperial propaganda, Percier's innovative motifs had a lasting impact outside of France. Like England's William Kent, Percier helped establish a new visual language, the Empire style. As Tom Stammers writes, Percier's ideas were reproduced "in interiors from Charlottenburg in Berlin to Hampton House in Baltimore, from Rosendal Palace in Sweden to Capodimonte outside Naples."[49]

The politically savvy Fontaine continued working during the Restoration, building the neoclassical Chapelle Expiatoire in Paris for Louis XVIII and the Palais Royal in Neuilly and other residences for Louis-Philippe. Fontaine finally retired with the Revolution of 1848. During the last five years of his life, he held the ceremonial post of president of the Conseil des bâtiments civils.[50] Fontaine died at age ninety-one in October 1853. Per his wish, he was buried at Père Lachaise Cemetery, sharing the tomb he designed with both Charles Percier and Claude-Louis Bernier, their friend from Rome. Per Fontaine's instructions, the tomb's octagonal stele was engraved with the inscription "*Hi tres in unum sunt*," these three are one.[51]

⚜

After the fall or death of a Roman emperor, his family was often wiped out. After Napoleon's defeat, several members of the Bonaparte family took refuge in Rome, thanks to Pius VII. Madame Mère and her stepbrother Cardinal Fesch lived one floor apart at the Palazzo Falconieri, surrounded by his art collection.

In 1818, Napoleon's mother moved to the Palazzo Rinuccini where her bedroom became a kind of shrine to the family's past glory. With her vision failing, she was read Alexandre Dumas's new play *Napoleon Bonaparte* and convinced herself that her son had escaped from St. Helena.[52]

Shortly before his death, Napoleon acknowledged her influence. "My excellent mother is a woman of courage and great talent, more of a masculine than feminine nature, proud and high minded . . ." he wrote. "To the manner in which she formed me at an early age, I principally owe my subsequent elevation."[53]

The abduction of Pius VII put a strain on the relationship between Napoleon and his uncle. Stripped of duties as Grand Chaplain in 1809, Cardinal Fesch was sent into exile in Lyon in 1812. Welcomed to Rome by Pius, the Cardinal announced Napoleon's death to his family in May 1821. Fesch died in 1839, three years after his sister. Napoleon's nephew Louis Napoleon built a family funerary chapel on Ajaccio. The gold engraved inscription on Letizia Bonaparte's black stone tomb reads *Mater regum*, mother of kings.[54]

Pauline Borghese proved the most loyal of Napoleon's siblings. After selling her jewelry, she brought the cash to Elba, where she encouraged her brother to try to get his throne back. After Waterloo, Pauline was blamed for her husband's sale of the Borghese antiquities to Napoleon. Thanks to Pius, Pauline continued to use the Palazzo Borghese while Camillo lived with his mistress. She also lived royally in Villa Paolina near the Porta Pia. After a long illness, Pauline died in June 1825 in Florence.

After Napoleon's decisive defeat at Leipzig, the Murats went rogue, allying themselves with the Austrians in an attempt to hold onto power. About the duplicity, Napoleon wrote: "I was well aware that Murat was a fool, but I thought he loved me. It is his wife who is the cause of his desertion. To think that Caroline, my own sister, should betray me!" During the Hundred Days, Murat rallied back to his brother-in-law's side.

Inspired by Napoleon's escape from Elba, Murat attempted his own comeback in Naples. But backed by a small force, he was outmanned by the Austrians and English. After Waterloo, Murat left for Corsica hoping to stage a return to Italy. Instead, he was imprisoned and sentenced to death in Pizzo, Calabria. Days before Napoleon arrived at St. Helena, Murat reportedly told his firing squad: "Soldiers, respect the face and aim at the heart . . . Fire!"[55]

Following her husband's execution, Caroline Murat and her four children were exiled in Trieste and Vienna. In 1830, she married Francesco Macdonald, former war minister of Naples. At the end of her life, she called herself the countess of Lipona, an anagram of Napoli. The couple moved to Florence where she died at age fifty-seven of stomach cancer in 1839.

Elisa Bonaparte left Florence to join Jérôme and his family in Trieste. In 1820, after inspecting excavations at Aquileia, the forty-three-year-old caught a fever and died. Though he was estranged from his powerful brother throughout his rule, Lucien Bonaparte supported him during the Hundred Days. Lucien died in Viterbo, Italy, in 1840.[56] Joseph Bonaparte fled to New Jersey with his art collection and several pieces from the Spanish crown jewels. He died in Florence in 1844.

An avid art collector, Joseph Bonaparte hung the finest paintings in his apartments at the royal palace, the Palacio Real. By spring 1813, the Spanish Royal Collection was one of the finest in Europe. After learning that Wellington's troops were again on the march into Spain (over one hundred thousand men, double the number of French troops in Spain), Joseph fled north with his treasure, ordering everything valuable packed and loaded. Within days, Spain's cultural patrimony filled one-hundred-plus wagons.

More than 150 of Joseph's favorite paintings from the Palacio Real had not been packed. Joseph ordered the pictures removed from their frames, cut from their stretchers, and rolled. They were added to his personal baggage, atop his coach. Many more valuable personal items were loaded into the boot of the coach, or into large trunks strapped to the outside. On May 26, 1813, Joseph, his own contingent of soldiers, and his baggage train began north, under the command of Victor Hugo's father, General

Joseph Léopold Sigisbert Hugo. The paintings wound up with Wellington, installed in his London residence, Apsley House.

After commanding a division at Waterloo, Napoleon's youngest brother Jérôme lived for stints in Trieste, Switzerland, and Italy. In 1847, he returned to France where he became Governor of Les Invalides, a marshal of France, and president of the Senate before his death in 1860.[57] Eugène de Beauharnais left Italy for Munich where his father-in-law Maximilian I made him duke of Leuchtenberg and prince of Eichstadt. The widowed Eugène died there in 1824 at age forty-three. His oldest child became queen consort to Sweden's Oscar I; his youngest married the daughter of Russian tsar Nicholas I.

When Napoleon forced him to abdicate as king of Holland, Louis Bonaparte lived in Bohemia, Austria, and Switzerland where he died in 1846. Separated from her husband, Hortense de Beauharnais secretly gave birth to a son in 1811 (the 1st Duc de Morny), fathered by her lover the Comte de Flahaut, rumored to be Talleyrand's illegitimate son. Hortense bought the Arenenberg Castle on Lake Constance, Switzerland where she died at age fifty-four in 1837. She is buried in the Church of Saint Pierre and Saint Paul in Rueil-Malmaison by her mother Joséphine.

Renamed the duke of Reichstadt, Napoleon's son was raised by his Habsburg relatives at Vienna's Schönbrunn Palace. From St. Helena, Napoleon received no news of the boy, who he had last seen at age three. The former king of Rome was not even allowed to visit his mother in Parma and only learned in 1829 that he had two stepsiblings from her liaison with Austrian general Adam Albert von Neipperg, who she married after Napoleon's death. Widowed again in 1829, Marie Louise married the Grand Master of her court, French Count Charles de Bombelles. In 1832, she was at her son's side when the twenty-one-year-old died at Schönbrunn Palace of tuberculosis. Fifteen years later, Marie Louise was buried at Vienna's Capuchin Church beside her son and father.

THREE

RES GESTAE

For the ancient Egyptians, a name was everything. Obliterating a person's name was the equivalent of destroying that person's hope for an afterlife. In the fifteenth century B.C.E., the female pharaoh Hatshepsut ruled for some two decades. Her prosperous reign was remarkable for a building spree that included a mortuary temple complex (the future site for the Valley of the Kings). After Hatsheput's death, she was targeted either by her stepson Thutmose III or his son Amenhotep II. Public references to her as king disappeared from reliefs, statues, cartouches, and the official list of Egyptian rulers.

About a century and a half later, when military commander Horemheb became pharaoh, he ordered the cartouches of the monotheistic pharaoh Akhenaten and his eighteenth-dynasty successors like Tutankhamun defaced. The husband of Nefertiti, Akhenaten established a new cult dedicated to the Aton, the sun's disk. He himself erased the name and image of the rival Theban god Amon from Egypt's monuments. In the fourth century B.C.E., a notoriety-seeking Greek named Herostratus set fire to Ephesus's

Temple of Artemis, one of the Seven Wonders of antiquity. Under penalty of death, the arsonist's name could never be repeated.

The Romans, familiar with both Egyptian and Hellenistic cultures, adopted this severe dishonor that later came to be known by the Latin term, *damnatio memoriae,* or damnation of memory. "Like the Greeks before them, Romans also traveled to the East and especially to Egypt, where the grandeur and antiquity of pharaonic civilization conveyed its own messages about memory and monuments over a much longer time span . . . it would have been virtually impossible for individual elite Romans not to bring home new ideas about memory and erasure, interpreted within their own frames of reference," writes Harriet Flower.[1]

In Republican Rome, sanctions limited or destroyed the memory of citizens deemed unworthy members of the community. The practice continued to evolve throughout the Republic and Empire, with names scratched from inscriptions, faces chiseled off statues, images on frescoes overpainted, coins defaced, and wills annulled.[2] According to Flower, Augustus introduced a less punitive type of memory sanction, epitomized by his treatment of his defeated rival Mark Antony who had been attacked by the senate after Actium.[3]

During major regime changes, the violent transitions between dynasties, deposed emperors were subject to memory sanctions of varying degrees. Rome's most notorious imperators, Nero, Domitian, and Commodus, were declared enemies of the state. Following the 96 C.E. assassination of Domitian, the dictatorial younger brother of Titus and son of Vespasian, Suetonius writes that his images were "torn down . . . and dashed upon the ground;" the senate ordered his inscriptions erased and "all record of him obliterated."[4]

Suetonius also tells us that after Caligula's assassination in 41 C.E., "some wanted all memory of the Caesars obliterated, and their temples destroyed." The sadistic emperor was spared from a damnatio morae by his successor Claudius, though his coinage was melted down. During the late imperial period, damnatio memoriae continued to be the ultimate disgrace. In the early fourth century, Diocletian reportedly was so upset by the condemnation of his co-ruler Maximian that he died shortly after.[5]

Though damnatio memoriae was meant to punish emperors who discredited Rome, the practice was also abused, as in ancient Egypt. On his deathbed in 211, Septimius Severus instructed his sons and co-heirs Geta and Caracalla to get along with each other. Instead, Caracalla murdered Geta and issued a damnatio memoriae against his slain brother. After the fratricide, Caracalla erased Geta's name from the inscription on the attic of their father's triumphal arch, and removed his face from the family portrait, the Severan Tondo.

Defaced sculptures and reliefs were often repurposed with images of the new emperor. Nerva, for example, reused the defaced stone statues of Domitian. Rather than melting down Nero's one-hundred-foot-tall bronze Colossus, Vespasian, founder of the new Flavian dynasty, changed it into the sun god with a crown of rays. Hadrian moved the giant statue from the entrance of Nero's Golden House, reportedly with twenty-four elephants. Commodus later turned it into a self-portrait, adding the attributes of Hercules, a club, and lion skin. After Commodus's fall, the statue reverted to a sun god.

Despite the many alterations to his statue, Nero wasn't forgotten, posits Mary Beard. "It was always the statue that once had been Nero. . . . The line drawn in the Roman world between the destruction and preservation of images of emperors, between remembering and forgetting them, destruction or partial destruction was a very powerful strategy of memorialization. It wasn't always and it certainly wasn't necessarily about forgetting."[6] Eventually destroyed, the Colossus lent its name to the Colosseum.

The practice of memory sanctions continued through the centuries. During the French Revolution, a kind of damnatio memoriae was imposed on the despised Bourbon monarchs. Statues of Louis XIV, XV, and XVI were razed; the royal necropolis at Saint Denis was desecrated. One of Louis XVIII's first acts as king was to transfer the remains of his guillotined brother Louis XVI and sister-in-law Marie Antoinette to Saint Denis and commission praying statues of the couple. He also ordered fragments from some 158 royal bodies removed from the mass graves and placed into an ossuary in Saint Denis's crypt.

Aware that Louis XVIII would try to erase the memory of his reign, Napoleon wrote from St. Helena on December 9, 1815: "I am so closely identified with our prodigious deeds, our monuments, our institutions, in short, all of our nation's acts, that I can never be removed from them without harming France; her glory is to confess my name. And whatever sophism, whatever circumlocution, whatever lie they may employ to prove the opposite, they cannot alter the fact that I will remain all this in the eyes of that nation."

After the One Hundred Days and Waterloo, Louis XVIII tried to reestablish the Bourbon dynasty's political legitimacy amid widespread fear that France was reverting to the ancien régime. Restoration authorities embarked on a smear campaign, depicting Napoleon as a Corsican ogre and devil. But as Sudhir Hazareesingh notes, the effort to vilify Napoleon was unsuccessful, hurt by a battered economy and the continued presence of Allied troops.[7]

If anything, Napoleon's legend grew stronger. ". . . despite Waterloo, the events of 1815 resurrected the myth of the Napoleonic Prometheus, of the glorious man who could succeed against all odds and defy the political and physical laws of the universe," writes Hazareesingh.[8] Between 1816 and 1825, rumors persisted that Napoleon would pull off another herculean escape and raise a vast army like those of Alexander or Caesar.

March, the month of Napoleon's escape from Elba, took on "almost mystical properties."[9] A clandestine cottage industry sprung up of Napoleonic memorabilia in the form of coins and medals, statuettes, and portraits. In addition to Napoleon, commemorative coins featured dynastic images of family members Marie Louise, Napoleon II, Joséphine, and Eugène de Beauharnais. Saint Napoleon not only remained a French tradition, it grew stronger. ". . . observance of this tradition intensified after the death of the emperor and his mortal remains' subsequent (though not immediate) return to France," writes Fiona Parr. "Celebrated by various groups of Bonaparte sympathizers, it was a day in the year for the emperor's admirers to come together and honour his life and death."[10]

Like the Romans' damnatio memoriae, Louis XVIII instigated a nationwide purge of objects to erase the public memory of Napoleon. For starters, Lorenzo Bartolini's colossal bronze bust of Napoleon at the entrance of the Louvre was replaced with a bust of the Bourbon king. In 1815, Napoleon's coronation and wedding carriage was cut up "as a loathsome relic of Bonaparte."[11] Ironically in 1794, the National Convention ordered the destruction of Louis XVI's coronation carriage. Painter Jacques-Louis

David was allowed to scratch the panel paintings destined for the fire with the tip of his penknife. From the top of the Vendôme Column, Antoine-Denis Chaudet's monumental statue of Napoleon crowned with a laurel wreath was replaced by a fleur-de-lys flag.

In 1819, Louis XVIII had Napoleon's spectacular coronation crown with its dozens of gold leaves melted down. Empire-inspired reliefs from Napoleon's Arc du Carrousel were removed, with the intention of replacing them with scenes from the Duc d'Angoulême's Spanish campaign of 1823. In 1828, a new bronze chariot and horses by François Joseph Bosio were installed on top of the arch, replacing the famous horses returned to St. Mark's Basilica. At the French Academy in Rome, Louis XVIII's head was added to a statue that began as Napoleon.

On August 21, 1815, Louis XVIII ordered Vivant Denon to "make all the paintings with the effigy of Bonaparte disappear from the royal palaces and houses."[12] The city of Orléans publicly burnt François Gérard's portrait of Napoleon. Sculptures of Napoleon were also targeted. In Maine-et-Loire, Antonio Canova's marble portrait bust of Napoleon was saved from destruction in 1816 by an official who hid it in an attic.[13] The same year, Louis XVIII sold Canova's monumental *Napoleon as Mars the Peacemaker* to the British government.

Canova had tried to buy back his sculpture while negotiating for Rome's artworks in Paris, but Denon demanded the Vatican's *Nile* in exchange. On behalf of the British government, William Richard Hamilton negotiated a price of 66,000 francs or 3,000 pounds sterling with the French government.

Napoleon as Mars the Peacemaker left Paris on April 1, 1816. Hamilton wrote Canova on July 15 to let him know that the work had arrived safely in London. In September, Hamilton wrote the sculptor again, to dispel a rumor about the statue being a gift for the Prince Regent. According to Hamilton, the marble was always intended for the Duke of Wellington.[14]

The work was initially stored in the Duke of Richmond's gardens, the former privy gardens of Whitehall Palace. This was also where the Elgin Marbles were first kept after arriving from Athens a few years earlier.[15] In 1817, the year after buying Apsley House at Hyde Park Corner from his brother, the Duke of Wellington commissioned Canova's friend, sculptor

John Flaxman, to install *Napoleon as Mars the Peacemaker*. According to Flaxman, it took six men twelve days to position the thirteen-ton marble at the base of a Robert Adam designed staircase. To support the tremendous weight, the floor had to be strengthened by adding a brick pier to the basement below (in 1828, the staircase was redesigned and extended to the third floor).[16]

According to Susan Jenkins, critics thought that the placement of Napoleon's statue in the stairwell of Apsley House was a conscious slight by Wellington to his archnemesis. But as it turns out, the staircase was the residence's central location at the time. "Napoleon's place at the heart of Wellington's house reflects his importance as the indirect architect of Wellington's fortunes," writes Jenkins.[17] When asked to name the greatest captain of the age, Wellington replied: "In this age, in past ages, in any age, Napoleon."[18]

Starting in 1820, Wellington hosted an annual celebratory Waterloo Banquet in the dining room of Apsley House. George IV and other A-list guests dined on the Prussian service, a gift from Frederick William III. Between 1829 and Wellington's death in 1852, the banquet moved to the ninety-foot-long Waterloo Gallery.

Louis XVIII presented Wellington with a souvenir from Napoleon's One Hundred Days—embroidered flags of the French departments paraded on the Champ de Mars in June 1815. In 1818, Louis also gave the British war hero a spectacular Sèvres Egyptian-style service commissioned by Napoleon for Joséphine. To complement Canova's colossal marble of Napoleon, Wellington assembled painted portraits of the emperor and family members, including Joséphine and siblings Joseph and Pauline Bonaparte.

Ironically, another highly symbolic artwork ordered by Napoleon wound up in the hands of his enemy. In May 1817, the Sèvres Commander's Table arrived at London's Carlton House, a gift from Louis XVIII. "Is there anything more amiable in the world? Yes, assuredly I accept with warmest gratitude this testimony of the king's goodness, and I shall devote myself to it all my life," said the delighted Prince Regent.[19] The prestigious table featuring a central image of Alexander the Great surrounded by celebrated commanders of antiquity became one of George IV's most treasured possessions. For his coronation and state portraits, the king insisted on being depicted standing next to the table.

George IV's artistic taste was formed after the French Revolution when paintings and furniture from French aristocratic collections flooded London. As Prince of Wales, he took full advantage of the market, snatching up Dutch and Flemish paintings, including pictures by Rembrandt, Cuyp, and de Hooch. Among the magnificent French furniture adorning Buckingham Palace's state rooms was a writing desk by Jean-Henri Riesener, supplier to the French court. George also commissioned art. To celebrate Napoleon's defeat, he hired Thomas Lawrence to produce a series of battlefield portraits for Windsor's new Waterloo Chamber.

In 1824, Louis XVIII died and was succeeded by his younger brother Charles X. Except for Napoleon's Hundred Days, he had ruled for a decade. He would be the last king to be buried at Saint Denis. Despite the Bourbon effort to expunge Napoleon's memory, he remained woven into the very fabric of the capital. An imperial cult arose with new symbols and images. Like Julius Caesar after his assassination, France's authoritarian emperor was recast in exile and death as a defender of revolutionary principles and a symbol of patriotism. Throughout France, Napoleon's birthday and Saint Napoleon's day continued to be celebrated as an anti-royalist gesture.

Though many Napoleonic artworks were destroyed, some valuable objects were just too beautiful and valuable. Like the Colossus of Nero reworked by his successors, some of Napoleon's commissions were physically altered to remove references to the emperor. This was the case with the *Table of the Imperial Palaces*, the last of the Sèvres gueridons ordered in January 1811. On the green porcelain table top, landscape painter Jean-François Robert created nine panels representing palaces tied to Napoleon including the Tuileries, Saint-Cloud, Fontainebleau, Rambouillet, and Compiègne.

According to Gillian Arthur, the table was "de-Napoleonized" and "Bourbonized" during the Restoration. The features of Napoleon in a hunting costume with his family were replaced by those of Louis XVIII's son, the duc de Berry. Paintings of Versailles, St. Germain, and Meudon replaced three of Napoleon's palaces; Bourbon fleurs-de-lys were subbed for Napoleonic eagles.[20] Completed in April 1817, the table was presented eight years later by Charles X to Francis I, king of the Two Sicilies, the father-in-law of his assassinated son.[21]

From St. Helena, Napoleon wrote prophetically that "... sooner or later a volcanic eruption would engulf the throne, its surroundings and its followers." That eruption came in 1830, when Charles X was ousted in the July Revolution. During the Paris insurrection, many participants shouted "Long Live Napoleon!" and "Long Live Napoleon II!"[22] Following Charles's abdication, the Duc d'Orléans was named King Louis-Philippe. A cousin of Louis XVI whose father was killed during the French Revolution, Louis-Philippe faced a sharply divided France.

A year before Augustus's death on August 9, 14 C.E., he deposited four documents for safekeeping with the Vestal Virgins. These included his will, funeral instructions, a balance sheet of Rome's financial and military readiness, and a detailed, biased account of his achievements, known as the *Res Gestae Divi Augusti*, or the *Deeds of the Divine Augustus*.

After Augustus's death, the senate decreed he should be divinized. His will was read aloud and per his wishes, the *Res Gestae* was inscribed on a pair of bronze pillars placed in front of his mausoleum. It's believed that Augustus penned the first-person résumé years before his death and that Tiberius made some later edits.[23]

A brief introduction was followed by thirty-five paragraphs organized in four sections plus a third-person posthumous addendum. Section one details Augustus's political career; section two his public benefactions, donations of money, land and grain to the citizens of Italy and his soldiers, along with the public works and gladiator contests he ordered. Section three describes Augustus's military feats and alliances.

The finale reads: "In my thirteenth consulship [2 B.C.E.] the senate, the equestrian order and the whole people of Rome gave me the title of Father of my Country, resolved that this should be inscribed in the porch of my house and in the Curia Julia and in the Forum Augustum below the chariot which had been set there in my honour by decree of the Senate. At the time of writing I am in my seventy-sixth year."[24]

Interestingly, Augustus's opponents remain nameless throughout the document. Marc Antony is a "faction," Brutus and Cassius are "enemies of Rome," and Sextus Pompeius is implied to be a "pirate."[25] The appendix details Augustus's building spree, recording that the emperor spent six hundred million silver denarii (six hundred thousand gold denarii) from his own money on public works.

Augustus's funerary inscription proved to be an effective form of propaganda, immortalizing his reign and and serving as a monument to his Julio-Claudian successors. Though the original *Res Gestae* was lost, many copies were carved in stone on monuments and temples across the Empire. Almost a full copy written in the original Latin with a Greek translation was preserved on a temple to Roma and Augustus in Ankara (today's Turkey). Several other copies have been found in Asia Minor.

Like the mausoleum of Augustus, writes Valérie Huet, Trajan's columnar funerary monument along with the rest of his Forum functioned as his *res gestae.*[26] Trajan's literal res gestae was housed in the library flanking the column. Trajan outdid Augustus by also immortalizing his military actions in the marble reliefs of his column. As Huet puts it, the Austerlitz Column was Napoleon's res gestae, documenting his greatest military achievements.[27] Unlike Trajan's Column, the Austerlitz Column would not be Napoleon's funeral monument.

"Death is sleep without dreams, and perhaps without an awakening," Napoleon said on St. Helena.[28] Confined to bed, he dictated a lengthy statement for his son who he had never heard from. "My son should read much history and meditate upon it; it is the only true philosophy," he dictated on April 17, 1821. "Let him read and meditate upon the wars of the great captains: it is the only way to learn the art of war. Yet no matter what you say to him, no matter what he learns, he will profit little from it if in his innermost heart he lacks that sacred flame, that love of the good which alone inspires great deeds."[29]

On the evening of May 5, 1821, fifty-one-year-old Napoleon Bonaparte died, probably from stomach cancer. He was buried in the green uniform of a colonel of the Chasseurs de la garde in the Sane Valley by two willow trees. The French wanted the inscription "Napoleon. Born in Ajaccio on 15 August, 1769, died on St Helena, 5 May, 1821" inscribed on the flagstones.

The British would only permit "General Buonaparte." In the end, his gravesite went unmarked.

Emmanuel Las Cases, who had started taking notes aboard the *Northumberland*, continued his journal on St. Helena where he became Napoleon's confidant. After every conversation with Napoleon, Las Cases transcribed his notes; his fifteen-year-old son, also named Emmanuel, put the notes into a legible form.[30] Las Cases was expelled from St. Helena in December 1816, and his notes were confiscated by the British. In 1821, Las Cases retrieved the journal and published the first edition of *Le Mémorial de Sainte-Hélène* the following year. It was a best-seller, sending political shock waves through Europe.

Napoleon's death on St. Helena enhanced his legend. Writers and artists portrayed his death and burial in wildly romantic terms. Napoleon became a hero of mythology. Edgar Quinet suggested immortality in his 1836 poem *Napoleon*: "He is not dead! He is not dead! From his slumber/ The giant will emerge even stronger at his awakening."[31] Some refused to believe Napoleon had died.

Napoleon's will, dated April 15, 1821, included this request: "It is my wish that my ashes repose on the banks of the Seine, in the midst of the French people, whom I have loved so well." For two decades after Napoleon's death, a movement grew for the British to allow him to be buried in Paris.[32]

With support fading for his own regime, Louis-Philippe took advantage of Napoleon's popularity. The statue of Napoleon was put back on top of the Austerlitz Column; the Arc de Triomphe was finally finished and the original reliefs were reinstalled at the Arc du Carrousel. Now the "citizen king" began negotiating with the British to repatriate Napoleon's remains from St. Helena.

The location of Napoleon's tomb was a topic of intense debate. "The choosing of the location of the tomb and the competition for the construction of it were of such great importance to the French nation that any decision was not taken lightly by the government," writes Fiona Parr. "Feelings towards Napoleon were so strong—both positive and negative—that every step of the way during the construction of his tomb there were debates and arguments."[33]

Not wanting to incite unrest, the government of the July Monarchy rejected burial sites with strong Napoleonic associations like the Church of the Madeleine, Arc de Triomphe, Saint Denis, and Chaillot hill. A petition called for the reburial of Napoleon's remains in the base of the Austerlitz Column—like the ashes of Trajan in the base of his column in Rome. The proposal was quickly defeated by the Chamber of Deputies.

Adolphe Thiers, président du conseil under Louis-Philippe, spearheaded a plan for a different site. In mid-1840, a law passed ordering construction of Napoleon's tomb at the Church of the Invalides. The royal chapel at Invalides was built at the end of the seventeenth century by Jules Hardouin-Mansart. Reportedly given just one week to submit the chapel plan, the ambitious young architect seems to have repurposed his great-uncle François Mansart's unrealized design for a Bourbon funerary chapel at Saint Denis, adding his own touches to the French baroque building.[34] Louis XIV had ordered construction of the adjacent Hôtel des Invalides in 1670 to provide shelter and hospital care for old and wounded veterans. Napoleon paid three visits to his own soldiers here in 1808, 1813, and 1815.

A contest for the design of Napoleon's tomb led to a major brouhaha. Over eighty submissions were exhibited to the public. Architects submitted almost half of the entries; sculptors another thirty percent. Ultimately, Louis Visconti's design was chosen—a sarcophagus below ground level in a crypt lit from the church's dome. The excavation of the opening for the sarcophagus directly below the dome destroyed much of the original seventeenth-century marble floor.[35] The circular opening, nearly fifty feet in diameter and twenty feet deep, was adorned with neoclassical art—winged Victories and bas-reliefs of key events in Napoleon's reign.

In 1840, a delegation including Napoleon's loyal valet Louis Marchand and Generals Gourgaud and Bertrand sailed to St. Helena to bring back his body. In addition, the delegation collected fragments of wood and rocks on the island which were treated like religious relics. When Napoleon's body was exhumed, it was practically intact and he seemed to be sleeping, like Alexander the Great, writes Paul Rapelli.[36] On October 15, Napoleon's coffin was transferred onto the French frigate *La Belle Poule*.

After landing at Cherbourg, France on November 30, Napoleon's casket traveled by steamboat up the Seine. On the bitterly cold morning of December 15, his funeral procession left Courbevoie, four miles north of Paris. Accompanied by drums and trumpets, hundreds of mounted soldiers led the march followed by Grande Armée veterans in their Napoleonic uniforms. Behind a six-hundred-member choir, a grenadier led a white stallion wearing Napoleon's saddle and draped in purple velvet. Sixteen black horses with ivory plumes pulled the towering funeral chariot accompanied by five hundred sailors.[37] Napoleon's heart lay in an urn at his feet. He requested it be sent to Marie Louise, but she refused to accept it.[38]

The magnificent cortege traveled south through Neuilly toward Paris where some one hundred thousand gathered to see Napoleon's hearse. As the horses bearing the casket stopped below the 160-foot-tall Arc de Triomphe de l'Etoile, the music stopped. The eerie silence was shattered with a deafening roar of "Vive l'Empereur!" and a spontaneous singing by the National Guard of the patriotic anthem, "La Marseillaise."

Napoleon hadn't lived to see his triumphal arch finished, but it became his greatest monument. Work stopped with the fall of the Empire and resumed in 1824. After thirty years and many changes in design and architects, the arch finally opened in July 1836.

Thirty shields engraved with the names of major French victories in the French Revolution and Napoleonic wars adorned the attic. On the shorter sides of the four columns are the names of Napoleon's thirty major victories. Allegorical figures representing characters from Roman mythology adorn the arcades. Four of the six reliefs on the façades mark Napoleonic victories: The Battle of Aboukir, The Battle of Arcole, The Fall of Alexandria, and The Battle of Austerlitz.

Napoleon wanted the names of his generals, marshals, and colonels from the campaign of 1805 represented on the monument. Instead, as Anne Muratori-Philip describes, a "battle of the inscriptions" was waged throughout the nineteenth century. By 1895, 697 names and 174 battles were inscribed on the interior of the arch.[39]

On the frigid winter morning of Napoleon's funeral, his triumphal arch was finally consecrated. Underneath the soaring arch, his casket was surrounded with the names of 386 generals; those killed in battle were underlined. On the left side, facing the Champs-Élysées was Jean-Pierre Cortot's relief, *The Triumph of Napoleon* celebrating the Treaty of Schönbrunn with Napoleon crowned by the goddess of Victory.[40]

Among the throngs that day was Victor Hugo, whose father had served under Napoleon. The novelist recalled that the sun suddenly appeared at the same time as Napoleon's hearse. Before the funeral, he had written "The Emperor's Return" in 1840: "*Sire, you will return to your capital, Without fighting or fury, Drawn by eight black horses through the Arch Triumphal, Dressed like an Emperor.*"[41] (During Hugo's own funeral in 1885, his body lay in state under the Arc de Triomphe.)

The streets were filled with red, white, and blue flags decorated with eagles and Napoleonic battles; statues representing his victories ran from the Arc de Triomphe to the Pont de la Concorde.[42] From the Arc de Triomphe, the cortege continued down the icy Champs-Élysées and across the Place de la Concorde before finally arriving at Les Invalides to the roar of cannons. In the esplanade, statues of France's heroes surrounded a huge plaster likeness of Napoleon. Over a million people braved the piercing cold in tribute to the former emperor.[43]

Three dozen sailors covered the coffin draped with a red cross and Napoleon's crown. Louis-Philippe accepted Napoleon's remains "in the name of France" and ordered Napoleon's Austerlitz sword and signature bicorn hat from Eylau placed atop his coffin in the center of the church below the dome. Over the next two days, a quarter of a million people paid their respects. From there, Napoleon's body was moved to the nearby chapel of Saint-Jérôme, one of the church's four circular side chapels some fifteen feet in diameter and eighty-two feet tall.

With the death in 1832 of Napoleon's son, his cousin Louis Napoleon Bonaparte, son of Louis Bonaparte and Hortense de Beauharnais, became heir presumptive to the imperial throne. In December 1848, Napoleon's nephew was elected president of the Second Republic. Two years later on the anniversary of his uncle's coronation, Louis Napoleon staged a coup d'état. Exactly one year later, on December 2, 1851, he established the Second Empire with himself as Napoleon III.

The inauguration of Napoleon's funerary monument was originally set for May 5, 1853, the thirty-first anniversary of his death. But eight more years transpired before the ceremony took place. Like his uncle, Napoleon III considered creating a family burial vault at Saint Denis near the tombs of France's royals.

Almost forty years after his death, in an April 2, 1861, ceremony attended by his nephew, Napoleon's body was transferred from Invalides' Saint-Jerôme chapel to the dramatic crypt below the church dome. Bronze doors forged from enemy cannons at Austerlitz flanked by allegories of Military Force and Civil Force led to the uncovered crypt, circular in shape like the mausoleums of Roman emperors Augustus and Hadrian. Above the lintel was the inscription from Napoleon's will: "I wish my ashes to rest on the banks of the Seine among the people of France whom I haved loved so well."

Napoleon's tomb was a marble res gestae. A circular gallery of austere white marble bas-reliefs illustrating Napoleon's major achievements adorned the peristyle. Sculptor Pierre-Charles Simart, a student of Ingres, created the classically-inspired models for all ten works and executed seven. Featuring inscriptions from de Las Cases's *Mémorial de Sainte-Hélène*, they include the *Creation of the Legion of Honor*, *The Civil Code*, and *Great Public Works*.

A visitor to the crypt in 1853 described the newly installed Public Works relief: "Napoleon, who is seated and whose head is surrounded by a crown of rays, is stretching forth his two arms toward tablets bearing the names and purposes of the various monuments and works of public utility, executed during his reign and by his order. . . . Two Glories are seated on the steps of the throne to the right and to the left."[44]

Encircling the sarcophagus were a dozen monumental winged Victories, each about fifteen feet tall, representing Napoleon's military triumphs. From the entry of the crypt, the figures run chronologically from the Italian campaign to the Belgium campaign. Carved in white marble by Jean-Jacques Pradier, the female figures hold palm branches and wreaths; the two flanking the door, guardians of the tomb, hold keys.

With his taste for the monumental, Napoleon would have especially liked this contemporary description: "Each caryatis, together with the pillar against which it placed, consists of a single [marble] block. This . . . imparts an air of great magnificence to the mausoleum, and gives it that peculiar character of grandeur which is found in the gigantic constructions of Egypt and ancient Nineveh."[45]

The military theme continued beneath Napoleon's sarcophagus with a round floor mosaic featuring the names of Napoleonic battles and a border of laurel. Red quartzite from Russia was chosen for the antique-style sarcophagus because of its resemblance to porphyry, antiquity's most prized stone.[46] Roman emperors like Hadrian and their family members coveted the polished purple-red imperial variety, quarried in Egypt. Difficult to work, the prestigious stone was used for vases, columns, and sarcophagi.

Resting on a green granite pedestal, the sarcophagus measures nearly thirteen feet long and over six and a half feet wide. It contains six coffins: one made of soft iron, another of mahogany, two of lead, one of ebony (from the national funeral on December 15, 1840), and one of oak. Napoleon is dressed in his colonel's uniform (of the cavalry of the Guard) with his sash of the Legion of Honor. His bicorn hat rests on his legs.[47]

A year after the tomb's opening, Jérôme Bonaparte was buried in the chapel of Saint-Jerôme, which had housed Napoleon's coffin for over two decades. Joseph Bonaparte was also buried at Invalides, as were two of Napoleon's most trusted aides—Grand Marshals of the Palace General Geraud-Christophe-Michel Duroc who died at Bautzen in 1813, and General Henri Gatien Bertrand who accompanied Napoleon to Elba and St. Helena and died in 1844.

During his triumphant tour of Paris in June 1940, Adolf Hitler visited Napoleon's tomb. As a tribute to the French emperor who he admired, Hitler ordered the remains of Napoleon's son transferred from Vienna to the Invalides crypt that December. In 1969, the king of Rome was reinterred under a marble slab near his father's sarcophagus. Looming over the tombstone is Simart's marble statue of Napoleon as a Roman emperor. The Caesar of Paris is shown wearing a Roman laurel wreath and holding an orb and scepter topped with Jupiter's eagle.

POSTSCRIPT

After Napoleon's fall, France continued to experience revolts, revolutions, and wars. In the course of the ensuing violence, the Tuileries Palace and Château de Saint-Cloud were destroyed. Napoleon's emblematic Austerlitz Column was toppled and rebuilt; the original statue on top melted down and remade twice, first with Napoleon in his bicorn and frock coat, later as a Roman emperor again. The giant plaster elephant at the Place de la Bastille was joined by a column honoring those killed in the 1830 Revolution.

Other Napoleonic buildings and monuments were repurposed, including the Temple to the Glory of the Grande Armée, the supersized version of the Roman temple in Nîmes, Maison-Carrée. Louis XVIII turned Napoleon's military shrine into the Church of the Madeleine, consecrated to the memory of his family members guillotined in the nearby Place de la Concorde.

The Madeleine's imposing neoclassical exterior was a stark contrast to its gilded interior. Lit by oculi in the center of three coffered domes, the church was adorned with paintings, mosaics, and sculptures, including Carlo Marochetti's theatrical statue *Magdalene exalted by Angels* behind the altar.

In October 1849, Frédéric Chopin's funeral was held at the Madeleine. To the strains of Chopin's own haunting *Funeral March* on the pipe organ, pallbearers including Eugène Delacroix carried the composer's casket down the long nave. At the north end of the church, they placed his casket by the high altar. Overhead, mourners saw the cupola of the apse filled with a colorful semicircular fresco.

King Louis-Philippe himself had presided at the mural's unveiling in July 1838, the anniversary of his monarchy. One of France's largest mural paintings, *The History of Christianity* by Jules-Claude Ziegler covers nearly three hundred square yards. Three angels bear Mary Magdalene up toward the figure of Christ at the top of a pyramid while popes, saints, martyrs, and artists form an enormous semicircle. A bishop holds a scroll marked "Concordat" while cardinals look on.

Standing front and center in an ermine-trimmed red velvet coronation robe is Napoleon receiving a crown from Pius VII. Behind him, a large imperial eagle perches menacingly in the clouds.

Depicting Napoleon as a friend of the Church was a deliberate gambit by Louis-Philippe and Adolphe Thiers, his interior minister. In Ziegler's colorful revision of history, Napoleon saves the Church and by association France's Catholic monarchy.[1]

A decade after the mural's installation, in February 1848, Louis-Philippe abdicated and fled to England. Another revolution had begun.

BIBLIOGRAPHY

Adams, John Paul. "Sede Vacante 1799–1800." California State University Northridge, September 29, 2015. https://www.csun.edu/~hcfll004/SV1800.html.

"Alexander How Great? Ancient History and Civilization: Confronting the Classics." Erenow. https://erenow.com/ancient/confronting-the-classics-traditions-adventures-and-innovations/5.html.

Alexander, Edward P. *Museum Masters: Their Museums and their Influence.* Nashville, Tenn.: American Association for State and Local History, 1983.

Alexander, Napoleon & Joséphine: A Story of Friendship, War & Art from the Hermitage. Zwolle, The Netherlands: WBOOKS, 2015.

Allard, Sebastian, et al., eds. *Citizens and Kings: Portraits in the Age of Revolution 1760–1830.* London: Royal Academy of Arts, 2007.

Allegret, Marc, and Peter Hicks. "Lesueur, Jean-François." Napoleon Foundation. https://www.napoleon.org/en/history-of-the-two-empires/biographies/lesueur-jean-francois/.

Almoguera, Adrián. "Project for the Bonaparte Forum in Madrid." Napoleon Foundation. Translated by Leyly Moridi and Peter Hicks. September 2016. https://www.napoleon.org/en/history-of-the-two-empires/objects/projet-for-the-bonaparte-forum-in-madrid/.

Ambrosini, Maria Luisa. *The Secret Archives of the Vatican.* Boston: Little, Brown, 1969.

Anderson, James C. Jr. "Anachronism in the Roman Architecture of Gaul: The Date of the Maison Carrée at Nîmes." *Journal of the Society of Architectural Historians* 60, no. 1 (March 2001): 68–79.

Anderson, Robin. *Pope Pius VII (1800–1823): His Life, Reign and Struggle with Napoleon in the Aftermath of the French Revolution.* Charlotte, N.C.: TAN Books, 2001.

Anderson, Sam."The Majestic Marble Quarries of Northern Italy." *New York Times Magazine,* July 26, 2017.

Andrews, Even. "8 Legendary Ancient Libraries." History.com. November 17, 2016. http://www.history.com/news/history-lists/8-impressive-ancient-libraries.

BIBLIOGRAPHY

Androsov, Sergei, Mario Guderzo, and Giuseppe Pavanello. *Canova*. Milan, Italy: Skira, 2003.

Antoni-Komar, I. "Zur Rezeption der Frisur a la Titus am Ende des 18. Jahrhunderts." In *Haar Tragen. Eine kulturwissenschaftliche Annaherung*, edited by C. Janecke, 209–31. Cologne, Germany: Böhlau Verlag, 2004.

"The Apartment of the Empress." Palais de Compiègne. http://en.palaisdecompiegne.fr/one-palace-three-museums/historic-apartments/apartment-empress.

Apolloni, Marco Fabio. *Napoleone e le arti*. Florence and Milan, Italy: Giunti Editore, 2004.

Ardiet, Vincent, Elisabeth Caude, et al. *La pourpre et l'exil: L'Aiglon et le Prince impérial*. Paris: Réunion des musées nationaux, 2004. Exhibition catalog.

Asuni, Michele. "Jupiter and Eagle." Johns Hopkins Archeological Museum. http://archaeologicalmuseum.jhu.edu/the-collection/object-stories/the-roman-house-at-hopkins/the-art-of-light/jupiter-and-eagle/.

Augustus. *Res gestae divi Augusti*. Introduction and commentary by P. A. Brunt and J. M. Moore. London: Oxford University Press, 1967.

Avrillion, Marie-Jeanne-Pierrette. *Mémoires de Mademoiselle Avrillion, première femme de chambre de l'impératrice Joséphine*. Edited by Maurice Dernelle. Paris: Mercure de France, 1986.

Ayers, Andrew. *The Architecture of Paris: An Architectural Guide*. Stuttgart, Germany, and London: Edition Axel Menges, 2004.

Baker, Malcolm. "Antonio Canova. Venice and Possagno." *Burlington Magazine* 134, no. 1072 (July 1992): 460–463.

Bakogianni, Anastasia, and Valerie M. Hope, eds. *War as Spectacle: Ancient and Modern Perspectives on the Display of Armed Conflict*. London and New York: Bloomsbury Academic, 2015.

Baltard, Victor. "École de Percier. Mémoire lu à la séance annuelle de l'Académie des beax-arts." *Institut de France* 43, no. 17 (November 15, 1873): 46.

Bargellini, Sante. "Paganini and the Princess." *Musical Quarterly* 20, no. 4 (October 1934): 408–418.

Barrillon, Béatrice Tupinier. "Cupid and Psyche." Louvre. http://www.louvre.fr/en/oeuvre-notices/cupid-and-psyche.

Barron, James. "Finally, From Italy, the Full George Washington." *New York Times*, April 23, 2017.

"Basilica of Saint Denis, The Role of Napoleon Bonaparte." Seine-Saint-Denis Tourisme. https://uk.tourisme93.com/basilica/the-role-of-napoleon-bonaparte-in-the-basilica-st-denis-restoration.html.

Baudez, Basile, and Nicholas Olsberg. *A Civic Utopia: Architecture and the City in France, 1795–1837*. Edited by Markus Lāhteenmāki. London: Drawing Matters Studio, 2016.

Bazin, Germain. *The Louvre*. New York: Harry M. Abrams, 1958.

Bazin, Germain. *The Museum Age*. Brussels: Desier S.A. Editions, 1967.

Beard, Mary. "Alexander: How Great?" *New York Review of Books*, October 27, 2011. http//:www.nybooks.com/articles/archives/2011/oct/27/alexander-how-great/?pagination=false.

Beard, Mary. *The Roman Triumph*. Cambridge, Mass., and London: Harvard University Press, 2007.

Beard, Mary. "The Twelve Caesars: Images of Power from Ancient Rome to Salvador Dali, Part 4: Caesar's Wife: Above Suspicion?" Lecture presented at the Sixtieth A. W. Mellon Lectures in the Fine Arts, National Gallery of Art, Washington, D.C., April 17, 2011.

Beauhaire, Matthieu, Mathilde Bejanin, and Hubert Naudeix. *L'Eléphant de Napoléon*. Arles, France: Honoré Clair Editions, 2014.

Becker, Jeffrey A. "Maison Carrée." Smarthistory, March 8, 2016. http://smarthistory.org/maison-carree/.

BIBLIOGRAPHY

Bedard, Jean-François. "Franks, Not Romans: Medieval Imagery and the Making of Imperial France." Paper presented at the Percier: Antiquity and Empire Symposium, Bard Graduate Center, New York, November 18, 2016.

Belozerskaya, Marina, and Kenneth Lapatin. "Antiquity Consumed: Transformations at San Marco, Venice." In *Antiquity and its Interpreters*, edited by Alina Payne, 83–95. Cambridge, U.K.: Cambridge University Press, 2000.

Beltrami, Costanza. Italian Art Society Blog, August 26, 2015. http://italianartsociety.tumblr.com/post/127642287447/by-costanza-beltrami-gem-engraver-and-medalist.

Bennington, Charles. *Luca Carlevarijs: Views of Venice*. San Diego, Calif.: Timken Museum of Art, 2001.

Bergvelt, Ellinoor. *Napoleon's Legacy: The Rise of National Museums in Europe 1794–1830*. Berlin: G+H Verlag, 2009.

Bernocchi, Ilaria. "'Inventing' Identity: Medals and Heroic Portraits in the Italian Renaissance." Paper presented at Full Circle: The Medal in Art History, A Symposium in Honor of Stephen K. Scher, The Frick Collection, New York, September 8, 2017.

Bertini, Giuseppe. "Works of art from Parma in Paris during Napoleon's time and their restitution." Paper presented at the Development of National Museums in Europe 1794–1830 International Conference, University of Amsterdam, January 31–February 2, 2008.

Bertrand, Pascal-François. "Louis XIV and Louis XV: Their Coronations and Their Tapestries." In *Woven Gold: Tapestries of Louis XIV*, edited by Charissa Bremer-David, 39–50. Los Angeles: The J. Paul Getty Museum, 2015.

Bertrand, Pascale, ed. *Napoleon at Les Invalides*. Paris: Societe Française de Promotion Artistique, Connaissance des Arts, 2007.

Bertrand, Pascale, ed. *The Château de Fontainebleau*. Paris: Société Française de Promotion Artistique, Connaissance des Arts, 2008.

Beyeler, Christophe. *Noces impériales: le mariage de Napoléon et Marie-Louise dessiné par Baltard*. Paris: Somogy; Fontainebleau: Château de Fontainebleau, 2010.

Beyeler, Christophe. *Pie VII face à Napoleon, la tiare dans les serres de l'Aigle*. Paris: Reunion des musées nationaux, 2015.

Beyeler, Christophe, and Vincent Cochet. *Enfance impériale: le roi de Rome, fils de Napoléon*. Dijon, France: Faton; Fontainebleau: Château de Fontainebleau, 2011.

Bianchi Bandinelli, Ranuccio. *Rome: The Center of Power: Roman Art to AD 200*. Translated by Peter Green. London: Thames and Hudson, 1970.

Bindman, David. "Canova and Color." Sydney J. Freedberg Lecture on Italian Art, National Gallery of Art, Washington D.C., November 2015. https://www.nga.gov/audio-video/video/freedberg-bindman.html.

Blaufarb, Rafe. *Napoleon: Symbol for an Age*. New York: Bedford/St. Martin's, 2008.

Blom, Phillip. *To Have and to Hold: An Intimate History of Collectors and Collecting*. New York: Overlook Press, 2002.

Blunt, Anthony, "Naples under the Bourbons." *Burlington Magazine* 121, no. 913 (April 1979): 207–208, 211.

Boime, Albert. *Art in an Age of Bonapartism, 1800–1815*. Chicago: University of Chicago Press, 1990.

Bonaparte, Napoleon. *Aphorisms*. Collected by Honoré de Balzac. Richmond, U.K.: Oneworld Classics Ltd., 2008.

BIBLIOGRAPHY

Bonaparte, Napoleon. *A Selection from the Letters and Dispatches of the First Napoleon: With Explanatory Notes*. London: Chapman and Hall, 1884.

Bonaparte, Napoleon. *Letters and Documents of Napoleon, Volume I: The Rise to Power.* Selected and translated by John Eldred Howard. London: Cresset Press, 1961.

Bonaparte, Napoleon. *The Napoleon Calendar: A Quotation from the Works and Sayings of Napoleon for Every Day in the Year.* Edited by John McErlean. Mississauga, Canada: Poniard Publishing, 1996.

Bonaparte, Napoleon. *The Opinions and Reflections of Napoleon*. Edited by Lewis Claflin Breed. Boston: Four Seas Company, 1926.

Bond, Sarah E. "Erasing the Face of History." *New York Times,* May 14, 2011. http://www.nytimes.com/2011/05/15/opinion/15bond.html?_r=1&.

Bondanella, Peter E. *The Eternal City: Roman Images in the Modern World*. Chapel Hill: University of North Carolina Press, 1987.

Bonde, Sheila. "Renaissance and Real Estate: The Medieval Afterlife of the 'Temple of Diana' in Nîmes." In *Antiquity and Its Interpreters*, edited by Alina Payne, Ann Kuttner, and Rebekah Smick, 57–69. Cambridge, U.K.: Cambridge University Press, 2000.

Bonfante, Larissa. "Nudity as a Costume in Classical Art." *American Journal of Archeology* 93, no. 4 (October 1989): 543–570.

Booth, David W. "Some Little-Known Designs by Louis-Pierre Baltard and Jean-Baptiste Rondelet for the Transformation of the Church of the Madeleine into a Temple of Glory." *Canadian Art Review* 16, no. 2 (1989): 147–154, 251–261.

Bordaz, Robert, and Claude Mollard. "Napoleon et l'Architecture." *Nouvelle Revue des Deux Mondes* (July 1, 1973): 98.

Bordes, Philippe. *Jacques-Louis David: Empire to Exile*. New Haven, CT, and London: Yale University Press, 2005.

de Bourrienne, Louis-Antoine Fauvelet. *Memoirs of Napoleon Bonaparte.* Edited by R. W. Phipps. London: Richard Bentley and Son, 1885.

Boutry, Phillipe. *Pius VII in the Papacy: An Encyclopedia*, Vol. 2. Edited by Philippe Levillain. New York and London: Routledge, 2002.

Boyer, Ferdinand. *Le monde des arts en Italie et la France de la Révolution et de l'Empire. Études et recherché.* Turin, Italy: Società editrice internazionale, 1970.

Bradley, Mark. *Colour and Meaning in Ancient Rome*. Cambridge, U.K., and New York: Cambridge University Press, 2009.

Brenk, Beat. "Spolia from Constantine to Charlemagne: Aesthetics Versus Ideology." *Dumbarton Oaks Papers* 41 (1987): 103–109.

Briant, Pierre. *The First European: A History of Alexander in the Age of Empire*. Translated by Nicholas Elliott. Cambridge, Mass.: Harvard University Press, 2017.

Brier, Bob. "Napoleon in Egypt." *Archeology* 52, no. 3 (May/June 1999): 44–53.

Brilliant, Richard. "The Arch of Septimius Severus in the Roman Forum." *Memoirs of the American Academy in Rome* 29 (January 1967): 5–271.

Brilliant, Richard. "Hairiness: A Matter of Style and Substance in Roman Portraits." *Studies in the History of Art* 43 (1993): 302–312. http://www.jstor.org/stable/42622078.

Brooks, Peter. "Napoleon's Eye." *New York Review of Books*, November 19, 2009. http://www.nybooks.com/articles/2009/11/19/napoleons-eye/.

Burleigh, Nina. *Mirage: Napoleon's Scientists and the Unveiling of Egypt*. New York: Harper, 2007.

Buvelot, Quentin. "Nederlands eerste museum: De Galerij Prins Willem V in Den Haag." *Desipientia: Kunsthistorisch Tijdschrift* 20, no. 1 (2013): 4–8.

Buvelot, Quentin. "1785–1815: Intermezzo in Paris, Musée Napoléon." In *Royal Picture Gallery Mauritshuis: A Princely Collection*, Peter van der Ploeg and Quentin Buvelot, 30–31. The Hague: Royal Picture Gallery Mauritshuis and Zwolle, The Netherlands: Waanders, 2006.

de Buyer, Xavier. *Fontaines de Paris*. Paris: F. Bibal, 1987.

Byrne, Janet S. "The Best Laid Plans." *Metropolitan Museum of Art Bulletin, New Series* 17, no. 7 (March 1959): 182–195.

Cage, E. Claire. "The Sartorial Self: Neoclassical Fashion and Gender Identity in France, 1797–1804." *Eighteenth-Century Studies* 42, no. 2 (Winter 2009): 193–215.

Campbell, Duncan B. "Caesar's Invasions of Britain." The Landmark Julius Caesar. www.thelandmarkcaesar.com.

Canova, Antonio. *Napoleon and Canova: Eight Conversations Held at the Château of the Tuileries, in 1810*. London: Treuttel and Wurtz, Treuttel, jun. and Richter, Soho Square, 1825.

Caracciolo, Maria Teresa, ed. *Les Soeurs de Napoleon*. Paris: Musée Marmottan Monet, 2013.

"Caroline, Soeur de Napoleon, Reine des Arts," Ajaccio. Palais Fesch-musée des Beaux-Arts. June 2017. https://enfilade18thc.files.wordpress.com/2017/07/palais-fesch-exposition-caroline-murat-dp.pdf.

Carroll, Maureen. "*Memoria* and *Damnatio Memoriae*. Preserving and erasing identities in Roman funerary commemoration." In *Living through the Dead: Burial and Commemoration in the Classical World*, edited by Maureen Carroll and Jane Rempel, 65–89. Oxford, U.K.: Oxbow Books, 2011.

Casey, Hiram, ed. *Law, Love, and Religion of Napoleon Bonaparte*. New York: Carlton 1961.

Casson, Lionel. "Ptolemy II and the Hunting of African Elephants." *Transactions of the American Philological Association* 123 (1993): 247–260.

"Cathedral of Notre Dame in Paris." Napoleon Foundation. https://www.napoleon.org/en/magazine/places/cathedral-of-notre-dame-in-paris/.

Caulaincourt, Armand-Augustin-Louis. *With Napoleon in Russia*. Edited and translated by Jean Hanoteau. 1935. Reprint, Mineola, N.Y.: Dover, 2005

Cavendish, Richard. "Napoleon Divorces Joséphine." *History Today* 59, no. 12 (December 2009). http://www.historytoday.com/richard-cavendish/napoleon-divorces-josephine.

Charles, Michael B., and Peter Rhodan. "Magister Elephantorvm: A Reappraisal of Hannibal's Use of Elephants." *Classical World* 100, no. 4 (Summer 2007): 363–389.

Charney, Noah. *Stealing the Mystic Lamb: The True Story of the World's Most Coveted Masterpiece*. New York: Public Affairs, 2010.

Chevalier, Bernard, Andrzej Rottermund, Jean-Pierre Samoyault, and Emmanuel Starcky. *Napoléon Ier ou la légende des Arts, 1800–1815*. Paris: Éditions de la Reunion des musées nationaux-Grand Palais, 2015.

Claridge, Amanda. *Rome: An Oxford Archaeological Guide*. Oxford, U.K., and New York: Oxford University Press, 1998.

Coarelli, Filippo. *The Column of Marcus Aurelius*. Translated by Helen Patterson. Rome: Editore Colombo, 2008.

Coarelli, Filippo. *Monuments of Civilization: Rome*. London: Cassell, 1973.

Cocke, Richard. *Paolo Veronese: Piety and Display in an Age of Religious Reform.* Burlington, Vt.: Ashgate, 2001.

Coignet, Jean-Roche. *Memoires.* London: Peter Davis Limited, 1928.

Coignet, Jean-Roche. *The Note-Books of Captain Coignet, Soldier of the Empire.* With an introduction by the Hon. Sir John Fortescue. London: Peter Davies, 1928.

Coliva, Anna, and Fernando Mazzocca, eds. *Canova e la Venere vincitrice.* Milan, Italy: Electa, 2007.

Collins, Jeffrey. "Obelisks as Artifacts in Early Modern Rome: Collecting the Ultimate Antiques." *Richerche di Storia dell'Arte*, no. 72 (2000): 49–68.

Collins, Jeffrey Laird. *Papacy and Politics in Eighteenth-Century Rome: Pius VI and the Arts.* Cambridge, U.K., and New York: Cambridge University Press, 2004.

Connelly, Owen. *Napoleon's Satellite Kingdoms.* Malabar, Fla.: Robert E. Krieger, 1990.

Conner, Susan P. "Napoleon's Courtesans, Citoyennes, and Cantinières." *Members' Bulletin of the Napoleonic Society of America* 73 (Spring 2003): 21–25.

Conti, Flavio. *A Profile of Ancient Rome.* Los Angeles: J. Paul Getty Museum, 2003.

Coppa, Frank J., ed. *Controversial Concordants: The Vatican's Relations with Napoleon, Mussolini, and Hitler.* Washington, D.C.: Catholic University of America Press, 1990.

Coppa, Frank J. *The Modern Papacy Since 1789.* London and New York: Longman, 1998.

Cordier, Sylvain. *Napoleon: The Imperial Household.* New Haven, CT: Yale University Press, 2018.

Coulston, J.C.N. "Three new books on Trajan's Column." *Journal of Roman Archeology* (1990): 290–309.

"The Cradle of the King of Rome Napoleon II." Imperial Treasury Museum, Vienna. http://wiener-schatzkammer.at/cradle-king-rome.html.

Crichton-Miller, Emma. "Portrait medals." *Apollo* (September 2017): 96–97.

Cuccia, Phillip. "Controlling the Archives: The Requisition, Removal, and Return of the Vatican Archives during the Age of Napoleon." *Napoleonica. La Revue,* no. 17 (February 2013): 66–74.

Cunial, Giancarlo, and Massimiliano Pavan. *Antonio Canova, Museum and Gipsoteca.* Possagno, Italy: Fondazione Canova Onlus, 2009.

Curry, A. "A War Diary Soars Over Rome." *National Geographic Magazine*, March 2015. https://www.nationalgeographic.com/trajan-column/article.html.

Curzi, Valter, Carolina Brook, Claudio Parisi Presicce, eds. *Il museo universale: dal sogno di Napoleone a Canova.* Milan, Italy: Skira, 2016.

Dalby, Andrew. *Empire of Pleasures: Luxury and Indulgence in the Roman World.* New York: Routledge, 2000.

Daniels, Margaret H. "M. Le Baron Vivant Denon." *Metropolitan Museum of Art Bulletin* 20, no. 11 (November 1925): 264–268.

Davies, Elliott, and Emanuela Tarizzo. *Canova and His Legacy.* Verona, Italy: Paul Holberton Publishing, 2017.

Davies, G.A.T. "Topography and the Trajan Column." *Journal of Roman Studies* 10 (1920): 1–28.

Davies, G.A.T. "Trajan's First Dacian War." *Journal of Roman Studies* 7 (1917): 74–97.

Davies, Penelope J. E. *Death and the Emperor: Roman Imperial Funerary Monuments, from Augustus to Marcus Aurelius.* Cambridge, U.K., and New York: Cambridge University Press, 2000.

Davies, Penelope J. E. "The Politics of Perpetuation: Trajan's Column and the Art of Commemoration." *American Journal of Archeology* 101, no. 1 (January 1997): 41–65.

Davis, Blair Hixson. "The Roman Drawings of Charles Percier." PhD diss., University of California, Santa Barbara, 2009.

"The Day of Napoleon's Coronation." Napoleon Foundation. https://www.napoleon.org/en/history-of-the-two-empires/timelines/the-day-of-napoleons-coronation-11-frimaire-an-xiii-2-december-1804/.

De Albentiis, Emidio. "Art, Power, and Consensus: From Trajan to Constantine." In *Rome: Art & Architecture*, edited by Marco Bussagli, 102–153. Cologne, Germany: Könemann, 1999.

De Beer, Gavin. *Alps and Elephants*. Boston: Dutton, 1957.

De Bellaigue, Geoffrey. *French porcelain in the collection of her Majesty the Queen*. London: Royal Collection Enterprises, 2009.

De Bellaigue, Geoffrey, "A Royal Keepsake: The Table of the Grand Commanders." *Furniture History* 34 (1998): 112–141.

De Feo, Roberto. *Giuseppe Borsato 1770–1849*. Verona, Italy: Scripta Edizioni, 2016.

DeLorme, Eleanor P., ed. *Joséphine and the Arts of the Empire*. Los Angeles: J. Paul Getty Museum, 2005.

Delors, Catherine. "Imperial wedding: Napoléon and Marie Louise." May 2011. http://blog.catherinedelors.com/imperial-wedding-napoleon-and-marie-louise/.

De Méneval, Claude-François. *Memoirs of Napoleon Bonaparte*, Vol. 2. New York: P. F. Collier & Son, 1910.

De Nanteuil, Luc. *David*. New York: Henry N. Abrams, 1990.

Denon, Vivant. *Travels in Upper and Lower Egypt*. 1803. Reprint, New York: Arno Press, 1973.

"Denon Discovers Ancient Egypt." Napoleon and the Scientific Expedition to Egypt. http://napoleon.lindahall.org/denon.shtml#top.

Denoyelle, Martine, and Sophie Descamps-Lequime. *The Eye of Joséphine: the antiquities collection of the Empress in the Musée du Louvre*. Atlanta, Ga.: High Museum of Art and Paris: Musée du Louvre, 2008.

"Diamond in the crown: Le Grand Mazarin." Christie's, October 18, 2017. http://www.christies.com/features/Le-Grand-Mazarin-Diamond-in-the-Crown-8625-3.aspx?pid=en_homepage_row1_slot2_1.

Dietz, Paula. "Recultivating the Tuileries." *Design Quarterly* 155 (Spring 1992): 6–12.

Dion-Tenenbaum, Anne. *L'orfèvre de Napoléon: Martin-Guillaume Biennais*. Paris: Reunion des musées nationaux, 2003.

Dorbani, Malika Bouabdellah. "The Consecration of the Emperor Napoleon and the Coronation of Empress Joséphine on December 2, 1804." Louvre. https://www.louvre.fr/en/oeuvre-notices/consecration-emperor-napoleon-and-coronation-empress-josephine-december-2-1804.

Draper, James David, "The Fortunes of Two Napoleonic Sculptural Projects." *Metropolitan Museum Journal* 14 (1979): 173–184.

Draper, James David, and Clare Le Corbeiller. *The Arts Under Napoleon*. New York: Metropolitan Museum of Art, 1978.

Driault, Edouard. "The Coalition of Europe Against Napoleon." *American Historical Review* 24, no. 4 (July 1919): 606.

Driskel, Michael Paul. *As Befits a Legend: Building a Tomb for Napoleon, 1840–1861*. Kent, Ohio: Kent State University Press, 1993.

Driskel, Michael Paul. "Eclecticism and Ideology in the July Monarchy: Jules-Claude Ziegler's Vision of Christianity at the Madeleine." *Arts Magazine* 56, no. 9 (May 1982): 119–129.

Dupuy, Marie-Anne, ed. *Dominique-Vivant Denon, L'oeil de Napoleon*. Paris: Editions de la Reunion des Musées Nationaux, 1999.

Durrell, Lawrence. "Provence Entire?" *Twentieth Century Literature* 33, no. 3 (Autumn 1987): 416–430.

Dwyer, Philip G. *Citizen Emperor: Napoleon in Power 1799–1815*. London: New York: Bloomsbury, 2013.

Dwyer, Philip G. "Napoleon and the Foundation of the Empire." *Historical Journal* 53, no. 2 (2010): 339–358.

Dwyer, Philip G., "Napoleon and the Universal Monarchy." *History* 95, no. 319 (July 2010): 293–307.

Edmondson, Jonathan, and Alison Keith, eds. *Roman Dress and the Fabrics of Roman Culture*. Toronto and Buffalo, N.Y.: University of Toronto Press, 2008.

Ehrlich, Blake. "Notre Dame: A Pageant of 800 Years." *New York Times Magazine*, May 5, 1963.

Ellis, Geoffrey James. *Napoleon*. London and New York: Longman, 1997.

Englund, Steven. *Napoleon: A Political Life*. Cambridge, Mass.: Harvard University Press, 2004.

Eustace, Katharine. *Canova Ideal Heads*. Oxford, U.K.: Ashmolean Museum, 1997.

Eustace, Katharine. "The Fruits of War: How Napoleon's Looted Art Found its Way Home." *Art Newspaper* 269 (June 2015). http://oldtheartnewspaper.com/features/the-fruits-of-war-how-napoleon-s-looted-art-found-its-way-home/.

Everitt, Anthony. *Augustus: The Life of Rome's First Emperor*. New York: Random House, 2007.

Fabre, Guilhem. *The Pont du Gard: Water and the Roman Town*. Paris: Presses du CNRS, 1992.

Fabréga-Dubert, Marie-Lou. *La collection Borghèse au musée Napoléon*. Paris: Musée du Louvre: École nationale supérieure des beaux-arts, 2009.

Farington, Joseph. *The Farington Diary*, Vol. 8. Edited by James Greig. London: Hutchinson & Co., Ltd., 1922.

Feeney, Denis C. *Caesar's Calendar: Ancient Time and the Beginnings of History*. Berkeley: University of California Press, 2007.

Feigenbaum, Gail, ed. *Display of Art in the Roman Palace, 1550–1750*. Los Angeles: J. Paul Getty Museum, 2014.

Fenby, Jonathan. *France: A Modern History from the Revolution to the War with Terror*. New York: St. Martin's Press, 2016.

Ferando, Christina. "Canova and the writing of art criticism in 18th century Naples." *Word & Image: A Journal of Verbal/Visual Inquiry* 30, no. 4 (2014): 362–376.

Ffoulkes, Fiona. "'Quality always distinguishes itself': Louis Hippolyte LeRoy and the luxury clothing industry in early nineteenth-century Paris." In *Consumers and Luxury: Consumer Culture in Europe 1650–1850*, edited by Maxine Berg and Helen Clifford, 183-205. Manchester, U.K.: Manchester University Press, 1999.

Fisher, Annika Elisabeth, "Sensing the Divine Presence: the Ottonian Golden Altar in Aachen." In *Image and Altar 800–1300*, Vol. 23, edited by Poul Grinder-Hansen, 65–80. Copenhagen: National Museum Studies in Archeology and History, 2014.

Fischer, Julia C., ed. *More than Mere Playthings: the Minor Arts of Italy*. Newcastle upon Tyne, U.K.: Cambridge Scholars Publishing, 2016.

Flower, Harriet I. *The Art of Forgetting: Disgrace and Oblivion in Roman Political Culture*. Chapel Hill: University of North Carolina Press, 2006.

Folz, Robert. *The Coronation of Charlemagne: 25 December 800*. Translated by J. E. Anderson. London: Routledge & Kegan Paul, 1974.

Font, Lourdes, and Michele Majer. "La Quatrieme Unité: Costume and Fashion in Genre Historique Painting." In *Romance and Chivalry: History and Literature Reflected in Early Nineteenth Century French Painting*, edited by Nadia Tscherny and Guy Stair Sainty, 198–199, 202. London and New York: Matthiesen Gallery and Stair Sainty Matthiesen Inc., 1996.

Fontaine, Pierre-François-Léonard. *Journal 1799–1853*. Paris: Société de l'histoire de l'art français, 1987.

Forrest, Alan I., and Peter H. Wilson, eds. *The Bee and the Eagle: Napoleonic France and the End of the Holy Roman Empire, 1806*. Basingstoke, U.K.: Palgrave Macmillan, 2009.

Fraser, Flora. *Pauline Bonaparte*. New York: Anchor Books, 2009.

Freeman, Charles. *The Horses of St. Mark's: A Story of Triumph in Byzantium, Paris, and Venice*. London: Little, Brown, 2004.

Frey, Katia. "L'enterprise napoléonienne." In *Paris et ses fontaines: de la Renaissance à nos jours*, edited by Dominique Massounie, Pauline Prévost-Marcilhacy, and Daniel Rabreau, 104–123. Paris: Délégation à l'action artistique de la ville de Paris, 1995.

Fried, Johannes. *Charlemagne*. Translated by Peter Lewis. Cambridge, Mass.: Harvard University Press, 2016.

Friedlaender, Walter. "Napoleon as 'Roi Thaumaturge.'" *Journal of the Warburg and Courtauld Institutes* 4, no. 3/4 (April 1941–July 1942): 139–141.

Fritze, Ronald H. *Egyptomania: A History of Fascination, Obsession and Fantasy*. London: Reaktion Books, 2016.

Gaborit-Chopin, Danielle. *Regalia: les instruments du sacre des rois de France, les "Honneurs de Charlemagne."* Paris: Ministère de la culture et de la communication, Editions de la Réunion des musées nationaux, 1987.

Gaehtgens, Thomas W. *Napoleon's Arc de Triomphe*. Gottingen, Germany: Vandenhoeck & Ruprecht, 1974.

Gaillard, Marc. *Les Fontaines de Paris: Guide historique*. Amiens, France: Martelle Editions, 1995.

Galinsky, Karl, and Kenneth Lapatin, eds. *Cultural Memories in the Roman Empire*. Los Angeles: J. Paul Getty Museum, 2015.

Galitz, Kathryn Calley. "François Gerard: Portraiture, Scandal, and the Art of Power in Napoleonic France." *Metropolitan Museum of Art Bulletin* 71, no. 1 (Summer 2013): 1, 4–48.

Garric, Jean-Philippe. *Charles Percier: Architecture and Design in an Age of Revolutions*. New York: Bard Graduate Center, 2016.

Giard, Jean-Baptiste. *Le Grand Camée de France*. Paris: Biblioteque nationale de France, 1998.

Gichon, Mordechai. "Jaffa, 1799." *Journal of the International Napoleonic Society* 1, no. 2 (December 1998). http://www.napoleon-series.org/ins/scholarship98/c_jaffa.html.

Gnecchi, Francesco. *The Coin-Types of Imperial Rome*. Translated by Emily A. Hands. London: Spink & Son Ltd, 1908.

Godart, Louis. *The Quirinale Palace: The History, the Rooms and the Collections*. Rome: Treccani, 2016.

Godlewska, Anne. "Map, Text and Image. The Mentality of Enlightened Conquerors: A New Look at the Description de l'Egypte." *Transactions of the Institute of British Geographers* 20, no. 1 (1995): 5–28.

Goldfarb, Stephanie. "Lessons in Looting." ARCA, July 2009. http://art-crime.blogspot.com/2009/07/lessons-in-looting.html.

Gontar, Cybele. "Empire Style, 1800–1815." Metropolitan Museum of Art, October 2004. http://www.metmuseum.org/toah/hd/empr/hd_empr.htm.

Gonzalez-Palacios, Alvar. *The Art of Mosaics: Selections from the Gilbert Collection*. Los Angeles: LACMA, 1977.

Gorse, George. "An Unpublished Description of the Villa Doria during Charles V's Entry into Genoa, 1533." *Art Bulletin* 68 (1986): 319–322.

Gould, Cecil. *Trophy of Conquest; the Musée Napoléon and the creation of the Louvre*. London: Faber and Faber, 1965.

Graham-Dixon, Andrew. *Art of France: There Will Be Blood*. Aired February 2017, on BBC4.

Grandjean, Serge. "Napoleonic Tables from Sèvres." *Connoisseur* 143 (January 1, 1959): 147–153.

Grafton, Anthony, Glenn W. Most, Salvatore Settis, eds. *The Classical Tradition*. Cambridge, Mass.: Harvard University Press, 2010.

Griffiths, Antony, "The Design and Production of Napoleon's Histoire Metallique," Parts I–III. *Medal*, no. 16 (Spring 1990): 16–30; no. 17 (Autumn 1990): 28–38; no. 18 (Spring 1991): 35–49.

Griffiths, Antony. "Drawings for Napoleonic Medals." In *Designs on Posterity: Drawings for Medals*, edited by Mark Jones. London: British Art Medal Trust, 1994.

Grossman, Ira. "Napoleon the Reader: The Imperial Years." http://www.napoleon-series.org/research/napoleon/c_read2.html.

Grossman, Janet Burnett. *Looking at Greek and Roman Sculpture in Stone*. Los Angeles: J. Paul Getty Museum, 2003.

Guderzo, Mario. *Napoleone e Canova: il Pantheon dell' Imperatore a Marengo*. Alessandria, Italy: LineLab, 2016.

Guffey, Elisabeth E. "Reconstructing the Limits of Propaganda: Pierre-Paul Prud'hon and the Art of Napoleon's Remarriage." *Visual Resources* 16, no. 3 (2000): 259–274.

Guffey, Elizabeth E. "The Toilette Berceau of Marie Louise: Napoleonic Imagery in Furniture." *Apollo* 143, no. 407 (January 1996): 3–8.

Gustavson, Natalia. "Retracing the restoration history of Viennese paintings in the Musée Napoléon (1809–1815). *CeROArt*, April 12, 2012. https://ceroart.revues.org/2325.

Gwilt, Joanna. *French Porcelain for English Palaces: Sèvres from the Royal Collection*. London: Royal Collection Publications, 2009.

Haag, Sabine. *Zuhanden Ihrer Majestät: Medaillen Maria Theresias*. Vienna: Kunsthistorisches Museum-Museumsverband, 2017.

Haas, Norbert. "Hairstyles in the Arts of Greek and Roman Antiquity." *Journal of Investigative Dermatology Symposium Proceedings* 10, no. 3 (December 2005): 298–300.

Haig, Diana Reid. *Walks Through Napoleon and Joséphine's Paris*. New York: The Little Bookroom, 2004.

Hale, Sheila. *Titian, His Life*. New York: Harper Press, 2012.

Hales, Edward Elton Young. *Napoleon and the Pope: The Story of Napoleon and Pius VII*. London: Eyre & Spottiswoode, 1962.

Hales, Shelley. "Men are Mars, Women are Venus: Divine Costumes in Imperial Rome." In *The Clothed Body in the Ancient World*, edited by Liza Cleland, Mary Harlow, and Lloyd Llewellyn-Jones, 131–142. Oxford, U.K.: Oxbow, 2005.

Hamilton, Edith. "A Star Shines over Egypt: How Baron Dominique-Vivant Denon Brought the Art of the Pharaohs into the Drawing Rooms of Napoleonic France." *Art and Antiques* (May 1987): 88–93, 112.

Hanson, Kate H. "The Language of the Banquet: Reconsidering Paolo Veronese's Wedding at Cana." *InVisible Culture*, no. 14 (Winter 2010): 32–50. https://ivc.lib.rochester.edu/the-language-of-the-banquet-reconsidering-paolo-veroneses-wedding-at-cana/.

Hallett, Christopher H. *The Roman Nude: Heroic Portrait Statuary 200 B.C.–A.D. 300*. Oxford, U.K., and New York: Oxford University Press, 2005.

Hanley, Wayne. *The Genesis of Napoleonic Propaganda, 1796 to 1799*. New York: Columbia University Press, 2005. http://www.gutenberg-e.org/haw01/frames/fhaw05.html.

Hansen, Maria Fabricius. *The Spolia Churches of Rome: Recycling Antiquity in the Middle Ages*. Translated by Barbara J. Haveland. Aarhus, The Netherlands: Aarhus University Press, 2015.

Haot, Giorgia. "The Divorce of Napoleon and Joséphine." History and Other Thoughts, January 2014; http://historyandotherthoughts.blogspot.com/2014/01/the-divorce-of-napoleon-and-josephine.html.

Harlow, Frederica Todd. "A Star Shines over Egypt." *Art & Antiques* (May 1987): 89–93, 112.

Harris, Judith. *Pompeii Awakened: A Story of Rediscovery*. London and New York: I. B.Tauris, 2007.

Harvey, Mary Jackson. "Death and Dynasty in the Bouillon Tomb Commissions." *Art Bulletin* 74, no. 2 (1992): 271–296.

Haskell, Francis, and Nicholas Penny. *Taste and the Antique: The Lure of Classical Sculpture, 1500–1900*. New Haven, CT, and London: Yale University Press, 1981.

Haughton, Brian. "What happened to the Great Library at Alexandria?" Ancient History Encyclopedia, February 1, 2011. https://www.ancient.eu/article/207/what-happened-to-the-great-library-at-alexandria/.

Haydu, Mark. *Meditations on Vatican Art*. Liguori, Mo.: Liguori, 2013.

Hazareesingh, Sudhir. *The Legend of Napoleon*. London: Granta Books, 2004.

Hazareesingh, Sudhir. *The Saint Napoleon: Celebrations of Sovereignty in Nineteenth Century France*. Cambridge, Mass.: Harvard University Press, 2004.

Heckscher, William. "Bernini's Elephant and Obelisk." *Art Bulletin* 29 (1947): 155–182.

Hedin, Thomas. "The Northern Axis: Discovery in the Gardens of the Premier Versailles." *Studies in the History of Gardens & Designed Landscapes* 37, no. 3 (2017): 191–230.

Hemmerle, Oliver Benjamin. "Crossing the Rubicon into Paris: Caesarian Comparisons from Napoleon to de Gaulle." In *Julius Caesar in Western Culture*, edited by Maria Wyke, 285-302. Malden, Mass., and Oxford, U.K.: Blackwell, 2006.

Henig, Martin. *Handbook of Roman Art: A Comprehensive Survey of all the Arts of the Roman World*. Ithaca, N.Y.: Cornell University Press, 1983.

Herold, J. Christopher, ed. and trans. *The Mind of Napoleon*. New York: Columbia University Press, 1955.

Hibbert, Christopher. *Napoleon's Women*. New York and London: W. W. Norton, 2002.

Hicks, Carola. *The Bayeux Tapestry: The Life Story of a Masterpiece*. London: Chatto & Windus, 2006.

Hicks, Peter. "The Celebration of the Baptism of the Roi de Rome." Napoleon Foundation, May 31, 2011. https://www.napoleon.org/en/history-of-the-two-empires/articles/the-celebration-of-the-baptism-of-the-roi-de-rome/.

Hicks, Peter. "Napoleon and the Pope: from the Concordat to the Excommunication." Napoleon Foundation. https://www.napoleon.org/en/history-of-the-two-empires/articles/napoleon-and-the-pope-from-the-concordat-to-the-excommunication/.

Hicks, Peter. "What did Napoleon do with the Horses on the Brandenburg Gate, Berlin?" Napoleon Foundation. https://www.napoleon.org/en/history-of-the-two-empires/articles/what-did-napoleon-do-with-the-horses-on-the-brandenburg-gate-berlin/.

Hiesinger, Ulrich. "The Paintings of Vincenzo Camuccini, 1771–1844." *Art Bulletin* 60, no. 2 (June 1978): 297–320.

Hirsch, Martin. "Papal Medals and the interplay of Prints, Paintings, and Numismatics." Paper presented at Full Circle: The Medal in Art History, A Symposium in Honor of Stephen K. Scher, The Frick Collection, New York, September 8, 2017.

"History and Architecture of the Great Fenice Opera House." BV Events. https://www.bvevents.com/more-info-venues-italy/History-and-architecture-of-the-great-Fenice-Opera-house-in-Venice-great-conductors-indications.

"History of the Vatican Medagliere." Vatican Library. https://www.vatlib.it/home.php?pag=dipartimento_numismatico&ling=eng.

Hochel, Marian. "Dominique-Vivant Denon (1747–1825): Napoleon's Chief Arts Adviser." Napoleonic Society. http://www.napoleonicsociety.com/english/pdf/j2011hochel.pdf.

Hodge, A. Trevor. *Roman Aqueducts & Water Supply*. London: Duckworth, 1992.

Holmberg, Tom. "Napoleon's Addresses: The Italian Campaigns." Napoleon Series. http://www.napoleon-series.org/research/napoleon/speeches/c_speeches1.html.

Holt, Frank L. *Alexander the Great and the Mystery of the Elephant Medallions*. Berkeley, Los Angeles, and London: University of California Press, 2003.

Honour, Hugh. "Canova's Napoleon." *Apollo* 98, no. 139 (September 1, 1973): 180–184.

Honour, Hugh. "Canova's Statues of Venus." *Burlington Magazine* 114, no. 835 (October 1972): 658–672.

Honour, Hugh. "Canova's Studio Practice" Parts I and II. *Burlington Magazine* 114, no. 829 (March and April 1972): 146–159, 214, 216–229.

Honour, Hugh. "The Italian Empire Style." *Apollo* 80, no. 31 (September 1, 1964): 226–236.

Hortense, Consort of Louis Bonaparte, King of Holland. *Mémoires de la Reine Hortense*, Vol. 2. Paris: Plon, 1927.

Hourihane, Colum, ed. *The Grove Encyclopedia of Medieval Art and Architecture*, Vol. 2. New York: Oxford University Press, 2012.

Hubert, Gérard, and Guy Ledoux-Lebard. *Napoléon, portraits contemporains, bustes et statues*. Paris: Arthena, 1999.

Huet, Valérie. "Napoleon I: A New Augustus?" In *Roman Presences: Receptions of Rome in European Culture, 1789–1945*, edited by Catharine Edwards, 53-69. Cambridge, U.K., and New York: Cambridge University Press, 1999.

Huet, Valérie. "Stories one might tell of Roman art: reading Trajan's column and the Tiberius cup." In *Art and Text in Roman Culture*, edited by Jaś Elsner, 9–31. Cambridge, U.K,. and New York: Cambridge University Press, 1996.

Hughes, Robert. *Rome*. London: Weidenfeld & Nicolson, 2011.

Hugo, Victor. *The Hunchback of Notre Dame*. Translated by Isabel F. Hapgood. Digireads.com Publishing, 2017.

Hugo, Victor. *Poems in Three Volumes*. Vol. 1 (Boston: Estes and Lauriat, n.d.).

Huguenaud, Karine. "Ala Napoleonica in Piazza San Marco Venice." Napoleon Foundation, https://www.napoleon.org/en/magazine/places/ala-napoleonica-in-piazza-san-marco-venice/.

Huguenard, Karine. "Les Invalides, the Military Museum and the Tomb of Napoleon." Napoleon Foundation. https://www.napoleon.org/en/magazine/places/les-invalides-the-military-museum-and-tomb-of-napoleon/.

Huguenaud, Karine. "A Mamluk's Harness." Translated by Peter Hicks. Napoleon Foundation, October 2003. https://www.napoleon.org/en/history-of-the-two-empires/objects/a-mamluks-harness/.

Huguenaud, Karine. "The Roi de Rome's Cradle." Napoleon Foundation, February 2004. https://www.napoleon.org/en/history-of-the-two-empires/objects/the-roi-de-romes-cradle/.

Huguenaud, Karine. "Star of the Legion d'Honneur." Napoleon Foundation, May 2002. https://www.napoleon.org/en/history-of-the-two-empires/objects/star-of-the-legion-dhonneur/.

Humbert, Jean-Marcel, Michael Pantazzi, and Christiane Ziegler. *Egyptomania: Egypt in Western art 1730–1930.* Ottawa: National Gallery of Canada, 1994.

Il Conclave di San Giorgio Maggiore di Venezi e l'elezione di Pio VII Chiaramonti. Venice, Italy: Benedetinni de San Giorgio Maggiore, Biblioteca Nazionale Marciana, 1800. https://marciana.venezia.sbn.it/mostre/il-conclave-di-s-giorgio-maggiore-di-venezia.

Ingholt, Harald. "The Prima Porta Statue of Augustus." *Archeology* 22, no. 3 (June 1969): 177–187.

Jacob-Desmalte, François-Honoré-Georges. *Coin Cabinet.* 1809-1819. Mahogany, applied and inlaid silver, 35 ½ x 19 ¾ x 14 ¾" (90.2 x 50.2 x 37.5 cm), The Metropolitan Museum of Art. http://www.metmuseum.org/art/collection/search/195473.

Jacobsen, Helen. *Gilded Interiors: Parisian Luxury and the Antique.* London and New York: Philip Wilson Publishers, 2017.

Jarry, Madeleine. *The Carpets of the Manufacture de la Savonnerie.* Translated by C. Magdalino. Leigh-on-Sea, U.K.: F. Lewis, 1966.

Jeffreys, David, ed. *Views of Ancient Egypt since Napoleon Bonaparte: Imperialism, Colonialism and Modern Appropriations.* London: UCL Press, 2003.

Jenkins, Susan. "Arthur Wellesley, first Duke of Wellington, Apsley House and Canova's Napoleon as Mars the Peacemaker." *Sculpture Journal,* no. 19 (2010): 115–121.

Jenkins, Susan. "Buying Bonaparte." *Apollo* (November 2010): 50–55.

Jenkins, Tiffany. *Keeping Their Marbles: How the Treasures of the Past Ended up in Museums . . . and Why They Should Stay There.* Oxford, U.K., and New York: Oxford University Press, 2016.

"Joachim Murat by Antonio Canova." Christie's, November 2017. http://www.christies.com/lotfinder/Lot/antonio-canova-1757-1822-1813-joachim-murat-1767-1815-6113947-details.aspx.

Johns, Christopher M. S. *Antonio Canova and the Politics of Patronage in Revolutionary and Napoleonic Europe.* Berkeley: University of California Press, 1998.

Johns, Christopher M. S. "Canova's Portraits of Napoleon: Mixed Genre and the Question of Nudity in Revolutionary Portraiture." *Consortium on Revolutionary Europe, 1750–1850: Proceedings* 20 (1990): 368–382.

Johns, Christopher M. S. "Empress Joséphine's Collection of Sculpture by Canova at Malmaison." *Journal of the History of Collections* 16 (2004): 19–33.

Johns, Christopher M. S. "Portrait Mythology: Antonio Canova's Portraits of the Bonapartes." *Eighteenth-Century Studies* 28, no. 1 (Autumn 1994): 115–129.

Johns, Christopher M. S. "Subversion through Historical Association: Canova's Madame Mère and the Politics of Napoleonic Portraiture." *Word & Image* 13, no. 1 (January 1997): 43–57.

Johnson, Dorothy, ed. *Jacques-Louis David: New Perspectives.* Newark, Del.: University of Delaware Press, 2006.

Jones, Mark. *The Art of the Medal.* London: British Museum Publications, 1979.

Jones, Mark. "The Medal as Instrument of Propaganda in Late Seventeenth and Early Eighteenth Century Europe." *Numismatic Chronicle* 143 (1983): 202–213.

Jones Mark. *Medals of the Sun King.* London: British Museum Publications, 1979.

Jones, Mark Wilson. "Genesis and Mimesis: The Design of the Arch of Constantine in Rome." *Journal of the Society of Architectural Historians* 59, no. 1 (March 2000): 50–77.

Jones, Mark Wilson. "One Hundred Feet and a Spiral Stair: Designing Trajan's Column." *Journal of Roman Archaeology* 6 (1993): 23–38.

Josephus, Flavius. *The Jewish War.* Edited by Betty Radice, E. Mary Smallwood. Translated by G. A. Williamson. London: Penguin Classics, 1981.

Jourdan, Annie. "The Grand Paris of Napoleon: From a Dream of Magnificence to a Dream of Unity." *Journal of the International Napoleonic Society,* November 2011.

Kane, Kathryn. "Bagging Bonaparte's Baggage." The Regency Redingot, June 2013. https://regencyredingote.wordpress.com/2013/06/28/regency-bicentennial-bagging-bonapartes-baggage/.

Kent, John P. C., Bernhard Overbeck, and Armin U. Stylow. *Die römische Münze.* Munich, Germany: Hirmer, 1973.

Kerautret, Michel. "The Meeting at Erfurt." Edited and translated by Hamish Davey Wright. Napoleon Foundation. https://www.napoleon.org/en/history-of-the-two-empires/articles/the-meeting-at-erfurt/.

Kiefer, Carol Solomon. *The Empress Joséphine: Art & Royal Identity.* Amherst, Mass.: Mead Art Museum, 2005.

Kimmelman, Michael. "In Venice, Viewers Are Becoming Voyeurs." *New York Times,* July 19, 1992. http://www.nytimes.com/1992/07/19/arts/art-view-in-venice-viewers-are-becoming-voyeurs.html.

King, David. *Vienna: 1814.* New York: Random House, 2008.

Kirsch, Edith W. "An early reliquary of the holy nail in Milan." *Mitteilungen des Kunsthistorischen Institutes in Florenz* 30 (1986): 569–576.

Klein, Bruno. "Napoleons Triumphbogen in Paris und der Wandel der offiziellen Kunstanschauungen im Premier Empire." *Zeitschrift fur Kunstgeschichte* 59, no. 2 (January 1, 1996): 244–269.

Kleinbauer, Eugene W. "Charlemagne's Palace Chapel at Aachen and Its Copies." *Gesta* 4 (Spring 1965): 2–11.

Kleiner, Diana E. E. *Roman Sculpture.* New Haven, CT, and London: Yale University Press, 1992.

Kleiner, Diana E. E. "Women and Family Life on Roman Imperial Altars." *Latomus* 46 (July–September 1987): 545–554.

Knapton, Ernest John. *Empress Joséphine.* Cambridge, Mass.: Harvard University Press, 1963.

Kobler, Franz. *Napoleon and the Jews.* New York: Schocken Books, 1976.

Koeppe, Wolfram. *Washstand.* 1800-1814. Yew wood, gilt bronze, and iron plate, 36 ⅜ x 19 ½" (92.4 x 49.5 cm), The Metropolitan Museum of Art. https://www.metmuseum.org/art/collection/search/195518.

Koloski-Ostrow, Ann Olga. *The Archeology of Sanitation in Roman Italy.* Chapel Hill: University of North Carolina Press, 2015.

Kurzel-Runtscheiner, Monica. "First meeting and Wedding in Paris." The World of the Habsburgs. http://www.habsburger.net/en/chapter/first-meeting-and-wedding-paris.

Kurzel-Runtscheiner, Monica. "Napoleon and Marie Louise: Courtship and Wedding in Vienna." The World of the Hapsburgs. http://www.habsburger.net/en/chapter/napoleon-and-marie-louise-courtship-and-wedding-vienna.

Lancaster, Lynne. "Building Trajan's Column." *American Journal of Archaeology* 103, no. 3 (July 1999): 419–439.

Lapatin, Kenneth, ed. *The Berthouville Silver Treasure and Roman Luxury.* Los Angeles: J. Paul Getty Museum, 2014.

Lapatin, Kenneth. *Luxus: The Sumptuous Arts of Greece and Rome.* Los Angeles: J. Paul Getty Museum, 2015.

La Regina, Adrino, ed. *Archeological Guide to Rome.* Milan, Italy: Electa, 2016.

Lady Mary Lloyd. *New Letters of Napoleon I.* Edited by Léon Lecestre. New York, 1898.

Las Cases, Emmanuel-Auguste-Dieudonné. *Memorial de Sainte Hélène: Journal of the Private Life and Conversations of the Emperor Napoleon at Saint Helena*, Vol. I and II. London: H. Colburn and Co., 1823.

Lascelles, Christopher. *Pontifex Maximus: A Short History of the Popes.* London: Crux Publishing, 2017.

Laveissière, Sylvain. *Le Sacre de Napoleon peint par David.* Paris: Louvre, 2004.

Lefebure, Amaury, and Bernard Chevallier. *National Museum of the Chateaux de Malmaison et de Bois-Preau.* Cesson-Sevigne, France: Artlys, 2001.

Legacey, Erin-Marie. "The Paris Catacombs: Remains and Reunion beneath the Post-revolutionary City." *French Historical Studies* 40, no. 3 (August 2017): 509–536.

Leitch, Alison. "The Life of Marble." *Australian Journal of Anthropology* 7, no. 1 (April 1996): 235–237.

Leivick, Joel. *Carrara: The Marble Quarries of Tuscany.* Stanford, Calif.: Stanford University Press, 1999.

Lemaistre, Isabelle, Emilie Leverrier, Béatrice Tupinier. "A sculptural group to top the Arc de Triomphe." Louvre. http://www.louvre.fr/en/oeuvre-notices/napoleon-triumph.

Leniaud, Jean-Michel. *La basilique royale de Saint-Denis: De Napoléon à la république.* Paris: Picard, 2012.

Lentz, Thierry. "Napoleon and Charlemagne." Translated by E. Da Prati. Napoleon Foundation. https://www.napoleon.org/en/history-of-the-two-empires/articles/napoleon-and-charlemagne/.

Leonardo da Vinci's Inventions. http://www.leonardodavincisinventions.com/.

Leoni, Daniele. *The Coins of Rome: Trajan.* Verona, Italy: lemonetediroma, 2009.

Lepie, Herta, and Georg Minkenberg. *The Cathedral Treasury of Aachen.* Translated by Manjula Dias Hargarter. Regensburg, Germany: Schnell & Steiner, 2010.

Les Maisons des Bonaparte à Paris 1795-1804. Aquarelles by Christian Benilan, Musée national de la Maison Bonaparte, 2013.

Licht, Fred. *Canova.* New York: Abbeville Press, 1983.

Lichtscheidl, Olivia. "Emperor Franz II/I and Napoleon." The World of the Habsburgs. http://www.habsburger.net/en/chapter/emperor-franz-iii-and-napoleon.

Lightfoot, Christopher. "Luxury Arts of Rome." In *Heilbrunn Timeline of Art History.* New York: Metropolitan Museum of Art, 2000. http://www.metmuseum.org/toah/hd/luxu/hd_luxu.htm.

Lindsay, Suzanne Glover. "Mummies and Tombs: Turenne, Napoleon and Death Ritual." *Art Bulletin* 82, no. 3 (September 2000): 476–502.

Lindsay, Suzanne Glover. "The Revolutionary Exhumations at St-Denis, 1793." In *Conversations: An Online Journal of the Center for the Study of Material and Visual Cultures of Religion* (2014). https://doi.org/10.22332/con.ess.2015.2.

Lord Byron. "On the Bust of Helen by Canova." In *The Poetical Works of Lord Byron*. London: John Murray, 1845: 568.

Lozier, Jean-François. *Napoleon and Paris*. Gatineau, Canada: Canadian Museum of History, 2016.

Ludwig, Emil. *Napoleon*. Translated by Eden and Cedar Paul. New York: Boni & Liveright, 1926.

Lusnia, Susann. "Battle Imagery and Politics on the Severan Arch in the Roman Forum." In *Representations of War in Ancient Rome*, edited by Sheila Dillon and Katherine E. Welch, 272-299. Cambridge, U.K., and New York: Cambridge University Press, 2006.

Macey, Samuel L. "The Concept of Time in Ancient Rome." *International Social Science Review* 65, no. 2 (Spring 1990): 72–79.

MacDonald, William L. *The Architecture of the Roman Empire*, Vol. 1. New Haven, CT, and London: Yale University Press, 1982.

MacGregor, Neil. "The Battle for Charlemagne." *Germany: Memories of a Nation*. Aired on October 13, 2014, on BBC Radio 4. http://www.bbc.co.uk/programmes/b04dwbwz/episodes/downloads.

Mack, Charles R. "Metaphorically Speaking: A Grand Tour Souvenir of the Vendome Column." *Southeastern College Art Conference Review* 9, no. 4 (2014): 443–458.

Mackay Quynn, D. "The Art Confiscations of the Napoleonic Wars." *American Historical Review* 3 (1945): 437–460.

Madelin, Louis. *The Consulate and the Empire*, Vol. 2. Translated by E. F. Buckley. New York: AMS Press, 1967.

Mainardi, Patricia. "Assuring the Empire of the Future: The 1798 Fête de la Liberté." *Art Journal* 48, no. 2 (Summer 1989): 155–163.

Majanlahti, Anthony. *The Families Who Made Rome: A History and a Guide*. London: Pimlico, 2006.

Malacrino, Carmelo G. *Constructing the Ancient World: Architectural Techniques of the Greeks and Romans*. Translated by Jay Hyams. Los Angeles: J. Paul Getty Museum, 2010.

Malkin, Elisabeth. "An Insect's Colorful Gift, Treasured by Kings and Artists." *New York Times*, November 27, 2017. https://www.nytimes.com/2017/11/27/arts/design/red-dye-cochineal-treasure-mexico-city-history.html?smprod=nytcore-ipad&smid=nytcore-ipad-share.

Mangia, Paola. *Canova. Artists and Collectors: A Passion for Antiquity*. Rome: De Luca Editori D'Arte, 2009.

Mansel, Philip. *Dressed to Rule: Royal and Court Costume from Louis XIV to Elizabeth II*. New Haven, CT: Yale University Press, 2005.

Mansel, Philip. *The Eagle in Splendour: Napoleon I and His Court*. London: G. Philip, 1987.

"Marie Antoinette at Rambouillet." Chateau de Rambouillet website. http://www.chateau-rambouillet.fr/en/Explore/MARIE-ANTOINETTE-AT-RAMBOUILLET.

Markham, J. David. *Imperial Glory: The Bulletins of Napoleon's Grande Armée, 1805–1814*. London: Greenhill and Mechanicsburg, Pa.: Stackpole, 2003.

Markham, J. David. *Napoleon for Dummies*. Hoboken, N.J.: Wiley Publishing, 2005): 189.

Markowitz, Mike. "Elephants on Ancient Coinage." Coin Week, February 6, 2017. https://coinweek.com/ancient-coins/elephants-ancient-coins/.

Marlowe, Elizabeth. "Framing the Sun: The Arch of Constantine and the Roman Cityscape." *Art Bulletin* 88, no. 2 (June 2006): 223–242.

Marsden, Jonathan. "Napoleon's Bust of 'Malbrouk'." *Burlington Magazine* 142, no. 1166 (May 2000): 303–306.

Marsden, Rhodri. "Pope Pius VII's Paper Crown." *Independent,* March 20, 2015. http://www.independent.co.uk/news/world/europe/rhodri-marsdens-interesting-objects-pope-pius-viis-paper-crown-10116494.html.

Martin, Marie. *Maria Féodorovna en son temps (1759–1828): Contribution à l'histoire de la Russie et de l'Europe.* Paris: L'Harmattan, 2003.

Matthews, Kenneth D. Jr. "The Embattled Driver in Ancient Rome." *Expedition* (Spring 1960): 22–27. https://www.penn.museum/documents/publications/expedition/PDFs/2-3/The%20 Embattled.pdf.

Martindale, Andrew. *The Triumphs of Caesar by Andrea Mantegna in the collection of Her Majesty the Queen at Hampton Court.* London: Harvey Miller, 1979.

Masson, Frédéric. *Napoléon et son fils.* Paris: Alben Michel, 1929.

McClellan, Andrew. *Inventing the Louvre: Art, Politics, and the Origins of the Modern Museum in Eighteenth-Century Paris.* Berkeley, Los Angeles, and London: University of California Press, 1994.

McClellan, Andrew. "Musée du Louvre, Paris: Palace of the People, Art for All." In *The First Modern Museums of Art,* edited by Carole Paul, 213–235. Los Angeles: J. Paul Getty Museum, 2012.

McDowall, Carolyn. "Empress Joséphine at Chateau Malmaison—Woman of Influence." Culture Concept Circle, March 14, 2013. http://www.thecultureconcept.com/empress-josephine-at-chateau-malmaison-woman-of-influence.

McDowall, Carolyn. "French Garden Style—Joséphine at Chateau de Malmaison." Culture Concept Circle, June 19 2013. http://www.thecultureconcept.com/french-garden-style-josephine-at-chateau-de-malmaison.

McGowan, Margaret M. *The Vision of Rome in Late Renaissance France.* New Haven, CT: Yale University Press, 2000.

McCoubrey, John Walker. "Gros' Battle of Eylau and Roman Imperial Art." *Art Bulletin* 43, no. 2 (June 1961): 135–139.

McKitterick, Rosamond, ed. *Carolingian Culture: Emulation and Innovation.* Cambridge, U.K.: Cambridge University Press, 1994.

McLynn, Frank. *Napoleon.* New York: Arcade Publishing, 2002.

Melchior-Bonnet, Bernardine. *Napoléon et le Pape.* Paris: Amiot Dumont, 1958.

Melikian, Souren. "Behind the Borghese Collection." *New York Times,* August 28, 2009. http://www.nytimes.com/2009/08/29/arts/29iht-melik29.html.

Montanaro, Caroline Vincenti, and Andrea Fasolo. *Palazzi and Villas of Rome.* Verona, Italy: Arsenale Editrice, 2001.

Montesquiou-Fezensac, Blaise de, and Danielle Gaborit-Chopin. *Le Trésor de Saint-Denis,* Vol. 3. Paris: Editions A. et J. Picard, 1973.

Moon, Iris. *The Architecture of Percier and Fontaine and the Struggle for Sovereignty in Revolutionary France.* New York: Routledge, 2017.

Moon, Iris. "Athénienne, or Washstand." Bard Research Forum, November 2016. https://www.bgc.bard.edu/research-forum/articles/98/athnienne-or-washstand.

Moonan, Wendy. "Napoleonic Style, in All Its Imperial Self-Promotion." *New York Times,* November 2, 2007. http://www.nytimes.com/2007/11/02/arts/design/02anti.html.

Moore, Susan. "Canova's lost portrait bust of Joachim Murat has come to light." *Apollo* (November 12, 2017). https://www.apollo-magazine.com/canovas-portrait-bust-of-joachim-murat-has-come-to-light-at-last/amp/.

Morel, Bernard. *The French Crown Jewels: The Objects of the Coronations of the Kings and Queens of France*. Antwerp, Belgium: Fonds Mercator, 1988.

Morrissey, Robert. *Charlemagne & France: A Thousand Years of Mythology*. Translated by Catherine Tihanyi. Notre Dame, Ind.: University of Notre Dame Press, 2003.

Morton, H. V. *The Fountains of Rome*. London: 'The Connoisseur,' Joseph, 1970.

Munger, Jeffrey. "Sèvres Porcelain in the Nineteenth Century." In *Heilbrunn Timeline of Art History*. New York: Metropolitan Museum of Art, 2000. http://www.metmuseum.org/toah/hd/sevr/hd_sevr.htm.

Muratori-Philip, Anne. *Arc de Triomphe*. Paris: Editions du patrimoine, Centre des monuments nationaux, 2007.

Musetti, Barbara. "Lorenzo Bartolini and the Banca Elisiana, or the 'Sculpture Factory.'" In *Lorenzo Bartolini: Beauty and Truth in Marble*, edited by Franca Falletti, Silvestra Bietoletti, and Annarita Caputo, 147–151. Florence, Italy: Galleria dell'Accademia, 2011.

Mutschlechner, Martin. "The double-headed eagle: the omnipresent emblem of the Habsburgs." The World of the Habsburgs. http://www.habsburger.net/en/chapter/double-headed-eagle-omnipresent-emblem-habsburgs.

Mutschlechner, Martin. "The Handover of the Bride." The World of the Habsburgs. http://www.habsburger.net/en/chapter/handover-bride.

Mutschlechner, Martin. "Marie Louise—A dutiful daughter sacrificed on the altar of political expediency." The World of the Habsburgs. http://www.habsburger.net/en/chapter/handover-bride.

Myssok, Johannes. "Modern Sculpture in the Making: Antonio Canova and the Plaster Casts." In *Plaster casts: making, collecting, and displaying from classical antiquity to the present*, edited by Rune Frederiksen and Eckhart Marchand, 269–288. Berlin: Walter de Gruyter, 2010.

"Napoleon becomes emperor—again." *Observer*, April 1, 2017. https://www.theguardian.com/news/2017/apr/01/from-the-observer-archive-napoleon-becomes-emperor-again.

"Napoleon's Consecration and Coronation in Milan." Napoleon Foundation. https://www.napoleon.org/en/history-of-the-two-empires/timelines/napoleons-consecration-and-coronation-in-milan-26-may-1805/.

"Napoleon Enters Moscow." History.com, 2010. http://www.history.com/this-day-in-history/napoleon-enters-moscow.

"Napoleon's Library." Napoleon Foundation. https://www.napoleon.org/en/history-of-the-two-empires/images/napoleons-library/.

"Napoleon and Paris: Dreams of a Capital." Musée Carnavelet, April 8, 2015. http://www.carnavalet.paris.fr/sites/default/files/pk_napoleon_and_paris.pdf.

"Napoleon I at Rambouillet." Chateau Rambouillet. http://www.chateau-rambouillet.fr/en/Explore/Napoleon-I-at-Rambouillet.

"Napoleon in Saint Helena: The Conquest of Memory." Musée de l'Armee, Paris, 2016. http://www.musee-armee.fr/ExpoNapoleonSainteHelene/from-shadow-to-light.html.

"Napoleon Was Here!" The National Library of Israel. http://napoleon.nli.org.il/eng/.

Nelson, Janet. "Kingship and Empire in the Carolingian World." In *Carolingian Culture: Emulation and Innovation*, edited by R. McKitterick, 52–87. Cambridge, U.K.: Cambridge University Press, 1994.

Ng, Aimee. "Portrait Medals from the Scher Collection Come to the Frick." The Frick Collection. http://www.frick.org/blogs/curatorial/portrait_medals_scher_collection.

Ng, Aimee. *The Pursuit of Immortality: Masterpieces from the Scher Collection of Portrait Medals*. New York: The Frick Collection in association with D. Giles Limited, 2017.

Nicassio, Susan Vandiver. *Imperial City: Rome, Romans and Napoleon, 1796–1815*. Welwyn Garden City, U.K.: Ravenhall Books, 2005.

Nousek, Debra L. "Turning Points in Roman History: The Case of Caesar's Elephant Denarius." *Phoenix* 62, no. 3/4 (Fall–Winter 2008): 290–307.

Nouvel-Kammerer, Odile. *Symbols of Power: Napoleon and the Art of the Empire Style 1800–1815*. New York: Abrams in association with the American Federation of Arts and Paris: Les Arts Décoratifs, 2007.

Novillo, Miguel Angel, and Juan Luis Posadas. "Octavian: The Last Man Standing." *National Geographic History* (July/August 2017): 62–73.

Nowinski, Judith. *Baron Dominique Vivant Denon*. Cranbury, N.J.: Fairleigh Dickinson University Press, 1970.

O'Brien, David. *After the Revolution: Antoine-Jean Gros, Painting and Propaganda Under Napoleon*. University Park: Pennsylvania State University Press, 2006.

O'Brien, David. "Antoine-Jean Gros in Italy." *Burlington Magazine* 137, no. 1111 (October 1995): 651–660.

O'Brien, David, "Antonio Canova's Napoleon as Mars the Peacemaker and the Limits of Imperial Portraiture." *French History* 18, no. 4 (December 2004): 354–378.

O'Dwyer, Margaret M. *The Papacy in the Age of Napoleon and the Restoration*. Lanham, Md., and London: University Press of America, 1985.

Oliver, Bette Wyn. *From Royal to National: The Louvre Museum and the Bibliotheque Nationale*. Lanham, Md.: Lexington Books, 2007.

Olson, Roberta J. M. "Representations of Pope Pius VII: The First Risorgimento Hero." *Art Bulletin* 68, no. 1 (March 1986): 77–93.

Östenberg, Ida. "Grief and Glory: Triumphal Elements in the Roman Funeral Procession." Paper presented at the Classical Association Conference, Edinburgh, April 6–9, 2016.

Östenberg, Ida, Simon Malmberg, and Jonas Bjørnebye, eds. *The Moving City: Processions, Passages and Promenades in Ancient Rome*. London: Bloomsbury Academic, 2015.

Östenberg, Ida. *Staging the World: Spoils, Captives, and Representations in the Roman Triumphal Procession*. Oxford, U.K., and New York: Oxford University Press, 2009.

Ottomeyer, Hans. "The Empire Style: Ideals, Methods and Objectives." In *Empire Style: The Hôtel de Beauharnais in Paris*, edited by Jörg Ebeling and Ulrich Leben, 69–76. Paris: Flammarion, 2016.

Packard, David. Art of the Vatican Collections. http://yourmovechessarthist.blogspot.com/2013/05.

Pacca, Bartolomeo. *Historical Memoirs of Cardinal Pacca*. Translated by Sir George Head. London: Longman, Brown, Green, and Longmans, 1850.

Packer, James E. *The Forum of Trajan in Rome: A Study of the Monuments in Brief*. Berkeley: University of California Press, 2001.

"Paolina Borghese e la storia della sua visita a Torino." Mole 24, December 9, 2013. http://www.mole24.it/2013/12/09/paolina-borghese-visita-torino/.

Papot, Emmanuelle. "Marie Louise of Austria." Napoleon Foundation. https://www.napoleon.org/en/history-of-the-two-empires/biographies/marie-louise-of-austria/.

Parks, Tiffany. "The Borghese Gallery and the Fate of an Ill-gotten Collection," Part 1. Tiffany-Parks.com, December 8, 2011. https://www.tiffany-parks.com/blog/2011/12/08/the-borghese-gallery-and-the-fate-of-an-ill-gotten-collection-part-1?rq=Borghese.

Parr, Fiona. "The Death of Napoleon Bonaparte and the Retour des Cendres: French and British Perspectives." Napoleon Foundation. https://www.napoleon.org/en/history-of-the-two-empires/articles/the-death-of-napoleon-bonaparte-and-the-retour-des-cendres-french-and-british-perspectives/.

Parton, Frances. "Charlemagne." *Burlington Magazine* 156, no. 1338 (September 2014): 625.

Pastoureau, Michel. *Red: The History of a Color.* Translated by Jody Gladding. Princeton, N.J.: Princeton University Press, 2017.

Pater, Walter. "The Poetry of Michelangelo." In *Michelangelo: the Sistine Chapel Ceiling*, edited by Charles Seymour Jr., 164–166. London: Thames and Hudson, 1972.

Paul, Carole. *The Borghese Collections and the Display of Art in the Age of the Grand Tour.* Aldershot, U.K., and Burlington, Vt.: Ashgate, 2008.

Paul, Carole. *Making a Prince's Museum: Drawings for the Late-Eighteenth-Century Redecoration of the Villa Borghese.* Los Angeles: Getty Research Institute, 2000.

Pauwels, Yves. "Le theme de l'arc de triomphe dans l'architecture urbaine à la Renaissance, entre pouvoir politique et pouvoir religieux." In *Marquer la ville: Signes, traces, empreintes du pouvoir*, 188. Paris and Rome: Editions de la Sorbonne, 2013.

Pavageau, Pascale. "An exceptional portrait of Madame Mère by Gerard up for Auction at Sotheby's." Napoleon Foundation. https://www.napoleon.org/en/history-of-the-two-empires/articles/an-exceptional-portrait-of-madame-mere-by-gerard-up-for-auction-at-sothebys/.

Pavanello, Giuseppe, and Giandomenico Romanelli, eds. *Canova.* Venice, Italy: Marsilio Publishers, 1992.

Pavanello, Giuseppe. *La Biblioteca di Antonio Canova.* Possagno and Verona, Italy: Cierre edizioni, Fondazione Canova, 2007.

Peck, William H. "'Description de l'Égypte': A Major Acquisition from the Napoleonic Age." *Bulletin of the Detroit Institute of Arts* 51, no. 4 (1972): 112–121.

"Père Lachaise Cemetery." Napoleon Foundation. https://www.napoleon.org/en/magazine/places/pere-lachaise-cemetery/.

Pérouse de Montclos, Jean-Marie. *Fontainebleau.* Translated by Judith Hayward. Paris: Editions Scala, 1998.

Pesando, Fabrizio. "Roman Coins." In *Rome: Art & Architecture*, edited by Marco Bussagli, 98–101. Cologne, Germany: Könemann, 1999.

Peters, H. K. "The Music at the Coronation of Napoleon and Joséphine." Napoleon Foundation. https://www.napoleon.org/en/history-of-the-two-empires/articles/the-music-at-the-coronation-of-napoleon-and-josephine.

Petrelli, Felix. "Visiting Carrara Marble Quarries—Apuan Alps' Eternal Snow." *Italy Magazine*, February 21, 2014. http://www.italymagazine.com/featured-story/visiting-carrara-marble-quarries-apuan-alps-eternal-snow.

Picon, Guillaume. *A Day at Chateau de Fontainebleau.* Paris: Flammarion, 2015.

"Pie VII et le Docteur Claraz." La Trace Claraz. http://www.latraceclaraz.org/pie-vii-et-le-docteur-claraz.html#comment.

Pietrangeli, Carlo. *The Vatican Museums: Five Centuries of History.* Translated by Peter Spring. Rome: Quasar, Biblioteca Apostolica Vaticana, 1993.

Piperno, Roberto. "Pope Pius VII." Rome Art Lover. https://www.romeartlover.it/Storia28.html.

Plant, Margaret. *Venice: Fragile City, 1797–1997.* New Haven, CT, and London: Yale University Press, 2002.

Plum, Gilles, with Dominique Fernandes and Isabelle Rouge-Ducos. *Arc de Triomphe de l'Étoile.* Paris: Centre des monuments nationaux/Editions du patrimoine, 2000.

Poisson, Georges. *Napoléon et Paris.* Paris: Berger-Levrault, 1964.

Popkin, Maggie L. *The Architecture of the Roman Triumph: Monuments, Memory, and Identity.* New York: Cambridge University Press, 2016.

Popkin, Maggie L. "Symbiosis and Civil War: The Audacity of the Arch of Constantine." *Journal of Late Antiquity* 9, no. 1 (Spring 2016): 42–88.

Porterfield, Todd B. *The Allure of Empire: Art in the Service of French Imperialism 1798–1836.* Princeton, N.J.: Princeton University Press, 1998.

Porterfield, Todd and Susan L. Siegfried. *Staging Empire: Napoleon, Ingres, and David.* University Park: Pennsylvania State University Press, 2006.

Pothecary, Sarah. "Strabo the Geographer," September 2007. http://www.strabo.ca/when.html.

Potts, Alex. "The Classical Ideal on Display." *Richerche di Storia dell'Arte* 72 (2000): 29–36.

Potts, Alex. "Colors of Sculpture." In *The Color of Life: Polychromy in Sculpture from Antiquity to the Present,* edited by Roberta Panzanelli with Eike Schmidt and Kenneth Lapatin, 78–97. Los Angeles: J. Paul Getty Museum and the Getty Research Institute, 2008.

Préaud, Tamara, et al. *Sèvres Porcelain Manufactory: Alexandre Brongniart and the Triumph of Art and Industry, 1800–1847.* Edited by Derek E. Ostergard. New Haven, CT: Yale University Press for The Bard Graduate Center for Studies in the Decorative Arts, 1997.

Prendergast, Christopher. *Napoleon and History Painting: Antoine-Jean Gros's La Bataille d'Eylau.* Oxford, U.K.: Clarendon Press and New York: Oxford University Press, 1997.

Prochaska, David. "Art of Colonialism, Colonialism of Art: the 'Description de l'Égypte' 1809–1828." *L'Esprit Createur* 34, no. 2 (Summer 1994): 69–91.

Quatremère de Quincy, M. *Letters to Miranda and Canova on the Abduction of Antiquities from Rome and Athens.* Introduction by Dominique Poulot. Translated by Chris Miller and David Gilks. Los Angeles: Getty Research Institute, 2012.

Quynn, Dorothy Mackay. "The Art Confiscations of the Napoleonic Wars." *American Historical Review* 50, no. 3 (April 1945): 437–460.

Rabb, Theodore K. *The Artist and the Warrior: Military History through the Eyes of the Masters.* New Haven, CT: Yale University Press, 2011.

Rapelli, Paola. *Symbols of Power in Art: A Guide to Imagery.* Translated by Jay Hyams. Los Angeles: J. Paul Getty Museum, 2011.

Raza, Roustam. *The Memoirs of Roustam: Napoleon's Mamluk Imperial Bodyguard.* Edited by Ara Ghazarians. Translated by Catherine Carpenter. London: Bennett & Bloom, 2014.

Reinhold, Meyer. *History of Purple as a Status Symbol in Antiquity.* Brussels: Latomus, r. Colonel Chaltin 60, 1970.

Ribeiro, Aileen. *The Art of Dress: Fashion in England and France 1750 to 1820.* New Haven, CT: Yale University Press, 1995.

Ribeiro, Aileen. *Clothing Art: The Visual Culture of Fashion.* New Haven, CT, and London: Yale University Press, 2017.

Richardson, Herbert. "Costume in History." *Journal of the Royal Society of Arts* 82, no. 4242 (March 9, 1934): 470–485.

Richmond, Ian, and M. Hassall. *Trajan's Army on Trajan's Column*. London: British School at Rome, 1982.

Ridley, Ronald T. *The Eagle and the Spade: The Archaeology of Rome during the Napoleonic Era 1809–1814*. Cambridge, U.K., and New York: Cambridge University Press, 1992.

Rinne, Katherine Wentworth. "The Secret Life of Roman Fountains." *Places: Forum of Design for the Public Realm* 12, no. 2 (Winter 1999): 76–81.

Rinne, Katherine Wentworth. *The Waters of Rome: Aqueducts, Fountains, and the Birth of the Baroque City*. New Haven, CT, and London: Yale University Press, 2010.

Robb, Graham. *Parisians: An Adventure History of Paris*. New York: W. W. Norton & Co., 2010.

Roberts, Andrew. *Napoleon: A Life*. New York: Penguin Books, 2015.

Robinson, H. Russell. *The Armour of Imperial Rome*. London: Arms and Armour Press, 1975.

Rodriguez, Cecelia. "Secret Island to Open after 500 Years." *Forbes*, December 30, 2016. http://www.forbes.com/sites/ceciliarodriguez/2016/12/30/secret-island-to-open-after-500-years-napoleons-saint-helena-will-be-a-2017-hot-destination/#569ff5a87038.

Rollason, David W. *The Power of Place: Rulers and their Palaces, Landscapes, Cities, and Holy Places*. Princeton, N.J.: Princeton University Press, 2016.

Rossi, Lino. *Trajan's Column and the Dacian Wars*. Translated by J.M.C. Toynbee. London: Thames and Hudson, 1971.

Rowell, Diana. "On the Road to Domination: The Reinvention of the Roman Triumph in Napoleonic Paris." Paper presented at the Classical Association Conference, Edinburgh, April 6–9, 2016.

Rowell, Diana. *Paris: The "New Rome" of Napoleon I*. London: Bloomsbury, 2012.

Rubin, Patricia. "Hierarchies of Vision: Fra Angelico's 'Coronation of the Virgin' from San Domenico, Fiesole." *Oxford Art Journal* 27, no. 2 (2004): 139–153.

Russell, Terence M. *The Discovery of Egypt: Vivant Denon's Travels with Napoleon's Army*. Stroud, U.K.: Sutton, 2005.

Salomon, Xavier F., with Guido Beltramini and Mario Guderzo. *Canova's George Washington*. New York: The Frick Collection, 2018.

Samoyault, Jean-Pierre. "Furniture and Objects designed by Percier for the Palace of Saint-Cloud." *Burlington Magazine* 117, no. 868 (July 1975): 457–463, 465.

Sandholtz, Wayne. *Prohibiting Plunder: How Norms Change*. New York: Oxford University Press, 2007.

Sani, Jean-Marie, et al. *1810 politique de l'amour: Napoléon Ier et Marie Louise à Compiègne*. Paris: Éditions de la Réunion des musées nationaux, 2010.

Sapio, Maria, ed. "The Museum of Capodimonte." Issuu. https://issuu.com/arte-m/docs/guida_capodimonte_inglese.

Sarmant, Thierry, et. al, eds. *Napoléon et Paris: rêves d'une capital*. Paris: Paris-Musées: Musée Carnavalet, 2015.

Savoy, Bénédicte. *Patrimoine annexé: Les siasies de bien culturels pratiqués par la France en Allemagne autour de 1800*, Vol. 2. Paris: Editions de la Maison des Sciences de l'Homme, 2003.

Scarborough, John. "Review: The Elephant in the Greek and Roman World." *Classical Journal* 72, no. 2 (December 1976–January 1977): 174–176.

Scarisbrick, Diana. *Chaumet: Master Jewellers since 1780*. Paris: A. de Gourcuff, 1995.

Schaffer, Jenny H. "Restoring Charlemagne's Chapel: Historical consciousness, material culture, and transforming images of Aachen in the 1840s." *Journal of Art Historiography*, no. 7 (December 2012): 1–38.

Schama, Simon. *Citizens: A Chronicle of the French Revolution*. New York: Vintage Books, 1990.

Scheurleer, T. H. Lunsingh, A. B. de Vries, L. Brummel, and H. E. van Gelder. *150 jaar Koninklijk Kabinet van Schilderijen/Koninklijke Bibliotheek, Koninklijk Penningkabinet*. 'S-Gravenhage: Staatsdrukkerij, 1967.

Scigliano, Eric. *Michelangelo's Mountain: The Quest for Perfection in the Marble Quarries of Carrara*. New York: Free Press, 2005.

Scott, Barbara. "'Cloth of Gold and Satins Rare': Silks Made at Lyons for Napoleon I." *Country Life* 169, no. 4372 (June 4, 1981): 1559–1561.

Scullard, Howard Hayes. *The Elephant in the Greek and Roman World*. Ithaca, N.Y.: Cornell University Press, 1974.

Sear, David R. *Roman Coins and their Value*. London: Seaby, 1988.

Selin, Shannon. "Caroline Bonaparte Murat, Napoleon's Treasonous Sister." Madame Dilflurt, July 2014. http://www.madamegilflurt.com/2014/07/a-salon-guest-caroline-bonaparte-murat.html.

Selin, Shannon. "The Marriage of Napoleon and Marie Louise." Shannon Selin: Imagining the Bounds of History, April 2016. http://shannonselin.com/2016/04/marriage-napoleon-marie-louise/.

Sérullaz, Arlette. *Gérard, Girodet, Gros: David's Studio*. Milan: 5 Continents and Paris: Musée du Louvre, 2005.

Sgarbi, Vittorio. "Appiani, the total artist crowned by Napoleon." Il Giornale, March 9, 2017. http://www.ilgiornale.it/news/appiani-lartista-totale-incoronato-napoleone-1436906.html.

Shaffer, Jenny H. "Restoring Charlemagne's Chapel: historical consciousness, material culture, and transforming images of Aachen in the 1840s." *Journal of Art Historiography* 7 (December 2012): 1–38.

Sheehan, Edward. "When Napoleon Captured the Pope." *New York Times*, December 13, 1981. http://www.nytimes.com/1981/12/13/theater/when-napoleon-captured-the-pope.html?pagewanted=all.

Sicca, Cinzia, and Alison Yarrington, eds. *The Lustrous Trade: Material Culture and the History of Sculpture in England and Italy, c.1700–c.1860*. London and New York: Leicester University Press, 2000.

Siegel, Jonah, "Owning Art after Napoleon: Destiny or Destination at the Birth of the Museum," *PMLA* 125, no. 1 (January 2010): 142–151.

Silverio, Francesco. *Trajan's Column*. Translated by Rebecca Amen. Rome: Quasar, 1989.

Simonetta, Marcello, and Noga Arikha. *Napoleon and the Rebel: A Story of Brotherhood, Passion and Power*. New York: Palgrave Macmillan, 2011.

Smith, Hazel. "Joséphine and Juliette: Neoclassical Goddesses of Paris Fashion." *Bonjour Paris*, October 4, 2016. https://bonjourparis.com/fashion/josephine-and-juliette-neoclassical-goddesses-of-paris-fashion/.

Smith, Philip. *A Dictionary of Greek and Roman Antiquities*. Edited by William Smith. London: John Murray, 1875.

Solari, Catherine Hyde Govion Broglio. *Private Anecdotes of Foreign Courts*, Vol. 1. London: H. Colburn, 1827.

Sondhaus, Lawrence. "Napoleon's Shipbuilding Program at Venice and the Struggle for Naval Mastery in the Adriatic." *Journal of Military History* 53, no. 4 (October 1989): 349–362.

Sood, Suemedha. "Exploring the History of Catacombs." BBC.com, October 26, 2012. http://www.bbc.com/travel/story/20121025-exploring-the-history-of-catacombs.

Sorabella, Jean. "Art of the Roman Provinces, 1–500 A.D." In *Heilbrunn Timeline of Art History*. New York: Metropolitan Museum of Art, 2000.

Sorek, Susan. *The Emperors' Needles: Egyptian Obelisks and Rome*. Exeter, U.K.: Bristol Phoenix Press, 2010.

Spence, Rachel. "Canova and the Victorious Venus, Galleria Borghese, Rome." *Financial Times*, January 3, 2008. https://www.ft.com/content/e7a22c8c-ba1f-11dc-abcb-0000779fd2ac.

Spier, Jeffrey, Timothy Potts, and Sara E. Cole, eds. *Beyond the Nile: Egypt and the Classical World*. Los Angeles: J. Paul Getty Museum, 2018.

Spivey, Nigel. *Classical Civilization: Greeks & Romans in 10 Chapters*. London: Head of Zeus Ltd., 2015.

Squire, Michael. "Embodied Ambiguities on the Prima Porta Augustus." *Art History* 36, no. 2 (April 2013): 242–279.

Squires, Nick. "Chemical analysis shows Medici Venus was once far gaudier." *Telegraph*, March 5, 2012. http://www.telegraph.co.uk/culture/art/9124246/Chemical-analysis-shows-Medici-Venus-was-once-far-gaudier.html.

Stagno, Laura. *Palazzo del Principe: The Villa of Andrea Doria, Genoa*. Genoa, Italy: Sagep, 2005.

Stammers, Tom. "The man who created 'dictator chic'." *Apollo* 185, no. 651 (March 16, 2017): 154–160.

Starck, Jeff. "Charlemagne, king father of Europe, ushers in coinage reform." Coin World, June 1, 2015. https://www.coinworld.com/news/world-coins/2015/05/charlemagne---king-father-of-europe--ushers-in-coinage-reform.all.html#.

Steiner, Frances H. "Building with Iron: A Napoleonic Controversy." *Technology and Culture* 22, no. 4 (October 1981): 700–724.

Stendhal. *The Charterhouse of Parma*. Translated by Richard Howard. Illustrations by Robert Andrew Parker. 1839. Reprint, New York: Modern Library, 1999.

Stephany, Erich. *Aachen Cathedral*. Translated by Pauline and Bernd Nutsch. Aachen, Germany: Arend und Ortmann, 1986.

Steward, W. Augustus. "Goldsmiths' and Silversmiths' Work—Past and Present: II." *Journal of the Royal Society of Arts* 81, no. 4210 (July 28, 1933): 853–863.

Stoltzfus, Zachary M. "Napoleon's Kindle: Libraries, Literature, and the Legacy of the Napoleonic Era." *Journal of the International Napoleonic Society* (December 2016): 75–85.

Suetonias. "The Lives of the Twelve Caesars." Wikisource. https://en.wikisource.org/wiki/The_Lives_of_the_Twelve_Caesars/Vitellius.

Sutherland, Carol Humphrey Vivian. *Ancient Numismatics: A Brief Introduction*. New York: American Numismatics Society, 1958.

Tadgell, Christopher. *Antiquity: Origins, Classicism and the New Rome*. New York: Routledge, 2007.

Tarbell, Ida M., ed. *Napoleon's Addresses: Selections from the Proclamations, Speeches and Correspondence of Napoleon Bonaparte*. Boston: Joseph Knight, 1896.

Tassinari, Gabriella. "Glyptic Portraits of Eugène de Beauharnais." *Journal of the Walters Art Museum* 60/61 (2002/2003): 43–64.

Taylor, Francis Henry. *The Taste of Angels: A History of Art Collecting from Ramses to Napoléon*. Boston: Little, Brown and Co., 1948.

"Tea Service of the Emperor Napoleon," National Museums Scotland. https://www.nms.ac.uk/explore-our-collections/stories/art-and-design/tea-service-of-the-emperor-napoleon/.

Teitler, Hans. "Raising on a Shield: Origin and Afterlife of a Coronation Ceremony." *International Journal of the Classical Tradition* 8, no. 4 (Spring 2002): 501–521.

Thate, Heidrun. "The creation of French satellite-museums in Mainz." Paper presented at the Development of National Museums in Europe 1794–1830 International Conference, University of Amsterdam, January 31–February 2, 2008.

Thibadeau, A. C. *Bonaparte and the Consulate.* New York: MacMillan, 1908.

Thomas, Edmund. *Monumentality and the Roman Empire: Architecture in the Antonine Age.* Oxford, U.K.: Oxford University Press, 2007.

Three hundred unpublished letters from Napoleon I to Marie Louise. London: Sotheby & Co., 1934.

Tolstoy, Leo. *War and Peace.* Translated by Anthony Briggs. London: Penguin Books, 2005.

Toynbee, Jocelyn M. C. *Roman Medallions.* New York: American Numismatic Society, 1986.

Treggiari, Susan M. *Roman Marriage: Iusti Coniuges from the Time of Cicero to the Time of Ulpian.* Oxford, U.K.: Oxford University Press, 1993.

Treue, Wilhelm. *Art Plunder: The Fate of Works of Art in War and Unrest.* Translated by Basil Creighton. New York: John Day Co., 1961.

Tuck, S. "The Origins of Roman Imperial Hunting Imagery: Domitian and the Redefinition of Virtus under the Principate." *Greece & Rome* 52 (2005): 221–245.

Van Uffelen, Chris, and Markus Golser. *Paris: The Architecture Guide.* Schweiz, Switzerland: Braun Publishing AG, 2013.

Van Zanten, David. "Fontaine in the Bumham Library." Arts Institute of Chicago. http://www.artic.edu/sites/default/files/fontaine_burnham.pdf.

The Vatican Collections: The Papacy and Art. New York: Metropolitan Museum of Art and Abrams, 1982.

Vilinbachov, George, and Magnus Olausson. *Staging Power: Napoleon, Charles John, Alexander.* Stockholm: Nationalmuseum, 2010.

Villa Medici, French Academy in Rome. https://www.villamedici.it/en/history-and-heritage/.

Voltaire. *Siècle de Louis XIV,* Vol. 1. Edited by Charles Louandre. Paris: Biblioteque-Charpentier, 1865.

Walton, Geri. "Victorian Paris Street Cries." Geri Walton: Unique Histories from the 18th and 19th Centuries, April 14, 2017. https://www.geriwalton.com/victorian-paris-street-cries.

Ward-Perkins, John Bryan. *Roman Architecture.* New York: Harry N. Abrams, 1977.

Wasserman, Jack. "The Quirinal Palace in Rome." *Art Bulletin* 45, no. 3 (September 1963): 205–244.

Wazer, Caroline. "The Cutthroat Politics of Public Health in Ancient Rome and What We Can Learn from It Today." *Atlantic,* April 22, 2016. https://www.theatlantic.com/health/archive/2016/04/the-tricky-politics-of-ancient-romes-aqueducts/479298/.

Werckmeister, Otto Karl. "The Political Ideology of the Bayeux Tapestry." *Studi Medievali,* 3rd Series 17, no. 2 (1976): 535–595.

Wescher, Paul. "Vivant Denon and the Musée Napoléon." *Apollo* 80, no. 31 (September 1, 1964): 178–186.

Weygand, Max. *Turenne Marshall of France.* Translated by George B. Ives. Boston: Houghton Mifflin, 1930.

Whaley, Joachim. "The Holy Roman Empire: From Charlemagne to Napoleon." British Museum, October 13, 2014. https://blog.britishmuseum.org/the-holy-roman-empire-from-charlemagne-to-napoleon/.

Whistler, Catherine. *Venice and Drawing, 1500–1800: Theory, Practice, and Collecting.* New Haven, CT: Yale University Press, 2016.

Whitely, Jon. "Vivant Denon. Paris." *Burlington Magazine* 142, no. 1166 (May 2000): 324–326.

Whitlum-Cooper, Francesca. "The Oath," Napoleon Foundation, August 2014. https://www.napoleon.org/en/history-of-the-two-empires/paintings/the-oath-napoleons-coronation-2-december-1804/.

Williams, Kate. *Ambition and Desire: The Dangerous Life of Joséphine Bonaparte*. Toronto: McClelland & Stewart, 2014.

Wilson-Smith, Timothy. *Napoleon and His Artists*. London: Constable and Company, 1996.

Wirsching, Armin. "How the Obelisks Reached Rome: Evidence of Roman Double-Ships." *International Journal of Nautical Archaeology* 29, no. 2 (October 2000): 273–283. http://onlinelibrary.wiley.com/doi/10.1111/j.1095-9270.2000.tb01456.x/epdf.

Worsdale, Derrick. "Later Neo-Classical Florentine Furniture at Palazzo Pitti." *Furniture History* 14 (1978): 49–57.

Wrathall, Claire. "What Napoleon's hat tells us about the power of branding." Christie's, June 17, 2015. http://www.christies.com/features/what-napoleons-hat-tells-us-about-the-power-of-branding-6280-3.aspx.

Wright, Hamish Davey. "The Marriage of Napoleon I and Marie Louise of Austria." Napoleon Foundation, March 2010. https://www.napoleon.org/en/history-of-the-two-empires/timelines/the-marriage-of-napoleon-i-and-marie-louise-of-austria/.

Wright, Hamish Davey. "Napoleon's 'Divorce.'" Napoleon Foundation, December 2009. https://www.napoleon.org/en/history-of-the-two-empires/timelines/napoleons-divorce/.

Wyke, Maria. *Caesar: A Life in Western Culture*. Chicago and London: University of Chicago Press, 2008.

Zanella, Andrea. *Canova in Rome*. Rome: Fratelli Palombi, 1993.

Zanker, Paul. *Roman Art*. Translated by Henry Heitmann-Gordon. Los Angeles: J. Paul Getty Museum, 2010.

Zarzeczny, Matthew D. *Meteors that Enlighten the Earth: Napoleon and the Cult of Great Men*. Newcastle upon Tyne, U.K.: Cambridge Scholars Publishing, 2013.

Ziolkowski, John E. *Classical Influence on the Public Architecture of Washington and Paris: A Comparison of Two Capital Cities*. New York: P. Lang, 1988.

ENDNOTES

INTRODUCTION

1 Matthew D. Zarzeczny, *Meteors that Enlighten the Earth: Napoleon and the Cult of Great Men* (Newcastle upon Tyne, U.K.: Cambridge Scholars Publishing, 2013), 46.

2 Ira Grossman, "Napoleon the Reader: The Early Years," https://www.napoleon-series.org/research/napoleon/c_read1.html.

3 Napoleon Bonaparte, *Aphorisms*, collected by Honoré de Balzac (Richmond, U.K.: Oneworld Classics Ltd., 2008), 30.

4 Zarzeczny, *Meteors*, 63.

5 Alex Potts, "The Classical Ideal on Display," *Richerche di Storia dell'Arte*, no. 72 (2000): 35.

6 Peter Hicks, "Napoleon and the Theatre," Napoleon Foundation, https://www.napoleon.org/en/history-of-the-two-empires/articles/napoleon-and-the-theatre/.

7 Mara Fazio, *François Joseph Talma, Primo Divo* (Milan: Electa, 1999), 167–68.

8 Diana Rowell, "On the Road to Domination: The Reinvention of the Roman Triumph in Napoleonic Paris" (paper presented at the Classical Association Conference, Edinburgh, April 6–9, 2016).

9 Zarzeczny, *Meteors*, 100.

10 Allard, Sebastian, et al., eds., *Citizens and Kings: Portraits in the Age of Revolution 1760–1830* (London: Royal Academy of Arts, 2007), 63.

11 Bette Wyn Oliver, *From Royal to National: the Louvre Museum and the Bibliothèque Nationale* (Lanham, Md.: Lexington Books, 2007), 78.

12 J. Christopher Herold, *The Mind of Napoleon* (New York: Columbia University Press, 1955), 281.

PART ONE: DIRECTORY

ONE: TRIUMPHUS

1 Nigel Spivey, *Classical Civilization* (London: Head of Zeus Ltd, 2015), 243.

2 Ida Östenberg, *Staging the World: Spoils, Captives, and Representations in the Roman Triumphal Procession* (Oxford, U.K., and New York: Oxford University Press, 2009), 45.

3 Mary Beard, *The Roman Triumph* (Cambridge, Mass., and London: Harvard University Press, 2007), 145.

4 Maria Wyke, *Caesar: A Life in Western Culture* (Chicago and London: University of Chicago Press, 2008), 125.

5 Beard, *The Roman Triumph*, 8.

6 Wyke, *Caesar*, 126.

7 Robert Hughes, *Rome* (London: Weidenfeld & Nicolson, 2011), 56.

8 John Henry Merryman, ed., *Imperialism, Art and Restitution* (New York: Cambridge University Press, 2006), 4.

9 Maggie Popkin, *The Architecture of the Roman Triumph: Monuments, Memory, and Identity* (New York: Cambridge University Press, 2016), 5.

10 Miguel Angel Novillo and Juan Luis Posadas, "Octavian: the Last Man Standing," *National Geographic History*, July/August 2017, 72.

11 Peter J. Holliday, *The Origins of Roman Historical Commemoration in the Visual Arts* (Cambridge, U.K., and New York: Cambridge University Press, 2002), 196.

12 Östenberg, *Staging*, 80.

13 Kenneth Lapatin, *Luxus: The Sumptuous Arts of Greece and Rome* (Los Angeles: The J. Paul Getty Museum, 2015), 36.

14 Paul Zanker, *Roman Art*, trans. Henry Heitmann-Gordon (Los Angeles: J. Paul Getty Museum, 2010), 3.

15 Ida Östenberg, Simon Malmberg, and Jonas Bjørnebye, eds., *The Moving City: Processions, Passages and Promenades in Ancient Rome* (London: Bloomsbury Academic, 2015), 137.

16 Ranuccio Bianchi Bandinelli, *Rome the Centre of Power: Roman Art to AD 200*, trans. Peter Green (London: Thames and Hudson, 1970), 38.

17 Ibid., 42.

18 Zanker, *Roman Art*, 42.

19 Östenberg, *Staging*, 114.

20 Merryman, *Imperialism*, 4.

21 Noah Charney, *Stealing the Mystic Lamb: The True Story of the World's Most Coveted Masterpiece* (New York: Public Affairs, 2010), 118.

22 Beard, *The Roman Triumph*, 31.

23 Ibid., 343.

24 Stephanie Goldfarb, "Lessons in Looting," ARCA, July 2009, http://art-crime.blogspot.com/2009/07/lessons-in-looting.html.

25 Patricia Mainardi, "Assuring the Empire of the Future: The 1798 Fête de la Liberté," *Art Journal* 48, no. 2 (Summer 1989): 158.

26 Charles Freeman, *The Horses of St. Mark's: A Story of Triumph in Byzantium, Paris, and Venice* (London: Little, Brown, 2004), 5.

27 Ian McClellan, *Inventing the Louvre: Art, Politics, and the Origins of the Modern Museum in Eighteenth-Century Paris* (Berkeley, Los Angeles, and London: University of California Press, 1994), 123.
28 Mainardi, "Assuring the Empire," 159.
29 Mark Haydu, *Meditations on Vatican Art* (Liguori, Mo.: Liguori, 2013), 73.
30 Paul Wescher, "Vivant Denon and the Musée Napoléon," *Apollo* 80, no. 31 (Sept. 1, 1964): 180.
31 Mainardi, "Assuring the Empire," 159.
32 Francis Haskell and Nicholas Penny, *Taste and the Antique: The Lure of Classical Sculpture, 1500–1900* (New Haven, CT, and London: Yale University Press, 1981), 108.
33 Stendhal, *The Charterhouse of Parma*, trans. Richard Howard; illustrations by Robert Andrew Parker (New York: Modern Library, 1999), 3.
34 Charney, *Stealing the Mystic Lamb*, 87.
35 Ibid., 88.
36 Mainardi, "Assuring the Empire," 156.
37 Jeffrey Laird Collins, *Papacy and Politics in Eighteenth-Century Rome: Pius VI and the Arts* (Cambridge, U.K., and New York: Cambridge University Press, 2004), 29.
38 Ibid., 70.
39 Anthony Grafton, Glenn W. Most, Salvatore Settis, eds., *The Classical Tradition* (Cambridge, Mass.: Harvard University Press, 2010), 56.
40 Haskell and Penny, *Taste and the Antique*, 146.
41 McClellan, *Inventing the Louvre*, 119.
42 Mainardi, "Assuring the Empire," 156.
43 Quatremère de Quincy, *Letters to Miranda and Canova on the Abduction of Antiquities from Rome and Athens*, trans. Chris Miller and David Gilks (Los Angeles: Getty Publications, 2012), 19.
44 Carlo Pietrangeli, *The Vatican Museums: Five Centuries of History*, trans. Peter Spring (Rome: Quasar, Biblioteca Apostolica Vaticana, 1993), 125.
45 Popkin, *Architecture of the Roman Triumph*, 21.
46 Mainardi, "Assuring the Empire," 157.
47 Ibid., 156.
48 Freeman, *Horses of St. Mark's*, 7.

TWO: THE LAND OF THE NILE

1 Nina Burleigh, *Mirage: Napoleon's Scientists and the Unveiling of Egypt* (New York: HarperCollins, 2007), 2.
2 Bob Brier, "Napoleon in Egypt," *Archeology* 52, no. 3 (May/June 1999): 46.
3 Burleigh, *Mirage*, 10.
4 Emil Ludwig, *Napoléon*, trans. Eden and Cedar Paul (New York: Boni & Liveright, 1926), 120.
5 Burleigh, *Mirage*, 241–42.
6 Ludwig, *Napoléon*, 11.
7 Spivey, *Classical Civilization*, 249.
8 Anthony Everitt, *Augustus: The Life of Rome's First Emperor* (New York: Random House, 2007), 196.

9 Frank L. Holt, *Alexander the Great and the Mystery of the Elephant Medallions* (Berkeley, Los Angeles, and London: University of California Press, 2003), 1.

10 Susan Sorek, *The Emperors' Needles: Egyptian Obelisks and Rome* (Exeter, U.K.: Bristol Phoenix Press, 2010), 36.

11 Ronald H. Fritze, *Egyptomania: A History of Fascination, Obsession and Fantasy* (London: Reaktion Books, 2016), 16.

12 Jeffrey Spier, Timothy Potts, and Sara E. Cole, eds., *Beyond the Nile: Egypt and the Classical World* (Los Angeles: J. Paul Getty Museum, 2018), 4.

13 Armin Wirsching, "How the Obelisks Reached Rome: Evidence of Roman Double-Ships," *The International Journal of Nautical Archaeology* 29, no. 2 (2000): 280.

14 Sorek, *The Emperors' Needles*, 49.

15 Ibid., xiii.

16 Pierre Briant, *The First European: A History of Alexander in the Age of Empire,* trans. Nicholas Elliott (Cambridge, Mass.: Harvard University Press, 2017), 250.

17 Zarzeczny, *Meteors*, 83.

18 Burleigh, *Mirage*, 15.

19 Fritze, *Egyptomania*, 158.

20 Burleigh, *Mirage*, 24.

21 "Napoleon Was Here!" The National Library of Israel, http://napoleon.nli.org.il/eng/.

22 Ibid.

23 Karine Huguenaud, "A Mamluk's Harness," trans. Peter Hicks, Napoleon Foundation, October 2003, https://www.napoleon.org/en/history-of-the-two-empires/objects/a-mamluks-harness/.

24 Walter Friedlaender, "Napoleon as Roi Thaumaturge," *Journal of the Warburg and Courtauld Institutes* 4, no. 3/4 (April 1941): 139.

25 Fritze, *Egyptomania*, 162.

26 Frederica Todd Harlow, "A Star Shines over Egypt," *Art & Antiques* (May 1987): 90.

27 Jean-Marcel Humbert, Michael Pantazzi, and Christiane Ziegler, *Egyptomania: Egypt in Western Art 1730–1930* (Ottawa: National Gallery of Canada, 1994), 202.

28 Vivant Denon, *Travels in Upper and Lower Egypt*, Vol. II (1803; repr. New York: Arno Press, 1973), 83–84.

29 Humbert, *Egyptomania*, 202.

30 "Denon Discovers Ancient Egypt," Napoleon and the Scientific Expedition to Egypt, http://napoleon.lindahall.org/denon.shtml#top.

31 Ibid.

32 Fritze, *Egyptomania*, 162.

33 Louis-Antoine Fauvelet de Bourrienne, *Memoirs of Napoleon Bonaparte*, Vol. 1 (London: R. Bentley, 1836), 351.

34 Frank McLynn, *Napoleon* (New York: Arcade Publishing, 2002), 290.

35 Christopher Hibbert, *Napoleon's Women* (New York and London: W. W. Norton, 2002), 96.

THREE: PONTIFEX MAXIMUS

1 Charles Bennington, *Luca Carlevarijs: Views of Venice* (San Diego, Calif.: Timken Museum of Art, 2001), 2.

2 Robin Anderson, *Pope Pius VII (1800–1823): His Life, Reign and Struggle with Napoleon in the Aftermath of the French Revolution* (Charlotte, N.C.: TAN Books, 2001).

3 Kate H. Hanson, "The Language of the Banquet: Reconsidering Paolo Veronese's Wedding at Cana," *InVisible Culture*, no. 14 (Winter 2010): 40.

4 Germain Bazin, *The Louvre* (New York: Harry M. Abrams, 1958), 148.

5 Hanson, "The Language of the Banquet," 35.

6 Richard Cocke, *Paolo Veronese: Piety and Display in an Age of Religious Reform* (Burlington, Vt.: Ashgate, 2001), 173.

7 *Il Conclave di San Giorgio Maggiore di Venezi e l'elezione di Pio VII Chiaramonti* (Venice: Biblioteca Nazionale Marciana), 42.

8 John Paul Adams, "Sede Vacante 1799–1800," California State University Northridge, September 29, 2015, https://www.csun.edu/~hcfll004/SV1800.html.

9 Anderson, *Pope Pius VII.*

10 Philippe Boutry, "Pius VII," in *The Papacy: an Encyclopedia*, Vol. 2, ed. Philippe Levillain, (New York and London: Routledge, 2002), 1183.

11 Spivey, *Classical Civilization*, 249.

12 Christopher Lascelles, *Pontifex Maximus: A Short History of the Popes* (London: Crux Publishing, 2017), viii.

13 Ibid.

14 Christophe Beyeler, *Pie VII face à Napoleon, la tiare dans les serres de l'Aigle* (Paris: Reunion des musées nationaux, 2015), 125.

15 Boutry, "Pius VII," 1184.

16 Anderson, *Pope Pius VII.*

17 Marisa Ciceran, *Bucintoro: The State Galley of the Doges of Venice*, Istria on the Internet, July 6, 2007, istrianet.org/istria/navigation/sea/navy/bucintoro/bucintoro-history.htm.

18 Bonaparte, *Aphorisms,* 56.

19 Ibid., 40.

20 Anderson, *Pope Pius VII.*

21 Diana Reid Haig, *Walks Through Napoleon and Joséphine's Paris* (Oxford, U.K.: The Little Bookroom, 2004), 71.

22 Andrew Roberts, *Napoleon: A Life* (New York: Penguin, 2015), 350.

23 Jean-François Lozier, *Napoleon and Paris* (Quebec: Canadian Museum of History, 2016), 57.

24 Lascelles, *Pontifex Maximus,* 240.

PART TWO: CONSULATE

ONE: THE ETRUSCANS

1 Haig, *Walks Through*, 17.

2 Hibbert, *Napoleon's Women*, 49.

3 *Les Maison des Bonaparte à Paris 1795-1804*. Aquarelles by Christian Benilan. (Musée National de la Maison Bonaparte, 2013), 36.

4 Iris Moon, *Architecture of Percier and Fontaine and the Struggle for Sovereignty in Revolutionary France* (New York: Routledge, 2017), 131.

5 Ibid., 132.

6 Helen Jacobsen, *Gilded Interiors: Parisian Luxury and the Antique* (London and New York: Philip Wilson Publishers, 2017), 1.

7 Moon, *Architecture of Percier and Fontaine*, 23.

8 Valérie Huet, "Napoleon I: A New Augustus?" in *Roman Presences: Receptions of Rome in European Culture*, 1789–1945, ed. Catharine Edwards (Cambridge, U.K., and New York: Cambridge University Press, 1999), 63–65.

9 Jean-Philippe Garric, ed., *Charles Percier: Architecture and Design in an Age of Revolutions* (New York: Bard Graduate Center, 2016), 78.

10 Victor Baltard, "École de Percier. Mémoire lu à la séance annuelle de l'Académie des beax-arts," *Institut de France* 43, no. 17 (November 15, 1873): 46.

11 Tom Stammers, "The man who created 'dictator chic'." *Apollo* 185, no. 651 (March 16): 155.

12 Eleanor P. DeLorme, ed., *Joséphine and the Arts of the Empire* (Los Angeles: J. Paul Getty Museum, 2005), 70.

13 Amaury Lefebure and Bernard Chevalier, *National Museum of the Château de Malmaison et de Bois-Preau* (Paris: Artlys, 2001), 10.

14 Alain Pougetoux, conversation with author, September 26, 2016.

15 "Napoleon's Library," Napoleon Foundation, https://www.napoleon.org/en/history-of-the-two-empires/images/napoleons-library/.

16 Garric, *Charles Percier*, 154.

17 Martine Denoyelle and Sophie Descamps-Lequime, *The Eye of Joséphine: the antiquities collection of the Empress in the Musée du Louvre* (Atlanta, Ga.: High Museum of Art and Paris: Musée du Louvre, 2008), 17.

18 Kate Williams, *Ambition and Desire: The Dangerous Life of Joséphine Bonaparte* (Toronto: McClelland & Stewart, 2014), 165.

19 Stammers, "The man," 156.

20 A. C. Thibudeau, *Bonaparte and the Consulate* (New York: MacMillan, 1908), 3.

21 James David Draper, *The Arts Under Napoleon* (New York: Metropolitan Museum of Art, 1978).

22 Jonathan Marsden, "Napoleon's Bust of 'Malbrouk'," *The Burlington Magazine* 142, no. 1166 (May 2000): 303.

23 *Alexander, Napoleon & Joséphine: a story of friendship, war & art from the Hermitage* (Zwolle: WBOOKS, 2015), 52.

24 Pierre-François-Léonard Fontaine, *Journal 1799–1853*, Vol. 1. (Paris: Société de l'histoire de l'art français, 1987), 35.

25 Wolfram Koeppe, *Washstand*, 1800–1814, yew wood, gilt bronze, and iron plate, 36 ⅜ x 19 ½" (92.4 x 49.5 cm), The Metropolitan Museum of Art, New York, https://www.metmuseum.org/art/collection/search/195518.

26 Anne Dion-Tenenbaum, *L'orfèvre de Napoléon: Martin-Guillaume Biennais* (Paris: Musée du Louvre, 2003), 14.

27 Fontaine, *Journal*, 34.

28 Garric, *Charles Percier*, 231.

29 Jean-Pierre Samoyault, "Furniture and Objects designed by Percier for the Palace of Saint-Cloud," *Burlington Magazine* 117, no. 868 (July 1975): 465.

30 Ibid.

31 Garric, *Charles Percier*, 228.

32 Thibaudeau, *Bonaparte*, 8.

33 Ibid., 10.

34 Hans Ottomeyer, "The Empire Style: Ideals, Methods and Objectives," in *Empire Style: The Hôtel de Beauharnais in Paris*, eds. Jörg Ebeling and Ulrich Leben (Paris: Flammarion, 2016), 74.

35 Iris Moon, "Athénienne, or Washstand," Bard Research Forum, November 2016, https://www.bgc.bard.edu/research-forum/articles/98/athnienne-or-washstand.

36 Stammers, "The man," 157.

37 David Van Zanten, "Fontaine in the Burnham Library," Art Institute of Chicago, http://www.artic.edu/sites/default/files/fontaine_burnham.pdf.

38 Stammers, "The man," 155.

39 Garric, *Charles Percier*, 36.

TWO: CAESAR'S FRIEND

1 Roberts, *Napoleon: A Life*, 305–06.

2 Barbara Scott, "'Cloth of Gold and Satins Rare': Silks Made at Lyons for Napoleon I," *Country Life* 169, no. 4372 (June 4, 1981): 1559.

3 Draper, *The Arts Under Napoleon*, 1.

4 Scott, "Cloth of Gold," 1559.

5 Thierry Sarmant, et al., eds., *Napoléon et Paris: rêves d'une capitale* (Paris: Paris-Musées: Musée Carnavalet, 2015), 203.

6 Michael Kimmelman, "In Venice, Viewers Are Becoming Voyeurs," *New York Times*, July 19, 1992, http://www.nytimes.com/1992/07/19/arts/art-view-in-venice-viewers-are-becoming-voyeurs.html.

7 Freeman, *Horses of St Mark's*, 213.

8 Giancarlo Cunial and Massimiliano Pavan, *Antonio Canova, Museum and Gipsoteca* (Possagno: Fondazione Canova Onlus, 2009), 77.

9 Catherine Whistler, *Venice and Drawing, 1500–1800: Theory, Practice, and Collecting* (New Haven, CT: Yale University Press, 2016), 231.

10 Rachel Spence, "Canova and the Victorious Venus, Galleria Borghese, Rome," *Financial Times*, Jan. 3, 2008.

11 Johannes Myssok, "Modern Sculpture in the Making: Antonio Canova and the plaster casts," in *Plaster casts: making, collecting, and displaying from classical antiquity to the present*, ed. Rune Frederiksen and Eckhart Marchand (Berlin: Walter de Gruyter, 2010), 133.

12 Xavier F. Salomon, with Guido Beltramini and Mario Guderzo, *Canova's George Washington* (New York: The Frick Collection 2018), 93.

13 Janet Burnett Grossman, *Looking at Greek and Roman Sculpture in Stone* (Los Angeles: J. Paul Getty Museum, 2003), 1.

14 Hughes, *Rome*, 366.

15 Elliott Davies and Emanuela Tarizzo, *Canova and His Legacy* (Verona, Italy: Paul Holberton Publishing, 2017), 12.

16 Ibid., 12.

17 Roberts, *Napoleon: A Life*, 349–50.

18 Huet, "Napoleon I," 55.

19 Lozier, *Napoleon and Paris*, 13.

20 Hugh Honour, "Canova's Napoleon," *Apollo* (Sept. 1, 1973): 180.

21 Irene Antoni-Komar, "Zur Rezeption der Frisur a la Titus am Ende des 18. Jahrhunderts," in *Haar Tragen. Eine kulturwissenschaftliche Annaherung*, ed. C. Janecke (Cologne, Germany: Böhlau Verlag, 2004), 224.

22 Philippe Bordes, *Jacques-Louis David: Empire to Exile* (New Haven, CT, and London: Yale University Press, 2005), 37.

23 David O'Brien, "Antonio Canova's Napoleon as Mars the Peacemaker and the Limits of Imperial Portraiture," *French History* 18, no. 4 (Dec. 2004): 357.

24 Huet, "Napoleon I," 60.

25 Christopher M. S. Johns, "Portrait Mythology: Antonio Canova's Portraits of the Bonapartes," *Eighteenth-Century Studies* 28, no. 1 (Autumn 1994): 122.

26 Huet, "Napoleon I," 58.

27 Gerard Hubert and Guy Ledoux-Lebard, *Napoleon: portraits contemporains, bustes et statues* (Paris: Arthena, 1999), 63.

28 DeLorme, *Joséphine*, 48.

29 Ibid., 49.

30 Béatrice Tupinier Barrillon, "Cupid and Psyche," Musée du Louvre, http://www.louvre.fr /en/oeuvre-notices/cupid-and-psyche.

31 DeLorme, *Joséphine*, 49.

32 Laurence Posselle, ed., *Dominique-Vivant Denon, L'oeil de Napoleon* (Paris: Editions de la Reunion des Musees Nationaux, 1999), 130.

33 Nick Squires, "Chemical analysis shows Medici Venus was once far gaudier," *Telegraph*, March 5, 2012, http://www.telegraph.co.uk/culture/art/9124246/Chemical-analysis-shows -Medici-Venus-was-once-far-gaudier.html.

34 Hugh Honour, "Canova's Statues of Venus," *Burlington Magazine* 114, no. 835 (Oct. 1972): 668.

35 Ibid., 661.

THREE: NAPOLEON'S EYE

1 Germain Bazin, *The Museum Age* (Brussels: Desier S.A. Editions, 1967), 180.

2 Enrico Bruschini, *The Vatican Masterpieces* (Florence, Italy and London: Scala, 2004), 30.

3 Mainardi, *Assuring the Empire*, 159.

4 Harlow, "A Star Shines," 90.

5 Ibid.

6 Humbert, *Egyptomania*, 204.

7 Marian Hochel, "Dominique-Vivant Denon (1747–1825): Napoleon's Chief Arts Adviser," International Napoleonic Society, http://www.napoleonicsociety.com /english/pdf/j2011hochel.pdf.

8 Thomas W. Gaehtgens, *Napoleon's Arc de Triomphe* (Gottingen: Vandenhoeck & Ruprecht, 1974), 52.

9 Bazin, *The Museum Age*, 176.

10 Ibid., 177.

11 Andrew McClellan. "Musée du Louvre, Paris: Palace of the People, Art for All," in *The First Modern Museums of Art*, ed. Carole Paul (Los Angeles: The J. Paul Getty Museum, 2012), 222.
12 McClellan, *Inventing the Louvre*, 121.
13 Ibid., 141.
14 Ibid., 140.
15 Charney, *Stealing the Mystic Lamb*, 95.
16 Ibid.
17 Barbara Musetti. "Lorenzo Bartolini and the Banca Elisiana, or the 'Sculpture Factory,'" in *Lorenzo Bartolini: Beauty and Truth in Marble*, ed. Franca Falletti, Silvestra Bietoletti, and Annarita Caputo (Florence, Italy: Galleria dell'Accademia, 2011), 172.
18 Elliott Davies and Emanuela Tarizzo, *Canova and His Legacy* (Verona, Italy: Paul Holberton Publishing, 2017), 74.
19 Musetti, "Lorenzo Bartolini," 172.
20 Arlette Sérullaz, *Gérard, Girodet, Gros: David's Studio* (Milan, Italy: 5 Continents and Paris: Musée du Louvre, 2005), 10.
21 David O'Brien, "Antoine-Jean Gros in Italy," *Burlington Magazine* 137, no. 1111 (Oct. 1995): 653.
22 Ibid., 654.
23 Walter Friedlaender, "Napoleon as Roi Thermaturge," *Journal of the Warburg and Courtauld Institutes*, 4, no. 3/4 (April 1941–July, 1942): 140.
24 O'Brien, "Antoine-Jean Gros in Italy," 660.
25 Timothy Wilson-Smith, *Napoleon and His Artists* (London: Constable and Company, 1996), 160.
26 Mordechai Gichon, "Jaffa, 1799," *The Journal of the International Napoleonic Society* 1, no. 2 (December 1998).
27 Theodore K. Rabb, *The Artist and the Warrior* (New Haven, CT, and London: Yale University Press, 2011), 158.
28 Heidrun Thate, "The Creation of French Satellite-Museums in Mainz" (paper presented at the Development of National Museums in Europe 1794–1830, International Conference, University of Amsterdam, January 31–February 2, 2008).
29 Ellinoor Bergvelt, *Napoleon's Legacy: The Rise of National Museums in Europe* (Berlin: G+H Verlag, 2009), 25.
30 James David Draper, "The Fortunes of Two Napoleonic Sculptural Projects," *Metropolitan Museum Journal* 14 (1979): 182.
31 DeLorme, *Joséphine*, 177.
32 Ibid., 178.
33 Ernest Knapton, *Empress Joséphine* (Cambridge, Mass.: Harvard University Press, 1963), 154–56.
34 Kenneth Lapatin, ed., *The Berthouville Silver Treasure and Roman Luxury* (Los Angeles: The J. Paul Getty Museum, 2014), 133.
35 Hazel Smith, "Joséphine and Juliette: Neoclassical Goddesses of Paris Fashion," Bonjour Paris, Oct. 4, 2016, https://bonjourparis.com/fashion/josephine-and-juliette-neoclassical-goddesses-of-paris-fashion/.
36 Lapatin, *Luxus*, 121.
37 E. Claire Cage, "The Sartorial Self: Neoclassical Fashion and Gender Identity in France, 1797–1804," *Eighteenth-Century Studies* 42, no. 2 (Winter 2009): 204.

38 DeLorme, *Joséphine*, 167.

39 Susan P. Conner, "Napoleon's Courtesans, Citoyennes, and Cantinieres," *Members' Bulletin of the Napoleonic Society of America*, 73 (Spring 2003): 23.

40 Aileen Ribeiro, *Clothing Art: the Visual Culture of Fashion* (New Haven, CT, and London: Yale University Press, 2017), 246.

41 Shelley Hales, "Men are Mars, Women are Venus: Divine Costumes in Imperial Rome," in *The Clothed Body in the Ancient World*, ed. Liza Cleland, Mary Harlow, and Lloyd Llewellyn-Jones (Oxford, U.K.: Oxbow, 2005), 131.

42 Ibid., 134.

43 Ibid., 138.

44 Jonathan Edmondson and Alison Keith, eds., *Roman Dress and the Fabrics of Roman Culture* (Toronto and Buffalo, N.Y.: University of Toronto Press, 2008), 33.

45 Ibid., 24.

46 DeLorme, *Joséphine*, 161.

47 Philip Mansel, *Dressed to Rule* (New Haven, CT, and London: Yale University Press, 2005), 79.

FOUR: PARISII

1 Basile Baudez and Nicholas Olsberg, *A Civic Utopia: Architecture and the City in France, 1795–1837* (London: Drawing Matters Studio, 2016), 1.

2 Geri Walton, "Victorian Paris Street Cries," April 14, 2017, Geri Walton: Unique Histories from the 18th and 19th Centuries, https://www.geriwalton.com/victorian-paris-street-cries.

3 Gaehtgens, *Napoleon's Arc de Triomphe*, 11.

4 Flavio Conti, *A Profile of Ancient Rome* (Los Angeles: J. Paul Getty Museum, 2003), 192.

5 Hughes, *Rome*, 65.

6 Ibid., 65.

7 Ibid., 67.

8 Caroline Wazer, "The Cutthroat Politics of Public Health in Ancient Rome and What We Can Learn from It Today," *The Atlantic*, April 22, 2016, https://www.theatlantic.com/health/archive/2016/04/the-tricky-politics-of-ancient-romes-aqueducts/479298/.

9 A. Trevor Hodge, *Roman Aqueducts and Water Supply* (London: Duckworth, 1992), 93.

10 H. V. Morton, *The Fountains of Rome* (London: The Connoisseur, Joseph, 1970), 31.

11 Ibid., 45.

12 Guilhem Fabre, *The Pont du Gard: Water and the Roman Town* (Paris: Presses du CNRS, 1992), 116.

13 Andrew Dalby, *Empire of Pleasures: Luxury and Indulgence in the Roman World* (London and New York: Routledge, 2000), 237.

14 Daniele Leoni, *The Coins of Rome*: *Trajan* (Verona, Italy: lemonetediroma, 2009), 35.

15 Frances H. Steiner, "Building with Iron: a Napoleonic Controversy," *Technology and Culture* 22, no. 4 (Oct. 1981): 710.

16 "Pont des Arts Bridge," Napoleon Foundation, https://www.napoleon.org/en/magazine/places/pont-des-arts-bridge/.

17 Edmund Thomas, *Monumentality and the Roman Empire: Architecture in the Antonine Age* (Oxford, U.K.: Oxford University Press, 2007), 121.

18 Steiner, "Building with Iron," 718.

19 Ibid., 724.

20 John E. Ziolkowski, *Classical Influence on the Public Architecture of Washington and Paris: A Comparison of Two Capital Cities* (New York: P. Lang, 1988), 59.

21 Garric, *Charles Percier*, 234.

22 Ibid., 242.

23 Helen Borowitz, *The Impact of Art on French Literature* (Newark, Del.: University of Delaware Press, 1985), 57.

24 Steven Englund, *Napoleon* (Cambridge, Mass.: Harvard University Press, 2004), 228.

25 Philip G. Dwyer, "Napoleon and the Foundation of the Empire," *Historical Journal* 53, no. 2 (2010): 340.

26 Alan I. Forrest and Peter H. Wilson, eds., *The Bee and the Eagle: Napoleonic France and the End of the Holy Roman Empire, 1806* (Basingstoke, U.K.: Palgrave Macmillan, 2009), 92.

27 Hibbert, *Napoleon's Women*, 127.

28 Williams, *Ambition and Desire*, 215.

29 Matthieu Beauhaire, Mathilde Béjanin, and Hubert Naudeix, *L'Elephant de Napoleon* (Arles: Honore Clair, 2014), 10.

30 Geoffrey James Ellis, *Napoleon* (London and New York: Longman, 1997), 157.

31 Paula Rapelli, *Symbols of Power in Art*, trans. Jay Hyams (Los Angeles: J. Paul Getty Museum, 2011), 50.

32 Carol Solomon Kiefer, *The Empress Joséphine: Art and Royal Identity* (Amherst, Mass.: Mead Art Museum, 2005), 12.

33 Rapelli, *Symbols of Power*, 50.

34 Thierry Lentz, "Napoleon and Charlemagne," trans. E. Da Prati, Napoleon Foundation, https://www.napoleon.org/en/history-of-the-two-empires/articles/napoleon-and-charlemagne/.

35 Martin Mutschlechner, "The double-headed eagle: the omnipresent emblem of the Habsburgs," The World of Habsburgs, http://www.habsburger.net/en/chapter/double-headed-eagle-omnipresent-emblem-habsburgs.

36 Odile Nouvel-Kammerer, *Symbols of Power: Napoleon and the Art of the Empire Style* (New York: Abrams, 2007), 153.

37 Ibid., 150.

38 Karine Huguenaud, "Star of the Legion d'Honneur," Napoleon Foundation, May 2002, https://www.napoleon.org/en/history-of-the-two-empires/objects/star-of-the-legion-dhonneur/.

39 *Napoleon Ier ou le Legend des arts* (Paris: Editions de la Reunion des musees nationaux, 2015), 150.

40 Todd Porterfield and Susan L. Siegfried, *Staging Empire: Napoleon, Ingres, and David* (University Park: Pennsylvania State University Press, 2006), 30.

41 Ibid.

PART THREE: IMPERIUM

ONE: CAROLUS MAGNUS

1 "Karl schätzte die Aachener Quellen," Route Charlemagne Aachen, http://www.route-charlemagne.eu/Charlemagne/Karl/Karl_badend_19/index.html.

2 Ibid.

3 Janet Nelson, "Kingship and Empire in the Carolingian World," in *Carolingian Culture: Emulation and Innovation*, ed. R. McKitterick (Cambridge, U.K.: Cambridge University Press, 1994), 69.

4 Neil MacGregor, "The Battle for Charlemagne," *Germany: Memories of a Nation*, aired on October 13, 2014, on BBC Radio 4, http://www.bbc.co.uk/programmes/b04dwbwz /episodes/downloads.

5 Erich Stephany, *Aachen Cathedral*, trans. Pauline and Bernd Nutsch (Aachen, Germany: Arend und Ortmann, 1986), 3–4.

6 Johannes Fried, *Charlemagne*, trans. Peter Lewis (Cambridge, Mass.: Harvard University Press, 2016), 354.

7 Maria Fabricius Hansen, *Spolia Churches of Rome: Recycling Antiquity in the Middle Ages*, trans. Barbara J. Haveland (Aarhus, Netherlands: Aarhus University Press, 2015), 65.

8 Fried, *Charlemagne*, 149.

9 W. Eugene Kleinbauer, "Charlemagne's Palace Chapel at Aachen and its Copies," *Gesta* 4 (Spring 1965): 2.

10 Beat Brenk, "Spolia from Constantine to Charlemagne: Aesthetics Versus Ideology," *Dumbarton Oaks Papers* 41 (1987): 107.

11 Ibid.

12 Ibid., 109.

13 Herta Lepie and Georg Minkenberg, *The Cathedral Treasury of Aachen*, trans. Manjula Dias Hargarter (Regensburg, Germany: Schnell & Steiner, 2010), 12.

14 David Rollason, *The Power of Place* (Princeton, Pa., and Oxford, U.K.: Princeton University Press, 2016), 279.

15 Colum Hourihane, ed., *The Grove Encyclopedia of Medieval Art and Architecture* 2 (New York: Oxford University Press, 2012), 532.

16 Lepie and Minkenberg, *The Cathedral Treasury of Aachen*, 13.

17 Robert Folz, *The Coronation of Charlemagne* (London: Routledge, 1974), 146.

18 Ibid., xi.

19 Fried, *Charlemagne*, 405–06.

20 Rollason, *Power of Place*, 324.

21 Lepie and Minkenberg, *The Cathedral Treasury of Aachen*, 44.

22 Ibid., 15.

23 Ibid., 32.

24 Lentz, "Napoleon and Charlemagne."

25 Annika Elisabeth Fisher, "Sensing the Divine Presence: the Ottonian Golden Altar in Aachen," in *Image and Altar*, ed. Poul Grinder-Hansen, *Copenhagen: National Museum Studies in Archeology and History* 23 (2014): 74.

26 Jenny H. Schaffer, "Restoring Charlemagne's Chapel: Historical Consciousness, Material Culture, and Transforming Images of Aachen in the 1840s," *Journal of Art Historiography*, no. 7 (Dec. 2012): 7.

27 Stephany, *Aachen Cathedral*, 13.

28 Lentz, "Napoleon and Charlemagne."

29 Philip Dwyer, "Napoleon and the Universal Monarchy," *History* 95, no. 3 (July 2010): 297.

30 Lentz, "Napoleon and Charlemagne," 40.

31 Robert Morrissey, *Charlemagne and France: a Thousand Years of Mythology*, trans. Catherine Tihanyi (Notre Dame, Ind.: University of Notre Dame Press, 2003), 258.
32 Fried, *Charlemagne*, 529.
33 Lentz, "Napoleon and Charlemagne," 32.
34 Zarzeczny, *Meteors*, 18.
35 Franz Kobler, *Napoleon and the Jews* (New York: Schocken Books, 1976), 174–75.
36 Sylvain Cordier, *Napoleon: The Imperial Household* (Paris: Hazan, 2018), 326.
37 Morrissey, *Charlemagne and France*, 261.
38 Frances Parton, "Charlemagne," *Burlington Magazine* 156, no. 1338 (Sept. 2014): 625.
39 Lepie and Minkenberg, *The Cathedral Treasury of Aachen*, 64.
40 Lentz, "Napoleon and Charlemagne," 54.
41 Frank Pohle, email message to author, June 9, 2017.
42 "Alexander How Great?" in Ancient History and Civilisation: Confronting the Classics, Erenow, https://erenow.com/ancient/confronting-the-classics-traditions-adventures-and-innovations/5.html.
43 Morrissey, *Charlemagne and France*, 259.
44 Hibbert, *Napoleon's Women*, 131.
45 Philip Dwyer, *Citizen Emperor: Napoleon in Power 1799–1815* (London and New York: Bloomsbury, 2013), 151.
46 Lentz, "Napoleon and Charlemagne," 55.

TWO: CHARLEMAGNE'S HONORS

1 MacGregor, "The Battle for Charlemagne."
2 Rapelli, *Symbols of Power*, 23.
3 Joachim Whaley, "The Holy Roman Empire: from Charlemagne to Napoleon," The British Museum, http://blog.britishmuseum.org/the-holy-roman-empire-from Charlemagne-to-napoleon.
4 Danielle Gaborit-Chopin, *Regalia: les instruments du sacre des rois de France, les "Honneurs de Charlemagne"* (Paris: Ministère de la culture et de la communication, Editions de la Réunion des musées nationaux, 1987), 82.
5 Rapelli, *Symbols of Power*, 26.
6 Blaise de Montesquiou-Fezensac and Danielle Gaborit-Chopin, *Le Trésor de Saint-Denis*. Vol. 3 (Paris: Editions A. et J. Picard, 1973), 73.
7 Ibid., 37.
8 Ibid.
9 Gaborit-Chopin, *Regalia*, 114.
10 Rapelli, *Symbols of Power*, 20.
11 Ibid., 22.
12 Knapton, *Empress Joséphine*, 239.
13 Fried, *Charlemagne*, 529.
14 Forrest and Wilson, *The Bee and the Eagle*, 118.
15 Pascal-François Bertrand, "Louis XIV and Louis XV: Their Coronations and Their Tapestries, 1654 and 1722," in *Woven Gold: Tapestries of Louis XIV*, ed. Charissa Bremer-David (Los Angeles: The J. Paul Getty Museum, 2015), 39.

16 Victor Hugo, *The Hunchback of Notre Dame*, trans. by Isabel F. Hapgood (Digireads.com Publishing, 2017), 81–82.

17 Blake Ehrlich, "Notre Dame: A Pageant of 800 Years," *New York Times Magazine*, May 5, 1963, 234.

18 Jean-François Bédard, "Franks, Not Romans: Medieval Imagery and the Making of Imperial France" (paper presented at Percier: Antiquity and Empire Symposium, Bard Graduate Center, New York, November 18, 2016).

19 Forrest and Wilson, *The Bee and the Eagle*, 119.

20 Bédard, "Franks, Not Romans."

21 Knapton, *Empress Joséphine*, 239.

22 "Cathedral of Notre Dame in Paris," Napoleon Foundation, https://www.napoleon.org/en/magazine/places/cathedral-of-notre-dame-in-paris/.

23 Hibbert, *Napoleon's Women*, 129.

24 Ibid., 132.

25 Knapton, *Empress Joséphine*, 236.

26 Herbert Richardson, "Costume in History," *Journal of the Royal Society of Arts* 82, no. 4242 (March 9, 1934): 476.

27 "The Day of Napoleon's Coronation," Napoleon Foundation, https://www.napoleon.org/en/history-of-the-two-empires/timelines/the-day-of-napoleons-coronation-11-frimaire-an-xiii-2-december-1804/.

28 Aileen Ribeiro, *The Art of Dress* (New Haven, CT, and London: Yale University Press, 1995), 157.

29 Michel Pastoureau, *Red: The History of a Color*, trans. Jody Gladding (Princeton, N.J.: Princeton University Press, 2017), 40.

30 Ibid., 42.

31 Ibid., 43.

32 Nouvel-Kammerer, *Symbols of Power*, 166.

33 DeLorme, *Joséphine*, 163.

34 Marie-Jeanne-Pierrette Avrillion, *Memoires de Mlle Avrillion, premiere femme de chamber de l'imperatrice Joséphine*, ed. Maurice Dernelle (Paris: Mercure de France, 1986), 98.

35 "The Day of Napoleon's Coronation," Napoleon Foundation.

36 Bernard Morel, *French Crown Jewels: The Objects of the Coronations of the Kings and Queens of France* (Antwerp: Fonds Mercator, 1988), 254.

37 G. Randall Jensen, "The Talisman of Napoleon Bonaparte," 2011, http://www.napoleon-series.org/research/napoleon/Napoleonsphinx.pdf.

38 Lourdes Font and Michele Majer, "La Quatrieme Unite: Costume and Fashion in Genre Historique Painting," in *Romance and Chivalry: History and Literature Reflected in Early Nineteenth Century French Painting*, eds. Nadia Tscherny and Guy Stair Sainty (London and New York: Matthiesen Gallery and Stair Sainty Matthiesen), 197.

39 Janet S. Byrne, "The Best Laid Plans," *Metropolitan Museum of Art Bulletin*, New Series 17, no. 7 (March 1959): 191.

40 Bertrand, "Louis XIV and Louis XV," 39.

41 Knapton, *Empress Joséphine*, 237.

THREE: THE SACRE

1 Ida M. Tarbell, ed., *Napoleon's Addresses: Selections from the Proclamations, Speeches and Correspondence of Napoleon Bonaparte* (Boston: Joseph Knight, 1896).
2 Cordier, *Napoleon: The Imperial Household,* 90.
3 *Napoleon et Paris* (Paris: Musee Carnavalet, 2015), 203.
4 Carolyn McDowall, "Empress Joséphine at Château Malmaison—Woman of Influence," Culture Concept Circle, March 14, 2013, http://www.thecultureconcept.com/empress-josephine-at-chateau-malmaison-woman-of-influence.
5 Rollason, *Power of Place*, 39.
6 Allard, *Citizens and Kings*, 299.
7 Ibid.
8 Alvar Gonzalez-Palacios, *The Art of Mosaics: Selections from the Gilbert Collection* (Los Angeles: LACMA, 1977), 58.
9 H. K. Peters, "The Music at the Coronation of Napoleon and Joséphine," Napoleon Foundation, https://www.napoleon.org/en/history-of-the-two-empires/articles/the-music-at-the-coronation-of-napoleon-and-josephine.
10 Knapton, *Empress Joséphine*, 241.
11 Cordier, *Napoleon: The Imperial Household,* 240.
12 Knapton, *Empress Joséphine*, 242.
13 DeLorme, *Joséphine*, 165.
14 Dwyer, *Citizen Emperor*, 167.
15 Hiram Casey, ed., *Law, Love, and Religion of Napoleon Bonaparte* (New York: Carlton, 1961), 61.
16 Hibbert, *Napoleon's Women*, 135.
17 Knapton, *Empress Joséphine*, 246.
18 Francesca Whitlum-Cooper, "The Oath," Napoleon Foundation, August 2014, https://www.napoleon.org/en/history-of-the-two-empires/paintings/the-oath-napoleons-coronation-2-december-1804/.
19 Nouvel-Kammerer, *Symbols of Power*, 146.
20 Haig, *Walks Through,* 109.
21 Roberts, *Napoleon: A Life*, 357.
22 Hans Teitler, "Raising on a Shield: Origin and Afterlife of a Coronation Ceremony," *International Journal of the Classical Tradition* 8, no. 4 (Spring 2002): 512.
23 Ibid., 506.
24 Bédard, "Franks, Not Romans."
25 Draper, *The Arts under Napoleon*, 7.
26 Marcello Simonetta and Noga Arikha, *Napoleon and the Rebel: A Story of Brotherhood, Passion and Power* (New York: Palgrave Macmillan, 2011), 69.
27 Philippe Bordes, *Jacques-Louis David: Empire to Exile* (New Haven, CT: Yale University Press, 2005), 50.
28 Sylvain Laveissiere, *Le Sacre de Napoleon peint par David* (Paris: Louvre, 2004), 29.
29 Dorothy Johnson, ed., *Jacques-Louis David: New Perspectives* (Newark, Del.: University of Delaware Press, 2006), 137.
30 Huet, "Napoleon I," 68–69.

31 Malika Bouabdellah Dorbani, "The Consecration of the Emperor Napoleon and the Coronation of Empress Joséphine on December 2, 1804," Musée du Louvre, https://www.louvre.fr/en/oeuvre-notices/consecration-emperor-napoleon-and-coronation-empress-josephine-december-2-1804.

32 Bordes, *Jacques-Louis David*, 45.

33 Dorbani, "The Consecration of the Emperor."

34 Maria Wyke, ed., *Julius Caesar in Western Culture* (Malden, Mass., and Oxford, U.K.: Blackwell Publishing, 2006), 289.

35 Luc de Nanteuil, *David* (New York: Henry N. Abrams, 1990), 102.

36 Bordes, *Jacques-Louis David*, 36.

37 Allard, *Citizens and Kings*, 299.

FOUR: KING OF ITALY

1 Edward Hale, *Napoleon and the Pope: The Story of Napoleon and Pius VII* (London: Eyre & Spottiswoode, 1962), 79.

2 Tom Holmberg, "Napoleon's Addresses: The Italian Campaigns," The Napoleon Series, http://www.napoleon-series.org/research/napoleon/speeches/c_speeches1.html.

3 W. Augustus Steward, "Goldsmiths' and Silversmiths' Work—Past and Present: II," *Journal of the Royal Society of Arts* 81, no. 4210 (July 28, 1933): 862.

4 Phillip Blom, *To Have and to Hold: an Intimate History of Collectors and Collecting* (New York: Overlook Press, 2002), 146.

5 Ibid., 147.

6 Lentz, "Napoleon and Charlemagne."

7 Edouard Driault, "The Coalition of Europe Against Napoleon," *American Historical Review* 24, no. 4 (July 1919): 606.

8 Knapton, *Empress Joséphine*, 248.

9 Gabriella Tassinari, "Glyptic Portraits of Eugène de Beauharnais," *Journal of the Walters Art Museum* 60/61 (2002/2003): 45.

10 Karine Huguenaud, "Napoleon I: King of Italy," trans. Peter Hicks, Napoleon Foundation, September 2012, https://www.napoleon.org/en/history-of-the-two-empires/paintings/napoleon-i-king-of-italy/.

11 Maria Louisa Ambrosino, *Secret Archives of the Vatican* (Boston: Little, Brown, 1969), 290–91.

12 Diana Scarisbrick. *Chaumet: Master Jewellers since 1780* (Paris: A. de Gourcuff, 1995), 18.

13 Beyeler, *Pie VII*, 124.

14 Ibid.

15 Sudhir Hazareesingh, *The Saint Napoleon: Celebrations of Sovereignty in Nineteenth Century France* (Cambridge, Mass.: Harvard University Press, 2004), 4.

16 Oliver Benjamin Hemmerle, "Crossing the Rubicon into Paris," in *Julius Caesar in Western Culture*, ed. Maria Wyke (Malden, Mass., and Oxford, U.K.: Blackwell Publishing, 2006), 291.

17 Dwyer, *Citizen Emperor*, 213.

18 Knapton, *Empress Joséphine*, 248.

19 Roberts, *Napoleon: A Life*, 142–43.

20 Laura Stagno, *Palazzo del Principe: The Villa of Andrea Doria* (Genoa: Sagep, 2005), 7.

21 Ilaria Bernocchi, "'Inventing' Identity: Medals and Heroic Portraits in the Italian Renaissance" (paper presented at Full Circle: The Medal in Art History, A Symposium in Honor of Stephen K. Scher, The Frick Collection, New York, September 8, 2017).

22 Stagno, *Palazzo*, 85.

23 Ibid., 18.

24 Louis Antoine Fauvelet de Bourrienne, *Memoirs of Napoleon Bonaparte*, ed. R. W. Phipps (London: Richard Bentley and Son, 1885), 238.

25 Zarzeczny, *Meteors*, 126.

26 Ibid., 126.

27 Stagno, *Palazzo*, 28.

28 Duncan B. Campbell, "Caesar's Invasion of Britain," in *The Landmark Julius Caesar Web Essay*, ed. Kurt A. Raaflaub, www.thelandmarkcaesar.com, 283.

29 Otto Karl Werckmeister, "The Political Ideology of the Bayeux Tapestry, *Studi Medievali*, Series 3, 17, no. 2 (1976): 537.

30 Jean-Michel Leniaud, *La basilique royale de Saint Denis: de Napoleon a la Republique* (Paris: Picard, 2012), 52.

31 Werckmeister, "The Political Ideology," 539.

32 Carola Hicks, *The Bayeux Tapestry: The Life Story of a Masterpiece* (London: Chatto & Windus, 2006), 96.

33 Ibid., 113.

34 Hicks, *Bayeux Tapestry*, 94.

35 Zarzeczny, *Meteors*, 85.

36 Roberts, *Napoleon: A Life*, 390.

PART FOUR: A NEW ROME

ONE: COLUMNS OF CONQUEST

1 Lino Rossi, *Trajan's Column and the Dacian Wars*, trans. J.M.C. Toynbee (London: Thames and Hudson, 1971), 68.

2 Andrew Curry, "A War Diary Soars over Rome," *National Geographic*, March 2015, 129.

3 Encyclopaedia Romana, "Apollodorus of Damascus," http://penelope.uchicago.edu/~grout/encyclopaedia_romana/imperialfora/trajan/apollodorus.html.

4 Giuliana Calcani, ed., *Apollodorus of Damascus and Trajan's Column: from Tradition to Project* (Rome: "L'Erma" di Bretschneider, 2003), 28.

5 Lynne Lancaster, "Building Trajan's Column," *American Journal of Archeology* 103, no. 3 (July 1999): 437.

6 Ibid., 423.

7 J.C.N. Coulston, "Three new books on Trajan's Column," *Journal of Roman Archeology* (1990): 303.

8 Rossi, *Trajan's Column and the Dacian Wars*, 219.

9 Calcani, *Apollodorus of Damascus*, 36.

10 Diana E. E. Kleiner, *Roman Sculpture* (New Haven, CT: Yale University Press, 1992), 217.

11 Filippo Coarelli, *The Column of Marcus Aurelius*, trans. Helen Patterson (Rome: Editore Colombo, 2008), 17.

12 Kleiner, *Roman Sculpture*, 215.

13 James E. Packer, *The Forum of Trajan in Rome: A Study of the Monuments in Brief* (Berkeley: University of California Press, 2001), 191.
14 Ibid., 187.
15 Adriano La Regina, ed., *Archeological Guide to Rome* (Milan, Italy: Electa, 2016), 188.
16 Carmelo G. Malacrino, *Constructing the Ancient World* (Los Angeles: J. Paul Getty Museum, 2010), 137.
17 Kleiner, *Roman Sculpture*, 214.
18 Hughes, *Rome*, 259.
19 Margaret McGowan, *The Vision of Rome in Late Renaissance France* (New Haven, CT: Yale University Press, 2000), 335.
20 Thomas Hedin, "The Northern Axis: Discovery in the Gardens of the Premier Versailles," *Studies in the History of Gardens & Designed Landscapes* 37, no. 3 (2017): 211.
21 Hughes, *Rome*, 118.
22 Samuel L. Macey, "The Concept of Time in Ancient Rome," *International Social Science Review* 65, no. 2 (Spring 1990): 74.
23 Denis C. Feeney, *Caesar's Calendar. Ancient Time and the Beginnings of History* (Berkeley, Los Angeles, and London: University of California Press, 2007) 174, 185.
24 Ibid., 185.
25 Steiner, "Building with Iron," 701.
26 Charles R. Mack, "Metaphorically Speaking: A Grand Tour Souvenir of the Vendôme Column," *Southeastern College Art Conference Review* XVI no. 4 (Jan. 2014): 446.
27 David Markham, ed., *Imperial Glory: the Bulletins of Napoleon's Grande Armée 1805–1814* (London: Greenhill Books, 2003), 226.
28 W. Jeffrey Tatum, *Always I Am Caesar* (Malden, Mass., and Oxford, U.K.: Blackwell Publishing, 2008), 86.
29 Mack, "Metaphorically Speaking," 446.
30 Huet, "Napoleon I" 66.
31 Ibid., 64.
32 Mack, "Metaphorically Speaking," 447.
33 Ibid.
34 Zarzeczny, *Meteors*, 105.
35 Steiner, "Building with Iron," 702.
36 Novillo and Posadas, "Octavian: the Last Man Standing," 73.
37 Anthony Grafton, Glenn W. Most, Salvatore Settis, eds., *The Classical Tradition* (Cambridge: Mass.: Harvard University Press, 2010), 148.
38 Mack, "Metaphorically Speaking," 447.
39 Ziolkowski, *Classical Influence*, 63.
40 Mack, "Metaphorically Speaking," 446.

TWO: ARCHES OF TRIUMPH

1 Gaehtgens, *Napoleon's Arc de Triomphe*, 11.
2 Geoffrey Ellis, *Napoleon* (Harlow: Pearson Education Limited, 1997), 166.
3 Diana Rowell, *Paris: the New Rome of Napoleon I* (London: Bloomsbury, 2012), 43.
4 Paula Dietz, "Recultivating the Tuileries," *Design Quarterly*, no. 155 (Spring 1992): 7.

5 Christopher Tadgell, *Antiquity: Origins, Classicism, and the New Rome* (New York: Routledge, 2007), 561.

6 Jaś Elsner, *Imperial Rome and Christian Triumph* (Oxford, U.K., and New York: Oxford University Press, 1998), 60.

7 Susann Lusnia, "Battle Imagery and Politics on the Severan Arch in the Roman Forum," in *Representations of War in Ancient Rome,* eds. Sheila Dillon and Katherine Welch (Cambridge, U.K., and New York: Cambridge University Press, 2006), 293.

8 Amanda Claridge, *Rome* (Oxford, U.K., and New York: Oxford University Press, 1998), 75.

9 Ibid., 76.

10 Popkin, *Architecture of the Roman Triumph*, 151.

11 Lusnia, "Battle Imagery," 294.

12 Ibid., 295–96.

13 Popkin, *Architecture of the Roman Triumph*, 146.

14 Richard Brilliant, "The Arch of Septimius Severus in the Roma Forum," *Memoirs of the American Academy in Rome* 29 (1967): 30.

15 Emidio De Albentiis, "Art, Power, and Consensus: From Trajan to Constantine," *Rome: Art & Architecture*, ed. Marco Bussagli (Cologne: Könemann, 1999), 140.

16 Elizabeth Marlowe, "Framing the Sun: The Arch of Constantine and the Roman Cityscape," *Art Bulletin* 88, no. 2 (June 2006): 237.

17 Filippo Coarelli, *Monuments of Civilization: Rome* (London: Cassell, 1973), 166.

18 De Albentiis, "Art, Power, and Consensus," 150.

19 Maggie L. Popkin, "Symbiosis and Civil War: The Audacity of the Arch of Constantine," *Journal of Late Antiquity* 9, no. 1 (Spring 2016): 44.

20 Yves Pauwels, "Le theme de l'arc de triomphe dans l'architecure urbaine à la Renaissance, entre pouvoir politique et pouvoir religieux," in *Marquer la ville: Signes, traces, empreintes du pouvoir* (Paris-Rome: Editions de la Sorbonne, 2013), 188.

21 Blair Hixson Davis, "The Roman drawings of Charles Percier" (PhD diss., University of California, Santa Barbara, 2009), 49–52.

22 Garric, *Charles Percier*, 241.

23 Beauhaire, Béjanin, and Naudeix, *L'Elephant de Napoleon*, 13.

24 Pierre Rosenberg, *Dominique-Vivant Denon: L'oeil de Napoleon* (Paris: editions de la Reunion des musees nationaux, 1999), 19.

25 Clifford Ando, *Imperial Ideology and Provincial Loyalty in the Roman Empire* (Berkeley and Los Angeles: University of California Press, 2000), 137.

26 *The Tuileries: From the Louvre to Place de la Concorde* (Paris: Editions du Patrimoine, 2001), 32.

27 *Napoleon et Paris,* 91.

28 Isabelle Lemaistre, Emilie Leverrier, Béatrice Tupinier, "A sculptural group to top the Arc de Triomphe," Louvre, http://www.louvre.fr/en/oeuvre-notices/napoleon-triumph.

29 Anne Muratori-Philip, *Arc de Triomphe* (Paris: Editions du patrimoine, Centre des monuments nationaux, 2007), 4.

30 Ibid.

31 Ibid.

32 Karine Huguenaud, "Arc de Triomphe d' l'Étoile—Paris," Napoleon Foundation, https://www.napoleon.org/magazine/lieux/arc-de-triomphe-de-letoile-paris/.

33 Bruno Klein, "Napoleons Triumphbogen in Paris und der Wandel der offiziellen Kunstanschauungen im Premier Empire," *Zeitschrift fur Kunstgeschichte* 59, no. 2 (Jan. 1, 1996): 253.

34 Muratori-Philip, *Arc de Triomphe*, 5.

35 Andrew Ayers, *The Architecture of Paris: An Architectural Guide* (Stuttgart and London: Edition Axel Menges, 2004), 236.

36 Claridge, *Rome*, 118.

37 Flavius Josephus, *The Jewish War*, eds. Betty Radice and E. Mary Smallwood, trans. G. A. Williamson (London: Penguin, 1981), 304.

38 Catherine Edwards, ed., *Roman Presences: Receptions of Rome in European Culture* (Cambridge, U.K., and New York: Cambridge University Press, 1999), 22.

THREE: TEMPLE TO THE GRANDE ARMÉE

1 Olivia Lichtscheidl, "Emperor Franz II/I and Napoleon," The World of the Habsburgs, http://www.habsburger.net/en/chapter/emperor-franz-iii-and-napoleon.

2 Clare Elisabeth Jeanne Gravier de Vergennes Rémusat, *Memoirs of Madame de Rémusat: 1802–1808* (London: S. Low, Marston, Searle & Rivington, 1880), 201–05.

3 Ricky D. Phillips, "Twelve things you didn't know about Frederick the Great," Making History: The Military History blog of Author Ricky D Phillips, June 5, 2015, https://rickydphillipsauthor.wordpress.com/2015/06/05/twelve-things-you-didnt-know-about-frederick-the-great/.

4 James W. Shosenberg, "Battle of Jéna: Napoleon's Double Knock-out Punch," historynet, http://www.historynet.com/battle-of-jena-napoleons-double-knock-out-punch.html.

5 Herold, *The Mind of Napoleon*, 229.

6 Mansel, *Dressed to Rule*, 80–81.

7 H. Russell Robinson, *The Armour of Imperial Rome* (London: Arms and Armour Press, 1975), 9.

8 Claire Wrathall, "What Napoleon's hat tells us about the power of branding," Christie's, June 17, 2015, http://www.christies.com/features/what-napoleons-hat-tells-us-about-the-power-of-branding-6280-3.aspx.

9 Jean-Roche Coignet, *Memoires* (London: Peter Davis Limited, 1928).

10 Walter Friedlaender, "Napoleon as 'Roi Thaumaturge,'" *Journal of the Warburg and Courtauld Institutes* 4, no. 3/4 (April 1941–July 1942): 141.

11 Wrathall, "Napoleon's hat."

12 Nouvel-Kammerer, *Symbols of Power*, 138.

13 Michael Squire, "Embodied Ambiguities on the Prima Porta Augustus," *Art History* 36, no. 2 (April 2013): 244.

14 Emmanuel-Auguste-Dieudonne Las Cases, *Le Mémorial de Sainte-Hélène: Journal of the Private Life and Conversations of the Emperor Napoleon at Saint Helene,* Vol. II (London: J. Colburn and Co., 1823), 3.

15 Zarzeczny, *Meteors*, 127–28.

16 Dwyer, *Citizen Emperor*, 232.

17 Lukas de Blois, "Caesar the General and Leader," in *The Landmark Julius Caesar Web Essay*, ed. Kurt A. Raaflaub, www.thelandmarkcaesar.com, 107.

18 James Harvey Robinson, ed., *Readings in European History*, Vol. II (Boston: Ginn and Co., 1904–1906), 487–88.

19 Wescher, "Vivant Denon," 185.

20 Ibid., 184.

21 Bénédicte Savoy, *Patrimoine annexé: Les siasies de bien culturels pratiqués par la France en Allemagne autour de 1800*, Vol. 2 (Paris: Editions de la Maison des Sciences de l'Homme, 2003), 117.

22 Wescher, "Vivant Denon," 184.

23 Ibid., 185.

24 Wrathall, "Napoleon's hat."

25 David W. Booth, "Some Little Known Designs by Louis-Pierre Baltard and Jean Baptiste Rondelet for the Transformation of the Church of the Madeleine into a Temple of Glory," *Canadian Art Review* 16, no. 2 (1989): 149.

26 Ibid., 150.

27 Ibid., 151.

28 Robert Bordaz and Claude Mollard, "Napoleon et l'Architecture," *La Nouvelle Revue des Deux Mondes* (July 1973): 98.

29 Booth, "Some Little Known Designs," 153.

30 Zarzeczny, *Meteors*, 157.

31 Tadgell, *Antiquity*, 571.

32 Jeffrey A. Becker, "Maison Carrée," Smarthistory, March 8, 2016, http://smarthistory.org/maison-carree/.

33 James Anderson, *Roman Architecture in Provence* (Cambridge, U.K.: Cambridge University Press, 2012), 53.

34 Sheila Bonde, "Renaissance and Real Estate: The Medieval Afterlife of the 'Temple of Diana' in Nimes," in *Antiquity and its Interpreters*, eds. Alina Payne, Ann Kuttner, and Rebekah Smick (Cambridge, U.K.: Cambridge University Press, 2000), 58.

35 Anderson, *Roman Architecture*, 109.

36 Ibid., 104.

37 Lawrence Durrell, "Provence Entire? Chapter One," *Twentieth Century Literature* 33 (Autumn 1987): 27.

38 Annie Jourdan, "The Grand Paris of Napoleon: From a Dream of Magnificence to a Dream of Unity," *Journal of the International Napoleonic Society* (Nov. 2011).

39 Bordaz and Mollard, "Napoleon et l'Architecture," 99.

40 *Napoleon et Paris*, 206.

41 Ibid., 198.

42 La Regina, *Archeological Guide to Rome*, 156.

FOUR: COINING AN EMPIRE

1 Draper, *Arts Under Napoleon*, 1.

2 Kleiner, *Roman Sculpture*, 26.

3 Fabrizio Pesando, "Roman Coins," in *Rome: Art and Architecture*, ed. Marco Bussagli (Cologne: Konemann, 1999), 100.

4 Daniele Leoni, *Coins of Rome: Trajan* (Verona: lemonetediroma, 2009), 3.

5 Kleiner, *Roman Sculpture*, 61.

6 Carol Humphrey Vivian Sutherland, *Ancient Numismatics: A Brief Introduction* (New York: The American Numismatic Society, 1958), 26.

7 Kleiner, *Roman Sculpture*, 61.

8 Novillo and Posadas, "Octavian: the Last Man Standing," 70–71.

9 Ibid.

10 David R. Sear, *Roman Coins and their Value* (London: Seaby, 1988), 95.

11 Pesando, "Roman Coins," 101.

12 Kleiner, *Roman Sculpture*, 62.

13 Francesco Gnecchi, *The Coin-Types of Imperial Rome*, tr. Emily A. Hands (London: Spink & Son Ltd, 1908), 74.

14 Leoni, *Coins of Rome: Trajan*, 4.

15 Ibid., 60.

16 Jocelyn M. C. Toynbee, *Roman Medallions* (New York: The American Numismatic Society, 1986), 17.

17 Ibid., 95.

18 *Roman Medallions* (Boston: Museum of Fine Arts, 1975), 3.

19 Toynbee, *Roman Medallions*, 15.

20 Ibid., 143.

21 Gnecchi, *The Coin-Types of Imperial Rome*, 54.

22 Jeff Starck, "Charlemagne, king father of Europe, ushers in coinage reform," Coin World, June 1, 2015, https://www.coinworld.com/news/world-coins/2015/05/charlemagne---king-father-of-europe--ushers-in-coinage-reform.all.html#.

23 Aimee Ng, *The Pursuit of Immortality: Masterpieces from the Scher Collection of Portrait Medals* (New York: The Frick Collection in association with D. Giles Limited, 2017), 15.

24 Ibid., 15.

25 Aimee Ng, "Portrait Medals from the Scher Collection Come to the Frick," The Frick, http://www.frick.org/blogs/curatorial/portrait_medals_scher_collection

26 Ibid.

27 Mark Jones, *Medals of the Sun King* (London: British Museum Publications, 1979), 2.

28 Mark Jones, "The Medal as an Instrument of Propaganda in late 17th and early 18th Century Europe," *The Numismatic Chronicle* 142 (1982): 117.

29 Sabine Haag, *Zuhanden Ihrer Majestät: Madaillen Maria Theresias* (Vienna: Kunsthistoriches Museum-Museumsverband, 2017), 10.

30 Draper, *Arts Under Napoleon*, 7.

31 Wayne Hanley, *The Genesis of Napoleonic Propaganda, 1796 to 1799*, (New York: Columbia University Press, 2008).

32 Antony Griffiths, "The Design and Production of Napoleon's Histoire Metallique," Part I, *The Medal*, no. 16 (Spring 1990): 16.

33 Hanley, *Genesis*.

34 Stephen Scher, *Commentary on Napoleonic Commemorative Medals*, Yale Center for British Art, http://interactive.britishart.yale.edu/critique-of-reason/528/commentary-by-stephen-scher.

35 Hanley, "Genesis."

36 Antony Griffiths, "Drawings for Napoleonic Medals," in *Designs on Posterity: Drawings for Medals*, ed. Mark Jones (London: British Art Medal Trust, 1994).

37 Karine Huguenaud, "5 Franc Piece, Napoleon Emperor, 1806," trans. Peter Hicks, January 2002, http://www.napoleon.org/en/history-of-the-two-empires/objects/5-franc-piece-napoleon-emperor-1806/.

38 Mark Jones, *The Art of the Medal* (London: British Museum Publications, 1979), 101.

39 Ibid., 100–01.

40 Daniela Gallo, ed., *Les Vies de Dominique-Vivant Denon* (Paris: Louvre, 2001), 386.

41 Beyeler, *Pie VII*, 117.

42 *Les Vies de Dominique-Vivant Denon*, 386.

43 Griffiths, "Design and Production," 23.

44 Ibid., 20.

PART FIVE: PRINCIPATE

ONE: CURIA REGIS

1 Cordier, *Napoleon: The Imperial Household*, 24.

2 Philip Mansel, *The Eagle in Splendour: Napoleon I and His Court* (London: G. Philip, 1987), 27.

3 Herold, *The Mind of Napoleon*, xxxiii.

4 Mansel, *Eagle*, 47.

5 Cordier, *Napoleon: The Imperial Household*, 248.

6 Ibid., 234.

7 Mansel, *Eagle*, 21.

8 Cordier, *Napoleon: The Imperial Household*, 34.

9 Ibid., 121.

10 Fiona Ffoulkes, "'Quality always distinguishes itself': Louis Hippolyte LeRoy and the luxury clothing industry in early nineteenth-century Paris," in *Consumers and Luxury: Consumer Culture in Europe 1650–1850*, ed. Maxine Berg and Helen Clifford (Manchester, U.K.: Manchester University Press, 1999), 193.

11 DeLorme, *Joséphine*, 166.

12 Mansel, *Eagle*, 27.

13 Las Cases, *Le Mémorial de Sainte-Hélène*, 124.

14 Mansel, *Eagle*, 17.

15 Rafe Blaufarb, *Napoleon: Symbol for an Age* (New York: Bedford/St. Martin's, 2008), 114.

16 Cordier, *Napoleon: The Imperial Household*, 62.

17 Mansel, *Eagle*, 61.

18 DeLorme, *Joséphine*, 114.

19 Blaufarb, *Napoleon*, 110.

20 Lapatin, *Luxus*, 221.

21 Ibid., 4.

22 "Dinner Plate from the Emperor's Personal Service: Schonbrunn Palace," Napoleon Foundation, https://www.napoleon.org/en/history-of-the-two-empires/images/dinner-plate-from-the-emperors-personal-service-schonbrunn-palace/.
23 Cordier, *Napoleon: The Imperial Household*, 216.
24 Joanna Gwilt, *French Porcelain for English Palaces: Sèvres from the Royal Collection* (London: Royal Collection Publications, 2009), 178.
25 Ibid., 1067.
26 Ibid.
27 Scott, "Cloth of Gold," 1561.
28 Katia Frey, "L'enterprise napoléonienne," in *Paris et ses fontaines: de la Renaissance à nos jours*, eds. Dominique Massounie, Pauline Prévost-Marcilhacy, and Daniel Rabreau (Paris: Délégation à l'action artistique de la ville de Paris, 1995), 104–23.
29 Ibid., 105.
30 Philip Smith, *A Dictionary of Greek and Roman Antiquities*, ed. William Smith (London: John Murray, 1875), 544.
31 Morton, *Fountains*, 31.
32 Katherine W. Rinne, "The Secret Life of Roman Fountains," *Places: Forum of Design for the Public Realm* 12, no. 2 (Winter 1999): 76.
33 Ibid., 266.
34 Ibid., 68.
35 Kenneth D. Matthews Jr., "The Embattled Driver in Ancient Rome," *Expedition* (Spring 1960): 26, https://www.penn.museum/documents/publications/expedition/PDFs/2-3/The%20Embattled.pdf.
36 Ayers, *The Architecture of Paris*, 27.
37 Frey, "L'enterprise napoléonienne," 109.
38 Marc Gaillard, *Les Fontaines de Paris* (Amiens: Martelle, 1995), 15–16.

TWO: A FAMILY OF KINGS

1 Jean Sorabella, "Art of the Roman Provinces, 1–500 A.D.," in *Heilbrunn Timeline of Art History* (New York: Metropolitan Museum of Art, 2000).
2 La Regina, *Archeological Guide to Rome*, 164.
3 Ibid., 16.
4 Dwyer, *Citizen Emperor*, 221.
5 Lady Mary Lloyd, *New Letters of Napoleon I*, ed. M. Léon Lecestre (New York: D. Appleton, 1898), 150.
6 Herold, *The Mind of Napoleon*, 257.
7 Zarzeczny, *Meteors*, 105.
8 Bonaparte, *Aphorisms*, 97.
9 Susan Vandiver Nicassio, *Imperial City: Rome, Romans and Napoleon, 1796–1815* (Welwyn Garden City, U.K.: Ravenhall Books, 2005), 229.
10 Mansel, *Dressed to Rule*, 84.
11 Cordier, *Napoleon: The Imperial Household*,, 43.
12 Hugh Honour, "The Italian Empire Style," *Apollo* 80, no. 31 (Sep. 1, 1964): 229.
13 Bazin, *The Museum Age*, 183.

14 Bazin, *The Louvre*, 55.

15 "The Marriage of the Virgin," Pinacoteca di Brera, http://pinacotecabrera.org/en/collezione-online/opere/the-marriage-of-the-virgin/.

16 Catherine Hyde Govion Broglio Solari, *Private Anecdotes of Foreign Courts*, Vol. 1 (London: H. Colburn, 1827), 456.

17 Shannon Selin, "Caroline Bonaparte Murat, Napoleon's Treasonous Sister," July 2014. A Covent Garden Gilflurt's Guide to Life, http://www.madamegilflurt.com/2014/07/a-salon-guest-caroline-bonaparte-murat.html.

18 Rémusat, *Memoirs of Madame de Rémusat*, 488.

19 Anthony Blunt, "Naples under the Bourbons," *The Burlington Magazine* 121, no. 913 (April 1979): 208.

20 "Caroline, Soeur de Napoleon, Reine des Arts," Ajaccio, Palais Fesch-musée des Beaux-Arts, June 2017, https://enfilade18thc.files.wordpress.com/2017/07/palais-fesch-exposition-caroline-murat-dp.pdf.

21 Costanza Beltrami, Italian Art Society, August 26, 2015, http://italianartsociety.tumblr.com/post/127642287447/by-costanza-beltrami-gem-engraver-and-medalist.

22 Judith Harris, *Pompeii Awakened: A Story of Rediscovery* (London and New York: I. B.Tauris, 2007), 149.

23 Joan R. Mertens, "A Drawing by Chassériau," *Metropolitan Museum Journal* 15 (1980): 153.

24 Harris, *Pompeii Awakened*, 149.

25 Ibid., 151.

26 Maria Sapio, ed., The Museum of Capodimonte, Issuu, https://issuu.com/arte-m/docs/guida_capodimonte_inglese.

27 Marianna van der Zwaag, ed., *King Louis Napoleon & his Palace in Dam Square, Amsterdam Royal Palace*, Issuu, July 24, 2012, https://issuu.com/koninklijkpaleisamsterdam/docs/napoleon_eng_final, 53.

28 Ibid., 81.

29 Ibid., 48.

30 Ibid., 70.

31 Adrián Almoguera, "Project for the Bonaparte Forum in Madrid," trans. Leyly Moridi and Peter Hicks, Napoleon Foundation, September 2016, https://www.napoleon.org/en/history-of-the-two-empires/objects/projet-for-the-bonaparte-forum-in-madrid/.

32 Ibid.

33 Kathryn Kane, "Bagging Bonaparte's Baggage," The Regency Redingote, June 2013, https://regencyredingote.wordpress.com/2013/06/28/regency-bicentennial-bagging-bonapartes-baggage/.

34 Wescher, "Vivant Denon," 186.

THREE: VENUS VICTRIX

1 "Paolina Borghese e la storia della sua visita a Torino," Mole 24, December 9, 2013, http://www.mole24.it/2013/12/09/paolina-borghese-visita-torino/.

2 Ibid., 122.

3 Ibid., 136.

4 Flora Fraser, *Pauline Bonaparte* (New York: Anchor Books, 2009), 112.
5 Anthony Majanlahti, *The Families Who Made Rome: A History and a Guide* (London: Pimlico, 2006), 80.
6 "Paolina Borghese e la storia."
7 Andrea Zanella, *Canova in Rome* (Rome: Fratelli Palombi, 1993), 63.
8 Anna Coliva and Fernando Mazzocca, eds., *Canova e la Venere vincitrice* (Milan: Electa, 2007), 39.
9 Paola Mangia, *Canova. Artists and Collectors: A Passion for Antiquity* (Rome: De Luca Editori D'Arte, 2009), 116.
10 Ibid., 104.
11 Coliva and Mazzocca, *Canova,* 19.
12 Carole Paul, *Making a Prince's Museum* (Los Angeles: Getty Research Institute, 2000), 47.
13 Coliva and Mazzocca, *Canova,* 92.
14 David Bindman, "Lost Surfaces: Canova and Color," *Oxford Art Journal* 39, no. 2 (Aug. 2016): 229–41.
15 Da Sesso, *Antonio Canova*, 27.
16 Christina Ferando, "Canova and the writing of art criticism in 18th century Naples," *Word & Image: A Journal of Verbal/Visual Inquiry* 30, no. 4 (2014): 362.
17 Giuseppe Pavanello, *La Biblioteca de Antonio Canova* (Verona: Cierre edizioni, 2007), 7.
18 Ibid., 10.
19 Ben Pollitt, "Canova, Paolina Borghese as Venus Victorius," Khan Academy, https://www.khanacademy.org/humanities/monarchy-enlightenment/neo-classicism/a/canova-paolina-borghese-as-venus-victorius.
20 Mary Beard, "The Twelve Caesars: Images of Power from Ancient Rome to Salvador Dali, Part 4, Caesar's Wife: Above Suspicion?" (Lecture at the Sixtieth A. W. Mellon Lectures in the Fine Arts, National Gallery of Art, Washington, D.C., April 17, 2011).
21 Ibid.
22 Cordier, *Napoleon: The Imperial Household,* 43.
23 Ibid., 68.
24 Dwyer, *Citizens and Kings*, 324.
25 Coliva and Mazzocca, *Canova,* 221.
26 Ibid., 90.
27 Hughes, *Rome*, 366.
28 Francis Henry Taylor, *The Taste of Angels* (Boston: Little, Brown, 1948), 556.
29 Ambrosino, *Secret Archives*, 290.
30 Majanlahti, *Families*, 177.
31 Caroline Vincenti Montanaro and Andrea Fasolo, *Palazzi and Villas of Rome* (Verona: Arsenale Editrice, 2001), 38.
32 Tiffany Parks, "The Borghese Gallery and the Fate of an Ill-gotten Collection," Part 1, Tiffany-Parks.com, Dec. 8, 2011, https://www.tiffany-parks.com/blog/2011/12/08/the-borghese-gallery-and-the-fate-of-an-ill-gotten-collection-part-1?rq=Borghese.
33 Gail Feigenbaum, ed., with Francesco Freddolini, *Display of Art in the Roman Palace* (Los Angeles: The Getty Research Institute, 2014), 44.

34 Paul, *Making a Prince's Museum*, 12.

35 Souren Melikian, "Behind the Borghese Collection," *New York Times*, Aug., 28, 2009, http://www.nytimes.com/2009/08/29/arts/29iht-melik29.html.

36 Parks, "The Borghese Gallery."

37 Mangia, *Canova*, 25.

38 Melikian, "Behind the Borghese Collection."

39 Coliva and Mazzocca, *Canova*, 19.

40 Marie-Lou Fabréga-Dubert, *La collection Borghese au musée Napoléon* (Paris: Musée du Louvre: École nationale supérieure des beaux-arts, 2009), 13.

41 Ibid., intro.

FOUR: CARRARA

1 Hibbert, *Napoleon's Women*, 166.

2 Ibid., 167–68.

3 Maria Teresa Caracciolo, ed., *Les Soeurs de Napoleon* (Paris: Musée Marmottan Monet, 2013), 10.

4 Ibid.

5 Sante Bargellini, "Paganini and the Princess," *Musical Quarterly* 20, no 4 (Oct. 1934): 4122.

6 Ibid., 409.

7 Joel Leivick, *Carrara: The Marble Quarries of Tuscany* (Stanford, Calif.: Stanford University Press, 1999), 10–11.

8 Leonardo da Vinci's Inventions, http://www.leonardodavincisinventions.com/.

9 Leivick, *Carrara*, 10–11.

10 Felix Petrelli, "Visiting Carrara Marble Quarries—Apuan Alps' Eternal Snow," *Italy Magazine*, Feb. 2014.

11 Christopher Tadgell, *Antiquity: Origins, Classicism and the New Rome* (New York: Routledge, 2007), 564.

12 Sarah Pothecary, "When was the *Geography* written?" Strabo the Geographer, September 2007, http://www.strabo.ca/when.html.

13 Malacrino, *Constructing the Ancient World*, 24.

14 Ibid., 39.

15 Ibid., 25.

16 Grossman, *Looking*, 8, 18, 25.

17 Ibid., 74–75, 85.

18 Ibid., 94, 105.

19 William L. MacDonald, *The Architecture of the Roman Empire*, Vol. 1 (New Haven, CT, and London: Yale University Press, 1982), 148.

20 Alison Leitch, "The Life of Marble," *Australian Journal of Anthropology* 7, no. 1 (April 1996): 235–37.

21 Walter Pater, "The Poetry of Michelangelo," in *Michelangelo: The Sistine Chapel Ceiling*, ed. Charles Seymour, Jr. (London: Thames and Hudson, 1972), 164.

22 Sam Anderson, "The Majestic Marble Quarries of Northern Italy," *New York Times Magazine*, July 26, 2017.

23 Pater, "The Poetry of Michelangelo," 164.

24 Mario Guderzo, email message to author, January 18, 2018.

25 Alison Yarrington, "Anglo-Italian Attitudes: Chantrey and Canova," in *The Lustrous Trade: Material Culture and the History of Sculpture in England and Italy, c.1700–c.1860*, eds. Cinzia Sicca and Alison Yarrington (London and New York: Leicester University Press, 2000), 143.

26 Eric Scigliano, *Michelangelo's Mountain* (New York: Free Press, 2005), 129.

27 Caracciolo, *Les Soeurs de Napoleon*, 27.

28 Hubert and Ledoux-Lebard, *Napoléon*, 100.

29 Ibid., 56.

30 Lawrence Sondhaus, "Napoleon's Shipbuilding Program at Venice and the Struggle for Naval Mastery in the Adriatic," *Journal of Military History* 53, no. 4 (Oct. 1989): 353.

31 "The Arrival of Napoleon," Teatro La Fenice di Venezia, http://www.teatrolafenice.it/site/index.php?pag=73&blocco=168&lingua=eng.

32 Mansel, *Eagle*, 32.

33 Bargellini, "Paganini," 415.

34 Ibid.

35 Derrick Worsdale, "Later Neo-Classical Florentine Furniture at Palazzo Pitti," *Furniture History* 14 (1978): 50.

36 Hibbert, *Napoleon's Women*, 169.

37 Caracciolo, *Les Soeurs de Napoleon*, 73.

38 Hibbert, *Napoleon's Women*, 167.

39 Caracciolo, *Les Soeurs de Napoleon*, 32.

40 Ibid., 32.

PART SIX: CAPITAL OF THE UNIVERSE

ONE: ABDUCTION

1 Morton, *Fountains*, 142.

2 Ibid., 144.

3 Louis Godart, *The Quirinale Palace: The History, the Rooms and the Collections* (Rome: Treccani, 2016), 110.

4 Lascelles, *Pontifex Maximus*, 242.

5 Peter Hicks, "Napoleon and the Pope: From the Concordat to the Excommunication," Napoleon Foundation, https://www.napoleon.org/en/history-of-the-two-empires/articles/napoleon-and-the-pope-from-the-concordat-to-the-excommunication/.

6 Ambrosini, *Secret Archives*, 291.

7 Bernardine Melchior-Bonnet, *Napoléon et le Pape* (Paris: Amiot Dumont, 1958), 126.

8 Herold, *The Mind of Napoleon*, 109.

9 Ibid.

10 Melchior-Bonnet, *Napoléon et le Pape*, 122.

11 Felix Markham, *Napoleon* (London: Weidenfeld and Nicolson, 1963), 139.

12 Anderson, *Pope Pius VII*.

13 Ibid.

14 Herold, *The Mind of Napoleon*, 109.

15 Ibid., 109.

16 Englund, *Napoleon*, 355.

17 Herold, *The Mind of Napoleon*, 270.

18 Bette Wyn Oliver, *From Royal to National: the Louvre Museum and the Bibliotheque Nationale* (Lanham, Md.: Lexington Books, 2007), 62.

19 Napoleon Bonaparte, *A Selection from the Letters and Dispatches of the First Napoleon: With Explanatory Notes* (Chapman and Hall, 1884), 54–55.

20 "History of the Vatican Medagliere," Vatican Library, https://www.vatlib.it/home.php?pag=dipartimento_numismatico&ling=eng.

21 Ambrosini, *Secret Archive*, 292.

22 Brian Haughton, "What happened to the great library at Alexandria?" Ancient History Encyclopedia, February 1, 2011, https://www.ancient.eu/article/207what-happened-to-the-great-library-at-alexandria/.

23 Evan Andrews, "8 Legendary Ancient Libraries," History.com, November 17, 2016, http://www.history.com/news/history-lists/8-impressive-ancient-libraries.

24 Ibid.

25 Ibid.

26 Tarbell, *Napoleon's Addresses.*

27 Mansel, *Eagle*, 61.

28 Zachary M. Stoltzfus, "Napoleon's Kindle: Libraries, Literature, and the Legacy of the Napoleonic Era," *Journal of the International Napoleonic Society* (December 2016): 80.

29 Ibid.

30 "Schönbrunn Palace," Napoleon Foundation, https://www.napoleon.org/en/magazine/places/schoenbrunn-palace/.

31 Natalia Gustavson, "Retracing the restoration history of Viennese paintings in the Musée Napoléon (1809-1815)," *CeROArt*, April 10, 2012, https://ceroart.revues.org/2325.

32 Wilhelm Treue, *Art Plunder: The Fate of Works of Art in War and Unrest*, trans. Basil Creighton (New York: John Day Co., 1961), 168.

33 Nouvel-Kammerer, *Symbols of Power*, 171.

34 William H. Peck, "'Description de l'Égypte': A Major Acquisition from the Napoleonic Age," *Bulletin of the Detroit Institute of Arts* 51, no. 4 (1972): 116.

35 Anne Godlewska, "Map, Text and Image. The Mentality of Enlightened Conquerors: A New Look at the Description de l'Egypte," *Transactions of the Institute of British Geographers* 20, no. 1 (1995): 7.

36 Ibid., 22.

37 Peck, "Description de l'Égypte," 112.

38 Godlewska, "Map, Text and Image," 7.

TWO: TROPHY WIFE

1 Emmanuel de Waresquiel, ed., *Mémoires du Prince de Talleyrand* (Paris: R. Laffont, 2007), 330–31.

2 Hamish Davey Wright, "Napoleon's 'Divorce,'" Napoleon Foundation, December 2009, https://www.napoleon.org/en/history-of-the-two-empires/timelines/napoleons-divorce/.

3 Hortense, consort of Louis Bonaparte, King of Holland, *Mémoires de la Reine Hortense* Vol. II (Paris: Plon, 1927), 44–45.

4 Cordier, *Napoleon: The Imperial Household,*, 90.

5 Giorgia Haot, "The Divorce of Napoleon and Joséphine," History and Other Thoughts, January 2014, http://historyandotherthoughts.blogspot.com/2014/01/the-divorce-of-napoleon-and-josephine.html.

6 Fraser, *Pauline Bonaparte,* 178.

7 Kleiner, *Roman Sculpture*, 60.

8 Susan M. Treggiari, *Roman Marriage: Iusti Coniuges from the Time of Cicero to the Time of Ulpian* (Oxford: Oxford University Press, 1993), 594.

9 Marie Martin, *Maria Féodorovna en son temps (1759–1828): Contribution a l'histoire de la Russie et de l'Europe* (Paris: L'Harmattan, 2003).

10 Shannon Selin, "The Marriage of Napoleon and Marie Louise," Shannon Selin: Imagining the Bounds of History, April 2016, http://shannonselin.com/2016/04/marriage-napoleon-marie-louise/.

11 Hamish Davey Wright, "The Marriage of Napoleon I and Marie Louise of Austria," Napoleon Foundation, March 2010, https://www.napoleon.org/en/history-of-the-two-empires/timelines/the-marriage-of-napoleon-i-and-marie-louise-of-austria/.

12 Monica Kurzel-Runtscheiner, "Napoleon and Marie Louise: Courtship and Wedding in Vienna," The World of the Habsburgs, http://www.habsburger.net/en/chapter/napoleon-and-marie-louise-courtship-and-wedding-vienna.

13 Martin Mutschlechner, "The Handover of the Bride," The World of the Habsburgs, http://www.habsburger.net/en/chapter/handover-bride.

14 Monica Kurzel-Runtscheiner, "First meeting and wedding in Paris," The World of the Habsburgs, http://www.habsburger.net/en/chapter/first-meeting-and-wedding-paris.

15 Hibbert, *Napoleon's Women,* 181.

16 Martin Mutschlechner, "Marie Louise—A dutiful daughter sacrificed on the altar of political expediency," The World of the Habsburgs, http://www.habsburger.net/en/chapter/handover-bride.

17 "The Apartment of the Empress," Palais de Compiègne, http://en.palaisdecompiegne.fr/one-palace-three-museums/historic-apartments/apartment-empress.

18 Edward P. Alexander, *Museum Masters: Their Museums and their Influence* (Nashville, Tenn.: American Association for State and Local History, 1983), 95.

19 Nouvel-Kammerer, *Symbols of Power*, 166.

20 Meyer Reinhold, *History of Purple as a Status Symbol in Antiquity* (Brussels: Latomus Revue D'Etudes Latines, 1970), 38.

21 Rapelli, *Symbols of Power*, 46.

22 Ibid., 46.

23 Reinhold, *History of Purple*, 70.

24 Elisabeth Malkin, "An Insect's Colorful Gift, Treasured by Kings and Artists," *New York Times*, Nov. 27, 2017, https://www.nytimes.com/2017/11/27/arts/design/red-dye-cochineal-treasure-mexico-city-history.html?smprod=nytcore-ipad&smid=nytcore-ipad-share.

25 Cordier, *Napoleon: The Imperial Household*, 274.

26 Jean-Roch. Coignet, *The Note-Books of Captain Coignet, Soldier of the Empire*, with an introduction by the Hon. Sir John Fontescue (London: Peter Davies, 1928), 192–94.

27 Marie-Anne Dupuy, *Dominique-Vivant Denon: L'oeil de Napoleon* (Paris: Editions de la Reunion des Musées Nationaux, 1999), 55.

28 Hibbert, *Napoleon*, 186.

29 Dupuy, *Dominique-Vivant Denon*, 1999, 54.

30 Martin Hirsch, "Papal Medals and the Interplay of Prints, Paintings, and Numismatics," in *Full Circle: The Medal in Art History, A Symposium in Honor of Stephen K. Scher*, The Frick Collection, New York, September, 8, 2017, https://www.frick.org/interact/video/scher_medals.

31 "Napoleon and Paris: Dreams of a Capital," Musee Carnavelet, April 2015, http://www.carnavalet.paris.fr/sites/default/files/pk_napoleon_and_paris.pdf.

32 Catherine Delors, "Imperial wedding: Napoléon and Marie-Louise," Versailles and More, May 2011, http://blog.catherinedelors.com/imperial-wedding-napoleon-and-marie-louise/.

33 Imbert de Saint-Amand, *The Happy Days of the Empress Marie Louise*, (New York: C. Scribner's Sons, 1890).

34 "Tea Service of the Emperor Napoleon," National Museums Scotland, https://www.nms.ac.uk/explore-our-collections/stories/art-and-design/tea-service-of-the-emperor-napoleon/.

35 "Diamond in the crown: Le Grand Mazarin," Christies, October 18, 2017, http://www.christies.com/features/Le-Grand-Mazarin-Diamond-in-the-Crown-8625-3.aspx?pid=en_homepage_row1_slot2_1.

36 *Napoleon Ier ou le legend des arts,* 2015, 150.

37 Lapatin, *Berthouville Silver*, 131.

38 Ibid., 133.

39 DeLorme, *Joséphine,* 115.

THREE: BREAKFAST WITH NAPOLEON

1 Valerie Huet, "Stories one might tell of Roman art: reading Trajan's column and the Tiberius cup," in *Art and Text in Roman Culture, ed. Jaś Elsner* (Cambridge, U.K. and New York: Cambridge University Press, 1996), 13.

2 Hochel, "Dominique-Vivant Denon."

3 Elisabeth E. Guffey, "Reconstructing the Limits of Propaganda: Pierre-Paul Prud'hon and the Art of Napoleon's Remarriage," *Visual Resources* 16, no. 3 (2000): 259.

4 Ibid., 264.

5 Elisabeth E. Guffey, "The Toilette Berceau of Marie Louise: Napoleonic Imagery in Furniture," *Apollo* 143, no. 407 (Jan. 1996): 4.

6 Alexander, *Museum Masters*, 99.

7 Dupuy, *Dominqiue-Vivant Denon*, 54.

8 Mario Guderzo, *Napoleone e Canova: Il Pantheon dell' Imperatore a Marengo* (Alessandria: LineLab.edizioni, 2016), 24.

9 Ibid., 14–15.

10 Guderzo, *Napoleone e Canova*, 15.

11 Christopher M. S. Johns, *Antonio Canova and the Politics of Patronage in Revolutionary and Napoleonic Europe* (Berkeley: University of California Press, 1998).

12 Ibid., 107.

13 Mansel, *Eagle,* 51.

14 Guderzo, *Napoleone e Canova*, 14.

15 Antonio Canova, *Napoleon and Canova: eight conversations held at the Château of the Tuileries, in 1810* (London: Printed for Treuttel and Wurtz, Treuttel, jun. and Richter, Soho-Square, 1825), 1–9.

16 Johns, *Politics and Patronage*, 136.

17 Ibid., 130.
18 Ibid., 123.
19 Cunial and Pavan, *Antonio Canova*, 237.
20 Canova, *Napoleon and Canova: eight conversations*, 10–15.
21 Ibid., 16–24.
22 Ibid., 30–33.
23 Ibid., 34–38.
24 Guderzo, *Napoleon e Canova*, 24.
25 Canova, *Napoleon and Canova: eight conversations*, 39–40.
26 Ibid., 41–43.
27 Cordier, *Napoleon*, 43.
28 DeLorme, *Joséphine*, 172.
29 Ibid., 48.
30 Christopher M. S. Johns, "Empress Joséphine's collection of sculpture by Canova at Malmaison," *Journal of the History of Collections* 16, no. 1 (2004): 31.
31 DeLorme, *Joséphine*, 49.
32 Johns, "Empress Joséphine's collection," 27.
33 DeLorme, *Joséphine*, 86.
34 Ibid., 87.
35 Johns, "Empress Joséphine's collection," 30–31.
36 Louis Madelin, *The Consulate and the Empire*, Vol. II, trans. E. F. Buckley (New York: AMS Press, 1967), 35.

PART SEVEN: DYNASTY

ONE: THE EAGLET

1 George Vilinbachov and Magnus Olausson, *Staging Power: Napoleon, Charles John, Alexander* (Stockholm: Nationalmuseum, 2010), 302.
2 Ibid., 301.
3 Karine Huguenaud, "The Roi de Rome's Cradle," Napoleon Foundation, February 2004, https://www.napoleon.org/en/history-of-the-two-empires/objects/the-roi-de-romes-cradle/.
4 "The Cradle of the King of Rome," Imperial Treasury Museum, Vienna, http://wiener-schatzkammer.at/cradle-king-rome.html. Even the infant's gilt silver and coral rattle sported an image of the she-wolf suckling Romulus and Remus (Vilinbachov and Olausson, *Staging Power*, 310).
5 Beyeler, *Pie VII*, 166.
6 Diana Kleiner, "Women and Family Life on Roman Imperial Altars," *Latomus* 46 (July–Sept. 1987): 545.
7 Kleiner, *Roman Sculpture*, 98.
8 Christophe Beyeler and Vincent Cochet, *Enfance impériale: Le Roi de Rome, Fils de Napoleon* (Dijon: Faton; Fontainebleau: Château de Fontainebleau, 2011), 124–25.
9 Marco Fabio Apolloni, *Napoleone et le Arti* (Florence and Milan: Giunti Editore, 2004), 25.
10 Vilinbachov and Olausson, *Staging Power*, 304.
11 Vincent Ardiet, Elisabeth Caude, et al., *La pourpre et l'exil: l'Aiglon et le Prince impérial*, exposition au Musée national du château de Compiègne, Nov. 25, 2004–Mar. 7, 2005. (Paris: Réunion des musées nationaux, 2004), 45–46.

12 Mansel, *Eagle*, 173.

13 Ardiet, *La pourpre et l'exil*, 46.

14 Ibid., 47.

15 Peter Hicks, "The Celebration of the Baptism of the Roi de Rome," Napoleon Foundation, May 31, 2011, https://www.napoleon.org/en/history-of-the-two-empires/articles/the-celebration-of-the-baptism-of-the-roi-de-rome/.

16 Ardiet, *La pourpre et l'exil*, 51.

17 Beyeler and Cochet, *Enfance impériale*, 132.

18 John P. C. Kent, Bernhard Overbeck, and Armin U. Stylow, *Die römische Münze* (Munich: Hirmer Verlag, 1973).

19 Beyeler and Cochet, *Enfance impériale*, 133–34.

20 Benjamin Hemmerle, "Crossing the Rubicon into Paris: Caesarian Comparisons from Napoleon to de Gaulle," in *Julius Caesar in Western Culture*, ed. Maria Wyke (Malden, Mass., and Oxford, U.K.: Blackwell, 2006), 291.

21 Frédéric Masson, *Napoléon et son fils* (Paris: Alben Michel, 1929), 83–84.

22 Hibbert, *Napoleon's Women*, 195.

23 Ibid., 25.

24 Martin Henig, *Handbook of Roman Art: A Comprehensive Survey of all the Arts of the Roman World* (Ithaca, N.Y.: Cornell University Press, 1983), 153.

25 Lapatin, *Luxus*, 253.

26 Ibid., 254.

27 Henig, *Handbook of Roman Art*, 155.

28 Christopher H. Hallett, *The Roman Nude: Heroic Portrait Statuary 200 B.C.–A.D. 300* (Oxford, U.K., and New York: Oxford University Press, 2005), 257.

29 Hallett, *The Roman Nude*, 257–58.

30 Lapatin, *Luxus*, 252.

31 Henig, *Handbook of Roman Art*, 156.

32 Julia C. Fischer, ed., *More than Mere Playthings: The Minor Arts of Italy* (Newcastle upon Tyne, U.K.: Cambridge Scholars Publishing, 2016), 50.

33 Hallett, *The Roman Nude*, 339.

34 Jean-Baptiste Giard, *Le Grand Camée de France* (Paris: Bibliothèque nationale de France, 1998), 38.

35 Nouvel-Kammerer, *Symbols of Power*, 164.

36 Giard, *Le Grand Camée*, 37.

37 DeLorme, *Joséphine*, 178.

38 Beyler and Cochet, *Enfance impériale*, 140.

39 Ibid., 140.

40 Vilinbachov and Olausson, *Staging Power*, 369.

41 Cordier, *Napoleon*, 73.

42 Beyeler and Vincent Cochet, *Enfance impériale*, 63.

43 Garric, *Charles Percier*, 245.

44 Ibid., 254–55.

45 Charles Percier and Pierre Fontaine, "Napoléon Architecte," *Revue de Paris* 52, (July 1833): 39–40.

46 Garric, *Charles Percier*, 255–56.

47 "Napoleon and Paris: Dreams of a Capital," Musée Carnavelet, April 2015, http://www.carnavalet.paris.fr/sites/default/files/pk_napoleon_and_paris.pdf.
48 Cordier, *Napoleon: The Imperial Household*, 73.
49 Ibid.
50 Garric, *Charles Percier*, 213.
51 Cordier, *Napoleon: The Imperial Household*, 68.
52 Ibid., 43.
53 "Marie Antoinette at Rambouillet," Chateau Rambouillet, http://www.chateau-rambouillet.fr/en/Explore/Marie-Antoinette-at-Rambouillet.
54 "Napoleon I at Rambouillet," Chateau Rambouillet, http://www.chateau-rambouillet.fr/en/Explore/Napoleon-I-at-Rambouillet.
55 Ibid.

TWO: IN MEMORIUM

1 Jean-Michel Leniaud, *La basilique royale de Saint-Denis*, 13.
2 Penelope J. E. Davies, *Death and the Emperor: Roman Imperial Funerary Monuments, from Augustus to Marcus Aurelius* (Cambridge, U.K., and New York: Cambridge University Press, 2000), 1.
3 Rollason, *Power of Place*, 351.
4 Davies, *Death and the Emperor*, 19.
5 Ibid., 15.
6 Rollason, *Power of Place*, 345.
7 Ibid., 351.
8 Davies, *Death and the Emperor*, 35.
9 "History of the Monument," Centre des Monuments Nationaux, http://www.saint-denis-basilique.fr/en/Explore/History-of-the-monument.
10 Ibid.
11 Ibid.
12 Leniaud. *La basilique royale de Saint-Denis*, 49.
13 Sérullaz, *Gérard, Girodet, Gros*, 84.
14 Basilica of Saint Denis, "The Role of Napoleon Bonaparte,"Seine-Saint-Denis Tourisme, https://uk.tourisme93.com/basilica/the-role-of-napoleon-bonaparte-in-the-basilica-st-denis-restoration.html.
15 David O'Brien, *After the Revolution, Antoine-Jean Gros, Painting and Propaganda under Napoleon* (University Park: Pennsylvania State University Press, 2006), 183.
16 Voltaire, *Siècle de Louis XIV*, Vol. 1, ed. Charles Louandre (Paris: Biblioteque-Charpentier, 1865), 133.
17 Max Weygand, *Turenne Marshall of France*, trans. George B. Ives (Boston: Houghton Mifflin, 1930), 246.
18 Mary Jackson Harvey, "Death and Dynasty in the Bouillon Tomb Commissions," *Art Bulletin* 74, no. 2, (1992): 273.
19 Suzanne Glover Lindsay, "Mummies and Tombs: Turenne, Napoleon, and the Death Ritual," *Art Bulletin* 82, no. 3 (Sept. 2000): 490.
20 Lindsay, "Mummies and Tombs," 491.
21 Zarzeczny, *Meteors*, 105.

22 Ida Östenberg, "Grief and glory: Triumphal Elements in the Roman Funeral Procession" (paper presented at the Classical Association Conference, Edinburgh, April 6–9, 2016).
23 Augustus, *Res Gestae Divi Augusti* (London: Oxford University Press, 1967), 3.
24 Suetonius, "The Lives of the Twelve Caesars," Wikisource, https://en.wikisource.org/wiki/The_Lives_of_the_Twelve_Caesars/Vitellius.
25 Karl Galinsky and Kenneth Lapatin, eds., *Cultural Memories in the Roman Empire* (Los Angeles: J. Paul Getty Museum, 2015), 70.
26 Ibid., 223.
27 Ibid., 70–71.
28 Ibid., 66.
29 Bonaparte, *Aphorisms*, 56.
30 Suemedha Sood, "Exploring the History of Catacombs," BBC.com, October 26, 2012, http://www.bbc.com/travel/story/20121025-exploring-the-history-of-catacombs.
31 Hughes, *Rome*, 185.
32 Zanker, *Roman Art*, 153.
33 Ibid., 155.
34 Grafton, *The Classical Tradition*, 178.
35 Les Catacombes, Histoire de Paris, http://www.catacombes.paris.fr/en/catacombs.
36 Graham Robb, *Parisians: an Adventure History of Paris* (New York: W. W. Norton & Co., 2010), 40.
37 Ibid.
38 Les Catacombes.
39 Ibid.
40 Erin-Marie Legacey, "The Paris Catacombs: Remains and Reunion beneath the Postrevolutionary City," *French Historical Studies* 40, no. 3 (August 2017): 516.
41 Ibid., 523.
42 Ibid., 522.
43 "Père Lachaise Cemetery," Napoleon Foundation, https://www.napoleon.org/en/magazine/places/pere-lachaise-cemetery/.
44 Ibid.

THREE: MARS THE PEACEMAKER

1 O'Brien, "Napoleon as Mars the Peacemaker," 358.
2 Klein, "Napoleons Triumphbogen," 244.
3 Johns, *Politics of Patronage*, 100.
4 Hugh Honour, "Canova's Napoleon," *Apollo* (Sept. 1, 1973): 183.
5 Grafton, *The Classical Tradition*, 646.
6 Honour, "Canova's Napoleon," 183.
7 Edward P. Alexander, *Museum Masters: their Museums and their Influence* (Nashville, Tenn.: The American Association for State and Local History, 1983), 99.
8 Huet, "Napoleon I," 58.
9 Grafton, *The Classical Tradition*, 646.
10 Huet, "Napoleon I," 59.
11 Johns, *Antonio Canova*, 95.

12 Fred Licht, *Canova* (New York: Abbeville Press, 1983), 97.

13 O'Brien, "Napoleon as Mars the Peacemaker," 356.

14 Ibid., 366.

15 Johns, *Antonio Canova*, 99.

16 Ferdinand Boyer, *Le monde des arts en Italie et la France de la Révolution et de l'Empire*. (Biblioteca di studi francesi, Torino: Società editrice internazionale, 1970), 136.

17 Honour, *Canova's Napoleon*, 182.

18 Huet, "Napoleon I," 59.

19 Margaret Plant, Venice: Fragile City, 1797–1997 (New Haven, CT, and London: Yale University Press, 2002), 72.

20 Johns, "Portrait Mythology," 126.

21 Judith Nowinski, *Baron Dominique-Vivant Denon* (Cranbury, N.J.: Fairleigh Dickinson University Press, 1970), 74.

22 O'Brien, "Napoleon as Mars the Peacemaker," 371.

23 Licht, *Canova*, 101.

24 Johns, *Antonio Canova*, 104.

25 Huet, "Napoleon I," 64.

26 Johns, "Portrait Mythology," 124.

27 Johns, *Antonio Canova*, 101.

28 O'Brien, "Napoleon as Mars the Peacemaker," 359.

29 Ibid., 365.

30 Johns, "Portrait Mythology," 125.

31 Andrew Graham-Dixon, *Art of France: There Will Be Blood*, aired in February 2017 on BBC4.

32 Grafton, *The Classical Tradition*, 643.

33 Michael Squire, "Embodied Ambiguities on the Prima Porta Augustus," *Art History* (April 2013): 257.

34 Larissa Bonfante, "Nudity as a Costume in Classical Art," *American Journal of Archeology* 93, no. 4 (Oct. 1989): 569.

35 Johns, *Politics of Patronage*, 97.

36 Squire, "Embodied Ambiguities," 260.

37 Christopher H. Hallett, *The Roman Nude* (Oxford, U.K.: Oxford University Press, 2005), 100.

38 Ibid., 98–99.

39 Ibid., 100.

40 Ibid., 160.

41 Shelley Hales, "Men are Mars, Women are Venus: Divine Costumes in Imperial Rome," in *The Clothed Body in the Ancient World*, ed. Liza Cleland, Mary Harlow, and Lloyd Llewellyn-Jones (Oxford, U.K.: Oxbow, 2005), 136.

42 Ibid., 134.

43 Hallett, *The Roman Nude*, 339.

44 Benjamin Hemmerle, "Crossing the Rubicon into Paris: Caesarian Comparisons from Napoleon to de Gaulle," in *Julius Caesar in Western Culture*, ed. Maria Wyke (Malden, Mass., and Oxford, U.K.: Blackwell, 2006), 289.

45 Melchior Missirini, *Della vita di Antonio Canova: libri quattro*, ed. Francesco Leone, trans. Francesco Mazzaferro (Bassano del Grappa: Istituto per gli Studi su Canova e il Neoclassicismo, 2004), 173, 175.

46 "ROME–PARIS. Academies face to face. The Accademia di San Luca and the French artists," Artsy, Oct. 13, 2016, https://www.artsy.net/show/accademia-nazionale-di-san-luca-rome-paris-academies-face-to-face-the-accademia-di-san-luca-and-the-french-artists.

47 Zanella, *Canova in Rome*, 45.

48 Nicassio, *Imperial City*, 185.

49 Ronald T. Ridley, *The Eagle and the Spade: The Archaeology of Rome During the Napoleonic Era 1809–1814* (Cambridge, U.K., and New York: Cambridge University Press, 1992), 86.

50 Ibid., 85.

51 Johns, *Politics Patronage*, 110.

52 Jean-Marie Sani, et al.,*Politique de l'amour: Napoléon Ier et Marie-Louise à Compiègne, Musée national du Palais Impérial de Compiègne* (1810; repr., Paris: Éditions de la Réunion des musées nationaux, 2010), 151.

53 Nicassio, *Imperial City,* 189–90.

54 Ibid., 34.

55 Ibid., 184.

56 Ibid., 184.

57 Huet, "Napoleon I," 59.

58 Nicassio, *Imperial City*, 32.

59 Ibid., 203, 205.

60 Rubin, *Hierarchies of Vision*, 139.

PART EIGHT: THE FALL

ONE: THE GOLDEN PRISON

1 Edward Sheehan, "When Napoleon Captured the Pope," *New York Times*, Dec. 13, 1981, http://www.nytimes.com/1981/12/13/theater/when-napoleon-captured-the-pope.html?pagewanted=all.

2 Anderson, *Pope Pius VII.*

3 "Doctor Claraz and Pope Pius VII," La Trace Claraz, http://www.latraceclaraz.org/pie-vii-et-le-docteur-claraz.html#montcenis.

4 Ibid.

5 Ibid.

6 Ibid.

7 Beyeler, *Pie VII*, 11.

8 Guillaume Picon, A *Day at château de Fontainebleau* (Paris: Flammarion, 2015), 156.

9 Christophe Beyeler, *The Château de Fontainebleau* (Paris: Connaissance des Arts, 2008), 40.

10 Jonathan Marsden, "Napoleon's Bust of 'Malbrouk'," *Burlington Magazine* 142, no. 1166 (May 2000): 305.

11 Picon, *A Day at Château de Fontainebleau*, 208.

12 Haig, *Walks Through*, 79.

13 Picon, *A Day at Château de Fontainebleau*, 177.

14 Beyeler, *Pie VII*, 177.
15 Louis Godart, *The Quirinale Palace: The History, the Rooms and the Collections* (Rome: Treccani, 2016), 47.
16 Ulrich Hiesinger, "The Paintings of Vincenzo Camuccini, 1771–1844," *Art Bulletin* 60, no. 2 (June 1978): 305.
17 Cordier, *Napoleon: The Imperial Household*, 108.
18 Ibid.
19 Godart, *The Quirinale Palace*, 181.
20 Ibid., 186.
21 Ibid., 184–85.
22 Ibid., 207.
23 Ibid., 115.
24 Beyeler, *Pie VII*, 162.
25 Susan L. Siegfried, *Ingres: Painting Reimagined* (New Haven, CT, and London: Yale University Press, 2009), 24.
26 Ibid., 120.
27 Ibid., 127.
28 Mansel, *Eagle*, 77.
29 Nicassio, *Imperial City*, 195.
30 Hugh Honour, *Canova's Statues of Venus*, 666.
31 Ibid., 670.
32 Bonaparte, *Aphorisms*, 97.
33 Mansel, *Splendour*, 173.
34 J. David Markham, *Napoleon for Dummies* (Hoboken, N.J.: Wiley Publishing, 2005), 189.
35 Mansel, *Splendour*, 173.
36 *Napoleon et Paris*, 153.
37 Leo Tolstoy, *War and Peace*, trans. Anthony Briggs (1868–9; repr, London: Penguin Books, 2005), 865.
38 Mansel, *Splendour*, 57.
39 *Napoleon Enters Moscow*, History.com, 2010, http://www.history.com/this-day-in-history/napoleon-enters-moscow.

TWO: RETRENCHMENT

1 Armand-Augustin-Louis Caulaincourt, *With Napoleon in Russia*, ed. Jean Hanoteau (Mineola, N.Y.: Dover, 2005), 259.
2 Lozier, *Napoleon & Paris*, 40.
3 Nicassio, *Imperial City*, 217.
4 Beyeler, *Pie VII face à Napoleon*, 177.
5 Ibid., 208.
6 Anderson, *Pope Pius VII*.
7 Stammers, "The man," 154.
8 Ibid., 159.
9 David Van Zanten, "Le Fonds Fontaine a l'Art Institute a Chicago," Northwestern University, http://www.artic.edu/sites/default/files/fontaine_rome.pdf.

10 Beauhaire, Béjanin and Naudeix, *L'Elephant de Napoleon*, 14.

11 Simon Schama, *Citizens: A Chronicle of the French Revolution* (New York: Vintage Books, 1990), 3.

12 Beauhaire, Béjanin and Naudeix, *L'Elephant de Napoleon*, 13.

13 Ibid.

14 John Scarborough, Review, "The Elephant in the Greek and Roman World," *Classical Journal* 72, no. 2 (Dec. 1976–Jan. 1977): 175.

15 William Heckscher, "Bernini's Elephant and Obelisk," *Art Bulletin* 29 (1947): 155–182.

16 Picon, *A Day at Château de Fontainebleau*, 28, 77.

17 Howard Hayes Scullard, *The Elephant in the Greek and Roman World* (Ithaca, N.Y.: Cornell University Press, 1974), 215.

18 Scullard, *The Elephant*, 75.

19 Ibid., 76.

20 Lionel Casson, "Ptolemy II and The Hunting of African Elephants," *Transactions of the American Philological Association* 123 (1993): 253.

21 Michael B. Charles and Peter Rhodan, "Magister Elephantorum: A Reappraisal of Hannibal's Use of Elephants," *Classical World* 100, no. 4 (Summer 2007): 380.

22 Scullard, *The Elephant*, 169.

23 Charles and Rhodan, "Magister Elephantorum," 388.

24 Debra L. Nousek, "Turning Points in Roman History: The Case of Caesar's Elephant Denarius," *Phoenix* 62, no. 3/4 (Fall–Winter 2008): 290.

25 Ibid., 292.

26 Ibid., 298.

27 Mike Markowitz, "Ancient Coins—Elephants on Ancient Coinage," Coin Week, February 6, 2017, https://coinweek.com/ancient-coins/elephants-ancient-coins/.

28 Beauhaire, Béjanin and Naudeix, *L'Elephant de Napoleon*, 19.

29 Ibid., 24.

30 Ibid., 14.

31 Suetonias, "The Lives of the Twelve Caesars."

32 Ibid.

33 François Houdecek, *The Collapse of the Grand Empire*, Vol. 14, Correspondance Generale de Napoleon Bonaparte, trans. Peter Hicks and R. Young (Paris: Fondacion Napoleon, 2017), intro.

34 Robert, *Napoleon*, 674.

35 Ibid., 683.

36 Ibid., 675.

37 Ibid., 683.

38 Ibid., 685.

39 Michel Kerautret, "The Meeting at Erfurt," trans. and ed. Hamish Davey Wright, Napoleon Foundation, https://www.napoleon.org/en/history-of-the-two-empires/articles/the-meeting-at-erfurt/.

40 Robert, *Napoleon*, 685.

THREE: FUNERAL OF THE EMPIRE

1 Hibbert, *Napoleon's Women*, 207.

2 Picon, *A Day at Château de Fontainebleau*, 132.

3 Haig, *Walks Through*, 85.
4 Roberts, *Napoleon: A Life*, 720.
5 Ibid.
6 Mansel, *Eagle*, 57.
7 Patricia Rubin. "Hierarchies of Vision: Fra Angelico's 'Coronation of the Virgin' from *San Domenico, Fiesole*," *Oxford Art Journal* 27, no. 2 (2004): 139.
8 Ibid.
9 *Three hundred unpublished letters from Napoleon I to Marie Louise* (London: Sotheby & Co., 1934), 36–37.
10 Haig, *Walks Through*, 91.
11 Johns, *Antonio Canova and the Politics of Patronage*, 117.
12 Johns, "Empress Joséphine's Collection," 31.
13 Ibid., 30.
14 *Alexander, Napoleon and Joséphine*, 112.
15 Rémusat, *Memoires de Madame de Remusat*, 272.
16 DeLorme, *Joséphine*, 54.
17 Rosenthal, *Citizens and Kings*, 324.
18 Louis Marchand, *Memoires de Marchand* (Paris: Tallandier, 2003), 169.
19 Sudhir Hazareesingh, *The Legend of Napoleon* (London: Granta Books, 2004), 19.
20 "Napoleon becomes emperor—again," Observer Archive, April 1, 2017, https://www.theguardian.com/news/2017/apr/01/from-the-observer-archive-napoleon-becomes-emperor-again.
21 Haig, *Walks Through*, 87.
22 Hazareesingh, *Legend*, 16.
23 Mansel, *Dressed to Rule*, 90.
24 John Cam Hobhouse, *The Substance of some Letters written by an Englishman resident at Paris during the Last Reign of the Emperor Napoleon*, (Philadelphia: M. Thomas, 1816), 415.
25 Hazareesingh, *Legend*, 35.
26 Ibid., 36.
27 Hibbert, *Napoleon's Women*, 257.
28 Haig, *Walks Through*, 93.
29 *Alexander, Napoleon and Joséphine*, 50.
30 Hibbert, *Napoleon's Women*, 262.
31 Cecelia Rodriguez, "Secret Island To Open Its Treasures: Napoleon's Saint Helena, A Hot Destination For 2017," *Forbes*, December 30, 2016, http://www.forbes.com/sites/ceciliarodriguez/2016/12/30/secret-island-to-open-after-500-years-napoleons-saint-helena-will-be-a-2017-hot-destination/#569ff5a87038.
32 "Island of St Helena," Napoleon Foundation, https://www.napoleon.org/en/magazine/places/island-of-st-helena/.
33 Zarzeczny, *Meteors*, 170.
34 Las Cases, *Le Mémorial de Sainte-Hélène*, 260–61.
35 Ibid., 3.
36 Mansel, *Dressed to Rule*, 91.
37 Napoleon, *Aphorisms*, 87.
38 Herold, *The Mind of Napoleon*, 58.

39 Ibid., 227.

40 Debra Nousek, "Caesar, Man of Letters," in *The Landmark Julius Caesar Web Essay*, ed. Kurt A. Raaflaub, www.thelandmarkcaesar.com.

41 Herold, *The Mind of Napoleon*, xvii.

42 Ibid., 279.

43 Ibid., 110.

44 Caracciolo, *Les Soeurs de Napoleon*, 22.

PART NINE: LEGACY

ONE: A MORAL LESSON

1 Haskell and Penny, *Taste & the Antique*, 114.

2 Katharine Eustace, "The Fruits of War: How Napoleon's Looted Art Found its Way Home," *The Art Newspaper* 269 (June 2015).

3 Oliver, *From Royal to National*, 66.

4 Jonah Siegel, "Owning Art after Napoleon: Destiny or Destination at the Birth of the Museum," *PMLA* 125, no. 1 (Jan. 2010): 145.

5 Gould, *Trophy of Conquest*, 134–35.

6 Mainardi, *Assuring the Empire of the Future*, 156.

7 Katharine Eustace, *Ideal Heads*, 12.

8 Johns, *Politics of Patronage*, 177.

9 T. H. Lunsingh Scheurleer, A. B. de Vries, L. Brummel, H. E. van Gelder, *150 jaar Koninklijk Kabinet van Schilderijen/Koninklijke Bibliotheek, Koninklijk Penningkabinet* ('S-Gravenhage: Staatsdrukkerij, 1967), 38.

10 Nowinski, *Baron Dominique Vivant Denon*, 104.

11 Quentin Buvelot, "1785–1815: Intermezzo in Paris, Musée Napoléon," in *Royal Picture Gallery Mauritshuis: A Princely Collection*, eds. Peter van der Ploeg and Quentin Buvelot (The Hague: Royal Picture Gallery Mauritshuis; Zwolle: Waanders, 2006), 30–31.

12 Buvelot, *Intermezzo*, 31.

13 Eustace, *The Fruits of War.*

14 Pietrangeli, *Vatican Museums*, 149.

15 Ibid.

16 Nowinski, *Baron*, 105.

17 Plant, *Venice*, 210.

18 David Packard, Art of the Vatican Collections. http://yourmovechessarthist.blogspot.com/2013/05.

19 Eustace, *The Fruits of War.*

20 Eustace, *Canova Ideal Heads,* 10.

21 Mainardi, *Assuring the Empire*, 160.

22 Pietrangeli, *The Vatican Museums*, 151.

23 Ibid., 153.

24 Bazin, *Museum Age*, 180.

25 Alexander, *Museum Masters*, 92.

26 Oliver, *From Royal to National*, 67.

27 McClellan, *Inventing the Louvre*, 200.

28 Pietrangeli, *The Vatican Museums*, 153.

29 Ibid., 154.
30 *The Vatican Collections: The Papacy and Art* (New York: Metropolitan Museum of Art: H. N. Abrams, 1982).
31 Ambrosini, *Secret Archives*, 295.
32 Ibid.
33 "History of the Vatican Medagliere," Vatican Library, https://www.vatlib.it/home.php?pag=dipartimento_numismatico&ling=eng.
34 Giuseppe Bertini, "Works of art from Parma in Paris during Napoleon's time and their restitution" (presentation at the Development of National Museums in Europe 1794–1830 International conference, University of Amsterdam Geneva and Brussels, January 31–February 2, 2008).
35 "Diamond in the crown: The Grand Mazarin," Christie's, October 18. 2017, https://www.christies.com/features/Le-Grand-Mazarin-Diamond-in-the-Crown-8625-3.aspx.
36 Tomas Macsotay, ed., *Rome, Travel and the Sculpture Capital* (New York: Routledge, 2017), 98.
37 *Alexander, Napoleon & Joséphine*, 115.
38 Plant, *Venice*, 210
39 Ibid.
40 Mainardi, "Assuring the Empire of the Future," 160.
41 Plant, *Venice*, 82.
42 Ibid., 81.

TWO: EXILES AND HEROES

1 Roberta J. M. Olson, "Representations of Pope Pius VII: The First Risorgimento Hero," *Art Bulletin* 68, no. 1 (March 1986): 93.
2 Grafton, *The Classical Tradition*, 956.
3 Nicassio, *Imperial City*, 223.
4 Ibid., 223.
5 Lascelles, *Pontifex Maximus*, 233.
6 Olson, "Representations," 77.
7 Nicassio, *Imperial City*, 224.
8 Olson, "Representations," 91.
9 Ibid.
10 Pietrangeli, *Vatican Museums*, 165.
11 *The Vatican Collections*, 20.
12 Valter Curzi, Carolina Brook, Claudio Parisi Presicce, ed., *Il museo universale: dal sogno di Napoleone a Canova* (Milan, Italy: Skira, 2016).
13 Rhodi Marsden, "Pope Pius VII's Paper Crown," *Independent*, March 20, 2015, http://www.independent.co.uk/news/world/europe/rhodri-marsdens-interesting-objects-pope-pius-viis-paper-crown-10116494.html.
14 Roberto Piperno, "Pope Pius VII," *Romeartlover*, https://www.romeartlover.it/Storia28.html accessed 12/15/17.
15 Plant, *Venice*, 221.
16 Grossman, *Looking*, 77.
17 Cunial and Pavan, *Canova*, 274.

18 Joseph Farington, *The Farington Diary*, Vol. 8, ed. James Greig (London: Hutchinson & Co., Ltd. 1922), 49.
19 Pietrangeli, *Vatican Museums*, 153.
20 Cunial and Pavan, *Antonio Canova: Museum and Gipsoteca*, 257.
21 Ibid., 154.
22 James Barron, "Finally, From Italy, the Full George Washington," *New York Times*, April 23, 2017.
23 Ibid.
24 Ibid.
25 Salomon, *Canova's George Washington*, 34–35.
26 Ibid., 108.
27 Ibid., 60.
28 Licht, *Canova*, 113.
29 Mario Guderzo, email message to author, January 16, 2018.
30 Sheila Hale, *Titian, His Life* (New York: Harper Press, 2012), 160.
31 Freeman, *Horses of St Mark's*, 213.
32 Elliott Davies and Emanuela Tarizzo, *Canova and His Legacy* (Verona: Paul Holberton Publishing, 2017), 14.
33 Johns, *Antonio Canova and the Politics of Patronage*, 93.
34 Hughes, *Rome*, 368.
35 Plant, *Venice*, 74.
36 Ibid.
37 *Canova and his Legacy*, 2017, 60.
38 Hughes, *Rome*, 369.
39 Charney, *Stealing*, 93.
40 Siegfied, *Ingres*, 265.
41 Ibid., 273.
42 Rosenberg, *Dominique-Vivant Denon: L'oeil de Napoléon*, 279.
43 Ibid., 280.
44 Ibid., 16.
45 Michel Kimmelman, "Ingres at the Louvre: His Pursuit of a Higher Reality," *New York Times*, March 24, 2008, http://www.nytimes.com/2006/03/24/arts/design/ingres-at-the-louvre-his-pursuit-of-a-higher-reality.html.
46 Hochel, *Dominique-Vivant Denon*, 7.
47 Garric, *Charles Percier*, 71.
48 Ibid., 63.
49 Stammers, "The man."
50 Van Zanten, "Fontaine in the Burnham Library."
51 Garric, *Charles Percier*, 46.
52 Hibbert, *Napoleon's Women*, 316.
53 Ibid., 319.
54 Caracciolo, *Les Soeurs de Napoleon*.
55 Antonio Canova, *Joachim Murat*, 1813, marble, 19 7⁄10" (50 cm), Christie's, http://www.christies.com/lotfinder/Lot/antonio-canova-1757-1822-1813-joachim-murat-1767-1815-6113947-details.aspx

56 Hibbert, *Napoleon's Women*, 330.

57 Ibid., 329.

THREE: RES GESTAE

1 Harriet I. Flower, *The Art of Forgetting: Disgrace and Oblivion in Roman Political Culture* (Chapel Hill: University of North Carolina Press, 2011), 43–44.

2 Sarah E. Bond, "Erasing the Face of History," May 14, 2011, *New York Times*, http://www.nytimes.com/2011/05/15/opinion/15bond.html?_r=1&.

3 Flower, *The Art of Forgetting*, 116.

4 Maureen Carroll,"Memoria and Damnatio Memoriae. Preserving and erasing identities in Roman funerary commemoration," in *Living through the Dead: Burial and Commemoration in the Classical World,* ed. Maureen Carroll and Jane Rempel (Oxford, U.K.: Oxbow Books, 2011), 72.

5 Bond, *Erasing the Face of History.*

6 Beard, "The Twelve Caesars."

7 Hazareesingh, *Legend*, 59.

8 Ibid., 39.

9 Ibid., 47.

10 Fiona Parr, "The Death of Napoleon Bonaparte and the Retour des Cendres: French and British Perspectives," Napoleon Foundation, https://www.napoleon.org/en/history-of-the-two-empires/articles/the-death-of-napoleon-bonaparte-and-the-retour-des-cendres-french-and-british-perspectives/.

11 Cordier, *Napoleon: The Imperial Household*, 246.

12 Susan Jenkins, "Buying Bonaparte," *Apollo* (Nov. 2010): 50.

13 Hazareesingh, *Legend*, 73.

14 Susan Jenkins, "Arthur Wellesley, First Duke of Wellington, Apsley House and Canova's Napoleon as Mars the Peacemaker," *Sculpture Journal*, no. 19 (2010): 116.

15 Jenkins, *Arthur Wellesley*, 116.

16 Ibid.

17 Ibid., 120.

18 Roberts, *Napoleon: A Life*, 518.

19 De Bellaigue, *A Royal Keepsake*, 112.

20 Wendy Moonan, "Napoleonic Style, in All Its Imperial Self-Promotion," *New York Times,* Nov. 2, 2007, http://www.nytimes.com/2007/11/02/arts/design/02anti.html.

21 Cordier, *Napoleon: The Imperial Household*, 82.

22 Hazareesingh, *Legend*, 150.

23 Augustus, *Res Gestae,* 6.

24 Ibid., 37.

25 Ibid., 3.

26 Huet, *Stories,* 23.

27 Ibid., 13.

28 Bonaparte, *Aphorisms*, 76.

29 Herold, *The Mind of Napoleon*, 255.

30 "Who Exactly Was the Conte de Las Cases?" Napoleon Foundation, October, 2017, www.napoleon.org/en/magazine/interviews/exactly-las-cases-three-questions-francois-houdecek-october-2017-memorial-napoleon-st_helena/.

31 Hazareesingh, *Legend*, 69.
32 Haig, *Walks Through*, 99.
33 Parr, *The Death of Napoleon Bonaparte*.
34 Ayers, *The Architecture of Paris*, 145.
35 Ibid., 146.
36 Rapelli, *Symbols*, 375.
37 Haig, *Walks Through*, 101.
38 Ibid., 111.
39 Muratori-Philip, *Arc de Triomphe*, 11.
40 Haig, *Walks Through*, 100.
41 Victor Hugo, *Poems in Three Volumes*, Vol. 1 (Boston: Estes and Lauriat, n.d.).
42 Haig, *Walks Through*, 101.
43 Hazareesingh, *Legend*, 155.
44 "Napoleon's Tomb," *Illustrated Magazine of Art* 2, no. 10 (Jan. 1853): 231.
45 Ibid., 240.
46 Ayers, *The Architecture of Paris*, 146.
47 Karine Huguenard, "Les Invalides, the Military Museum and the Tomb of Napoleon," Napoleon Foundation, https://www.napoleon.org/en/magazine/places/les-invalides-the-military-museum-and-tomb-of-napoleon/Napoleon.org.

POSTSCRIPT

1 Ben Pollitt, "Vignon, Church of La Madeleine," *Smarthistory*, January 8, 2016.

ACKNOWLEDGMENTS

The idea for *The Caesar of Paris* came from reading Antonio Canova's *Napoleon and Canova: eight conversations,* published in London in 1825. In 1810, Napoleon strong-armed the Rome-based sculptor into modeling a portrait of his new wife at Fontainebleau. Canova did not expect to find Napoleon at every sitting. Fortunately he recorded their breakfast conversations, excerpts of which appear here. Pierre Fontaine's candid observations in his *Journal 1799–1853* were key to understanding the motivations behind Napoleon's building program, as was a 2016 exhibition/symposium on Fontaine's unsung partner, Charles Percier, organized by Jean-Philippe Garric at the Bard Graduate Center.

I owe a large debt of gratitude to the scholarship of many biographers, historians, and writers whose outstanding works are referenced. Again and again, works of two ancient writers lit the way: Pliny the Elder's *Natural History* and *The Lives of the Twelve Caesars* by Suetonius. Also indispensable: Matthew Zarzeczny's *Meteors that Enlighten the Earth: Napoleon and the Cult of Great Men*, Sylvain Cordier's *Napoleon: The Imperial Household,* and the Fondation Napoleon's encyclopedic website, napoleon.org.

ACKNOWLEDGMENTS

A number of people have been especially generous in helping me think about Napoleon's relationship with antiquity. Thomas W. Gaehtgens, former director of the Getty Research Institute, steered me toward looking at the impact of place on the itinerant emperor. Josephine Oxley, Keeper of the Wellington Collection, Apsley House and Wellington Arch, shared her insights on Canova's *Napoleon as Mars the Peacemaker.* Alain Pougetoux, Chief Curator of Château de Malmaison; Marc Desti, Conservateur of the Palais impérial de Compiègne; and Isabella Botti of the Galleria Borghese were invaluable guides.

Thanks too to Mario Guderzo, director of the Gypsotheca e Museo Antonio Canova; Alberto Craievich, director of the Ca' Rezzonico Museum in Venice; Jens Daehner, associate curator of antiquities at the Getty Villa; Nigel Spivey of the University of Cambridge; Jean François Bédard of Syracuse University; Quentin Buvelot, senior curator at the Royal Picture Gallery Mauritshuis in The Hague; Frank Pohle, history professor at RWTH Aachen University; and Martin Hirsch, curator at the Staatliche Münzsammlung, Munich.

From ancient civilizations to France's First Empire, the resources of the Getty Research Library were invaluable. For her help with translations, I am extremely grateful to my colleague Alex Wolfe. Thanks again to my agent, Alice Martell. It's been a true pleasure working with my insightful editor, Jessica Case, Maria Fernandez, and the team at Pegasus Books.

I would like to thank my wonderful family for their endless support and encouragement, especially my daughter, Clara, and husband, Doug, to whom this book is dedicated.

Susan Jaques
August 2018

ILLUSTRATION CREDITS

Fig. 1: Vase depicting Napoleon in front of Italian works of art being delivered to Louvre. Copyright © The De Agostini Picture Library / G. Dagli Orti / Bridgeman Images.

Fig. 2: *Laocoön and his sons.* By Jean-Pol Grandmont [CC BY-SA 3.0 (https://creativecommons.org/licenses/by-sa/3.0) or GFDL (http://www.gnu.org/copyleft/fdl.html)], via Wikimedia Commons.

Fig. 3: *Apollo Belvedere.* By Dennis Jarvis from Halifax (Italy-3104 - Apollo) [CC BY-SA 2.0 (https://creativecommons.org/licenses/by-sa/2.0)], via Wikimedia Commons.

Fig. 4: *Venus de' Medici.* By Wai Laam Lo [CC BY-SA 3.0 (https://creativecommons.org/licenses/by-sa/3.0) or GFDL (http://www.gnu.org/copyleft/fdl.html)], from Wikimedia Commons.

Fig. 5: *Alexander the Great.* By Carole Raddato from Frankfurt [CC BY-SA 2.0 (https://creativecommons.org/licenses/by-sa/2.0)], via Wikimedia Commons.

Fig. 6: Frontispiece to Volume 1 of the "Description of Egypt." Copyright © Private Collection / The Stapleton Collection / Bridgeman Images.

Fig. 7: Portrait of Gaius Julius Caesar, the Green Caesar. By Anagoria [Public domain] via Wikimedia Commons.

Fig. 8: Portrait Head of Augustus. Copyright © The J. Paul Getty Museum, Los Angeles.

Fig. 9: *Napoleon Crossing the Grand Saint-Bernard Pass.* Copyright © Bridgeman Images.

Fig. 10: *Portrait of Joséphine.* Copyright © Wellington Collection, Apsley House, London.

Fig. 11: Bonbonniere with portraits of Eugene (1781–1824), Hortense (1783–1837), Josephine Beauharnais (1763–1814), and Louis Bonaparte (1778–1846). Copyright © Musee National du Chateau de Malmaison, Rueil-Malmaison, France / Bridgeman Images.

Fig. 12: *Marie-Annuciade-Caroline Bonaparte, Queen of Naples with her daughter Laetitia-Joséphine Murat.* Public Domain via Wikimedia Commons.

Fig. 13: *Elisa Bonaparte (1777–1820) Grand Duchess of Tuscany and her Daughter Napoleone-Elisa.* Copyright © Bridgeman Images.

Fig. 14: *Bust of Joachim Murat*. From private collection, photo courtesy of Christie's Ltd, 2017.

Fig. 15: *Pauline Borghese as Venus Victrix*. Copyright © Leochen66, Dreamstime.com.

Fig. 16: *Letitia Ramolino Bonaparte*. Copyright © Devonshire Collection, Chatsworth / Reproduced by permission of Chatsworth Settlement Trustees / Bridgeman Images.

Fig. 17: *Marie Louise, Empress of the French*. By Dennis Jarvis from Halifax, Canada (Austria-03332 - Empress of the French) [CC BY-SA 2.0 (https://creativecommons.org/licenses/by-sa/2.0)], via Wikimedia Commons.

Fig. 18: *The Emperor Napoleon in His Study at the Tuileries*. From the Samuel H. Kress Collection, National Gallery of Art, Washington, D.C.

Fig. 19: *Napoleon as Mars the Peacekeeper*. Copyright © Wellington Collection, Apsley House, London.

Fig. 20: *Portrait of Pope Pius VII*. Copyright © Wellington Collection, Apsley House, London.

Fig. 21: *Portrait of Antonio Canova*. Copyright © The J. Paul Getty Museum, Los Angeles.

Fig. 22: *Portraits of Charles Percier, Pierre Fontaine, and Claude-Louis Bernier*. Gift of David Jenness in honor of Arthur F. Jenness. Image courtesy of the Clark Art Institute, Williamstown, Massachusetts.

Fig. 23: *David par lui-même*. Copyright © The J. Paul Getty Museum, Los Angeles.

Fig. 24: *Portrait of Dominique-Vivant Denon*. Copyright © De Agostini Picture Library / G. Dagli Orti / Bridgeman Images.

Fig. 25: Josephine's Bedroom, Malmaison. By Moonik [CC BY-SA 3.0 (https://creativecommons.org/licenses/by-sa/3.0)], via Wikimedia Commons.

Fig. 26: Gondola Chair from Chateau de Saint-Cloud. From [CC0], via Wikimedia Commons, photo by Jebulon.

Fig. 27: Athénienne. Bequest of James Alexander Scrymser, 1918. Metropolitan Museum of Art.

Fig. 28: Coin cabinet. Bequest of Collis P. Huntington, 1900. Metropolitan Museum of Art.

Fig. 29: Table of the Great Commanders. From the Royal Collection Trust © Her Majesty Queen Elizabeth II, 2018 / Bridgeman Images.

Fig. 30: Austerlitz Table. Copyright © Musee National du Chateau de Malmaison, Rueil-Malmaison, France / Bridgeman Images.

Fig. 31: Sword worn by Napoléon I at the Battle of Austerlitz. By Rama [CC BY-SA 2.0 fr (https://creativecommons.org/licenses/by-sa/2.0/fr/deed.en) or CeCILL (http://www.cecill.info/licences/Licence_CeCILL_V2-en.html)], via Wikimedia Commons.

Fig. 32: Bayeux Tapestry, scene 57, Harold's death. By Myrabella [Public domain or CC0], from Wikimedia Commons.

Fig. 33: Imperial Eagle on main portal of Fontainebleau. By dynamosquito [CC BY-SA 2.0 (https://creativecommons.org/licenses/by-sa/2.0)], via Wikimedia Commons.

Fig. 34: Eagle, A.D. 100–200. Copyright © The J. Paul Getty Museum, Los Angeles.

Fig. 35: Reliquary *Bust of Charlemagne*. Copyright © Hurza, Dreamstime.com.

Fig. 36: *Hand of Justice*. By Marie-Lan Nguyen [CC BY 2.5 (http://creativecommons.org/licenses/by/2.5)], via Wikimedia Commons.

Fig. 37: *Crown of Charlemagne*. By Faqscl (Own work) [CC BY-SA 4.0 (https://creativecommons.org/licenses/by-sa/4.0)], via Wikimedia Commons.

Fig. 38: *The Coronation of Napoleon*, detail. Copyright © Legacy1995, Dreamstime.com.

Fig. 39: Silver medallion, Napoleon and Charlemagne. Photo courtesy of Bonhams.

Fig. 40: *Portrait of Napoleon I as King of Italy*. By Dennis Jarvis from Halifax (Austria-03330 - Napoleon I) [CC BY-SA 2.0 (https://creativecommons.org/licenses/by-sa/2.0)], via Wikimedia Commons.

Fig. 41: *Joséphine in Coronation Costume*. Public domain, via Wikimedia Commons.

Fig. 42: The Arch of Septimus and Temple of Vespasian, Rome. Copyright © The J. Paul Getty Museum, Los Angeles.

Fig. 43: Arch of Constantine, Rome. Copyright © The J. Paul Getty Museum, Los Angeles.

Fig. 44: Arc de Triomphe du Carrousel, Paris. By Rafesmar [CC BY-SA 4.0 (https://creativecommons.org/licenses/by-sa/4.0)], from Wikimedia Commons.

Fig. 45: The Horses of St. Mark's Basilica. Copyright © Scaliger, Dreamstime.com.

Fig. 46: Interior of the Arch of Titus, Rome. Copyright © The J. Paul Getty Museum, Los Angeles.

Fig. 47: Arc de Triomphe de l'Étoile, Paris. By Dennis Jarvis, Halifax (France-000136 - Arc de Triomphe) [CC BY-SA 2.0 (https://creativecommons.org/licenses/by-sa/2.0)], via Wikimedia Commons.

Fig. 48: Arch of Titus, interior detail. Copyright © The J. Paul Getty Museum, Los Angeles.

Fig. 49: Triumph of 1810, Arc de Triomphe. By Dennis Jarvis, Halifax (France-000142 - Triumph of 1810) [CC BY-SA 2.0 (https://creativecommons.org/licenses/by-sa/2.0)], via Wikimedia Commons.

Fig. 50: Trajan's Column, detail, Rome. Copyright © The J. Paul Getty Museum, Los Angeles.

Fig. 51: Vendome Column, detail, Paris. By Gordon Gartrell (IMG_9428) [CC BY-SA 2.0 (https://creativecommons.org/licenses/by-sa/2.0)], via Wikimedia Commons.

Fig. 52: Trajan's Column, Rome, detail. Copyright © Tiziano Casalta, Dreamstime.com.

Fig. 53: Vendome Column, Paris, detail. Copyright © Daniele Longhi, Dreamstime.com.

Fig. 54: Maison Carrée, Nimes. By Dennis Jarvis, Halifax (France-002364 - Square House) [CC BY-SA 2.0 (https://creativecommons.org/licenses/by-sa/2.0)], via Wikimedia Commons.

Fig. 55: The Madeleine Church, Paris. Copyright © Rene Drouyer, Dreamstime.com.

Fig. 56: The Bourse of Paris. Copyright © Kovalenkov Petr, Dreamstime.com.

Fig. 57: View of the Elephant Fountain at the Place de la Bastille. Copyright © Musee de la Ville de Paris, Musee Carnavalet, Paris / Bridgeman Images.

Fig. 58: The Great Cameo of France, Roman. Copyright © Bibliotheque Nationale, Paris / Bridgeman Images.

Fig. 59: Marie-Louise of Austria (1791–1847) guiding her son, with the ribbon of a medal of the Legion of Honour, towards a bust of Napoleon Bonapart. Copyright © Musee National de la Legion d'Honneur, Paris, France / Bridgeman Images.

Figs. 60 and 61: *Napoleon, Baptism of the King of Rome*. Copyright © Metropolitan Museum of Art, Rogers Fund, New York, 1977.

Fig. 62: *Cradle of the King of Rome*. Photograph by Dennis Jarvis, Halifax, Canada (Austria-03324) [CC BY-SA 2.0 (https://creativecommons.org/licenses/by-sa/2.0)], via Wikimedia Commons.

Fig. 63: *Pope Pius VII in the Sistine Chapel*. Copyright © Samuel H. Kress Collection, National Gallery of Art, Washington, D.C.

Fig. 64: Temple Canoviano, Possagno, Italy. By mrlov (P1070329) [CC BY-SA 2.0 (https://creativecommons.org/licenses/by-sa/2.0)], via Wikimedia Commons.

Fig. 65: *The History of Christianity*, Madeleine Church. Copyright © Photogolfer, Dreamstime.com.

Fig. 66: Tomb of Napoleon. Copyright © Dennis Dolkens, Dreamstime.com.

INDEX

INDEX

D

E

Q

R